Stalin's Terror of 1937-1938
Political Genocide in the USSR

Vadim Z. Rogovin

Translated by Frederick S. Choate

2009

© 2009 Mehring Books
All rights reserved

Published by Mehring Books
P.O. Box 48377
Oak Park, MI 48237

Printed in the United States of America

Translation of: *Partiia rasstreliannykh*, M., 1997.

Library of Congress Cataloging-in-Publication Data

Rogovin, Vadim Zakharovich.

Stalin's terror of 1937-1938 : political genocide in the USSR / Vadim Z. Rogovin ; translated by Frederick S. Choate

   p. cm.

Includes bibliographical references and index.
ISBN 978-1-893638-04-4 (pbk. : alk. paper)
ISBN 978-1-893638-08-2 (cloth : alk paper)

1. Soviet Union--Politics and government--1917-1936. 2. Political purges--Soviet Union. 3. Stalin, Joseph, 1879-1953. 4. Trotsky, Leon, 1879-1940. 5. Moscow Trials, Moscow, Russia, 1936-1937. I. Title.

DK268.4.R64 2009

947.084'2--dc22

2008046730

Cover photographs
Left: Stalin; Right top to bottom: I. Reiss, Sergei Sedov, Leon Sedov, Bukharin, Rakovsky; Center: Delegates to the Eighth Extraordinary Congress of Soviets in December 1936

Contents

Foreword vii
Note from the Translator ix
Introduction 1
1. "Mass Operations" 7
2. The January Plenum of the Central Committee:
"On the Errors of Party Organizations" 15
3. The January Plenum of the Central Committee:
The Postyshev Affair 21
4. Preparation for the Third Show Trial 27
5. The Episode with Krestinsky 39
6. Bukharin and Vyshinsky 43
7. The "Conspiracy" of 1918 49
8. The Mystery of Bukharin 55
9. Yagoda's Orbit 61
10. Poisonings and Poisoners 67
11. What Was True at the Trial? 73
12. The Main Defendant 79
13. The Trial's Domestic Political Goals 83
14. Foreign Policy Goals of the Moscow Trials 87
15. The General Prosecutor 93
16. The Sentence 99

17. International Response to the Trial 103
18. Trotsky on the Moscow Trials 111
19. The Historical Fate of the Moscow Trials 119
20. Stalin and His Intimate Circle 129
    1. Molotov 134
    2. Kaganovich 142
    3. Voroshilov 149
    4. Mikoyan 152
    5. Andreev 154
    6. Kalinin 156
    7. Zhdanov 157
    8. Khrushchev 158
    9. Beria 161
    10. Malenkov 163
    11. Mekhlis 164
    12. Shkiriatov 166
21. In the Bowels of the Politburo 169
22. Liquidation of the Central Committee 173
23. The Party Apparatus 185
24. The Army 195
25. The NKVD 205
26. The Komsomol 213
27. The Non-Party Intelligentsia 219
28. The People 229
29. The Great Purge as Seen by Enemies of Soviet Power 237
30. The Great Purge as Seen by Russian Émigrés 241
31. The Great Purge as Seen by Communists 247
32. Was Anyone Guilty? 265
33. Oppositionists in the Camps 275
34. The Tragedy at Vorkuta 281
35. Who Benefited from the Great Purge? 287
36. The New Recruits of 1937 291
37. Who Was Punished, and in What Way, After Stalin's Death? 297
38. Terror against Foreign Communists 303

Table of Contents

39. Non-Returners of 1937 321
    1. Ignatii Reiss 321
    2. Walter Krivitsky 326
    3. Alexander Barmine 328
40. Non-Returners of 1938 333
    1. Alexander Orlov 333
    2. Fyodor Raskolnikov 336
41. The Verdict of the Dewey Commission 341
42. Bolshevism, Stalinism, Trotskyism 347
43. "Hue and Cry over Kronstadt" 357
44. "Their Morals and Ours" 365
45. "The Old Man Would Find It Hard Without Sonny" 381
46. An Agent Known as "Tulip" 385
47. The Death of Leon Sedov 391
48. Trotsky in Mexico 397
49. Murders Abroad 403
50. Paris Intrigues 407
51. The End of the "Yezhov Period" 413
52. The Falsification of History 421

Appendix I 429

Appendix II 441

Glossary.. 451

Dates of Party Congresses, Comintern Congresses and Trials.................... 455

Endnotes 457

Index.. 493

Foreword

The basic ideas in this book were outlined in lectures given by its author in 1995-1996 at universities in the USA, England, Australia, Argentina and Germany. The fruitful discussions which unfolded in the course of the lectures allowed a refinement of the book's overall conception and of several individual theses. The author would like to express his gratitude to the university personnel and to the members of the left political parties and movements who participated in the organization and presentation of these lectures.

Chapters 2 and 3 were co-authored with M. V. Goloviznin.

Note from the Translator

Transliterating Cyrillic always involves compromises. Throughout the main body of the text, I have adopted a modified version of the system used in the *Handbook of Russian Literature*. Thus, the familiar "–skii" ending of many surnames is rendered as "–sky." Soft and hard signs are omitted (Koltsov, not Kol'tsov). Where names are of Germanic origin, I have usually retained the Russian form (Erenburg, not Ehrenburg). An exception is Kronstadt, instead of Kronshtadt. Some other names that have become popularized over the years are used in their more familiar form, even if this violates stricter transliteration norms (Zinoviev, not Zinov'ev; Barmine, not Barmin). In the endnotes, however, I have adhered to the more formal rules. Names that begin with the Cyrillic "E-" are rendered as "Ye-" (Yeltsin, Yezhov, Yenukidze). Here I adopt the popularized form, even when the first syllable is unstressed.

A glossary of some of the acronyms and terms from the Soviet period follows the second appendix. For brevity's sake, I have used several of these terms in the text (e.g., "narkom" instead of "people's commissar"), even though they might seem strange to the non-Russian reader.

Vadim Rogovin frequently inserted parenthetical comments, signed with his initials. I have retained them in parentheses. All unsigned notes in square brackets belong to the translator, not to the author.

Many of the most difficult translation problems could not have been solved without the invaluable assistance of Vadim's wife, Galya. She made this book possible in countless ways, for which she deserves our deepest gratitude.

Introduction

The crimes committed in the two and one half years of the Great Purges (from July 1936 to the end of 1938) were so wide-ranging and monstrous that the publication of the entire truth about them threatened to undermine the post-Stalin political regime. Therefore, after the Twentieth Congress of the Communist Party of the Soviet Union [CPSU] in 1956, its leaders carefully measured out in doses the "admissible" truth about the tragic events of the 1930s, mixing this partial truth with untouched Stalinist myths and falsifications. The party leaders frequently retreated from self-exposure and, by the mid-1960s, the subject of the Stalinist terror was taboo.

The more than twenty-year ban on any mention of what lived on as an open wound in the consciousness of the Soviet people did not alleviate, but merely aggravated, the inescapable pain of this wound. The social atmosphere generated by attempts to control or erase the historical memory of the people is clearly described in A. Tvardovsky's poem, "By Right of Memory":

They tacitly order us to forget, forget,
They want to drown in oblivion
The living past. They want waves to close
Above it. Forget — the past! ...
They order us to forget, and softly beg us
Not to recall — memory is sealed so as not
To disturb accidentally the uninitiated with such words...
Others simply have said that all these stories
Of that black day, which cast shadows upon us,
Do us no good.
But all that was is unforgotten,
And unconcealed among the people.
Lies alone bring us loss.
And truth alone shall do us good.[1]

The official ideologues of the CPSU, never known for their historical imagination, were so sure of the stability and longevity of the dominant political regime with its hermetically sealed ideology, that they assumed truthful scholarly investigations and artistic works about the Stalinist terror would see the light of day only after centuries had passed. Indeed, Suslov suggested just such a time frame for the publication of V. Grossman's novel, *Life and Fate*.

But reality did not develop according to the scenarios envisioned by the shortsighted and conservative party bosses who were mired in Stalinist prejudices. The removal of the theme of mass repression from official Soviet historiography virtually handed it to foreign Sovietology and the domestic dissident movement. And insofar as it was impossible, after the Twentieth Congress of the CPSU, to remain so closed to the outside world and so ruthless toward dissident thought as in Stalin's time, the intellectual vacuum in the consciousness of the Soviet people began to be filled with the ideology that was spreading through "samizdat" [self-publishing] and "tamizdat" [publishing abroad]. A serious shift in mass consciousness was produced by the publication abroad in 1973-75 of Alexander Solzhenitsyn's book, *Gulag Archipelago*, which made its way secretly into the USSR and was widely distributed. This book was a revelation for Soviet readers mainly because it contained many "human eyewitness accounts" that had been denied publication in our country. It seemed that the whole truth about state terror in the USSR had finally been told. However, the very genre that Solzhenitsyn had chosen, "oral history" based exclusively on memoir sources, did not allow him to present a full and adequate picture of the events that had occurred in our land before Stalin's death. Moreover, Solzhenitsyn often altered and interpreted his sources in order to make them fit his preconception that Stalinist totalitarianism had arisen from the ideology and revolutionary practice of Bolshevism.

A new upsurge in public interest in the theme of Stalinist terror occurred during the years of political shocks officially known as "perestroika" [rebuilding]. The opening of the Soviet archives revealed that they contained all the documents gathered with bureaucratic precision by party and secret police officialdom. The fetishism with regard to products of not only the clerk's but the executioner's pen was so great under Stalin that the dossier of each prisoner was stamped with the mystical formula: "To be preserved forever."

The flood of publications containing documentary material and memoirs about the Great Purge provoked the liveliest response of the public, immersed at the end of the 1980s in a reevaluation of events occurring fifty years before. The press runs of periodical publications that opened their pages to previously forbidden memoirs, artistic works and analytical articles about the events of the 1920s and 1930s increased several times over. A further advance along these lines would have allowed the presentation of an adequate picture of the inner-party struggle in the VKP(b) [All-Russian Communist

Party (Bolshevik)] and of the terror that brought this struggle to a conclusion. However, the first honest investigations of the tragic pages of our history were rapidly overwhelmed by a massive wave of anticommunist propaganda. "Democratic" journalism moved from criticizing Stalinism to mechanically reproducing the historical versions presented by ideologues of the first Russian emigration and the most reactionary Western Sovietologists. These ideological operations served the same purpose as the historical falsifications produced by the Stalinist school: to cauterize, deceive, distort and poison the historical memory and social consciousness of the Soviet people.

During the still-unceasing ideological clamor, the "democrats" and their "national-patriotic" opponents paradoxically have closed ranks to reject Bolshevism and the October Revolution. The very concept of "Bolshevism" has become the most abusive word both in "right-" and "left-wing" journalism, even though their final conclusions are diametrically opposed. While the "democrats" deduce Stalinist totalitarianism from what is supposedly the inherently "utopian" and "criminal" nature of Bolshevik ideas, the "patriots" (including those who call themselves communists) ever more justify and extol Stalinism by juxtaposing it to Bolshevism.

Many Stalinists come close to an understanding of the social and political meaning of the Great Purge, since they consider it a dividing line in the development of Soviet society, signifying the final rupture of Stalinism with the ideological and political heritage of the October Revolution. A conception of this sort is advanced, for instance, in the works of the emigrant Alexander Zinoviev. In the not too distant past Zinoviev engaged in what may be the most significant vilification (after Solzhenitsyn) of the entire post-October history, and has now turned into an open apologist for Stalin and Stalinism. Zinoviev rejects the conception of the CPSU as a political party that arose before the October Revolution and was linked with Bolshevism as its ideological successor. He calls it Stalin's child, created "in a cruel struggle against the representatives of the Leninist guard."[2]

The journalist S. Kara-Murza has more sharply formulated similar ideas, typical of modern-day "great-power" and "strong state" advocates. He proceeds from the view of Russia as a special "traditional society," unlike the rest of the world, which was demolished by the October Revolution and restored by Stalin. On this basis, he openly proclaims that Stalinism is a "restoration after the revolution (accompanied by the cruel punishment of revolutionaries)."[3] As the reader of this book will see, similar statements were made during the 1930s, only with greater qualifications, by right-wing ideologists of the Russian emigration.

The ideological "renaissance of Stalinism" proved to be possible because over the past decade the "sorting out" of our historical past was conducted not as serious scholarly research, but as light-minded journalistic squabbles and escapades, in which true historical facts were either shamelessly ignored or distorted.

A juxtaposition of the historical versions of the "democratic" or "national-patriotic" persuasions confirms the correctness of Goethe's famous observation: "They say that midway between two opposing opinions lies the truth. By no means: between them lies the problem."[4]

The complexity of scientifically working on the problems connected with the Great Purge is determined primarily by the fact that neither its character nor scale has precedents or analogies in mankind's political history. The Great Purge is different, for example, from the Civil War of 1918-1920, in which one can find much in common with other great civil wars.

At the beginning of the 1930s, Trotsky proposed to write a book, *1918*, in which he intended to compare the civil war in Soviet Russia with the war between the Northern and Southern states in America. In an interview with the Associated Press of America, he said that American readers would be amazed by the analogies between these wars, just as they amazed him in studying the civil war in the U.S.A.[5]

Several generations of Soviet citizens were rightfully proud of the victory of the revolutionary people over the combined forces of the white armies and foreign interventionists, much as Americans even now are proud of the North's victory in the civil war of the 1860s. They considered the tragic period in the development of Soviet society to be the years of forced collectivization and the Great Purge. These, in fact, were two civil wars in which the number of victims was significantly greater than in the civil war of 1918-1920.

Whereas forced collectivization faced an armed response by the peasants, the Great Purge at first glance is a paroxysm of senseless and irrational violence. Even many serious researchers reduce the political function of the Great Purge exclusively to terrorizing the people and, thus, to warning against any resistance to the ruling authorities. Such a conception, leaving many blank spots in the history of Soviet society, reduces complex and contradictory historical events to a simplified schema: the all-powerful Stalin, the party which is fully subordinate to him, and the slavishly mute people.

The filling in of the blank spots results in the introduction into historical analysis of a new component — the resistance of genuinely communist forces to the Stalinist regime — and leads us to the conclusion that Stalinism was able to crush this growing resistance only through the application of state terror in forms and on a scale never before seen in human history.

Drawing on these ideas in my previous book, *1937*, I cast light on the mechanism of the origins and first stages of the Great Purge. As an independent historical investigation, the present book is a continuation of this work. It analyzes events from June 1937 to the end of 1938, and examines the political subjects and social objects of the Great Purge. It discusses the reaction to the purge by various social groups in the USSR and by political forces abroad.

As in my previous books devoted to the history of the inner-party struggle in the VKP(b) and the international communist movement, I have paid most attention to the opposition and struggle between Stalinism and Trotskyism. The logic of this struggle, in which the ideological strength of each of these political tendencies was inversely proportional to its material might, led not only to the physical extermination of the adherents of the Left Opposition, but also to the liquidation of at least two generations of Bolsheviks who had prepared and defended the October Revolution. A specific feature of this extermination campaign against Bolshevism was that the Stalinist clique conducted it under the guise of Bolshevik phraseology and symbolism. Innumerable judicial and extrajudicial frame-ups were constructed while keeping in mind the socialist elements predominant in the consciousness of the masses. In other words, to crush savagely a great revolutionary movement from within, the Stalinists employed political slogans that were borrowed from the movement itself.

The original Russian title of this book, *Party of the Executed*,* was the name acquired by the Communist Party of France after it became the main force in the antifascist resistance and the main object of Hitler's terror in that country. There is even greater foundation for applying this expression to the Bolshevik Party, whose members comprised no less than half of the victims of the Great Purge. The years 1936-1938 witnessed the final replacement of the Leninist party with its Stalinist successor, and the liquidation of Bolshevism as a mass political and ideological force.

---

* The editors of the English translation have chosen a new title, *Stalin's Terror of 1937-38, Political Genocide in the USSR*. We believe that this title suggests the content of the book more clearly to the English-speaking reader, who may not be familiar with the historical analogy inherent in the original title.

1. "Mass Operations"

One of the major milestones of the Great Purges was the June Plenum of the Central Committee in 1937, which crushed any opposition to the Stalinist terror in the party's Central Committee. This plenum, which invested the NKVD [People's Commissariat of Internal Affairs] with extraordinary powers, launched a series of "mass operations."

On 2 July 1937, the Politburo adopted the resolution "On Anti-Soviet Elements." According to a statement at the June 1957 Plenum of the Central Committee, a draft of this resolution written by Kaganovich had been found in the archives. In reply to the accusation that he had written this document, Kaganovich declared that, as often happened at Politburo sessions, he had written it down as Stalin dictated the contents.[1]

The resolution states: "It has been noted that the majority of former kulaks and criminals who were sent at some time from various provinces to northern and Siberian regions, and who returned to their provinces upon completing their term of exile, are the main instigators of all kinds of anti-Soviet crimes and sabotage both in the collective and Soviet farms, as well as in transport and several branches of industry." On this basis the party bodies were instructed "to keep track of all returning kulaks and criminals in order to arrest immediately and shoot the most hostile among them by submitting their cases administratively to troikas. The rest, who were less active but nevertheless hostile elements, were to be re-registered and exiled to regions according to NKVD directives."[2]

On 9 July, the Politburo approved the composition of provincial and republican troikas and the number of former kulaks and criminals who were to be subjected to extrajudicial execution and exile.

On 10 July, Khrushchev sent Stalin a report in which he said: "This is to inform you that altogether the number of criminals and kulak elements who finished their sentences and settled in the city of Moscow and in the Moscow area is 41,305. Among these the criminals make up 33,426 persons. Material at hand allows us to assign 6,500 to the first category of criminals and 26,939 to the second category ... The number of kulaks who completed their punishment and settled in Moscow and in the regions of Moscow is 7,869. Material we have allows us to assign 2,000 people to the first category and 5,869 to the second."[3]

On 31 July, the Politburo confirmed a directive from the People's Commissar of Internal Affairs that ordered the start of the operation "to repress former kulaks, active anti-Soviet elements and criminals." In the directive the contingents subject to extrajudicial repression were widened to include the following categories:

> Former kulaks, who continue to carry out active anti-Soviet activity after returning upon completion of their sentences, escaping from the camps or labor settlements, or concealing themselves during dekulakization;
> Members of anti-Soviet parties (SRs, Georgians, Mussavatists, Dashnaks, former Whites, policemen, enforcement officials, and re-emigrants who have hidden themselves from the places of punishment);
> The most active anti-Soviet elements, who are now contained in prisons, camps, work settlements and colonies;
> Criminals conducting illegal activity and linked to the criminal milieu.

The directive contained instructions on the scale of the repression throughout the republics, regions and areas. It proposed arresting 258,950 people, of whom 72,950 were to be convicted "according to the first category." The plan was to shoot 10,000 people in the camps.

The "operation" was to be carried out in a four-month time span, and the cases were to be investigated "in an expedited and streamlined manner." In accomplishing this task, the repression was extended to the families of those being persecuted. Those families, "the members of which are capable of active anti-Soviet activities," were subject to "transfer to camps or labor settlements." The families of those convicted according to the first category and who lived in large cities, border areas and the resort areas of the Caucasus were subject to resettlement "in other regions of their own choice."[4]

The vagueness and imprecision of the directive's formulations opened the way to the most unrestrained exercise of arbitrary behavior. Semionov, the chairman of the area-wide special troika, recounted during investigation how the "mass operation" was conducted in the Moscow area. He declared that "in the course of one evening we would go through up to 500 cases, and we tried people at the rate of several per minute, sentencing some to be shot, and others to various prison terms. ... We weren't able to read even the summons, let alone look at the material in the dossiers." Semionov's colleague testified, "I repeatedly happened to hear conversations like this between Semionov and Yakubovich after a session of the troika, when Semionov would say to Yakubovich, 'How many did you convict today?' Yakubovich would answer: 'About 500.' Semionov would then laugh, and say to Yakubovich, 'That's not many ... I convicted 600!'"

At the beginning of 1938, the "troika" for the Moscow area reviewed the cases of 173 invalids in prison; 170 of them were sentenced to be shot. As Semionov testified, "We shot these people only because they were invalids who were not being admitted to the camps."[5]

A similar situation existed in other areas, too. Shreider, the former deputy head of the Ivanovo NKVD directorate for the police, recalled the work of the troika in the area. They compiled an "album," every page of which contained the first name, patronymic and surname of the arrested and the "crime" he had committed. After this, the head of the NKVD directorate would write a large letter "R" and then sign his name. The remaining members of the troika usually signed the pages of the "album" for tomorrow — in advance.

As a result of this procedure, from July 1937 to January 1938 the NKVD in the area shot all former SRs; all communists having any, even the most indirect, relationship to the Trotskyists; many former anarchists and Mensheviks; and almost all the former personnel of the Chinese-Eastern Railway.[6]

Besides these categories, the special troikas reviewed the cases of criminals who had repeatedly been convicted of murder, banditry, robbery, escape from prison, and so forth. With such methods, Stalin also hoped to eliminate criminal recidivism during the feverish atmosphere of the Great Terror.

Having acquired a taste for such activities, the secretaries of area committees and heads of the NKVD repeatedly requested that Moscow increase the quotas they had been assigned. These requests were reviewed in the Politburo or decided personally by Stalin, who would give the corresponding directives to Yezhov. As a result, the "mass operation" was extended virtually until the end of 1938. In the second half of 1937, the Politburo sanctioned an increase of 40,000 people above the established quotas. On 31 January 1938, the Politburo affirmed "an additional number of former kulaks, criminals and active anti-Soviet elements subject to arrest" — 57,200 people. During the following eight months, the Politburo made decisions to raise even these quotas by an additional 90,000 people throughout various republics and areas. Thus, more than 400,000 people became victims of this "mass operation," which lasted almost one year.[7]

The second "mass operation" consisted of general reprisals against the representatives of a number of nationalities, primarily those having their own territories that had been part of the Russian Empire, but which had become independent states after the October Revolution (Poles, Finns, Latvians, Lithuanians, Estonians). The "foundation" of these repressions was the unspoken assumption that people who belonged to these nationalities (as well as people of other nations with their own state formations beyond the borders of the USSR), even if they were the most devoted revolutionaries, were inclined to engage in espionage for "their own" state.

The ethnic purges were conducted according to directives from the People's Commissar of Internal Affairs and confirmed by Politburo decrees. Thus, on 31 January 1938, the Politburo adopted the following resolution: "To permit the People's Commissar of Internal Affairs to continue until 15 April 1938 the operation of annihilating espionage and sabotage contingents among Poles, Latvians, Germans, Estonians, Finns, Greeks, Iranians, Kharbintsy,* Chinese and Rumanians, including foreign nationals as well as Soviet citizens. To leave in place until 15 April 1938 the existing extrajudicial procedure of reviewing the cases related to these operations... To propose that the NKVD conduct a similar operation until 15 April and to pogromize (sic — V. R.) the Bulgarian and Macedonian cadres..."[8]

These "mass operations," which had in fact turned into ethnic genocide, were distinguished by their extraordinarily crude and arbitrary actions. Thus, in Rostov, Latvians and Poles were arrested according to lists that had been drawn up on the basis of information from the address bureau. In February 1938, 300 Iranians were arrested here — the entire staff of the shoe-shine cooperative.[9]

In his testimony, Semionov, the chairman of the Special Troika of the NKVD for the Moscow area, said: "During the mass operations of 1937-1938 to remove Poles, Latvians, Germans and other nationalities, the arrests were conducted without the existence of any compromising material... Whole families were arrested and shot, among whom were absolutely illiterate women, minors, and even pregnant women; and all were shot as spies without any evidence, simply because they were nationals."[10]

The reprisals were especially ferocious against communists who belonged to the given nationalities. According to Radzivilovsky, one of Yezhov's closest stooges, local NKVD bodies received the following directive from Yezhov: "Don't stand on ceremony with this crowd, their cases will be reviewed according to the 'album' procedure. You must prove that the Latvians, Poles, Germans and others who are in the VKP(b) are spies and saboteurs."[11]

The greatest number of victims among the "nationals" were Poles and Latvians. The reprisals against them paralleled the liquidation of the social and cultural rights of these nationalities. For instance, at the beginning of

---

* By Kharbintsy they meant people [living in Harbin] who had voluntarily returned to the USSR after the Soviet government had sold the Chinese-Eastern Railway to Japan.

1. "Mass Operations"

Latvian journalists and writers in Moscow, January 1937. Of the twenty-six people in this photo, twenty were shot in 1937-1938 and two survived prison.

the 1930s in the Ukraine and Belorussia, there were 670 Polish schools, two Polish institutes of higher learning, and three theaters; one central, six republican and sixteen regional newspapers were issued in the Polish language. All were closed in 1937-1938. In Moscow, a Latvian theater, club and school were closed.[12]

In 1936, 35,820 Poles had already been victimized. As Khrushchev remembered, "When, in 1936, 1937 and 1938, the real 'witch-hunt' got under way, it was hard for any Pole to hold on, and there could no longer be any talk of promoting them to leading posts. All Poles in the USSR fell under suspicion."[13]

A large number of Latvians were in the USSR because a semi-fascist regime which conducted a merciless struggle against revolutionaries had been established in Latvia after the Civil War. This caused a significant influx of political emigrants from Latvia into the Soviet Union. All the fighters from the Latvian Rifle Division, which had played an enormous role in defending the Soviet regime, remained in the USSR.

In December 1937, the NKVD published an order for the mass arrests of Latvians. The majority of those arrested became victims of group executions. From 5 January through 20 July 1938 alone, there were fifteen instances of group executions in which 3,680 Latvians were shot.[14]

The "Yurasov Card Index"[15] contains the names of more than one thousand Latvian victims, the majority of whom were shot in 1937-1938. Among

V. A. Irbe, commandant of Trotsky's train. Shot on 2 October 1938

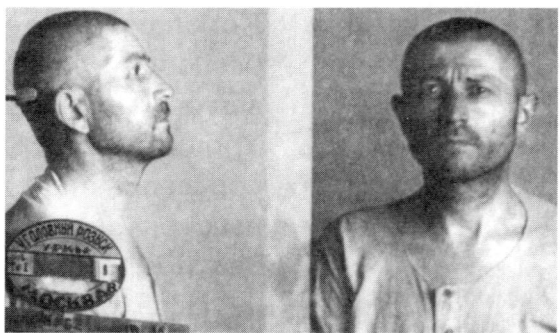

V. P. Zalman, head of security on Trotsky's train. Shot on 17 May 1938

Two of the 67 Latvian riflemen who had served on Trotsky's military train during the Civil War. Many were executed during the "mass operations."

them are no small number of rank-and-file workers, collective farmers, engineers, teachers and so forth. A significant portion is representatives of the qualified layers of the intelligentsia — professors, journalists, writers, economists, diplomats, officers, members of the secret police, etc. More than half of the list contains members of the VKP(b), and more than a third comprises Bolsheviks who had served in the underground, participants in the revolutions of 1905-1907, members of the societies of political prisoners and exiles, and delegates to congresses of the VKP(b). Almost all these people were shot because they were accused of spying for bourgeois Latvia.

Latvians, Lithuanians and Estonians without high social status were deported from Moscow, Leningrad and other major cities to areas containing special settlements.

Several thousand Finns were victimized in the Leningrad area alone, where, at the same time, the authorities closed all the active Finnish schools, technical institutes, houses of culture, churches, newspapers, and publishing houses, as well as the Finnish department at the Herzen Institute.[16]

The first mass deportations of entire nations were carried out in 1937-1938. The largest of these was the deportation of Koreans from the Far East.

1. "Mass Operations" 13

On 10 June 1924, Rykov, the chairman of the Council of People's Commissars, signed "The Charter of the Union of Koreans Living on the Territory of the USSR," according to which the Korean community received wide legal rights and the opportunity to develop their national culture.[17] In the Far East Territory, a national Korean region was created with fifty-five Korean village councils.[18]

In April 1937, an article in *Pravda* said that the Japanese secret services had sent many of its Korean and Chinese agents into the territory of the Far East, "disguising them as inhabitants of this region."[19]

On 21 August 1937, the Council of People's Commissars and Central Committee adopted a secret resolution, "On the Deportation of the Korean Population from the Border Regions of the Far East Territory." It assigned the NKVD the task of resettling, by 1 January 1938, Koreans from the Far East Territory to Kazakhstan and Uzbekistan. The Koreans were accused of mass espionage and readiness to act on behalf of Japan in the event the latter invaded the USSR. All those deported turned into "inhabitants of special settlements" who were forbidden to return to their native areas.[20]

On 11 September, Stalin sent a telegram to the Far East Territory in which he said: "From everything it is evident that the deportation of the Koreans is a pressing matter... We propose the adoption of harsh and timely measures in the precise execution of the calendar plan."[21]

In the course of the deportations carried out in October 1937, about 172,000 Koreans were deported from the Far East Territory. Twenty-five thousand Koreans and 11,000 Chinese were arrested.[22]

The deportation of several national minorities, primarily the Kurdish population, was conducted also in the republics of the Caucasus. Prior to 1937, a Kurdish national theater existed in Armenia; and in Armenia and Georgia there were Kurdish schools and Kurdish-language newspapers. All these establishments were closed in 1937-1938, when a significant part of the Kurdish population was resettled in the Central Asian republics and in Kazakhstan. Iranians were subjected to forced resettlement from Azerbaidzhan to Kazakhstan.[23]

These "mass operations" were carried out in the strictest secrecy, for reprisals against people who had already been punished once, not to mention subjected to ethnic genocide, could not be justified by any, even the most refined, sophistry.

The victims of the "mass operations" comprised approximately half the non-party figures victimized during the years of the Great Purge. For communists there were separate "quotas" (see Chapter 25), but as a rule, party sanctions and a more prolonged investigation preceded the reprisals against them. These reprisals became so widespread that, in January 1938, Stalin sought to camouflage them by creating the impression that the Central Committee was disturbed by the mass expulsions from the party and wanted to end them.

Passport of Van-Vy-Chan, one of many Chinese laundry workers rounded up and executed in Moscow during the purge of "nationals"

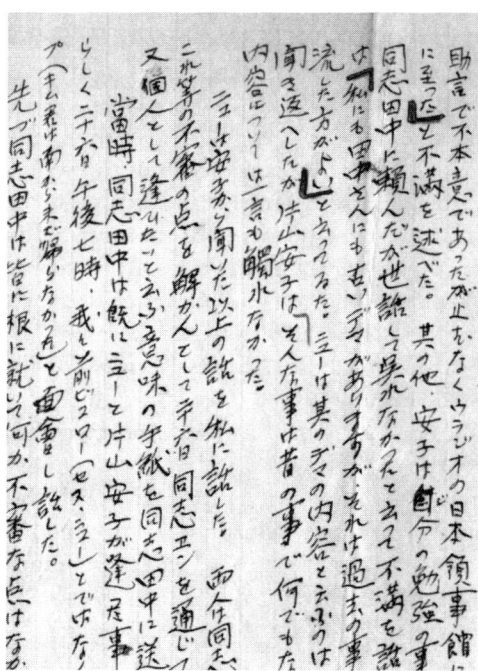

G. S. Kim (Yamasito), a teacher of Japanese at the Communist University of the Workers of the East. Shot on 29 May 1938

Part of a letter confiscated during Yamasito's arrest

2. The January Plenum of the Central Committee: "On the Errors of Party Organizations"

The regular plenum of the Central Committee met on 11, 14, 18 and 20 January 1938. Twenty-eight of the seventy-one members of the Central Committee elected at the Seventeenth Congress (1934) took part in its work. More than half were members or candidate-members of the Politburo.

Recalling Molotov's words at a session of the Supreme Council — "In all important questions the Council of People's Commissars turns for advice to the Central Committee" — the *Bulletin of the Opposition* wrote: "Molotov forgets to indicate which Central Committee he means. For the 'Stalinist' CC chosen at the Seventeenth Congress no longer exists. There is not even a quorum. Could it be that Molotov actually has in mind the majority of the CC, which now sits in the prisons of the GPU or has been shot?"[1]

The main item on the plenum's agenda was the question: "On the errors of party organizations in expelling communists from the party, on the formal-bureaucratic attitude to appeals of those expelled from the VKP(b), and on measures to eliminate these shortcomings." Malenkov, who was not even a candidate-member of the CC, delivered the report. This was an unprecedented occurrence in the party's history, one that had never happened before and would never happen again.

The report indicated that about 100,000 communists had been expelled from the party in 1937 (in the first six months, 24,000; in the second six months, 76,000), and no less than 65,000 unreviewed appeals had accumulated in the party committees. The majority of appeals had been submitted by people expelled during the period of exchanging and verifying party documents (in 1935 and 1936). Malenkov addressed the groundlessness of the majority of expulsions, and declared that after reviewing the appeals the Party Control Commission of the CC VKP(b) had reinstated from forty to seventy-five percent of those expelled in a number of areas.[2]

To demonstrate that the mass expulsions were instigated by "enemies of the people," Malenkov introduced the testimony of a number of arrested slanderers, in which they explained their actions by the desire to provoke dissatisfaction and bitterness among communists. Particularly striking was the testimony of a certain Tregub from Kiev, who told how he and his friends spread slanderous accusations at party meetings and sent written denunciations to all the party and soviet authorities. The report described their behavior as a desire on the part of the slanderers "to conceal their own crimes before the party." However, Tregub's testimony revealed not so much his personal intentions as the monstrous atmosphere that had developed in 1937. Tregub declared:

> I, for instance, would speak at the party meetings at Stankostroi, pointing my finger at the communists sitting there; I would call some Trotskyists, other Bukharinists, and others saboteurs. I would express my political distrust towards some, accuse others of ties with enemies, and, finally, I would write a list of no less than fifteen to twenty people. At the Stankostroi factory, I created such a situation that, in the party organization of eighty to eighty-five people, no less than sixty communists are under suspicion or are being investigated
> ...
> Fearing slander, the honest workers began to run away (from the factory). Others adopted all measures in order to avoid attacks from us, up to groveling before us ... Vorozheikin and I began to go to the party meetings of other organizations with prepared lists of people whom we intended to accuse of belonging to our enemies. We would suddenly appear at these meetings of party organizations with which we had no relations, we would make our way to the tribune out of order, and, without knowing anybody at all, we would label the communists enemies of the people. Everyone already knew Vorozheikin and me. Not only would confusion arise when we appeared at a meeting, but gradually members of the party who were afraid would run from the building, for it often happened that names that accidentally came into our heads right there at the meeting would be added to the existing lists. So it turned out that the party organizations were already terrorized by their own local pseudo-denunciations, and our appearance ... would decisively confirm the supposed truthfulness of their material.

Not only was the practice of denouncing people unconcealed, but on the contrary, it was elevated to the rank of party valor, as Tregub's testimony illustrates: "When I would send lists to the NKVD, I did so in such a way that everyone would know that I had sent the entire list to the NKVD."[3]

Malenkov's report gave many examples of the charges upon which rank-and-file communists were expelled from the party. Thus, Aminev was expelled and removed from work only because his brother had been expelled from the Komsomol for having ties with enemies of the people. After Aminev, all his relatives lost their jobs. Kushchev was expelled and fired from work because of a statement at lessons of his political circle. After giving the "correct" answers to three questions about the possibility of building "complete socialism" and "complete communism" in a single country, he replied to the fourth scholastic question, "And will we fully build communism?": "We will hardly do so fully without the world revolution. By the way, I will look in *Problems of Leninism* to see what Comrade Stalin has to say about this." After Kushchev, his wife was fired on charges of having ties with him. Bykov submitted a statement to his party organization about the arrest of his own brother, with whom "he had no ties," and was immediately expelled from the party. When he asked the party organizer why he had been expelled, the organizer replied, "You understand, we had to expel you. So you gather the evidence and submit an appeal."[4]

The published text of the plenum's resolution gave similar examples. For instance, at one of the enterprises in the Kursk area, the chairman of the factory trade union committee was expelled from the party and arrested only because a non-party worker, whom she had prepared to speak at a pre-election meeting, had become confused in his speech and forgot to name the candidate for deputy of the Supreme Soviet. In another region, a female worker who was summoned to the NKVD in the case of "an arrested Trotskyist," mentioned this to the head of the factory's special department. As a result, she was removed from her job for "ties with Trotskyists," and her sister's husband was fired because he "did not tell of his wife's ties with Trotskyists."[5]

The speakers who participated in the discussion tried to answer the question about why there had been such reprisals instigated under the most absurd pretexts. Mentioning that in the Ukraine there were many instances of expulsions "because of a single anonymous denunciation which said nothing," Kosior explained that "we had lived through a very stormy period, when enemies were being discovered and thrown out of the party in batches, in large and significant groups, when the question of exposing the enemy and forcing him into the open overshadowed all other questions." Kosior confessed that even he, a member of the Politburo, was often afraid to defend a person being expelled, although "there were insignificant grounds for expelling him. This is the way it was for us: here, let us say, rumors were circulating about the impending arrest of this or that party member, for he had been closely linked with others arrested. In the organization, we would say: before they arrest him, we should expel him from the party, because when they arrest him, they will ask us where we were and why we had overlooked him."6

At the plenum people spoke about the groundlessness of the expulsions, but not of the arrests, which they said confirmed the correctness of the expulsions. Moreover, Bagirov declared that he was prepared "to give facts, when even now several people deserve to be arrested, but are at liberty." At this point, even Malenkov felt it was necessary to interject: "Comrade Bagirov, these people have not been arrested since they are at liberty."7

Touching upon slanderous declarations, Bagirov talked about how in Baku there had been a certain Morozova, "a semi-literate person," who wrote denunciations with the help of other "enemies." As a result, "not a single senior employee remained (including Bagirov himself — V. R.), about whom she had not written a statement." In this regard, the following dialogue occurred between Bagirov and Stalin:

> *Stalin*: The authors of the declarations frightened the party leaders.
> *Bagirov*: If this had been the case, then we would have completely fallen apart (*general laughter*) ...
> *Stalin*: They fear the authors of declarations.8

Despite the airing at the plenum of such unseemly facts, its sessions proceeded in the customary major key of other CC plenums. Kaganovich, with particular bravura, declared: "I think that we can say without any exaggeration that the last year — a year of rooting out the party's enemies and enemies of the people — for honest Bolsheviks ... turned out to be a year of the type of Bolshevik education and tempering that we would not receive in ordinary times in decades." Kaganovich called the advancement over the last year of more than 100,000 new leaders "our great Stalinist victory."9 Yaroslavsky was just as optimistic as he evaluated the perspectives of "cadre policy": "It cannot be that ... it was impossible to promote thousands, tens and hundreds of thousands of people who could replace the enemies who appeared in our ranks."10

Kosarev's speech testifies to the existence of a plan for radically replacing arrested communists with "young cadres." He said that in June 1937, a resolution was adopted to bring into the party more than 140,000 Komsomol members, "tested in the struggle against enemies."11

The plenum reviewed two more questions: (1) the new composition of the Council of People's Commissars [Sovnarkom], scheduled to be confirmed during a session of the Supreme Council meeting at the same time, and (2) sabotage in agriculture. Molotov spoke on the changes in the Sovnar-

2. The January Plenum: "On the Errors of Party Organizations"

kom, proposing to "strengthen the Sovnarkom" with new deputies, including Chubar (first deputy), Kosior and Mikoyan. After mentioning that "the chairman of Gosplan, as you know, is not at liberty," Molotov announced the promotion to this post of the 35-year-old Voznesensky. A similar "rejuvenation" was proposed through the appointment of new People's Commissars. Thus, Chvialev was promoted to People's Commissar of Foreign Trade; a few months earlier he had worked as the head of the instructional division of the Academy of Foreign Trade.[12]

Eikhe gave the report on sabotage in the countryside. Two months earlier he had been appointed the People's Commissar of Agriculture. His announcement that "the agricultural system turned out to be particularly littered with enemies of the party and the people" evoked approval from Stalin, who interjected: "It stands in the first ranks." Eikhe's report, published in the main newspapers, was designed to fill in the gaps in the "sabotage" already uncovered, demonstrating that it involved branches of agriculture no less than those of industry. When Eikhe's time had expired, Stalin gave a positive assessment of his efforts when he declared: "It can be extended, the report is very good."[13]

The plenum's resolution on the main point of the agenda was published on 19 January. It gave a sufficient portrait of the scale of what was in fact a new party purge that had surpassed the number of victims from all previous official purges. For example, in Kiev, the secretary of the city committee continuously asked the communists there: "Haven't you written a statement at least against somebody?" As a result, "compromising statements" were submitted against half the members of the city's party organization. Several village schools in the Ukraine halted the teaching of basic academic disciplines because the majority of teachers had been fired.

Particularly striking was the announcement that the Party Control Commission for the Kuibyshev area had received statements from "many expelled by the regional committees of the VKP(b) as enemies of the people, *demanding that they either be arrested*, or have the shameful label removed from them" (emphasis added — V. R.).

The resolution, which did not hesitate to provide examples of illegality and arbitrary decisions, created the impression that injustice was being allowed, as a rule, when it came to party repression, but not when it came to arrests. To reinforce the widely circulated idea that the NKVD "makes no mistakes," a statement was issued: in a number of areas a large number of communists had been expelled from the party and declared enemies of the people, whereas the NKVD "finds no grounds to arrest these people who have been expelled."

The resolution recalled that as long ago as the Central Committee's letter from 24 April 1936, "On the Mistakes in Reviewing Appeals from Those

Expelled from the Party during the Verification and Exchange of Party Documents," a ban had been placed on removing those expelled from their jobs. Meanwhile, even before appeals had been sorted out, many organizations continued to deprive of work and living quarters not only those expelled, but also "people connected with them," such as acquaintances and relatives.

The resolution named two groups of people who participated in the slander campaigns. The first included "individual communist-careerists who were trying to distinguish themselves and gain promotion on the basis of expulsions from the party and repression directed against party members. Such people were trying to insure themselves against possible accusations of lacking vigilance by means of employing widespread repressions against party members." This real category of slanderers was joined by another, phantom category of "those elaborately camouflaged enemies" who were trying "to destroy our Bolshevik cadres, to sow uncertainty and excessive suspicion in our ranks, and to deflect the attention of the party organizations from exposure of genuine enemies of the people." These "saboteurs and double-dealers," who "in pursuit of provocative goals ... achieve the expulsions from the ranks of the VKP(b) of honest and decent communists, thereby fending off the blow to themselves and preserving their own positions in the party," had produced, according to the resolution, one more category of enemies — people who were dissatisfied and embittered by the widespread repression, and whom "Trotskyist double-dealers ... quickly latch onto and skillfully drag into the swamp of Trotskyist sabotage." In actual fact, the resolution aimed not at weakening, but at strengthening, the inner-party terror by demanding the "exposure and final extermination ... of deliberate and *involuntary* enemies of the people (emphasis added — V. R.)."

Just as in the previous campaigns to correct "excesses," blame was placed on local apparatchiks, who "approach ... the expulsions of communists from the party with criminal light-mindedness ... despite repeated directives and warnings from the Central Committee of the VKP(b)." The resolution juxtaposed rank-and-file communists, who had been subjected to "soulless and bureaucratic attitudes," to "certain leaders," who "consider it a trifle to expel thousands and tens of thousands of people from the party."[14]

3. The January Plenum of the Central Committee: The Postyshev Affair

The main scapegoat at the January 1938 plenum was Postyshev, whom Stalin had already led through several degrees of degradation and humiliation. At the beginning of 1937, Postyshev was removed from the post of first secretary of the Kiev area committee and city committee, and then, from the post of secretary of the Central Committee of the KP(b) of the Ukraine. On 30 March of the same year, he was elected first secretary of the Kuibyshev city committee, and in June, first secretary of the Kuibyshev area committee.

After his transfer to Kuibyshev, it was not difficult to foresee Postyshev's subsequent fate. In June 1937, Trotsky wrote: "Postyshev rose to secretary of the CC due to his zealous participation in the struggle against Trotskyism. In the Ukraine in 1933, Postyshev purged 'nationalists' in the party and state apparatus, and drove the Ukrainian People's Commissar Skrypnik to suicide by slandering him as 'a protector of nationalists.' Four years later, it turns out that Postyshev, who remained dictator in the Ukraine after his exploits, has been accused of protecting nationalists: as a satrap in disgrace, they recently transferred him to the Volga area. One must assume that this is not for long. Not only wounds, but even scratches no longer heal. Whether Postyshev resorts to suicide or confesses to crimes he has not committed, in either case he will find no salvation."[1]

At his new post, Postyshev tried to rehabilitate himself by increasing his "vigilance." In August 1937, the arrival in Kuibyshev of the CC secretary Andreev spurred ferocious reprisals against the party apparatus in the area. Andreev told Postyshev: "The Central Committee feels that you are conducting no struggle against enemies and that you must mobilize the

Pavel Postyshev
(1887-1939)

Kuibyshev party organization to do so." In the words of Ignatov, the second secretary of the Kuibyshev area committee (a recruit from 1937, who twenty years later would become a member of Khrushchev's Politburo), after feeling the whip, "[Postyshev's] style became different, everywhere he began to shout that there were no decent people... He began to shout that enemies were everywhere." As Ignatov related, "for two weeks all the secretaries of the city regional committees and the entire apparatus of the regional committees in the city of Kuibyshev ran about with magnifying glasses. Postyshev would take a magnifying glass, summon a representative of the regional committee and begin to examine notebooks. They tore up all our notebooks. On the covers, they found the fascist swastika and went so far as to find reindeer on cookies — fascist symbols, and on caramel candies they found a flower, which is also a fascist emblem."[2] Searching for fascist symbols or for Trotsky's silhouette on bookjackets and notebooks was not Postyshev's invention. People in other localities resorted widely to "investigations" of this sort, sometimes even including schoolchildren in the search for hostile emblems.

Postyshev's ruthless terror against party cadres was unprecedented even by the standards of 1937. Within a week after the re-elections of the Kuibyshev city committee, out of the forty-one newly elected members, seventeen people were arrested. At one of the sessions of the Kuibyshev city council, thirty-four of its deputies were removed on Postyshev's orders (and in his

3. The January Plenum of the Central Committee: The Postyshev Affair

presence). During the last five months of 1937 alone, 3,300 communists were expelled from the party in the Kuibyshev area.[3]

Postyshev turned directly to Stalin to receive approval for the arrest of the most important figures. On 29 November 1937, he sent Stalin a coded message asking him to sanction the arrest of Filippov, the head of the Penza department of the NKVD, for "a counter-revolutionary conversation," containing the following remarks: "We are expelling many from the party, communists are dropping like flies," and "shouldn't Comrade Stalin write a second article about dizziness from success." The coded message was marked with speedy resolve: "For the arrest. Stalin."[4]

Postyshev's innovation, which won him reproach even before the plenum, was the dissolving of more than 30 regional committees on the grounds that the majority of their leaders had turned out to be enemies of the people. This action was carried out so hastily that even the reports about it sent to the CC did not give an adequate picture of the scale of the pogrom against the party committees. As Malenkov said, "No one in the area committee understood how many regional committees had been dissolved. At first they said that it was thirteen; then they said that it was twenty; and when they were told that thirty of their regional committees had been disbanded, they were surprised. And now it turns out that thirty-four were dissolved."[5]

On 9 January 1938, the Politburo passed a resolution describing the decision of the Kuibyshev area committee to dissolve regional committees as "politically harmful" and "provocative." "For the widespread use of such an exceptional measure in the party leadership as the dissolution of party committees without any grounds and without the knowledge of the CC of the VKP(b)," Postyshev received a strong reprimand; he was removed from his post and "placed at the disposal of the CC."[6]

In this capacity Postyshev took the floor at the January plenum. His tale of terror against party cadres seemed so monstrous even in the eyes of CC members who had seen a lot, that they showered his entire speech with insistent questions: Could it possibly be that all the party personnel in the area were enemies? Even such inveterate executioners as Yezhov, Beria, and Bagirov were indignant and criticized Postyshev's explanations.

The following excerpt from the transcript shows the character of Postyshev's speech, which had virtually turned into an interrogation:

> *Postyshev*: The leadership there (in the Kuibyshev area), both party and soviet, was hostile, from the area leadership to the regional.
> *Mikoyan*: All of them?
> *Postyshev*: What's surprising here? ... I counted, and it turns out that enemies had sat there for twelve years. When it comes to the soviets, the same hostile leadership had been there. They sat there

and chose their own cadres. For instance, in our area executive committee, right down to the technical personnel, they are out-and-out enemies who have confessed to their destructive work and who behave rudely, starting with the chairman of the area executive committee, his deputy, consultants, secretaries — they are all enemies. Absolutely all the departments of the area executive committee were littered with enemies ... Now take the chairmen of the regional executive committees — they are all enemies. Sixty chairmen of the regional executive committees — are all enemies. The overwhelming majority of second secretaries, not to mention first, are enemies, and not simply enemies, but many have been spies: Poles, Latvians, they picked the most arrant scum ...

Bulganin: Weren't there any honest people there? ... It turns out that there was not a single honest person.

Postyshev: I am speaking about the leading big shots. Out of the leading big shots, out of the secretaries of the regional committees, and the chairmen of the regional executive committees, it turns out that there was hardly a single honest person. And why are you surprised?

Molotov: Aren't you exaggerating, Comrade Postyshev?

Postyshev: No, I am not exaggerating. Look, take the area executive committee. People sit there. There is evidence, and they confess, they give testimony about their own hostile work and espionage activity.

Molotov: We have to verify the evidence.

Mikoyan: It turns out that on the lower levels, in all the regional committees, there are enemies ...

Beria: Could it possibly be that all the members of the plenums of the regional committees turned out to be enemies? ...

Kaganovich: You can't base yourself on the fact that they all were crooks.[7]

Knowing that a total purge of party cadres was sweeping the land, Postyshev, who not long before had been accused of liberalism, could not understand why he was now being reproached for the exact opposite — for excessive zeal in "rooting out enemies of the people." Hence the refrain which recurs throughout his entire speech: "Why are you so surprised?"

However for Stalin, who had planned the complete destruction of the former party and state apparatus, the mass dissolution of party committees was nevertheless a dangerous step which could provoke mass protest from communists. Therefore, as the subsequent speakers mentioned Postyshev's initiative, Stalin tossed out threatening comments: "This amounts to shoot-

3. The January Plenum of the Central Committee: The Postyshev Affair

In December 1935, Postyshev suggested to Stalin that the elka, or New Year's tree, be brought back. Stalin agreed. In this cartoon by Boris Yefimov, Postyshev is portrayed as Father Frost, bringing toys to children. He was arrested on February 26, 1938 and shot on February 26, 1939.

ing the organization. They are soft on themselves, but they are shooting the regional organizations ... This means raising the party masses against the CC, there is no other way of interpreting it."[8]

After this remark, almost every speaker felt it was necessary to cast a stone at Postyshev. Kaganovich's contribution was particularly ferocious. He declared that Postyshev's excessive zeal in Kuibyshev was a continuation of his insufficient zeal in Kiev. "Comrade Postyshev's blindness which was evident in Kiev," Kaganovich explained, "borders on a crime, because he did not see the enemy even when all the sparrows were chirping on the rooftops ... His main sin is that he is incapable of distinguishing an enemy from a friend ... and a friend from an enemy. This is his original sin. If in Kiev he could not distinguish an enemy from a friend, if he took an enemy for a friend, then the same sin has led him in Kuibyshev to a state where he cannot distinguish a friend from an enemy, and he consigns friends to the enemy camp."

Kaganovich announced that before the plenum, Postyshev had been designated to be chairman of the Commission of Soviet Control, but after his speech at the plenum, "the Central Committee would hardly be able to entrust him with such a post."[9]

After this announcement, the completely demoralized and frightened Postyshev asked for the floor to make a statement in which he abjectly confessed to his mistakes. "How I gave this speech — I cannot understand myself," he said. "... I have made many mistakes. I did not understand them. Perhaps even now, I do not completely understand them. I will say only one thing, that I gave an incorrect, a non-party speech, and I beg the Plenum of the CC to forgive me for this speech."

Stalin concluded the discussion of the "Postyshev affair" with brief remarks. He said: "Here in the presidium of the CC or in the Politburo, as you wish, the opinion has formed that after all that has unfolded, we have to take some kind of measures with regard to Comrade Postyshev. And the opinion has formed that we must remove him from his position as candidate-member of the Politburo, while leaving him as a member of the CC."[10] This proposal was immediately adopted.

This slight ray of hope in Postyshev's fate lasted only about a month. On 10 February, the Politburo adopted a resolution: "In view of compromising material received from the NKVD and the Kuibyshev organization, transfer Comrade Postyshev's case for review by the Party Control Commission of the CC VKP(b)."[11] On 17 February, the Politburo sent the commission's findings to members of the CC for confirmation. In them Postyshev was charged not only with reprisals against honest communists, but also with sending the village regional committees "provocative and deleterious directives" about using collective farmers' cows for field work during sowing and harvesting time, etc. Postyshev was also indicted for the "excessive trust and support" that he had shown toward "enemies of the people." Basing itself on the testimony received from a number of people in Postyshev's entourage, the commission "established" that he "at the very least knew from them about the presence of a counter-revolutionary, right-Trotskyist organization, was informed about participation in it by his closest assistants and about the harmful and provocative work they had carried out."[12] On the basis of all these charges, Postyshev was expelled from the CC and the party by referendum, and arrested during the night of 21-22 February. A year later he was sentenced to the supreme penalty and shot on the same day.

In the eyes of rank-and-file party members, the decrees of the January plenum seemed to indicate a certain softening of the terror. However in 1938, no fewer people were arrested and shot than in the previous year, which is usually considered the culmination of the Great Purge. The signal for the further unfolding of mass repression was the third Moscow trial, which was a much more grandiose inner-party conspiracy than all the conspiracies mentioned in the previous trials.

4. Preparation for the Third Show Trial

The third open trial (March 1938) was prepared over a much longer period than the two previous ones. Its main defendants were under investigation for more than a year — sufficient time to extort the most fantastic testimony.

The defendants at the trial, twenty-one people, fell into four basic groups. The first contained two former members of the Politburo and leaders of the Right Opposition, Bukharin and Rykov. The second included three well-known former Trotskyists. Two of them, Krestinsky and Rozengolts, had broken from the Left Opposition in 1926-1927. Prior to their arrest in 1937, they had never been expelled from the party or subjected to repression. Rakovsky remained unbroken for a longer time; he capitulated only in 1934.

The third group contained five men charged with medical murders: three non-party Kremlin physicians, Gorky's secretary Kriuchkov, and Kuibyshev's secretary Maksimov-Dikovsky (whose entire "guilt," for which he was shot, was based on the fact that he allegedly did not summon physicians when Kuibyshev felt unwell, and did not prevent him from leaving work and heading home). The last and largest group comprised people's commissars, secretaries of republic party organizations and other highly-placed bureaucrats, who had never taken part in opposition groups and were selected from an enormous number of people arrested in 1937.

In speaking about the reasons for the confessions at the open trials, Avtorkhanov rejected Koestler's version that these confessions were dictated by a fetishistic devotion to the party, which was identified with Stalin. "At the Moscow Trials, we saw people who gave the confessions Stalin wanted under torture," wrote Avtorkhanov, "but there were no Rubashovs there (by which he meant figures resembling the main character in Koestler's novel — V. R.), although there were no enemies of Soviet power either. The Rubashovs nev-

Avel Yenukidze,
shot on 30 October 1937

ertheless could be found, and I met them myself, but only among the middle level of the elite. These were politically limited people. 'There is no revolution without sacrifices; in the interests of socialism I will carry out the party's orders and will confirm my testimony at the trial!' — that is how they reasoned. The secret police calmly put such simpletons on trial, and just as calmly shot them after the trial. And they dealt the same way with those who gave up and did not withstand the tortures. However we saw only dozens of people at the trials, but not the hundreds and thousands of others whom Stalin did not allow to appear at an open trial."[1]

The trial was preceded by a lengthy selection of people who were more submissive to the demands of the investigation. This is shown at the trial by the absence of people often mentioned by the defendants as leaders and active participants in the "right-Trotskyist bloc." Among these "invisible defendants" were Rudzutak and Antipov, the deputies of the Sovnarkom's chairman; Yenukidze, the secretary of the Central Executive Committee of the USSR [TsIK]; the famous diplomats Karakhan, Iurenev, and Bogomolov; the area committee secretaries Razumov and Rumiantsev, and many others. Some of them were shot before the trial and others, a few months after. Evidently, they all refused to provide false testimony at the open trial.

One of the most famous victims of the Stalinist terror was Yenukidze. Since 1918 he had worked as secretary of the All-Russian Central Executive Committee [VTsIK]. He was removed from this post in 1935, when he was accused of littering the Kremlin apparatus with anti-Soviet elements, of sheltering people hostile to Soviet power, and of leading an immoral life.

4. Preparation for the Third Show Trial

Yenukidze, Stalin, and Gorky

In 1937 Yenukidze was arrested. According to Orlov, he explained to the investigators the cause of his conflict with Stalin: "My entire crime consisted of this: when he told me (at the end of 1934 — V. R.), that he wanted to stage a trial and then shoot Kamenev and Zinoviev, I tried to talk him out of it. 'Soso,' I told him, 'there's no argument — they have done you a lot of harm, but they have long since paid enough for it: you have expelled them from the party, you hold them in prison, their children have nothing to eat... They are Old Bolsheviks, just like you and me' ... He looked at me as if I had murdered his father and said: 'Remember, Avel, he who is not with me is against me.'"[2]

Trotsky reacted to the persecution of Yenukidze with an article entitled, "Behind the Kremlin Walls." In it he wrote that after the victory in the Civil War, for Yenukidze as for many other bureaucrats, it seemed that "a quiet and carefree life lay before them. But history deceived Avel Yenukidze. The main difficulties lay ahead. In order to supply millions of large and small bureaucrats with beefsteaks, a bottle of wine and other comforts of life, a totalitarian regime was required. Of course Yenukidze — by no means a theoretician — could hardly deduce Stalin's autocratic rule from the bureaucracy's yearning for comfort. He was simply one of Stalin's instruments in establishing the new privileged caste. 'Immorality in everyday life,' with which he was personally charged, was in actual fact an organic element of official policy. It was not because of this that Yenukidze perished, but because he could not go all the way. He held out for a long time, was submissive and adaptive, but a limit appeared that he could not transgress."

At first, Stalin promised to give Yenukidze an honorary position as chairman of the Transcaucasian TsIK in exchange for his post as secretary of the TsIK of the USSR. Instead, Yenukidze's appointment as head of the Caucasian resorts, "which bore a note of mockery — fully in Stalin's style — foretold of nothing good." Following this appointment, the charges of everyday immorality, too grand a lifestyle, etc., meant that Stalin had decided to act in installments. However, after disgrace had befallen him, Yenukidze refused to yield. The second trial of Zinoviev-Kamenev, which ended in their execution, "evidently stiffened the resolve of old Avel ... Avel became indignant, grumbled, perhaps even swore. This was too dangerous. Yenukidze knew too much. It was necessary to act decisively."

Of course, Yenukidze entered into no conspiracies and prepared no terrorist acts. "He simply raised his grayed head with horror and despair ... Yenukidze tried to stay the hand which was raised over the head of the Old Bolsheviks. This proved to be enough." But Yenukidze did not yield even after his arrest. He refused to give any testimony that would allow them to include him among the defendants of a show trial. "A defendant without a voluntary confession is no defendant. Yenukidze was shot without a trial, as a 'traitor and enemy of the people.'"*

Noting that "Yezhov readily used a Mauser against anyone that Stalin pointed his finger at," Trotsky wrote: "Yenukidze was one of the last. With him, the old generation of Bolsheviks has left the stage, without, at least, self-humiliation."[3]

Nor did they manage to extort confessions, it seems, from former Georgian Oppositionists, especially Mdivani, whose "crimes" had been mentioned as early as the Radek-Piatakov trial. These people, whose struggle against Stalin over problems of national policy began in 1922, belonged subsequently to the Left Opposition, and after its defeat were sent into exile. From them, only Kote Tsintsadze remained irreconcilable to the very end; after refusing to sign a statement of capitulation, he died in Siberia from a serious illness. Mdivani, Okudzhava, and others capitulated in 1929 and, as a reward, were returned to responsible posts. Beria's words tell us something about their political moods in the 1930s. He bitterly wrote that Mdivani and his comrades "talked about a supposedly 'unbearable regime' ... about the use of some kind of 'secret police' methods, about how the situation of the workers in Georgia was supposedly deteriorating."[4]

On 9 July 1937, the Supreme Court of Georgia in a one-day closed session reviewed the cases of seven defendants, including Mdivani and Okud-

---

* Although it was announced in the press that Yenukidze and Sheboldaev had been shot with five others according to a court sentence received in December 1937, both had been shot two months earlier. – V. R.

zhava, and sentenced them to be shot for the usual charges of "spying, wrecking activity and sabotage," and for preparing terrorist acts.

Commenting on the results of the Tbilisi trial, L. Sedov wrote: "The old Georgian revolutionaries, unlike many of their former Moscow friends, did not allow themselves to be broken ... Besides, Stalin probably hopes to use the closed 'trials' to reinforce the inquisitional techniques of obtaining confessions, undermined by the outcome of the Moscow Trials. Future defendants will be presented with two alternatives: a secret trial followed by the executioner's bullet, or a false confession with the hope of receiving a 'chance,' à la Radek."[5]

Among the prominent Georgian Oppositionists, only Kavtaradze managed to survive. He passed through tortures in the cellars of the NKVD and mock executions, but in 1939 he was freed on Stalin's personal orders and even returned to a leading position. Kavtaradze's case was the single example of Stalin's "forgiveness" of a former active Oppositionist. Nevertheless, in the postwar period, when Kavtaradze was deputy minister of foreign affairs, at one of the government receptions Stalin suddenly called him to the side and said threateningly: "But still, you wanted to kill me."[6]

The NKVD intended to fabricate an open trial of the "reserve center of rightists," where they planned to include former members of the groups headed by Syrtsov-Lominadze, Riutin and A. P. Smirnov-Eismont.[7] However, these people, whose names were mentioned at the trial of the "Right-Trotskyist Bloc," refused to confess their guilt and were shot according to sentences at closed trials. For Syrtsov, such a trial occurred in September 1937, and for A. P. Smirnov (named at the trial of the "Right-Trotskyist Bloc" as a member of the "center" of rightists), in February 1938.

The greatest difficulties for the organizers of the trial were the extortion of confessions from the five main defendants whose presence at the trial Stalin considered mandatory (Bukharin, Rykov, Rakovsky, Krestinsky and Rozengolts). Several months before their arrest, they all knew it was inevitable. According to Barmine's testimony, when he talked at the beginning of 1937 with Krestinsky, who was still first deputy of the People's Commissar of Foreign Affairs, the latter was in such a depressed state that "with obvious effort he tried to answer business questions, but then he would forget about them... Krestinsky's sense of being doomed did not leave me during my conversation with him."[8]

In March 1937, Stalin told Krestinsky that it was awkward for a person who had been in the Opposition to remain at a post where he would have to come into frequent contact with foreigners. Krestinsky was transferred to the People's Commissariat of Justice and, after working there for two months, was arrested.[9]

Another person brought to a state of complete demoralization was Rozengolts. Before his arrest, he tried to meet with Stalin, wishing to convince

Khristian Rakovsky
(1873-1941)

him of his innocence. At the trial, his efforts were interpreted as proof that he intended to murder Stalin during their meeting.

It seems that obtaining a confession from Rakovsky — one of the oldest activists of the revolutionary movement and Trotsky's personal friend for three decades — presented particular difficulties for the trial's organizers. Although continuously transferred from 1928 on to ever more severe conditions of exile, Rakovsky capitulated later than other leaders of the Opposition. This surrender opened up the period of his profound political degeneration. After he was reinstated into the party in November 1935, he sent Stalin a humiliating letter with the following:

> I learned yesterday of my re-acceptance into the party and on the same day I received my party card.
> For me this was a great and joyful event.
> Allow me on this occasion to express to you my warm gratitude and my deep appreciation.
> I assure you, dear Iosif Vissarionovich, as the leader of our great party and as an old fighting comrade, that I will apply all my strength and abilities to show that your trust and the trust of the CC is justified.
> With Bolshevik greetings.
> Sincerely devoted to you,
> Kh. Rakovsky[10]

During the days of the first Moscow trial, Rakovsky wrote a disgraceful article demanding that the defendants be shot.[11]

Arrested in January 1937, Rakovsky presented voluminous written accounts about the motives that prompted his oppositional activity. In them he indicated, in particular, that he had arrived at the conclusion that the proletarian dictatorship had degenerated in the USSR. "While remaining socialist in its foundations, insofar as the land and other instruments and means of production are social property," he wrote, "the proletarian dictatorship has turned into a new form of state. The estate of functionaries has replaced the proletariat and the laboring masses (as the bearers of power — V. R.)."[12]

Of course, the investigators didn't need this testimony, which in fact was an indictment of the Stalinist regime, but testimony which would politically compromise the Opposition. Rakovsky began to give testimony of this kind only after several months in prison. He cautiously tried to refer to the reasons for this at the trial. He said:

> "I remember, and I never will forget this as long as I am alive, the circumstance that finally propelled me along the path of giving testimony. During one of the sessions of the investigation I learned ... that Japanese aggression had been launched against China, against the Chinese people, and I learned about the unconcealed aggression of Germany and Italy against the Spanish people. I learned about the feverish preparations of all the fascist states for the unleashing of world war. That which the reader usually reads every day in small doses in telegrams, I received all at once in a huge, massive dose. This news acted on me in an earthshaking manner. ... I felt that from now on my duty was to help in this struggle against the aggressor ... and I told the investigator that from the following day I would begin to give him full and exhaustive testimony."[13]

Of course, the investigation did not limit itself to playing on the military threat facing the Soviet Union and other sophisticated ideological and psychological devices.

The majority of the investigators who prepared the given trial were arrested in 1938. At interrogations, they declared that the testimony of the defendants was received as a result of Yezhov's promises to spare their lives, as well as brutal torture and indignities. In 1956, Rozenblium, the former head of the medical clinic at Lefortovo Prison, recounted that during the investigation they brought Krestinsky in an unconscious state from his interrogation to the clinic. He had been severely beaten, and his entire back was a mess.[14]

Long before the trial, Stalin had organized a series of provocations, which included sending Rakovsky on an official trip to Japan and Bukharin to Europe. In 1937, Trotsky suggested that these trips were arranged in order to later charge Rakovsky and Bukharin with having contact with foreign intelligence services.[15] And indeed, Rakovsky "confessed" at the trial that during his stay in Japan, he had been recruited by the special services there. From Bukharin, who stubbornly refused to acknowledge the espionage charges, they managed to extort only the confession that he had agreed with the Menshevik Nicolaevsky that, in the event that the "conspiracy" failed, the Second International would raise a campaign in defense of the "conspirators."[16] During the trial itself, Nicolaevsky announced that during his meeting with Bukharin about the purchase by the Soviet government of material from the archives of Marx and Engels, there had transpired "nothing even remotely resembling negotiations of a political character. The meetings did not bear the character of secret conferences and were well known to the organizers of today's Moscow Trial."[17]

Some of the defendants, it seems, were blackmailed with compromising facts contained in their biographies. Thus, Zelensky and Ivanov were charged with working prior to the revolution for the tsarist Okhrana (secret police). Commenting on these charges, Trotsky recalled that immediately after the October Revolution, the party committees and the Cheka had conducted a thorough study of the police archives to uncover provocateurs, who were then severely punished. All this work was completed in 1923. During the investigation, besides information about police agents, material was discovered which showed that several young revolutionaries had behaved faint-heartedly or with insufficient caution during interrogations, that they had renounced their views, etc. Stalin archived all such material and used it to blackmail the compromised people in order to achieve their complete obedience. Zelensky and Ivanov might belong to this category. Trotsky expressed his absolute certainty that they never were agents of the Okhrana; "but Stalin had some kind of documents that gave him the opportunity to break the will of his victims and to lead them to the final stage of moral degradation. Such is Stalin's system!"[18]

The procedure to which Postyshev was subjected is indirect confirmation that Trotsky's supposition is close to the truth. Eight months before his arrest, the Politburo passed a resolution in which "the fact was established that Comrade Postyshev submitted a humiliating appeal in 1910 to the commander of the Moscow military district about lessening his sentence from his trial." Attributing "this inadmissible act" to "Postyshev's youth and backwardness," the Politburo issued him a reprimand for not informing the Central Committee about the submission of this appeal.[19]

A much more complicated problem is bound up with Bukharin's behavior in prison. In his final statement at the trial, he said that he had "refused to speak" for about three months. A more relaxed regimen had been established for him than for his codefendants, as a result of which in prison he "worked, studied and preserved his mind."[20] At the beginning of the investigation, he was allowed to send his wife a letter with a request to select and send him books from his library that might be needed for his scientific research. Larina twice sent him books that Bukharin used for work on his manuscripts. Several books needed for work were also given to Bukharin by his investigator, Kogan.

In his prison cell, Bukharin wrote more than fifty printer's pages (about 1,250 pages). It is obvious that he could not have created such a quantity of relatively finished works of the most varied genres, written with the assistance of countless Russian and foreign sources, if he had been subjected to torture or even lesser torment.

All of Bukharin's prison writings were sent to Stalin, who kept them in his personal archive until his death. They saw the light of day only in 1994-1996. Among three large manuscripts that survived, the first chronologically is "Socialism and Culture," which is the second part of the work, "The Crisis of Capitalist Culture, and Socialism."[21] The first part, "The Degradation of Culture Under Fascism," written mostly before Bukharin's arrest, has not yet been found. Besides a sharp criticism of fascism, this book includes an apologetic picture of "the building of socialism" in the USSR.

After this, Bukharin wrote an incomplete biographical novel,[22] a theoretical work titled *Philosophical Arabesques*,[23] and a book of poems.[24]

Stalin's archives contain four letters from Bukharin sent from prison. Among them, we now know there was a wide-ranging letter, written three months before the trial and labeled with Bukharin's remarks: "Top secret. Personal. I ask that this *not be read* by anyone else without I. V. Stalin's permission." In this letter, Bukharin repeatedly returns to a depiction of his neurotic state ("I am now shaking from consternation and a thousand emotions and can hardly control myself"; "I have no idea what state I will be in tomorrow and the next day, etc. Perhaps, like a neurasthenic, I will be enveloped in such universal apathy, that I will not be able to move a finger"; "Lord, if only there were an instrument with which you could see my shattered and tormented soul!").

"Standing on the edge of an abyss, from which there is no return," wrote Bukharin, "I give you my word of honor, on the eve of my death, that I am not guilty of the crimes that I acknowledged during the investigation. ... I had no 'way out' except to acknowledge the charges and the testimony of others and then to develop them: otherwise, it would turn out that I 'was not laying down my arms.'"

In attempting to give theoretical grounds for such behavior, Bukharin "developed approximately the following conception": Stalin had "some kind of *grandiose and bold political idea* of a general purge (a) in connection with the pre-war period, (b) in connection with the transition to democracy. This purge embraces (a) those guilty, (b) those under suspicion, and (c) those potentially under suspicion. Here they could not pass me by. They neutralize some in a certain way, others in another way, and still others in a third way. Beseeching Stalin not to perceive these thoughts as if he were reproaching the leader "even in musings with myself," Bukharin wrote: "I have come such a long way from my diapers, that I understand that *grand* plans, *grand* ideas, and *grand* interests trump everything, and it would be petty to raise the question of myself *in the same breath with the universally-historic* tasks which lie primarily on your shoulders." According to Bukharin, the only paradox which tormented him was that Stalin might not be proceeding from this "universally-historic" idea, but might actually believe in his crimes. "*Then* what do we have? That I *myself* am helping to get rid of a number of people (starting with myself!), that is, I am committing a deliberate *evil! Then* nothing can justify this. And everything becomes confused in my mind, and I feel like letting out a scream and beating my head against the wall: for I am becoming the reason for the destruction of others. What, then, must be done? What is to be done?"

Trying to persuade Stalin that "in recent years I ... have learned to value you in an intelligent way and to love you," in the conclusion to his letter, Bukharin asked him for his "final forgiveness (sic! — V. R.)" and assured him: "Iosif Vissarionovich! In me you have lost one of your most capable generals, who is truly devoted to you."

Declaring that "I have no intention ... of asking you for anything, and I do not intend to implore you for anything that would make the cause swerve from the rails on which it is moving," Bukharin nevertheless did present a few requests: (1) To give him the chance to die before the trial, for "it is a thousand times easier for me to *die*, than to suffer through the impending trial"; (2) In case he received the death penalty, "not to shoot me, but allow me to take poison in my cell (give me morphine, so that I can fall asleep and never awaken) ... Give me the chance to spend my last seconds the way I want. Have pity! ... I beg for this ..."

Meanwhile, cherishing the hope that his life would be spared, Bukharin proposed in this case to send him to America, where he "would conduct a campaign about the trials, wage a mortal struggle against Trotsky, win over large layers of the vacillating intelligentsia, become what amounts to an Anti-Trotsky and conduct this matter both on a grand scale and with definite enthusiasm." Bukharin even offered guarantees which could be used in these endeavors: to send with him a qualified Chekist, to retain his wife in the USSR and so forth.

Feeling that such a scenario might interest Stalin, Bukharin proposed a second variant as well: to exile him "if only for 25 years to Pechora or to

Kolyma, to a camp: I would set up there a university there, a museum of local history, a technical station, and so forth, institutes, a picture gallery, an ethnographic museum, a zoological and botanical museum, a camp journal, or a newspaper."[25]

This letter was distributed in 1956 to members and candidate-members of the Presidium of the Central Committee and to secretaries of the CC of the CPSU. But even this document failed to prompt the members of the "collective leadership" to take some kind of steps with regard to Bukharin's rehabilitation.

Bukharin's letter, of course, could not have provoked anything but mocking satisfaction in Stalin. It only moved him to the extent that he continued his insidious game with Bukharin. With these goals in mind, Bukharin was allowed to write a letter to his wife one and a half months before the trial, in which he spoke about the works he had written in prison. Judging from the contents of this letter, Bukharin had been promised that all his manuscripts would be handed over to his wife. He even asked her to retype them "in triplicate."

Bukharin was also promised a meeting with his wife ("in all cases and no matter what the outcome of the trial, I will see you after it is finished"). Understanding that during such a meeting a candid conversation would be impossible, Bukharin wrote: "No matter what you read, no matter what you hear, no matter how horrible the things they say about me, no matter what I say, ... remember that the great cause of the USSR lives on, and this is the main thing, whereas the fate of individuals is transitory and miserable."[26]

Bukharin was deceived this time, as well. His wife was arrested and sent from Moscow in June 1937, and the letter, it goes without saying, did not reach her.

Having selected the defendants and applied every possible moral and physical torture during the pre-trial investigation (in various combinations), the organizers of the trial may have felt that the trial would proceed without any obstacles or glitches. However, problems started on the first day of the trial.

Nikolai Krestinsky (1883-1938)

5. The Episode with Krestinsky

In the indictment, the outlines of the conspiracy were presented in the following manner. In 1928, a center was formed for the underground organization of "rightists," and in 1933, they created a "contact center" for establishing links with the Trotskyists, as a result of which the "right-Trotskyist bloc" came into being. After the arrests of 1936, the "center" of this bloc was joined by Rozengolts and Krestinsky — from the Trotskyists; Bukharin, Rykov, Rudzutak and Yagoda — from the rightists; and Tukhachevsky and Gamarnik — from the military.[1]

This construction failed at the first session of the trial, however, when an episode occurred which was unforeseen and troublesome for its organizers. When Ulrikh asked the defendants whether they acknowledged their guilt, Krestinsky answered: "I am not a Trotskyist. I never was a participant in a 'right-Trotskyist bloc,' and I knew nothing about its existence. I did not commit a single one of the crimes with which I am personally charged."[2]

After several additional questions addressed to Krestinsky, Ulrikh was compelled to pass on to the interrogation of the other defendants, who obediently affirmed their testimony at the pre-trial investigation. Next Vyshinsky began to question Bessonov, an activity which soon turned into a cross examination of Bessonov and Krestinsky. Bessonov declared that while Krestinsky was the USSR's ambassador to Germany in 1933, he gave Bessonov, as an adviser to the embassy, directives "not to allow normal relations between the USSR and Germany." In response to the prosecutor's questions along these lines, Krestinsky rejected all of Bessonov's testimony and declared that in his conversations with the latter "there had not been a single reference to Trotskyist directives."[3]

When Vyshinsky asked Krestinsky why he had lied at the pre-trial investigation, thereby showing his "disrespect toward the investigation," Krestinsky responded that he hoped to discredit this testimony "at a trial session, if one were to take place." Then Vyshinsky went beyond the framework of

Nikolai Krestinsky

the examination of Bessonov and began to question Grinko and Rozengolts about their criminal ties with Krestinsky. Rozengolts confirmed that he had conducted "Trotskyist negotiations" with Krestinsky, and Grinko said that Krestinsky had helped him establish contact with foreign intelligence. However, Krestinsky continued stubbornly to state that his testimony at the pretrial investigation "from beginning to end was incorrect," and explained that he felt that "if I said what I am saying today... then my declaration (of his innocence – V. R.) would not reach the leaders of the party and government."[4]

In the course of the interrogation, Krestinsky kept mentioning his letter to Trotsky from 27 November 1927, where he spoke of his "break with Trotskyism." Vyshinsky declared that there was no such letter in his dossier. In reply, Krestinsky noted that this letter had been taken from him during a search.[5]

Vyshinsky began the evening session with an interrogation of Grinko, who announced that Krestinsky had put him in touch with "fascist circles of a state which is hostile to the Soviet Union." During this interrogation, the prosecutor turned to Rykov, who confirmed that he had repeatedly spoken with Krestinsky as "a member of an illegal organization."[6] However Krestinsky stubbornly denied all these facts, as he had done earlier.

At the morning session of 3 March, there was no mention of Krestinsky. However at the evening session of the same day, Vyshinsky started by questioning Krestinsky, and this procedure turned into a cross-examination between Krestinsky and Rakovsky. In response to a question about his relationship with Rakovsky, Krestinsky replied that after Rakovsky had been exiled,

5. The Episode with Krestinsky

he had corresponded with him and asked Kaganovich to transfer Rakovsky from Astrakhan, a city with an inclement climate, to Saratov. Rakovsky then declared that Krestinsky "never broke from Trotskyism" and, as confirmation of this, announced that in 1929 he had received a letter from Krestinsky in which the latter had tried to persuade him to return to the party, "naturally, in order to continue Trotskyist activity."[7]

After this exchange, Vyshinsky announced that on his orders "there has been a review of the documents taken in a search of Krestinsky's apartment." As a result, a letter to Trotsky had been found, the existence of which the prosecutor had earlier denied. Excerpts were read from this letter, in which Krestinsky wrote that the tactics of the opposition over the last six months had been "tragically wrong." Excerpts were also read from the statement of capitulation sent by Krestinsky to the CC, which had been published in April 1928 in the central newspapers.

Commenting on this episode in the trial, Trotsky noted: "In 1927 Krestinsky wrote me a letter from Berlin to Moscow in which he informed me of his intention to capitulate before Stalin, and he advised me to do the same. I replied with an open letter announcing the severing of all relations with Krestinsky as well as with all the other capitulationists... But the GPU continues to construct its show trials exclusively on capitulators, who for many years have been playthings in its hands. Hence the necessity for the prosecutor Vyshinsky to show that my break with Krestinsky had a 'fictitious character.' To prove this was the task of another capitulator, the 65-year-old Rakovsky, who declared the capitulations were 'a maneuver'... Rakovsky did not explain, however, and the prosecutor, of course, did not ask, why he, Rakovsky, did not carry out this 'maneuver' for seven years, but preferred to remain in the harsh conditions of exile in Barnaul (Altai), isolated from the entire world. Or why, in the fall of 1930, Rakovsky wrote his famous phrase in an indignant letter from Barnaul against the capitulators: 'The most terrible thing is neither exile nor prison, but capitulation.' And why, in conclusion, did he himself capitulate only in 1934, when his physical and moral strength had finally dissipated?"[8]

After the excerpts had been read from Krestinsky's letters of capitulation, he suddenly declared that he fully confirmed the testimony he had given at the pre-trial investigation. Then the prosecutor turned to him and asked how they were in that case supposed to understand his statement yesterday, which "can be seen in no other way than as a Trotskyist provocation at the trial." In response, Krestinsky said: "Yesterday, under the influence of a momentary and sharp feeling of false shame, evoked by the circumstance of sitting on the defendants' bench and by the painful impressions from the reading of the act of indictment, deepened by my state of illness, I was not in any condition to tell the truth... And instead of saying — Yes, I am guilty, I almost mechanically answered — No, I am not guilty."[9]

Of course one could hardly call "mechanical" the consistent denial by Krestinsky of all charges over the course of two court sessions.

Evidently, Krestinsky's "confession" was influenced by the conduct of the person "exposing" him, i.e., Rakovsky, who for many years had been considered the most irreconcilable of the opposition's leaders.

As for Rakovsky, in his further conduct at the trial it seems that he followed all the prosecutor's demands. Acknowledging that his ties as an agent with the "Intelligence service" began supposedly as far back as 1924, he added that Trotsky at that time "had given his blessing in this matter." In 1934, according to Rakovsky, this contact was reactivated through the famous English philanthropist Lady Paget.[10] However when it came to a concrete description of how he carried out the assignments given him from foreign intelligence services, Rakovsky virtually repudiated his confessions about espionage. He announced that he had given the Japanese information about the effect that cancelling the ration-card system had on the level of wages, and that he had given the English "an analysis of the latest construction from the standpoint of the relations of the republics on the periphery to the center."[11] It is clear that carrying out "assignments" of this kind, even if they had taken place, could in no way have been called espionage.

Characterizing Rakovsky's conduct at the trial, Victor Serge noted that "it is as if he deliberately compromised the trial with testimony, the falseness of which would be obvious to Europe... Rakovsky talks about Emile Bure, about Madeleine Paz, and Fyodor Dan (as people with whom he had espionage ties – V. R.), knowing that they would quickly expose the lie to the entire world." Rakovsky, Serge continued, could not directly uncover the "amalgam" of the trial, because in this case "they would have immediately shut his mouth and others would have lied about him and in his place... No, only two things are possible, either subtle sabotage of this kind, or a hysterical outburst as with Krestinsky."[12]

6. Bukharin and Vyshinsky

Vyshinsky had great difficulty with Bukharin's conduct at the trial.

At the beginning of his questioning, Bukharin addressed the court with an appeal: to give him the opportunity to freely deliver his testimony and to present an analysis of the ideological and political composition of the bloc. In doing this he wanted to avoid, if only for a short while, the unceremonious and mocking questions coming from the prosecutor. Vyshinsky, however, insisted on denying this appeal as something which impinged on the rights of the prosecutor. Nevertheless, even in the questioning that proceeded in the form insisted on by the prosecutor, Bukharin managed to say much that Vyshinsky did not want him to say, and to refute much of what Vyshinsky was demanding that he admit.

Thousands of his contemporaries in the USSR and abroad, and dozens of researchers of more recent times, have re-read with special attention and considered carefully the pages of the transcript that contain Bukharin's interrogation in order to find an explanation of his conduct at the trial — for his behavior differed significantly from that of all the other defendants.

Even in the first few minutes of the questioning, Bukharin admitted his guilt "for the entire totality of crimes committed by this counterrevolutionary organization ("the Right-Trotskyist Bloc"), independently of whether I knew or did not know, whether I participated or did not directly participate in this or that act, because I am responsible as one of the leaders and not as a minor figure in this counter-revolutionary organization."[1] However, after giving such a blanket confession, Bukharin then proceeded to systematically destroy all the concrete charges presented to him.

Bukharin adhered to these positions very tenaciously throughout the trial. Unlike Krestinsky and Yagoda, who first denied and then admitted the facts that were discrediting them, he never once abandoned his position of categorically denying his participation in espionage and murders. He categorically denied that he had known anything about the preparations for Kirov's murder, or about the espionage activity of the "bloc."[2] By doing all this, Bukharin led Vyshinsky to such a state that the latter declared he would be forced to stop the questioning, "because, you, obviously, are pursuing a definite tactic and do not want to tell the truth; instead you are hiding behind a flood of words, using chicanery, and retreating into the realm of politics, philosophy, theory, and so forth, which you should forget once and for all, for you are charged with espionage and are, obviously, according to all the evidence of the investigation, a spy for one of the intelligence services." However, even after this tirade, Bukharin continued to deny his ties with foreign intelligence, and pointed out that the prosecutor had not even asked him about this during the pre-trial investigation.* Then the thoroughly exasperated Vyshinsky turned to Bukharin with a question that was absurd, coming from the mouth of the prosecutor who had conducted the pre-trial investigation: "Would you be so kind as to confess before the Soviet court, which intelligence service recruited you: the English, German or Japanese?" Bukharin, of course, replied: "None whatsoever."[3]

The same tactic — decisive rejection of the charges that had not been mentioned during the pre-trial investigation — was used by Bukharin more than once at the trial. Apparently, Bukharin — who had been handed over to Vyshinsky on 1 December 1937 — had over the course of three months created such difficulties for the prosecutor that the latter was not able to extort from him many of the necessary confessions. Vyshinsky decided to rely on the testimony of the other defendants to discredit Bukharin.

A particularly generous number of charges against Bukharin were scattered throughout the testimony of Ivanov, who declared that as early as 1921 Bukharin had said that he was preparing cadres who, as soon as he gave the word, would be ready to "remove Lenin ... up to and including physical methods." Later, Ivanov asserted that in 1926, Bukharin (who was then in a bloc with Stalin – V. R.) told him that "it was necessary to prepare for a struggle in open combat with the party," and for this "to work in the underground to assemble cadres and to lure the most influential party members into our network." In Ivanov's words, from 1928 he worked on Bukharin's assignment to transform "the Northern Caucasus into a Russian Vendée," i.e., to prepare and organize kulak uprisings. Finally, Ivanov described his conversations with Bukharin at the end of 1936 and the beginning of 1937 (when Bukharin was under voluntary confinement in his apartment and did not meet with anyone except his own family – V. R.), in which Bukharin informed him of the measures being undertaken to accelerate the attacks of Germany and Japan on the

---

* These words were omitted in the newspaper account and restored in the full stenographic transcript of the trial after foreign journalists who were present in the courtroom included them in their correspondence from the trial.

6. Bukharin and Vyshinsky

Nikolai Bukharin
(1888-1938)

USSR and to murder the members of an illegal organization of "rightists," who were inclined to "repent before the Soviet authorities."[4]

As Ivanov was being questioned, Bukharin completely denied all his testimony. During further questioning, he challenged Vyshinsky's references to the damaging testimony given by Ivanov and Sharangovich on the grounds that they both were provocateurs.[5] Meanwhile Ivanov was accused at the trial of working for the Tsarist Okhrana before the revolution, and Sharangovich of working for Polish intelligence in 1920. But their names were mentioned by Bukharin in another context, which was obvious: he had in mind their provocative role at the present trial.

It seems that immediately before the trial Stalin demanded that Vyshinsky obtain Bukharin's confession at the trial about his ties with foreign intelligence services. Bukharin's intransigence on this point drove Vyshinsky into such a frenzy that he began to ask Bukharin questions which he knew could not receive a positive answer. Even at the beginning of the questioning, he began to list the countries in which Bukharin had lived in emigration and to ask whether Bukharin had been recruited there by the local police. In reply Bukharin noted that his ties with the police consisted of the fact that he repeatedly ended up in Russian and foreign jails. The last time the issue was raised, the following dialog ensued between the prosecutor and defendant:

> *Bukharin*: ... It would, of course, be preferable for you to say that I considered myself a spy, but I did not consider myself one and do not now.

Vyshinsky: That would be the most correct of all.
Bukharin: That is your opinion, but my opinion is different.⁶

Bukharin was just as thorough in destroying other charges made against him. In response to the prosecutor's insistent questions, he declared that he knew nothing about the "bloc's" ties with White émigré circles, German fascists, and Poland; that the question of weakening the USSR's defense capability was never discussed in his presence; that he did not adhere to a defeatist position; that he had spoken against opening a front in the event of war; and that he was against any territorial concessions to Germany.⁷ In rejecting the prosecutor's assertion that the leaders of the rightists discussed the question of separating Belorussia from the USSR, Bukharin told Vyshinsky: "I have the right to speak to the court not as you wish, but the way things are in actual fact."⁸ Finally, in response to the prosecutor's mocking attacks he declared angrily: "I do not consider the time and place to be particularly appropriate for witticisms. I, too, am capable of having a sharp tongue ..."⁹

Meanwhile, Bukharin named actual facts from his political activity, although sometimes he introduced them in exaggerated form. He said that as early as 1919-1920 "among my students at Sverdlov University a definite group arose which very quickly began to grow into a faction." He was referring to the so-called "Bukharin school," which during the period of the legal struggle against the Left Opposition was the main ideological weapon of the ruling faction headed by Stalin. Later Bukharin named the main groups which belonged in 1928-1929 to the Right Opposition, and announced that he came to Yagoda "for tendentiously selected material." Bukharin had already spoken about this matter — the study of GPU material about the hostile reaction of the peasants to emergency measures being taken — at the April Plenum of the CC in 1929. Finally, he described his negotiations at the end of the 1920s with Kamenev and Piatakov, at which they discussed the question of forming an anti-Stalinist bloc.¹⁰ These facts, too, had a basis in reality.

All these confessions, however, fell far short of laying the foundation for charging Bukharin with criminal conspiratorial activity, which was Vyshinsky's main assignment. Even less conducive to this assignment was Bukharin's testimony about the motives of the "rightists," who at the beginning of the 1930s allegedly wanted to "overthrow Stalin's leadership which had been so valiant." Bukharin declared that the "rightists" considered the collective farms the "music of the future," and they "pitied, out of so-called humanitarian considerations, the peasants who had been persecuted as kulaks." They had spoken against "over-industrialization" and excessive budgetary strains, and they looked "at our enormous factories, growing gigantically, as some kind of voracious monsters who would devour everything and deprive the broad masses of the means of consumption."¹¹ All these were the actual views of the "right-

6. Bukharin and Vyshinsky

Vasily Ulrikh
(1889-1951)

ists," who had outlined them in their declarations and in Bukharin's famous article, "Notes of an Economist."

Such a turn in the testimony provoked the wrath of Ulrikh, who interrupted Bukharin and declared: "It was proposed that you give testimony about your anti-Soviet counterrevolutionary activity, yet you are giving us a lecture." However Bukharin continued to speak about the ideological views of the "rightists" and in particular about their "slipping onto the rails of bourgeois-democratic freedom." Vyshinsky hastened to interpret this statement in a directly opposite sense: "In short, you slid into the camp of out-and-out fascism."[12]

Later Bukharin spoke about how the rightists worked on the "Riutin Platform" in 1932, which supposedly was named after Riutin in order "to conceal the rightist center and its leading figures." However this statement, too, upset Ulrikh, who said: "You still are beating around the bush; you are saying nothing about your crimes."[13]

Under pressure from the chairman of the court and from the prosecutor, Bukharin actually acknowledged only two crimes committed by the "bloc" in which he had participated. The first consisted of the intention "to arrest the Seventeenth Congress." There had been reference to the preparation of a "palace coup" and the "seizure of the Kremlin," as well as the arrest of the Seventeenth Congress, in the testimony of other defendants, too. However Bukharin, and then Rykov after him, declared that, before any concrete preparation of the action under consideration, the plan had been rejected by both the "rightist" and the "contact" centers.[14]

The second "crime" occurred when Bukharin sent Slepkov to the Northern Caucasus and Yakovenko to Siberia in order to organize kulak uprisings; in the last instance, moreover, the uprising was to be made with forces composed of former red partisans.[15] This confession was also striking for its obvious absurdity, although it was not completely invented out of thin air. Apparently, Bukharin had actually talked with these people, not of course for the purpose of orienting them toward organizing anti-Soviet uprisings, but to find out how far the insurgent moods among the peasants in these regions had gone (the social tension among them had reached such a degree in 1932-1933 that many communists feared the outbreak of peasant rebellions there). That was how Kaganovich interpreted the talks between Bukharin and Slepkov at the end of the 1980s: "They asked Slepkov at a face-to-face confrontation: did Bukharin send you to the Northern Caucasus? — Yes, he did. — What assignments did he give you? — He gave us assignments to find out the moods of the Don and Kuban Cossacks, to see if they were ready or not for something to happen."[16] In Vyshinsky's interpretation, these "assignments" turned into directives to lead peasant uprisings. However, it was obvious that any anti-Soviet Cossacks would by no means choose the Bolsheviks Bukharin and Slepkov to be their leaders.

Bukharin undoubtedly thought over the lessons of the preceding trials and, proceeding from them, constructed his own tactics in the courtroom. During the entire trial he repeatedly demonstrated his superiority over Vyshinsky, was impertinent and derisive toward him, and drove him into a blind alley. The sharpest exchange between Bukharin and Vyshinsky erupted during the review of the "conspiracy," which allegedly took place in 1918.

7. The "Conspiracy" of 1918

A significant innovation at the third trial in comparison to the previous ones was the shifting of the criminal activity of the defendants to the first years of the existence of the Soviet regime. To accomplish this shift, an investigation of the "conspiracy" of 1918 was launched that occupied several court sessions. According to the act of indictment, the majority of the members of the party's Central Committee at that time had taken part in this conspiracy.

Insofar as they had not managed to obtain a confession from Bukharin during the pre-trial investigation regarding this question, Vyshinsky arranged the courtroom investigation in such a way that, at first, the witnesses he called were questioned. Among them were two former leaders of the Left SRs (Kamkov and Karelin) and three former "Left Communists" (Yakovleva, Osinsky and Mantsev). Such a number of witnesses looked very imposing, all the more so since witnesses were not summoned with regard to all the remaining aspects of the indictment.

The starting point for returning to events that had happened twenty years earlier, and for casting them in "conspiratorial" tones, was a statement made by Bukharin in the course of the discussion of 1923. In defending the idea of not allowing factions inside the party, Bukharin then gave the following example as evidence: in 1918 the factional struggle over the conclusion of peace with Germany had become so sharp that the Left SRs came to him, as leader of the faction of "Left Communists," with a proposal to arrest Lenin for twenty-four hours and to form a coalition government; the opponents of the Brest Treaty would have thereby undermined the peace treaty and been able to launch a "revolutionary war."

Although Bukharin added that the matter had been limited to a passing conversation that had no political consequences, his allies of that time — Zinoviev and Stalin — set out to blow this episode out of proportion. In response, a group of "Left Communists" sent a letter to the editors of *Pravda*, in which they said that the issues under discussion could only be seen as "absolutely insignificant incidents." The authors of the letter announced that, at one time, the Left SR Proshian had laughingly said to Radek: "You are always writing resolutions. Wouldn't it be simpler to arrest Lenin for a day, to declare war against the Germans, and then, after this, to re-elect Lenin unanimously as chairman of the Sovnarkom?" "Proshian then said," the letter's authors continued, "that of course Lenin, as a revolutionary who found himself in a position of having to defend against the invading Germans, while scolding both us and you in every possible way ("you" being the Left Communists), would nevertheless conduct a defensive war better than anyone else... This proposal ... was not discussed, since it was seen to be a ridiculous fantasy and a joke on Proshian's part... Comrade Radek told Lenin about this incident, and the latter laughed with regard to the plan." A similarly light-hearted conversation, the letter's authors noted, had occurred between Kamkov, on the one side, and Bukharin and Piatakov on the other.[1]

As Bukharin himself would later say, immediately after his conversation with the SRs, he told Lenin about it. Lenin made him give his word of honor not to tell anyone else about the matter. However, six years later, at the height of the struggle against the Left Opposition, Bukharin broke his pledge, which would have painful consequences for him at the time of his first rupture with Stalin. At the April Plenum of the CC in 1929, Stalin gave a tendentious reinterpretation of the facts when he declared: "The history of our party knows examples such as Bukharin, who, during the time of the Brest Treaty, under Lenin, ended up in the minority on the question of the treaty, ran to the Left SRs, to the enemies of our party, and conducted behind-the-scenes negotiations with them, trying to form a bloc with them against Lenin and the CC. *What kind of arrangement he made back then with the Left SRs — unfortunately remains unknown to us.* But we do know that the Left SRs intended at that time to arrest Lenin and carry out an anti-Soviet coup... (my italics – V. R.)."[2]

One of the tasks of the trial was to fill in the "blank spot" in Bukharin's old confession in such as way that it would seem that Bukharin and other leaders of the "Left Communists" had made a deal with the Left SRs to arrest and murder Lenin, Stalin and Sverdlov.

In commenting on this phantasmagorical version, Trotsky wrote: "Whoever knows people and relationships will easily understand the absurdity of this charge. Bukharin displayed toward Lenin the devotion of a child to his mother. As for Stalin, he was in 1918 such a secondary figure that it would never have come into the head of the most inveterate terrorist to select him as a victim."[3]

Trotsky addressed in greater detail the reasons for such fantastic inventiveness in his article "Super-Borgia in the Kremlin," where he outlined a scenario in which Stalin may have poisoned Lenin. Recalling that Bukharin in camouflaged form had shared his suspicions in this regard, Trotsky stressed that charging Bukharin with the desire to kill Lenin was initiated by "the same aggressive-defensive 'reflex of Stalin,' which was so clearly displayed in the case of Gorky's death." "The naive and excitable Bukharin," wrote Trotsky, "was reverential toward Lenin … and if he was impertinent toward him in polemics, then it was in no other way than on his knees. Bukharin, who was as soft as wax, to use Lenin's expression, did not have and could not have independent and ambitious plans. If someone had predicted long ago that Bukharin would one day be charged with preparing an attempt on Lenin's life, each one of us (and Lenin would be the first) would have advised that the speaker be placed in a lunatic asylum. Why then did Stalin need such a completely absurd accusation? Knowing Stalin, we can say with certainty: this is his reply to the suspicions which Bukharin incautiously voiced regarding Stalin himself."[4]

At the trial, the witnesses from among the former "Left Communists" declared: the inner-party struggle over the question of the Brest Treaty had assumed such aggressive and irreconcilable forms that the "Left Communists" resorted to illegal methods and formed a conspiratorial bloc with the Left SRs. During the testimony of these witnesses, Bukharin conducted himself very aggressively, interrupting the questioning and causing no small amount of difficulty for the prosecutor. Thus, he asked Yakovleva a number of questions which suggested the patent absurdity of the version about the "conspiracy." Vyshinsky demanded that all these questions be struck since they "did not relate to the case." Then Bukharin turned to the chairman of the court with the request for clarification: "Do I have the right to ask the questions which I feel need to be asked, or is their character to be determined by someone else, namely, the citizen prosecutor?"[5] This statement pointed so demonstratively to the prosecutor's violation of the most elementary court procedures that, during the examination of the next witness, Vyshinsky declared he would no longer insist on striking Bukharin's questions if they were needed by the latter for his defense. At this point Ulrikh announced that the court was now objecting to the asking of these questions, and he accused Bukharin of obstructing the work of the court.[6]

In the course of cross examination, Bukharin nevertheless managed to say that he was rejecting the testimony of the witnesses who were presenting "arrant nonsense." He recalled that during the discussion of the Brest Treaty, the "Left Communists" and the "Trotskyists" held a majority in the CC, and that the party was holding an open polemic over this question. In the course of this, the "Left Communists" aimed at winning a majority by legal means, i.e., by voting at party meetings. Therefore, the intention to arrest "three party leaders" in this period "would have been absurd from every point of view."[7]

Announcing that the only discussion with the Left SRs about the arrest "of certain people" had taken place after the signing of the treaty, Bukharin stressed several times that, during this discussion, "in no case" did anyone propose the murder of these people, but, on the contrary, negotiations were held to secure and guarantee absolutely their complete "safety," and to see "that not a single hair on the head of the respective people would be harmed."[8]

During the cross-examinations, there were several sharp exchanges between Bukharin and Vyshinsky that clearly showed the prosecutor's exasperation and the readiness of the defendant to defend the truth to the last:

> *Vyshinsky*: How do you explain that they (the witnesses) are lying?
> *Bukharin*: You should ask them...
> *Bukharin*: ... I am saying what I knew, but as for what they know, that is a matter for their own conscience to speak about it.
> *Vyshinsky*: You have to explain somehow why it is that three people who were your former accomplices are speaking against you.
> *Bukharin*: Don't you see, I have neither enough material nor psychological evidence to clarify this question.
> *Vyshinsky*: You cannot explain.
> *Bukharin*: Not that I cannot, but that I simply refuse to explain.

Pointing to obvious contradictions in the testimony of the witnesses, Bukharin declared to the prosecutor, not without a note of mockery: "They should first reach an agreement among themselves."[9]

Finally, there was an unequivocal political aim in his reply to Vyshinsky's assertion that Bukharin, in several instances, had single-handedly decided questions concerning the activity of the "Left Communists." In this regard Bukharin said: "The times were such, citizen prosecutor, that this was absolutely unthinkable."[10]

The scenario developed by Stalin and Vyshinsky was designed to attribute criminal intentions not only to Bukharin, but to other members of the CC of that time. In this regard, Yakovleva declared that Bukharin had told her: "Trotsky also admits the possibility of developing the struggle to the point of ... the physical annihilation of leading figures in the government and in the party. He then named Lenin, Stalin and Sverdlov."[11]

According to the testimony given by Yakovleva and Osinsky, participants in the conspiratorial bloc with the "Left Communists" included not only Trotsky, but also Zinoviev and Kamenev. Insofar as it was well known that these people supported Lenin's position during the "Brest" discussion, Osinsky gave the following explanation: their defense of the Brest Treaty was "only a very sophisticated double game"; in actual fact they entered into a bloc with the "Left Communists," insisting while doing so on observing "extremely deep conspiratorial secrecy."[12]

7. The "Conspiracy" of 1918

Andrei Vyshinsky
(1883-1954)

It therefore followed from the testimony of the witnesses that the majority of party leaders and members of the October CC were already "traitors" and "conspirators" in 1918.

Both in the cross-examination and in his final words, Bukharin mentioned several times that the faction of "Left Communists" included "a number of famous names," among whom, however, he named only Kuibyshev, Menzhinsky and Yaroslavsky.[13] Mentioning Kuibyshev and Menzhinsky was understandable — they were people who had managed to die before the trial and they were officially held in honor, especially since at the trial they were declared to have been killed "by the right-Trotskyist bloc." It is less clear why, among the many people who remained at liberty during the trial, Bukharin named only Yaroslavsky, although, for instance, another former "Left Communist," S. Kosior, was a member of the Politburo at the time of the proceedings.

Following the "Left Communists," the Left SRs were summoned to a court session. Kamkov confirmed his conversation with Bukharin, but only in the variant which Bukharin himself had outlined in 1923. According to Kamkov, the CC of the Left SRs not only did not make a decision about coming to an agreement with the "Left Communists," they did not even discuss this question.[14]

Karelin behaved quite differently; his examination was preceded by a strange dialogue between Vyshinsky and Bukharin. In response to the prosecutor's question as to whether Bukharin recognized the witness as Karelin, Bukharin gave the following reply: "His bearing, which he now has, is very different from what it was... I had a hard time recognizing him when he was with you (at a face-to-face confrontation – V. R.), but after seeing him when he was with you, I now recognize in him the same person."[15]

Karelin significantly widened the time frame of the "conspiracy." He declared, first of all, that his party had already concluded a bloc with the "Left Communists" at the end of 1917, and secondly, that he had informed Bukharin not only about the preparation of the Left SR uprising, which occurred in July 1918, but about Kaplan's attempt on Lenin's life, whereupon Bukharin had demanded that they speed up this terrorist act.[16]

After these words, Vyshinsky turned to an examination of Osinsky, who confirmed that Kaplan's shot had been the result of directives and organizational measures that had been developed and carried out by the bloc, "starting with the 'Left Communists' and ending with the Right SRs." After this, Vyshinsky could not refrain from asking Bukharin: "Who gave you the assignment to prepare this crime, which intelligence service gave the orders?" He received Bukharin's reply: "I deny this fact entirely."[17]

Nevertheless, the version of Bukharin's participation in preparing an attempt on Lenin's life not only made its way into the *The Short Course of the History of the VKP(b)*, but found "artistic expression" in the film *Lenin in 1918*, directed by M. Romm and based on A. Kapler's film script.

8. The Mystery of Bukharin

In his indictment speech, Vyshinsky singled out Bukharin for special attention. For an entire hour he outlined the broad chronology of Bukharin's "crimes," including every instance of theoretical and political disagreement the latter had, first with Lenin and then with the Stalinist clique, enlarging and exaggerating these differences. Rather embittered by Bukharin's behavior at the trial, Vyshinsky tried to humiliate him as much as possible by using the most ignoble expressions and epithets. "With his hypocrisy and insidiousness," the prosecutor exclaimed bombastically, "this man has surpassed the most perfidious and monstrous crimes which human history has known."[1]

In his closing statement, Bukharin struck a few blows at Vyshinsky. It may be that the strongest blow was his phrase virtually equating the present trial, which had based all the charges on the confessions of the defendants, with the frame-ups of the Inquisition: "[Relying upon]confessions from the defendants is a legal principle of the Middle Ages."[2] Rejecting the testimony of the other defendants which Vyshinsky had presented in his indictment speech, Bukharin directed attention to the fact that the defendants — who had been accused of ties with the Tsarist Okhrana — had declared that they joined the underground organization of rightists "out of fear of being exposed... But where is the logic here? It is remarkable logic: out of fear of being exposed, to enter a terrorist organization where they might be caught the next day. It is difficult to imagine; I, in any case, cannot imagine this. But the citizen prosecutor believed them, even though everything sounds patently unpersuasive."[3]

Bukharin once again solemnly declared himself guilty for all the crimes of the "bloc," although he stated that personally he had never given any directives for sabotage, he had never had any ties with foreign intelligence services, and the charges of his participation in murders were "quite transparent." He acknowledged his guilt "in the perfidious plan to dismember the USSR" only on the grounds that "Trotsky had negotiated with regard to territorial concessions, and I was in a bloc with the Trotskyists."[4]

Finally, Bukharin virtually discredited the trial as a whole as one that had tied into a "bloc" people who had not had any relationship to each other. Ridiculing the explanation of complicity in the conspiracy advanced by Vyshinsky, he declared: "The citizen prosecutor explained in his indictment speech that members of a gang of thieves may rob people in various places and nevertheless be responsible for each other. That is true, but members of a gang of thieves must know each other in order to be a gang, and they must be in more or less close contact with each other." Meanwhile, Bukharin continued, for the first time at the trial he learned of the existence of several defendants; he had never been acquainted with, let alone "talked about counterrevolutionary matters" with, the majority of the others. Moreover the prosecutor had not once questioned him about these people during the pre-trial investigation.[5]

G. Fedotov, one of the most honest representatives of the centrist wing of the emigration, noted that Bukharin's behavior at the trial presented the most insoluble riddles. In his words, Bukharin had not been broken, and he energetically and skillfully defended himself, often driving the prosecutor into a ridiculous or stupid position. But this defense proceeded within a very limited framework and dealt only with the charges of terror and espionage. Fedotov rejected any "complicating assumption" (that Bukharin's defense had been foreseen by the organizers of the trial and had been played through in order to give the trial an air of verisimilitude), referring to "Vyshinsky's exasperation and rage, and his awkward attempts to shut Bukharin's mouth, which completely compromised Ulrikh's court."

After these comments, Fedotov raised a reasonable question: why did Bukharin "not defend, with the courage of a revolutionary, his position of fighting against Stalin; why did he not shift from a pitiful semi-defense to an offensive; why did he not expose, not only his own, but the common enemy on the eve of his death?" He rejected the arguments suggesting that Bukharin falsely accused himself because he accepted the Stalinist conception of party duty, which demanded the most severe sacrifice of his honor "for the good of the revolution." This hypothesis, in Fedotov's opinion, "was five years too late, if not more, and reflects that party mysticism of which not a trace could possibly remain any more. One could not think that Bukharin believed in Stalin's party as the embodiment of Leninist traditions. Stalin, who was killing all the Leninists and raising the flag of Russian nationalism, must be seen as a traitor by any true Bolshevik. Bukharin could not help but recognize that Lenin's party was seated on the defendants' bench, and that the final judgment of history on his party, which had already been annihilated, depended on his courage in the courtroom."[6]

Another explanation of the "Bukharin mystery" was given by Victor Serge, who noted that "Bukharin maintains himself (at the trial) along strictly party lines. In order to carry out the Politburo's directives and to perform

8. The Mystery of Bukharin

Nikolai Bukharin

the service he had promised to the party, he takes upon himself monstrous political accusations, but feels that he does not have the right to stain "the honor of a Bolshevik," that he cannot in any way admit to being a spy or an agent of the bourgeoisie. It is possible to exaggerate the inner-party debate, but that is all." "Bukharin's rebellion," his altercations with the prosecutor, were explained by Serge in the following manner: "The same agreement was made with Bukharin, undoubtedly, as with all the others. But he is a nervous person. In the atmosphere of the trial, of the fight against the judges, a certain reaction occurred. One must assume that haggling and exhortation would be renewed in the prison cell after each session. This explains the nervousness of the debate. They dealt with Krestinsky easily. With Bukharin, things were more difficult, because for many years he was the party's theoretician and it was he who established the line of party ethics and moral discipline... It is possible that Yezhov foresaw this. In the points of the indictment which Bukharin rejected, his comrades finished him off. For the court, this was sufficient."

Serge was examining Bukharin's behavior at the trial within the broad context of the political differentiation within the anti-Stalinist opposition. He indicated that this differentiation proceeded along the lines of one's attitude toward the party: "The left part (Sapronovists and Trotskyists) acknowledged the party's degeneration, and therefore rejected it, whereas the right part (the Zinovievists and Bukharinists), despite profound disagreements with Stalin (whom Bukharin compared to Genghis Khan), feels that outside the party there could not be any leadership for the country or salvation for the revolution." Proceeding from these premises, Serge declared: "If I occupied the position of the Zinovievists or Bukharinists within the party, then my conduct would be the same as theirs. Note that there were no genuine Trotskyists at a single one of the three trials. Yet more than 500 such people have been rotting in their prisons since 1928, including dozens of people with major revolutionary names. Why have they not been included in Yezhov's productions? Because they cannot be included. Not because they fear death and torture any less than the Zinovievists and Bukharinists. But because our opposition is *against the party of Stalin*, whereas the opposition led by Zinoviev and Bukharin is *within* the party of Stalin. Party law remains operative for the Zinovievists and Bukharinists, for us, however, it does not exist, because... the old party no longer exists! The party has degenerated into a bureaucratic apparatus."[7]

Later, Serge, like many researchers of more recent times (with Stephen Cohen in the forefront), tried to find in Bukharin's responses to questions and in his final remarks cunning subterfuges and Aesopian language, with which he was trying to express his own true attitude toward Stalin and the Stalinist regime. In his book, *The Life and Death of Leon Trotsky*, Serge voiced the opinion that, at the trial, Bukharin used "crystal clear and tortuous dialectical arguments" about degeneration, in order to express his shame, and not only for himself, but for the whole party which had bowed before Stalin.[8]

Such considerations are destroyed by the recent publication of the last document written by Bukharin, his appeal for clemency. This document shows that everything in Bukharin's behavior was both simpler and more complicated than in the behavior of the "steel people," as portrayed by Arthur Koestler, who borrowed his arguments from Serge. The main difference between Bukharin and Koestler's character Rubashov consists in the fact that Rubashov went to trial without a glimmer of hope that his life would be spared (the investigator who was conducting his case told him directly that there could be no such hope). Until the last hour of his life, Bukharin, however, submitted to the rules of a different game being played by Stalin. Stalin's final decision interested him much more than the judgment of history, for he continued to hope in the depths of his soul that Stalin would grant him his life in return for "completely laying down his arms." Therefore, to use Fedotov's words, at the trial Bukharin "defended himself, but helped Stalin bury the party in filth and shame."[9]

In the course of a single day, Bukharin and Rykov submitted two appeals for clemency. It is clear that after they had submitted the first variant, they were asked to present a new variant with a more detailed description of the motives for their appeal. But whereas Rykov limited himself to a virtual repetition of his previous formulations, Bukharin submitted a much more detailed statement which can essentially be reduced to the formulation of one thesis: "A year in jail has been such a school for me, that I have the right to speak to the Presidium about my complete reorientation."

Understanding that his fate would be decided not by the Presidium of the TsIK, in whose name the appeal was officially directed, but personally by Stalin, Bukharin essentially addressed his request and arguments to the latter. At the same time he knew that his statement would pass through the hands of many people. Therefore he was completely deprived of the secretly confidential tone that had permeated the personal letter he had sent to Stalin three months before. For these reasons the declaration contained no statements or hints whatsoever at the falseness or forced nature of his confessions. Repeating the phrase which had resounded in his final remarks, "I stand on my knees before the motherland, the party and the people," Bukharin then introduced a full panoply of high-flown, official clichés: "Our mighty country, our mighty party and government have carried out a general purge. The counter-revolution has been crushed and rendered harmless. The fatherland of socialism proceeds in its heroic march into the arena of the greatest and most victorious struggle in world history. Within the country, on the basis of the Stalinist constitution, broad inner-party democracy is developing. A great creative and fertile life is flourishing." Bukharin needed this selection of panegyrics and general passages resembling lead articles from *Pravda* in order to beg for the chance, "even if behind prison bars, to participate as much as he could in this life."

Trying to choose the most convincing expressions to show that he harbored "in his soul not a single word of protest" (evidently regarding what was happening in the country as well as what was happening to himself), Bukharin declared: "My more than year-long stay in prison has forced me to think over and review so many things that nothing remains from my criminal past, toward which I feel indignation and contempt... Internally I have laid down my arms and rearmed myself along new, socialist lines... What is old in me has died forever and irretrievably. I am glad that the power of the proletariat has destroyed everything criminal that saw in me its leader, and the leader of which I truly was."

It seems that Koestler's Rubashov, who carried out the role he was given at the trial but preserved remnants of his personal dignity, would hardly have resorted to such additional humiliation. Right until the last hour, however, Bukharin was concerned with preserving his life at any cost. To do this he chose one last dialectical device. Agreeing with Vyshinsky's arguments that "for my crimes I should be shot ten times over," he nevertheless tried to argue that he should not be shot, since "the former *Bukharin* has already died, he no longer exists on this earth... My knowledge and capabilities have been preserved, as has my entire intellectual mechanism, the activity of which was previously directed at criminal goals. Now this mechanism has been wound in a new key... Therefore may I be so bold as to appeal to you, as the highest organ of the government, for mercy; the motive for this is my work capability, and I appeal to your sense of revolutionary expediency... Give this new, second *Bukharin* a chance to grow — let it be even in the form of some *Petrov* — this new man will be the exact opposite of the one who has died. He has already been born — give him at least the opportunity to accomplish some work."

In this way, by announcing his "death" as a man possessing independent thoughts, Bukharin was assuring Stalin that he was ready to place himself at the latter's complete disposal as an "intellectual mechanism," capable of carrying out any of Stalin's commands. Since he harbored no far-reaching illusions about Stalin's inclination toward mercy, he offered the assurance: "If I am granted physical life, then it will be to the benefit of the socialist motherland, no matter the circumstances in which I would have to work: in solitary confinement in prison, in a concentration camp, at the North Pole, in Kolyma, wherever you like, in any location and under any conditions... I will try with all my strength to prove to you that this gesture of proletarian magnanimity was justified."[10]

In the light of this eloquent document, one can draw the following conclusions: first of all, Bukharin had engaged in the polemic with Vyshinsky at the trial in order to show Stalin the absurdity of the charges which were compromising Stalin's very "legal system." Second, it would remove any shadow of doubt that might arise in Stalin's mind that any of the crimes with which Bukharin was incriminated had ever actually occurred. Third, it would convince Stalin that he, Bukharin, was demonstrating obedience and consistency with regard to the main issue: the recognition that any oppositional activity would lead to the most terrible crimes. By doing so, he had carried out the role he had been assigned, for which he was justified in hoping that his life would be spared.

9. Yagoda's Orbit

One of the main sensations at the trial was the appearance on the defendants' bench of Yagoda, who for many years had led Stalin's secret police. Trotsky called Yagoda's presence among the conspirators "the most, if you will, fantastic part of the entire series of Moscow judicial phantasmagorias... If someone were to say that Goebbels was an agent of the Roman Pope, it would sound much less absurd than the claim that Yagoda has been Trotsky's agent."[1] Noting the striking nature of "Yagoda's orbit," Trotsky stressed that Yagoda "for the last ten years has been the person closest to Stalin. Not a single member of the Politburo has been entrusted by Stalin with the secrets that have been entrusted to the head of the GPU. That Yagoda was a scoundrel, everyone knew. ... As a consummate scoundrel he was just the person Stalin needed for carrying out the darkest assignments... And now this guardian of the state, who has exterminated the older generation of the party, turns out to be a gangster and traitor."[2]

Trotsky recalled that from the mid-1920s, Yagoda had directed the police persecution, arrest and exile of oppositionists. He was the organizer of the first executions of Trotskyists in 1929. Along with Vyshinsky he prepared the sensational trials which occurred after Kirov's murder, right up until the second trial of Zinoviev and Kamenev in August 1936. "The system of heartfelt confessions will go down in history as an invention of Genrikh Yagoda."[3]

Besides this, Yagoda's hands controlled the Kremlin security forces, including those for Stalin. Members of the Politburo could not take a step without the "personal bodyguards" assigned to them by Yagoda. In every department which they directed, Yagoda planted thousands of secret informers. He compiled for Stalin dossiers with compromising material about the biographies of all the highest leaders of the party; he placed hidden microphones in their apartments and dachas. It is natural that Stalin's "closest comrades-in-arms" could have no other attitude toward Yagoda than one of hatred. Voroshilov waged a prolonged battle with the special departments of the NKVD created by Ya-

Genrikh Yagoda
(1891-1938)

goda in all military units and conducting surveillance of the army commanders. According to Orlov, Kaganovich gave Yagoda the nickname "Fouché," indicating his resemblance to Napoleon's minster of the secret police. A translation of Stefan Zweig's book on Fouché was published in the Soviet Union in the 1930s, and it made a big impression on Stalin and his entourage. In his narrow circle, Stalin spoke admiringly about Fouché, who had survived four regimes — that of the Jacobins, the Directory, Napoleon and the restoration — remaining all the while at high posts. Of course, the official assessment of Fouché was quite different, and for that reason, Vyshinsky quoted generous passages from Zweig's book in his indictment speech in order to show that Yagoda followed "the old, treacherous and double-dealing school of the political careerist and dishonest scoundrel ... Joseph Fouché."[4]

According to Orlov, as early as the beginning of the 1930s, members of the Politburo had tried to convince Stalin to remove Yagoda. On their insistence in 1931, the Old Bolshevik Akulov had been sent into the OGPU, where they assumed that he would soon become head of this establishment. However Yagoda managed to persuade Stalin to transfer Akulov to other work.[5] In 1935, Stalin awarded Yagoda the title of General Commissar of State Security, equal in rank to marshal in the army, and settled him in the Kremlin. "In the figure of Yagoda," wrote Trotsky, "a nonentity known to all and despised by everyone was being elevated. The old revolutionaries looked at one another in indignation. Even in the submissive Politburo they tried to resist. But a secret of some kind linked Stalin with Yagoda, and did so, it would seem, forever."[6]

This secret link was broken after Yagoda was dismissed from his post as People's Commissar of Interior Affairs in September 1936 and arrested in

March 1937. The official announcement of Yagoda's fall was couched in lofty tones. It said that Yagoda "had been suspended" in view of recently discovered malfeasance in office of a criminal character.[7]

For the new judicial frame-up, Yagoda was no longer needed as an architect, but as raw material. It is true that right up until the trial of the "Right-Trotskyist Bloc," the Soviet press had uttered not a word about his participation in the combined conspiracy of Trotskyists, rightists and military figures. "Neither Yagoda nor public opinion had matured enough for that, nor was there any certainty that Vyshinsky would be able to show his new client to the public successfully." The announcement focused merely on his uncontrolled lifestyle, embezzlement, and so forth. "Were these charges true?" wrote Trotsky. "With regard to Yagoda we can allow this completely. A careerist, cynic and petty despot, he was, of course, no image of virtue in his personal life, either. We must only add that, if he allowed his instincts to run unchecked up to the point of criminality, then it was only because he was confident of being completely above the law. Yagoda's lifestyle, moreover, had long been known in Moscow, and to Stalin as well. All facts which discredit Soviet satraps are gathered by Stalin with scientific assiduousness and comprise a special archive, from which they are drawn selectively, in accordance with political necessity. The hour struck when Yagoda had to be morally broken. This was accomplished by using scandalous exposés of his personal life. After being worked over in this way for several months, the former head of the GPU stood before two alternatives: to be shot as an embezzler of state funds, or perhaps to save his life as a false conspirator. Yagoda made his choice and was added to the list of the 21 defendants. The world then learned, finally, that Yagoda has been shooting Trotskyists only to 'mask' himself; in actual fact he was their ally and agent."

Given all this, the question still remained: "Who needed, and why, however, such an improbable and compromising complication of an already confused judicial amalgam? ... There had to have been some kind of concrete, immediate and extremely sharp reason which forced Stalin not to halt before turning his own № 1 agent into an agent of Trotsky."[8]

Trotsky felt that this reason was disclosed by Yagoda himself when, during questioning at the trial, he announced that he had given his subordinates in Leningrad the directive "not to impede the execution of a terrorist act against Kirov." Such an order, coming from the head of the NKVD, would have been equivalent to a command to organize Kirov's assassination.

This assassination was the starting point for accusing the entire opposition of terrorism. The more trials were staged in connection with the case of Kirov's murder, the more insistently the question arose in everyone's mind: "Who needs this?" The circumstances of the murder which became known clearly pointed to the participation of the NKVD. Stalin at first tried to foist

Sergei Kirov
(1886-1934)

Сталин использовал убийство Кирова, чтобы узаконить массовые репрессии в стране, пик которых пришелся на 1937-й год

secondary figures onto public opinion — the leaders of the Leningrad administration of the NKVD. However, in the Moscow upper echelons, the suspicion took root that the affair could not have unfolded without Yagoda's participation, and he, in turn, could have acted only on Stalin's orders. "The suspicion spread to ever widening circles, turning into certainty. It became absolutely imperative for Stalin to separate himself from Yagoda, to create between himself and Yagoda a deep ditch, and if possible, to dump Yagoda's corpse into this ditch... This explains the most inexplicable aspect of the present trial: the testimony of the former chief of the GPU that he participated in Kirov's murder 'on instructions from Trotsky.' Whoever grasps this most hidden mainspring of the trial, will readily grasp all the rest."⁹

Once he had decided to sacrifice his chief collaborator who knew too much, Stalin achieved a few other advantages by doing so: "In return for a promise of clemency, Yagoda accepted personal responsibility at the trial for crimes that, rumor had it, belonged to Stalin. The promise, of course, was not kept: they shot Yagoda in order to better show Stalin's irreconcilability in questions of morality and justice."¹⁰

Trotsky pointed out that "of all the defendants, Yagoda alone undoubtedly deserved harsh punishment, although not at all for the crimes with which he is charged."* Vyshinsky unwittingly came close to characterizing Yagoda's actual crimes when he compared Yagoda to the famous American gangster Al

---

* In 1988, such a conclusion was actually drawn, without explanation, by the Politburo commission which rehabilitated all the defendants from the trial of the "Right-Trotskyist Bloc," with the exception of Yagoda.

Capone. "No saboteur could make a more dangerous comparison!" Trotsky noted in this regard. "Al Capone was not head of the police in the United States. Meanwhile, for more than ten years Yagoda headed the GPU and was Stalin's closest collaborator... And Yagoda's power was so great that even highly-placed Kremlin physicians did not dare to expose Capone, but submissively carried out his orders... It turns out that Capone wielded unlimited power over the Soviet Union. Of course it is true that Yezhov has now taken his place. But where is the guarantee that he is any better? Under conditions of totalitarian despotism, where public opinion is stifled and where there is a complete absence of control, only the names of the gangsters change, but the system remains."[11]

Of course, the prosecutor charged Yagoda with crimes he did not commit, that traditionally had been ascribed to victims of the Moscow Trials. However, when mention was made of these crimes, Yagoda's conduct frequently drove Vyshinsky into a blind alley. Thus, when Yagoda denied the accusation that he murdered Menzhinsky and Maksim Peshkov, the prosecutor asked repeatedly why he had confessed to these crimes at the pre-trial investigation. In response, Yagoda reiterated several times: "Allow me not to answer this question."[12]

When he refused to confess to espionage activities, Yagoda told the prosecutor: "If I had been a spy, then I assure you that dozens of states would have had to close their intelligence operations (in the Soviet Union – V. R.)."[13] These words were omitted in the newspaper account, and only after they were published by foreign correspondents who had been at the trial were they included in the trial transcript.

The "Yagoda affair" introduced a new group of charges — the villainous murder of prominent state and public figures.

D. D. Pletnev, Professor of Medicine

10. Poisonings and Poisoners

Sitting next to the famous political figures on the defendants' bench were Kremlin doctors charged with the "medical murders" of Kuibyshev, Menzhinsky, Gorky, and his son, Maksim.

Trotsky explained this selection of criminals and victims in the following way: "Even the most fantastic frame-up must be constructed from elements of reality ... Despite the many terrorist 'centers,' ... in reality, i.e., in the realm of three dimensions, the world did not observe coups, uprisings, and terrorist acts, but only arrests, exile, and shootings. It is true that the GPU was able to refer to a single terrorist act. ... Kirov's corpse has invariably figured in all the political trials for slightly more than the last three years. Everyone stood in line to kill Kirov: White-Guardists, Zinovievists, Trotskyists, rightists. This resource proved to have been exhausted. In order to support the contrived charges of conspiracy, new victims of "terror" were required. They had to be sought among the recently deceased satraps. And since satraps were dying in the Kremlin, i.e., under conditions excluding access by outside "terrorists," then it became necessary to resort to charging the Kremlin doctors with poisoning their patients, on instructions, of course, from Bukharin, Rykov, or, still worse, Trotsky."[1]

Among the doctor-poisoners and their assistants, the most significant were the figures of Pletnev and Levin. Pletnev was not only an outstanding therapist, but a world-renowned author of scientific works in the realm of medicine. Not long before his arrest, he was dragged through a shameful courtroom procedure as a rapist who had done violence to one of his patients. On 8 June 1937, *Pravda* published an article, "Professor — Rapist, Sadist," describing with unusual detail the "bestial rape" which had been committed by Pletnev against a certain "patient B." The article cited B.'s hysterical letter, in which she told how three years before, during a medical examination, the professor became seized with a paroxysm of sexual sadism and suddenly bit her breast. The sixty-six-year-old's bite proved to be so terrifying that the patient, in her own words, "lost her capacity for work, and became an invalid as a result of the wound and severe psychological shock." The letter from the "desecrated woman" ended with the words: "May you be damned, wretched criminal, for having rewarded me with an incurable illness and for having disfigured my body."

In medical circles it was well known that the mysterious patient B. was a certain Braude, a physically deformed and mentally disturbed woman, and a secret informer for the NKVD. She had blackmailed Pletnev even before the publication of the fantastic article in *Pravda*. Nevertheless, on a command from above the newspapers quickly began to publish letters from famous physicians and resolutions from doctors' meetings with demands for "the most severe sentence for this monster."

An article was soon printed about a closed session of the Moscow city court where Pletnev had received a suspended sentence of two years' confinement, i.e., he had in fact been freed without any punishment. Commenting on this decision, Trotsky wrote: "In the USSR, people are frequently sentenced to be shot for stealing a sack of flour. One could all the more expect a merciless sentence for the physician-rapist ... The sentence appeared just as unexpected as the accusation had earlier. ... The charge of sadism had been lodged with such overwhelming commotion ... only in order to break the will of the old physician, the father of a family, and to turn him into an obedient tool in the hands of the GPU for a future political trial."[2]

Having passed through the shock of monstrous intrigue and unbelievable disgrace, Pletnev was arrested a few months later. As he would later write in declarations from Vladimir prison, during his investigation "they used terrifyingly foul language, threats of the death penalty; they tossed me around by the scruff of my neck, they choked me. I was tortured with sleep deprivation. In the course of five weeks I was allowed sleep only two or three times. They threatened to rip out my throat and along with it a confession; they threatened to beat me with a rubber truncheon ... The combined effect of all this was to induce paralysis in half my body."[3]

The main murderer was declared to be Professor Levin, who since the first years of the revolution had occupied a leading position among the Kremlin doctors and was undoubtedly well-informed about the reasons for the truly enigmatic deaths which had befallen several of his patients. "This superb Kremlin physician," one of the *Bulletin's* articles about the trial said, "also knew too much, and he could have disclosed much at some time. He knew how Ordzhonikidze had died... Doctor Levin could have also spoken at some time about the suicide of Alliluyeva, Stalin's wife. He would have nothing to say to posterity about Kuibyshev's death, but he could say something about Frunze's operation."[4]

In Trotsky's opinion, the case of Doctor Levin served as a key "not only to the riddles of the Moscow Trials, but also to Stalin's entire regime as a whole...

This key opens all the Kremlin secrets and at the same time shuts once and for all the mouths of the lawyers for Stalinist justice throughout the world."

Levin was not accused of being a disguised Trotskyist who wanted to seize power in the USSR in an alliance with Hitler. He had no personal incentives to commit the most ignoble of all the crimes named at the trial — the treacherous murder of patients who trusted him. From his testimony it followed that he killed his patients on orders from Yagoda, who threatened, if he did not obey, to destroy not only him, but his family as well. "In the Moscow courtroom panorama, that's how the Stalinist regime looks," wrote Trotsky, "at its uppermost echelons, in the Kremlin, in the most intimate part of the Kremlin, in the hospital for members of the government! What then is happening in the rest of the country?"

At the time of the trial Trotsky considered the charge that Levin murdered Gorky to be a "nightmarish invention." He nevertheless directed attention to the fact that Stalin, Vyshinsky and Yezhov, in putting into circulation the present version, "of all the possible variants chose the most probable, i.e., that which corresponded most of all to the given conditions, relationships and morals. All the participants in the trial, the entire Soviet press, all the bearers of power silently acknowledged the complete likelihood that the head of the GPU might force any person to commit any crime, even when this person is at liberty, occupies a high post and enjoys the protection of the ruling elite." Given their bureaucratic impunity they had not taken into account the fact that after this any doubts would evaporate about the ability of the executioners from the NKVD to force any prisoner to "voluntarily" confess to crimes he had not committed.

Unlike the defenseless prisoners of the NKVD and the overwhelming majority of Soviet citizens at liberty, Levin was not under the exclusive power of the secret police and its powerful chief. He had the opportunity to expose Yagoda by turning to people occupying the highest positions in the land. "Levin is not an accidental person," Trotsky noted in this regard. "He treated Lenin, Stalin, and all members of the government… As with every authoritative physician, he established intimate, almost patronizing relations with highly-placed patients. He knows very well what the backbones of the leaders look like, and how their authoritarian kidneys function. Levin had free access to any dignitary. Couldn't he therefore have told Stalin, Molotov, or any member of the Politburo and government about Yagoda's bloody blackmail? It turns out that he could not."[5]

Trotsky found a more precise answer to this question when he partially revised his views of the Moscow Trials. In the article "Super-Borgia in the Kremlin," he wrote that at the time of the trial, the charges and confessions concerning the murder of the old and ill writer seemed to him to be phantasmagorical. "The latest information and a more attentive analysis of the cir-

Gorky and Yagoda

cumstances allow me to change this assessment. Not everything in the trials was a lie. There were those poisoned, and there were poisoners. Not all poisoners were sitting on the defendants' bench. The chief one among them was directing the trial by telephone."[6]

Trotsky recalled that in the last years of Gorky's life, his relations with Stalin had by no means been as cloudless as they were portrayed by Soviet propaganda. From 1929 through 1933 Gorky traveled yearly for prolonged stays abroad, but by 1934 such trips had been banned by Stalin. The correspondence between Gorky and Romain Rolland passed through careful censorship. The NKVD surrounded Gorky "with a ring of its own agents in the guise of secretaries and typists. Their task was to allow no unwelcome visitors to gain access to Gorky."[7]

Vivid accounts of Gorky's status and moods during his last years are contained in the testimony written by Babel when he was in prison. In March 1936, Gorky was staying in the Crimea. He was visited by André Malraux, who was accompanied by Koltsov, Kriuchkov (Gorky's secretary) and Babel (the last had been invited at Gorky's request). As Babel would write, "at this time we found [Gorky] in a miserable mood. The atmosphere of loneliness which had been created around him by Kriuchkov and Yagoda, who were zealously trying to isolate Gorky from all that was more or less fresh and interesting that could appear in his surroundings, proclaimed itself from the first day that I visited his dacha in Tesseli. Gorky's morale was very low, and notes crept into his conversation that he had been abandoned by everyone. Gorky repeatedly said that they were preventing him in every way from returning

10. Poisonings and Poisoners

Malraux and Babel, 1936

to Moscow, and to the work which he loved... The selection of people taken by Kriuchkov to see Gorky was deliberately designed so that Gorky would see no one except Chekists from Yagoda's entourage, and crack-pot inventors. These artificial conditions in which Gorky had been placed began to weigh ever more heavily on him; they caused the feeling of loneliness and sorrow in which we found him in Tesseli, not long before his death."[8]

Not knowing in such detail the blockade which had been established around Gorky, Trotsky nevertheless recalled that after the writer's death, "suspicions arose that Stalin had aided somewhat the destructive force of nature. Yagoda's trial had the secondary task of removing this suspicion from Stalin."[9] Therefore Bessonov declared that Trotsky had given him a directive about Gorky's physical annihilation, providing as a motivation the "extraordinary closeness" of the writer to Stalin and his exceptional influence on the Western intelligentsia, which had driven many supporters away from Trotsky.[10] Following Bessonov, Yagoda, Bukharin, Rykov, the physicians, and other defendants continuously reiterated that Gorky was "a defender of Stalin's policies," was Stalin's personal friend and "unswerving supporter," and always spoke of him "with exceptional admiration."[11] "If this were even halfway true," noted Trotsky, "Yagoda would never have decided to undertake Gorky's death and even less so dared to entrust such a plan to a Kremlin doctor who could destroy him with a simple telephone call to Stalin."[12]

Insofar as Gorky enjoyed tremendous authority in the USSR and abroad, he began to represent a serious danger for Stalin under conditions when dissatisfaction and repression had reached extreme limits in the country. It would have been possible to tighten control over him, but not to forbid him to correspond with European writers nor to completely isolate him from the visits of foreigners and the complaints of offended Soviet citizens. "There was no way to force him to remain silent. It was even less feasible to arrest him, exile him, let alone shoot him. The idea of hastening the liquidation of the sick Gorky 'without bloodshed' through the intermediary of Yagoda must have seemed under these conditions to be the only way out for the master of the Kremlin. Stalin's mind is constructed in such a way that such decisions arise within it with the force of a reflex."

Only this can explain the fact that Levin and other authoritative Kremlin doctors did not seek defenders against Yagoda from among their patients, who often belonged to the Kremlin's highest dignitaries. "The solution lies in the fact that Levin, as well as everyone in the Kremlin and around the Kremlin, knew very well whose agent Yagoda was. Levin subordinated himself to Yagoda because he was powerless in opposing Stalin."[13]

Trotsky felt that the frequent repetition by the defendants of the idea that certain "highly-placed people" were not satisfied with Gorky's moods and behavior was confirmation of this version, and of no small importance. Of course, this formula was interpreted at the trial in such a way that the "highly-placed people" were Bukharin, Rykov, Kamenev and Zinoviev. "But in this period the persons named were pariahs being persecuted by the GPU. Only the masters of the Kremlin could figure under the pseudonym of 'highly-placed people.' And this means Stalin, most of all."[14]

An analysis of Gorky's treacherous murder led Trotsky to the conclusion that "the basic elements of Stalin's frame-ups are drawn not from pure fantasy, but are taken from reality, and mainly from the affairs and schemes of the very master of spicy dishes."[15]

11. What Was True at the Trial?

Reference to "medical murders" was not the only thing that was true at the trial. Many other aspects of the trial were not pure falsification, but more precisely the weaving together of separate elements of truth with stunning and insidious lies.

First of all, many confessions were dictated by a desire to declare unforgettable "excesses" in the localities to be the work of "enemies of the people." Thus Zelensky told how in 1929 he presented the Central Committee of the VKP(b) a plan in which collectivization in the republics of Central Asia would encompass 52 percent of the peasant households by the end of the first Five-Year Plan. The CC rejected this plan and raised the projected collectivization to 68 percent. After this decision, Zelensky submitted to the demands for breakneck collectivization tempos handed down from above and advanced the slogan: "Catch up with and surpass the most advanced regions in the Soviet Union with regard to collectivization." At the trial this slogan was called a provocation directed at undermining the construction of collective farming in Central Asia and provoking mass reactions against collectivization in this region.[1]

Sharangovich "confessed" that he was guided by similarly hostile intentions when he issued a directive in Belorussia: "If an individual farmer does not go into the collective farm, then he is an enemy of Soviet power." By proceeding with this slogan, according to Sharangovich, such pressure was exerted through taxes on individual farmers that it generated discontent and rebellious moods among the peasants.[2]

Many of the defendants attributed to the "rightists" intentions which were diametrically opposed to their political views — to embitter the middle peasant and thereby provoke peasant unrest. In other words, the active response to which the peasants were driven by Stalin's merciless policy in the countryside was explained as the result of criminal actions by the "Right-Trotskyist Bloc."

In this regard, the trial was the forum where for the first time direct reference was made to the peasant uprisings which had occurred in 1928-1933. These uprisings, the mere mention of which had earlier been punished as anti-Soviet slander, were depicted, however, not as a spontaneous reaction of the peasantry to forced collectivization, but as the result of the activity of "rightists," who had acted in an alliance with SRs, White-Guardists, and so forth.

The selection of defendants was made in such a way that it included several of those who exhibited extreme cruelty in executing Stalin's orders. Victor Serge felt that Stalin "once again needed to stage a bloody farce," at least in part to "dump all the victims of forced collectivization onto the shoulders of those who carried out his directive of 1930." From this standpoint, Serge juxtaposed Sharangovich's confessions of excesses during collectivization in Belorussia with the announcement that Sheboldaev had been shot. The latter "had become famous in party circles for extraordinary cruelty in the Northern Caucasus... His name was deeply hated in the Don and Kuban, where he sent to the North whole Cossack villages, down to the last man."[3]

Secondly, the trial mentioned attempts of local leaders to conduct policies which in some way did not coincide with the aspirations of the Kremlin clique. Thus, Khodzhaev recalled the activities of the Uzbek leadership, which were aimed at reinforcing the republic's economic independence and developing its economy in many ways. He explained that these activities were dictated by the separatist designs "of bourgeois nationalists."[4]

Thirdly, the trial revealed several historical facts which were placed, however, in a false political context. Thus, for instance, information about Soviet-German military collaboration was provided for the first time, yet the collaboration was declared to be the result of the conspiratorial activity of the "bloc." Krestinsky and Rozengolts declared that Trotsky had given them directives about forming an alliance with Tukhachevsky and other military leaders in order to defeat the USSR in a future war with Germany. "The ghost of the executed Marshal Tukhachevsky apparently still hovers above the courtroom proceedings," Trotsky wrote in this regard. "Fearing the discontent of his best generals, Stalin beheaded the Red Army and thereby aroused indignation throughout the world. Now, in hindsight, he is trying to prove to the public opinion of the USSR and all mankind that the executed generals actually were traitors."[5]

With these goals in mind, the trial brought to light and then falsely interpreted facts which were connected with the defense pact signed at the beginning of the 1920s between the USSR and Germany and directed against the Entente and the Versailles Treaty. The reasoning behind this pact, according to Trotsky, was that "the officer corps of the Reichswehr (the German armed forces – V. R.), despite its political hatred for communism, felt that diplomatic and military collaboration with the Soviet republic was necessary ...

The 'Moscow' orientation of the Reichswehr began to influence government spheres as well."

The USSR had been interested in such collaboration because the Soviet government at that time could expect assistance only from Germany in developing modern military technology. In turn, the Reichswehr, which had been deprived according to the Versailles Treaty of producing the latest armaments in its own country, tried to use Soviet military industry for this purpose. "All this work," wrote Trotsky, "was conducted, it goes without saying, under the cover of secrecy, since the Damocles sword of Versailles obligations was hanging over Germany's head. Officially the Berlin government took no part in this matter, and supposedly did not even know about it: formal responsibility lay on the Reichswehr, on one hand, and on the Red Army, on the other."[6] In the Soviet Union, such policy was directed not by Trotsky alone, as head of the military establishment, but by the Politburo as a whole. Moreover, Stalin was the most insistent advocate of collaboration with the Reichswehr, and with Germany as a whole. Immediate supervision of the German military concessions was entrusted to Rozengolts as the representative of the People's Commissariat of War.

Trotsky pointed out that the secret archives of the Red Army and GPU contained documents concerning this military collaboration. The content of the relevant documents, written in very cautious and conspiratorial formulations, might have appeared baffling not only to Vyshinsky, but to the majority of members of Stalin's Politburo. According to Trotsky, at the beginning of 1938 their existence would be known only to Stalin, Molotov, Bukharin, Rykov, Yagoda, Rakovsky, Rozengolts, and no more than ten other people in the USSR.

Fourthly, evidence of the corruption that was widespread in the USSR in the 1930s found its reflection in the defendants' testimony. Thus, Kriuchkov confessed that he had embezzled large amounts of money belonging to Gorky for his own personal needs.[7] Even more significant were the claims that Yagoda "gave" Doctor Levin, as his personal physician, a luxurious dacha and also issued a directive to allow him to return from his foreign travels without submitting to a customs inspection.[8]

Fifth, several statements about "treacherous crimes" were not naked inventions, but the result of a provocation. Thus Bulanov, Yagoda's former secretary, said that he had prepared poison that was to be sprinkled about Yezhov's office immediately before Yezhov came to the NKVD.[9] At Yezhov's trial in 1940, it was established that this "terrorist act" was fabricated by Yezhov himself and the head of the counter-intelligence department of the NKVD, Nikolaev. The latter had consulted with the head of the chemical academy of the Red Army about how to use mercury as a poison, after which he rubbed mercury into the upholstery of the furniture in Yezhov's office.

At the trial, Bulanov declared that all these actions had been performed by the NKVD member Savolainen. After Savolainen's arrest, a jar of mercury was surreptitiously placed in the entrance way to his apartment building. It was then "discovered" and introduced into the case as material evidence.[10] The carpet, curtains, furniture upholstery and air in Yezhov's office were subjected to chemical analysis. On the basis of this analysis, "as well as analyses of his (Yezhov's) urine," a group of authoritative medical personnel brought in as expert witnesses indicated that, as a result of mercury poisoning, Yezhov's health "had been significantly damaged, and if the given crime had not been discovered in time, then the life of Comrade N. I. Yezhov would have been threatened by immediate danger."[11]

Sixth, at the trial, tangled up in a confusion of monstrous inventions, actual facts were mentioned which were connected with oppositional sentiments held by Stalin's opponents. An abundance of such facts was introduced by the defendants when they explained their motives for uniting with the "rightists." Chernov recounted how he had told Rykov in 1928 that the use of extraordinary measures had reduced the production of agricultural commodities and destroyed the peasants' interest in developing their farms. Rykov replied that these were the results of Stalin's policies, which were leading agriculture to ruin.[12]

Acknowledging that he had engaged in such conversations with Chernov, Rykov announced that Yagoda, too, had sympathized with the positions of the "rightists" concerning extraordinary measures; he had even expressed his feelings at a session of the Politburo.[13] And this evidence, it seems, corresponds to the truth, since in his conversation with Kamenev in July 1928, Bukharin named Yagoda as one of the people who shared the views of the "rightists."

Zubarev told how, in a conversation with him in 1929, A. P. Smirnov had given a detailed description of the political situation in the country, underscoring the discontent which had been growing in the countryside as a result of the use of extraordinary measures. In 1930, according to Zubarev, he had talked with Rykov, who declared that as a result of the rapid collectivization and elimination of the kulaks, spontaneous armed uprisings were breaking out in a number of regions. He said that the policy of eliminating the kulaks embraced not only the kulak upper strata, but also layers of middle peasants in the villages; and that "this great drama in the countryside had created a hostile attitude (on the part of the peasants) toward the policies of the party."[14]

When it came to more recent times, the defendants' assessments of the situation in the country were more cautious, but even from these it was possible to get an idea of the broad dissatisfaction with Stalin's policies. Thus, Levin announced that Yagoda had once told him: the dissatisfaction with Stalin's leadership is growing throughout the land, and "there is hardly a single major establishment which does not have people sitting there who are dissatisfied with this leadership and who feel that it is necessary to remove it and replace it with other people."[15]

One cannot allow that all the political figures in the USSR were so shortsighted and lacking in independence that they unreservedly endorsed the adventurist policy of the Stalinist clique without exchanging ideas about the need to overthrow Stalin. Noting that the political content of the trial could not be reduced simply to "the satisfaction of the personal and long-simmering vengeance of the party parvenu at the expense of the Leninist aristocracy," G. Fedotov correctly stated that it was impossible to reject the entire factual side of the defendants' confessions. "The general impression, in contrast to the previous trials, is that here there are many more elements of truth, lost in a sea of lies," he wrote. "In recent times the political struggle has sharpened in Russia... One might allow, although nothing can prove this, that some of the old, honest communists wanted a coup, Stalin's arrest, and a sharp change of course. Or, perhaps, they only dreamed of this. By compromising these unquestionably widespread moods with charges of espionage and with the perspective of dismembering Russia, Stalin wants to paralyze the popularity of conspiratorial activism."[16]

Victor Serge came to similar conclusions. He pointed out that the trial created the impression that there never had been an October Revolution and that Bolshevism had never existed, but instead a band of unscrupulous adventurists had been at work. Then the "leader of the peoples" saved the Soviet Union from this band and turned it into a flourishing nation. Such a conclusion, in Serge's opinion, might have seemed true to unsophisticated people because the trial was based not on naked falsifications, but on a mixture of lies and truths, of the plausible and improbable. Serge felt that it was entirely possible that Bukharin and Rykov, or Tukhachevsky and Gamarnik, watched the solidification of the monstrous Stalinist regime that was destroying the Old Bolsheviks, and began to think up a plan for a "palace revolution." "If these people had not developed such thoughts," Serge correctly noted, "they would have to possess the souls of sheep going submissively to slaughter." Serge noted that the organizers of the trial used "the phenomenon of rationalization, which is known to every psychologist under the name of projection or guilt transference."[17]

Despite all of Vyshinsky's attempts to prevent the defendants from describing their genuine political feelings, in much of the testimony evidence emerged about how disturbed they were by Stalin's policies and their consequences. Thus, Ikramov told how, in a conversation with him in 1933, Bukharin had compared the collective farms to the corvée system [barshchina] and had shared his stark impressions from a trip throughout the territory of Kazakhstan. "When it comes to Kazakhstan, he (Bukharin) is absolutely correct in what he says," declared Ikramov. "...He traveled, looked out the railcar window along the way, and what he saw was horrific. I confirmed this."[18] If we remember that, in 1933, mass starvation was raging in Kazakhstan, then Ikramov's words, which at first glance are not entirely intelligible, become rather clear.

Today, we still do not have a complete picture of the "conspiratorial activism" of the Bolsheviks. Nevertheless we agree with the comment of the French historian, P. Broué, that it is time for a new investigation into the Moscow Trials from the standpoint of establishing which of the claims made at the trials regarding opposition to Stalinism do in fact correspond to reality. To support this conclusion, Broué provides one characteristic example. At the trial of the "Right-Trotskyist Bloc," mention was made of the Trotskyist Raikh, who had emigrated from the USSR and adopted Danish citizenship under the name of Johansson.[19] In his responses to the trial, Trotsky denied that he knew anything about this person. However, in a list of Danish subscribers to the *Bulletin of the Opposition*, Broué found the name of Raikh-Johansson. Such facts, in Broué's opinion, show that a portion of the truth was hidden at the trial behind false charges.[20]

12. The Main Defendant

Many aspects of the third trial can be correctly understood only if one considers that the trial itself was part of a ruthless political struggle in which Stalin was continuously receiving devastating ideological blows from Trotsky.

Although Trotsky was thousands of kilometers from the courtroom, it was no secret to anyone that he was once again the main defendant. As at the previous trials, his name was repeated in the questioning of the defendants, in the indictment speech, in Vyshinsky's speech, and in the court's sentence hundreds of times. "Every one of the defendants," Orlov was justified in noting, "clearly sensed how Stalin's hatred and thirst for revenge, directed at the distant Trotsky, pulsated through the trial. The intensity of this hatred was comparable only to the envy which Stalin had felt years before toward the brilliant capabilities and revolutionary contributions of this man."[1]

Earlier, in response to the second show trial, the Menshevik journal *Socialist Herald* had written: "The maniacal and sadistic malice with which Trotsky is ascribed the role of demon-seducer, of Satan, holding in his hands the threads of all the conspiracies, assassination attempts, acts of sabotage, and both foreign and domestic political threats to the Stalinist regime, testifies only to what a *personal* imprint lies on all this bacchanalia of extermination, what uncertainty, fear and panic embrace the dictator, and how strongly two obsessions gnaw away at him: the thirst for revenge for offenses suffered in the past and hatred towards his possible opponent in the future, who is all the more dangerous because he is beyond reach."[2]

Trotsky understood all too clearly that the trial had been organized primarily as a new attempt to discredit him politically. "The present major trial, like the first two, revolves precisely around an invisible axis, around the author of these lines," he wrote. "All the crimes have been committed invariably on my orders... At my command, members of the Soviet government have become agents of foreign states, they have tried to 'provoke' war, they have been preparing the defeat of the USSR, caused train wrecks, and poisoned workers

Leon Trotsky

with poisonous gases... As if that's not enough, even the Kremlin doctors have been poisoning their patients for my benefit!"[3]

Trotsky noted once again that, according to the trial material, premiers, ministers, marshals, and ambassadors had invariably subordinated themselves to one person, and on his orders had been destroying the nation's productive forces and culture. He then added: "But here a difficulty arises. A totalitarian regime is the dictatorship of the apparatus. If all the key points of the apparatus are occupied by Trotskyists, who are at my command, why in this case is Stalin in the Kremlin, and I am in exile?"[4]

But even if one were to acknowledge, Trotsky continued, that his influence had spread to his former friends and co-thinkers, then how could one explain the behavior of Rykov and Bukharin? For these were people who, as members of the Politburo, had worked hand in hand for many years with Stalin in waging a bitter political campaign against Trotsky, producing hundreds of "anti-Trotskyist" speeches and articles. Then they had voted for his expulsion from the party, for his domestic exile and banishment abroad. But as soon as Trotsky ended up in emigration, they began not only to agree with his views, but proved to be ready to commit any crime according to his "instructions."

According to the designs of the trial's organizers, the most "fatal" testimony against Trotsky should have been that given by Rakovsky and Krestinsky. Rakovsky said that Trotsky himself had told him about his ties with British intelligence, which had begun as early as 1926.[5] Krestinsky moved Trotsky's espionage activity still further back — to 1921, when Trotsky supposedly came to an agreement with the German General Seeckt that the German Reichswehr would finance the "Trotskyist organization" in exchange for espionage information handed over by Trotskyists to the Reichswehr.[6] In this way, Trotsky's service to foreign powers was traced back to the period when he was a member of the Politburo and head of the Red Army.

One more "innovation" at the trial was information about the colossal resources which Trotsky and the Trotskyists were supposedly receiving simultaneously along several channels. Krestinsky testified that the Trotskyists received from the Reichswehr alone in 1923-30 two million marks in gold.[7] Rozengolts announced that, with the aid "of one of the foreign governments," Trotsky and the Trotskyist organization were given 300,000 dollars, 27,000 pounds sterling and 20,000 marks, all from the People's Commissariat of Foreign Trade.[8] Grinko said that he had helped Krestinsky finance the Trotskyists at the expense of the foreign currency reserves of the People's Commissariat of Foreign Affairs.[9] Even from the budget of the NKVD, according to the testimony given by Yagoda and Bulanov, Trotsky was handed over tens of thousands of dollars.[10]

Regarding this aspect of the trial, N. I. Sedova [Trotsky's wife] wrote: "Hundreds of people — it must have been over a thousand — knew the austere life Trotsky had led, how great his material difficulties had been ... Hundreds had seen Leon Sedov live and die in a state of poverty that at times deserved to be called something worse... When we arrived in Mexico, we owned practically nothing and American friends saw to our basic needs... And the Trotskyist movement? In every country where it existed... the government and anyone who had had anything to do with its groups knew how poor they were and at what great personal sacrifice their irregular publications were brought out."[11]

All this did not mean that the money which the defendants mentioned did not exist. Under the guise of the sums which Krestinsky supposedly received from Germany for the needs of the Trotskyist movement, the defendants had in mind the foreign currency deposits made by the Reichswehr to the Soviet government as payment for the training of German officers on the territory of the USSR. The resources from the People's Commissariat of Foreign Trade, the transfer of which to the Trotskyists was one of the charges against Rozengolts, were part of the enormous sums of foreign currency transferred on the orders of the Politburo to subsidize the foreign activity of the Comintern and secret operations of the OGPU-NKVD.

At the trial, new dates and addresses were given for conspiratorial meetings between Trotsky or Sedov and the defendants. On the first day of the trial's work, Bessonov declared that in October 1933, Trotsky had met with Krestinsky at the Italian resort of Merano, "despite the fact that it was extraordinarily difficult for Trotsky to disappear from France at this time."[12]

Krestinsky confirmed that at that time he had been in Merano for medical treatment, but he categorically denied meeting there with Trotsky. Two days later, Krestinsky not only confessed to this meeting, but added some details: Trotsky had arrived with Sedov under someone else's passport.[13] However, at the time named by Krestinsky and Bessonov, Trotsky had remained continuously in the city of Barbizon under the guard and watchful eye of the French police, which was soon documented.

A confusing fate also awaited Krestinsky's testimony about his meetings with Sedov in Germany in 1929 and 1930. Soon it was shown that until February 1931, Sedov had lived in Turkey without ever leaving. Rozengolts spoke about his conspiratorial meetings with Sedov in 1933 in Austria and in 1934 in Czechoslovakia. In these cases, too, it was easy to prove the falsity of the testimony, since from the time he arrived in France at the beginning of 1933, Sedov never left that country.

Just as fantastic was the testimony about secret correspondence between Trotsky and the defendants. Bessonov declared that in December 1936 or at the beginning of 1937, he sent a letter to Trotsky in Norway which was from Krestinsky, and after a few days he received Trotsky's reply to Krestinsky.[14] After this statement the world press carried an announcement from the Norwegian police: from the beginning of September 1936, all mail for Trotsky, who was interned at that time, was controlled by the head of Norway's passport office, and a copy was made of every incoming and outgoing letter. From 18 December 1936 until 9 January 1937, Trotsky was en route from Norway to Mexico, and during this ocean voyage was deprived of any opportunity to communicate with the outside world.

Of course, the goals of the trial went beyond the framework of compromising Trotsky politically, which was necessary in order to weaken his influence on left forces abroad. The trial pursued even broader goals, both of a domestic and foreign political nature.

13. The Trial's Domestic Political Goals

After the last capitalist class, the kulaks, had been liquidated in the USSR, it became impossible to explain the burdens and deprivations endured by the people by referring to the intrigues of hostile class forces. As a result, a new political and ideological task appeared on the agenda — to convince the Soviet people through massive ideological pressure that all their sacrifices during the terrible six years of forced collectivization (1928-1933) had been justified, and the country had entered into a period of "happy life." However, the majority of the population in their everyday activity by no means felt that "life has become better, life has become more joyful," as was incessantly repeated by official propaganda. Therefore what was demanded was the shifting of the blame for a "slowdown" in the betterment of the people's welfare onto arch-villains and conspirators who were consciously destroying the fruits of the labor of the Soviet people and impeding the flourishing of the nation; they were trying to enslave the people and to force them under the heel, not only of the land-owners and capitalists, but of the most brutal fascist regimes.

Stalin did not arrive at such a decision at the outset. During the first trial (of Zinoviev-Kamenev), mention was made only of terror against "leaders," and nothing was said about crimes directly aimed against the general population. At the second trial (of Radek-Piatakov), the circle of crimes committed by the "Trotskyists" was widened substantially to include deals with the fascist powers concerning the defeat of the USSR in a future war and the dismemberment of the country. It was there that significant attention was paid to sabotage, in particular, the organization of industrial catastrophes and railway accidents that claimed the lives of tens and then hundreds of simple people. The trial of the "Right-Trotskyist Bloc" laid blame on the "conspirators" for everything that contradicted the widespread assurances that "a happy life" had begun. Along these lines, the defendants confessed to criminal activities that supposedly had been causing all the suffering and burdens that the Soviet people had been forced to bear in the 1930s.

Noting that the totalitarian regime was capable of answering its economic failures only with cynical demagogy and ruthless repressive measures, Trotsky wrote: "What is called 'sabotage' in the language of Stalinist justice is in actual fact the ill-starred consequences of the bureaucratic methods of command. The phenomena of disproportions, wastefulness, and confusion, which are growing ever more, threaten to undermine the very foundations of the planned economy. The bureaucracy invariably is looking for someone who is "guilty." In the majority of cases, such is the hidden meaning of the Soviet trials against saboteurs."[1]

If the Radek-Piatakov trial intended to remove responsibility from Stalin and his clique for the mistakes and failures in the areas of heavy industry and transport, then the trial of the "Right-Trotskyist Bloc" spoke primarily of the deliberate disorganization of those branches of the economy most closely affecting the population: the municipal economy, trade, the production of commodities of mass consumption, and so forth. The defendants confessed to undermining these branches in order to embitter the population against the government. As was clear from their testimonies, with these goals in mind they did not shrink from engaging in even petty sabotage, for instance, interrupting the supply of school notebooks, in order "to provoke dissatisfaction in the broad masses."[2]

For years, Grinko, the People's Commissar of Finances, exerted enormous effort in order to follow a zigzag course between inflation and deflation, thereby obeying the contradictory orders emanating from the Politburo. Now he was confessing to the disorganization of financial matters and, in particular, to deliberately decreasing the number of local savings bank branches in order to cause long lines, which would in turn anger the population.

The trial paid special attention to blaming the crimes of the "Right-Trotskyist Bloc" for the severe failures in agriculture, which were a particularly painful burden for the population. The defendants cited figures which testified to the gigantic scale of the deliberate poisoning of livestock and of the spoilage of food reserves in order to create starvation in the country. Chernov, the People's Commissar of Agriculture, declared that, on the orders of German intelligence, he impeded the construction of warehouses and grain elevators in order to embitter the peasants over the senseless loss of grain that had been harvested.[3] Sharangovich "confessed" that, on orders from the center of "rightists" and Polish intelligence, 30,000 horses were infected with anemia in Belorussia, and an enormous number of pigs were infected with the plague.[4]

Characteristic in this vein was the questioning of Zelensky, who directed the system of consumer cooperatives. He said that phenomena with which

13. The Trial's Domestic Political Goals

Isaak Zelensky
(1890-1938)

the population collided every day in trade were the result of conscious sabotage: miscounting, mis-weighing and deceiving the customers, embezzlement, theft, and so forth. Zelensky explained that a desire to provoke dissatisfaction against the government lay behind the deliberate organization of holdups in trading, during which, according to him, "for about two weeks" in many shops there would be no sugar, cheap tobacco, salt, etc. When the prosecutor asked: "Was there an instance or instances when you tried periodically to leave Moscow without eggs," Zelensky replied that in 1936 he allowed "50 railway carloads of eggs to be spoiled through sabotage."[5] In a country tormented by every imaginable shortage and which only five years before had suffered through massive starvation, such "confessions" could not have failed to produce a strong impression on a population that had grown accustomed to seeing empty counters in the stores.

Not satisfied with all this, Vyshinsky asked Zelensky: "And how did things stand with butter because of your sabotage activity?" "A whole generation of children born after 1927," Orlov wrote in this regard, "was unfamiliar with even the taste of butter. From 1928 until 1935, Russian citizens could see butter only in the windows of so-called foreign-trade stores, where everything was sold only in exchange for gold or foreign currency. In 1935, when the card-ration system, which had been in effect for six straight years, was finally ended, butter appeared in commercial stores, however at a price which was absolutely beyond the reach of the populace."[6]

Surprised by the prosecutor's question, Zelensky said that the consumers' cooperative did not generally trade in butter. "I am not asking what it is you trade," Vyshinsky declared in response to this. "You traded away earlier than anyone the most important thing, the motherland, but I am speaking about what measures your organization undertook in order to disrupt the circulation of commodities and deprive the population of the most badly needed items of primary consumption. ... Do you know anything at all about butter?"

Since the defendant could not know beforehand what answer the prosecutor was demanding from him, Vyshinsky suggested to him that, on orders from the "Right-Trotskyist Bloc," "you did not release inexpensive kinds of butter." After this prompting, he forced Zelensky to confirm that "there were instances" when glass and nails were added to butter in order to "cut the throat and stomachs of our people."[7]

In his indictment speech, Vyshinsky mentioned the attempts of the defendants "to strangle the socialist revolution with the bony hand of hunger," and made a statement, the likes of which had not been seen in even the most apologetic and pharisaical articles in the Soviet press. From this statement it was clear that an abundance of products had already been achieved in the nation. The population could not enjoy the fruits of this abundance only because of the "saboteurs' organization," which had wanted "to take what we possess in abundance, and turn it into a deficit, to hold the market and the needs of the population in a state of tension." "In our country, rich with every kind of resource," Vyshinsky intoned, "there could not have been, and cannot be a situation where there is a deficit of one or another product... Now it is clear why, here and there, we have shortages, why suddenly, in conditions of wealth and the abundance of produce, we are missing this, that, or some other thing. The precise reason is because these traitors are to blame. All the more so because it gave them grounds for creating moods against the system of our economic regulation, against the entire system of Soviet power."[8]

Much was written in the commentaries of the Soviet press about mood swings of the masses under the impact of the trial. Thus, *Izvestiia* published the resolution of a collective farm meeting which said: "Now we know why our horses and livestock have been dying."[9]

Besides domestic political goals, the trial pursued far-reaching foreign policy goals.

14. Foreign Policy Goals of the Moscow Trials

Starting with 1933, the international status of the Soviet Union rapidly began to grow stronger. The western press often published statements of the type: "The Kremlin holds the fate of Europe in its hands," or "Stalin has become the international arbiter." Assessments of this kind originated in the presence of two objective factors: the sharpening of antagonisms between the major capitalist powers, and the strengthening of the industrial and military might of the USSR.

Under these conditions, the Moscow Trials were staged not only to mislead Soviet and foreign public opinion. They fulfilled important foreign policy functions, signaling whom at a given stage the Kremlin viewed as an ally, and whom as an enemy. In the feverish conditions of the 1930s, when the government of any capitalist power was afraid of facing a military alliance between the USSR and other states, the "confessions" of the defendants about their espionage activity were elicited to highlight changes in the foreign policy orientation of the Soviet government. Insofar as the diplomatic combinations of those years were constantly changing, the content of the accusations changed as well, particularly when it came to the defeatist activity and espionage of the arch-conspirator Trotsky. The governments of the capitalist countries were in no hurry to deny these charges. What explains this, most of all, is that they viewed Trotsky as a more dangerous opponent than Stalin, insofar as they legitimately saw in him the future leader of the world revolution, the possibility of which was looming throughout the 1930s. Even in August 1939, when diplomatic relations between Germany and France were at a point of rupture, the French ambassador Coulondre told Hitler that, in the event of a new world war, "the actual winner" would only be Trotsky, to which Hitler replied: "I know."[1]

After Trotsky's first articles abroad, the Soviet press called him nothing other than "Mister Trotsky." On 8 March 1929, *Pravda* carried an expansive article which stated that Trotsky was performing a service for Churchill and Wall Street by publishing his articles.

During the sharpening of relations with Poland, *Pravda* published a forged document which was supposed to convince readers that Trotsky was an ally of the Polish dictator Pilsudski.[2] Two years later, the Soviet ruling circles began to elaborate plans to establish a Soviet-Polish alliance. In 1933, on Stalin's orders Radek was sent to Poland, where he was triumphantly received by Pilsudski. He spoke of the beginning of friendly relations between the Soviet Union and Poland as "two countries emerging from revolution." After this statement, references to Trotsky's collaboration with Pilsudski disappeared from the pages of the Soviet press.

Until 1933, Germany was among the friends of the Soviet Union and the main enemy was considered to be France. Therefore at the trials of the "Industrial Party" (1930) and the "Union Bureau of Mensheviks" (1931), the defendants were charged with coming to an agreement with the French government as the center of hostile intrigues against the Soviet Union. When, in July 1933, Trotsky arrived in France, *L'Humanité* quickly declared: "From France, this center of anti-Soviet sentiment, Trotsky will attack the USSR — here is the strategic point, and that is why Mister Trotsky comes here."

After Hitler came to power, Stalin tried to maintain cordial relations with Germany. An expression of these intentions was the probing article in *Izvestiia* which stated that the USSR was the only country in the world that harbored no ill will toward Germany, "regardless of the form and composition of the Reich's government."[3] Therefore, in the Soviet and Comintern press, although Trotsky, as before, was not accused of deals with the German ruling circles, he continued to be called an agent of the Entente.

Right up until the Moscow Trials, such accusations suggested only that Trotsky was applying his literary efforts to "add grist to the mill" of states hostile to the USSR. Only non-party specialists and former Mensheviks were accused of deals with such states at the beginning of the 1930s.

The supposed treachery and defeatism of Trotsky and Trotskyists, all to the benefit of capitalist states, began to be mentioned only in 1936. With every trial the circle of these states widened, and the espionage contacts of Trotsky and the Trotskyists was moved ever further back into the past.

By the time of the second trial of Zinoviev-Kamenev in August 1936, it became clear that Stalin's plans to improve relations with the Third Reich were encountering resistance on Hitler's part. Therefore the defendants at this trial were accused of collaboration with the Nazis for the sake of preparing the assassination of Stalin and other Kremlin leaders. This scheme, which was not distinguished by an abundance of imagination, was reworked and rendered more complicated at the trial of Radek-Piatakov. Here there was talk of Trotsky's direct conspiracy with the governments of Germany and Japan, di-

14. Foreign Policy Goals of the Moscow Trials

1937 caricature by Deni of "Judas Trotsky" leading German and Japanese forces to war against the Soviet Union

rected at preparing the defeat of the USSR in a future war with these powers. "It was no accident," wrote Trotsky, "that this formulation of the charges coincided with the flourishing of the policy of the Popular Front. On the banner of Soviet diplomacy, and thereby the Comintern, was inscribed the creation of a military bloc of the democracies against the alliance of fascist countries. ... In their international intrigues, the defendants carefully adapted to the forms and calculations of Soviet diplomacy. They might make an attempt on Stalin's life, but not on Litvinov's* policy."[4]

The preparation of the third trial coincided with the strengthening of Germany's international positions, and the fading of hopes for Popular Fronts and a military alliance between the USSR and Great Britain. The replacement of the English Minister of Foreign Affairs, Eden, with the pro-Hitler Lord Halifax was a symptom of England's rapprochement with Germany. In light of this, new diplomatic ideas arose in Moscow that influenced the content of the defendants' "confessions." The previous scheme, according to which the Trotskyists served the German-Japanese bloc exclusively, was discarded. The defendants were declared agents of a whole synod of capitalist states: Germany, Japan, Poland, and England.

At the trial of the "Right-Trotskyist Bloc," the charges did not distinguish between the Weimar and Nazi regimes. The ties between the Trotskyists and Germany lost their purely fascist coloration; according to Krestinsky's testi-

---

* Litvinov, M. M.: People's Commissar of Foreign Affairs from 1930 to 1939.

mony, they began even in 1921. It turned out that, after Hitler seized power, the Trotskyists automatically transferred their services to the Nazis. In an attempt to make this nonsensical tale more credible, Bessonov declared that the opposition groups in the Soviet Union had already entered into an agreement with certain circles in the National Socialist Party in 1931, and that from 1933 they had tried to impede the normalization of German-Soviet relations. They did so in order to show the German industrial and military circles that good relations between Germany and the USSR were impossible under Stalin. In 1936, according to the testimony of this same Bessonov, Trotsky and his supporters tried to urge the ruling circle in Germany to hasten the start of war.[5]

The establishment of Trotsky's conspiratorial ties with England was placed in 1926, although at the previous trial, Radek, who according to Vyshinsky was the Trotskyist minister of foreign affairs, did not mention a word about these ties in his wide-ranging testimony. In explaining this paradox, Trotsky wrote that Moscow had considered England to be a peace-loving and democratic state at the beginning of 1937, but after Eden's retirement, Moscow once again relegated England to the camp of aggressive imperialist powers. "Litvinov decided to show his teeth to London. The defendants quickly take this into account... Rakovsky's testimony, which turns him and me into agents of the Intelligence Service, is in actual fact a diplomatic warning addressed to Chamberlain (the Prime Minister of Great Britain – V. R.)!"

The inclusion of Poland among the countries collaborating with the Trotskyists had a similar goal. After the shift of British policy toward Germany, the pro-German orientation of Poland also became much more manifest. Moscow therefore decided to "show Warsaw that it had no illusions about the latter's neutrality, and that in a future war Poland would have to be prepared to become an arena for the confrontation between the USSR and Germany. Through the mouths of the defendants, Litvinov threatened Colonel Beck (who was then Minister of Foreign Affairs for the Polish government – V. R.)."

By 1938, only the USA and France remained from the conception of the "bloc of democracies" as a counterweight to the fascist-militarist "axis." These countries were therefore not named among the states whose governments had been conspiring with the Trotskyists. Trotsky considered the silence about France to be eloquent in its absurdity. The Trotskyists, who had reputedly established ties with enemies of the USSR in 1921, "absolutely skipped over France, as if they had forgotten about her existence. No, they forgot nothing; they simply foresaw the future Franco-Russian pact and were wary of creating any difficulties for Litvinov in 1938." It is true that Rakovsky spoke at the trial of his espionage contacts with French industrialists and journalists. But all the people he named belonged to the opponents of the Popular Front,

14. Foreign Policy Goals of the Moscow Trials

which was in power in France. "The defendants, in any case, remained true to themselves: in their most 'treacherous' deals with foreign states they carefully protected the Kremlin's diplomatic plans."

In drawing the balance sheet of the discrepancies in the confessions of "betrayal" at the three Moscow Trials, Trotsky came to the conclusion that "the treacherous activities of the defendants are only the negative complement to the international machinations of the government." As the diplomatic calculations of the Kremlin changed, the content of the "treachery" of the Trotskyists changed also. In this process, "today's combinations and interests became empowered to completely refashion the events of the last twenty years." In particular, this retrospective adaptation to changes in the international situation had a telling effect on the versions about the treacherous activity of Trotsky himself. "In 1937 my old friendship with Winston Churchill, Pilsudski and Daladier was forgotten," wrote Trotsky. "I became the ally of Rudolf Hess and a cousin of the Mikado. For the indictment of 1938, my old calling as an agent of France and the United States proved to be absolutely inappropriate; however, my forgotten friendship with British imperialism became an exceptionally pressing matter... Thus, even in my 'betrayals,' I continue to fulfill a patriotic function."[6]

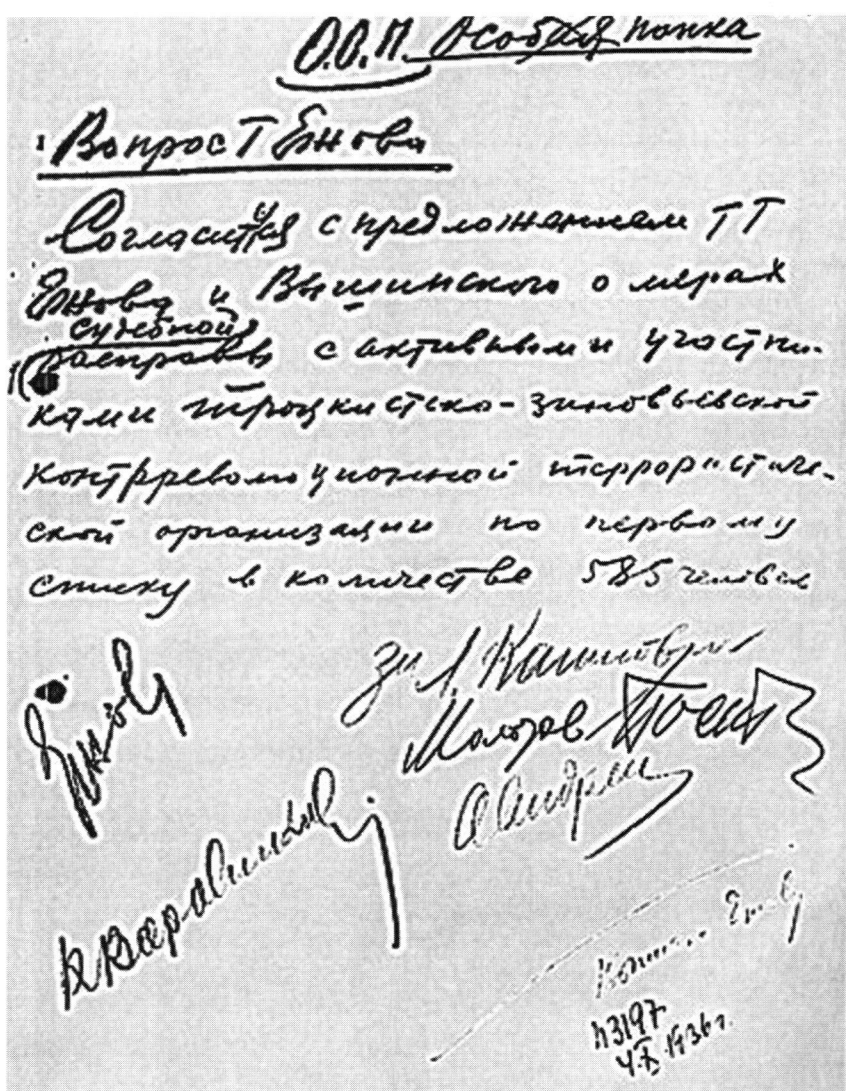

Yezhov polls members of the Politburo on 4 October 1936

The text reads: "Do you agree with the proposal of Comrades Yezhov and Vyshinsky concerning measures of judicial reprisal against active participants in the Trotskyist-Zinovievist counter-revolutionary terrorist organization according to the first list of 585 people."

The following people respond "For": Kaganovich, Molotov, Postyshev, Andreev, Voroshilov and Yezhov. [Stalin was on vacation].

The note was designated for a Special Folder [особая папка], but seems to have been filed under О.О.П [Separate (?) Special Folder].

15. The General Prosecutor

In the immediate conduct of the Moscow Trials, a key role belonged to Vyshinsky, which by itself was an insult to the defendants. Vyshinsky was a right-wing Menshevik who had occupied a high post during the Provisional Government. After the October Revolution he waited for a long time, and only in 1920, when the Civil War was coming to a close, did he apply to join the ruling party.

While the old Leninist guard maintained the leading role in the party, Vyshinsky was doomed to remain at secondary posts and await expulsion from the party at the time of party purges. Expelled in the course of the general purge of 1921, he was readmitted into the party a year later. In 1924, the commission to purge non-production party cells once again took away his party card, which was returned to him only upon intervention by the chairman of the Party Collegium of the Central Control Commission, Solts, after Vyshinsky went into hysterics in his office.[1]

From 1923, Vyshinsky worked as prosecutor in the judicial collegium of the Supreme Court of the USSR. His colleagues in this establishment were Krylenko, Karklin, Galkin and other Old Bolsheviks, who "did not consider the revolution and Soviet power to be the source of any privileges for themselves. They did not seek high posts or personal benefits. They dressed poorly, although they could have had any clothing they desired, and they limited themselves to meager nourishment at a time when many of them needed a special diet in order to restore their health which had been shattered in tsarist prisons."[2] They all despised Vyshinsky and considered him a wretched careerist.

As the persecution and defeat of the inner-party oppositions proceeded, Vyshinsky, much like several other former Mensheviks (for instance, Maisky and Troyanovsky), began to assume ever higher positions. From 1925 to 1931 he served as rector of MGU [Moscow State University] and chairman of the main directorate of professional education at the People's Commissariat of

Enlightenment of the RSFSR. Then he returned to legal work, rising within several years from Prosecutor of the RSFSR to General Prosecutor of the USSR.

Parallel with practical work, Vyshinsky served as a theoretician of criminal and procedural law. The widely held belief that he publicly defended the position describing the defendants' confession as the "tsarina of proof" is hardly true. M. S. Strogovich's book, *The Criminal Trial*, which was published in 1936 with Vyshinsky as editor, states: "In a system of formal evidence, the confession of one charged with a crime was considered 'the best evidence in the world,' and 'the tsarina of evidence.' Now, belief in the absolute truthfulness of a confession by the accused has to a significant degree been destroyed: the accused can make a false confession... Therefore the confession of the accused, as any other evidence, must be checked and evaluated according to the totality of all the circumstances of the case... Over-evaluating the evidentiary significance of the confessions by the accused does not to any degree correspond to the principles of the Soviet criminal trial, nor does relying on them as the fundamental and most important evidence: the testimony of the accused in a Soviet trial does not and cannot have such significance."[3] This point of view also found reflection in articles in the *Great Soviet Encyclopedia*. Thus, S. Prushitsky's article "Evidence" states the following: "Confession is viewed in bourgeois countries as evidence, and besides, as the most dependable evidence, as the 'tsarina of all evidence.' In order to receive this confession, the criminal police resorts to various methods, among which the most reliable during the Middle Ages, particularly in the practice of the Inquisition and religious trials... was considered to be torture."[4] In a more concise form, these views were repeated in the article, "Confession," published in 1940, when Vyshinsky was the main editor of the section on state and law in the encyclopedia.[5]

In his indictment speeches at the Moscow Trials, Vyshinsky introduced a number of substantive "correctives" into legal theory. Thus, in his speech at the trial of the "Right-Trotskyist Bloc," he rejected the standpoint commonly accepted among criminal scholars, according to which the general agreement and intent of each of the criminals serves as evidence of participation in a crime. He declared that this standpoint "could not be accepted by us, never has been adopted, and has not been accepted. It is narrow and scholastic. Life is broader than this point of view."[6] On these grounds, Vyshinsky demanded the conviction of the members of the illusory "centers" and "blocs," for crimes about which, even according to trial material, they knew nothing.

The Moscow Trials became the most prominent moment in Vyshinsky's life. He fulfilled the role he was offered as state prosecutor with sadistic satisfaction, replacing legal formulations with a flood of vulgar abuse, consisting of such expressions as "damned vermin," "stinking carrion," "watchdogs of imperialism," "wretched scum," "animals in human form," "stinking heap

15. The General Prosecutor

Andrei Vyshinsky

of human waste," and so forth. "Vyshinsky spoke with the defendants," wrote Trotsky, "not in the language of a lawyer, but in the conventional jargon of an accomplice, a conspirator, or a master of deception, using the jargon of thieves."[7] Characterizing Vyshinsky's style of behavior and his subjective motives at the trials, Trotsky noted that "every mediocre journalist is capable of writing beforehand the text of tomorrow's prosecutorial speech delivered by Vyshinsky, perhaps only with fewer terms of vulgar abuse. Vyshinsky combines his personal trial with the political trial. During the years of the revolution he was in the camp of the Whites. Changing his orientation after the Bolsheviks' decisive victory, he long felt oppressed and under suspicion. Now he is taking his revenge. He can mock Bukharin, Rykov, and Rakovsky, whose names for a number of years he pronounced with exaggerated respect."[8]

Vyshinsky understood that the defendants experienced particular humiliation from the fact that they were being accused of betraying the revolution by a man who was in the enemy camp during the revolution's crucial years. Knowing that none of them would dare to recall his own past, he displayed inexhaustible imagination in finding ways to mock his victims. "He fell upon the defenseless Stalinist prisoners with such sincere pleasure," wrote Orlov, "not only because Stalin was demanding that the score be settled with them, but because he himself was glad to have the chance to reckon with the Old Bolsheviks... Knowing that sitting before him on the defendants' bench were the innocent victims of the Stalinist regime, that in the next few hours they would be shot in the cellars of the NKVD, it seems he experienced sincere delight when he trampled on the last remnants of their human dignity, blackening everything in their biographies which he perceived to be the most outstanding and sublime."[9]

The more famous the personality of the defendant and the more significant his revolutionary deeds, the more frequently did Vyshinsky recall that he saw in him only a "counterrevolutionary bandit." At the trial of the "Right-Trotskyist Bloc," he said to Rakovsky, whom even the anti-communist Conquest calls a "legendary figure": "In your explanations today you have generally allowed a number of expressions, as if you are forgetting that we are talking about you as a member of a counterrevolutionary, bandit, espionage, and sabotage organization of traitors. I feel obliged... to ask you to stick more closely to the essence of the treacherous crimes you have committed, and to speak without philosophy or similar things, which are completely out of place here."[10]

According to Orlov, the leaders of the NKVD did not have the right to tell Vyshinsky about the Inquisitional methods applied to those under investigation. They showed him only some of their cards, and pointed to dangerous areas which must be avoided during the court sessions. The scenario of the future trial, the "crimes" to which the defendants would have to confess — all this was formulated without Vyshinsky's participation. They admitted him to interrogations during the pre-trial investigation only when the accused had already given a confession. Therefore "Vyshinsky wracked his brains trying to guess what extraordinary means the NKVD had used in managing to crush or paralyze the will of these leading Leninists and to force them to slander themselves. One thing was clear to Vyshinsky: the defendants were innocent. As an experienced prosecutor he saw that their confessions were supported by no objective evidence of guilt... The fate of the defendants not only did not depend on Vyshinsky, he did not even know what sentence had been prepared in advance for each of them."[11] All that he firmly knew was that the slightest misstep at the trial would reflect in a deadly manner on his own future.

The fate of Solts, who was known as the "conscience of the party," was tragically entwined with Vyshinsky's fate. For many years Solts headed the supreme party court — the party collegium of the Central Control Commission [CCC]. Although at that post he could not help but participate in the expulsion of Trotskyists from the party, according to Orlov, "only during the last years of his life, under the influence of the all-embracing terror, did he have to repeat the Stalinist slander against Trotsky."[12]

In 1937, Solts, who occupied the post of assistant to the prosecutor of the USSR in the judicial-civil sector, tried to gain access to the investigative dossiers of several Old Bolsheviks. Having known Vyshinsky while they were studying in law school, Solts demanded that he show him material from the case of Trifonov, his comrade in the Bolshevik underground and in exile at Narym. In response to Solts's expression of doubt over Trifonov's guilt, Vyshinsky repeated a phrase which was typical for those years: "If the organs

15. The General Prosecutor

Aron Solts
(1872-1945)

took him away, that means he is an enemy." To which Solts began to shout: "You are lying! I have known Trifonov for thirty years as a genuine Bolshevik, but I have known you as a Menshevik."

In the fall of 1937, Solts spoke at a conference of party activists from the Sverdlovsk region and demanded that a commission be created to investigate Vyshinsky's activity. After these words, part of the audience froze in horror, but the majority began to shout: "Down with him! Away from the tribune! A wolf in sheep's clothing!" Solts tried to continue his speech, but they dragged him from the tribune.[13]

In February 1938, Solts was removed from the prosecutor's office. He tried to arrange a meeting with Stalin, with whom he had shared a cot during work in the underground. When Stalin refused to receive him, Solts declared a hunger strike. After this, they placed him for two months in a psychiatric hospital. But even from there he emerged not entirely broken. In September 1939, he sent a letter to Ulrikh, with whom at one time he had worked in the amnesty commission of the TsIK. In this letter he declared: "On 21 April 1939, my niece, Anna Grigorievna Zelenskaia, was convicted by the collegium of the Supreme Court. She had separated from Zelensky ten years ago and has been living ... at my apartment, from where she was taken during those evil days when cases were being fabricated and charges were being formulated under Vyshinsky's leadership."

Noting that recently *Pravda* had often published articles about slanderers whose denunciations had caused the sentencing of many innocent people, Solts wrote: "I suppose that the guilt of the slanderers is not so great, if the court is such that it so readily listens to the slanders and bases its judgement upon them. Unfair judges and prosecutors, who allow such sentences, should be made to answer much more harshly."

With unconcealed sarcasm and indignation Solts mentioned that "not long ago, Goliakov, the chairman of the Supreme Court of the USSR, weighed in with an article in *Pravda*. In it he explains that the court should be just, and the rights of the defendant be protected. In actual fact, he admits, in many cases this is not observed, for which he provides many examples. Unfortunately, there are many more of them, there are many thousands of them, and Goliakov is a bit late in issuing the call to improve the work of the court."

In conclusion, Solts turned to Ulrikh with the following demands: "You must act on the judges with more decisive measures... I beg you to demand the case (of Zelenskaia) and to say what you think. If you do not do this, then in essence you, too, will bear responsibility for this unjust affair."[14]

During the war, Solts was one of a group of Old Bolsheviks evacuated to Tashkent. There he remained in a state of deep depression. Yuri Trifonov met him in evacuation and recalled that Solts "was continuously writing on long sheets of paper some kind of endless rows of figures. I do not know what this was. Perhaps he was writing something valuable in the old underground code."[15] Solts died a few days before the end of the war. Not a single newspaper carried his obituary.

As for Vyshinsky, he was generously rewarded by Stalin. In 1939, he was elected to the Central Committee of the VKP(b) and was made an academician, plus he was appointed to the post of deputy chairman of the Sovnarkom. Later, he worked as the First Deputy Minister and then Minister of Foreign Affairs until 1953, when this post was returned to Molotov. Vyshinsky died almost two years after Stalin's death, while occupying the post of permanent representative of the USSR to the United Nations.

Vyshinsky's political portrait would not be complete if we did not say that he derived not only career benefits from the repressions, but also mercenary and proprietary advantages. Thus, after the arrest of Serebriakov, one of the main defendants at the second Moscow trial, Vyshinsky obtained his share in a cooperative countryside home. Vyshinsky then transferred the dacha to the balance of the economic directorate of the Sovnarkom and built next to it another dacha which cost the government 600,000 rubles. In 1945, a decree of the Sovnarkom bearing Stalin's signature granted new dachas to "those who particularly distinguished themselves in the war"; as a beneficiary of this decree, Vyshinsky, put his former dacha up for rent, thereby receiving a steady source of non-labor income.[16]

16. The Sentence

Many people who were used to providing the ideological foundations of the trial assisted Vyshinsky's efforts at falsification as much as they could.

The memoirs of E. A. Gnedin are instructive in this regard. Among his duties was the censoring of articles filed by foreign journalists attending the trial. After the first few sessions of the trial, when Gnedin discovered that the foreign correspondents were noting the patent absurdities contained in Bessonov's testimony, he hastened to tell Vyshinsky about what was going on. The latter replied in "a purely businesslike manner": "Fine, I will have another word with Sergei Alekseevich [Bessonov]."

Gnedin sensed the precariousness of his own position because he had worked as first secretary in the embassy of the USSR in Berlin from 1935 to 1937, when Bessonov occupied an advisory post there. At the trial Bessonov mentioned Gnedin's "illegal ties" with Bukharin and Radek, although he added that "Gnedin was timid and took no part in anything."[1] These words did not find their way into the transcript of the trial, and Gnedin was arrested a year later in connection with the attempt to fabricate the "Litvinov case."

A whole cohort of journalists and writers was assigned to shed light on the trial in the pages of the Soviet press. The writer Avdeenko, who worked at that time in *Pravda*, recalled that after he had asked Koltsov for a pass to the trial, Koltsov looked at him "with a strange look of alarm" and confided to him:

"You're wrong to be in such a hurry to go there. Don't go! ... You can't imagine what is going on there. They are all saying the same thing: the Military Collegium, the state prosecutor, the defense, the witnesses and the defendants themselves. It's a strange trial. Very strange. I ran from there. I couldn't get over what I saw and heard."

Avdeenko reports that he listened to these words by Koltsov "in amazement, with growing indignation, although I had always trusted him with all my heart."[2] It should be noted that on the next day *Pravda* carried an article

Boris Yefimov's cartoon mocking Rykov, Bukharin, Trotsky and others as creatures fed by their Nazi masters

by Koltsov, who had "run from" the trial. The title of the article was "A Pack of Bloody Dogs."[3]

Koltsov's brother, Boris Yefimov, published his response to the trial in the form of caricatures. One of them depicts a two-headed creature (Trotsky's face is on one head, Bukharin's on the other) with animal paws and fur, held on a leash by an arm decorated with a swastika.[4]

After the trial, all the movie screens throughout the land showed the film, *The Sentence of the Trial Is the Sentence of the People*, which presents Vyshinsky's indictment speech. In it, Vyshinsky outdoes himself in demonstrating that the conspiracy unmasked at this trial was much more grandiose than the conspiracies mentioned at the earlier trials since it united innumerable underground groups of Trotskyists, Rightists and nationalists from all the republics. Pouring a torrent of the filthiest abuse on the defendants, Vyshinsky called them a "band of criminals... whom even criminals slight as the worst, lowest, most despicable, and most corrupt of them all."[5]

In their final remarks, the majority of the defendants described their crimes in almost the same terms Vyshinsky had used. Rykov stressed that he "had exposed and betrayed" all his former co-thinkers "who remained in my memory." He declared that he wanted to use his last words in order "to

16. The Sentence

Arkady Rozengolts
(1889-1938)

exert as much influence as possible on my former supporters who, perhaps, have not yet been arrested and who have not laid down their arms, and about whom I knew nothing or forgot... I would like ... them all to understand that laying down one's arms, even at the risk of incurring certain losses or even arrest, is the only thing that gives any degree of relief."[6] Ivanov reproached Bukharin for "not telling the entire truth here, ... because he wants to preserve the remnants of the hostile forces which still take refuge in their lairs."[7] In making such statements, the defendants let it be known unequivocally that the terror would not diminish after the present trial.

Rozengolts said that he would like in his "last address to the audience ... to recall what was good in my life, unreservedly good," and that in this regard he told about "the enormous support which Stalin always gave me during the civil war." After declaring that "we are on the rise in the Soviet Union unlike anywhere else in the world," he stressed this idea by starting to sing the song, "My Native Land Is Boundless."[8]

Rakovsky spoke of his personal friendship with Trotsky which had spanned 34 years and lamented to the court only that the prosecutor's demand to deprive him of his freedom for 25 years did not correspond to the "physiological limitations of the defendant who stands before you."[9]

The court spared the lives of only three defendants, but for two of them (Rakovsky and Pletnev), the prison sentences were so long that they could only emerge from prison after they had turned 90. All three were shot in October 1941 in the Orel prison, together with a large group of other political prisoners who were executed before Hitler's troops seized Orel. Half a year before this, Rakovsky told Aronson, a member of the NKVD: "I have decided to change my tactics: until now I have asked only for clemency, but I have not written about the case itself. Now I will write a declaration demanding the review of my case, with a description of all the 'secrets of the Madrid court,' of the Soviet investigators. At least let the people who handle this declaration know how they 'concoct' exaggerated cases and trials out of a desire for personal political revenge. Perhaps I will die, perhaps I am a corpse, but keep in mind ... sometimes even corpses begin to speak."[10]

Rakovsky did not know that "corpses" ... "had begun to speak" even during the time of the trial itself — through the voices of Trotsky and foreign left-wing activists who left not a single stone standing of the Moscow trial's fabrications. A sharp political struggle over the trial arose abroad, and the voices of witting and unwitting yes-men who supported Stalin were overcome by the voices of honest political figures and journalists.

17. International Response to the Trial

Stalin made sure that foreign society was informed about the trial in the shortest possible time. The publication of the English text of the court transcript was accomplished with such telegraphic speed that a day after the trial was finished, it had already appeared in book form. At the same time, many propaganda books about the trial were published in foreign languages. Among these was the pamphlet, *The Plot Against the Soviet Union and World Peace,* whose author was Ponomarev, the future academician and secretary of the Central Committee of the CPSU.[1]

Of course, books of such a nature were not intended for the heads of governments, general staffs and secret services of the fascist states, who knew better than anyone else that accusing Trotskyists and Soviet generals of state treason and conspiracy with German and Japanese military circles was the purest fabrication. As for the many short-sighted politicians from the bourgeois-democratic states, they arrived at such a conclusion only after the Second World War, when the publication of secret archives in Germany and Japan thoroughly demolished the false versions about negotiations between Trotsky or his supporters and the fascist powers.

In its assessments of the great purges, the bourgeois press responded in two basic ways to the question of whether Stalin had strengthened or weakened his reign with the purge. On the one hand, the obviously falsified Moscow Trials suggested that the very need to resort to judicial falsifications testified to the weakness of Stalin's regime. On the other hand, many foreign journalists accredited in Moscow helped Stalin in deceiving public opinion in the West by declaring that, as a result of dealing with the opposition and with the obstinate generals, the Stalinist leadership had become more powerful and domineering than ever before.

No small number of foreign observers attended the trial, including representatives of foreign Communist parties. When they returned home, they tried to convince the public in their respective countries that the trial was juridically irreproachable. A similar role was played by the English Labourite Pritt, whose credibility was reinforced by the fact that not long before he had been the chairman of the counter-trial organized in London by the German Communist Münzenberg concerning the case of the Reichstag fire. "The first thing that made a great impression on me, as an English lawyer," wrote Pritt, "was the free and unconstrained conduct of the prisoners. They all looked fine... The trial's sentence and the prosecutor of the Soviet Union gained the well-deserved praise of the major powers of the modern world."

Joseph Davies, the US ambassador to the USSR, also swallowed the bait supplied by the organizers of the trial. During the days of the trial, he wrote his daughter: "The trial has shown all the elementary weaknesses and flaws of human nature — personal ambition of the worst kind. What has become clear are the threads of a conspiracy which nearly led to the overthrow of the existing government."[2] Davies did not limit himself to providing impressions of the trial to those closest to him. He sent detailed accounts to the US Secretary of State, Cordell Hull, and during a trip to England shared his thoughts with Winston Churchill, after which the latter declared that Davies "revealed an absolutely new view of the situation." Davies wrote a book about his Moscow impressions; this book later served as the basis for the film, *Mission to Moscow,* a significant portion of which was devoted to the Moscow Trials.

Unlike Davies and Pritt, the majority of people in the West who knew the situation in the USSR and the personalities of the main defendants experienced extreme shock. The Swiss writer, Peter Weiss, author of the play *Trotsky in Exile,* recalled in the book *The Aesthetics of Resistance* that many fighters in the International Brigades in Spain considered the Moscow Trials to be phantasmagorical, and pondered with anguish the reasons for the confessions of the defendants. Without believing these confessions, they tried to discover a hidden meaning in them. "If Bukharin confesses that he made critical and slanderous speeches against the party leadership," some of them said, "then he wants to draw attention to the alternative which he represents; in doing so he is contrasting Bolshevism to the existing party structure."[3]

Romain Rolland, who had sent futile letters to Stalin about freeing the defendants, wrote during the trial to the French writer and communist J. P. Bloch:

> "For me the Moscow trial is torture... The response to this event throughout the world, and especially in France and America, will be catastrophic. Do the best friends of the USSR not think that we must as quickly as possible send the Soviet authorities a letter (closed,

not intended for publication), entreating them to think about what sorrowful consequences there will be for the People's Front, for the collaboration of the communist and socialist parties, and for the common defense of Spain if the decision is made to sentence the convicted prisoners to the death penalty? Precisely now, when the French CP is doing everything possible to establish a united front of the workers of various ideological tendencies, all efforts are at risk of being undermined as a result of the moral response which such a sentence will receive. After all, it is quite possible (and it would be necessary) to replace it with exile, which would render the defendants harmless without arousing public opinion, that is so deeply confused at the moment."[4]

The trial evoked a wave of protests throughout the world. Refutations were issued by all the people living abroad who were mentioned at the trial as "accomplices" of the defendants: the Mensheviks Dan and Nicolaevsky; the SR Vishniak; left political activists of France such as Rosmer, Paz, Rappoport, and Souvarine; the French industrialist Nicole; and others. A particularly large number of statements were made in defense of Rakovsky, who was well known and highly respected by socialists and diplomats of various countries. Rakovsky's confessions were disavowed by the people he named at the trial. The French journalist Bure announced that when he had visited Moscow he had not been allowed to meet with Rakovsky, despite a preliminary pledge from the authorities that they would organize such a meeting. The famous English philanthropist Paget declared that in 1934 she had met with Rakovsky in the USSR and in Japan, but that their conversations dealt only with questions connected with the activity of the International Red Cross.[5]

On the eve of the trial, the leaders of the Second International and the International Federation of Socialist Trade Unions sent a telegram to Moscow which said:

"We once again consider it our duty to direct the attention of the Soviet government to the harm which these trials and executions are doing to the workers' cause throughout the world. We do not wish to voice our opinion at this time about whether the charges are reasonable or groundless, regardless of how fantastic they may seem. But we cannot help but look with concern at the conduct of the official Soviet press, which condemns all the defendants without exception even before any evidence of their guilt has been presented. Such conduct appears to us to be absolutely opposed to the elementary principles of justice and is capable of creating an atmosphere detrimental to the impartial conduct of the trial."[6]

In response to the trial, F. Adler, the secretary of the Socialist International, pointed to the glaring contradiction which flowed from the actions of the Moscow falsifiers:

> "On the one hand, they accuse the defendants at the Moscow trials of the most despicable crimes, and they openly depict them as some kind of human degenerates; on the other hand, the same defendants are presented to the entire world as pillars and bearers of truth, not only when they accuse themselves, but also when they carry out the duties of slanderers for hire in testifying against others." Adler arrived at the conclusion that "our ideal has never been threatened with a danger as great as now, when fascist criminals are going on the offensive and, unfortunately, have the opportunity to use so widely in their plans the vile actions which are being committed by the dictatorship of madmen which has been established in Moscow."[7]

Vandervelde, the leader of Belgian socialists, stressed that "the working masses in Western Europe cannot fail to be disturbed when they see that the majority of the veterans of the October Revolution are being sent to the gallows."[8]

Pain and despair permeated the lead article of the newspaper of the French Socialist Party, *Populaire*, which was written by Léon Blum. In it he pointed out that the Moscow trial was damaging the Popular Front, giving nourishment to the campaign of French reaction against the Franco-Soviet Pact, and was creating in England and the USA a current of public opinion hostile to bringing these countries closer to the USSR. "People, whose names several months ago still figured among the most important in Soviet history," wrote Blum, "have confessed to committing acts, the reality of which reason cannot accept and the completion of which, much like at the previous trials, was simply physically impossible. Moreover, the falsity of these acts — and I have the right to add this — have been proven from a moral standpoint for us... These are the feelings which I cannot suppress within me. I know very well that tomorrow they will be exploited by the common enemies of both the Soviets and of socialism. But that is not my fault. Why are we forced to make a choice between the word, which becomes dangerous, and silence, which would be a disgrace?"[9]

Populaire showed that the Moscow trial had placed the world proletariat before a tragic alternative:

> "If the accused are truly guilty of the crimes with which they have been charged, then what is anyone to think about a regime which so systematically corrupts the leading circles of a state led by a work-

ers' party? Obviously, this regime suffers from some kind of internal organic defect and is rotting at the root... Or else — the accused are smearing themselves with nonsensical charges, they are innocent, they are honest revolutionaries. What then must we think about a government which instigates false trials, which places completely innocent people on the defendants' bench, and which exterminates all the best people of the revolution in the name of the dictatorship of one person?"[10]

In summarizing the responses of world opinion, Trotsky wrote: "If, at the time of the Radek-Piatakov trial, a significant part of the world press vacillated and remained perplexed, then at the time of the last trial the unanimous conclusions of public opinion stated: this is the most grandiose and most brazen frame-up in the political history of the world!"[11]

Similar conclusions were drawn by the left wing of the Russian emigration. In an article, "The International Significance of the Moscow Trial," R. Abramovich, one of the leaders of the Menshevik Party, wrote:

> "With unprecedented unanimity, the entire truly left press of the entire world, both socialist and liberal, with the exception of the official communist newspapers, have condemned the last trial as a weaving together of lies and slanders, as a historical frame-up, as a crime against all laws of proletarian morality, as the defilement of socialist honor, but most of all, as a shattering blow against worldwide socialism. All political groups without exception, apart from the official sections of the Comintern, all socialist and political organizations, even those which until now have clearly leaned in the direction of Bolshevism, ... now speak as a united front against the crime being committed by Stalin."[12]

Noting that the Moscow Trials presented a picture of diabolically evil deeds supposedly committed by the defendants on the orders of international capitalism and fascism, Abramovich wrote that "there is an infinitely more genuine, infinitely more refined, and most of all, immeasurably more effective method of striking a truly irreparable blow against the Russian revolution and the entire country." This method consisted in having Soviet justice declare before the entire world that the Bolshevik Party had been led by people without principles and convictions, and that "the October Revolution itself, this radiant sun of the world revolution, had been made by the hands of German, Japanese and English spies (Rakovsky, Bukharin, Trotsky and others)." Such a public discrediting of the Russian revolution, according to Abramovich, was weakening the Soviet Union more on the international arena and was causing greater harm to the prestige of the USSR and the cause of world socialism than could have been done by all the real or imaginary saboteurs and spies put together.[13]

F. Dan, another Menshevik leader, called the new judicial tragi-comedy infinitely more despicable than the earlier ones, insofar as it "too obviously bears the character of a simple 'head-hunt' — for the heads of the Old Bolsheviks, for the heads of all who in one way or another had served the revolution which Stalin was now burying ... Stalin is no longer satisfied with depicting his Bolshevik opponents as people who have descended to the lowest depths in fighting against him, the brilliant and wise 'leader of the peoples.' No, they drag out old twists and turns of the inner-Bolshevik struggles of 1917-1918 and later years, which have long ago been recounted even in the Soviet press, they dust off episodes of the pre-revolutionary or war-time periods in order to 'prove' that all the leaders of the old Bolshevism who have either already been shot or not yet shot, were from time immemorial, if not spies for the tsarist secret police, than at least the paid agents of counter-intelligence services around the world."[14]

G. Fedotov arrived at similar conclusions. He wrote that "during the trial of the 21, the mind simply refused to understand this political madness when the state publicly, before the entire world, tore itself to pieces to the joy of its enemies." Fedotov saw the reason for the trial's effect in the bungling which, he felt, was Stalin's defining characteristic. "In pursuing a direct and proximate goal, he forgets about everything else in the world. In order to destroy Yagoda, he doesn't hesitate to expose before the entire world the criminal secrets of the GPU... The leader of the peoples has added the name of poisoner to his historical epithets. And here Stalin heaps his own sins on his collaborators."[15]

Fedotov underscored that "this time Stalin placed on the defendants' bench the cream of the party — to be sure, mixing them with Chekists and provocateurs... Bukharin, principled and pure, the party's favorite, the keeper of ethical legacies. Rakovsky — whose entire life long before Russia and before 1917 passed in revolutionary struggle, whom even Korolenko favored with his friendship. Rykov, the most Russian 'native-son' of the Old Guard, defender of the service intelligentsia who in recent years paid him with their sympathy."[16] These impartial assessments by an émigré journalist are much closer to the historical truth than the evaluations of today's Russian "democrats" and "national-patriots," who paint all the leaders of Bolshevism with one color — black.

The most perceptive members of the Russian emigration detected one of the most dramatic consequences of the Moscow Trials — the compromising of the Bolshevik Party. In the previous trials, the beginning of the conspiratorial activity of the oppositionists was placed in 1932, when, embittered by

17. International Response to the Trial 109

their defeat, the Trotskyists and rightists allegedly embarked upon a path of state treason in order to return to power. Now, however, the threads of their "betrayal" were being extended to 1926, 1921 and even 1918, and the circle of the "traitors" had widened immeasurably. According to the material of the trial, the VKP(b), the government, the Comintern, the Red Army, and the GPU had all been headed for many years by conscious scoundrels, masked adherents of capitalism and fascism, venal hirelings of bourgeois intelligence services, provocateurs of the tsarist secret police, and so forth. Insofar as the profile of a political party is defined by its leaders and ideologists, then the Bolshevik Party was a kind of cesspool in which, from the moment it was founded, people wallowed who were capable of the most heinous crimes. The Moscow Trials indirectly cast a shadow on Lenin as well, since, according to their "revelations," almost all his closest collaborators proved to be the most abject criminals.

The lowering of the authority of Bolshevism and the destruction of its acknowledged leaders aroused profound satisfaction in the most reactionary political circles. During the trial, the Italian fascist semi-official organ, the newspaper *Popolo d'Italia*, wrote: "Has Stalin not become a secret fascist due to the catastrophe of the Leninist system?"[17] Mussolini himself declared gleefully that "until now no one has dealt such blows to the idea of communism (the proletarian revolution) and exterminated communists with such cruelty as Stalin."[18]

Realizing how the great purge was weakening the economic, political and military might of the USSR, Hitler's clique not only inspired articles in the German press about how well-founded the massive repression occurring in the USSR was, but it even sent Stalin forged documents through its secret services intended to convince him of the treachery of the Old Bolsheviks and generals.

In describing the wide spectrum of judgements in the world press about the events occurring in the USSR, Trotsky wrote: "Could there be anything more shameful, than the indifference which the bureaucracy displays with regard to the country's international prestige? ... The Moscow government emerges from the trials it has organized completely discredited. Enemies, as well as possible allies, place its strength and authority on an incomparably lower plane than before the last purge."[19]

10-ый год издания. — Апрель 1938 г. Пролетарии всех стран, соединяйтесь!

БЮЛЛЕТЕНЬ ОППОЗИЦИИ
(БОЛЬШЕВИКОВ-ЛЕНИНЦЕВ)
Bulletin de l'Opposition (Bolcheviks-Léninistes)

ЛЕВ СЕДОВ — РЕДАКТОР-ИЗДАТЕЛЬ С ИЮЛЯ 1929 г. ПО ФЕВРАЛЬ 1938 г.

№ 65

АДМИНИСТРАЦИЯ и РЕДАКЦИЯ — ADMINISTRATION ET REDACTION :
« BULLETIN DE L'OPPOSITION », Librairie du Travail
17, Rue de Sambre-et-Meuse - Paris (10e)
Подписная плата за 12 номеров — 34 фр. фр., за 6 номеров — 17 фр. фр.

Prix 3 fr.

СОДЕРЖАНИЕ:

Каин Джугашвили идет до конца.
Новые невозвращенцы.
Процесс 21-го (От редакции).
Л. Троцкий: Итоги процесса.
— Дипломатические планы Москвы в зеркале процесса.
— Статья Сталина о мировой революции и нынешний процесс.
Л. Т. Роль Генриха Ягоды

Л. Т. Случай с профессором Плетневым.
— Подсудимые Зеленский и Иванов.
— Сталин и Гитлер. (К заключительной речи Вышинского).
Л. Троцкий: Поправки и примечания к показаниям подсудимых.
Правда о «заговоре» на жизнь Ленина в 1918 году.
Из советской жизни: Завод. — ГПУ на заводе. — Выборы. — Московские слухи.

Каин Джугашвили идет до конца

Подлость последней судебной инсценировки моментами тускнеет рядом с ее глупостью. Сталин все еще думает, что при помощи изобретенного им вместе с Ягодой трюка он может обмануть все человечество. Общий замысел инсценировки, мнимые политические планы «заговорщиков», распределение ролей между ними, — как это все грубо и низменно, даже под углом зрения судебного подлога! Из-за спины «великого» Сталина глядит на человечество тифлисский мещанин Джугашвили, ограниченный и невежественный пройдоха. Механика мировой реакции вооружила его неограниченной властью. Никто не смеет критиковать его и даже подавать ему советы. Его помощники, Вышинские и Ежовы, до мозга костей развращенные ничтожества, не случайно заняли свои высокие посты в системе тоталитарного самодурства и разврата. Подсудимые, из которых большинство выше обвинителей несколькими головами, приписывают себе планы и идеи, порожденные гением современного Кречинского и разработанные кликой гангстеров. Гонимые логикой капитуляций и падений, физически и морально раздавленные, терроризованные страхом за близких, гипнотизированные политическим тупиком, в который их загнала реакция, Бухарин, Рыков, Раковский, Крестинский и другие играют страшные и жалкие роли по безграмотным шпаргалкам Ежова. А за стеной Каин Джугашвили потирает руки и злобно хихикает: какой трюк он придумал для обмана солнечной системы!

Но точно ли еще продолжает хихикать за кулисами Сталин? Не спирает ли у него дыханье от непредвиденного оборота событий? Правда, он огражден от мира стеной невежества и низкопоклонства. Правда, он привык думать, что мировое общественное мнение — ничто, а ГПУ все. Но множатся угрожающие симптомы, видимые и для него. Все меньше могут Трояновские, Майские, Сурицы и состоящие при них, в качестве контролеров, агенты Ежова доносить Кремлю отрадные вести из-за границы. Все более острая тревога охватывает рабочие массы всего мира. Все чаще и в все большем числе крысы, именуемые «друзьями», торопятся покинуть угрожаемый корабль. Сгущаются международные тучи. Фашизм одерживает победу за победой, и главным его помощником на всех мировых путях оказывается сталинизм. Грозные военные опасности стучатся во все ворота Советского Союза. А Сталин тем временем разрушает армию и попирает страну. Каин вынужден идти до конца. Он торопится окропить свои руки кровью Бухарина и Рыкова. Он еще может позволить себе сегодня эту роскошь. Но все меньше способен он вкушать «сладость» мести. Все труднее становится хихикать тифлисскому пройдохе, подброшенному мутной исторической волной на трон термидора. Безмерно накопляется вокруг него не-

April 1938 issue of the *Bulletin of the Opposition* with Trotsky's article "Cain-Dzhugashvili Goes All the Way"

18. Trotsky on the Moscow Trials

During the third Moscow trial, Trotsky wrote about twenty articles and comments for the world press. Describing his psychological state as he received regular reports from Moscow, he noted: "For almost a year and a half, I have been living virtually without respite in the atmosphere of the Moscow Trials. And nevertheless, each new telegram... seems to be delirious ravings. I must make an almost physical effort in order to separate my own thoughts from the nightmarish combinations of the GPU and to direct them to the questions: how and why is all this possible?"[1]

Trotsky's first responses to the trial bore the character of impassioned emotional invectives. It is hardly possible to find in any other article he wrote more angry and frenzied words about "the system of totalitarian tyranny and debauchery" than those which are contained in the article, "Cain-Dzhugashvili Goes All the Way." "Out from behind the back of the 'great' Stalin," it says, "the Tiflis philistine Dzhugashvili, a limited and ignorant scoundrel, gazes at humanity. The mechanics of world reaction have armed him with unlimited power... The accused, the majority of whom are several heads above their accusers, ascribe to themselves plans and ideas which have been fostered by the genius of a modern-day Krechinsky* and developed by a clique of gangsters. Driven by the logic of capitulation and collapse, physically and morally crushed, terrorized by fear for their closest ones, and hypnotized by the political impasse into which reaction has driven them, Bukharin, Rykov, Rakovsky, Krestinsky, and the others are playing horrific and pitiful roles according to Yezhov's illiterate cheat-sheets. And behind the wall, Cain Dzhugashvili rubs his hands and giggles maliciously: what a scam he has dreamed up to fool the solar system!"[2]

---

* Krechinsky: main character in A. V. Sukhovo-Kobylin's comic satire "Krechinsky's Wedding" (1854). A consummate con artist, Krechinsky is cynical, manipulative, and contemptuous of other people. As a literary type, Krechinsky served to debunk some of the demonic aspects of the early nineteenth century romantic hero.

Lev Karakhan,
shot 20 September 1937

Khristian Rakovsky,
shot 11 September 1941

Of course, Trotsky could not limit himself to emotional denunciations alone, despite their accuracy or the degree to which they had been tempered by the force of reason. In his responses to the trial he provided detailed argumentation which was capable of convincing any honest person that the trial was false and fabricated. A new act of the sharpest political confrontation was being played out. At one pole stood the absolute ruler of an enormous state, possessing colossal material resources and a gigantic slander apparatus. At the other stood a solitary exile, stripped of means, separated by thousands of kilometers from his friends and co-thinkers, and surrounded by an impenetrable barrier from his country.

Each time that Trotsky uttered a new word exposing him, Stalin answered with new political murders and falsifications, obediently disseminated by the servile Comintern press throughout the world. Encircled by a hostile ring, Trotsky was able to use the only resource which remained at his disposal — the weapon of logic and truth aimed at the common sense and moral sensitivity of thinking and honest people throughout the globe.

The third Moscow trial was a laboratory of the big lie which exceeded in its cynicism and shamelessness all the previous judicial stage adaptations. It confirmed Trotsky's prediction which had been made during the Radek-Piatakov trial: "Stalin resembles a man who tries to slake his thirst with salt water. He will be forced to stage further judicial frame-ups."[3] The next frame-up presented the Soviet state "as a centralized apparatus of state treason,"[4] and all the members of Lenin's Politburo, with the exception of Stalin, as conspirators and traitors — even when power was concentrated in their own hands. According to the picture presented at the trial, the greatest Soviet diplomats (Rakovsky, Krestinsky, Karakhan, Iurenev, Bogomolov) had served foreign intelligence services. The overwhelming majority of people's commissars of the USSR and all the heads of government for thirty union and autonomous republics, who had been advanced by national-liberation movements, had tried to dismember the Soviet Union and place its people under the yoke of

18. Trotsky on the Moscow Trials

Nikolai Krestinsky,
shot 15 March 1938

Konstantin Iurenev,
shot 1 August 1938

fascism. The heads of industry, transport, agriculture and finance were almost entirely saboteurs. People who had given the revolutionary movement thirty, forty, even fifty years (as had Rakovsky), had conducted subversive work for the sake of restoring capitalism. Taken together, all these charges that stained the honor of Bolshevism exceeded even the slander of the White emigration, which had accused Lenin, Trotsky, and other Bolshevik leaders of carrying out the October Revolution on behalf of the German general staff.

Summing up the innumerable absurdities of the Moscow Trials, Trotsky wrote: "As often happens in life, 'common sense' strains at mosquitoes, but swallows camels. Of course, it is not easy to believe that hundreds of people are slandering themselves. But is it really easier to believe that the same hundreds of people have been committing horrifying crimes which contradict their own interests, their psychology, and their entire life's cause? ... Which is more probable, we ask further: that a political exile, deprived of power and resources and separated from the USSR by a smokescreen of slander, with the wave of his little finger over a number of years has caused ministers, generals and diplomats to betray the state and themselves in the name of unrealizable and absurd goals; or, that Stalin, who has at his disposal unlimited power and... all the means of terrorizing and corrupting people ... has forced the defendants to give testimony which would correspond to his (Stalin's) goals? ... In order to finally overcome shortsighted doubts raised by 'common sense,' we can pose one more question, the last one: what is more probable — that witches in the Middle Ages were truly in contact with demonic forces and released cholera, pestilence, and cattle plague on their own villages after nightly consultations with the devil ('the enemy of the people'), or that the unfortunate women simply slandered themselves when faced with the red-hot poker of the Inquisition?"[5]

A return to medieval barbarism proved possible "only in the thoroughly poisoned atmosphere which has accumulated under the leaden lid of the totalitarian regime."[6] But not even the omnipotence of Stalin, who forced dozens of his helpless victims to confess to crimes they had not committed, could compel thinking people to believe in the series of judicial phantasmagorias. "Despite the extraordinary power of his craftiness, armed with all the resources of state power and the latest technology, the Moscow trials, taken as a whole, are striking for their grandiose absurdity, and the delirium of a limited man... It would not be an exaggeration to say that the main accusations of the trials have been permeated with the spirit of totalitarian idiocy."[7]

The only consolation which could be felt in the face of the last, terrible and nonetheless ridiculous trial, Trotsky emphasized, consisted in the radical shift in world public opinion, which accurately assessed the crudity of its conception and execution. This, however, could not diminish the damage done by the trials and the great purge as a whole to the Soviet Union. In anguish for his country and its heroic people who ended up under the unbounded power of a dictator who did not acknowledge even the semblance of personal and political morality, Trotsky insisted: no matter how one judged the defendants, no matter how one judged their behavior in the clutches of the GPU, with the content of their entire lives they had proven their selfless devotion to the Russian people and its struggle for liberation. "By shooting them and thousands of those who are lesser known but no less devoted to the cause of the workers, Stalin continues to weaken the moral powers of resistance of the country as a whole."[8]

Trotsky pointed out that for many years the extermination of witnesses to his own crimes had been an inherent characteristic of Stalin's state activity. With the Moscow Trials he was trying to "fill all the holes and cracks, and create a hermetic, or, to use a newer term, totalitarian environment for the most gigantic frame-up in world history."[9] The replacement of the entire diplomatic corps and the entire foreign espionage apparatus served the same goal — concealing crimes and failures in the realm of international politics. However, several "non-returners" emerged from this milieu (see chapters 39-40), who then gave testimony before world public opinion exposing the rotten underpinnings of Stalin's frame-ups.

In preparing for the massive purges, Stalin promoted the idea of a new "constitution, the most democratic in the world." His plan was to present world public opinion with the picture of a country which, after harsh years of struggle and deprivations, had finally begun to raise the welfare of its people and allow democracy to flourish. Against this optimistic background, the diabolical figures of the Trotskyists were supposed to appear sinister as they destroyed the economy, organized famine, poisoned the workers and prepared to hand over the happy land to be torn asunder by fascist thugs. "Resting on the totalitarian apparatus and unlimited material resources, Stalin conceived a unique plan: to do violence to the world's conscience and with the approval of all mankind to deal once and for all with any opposition to the Kremlin

18. Trotsky on the Moscow Trials

clique." At first, he was given the full support in this endeavor by the liberal "friends of the USSR," who competed in heaping praise on the opening of the era of democracy in the USSR. Trotsky emphasized that if a collection of their articles about the democratic turn-about in the Kremlin's politics were now to be published, then "many of the authors would have nothing left to do but burn with shame."

Recalling that many western journalists and writers had explained all his warnings about Stalin's plans for an Inquisition as arising from "personal hatred," Trotsky wrote: "Personal hatred is generally a petty and despicable feeling when dealing with questions and relations on an historical scale. Besides, hatred is blind. And in politics, just as in personal life, there is nothing more terrible than blindness. The more difficult the circumstances, the more necessary it is to follow the advice of old man Spinoza: 'Neither to cry nor to laugh, but to understand.'"[10]

Trotsky saw a tragic symbolism in the fact that the Moscow trial coincided in time with Hitler's entry into Austria. He felt that this coincidence was no accident. Hitler was growing much less fearful of a challenge to his expansionist pretensions coming from Moscow, because he was "extremely well informed of the demoralization which the ruling Kremlin clique had introduced in the army and the nation's population during its struggle for self-preservation."[11] Fascism was achieving victory after victory, and was creating an ever more ominous military threat to the Soviet Union at the very time when Stalin was weakening the nation with his barbaric purges.

Trotsky pointed out that no statistical calculations are able to give an exhaustive portrayal of the processes of the economy, politics and culture, which, in the final analysis, are relations between people and social groups. "The Moscow judicial tragedies have revealed that these relations are wretched, or, to be more precise, unbearable." The Stalinist regime had been fundamentally transforming the social relations generated by the October Revolution. "No class ever in history has concentrated in its hands in such a short time such wealth and power as the bureaucracy has done during the period of the two five-year plans. But by doing so it has placed itself in increasing contradiction to the people who have passed through three revolutions and overturned the tsarist monarchy, nobility and bourgeoisie. The Soviet bureaucracy is now concentrating within itself, in a certain sense, the traits of all these overthrown classes, without having either their social roots or their traditions. It can defend its monstrous privileges only through organized terror, just as it can base its terror only on false accusations and frame-ups."[12]

These words lead toward an explanation of the main historical paradox of the great purge and of one of the main questions that arises before those investigating it: why did the bureaucracy, which elevated Stalin to power and became the social foundation of his authoritarian rule, demonstrate its weakness in the face of the campaign of extermination that Stalin unleashed against it? Lacking support in property relations, being alienated from the people and sensing no support from the laboring masses, the bureaucracy proved incapable — if only out of a feeling of self-preservation — of opposing Stalin, and followed after him in pursuing its own annihilation.

"For two decades," Trotsky argued, "all spheres of government life witnessed a selection of the most outstanding, most appropriate, most capable and talented people for the most responsible posts."[13] To the extent that the proletarian dictatorship degenerated into the personal dictatorship of Stalin, there was an ever-increasing sharpening of the contradiction between the personal qualities of these people and the functional role of the social layer they comprised. Despite the fact that the degenerative processes had seized a significant part of the party, state, military and economic apparatus, toward the beginning of the great purge this apparatus consisted for the most part of talented people, capable of independent thought and creative activity — at least within the framework of their professional duties. But it was precisely these people who were slated to be swept away under conditions of an absolutist regime.

In the course of the great purge, the bureaucracy as a social layer kept losing ever more capable and honest people and found them being replaced with limited and morally deficient careerists. To an ever greater degree the bureaucracy was becoming the perpetrator of decline, demoralization, and degradation of the nation in all spheres of social and political life. This process was expressed most clearly of all in the realm of the economy. "Tossing charges of sabotage to the right and left," wrote Trotsky, "has led to dismay in the entire administrative apparatus. Every objective difficulty is explained as personal negligence. All negligence, whenever necessary, is equated with sabotage. Every district and every region has had its own Piatakov shot. The engineers of planning bodies, the directors of trusts and factories, the master — all are mortally frightened. No one wants to bear any responsibility for anything. Everyone is afraid of showing initiative. At the same time, one can end up being shot for showing insufficient initiative. The overexertions of despotism lead to anarchy. A regime of democracy is needed by the Soviet economy no less than high quality resources or good lubricants. The Stalinist system of management is nothing but the universal sabotage of the economy."[14]

This system, combined with the rise to leadership at all levels of unprepared, incompetent and unskillful people, led to a sharp decline in rates of economic growth. The growth of industrial production, which reached 28.8 percent in 1936, sank to 11.1 percent in 1937 and 11.8 percent in 1938. In 1939-1940, industry as a whole remained at the same level — the production of steel, iron, rolled iron, paper and oil practically failed to rise, and the production of automobiles, tractors and other types of farm machinery even fell in comparison to 1936.

It is significantly more difficult to express in figures the damage done by the great purge to the development of culture. The consequences of this destruction bore an even more painful and, more importantly, longer-lasting character. "The last trials, and in general the whole purge which is dishonest in its goals and methods," wrote Trotsky, "have finally established the domination of slander, baseness, denunciation and cowardliness... Scientists, teachers, writers or artists who are the least bit independent or talented are frightened, persecuted, arrested, and exiled, if not shot. The untalented scoundrel triumphs across the board. He prescribes the path that science is to take, and dictates the rules of creativity to art. A stifling stench of decay wafts from the Soviet press."[15] Such an intellectual atmosphere led to the sharp decline of the cultural and moral level of society, which in the post-Stalin period was only partially compensated by the successes of the Soviet educational system and by a certain broadening of intellectual freedom, a liberalization of cultural life.

Responding to the voices of Western liberals who had gone from positions of uncritical support for Stalin to positions of an equally uncritical rejection of Bolshevism, Trotsky wrote: "Let no one tell us: here is what the October Revolution has led to! This is almost the same as shouting when one sees a shattered bridge over Niagara: here is what waterfalls have led us to! ... The October Revolution led not only to judicial frame-ups. It gave a mighty impetus to the economic and cultural life of a great family of nations." But due to an intricate complex of foreign and domestic, objective and subjective reasons, new social antagonisms arose in Soviet society, and on their foundations a bureaucratic dictatorship grew up, possessing neither ideas, nor honor, nor conscience. In its struggle against the new society, this bureaucracy resorted to unprecedented crimes. This political regime, which came into ever greater contradiction with the social foundations of Soviet society laid down by the October Revolution, was capable of carrying "to the bottom of the historical abyss all the social gains which a number of generations of the Russian people had paid for with countless sacrifices."[16]

In the end, this more pessimistic variant of Trotsky's prognosis became a reality; no small role was played in this by the conduct of the post-Stalin bureaucracy, including its attitude toward the Moscow Trials.

Khrushchev and Stalin

Khrushchev speaking at the Twentieth Congress of the CPSU

19. The Historical Fate of the Moscow Trials

The discovery (and concealment) of the truth about the Moscow Trials followed complex and winding paths in the USSR.

Khrushchev's report to the Twentieth Congress of the CPSU in 1956 contained descriptions of "Trotskyists" which directly suggest that the charges made against them were fabricated. "Now, when a sufficient historical period has passed," Khrushchev declared, "we can speak absolutely calmly about the struggle against the Trotskyists, and investigate this matter with sufficient objectivity. After all, there were people around Trotsky who by no means had come from a bourgeois milieu (this "not guilty" passage is a typical example of the Stalinist vulgarization of a class approach. – V. R.). Some of them were party intelligentsia, and some of them were from the workers." Recalling that many Trotskyists had taken an active part in the struggle for the socialist revolution and the consolidation of its gains, Khrushchev expressed confidence that, if Lenin had remained alive, he would not have allowed their physical annihilation.[1]

These statements were an undoubted step forward in freeing the history of the inner-party struggle from Stalinist falsifications, although they continued to counterpose Trotskyism to Leninism; indulgence was given only to those oppositionists who "broke from Trotskyism." This corresponded to the entire spirit of the report, in which, as before, Stalin's services were underlined in the political struggle against Trotskyism and other "anti-party currents" whose line, according to Khrushchev, "led essentially to the restoration of capitalism, to capitulation before the world bourgeoisie." Stalin's "mistakes" were seen to lay in the fact that he had resorted to bloody repressions against his ideological opponents after they "had already long since been demolished politically."[2]

It would seem that raising the question even in this way should have led to an immediate review of the Moscow Trials. Even before the Twentieth

Congress, the Presidium of the Central Committee of the CPSU had created a commission to investigate them. However, as Khrushchev announced at the June 1957 Plenum of the Central Committee, Molotov and other stooges closest to Stalin had done "everything possible not to allow a serious investigation of these cases."[3]

After these individuals were driven from the Central Committee, Khrushchev's hands were freed for a serious and thorough-going investigation. On orders from the Central Committee of the CPSU, the security and party organs conducted a new and careful analysis of the material from the Moscow Trials. From 1959 to 1963, seven (out of seventeen) defendants of the second trial and ten (out of twenty-one) defendants of the third trial were rehabilitated. News of the innocence of several of them was widely circulated in the press, and a few were paid respectful tribute as leading members of the party. Thus, in Uzbekistan, many streets, enterprises and collective farms were named after F. Khodzhaev and A. Ikramov. In addition, 1957 witnessed the full rehabilitation in a juridical and political sense of all the participants of the "military organization," who, according to the material from the trial of the "Right-Trotskyist Bloc," had entered into that bloc.

By 1956 the members of the Presidium of the Central Committee already clearly understood that the main defendants of the Moscow Trials were innocent of the crimes with which they had been charged. In a meeting with Rykov's daughter, Mikoyan replied to her question about the rehabilitation of her father: "This is a political question. It is one we will decide, not the prosecutor. He, of course, never betrayed anyone and did not sell out ... If he had held out at the time, then he would be working now."[4]

By the time of the Twenty-Second Congress (1961), all the judicial information about the falsified character of the Moscow Trials had been assembled. In the prelude to the Congress, rumors spread widely in Moscow about the impending rehabilitation of all the victims of these trials. However, Khrushchev then decided not to take this next logical step along the path of destalinization. A factor here was the pressure of the Chinese leadership, who reproached him with the complaint that the exposure of Stalin's crimes had already delivered a blow to "the cause of world socialism." Another factor was the explosive consequences of the official re-examination of the show trials in the "countries of people's democracy," which had contributed to the tragic events in 1956 in Hungary and Poland. Under the influence of these factors Khrushchev acted like a pendulum: at times he would issue new exposures of Stalin, and then he would suddenly praise his contributions, including those in the fight against "enemies of the people."

According to Khrushchev himself, the leaders of the European Communist Parties, especially Maurice Thorez and Harry Pollitt, dissuaded him from carrying out what had been fully prepared: the exposure of the open trials. They insisted that revealing the truth about the trials would cause an even greater departure from their parties of communists who remembered well the assurances of their leaders that Stalin's legal system was just (a mass exodus from these communist parties had occurred under the influence of the exposures of Stalin's crimes at the Twentieth Congress of the CPSU). As a result of these inter-party negotiations, the decision was made not to raise the question of the trials at the Twenty-Second Congress.

As he searched in his memoirs for arguments to justify this cowardly and shameful decision, Khrushchev declared that "we took, as they say, a sin on our souls in the interests of our party, our ideology, our common workers' cause … If we had published true material about the open trials, then this would have become, if you will, an abstract truth (? — V. R.) … For what's been done can't be undone." In his words, the rehabilitation "of honest people, devoted to and very valuable for the USSR, but simply having some other views," was set aside by the leaders of the CPSU at that time until the day came when "all those who had lived (in the 1930s – V. R.) would leave, as they say, for another world."[5]

Khrushchev's claim that clearing the names of former oppositionists of deliberately false accusations would be beneficial "only to our enemies, the enemies of socialism, the enemies of the working class," masked the unwillingness of the ruling circles in the Soviet and foreign communist parties "to stir up the past," which was dictated by concern not for the interests of socialism, but for personal interests. After all, the judicial rehabilitation of former opposition leaders would have led to the restoration of their political names and would have prompted an analysis of the ideological alternative to Stalinism which they had advanced. Tarnished by their shameful past statements about the justice of reprisals against "enemies of the People," Khrushchev and other leading bureaucrats of the "thaw" period were neither ready for nor capable of reassessing the inner-party struggle. To do so would have unavoidably called into question not only the conception of party history which had been maintained since Stalin's time, but also the Stalinist conception of socialist construction which had been firmly deposited in their consciousness and which determined their current politics.

Khrushchev's explanation of the unwillingness to even approach the question of the historical fate and political role of Trotsky appears particularly deplorable. "We did not deal with Trotsky and the question of his death," he declared. "*We did not raise the curtain and did not even want to.* We had waged an ideological battle against Trotsky, we had condemned him, we had been and remained opponents of his ideology, of his conceptions. He brought no small harm to the revolutionary movement, and moreover he perished outside the territory of the USSR, he died without a trial and investigation" (my italics – V. R.).[6] Even in his memoirs, Khrushchev lacked the courage to mention the secret action taken during his rule: inviting Trotsky's assassin, Mercader, to Moscow after he had finished his twenty-year prison sentence. There he was presented with the Gold Star of Hero of the Soviet Union, a medal he had been granted during Stalin's time.

In the first chapters of his memoirs, Khrushchev proved to be incapable of going beyond the Stalinist interpretations of the inner-party struggle of the 1920s. As before, he claimed that this struggle had been waged "with Leninist party methods," using free democratic discussions and free voting in party organizations. However, the further Khrushchev proceeded in his reminiscences of the past, the more he subjected his earlier views and judgements to a critical rethinking, and the more frequently he noted the political merits of the leaders of the anti-Stalinist oppositions. In speaking about the way Stalin annihilated almost all the party leaders who had "fought in the ranks of the party for its consolidation," he added: "In the note before his death, Lenin mentioned that the two most outstanding men in the party were Trotsky and Stalin. And then he wrote about Stalin's negative characteristics."[7]

During the 1960s and 1970s, questions of the character of the Moscow Trials were widely discussed in the Western communist press. However, even in the book by a famous leader of the British Communist Party which came out after the Twenty-Second Congress of the CPSU, R. Palme Dutt stated that the enemies of communism "declare that all the legal trials conducted by the Soviet organs of state security... were, they say, frame-ups. These monstrous distortions and exaggerations of a serious fact — of a desire to correct what was done — are possible at the present time in the West only because the prolonged process of legally reviewing and investigating events of that period is still not complete. We still cannot counterpose precise and full information to these fabrications ... Historians must wait until the work of the legal system is complete."[8]

The legal system, however, during the time of stagnation, refused, in general, to investigate the Moscow Trials any further. The Brezhnev leadership ignored even the calls of foreign communist and socialist parties and prominent figures of Western culture to rehabilitate at least Bukharin, who was seen in the West as the bearer of a humanistic alternative to Stalinism.

The only statement about the innocence of Bukharin and Rykov was made in 1962 at a conference of historians. Replying to a note from the audience, the speaker Pospelov declared, as if it were obvious: "It is enough to study closely the documents of the Twenty-Second Congress of the CPSU to be able to say that, of course, neither Bukharin nor Rykov were spies or terrorists."[9] Such a categorical reference to the Twenty-Second Congress was obviously misplaced, however, for virtually nothing was said about Bukharin and Rykov at the congress. It is also noteworthy that this statement was made by a man who in 1937 had called "the Rightists," headed by Bukharin and Rykov, "a brazen band of enemies of the people, ready to commit any and all crimes against our motherland, a band of fascist scoundrels."[10]

In editions of the new textbook on the history of the CPSU that replaced the *Short Course*, the space devoted to criticizing Stalin and Stalinism sometimes shrinks, and sometimes expands. What is preserved throughout is a taboo against any mention of the Moscow Trials. Even more absurd was the silence regarding the main defendants of these trials in all Soviet reference books and encyclopedias published right until the end of the 1980s. They contained articles about Hitler, Mussolini, and other fascist leaders, but they were completely devoid of biographical material about Trotsky, Zinoviev, Bukharin, and other leaders of the anti-Stalin oppositions. The sole publication in which their lives found any place was Lenin's complete collected works. But even in volume 45 of this edition, which came out in 1964, the culminating moment in criticizing Stalinism, the content of this personal information was basically reduced to statements about their "anti-party activity."

Any positive or even neutral mention of the leaders of the anti-Stalinist oppositions in party histories or in works of imaginative literature was banned without exception. This tendency was reinforced in the 1970s, when a number of thick and pseudo-scientific works were published which were devoted to "the party's struggle against Trotskyism." They reproduced the traditional Stalinist conceptions of the inner-party battles, cleansed only of references to the Moscow Trials and the espionage or sabotage activities of the oppositionists.

The first years of "perestroika" [restructuring] added nothing substantially new to the evaluation of our historical past. Gorbachev's report devoted to the 70th Anniversary of the October Revolution reiterated the traditional Stalinist conception of the party's victorious struggle for the construction of socialism. The report's innovations included only a few critical phrases about Stalin and the first favorable mention of Bukharin, for whom a specific context, however, was chosen: along with Stalin and several other party leaders Bukharin was praised for his contribution in the fight against Trotskyism.

Only when the first failures of the widely advertised "restructuring" began to appear did the Gorbachev leadership decide to put into action a new "openness" which was directed at the past. A commission was created to further study the material connected with Stalinist repression, and this commission finally completed a review of the Moscow Trials. All the defendants (with the exception of Yagoda) were rehabilitated along party and judicial lines. Later, the commission rehabilitated other active oppositionists condemned by closed trials or decisions of Special Boards.

Nineteen eighty-eight witnessed the beginning of the publication of works by the most prominent oppositionists (Bukharin most of all), as well as works filling in the "white spots" of history, including instances of resistance by the communist oppositions to Stalinism.

In the middle of 1989, the first fragments of works by Trotsky appeared in the Soviet press, followed by the publication of several of his articles and books. However the impact of these publications on Soviet society was overwhelmed by the wave of anti-communist propaganda identifying Stalinism with Bolshevism. This tendency was also revealed in the first works about Trotsky which appeared in the USSR, written by the party apparatchik Vasetsky, who had made a party and scholarly career by criticizing "Trotskyism" during the years of "stagnation," and by General Volkogonov, who had achieved fame with his works in the same period by "exposing the ideological diversions of imperialism."* During the years of "restructuring" and "reform," Vasetsky turned into an ideologist of "national-patriotic forces," and Volkogonov — into an ideologist of the "democrats." Both of these tendencies joined in condemning the "utopian" and "criminal" nature of the theory and practice of Bolshevism.

Thus, the prognoses made by Trotsky in 1937-1938 had only partially come true: "The revolution will open all hidden safes... and cover the names of the executioners with eternal damnation. Stalin will leave the scene, weighed down by all the crimes he committed — not only as gravedigger of the revolution, but as the most odious figure in human history"[11]; "the monuments which he built to himself will be demolished or consigned to a museum of totalitarian gangsterism. On the other hand, the victorious working class will review all the trials, both public and closed, and erect on the squares of the liberated Soviet Union monuments to the unfortunate victims of the Stalinist system of baseness and dishonor."[12]

The monuments to Stalin were indeed demolished, and the trials were reviewed — not, however, by the revolutionary people, but by the post-Stalinist bureaucracy.

All of Trotsky's prognoses, however, were multi-faceted by nature. In his works we find a prediction of another kind, which turned out to be much closer to reality: "If the bureaucracy manages, after refashioning the forms of property ownership, to separate out a new propertied class from itself, this class will find other leaders not bound by a revolutionary past and — who are

---

* A criticism of the historical accounts by Vasetsky and Volkogonov, which are comparable in their fantastic and arbitrary manner to the products of the Stalinist school of falsification, is contained in my articles, "'Trotskyism,' Toward a History of the Problem," (*Literaturnoe obozrenie*, 1991, № 8) and "Volkogonov's Trotsky" (*IV International*, 1994, № 1).

more literate. In this case Stalin will hardly hear a word of thanks for the work he has done. The open counter-revolution will deal with him, most likely of all, by accusing him ... of Trotskyism. Stalin will become in this sense the victim of an amalgam of the kind he has already established."[13]

This prediction approximated Stalin's posthumous fate at the end of the 1980s, when the ruling bureaucracy, which had long since lost any consistent ideological connection to Bolshevism, actually did go over to refashioning property forms and producing a new propertied class from its own ranks. This process proceeded along complex and twisted paths, at first masked by calls to "restore the Leninist profile of socialism." During "perestroika" the new wave of exposures of Stalinism were accomplished by constructing the amalgams Trotsky had described. A whole mob of "democratic" journalists and quasi-scholarly writers resurrected not only the charge that Stalin was a Trotskyist (which had been advanced at the end of the 1920s by the "Rightists"), but also armed itself — by using a minus sign — with the thesis that Stalin was the "true continuator of Lenin's cause." These historical forgeries were a necessary condition for ideologically guaranteeing capitalist restoration in the USSR.

The victory of anti-communist forces was facilitated by the prolonged discrediting of Bolshevism which traces its roots back to the Moscow Trials. On their foundations, a sentence was passed on the Bolshevik Party, which was depicted as a cesspool filled with traitors, murderers and provocateurs. Of course, the Stalinist bureaucracy, which had itself in mind when it mentioned the party, continued to praise tirelessly the party which retained the Bolshevik name. It filled the ideological vacuum of a lost faith in Bolshevism by identifying the party with the all-powerful and infallible leader.

The Stalin cult, on which the Soviet people and foreign communists had been raised for decades, was destroyed at the Twentieth Party Congress. In Khrushchev's report, Stalin appeared as he was, as a state criminal (although the words "criminal" and "crime" were not used in the report; the facts, however, that were presented by Khrushchev literally cried out and relentlessly forced one to make such a conclusion).

For millions of people in the USSR and beyond its borders, Khrushchev's report was a shattering blow. Now both Stalin and the Bolshevik leaders he had destroyed (the evaluation of whom had not been reviewed) were acknowledged to be criminals, even though for different reasons. An even more complex problem arose, which the leaders of the CPSU simply dismissed. All the while new errors in the economy and in social life were accumulating, which were conditioned by the maintenance of the political structures and authoritarian methods of management developed under Stalin. By changing nothing in the mechanism of power, each successive leader copied the obvious errors in running the country committed by his predecessor. All this revealed even more the phariseeism of the official, stereotypical propaganda and did even more to destroy the prestige of the party, in whose name its recently glorified "leaders" had been brought down.

Meanwhile the socialist consciousness of the people separated the degenerated party from the ideas of Lenin and the October Revolution, adherence to which continued to live in the souls of millions of Soviet people. Gorbachev tried to play on these moods during the first years of "perestroika," once he had earned the people's trust by calling for the return to Leninist, Bolshevik traditions. However the failure of the "fateful transformations" he had promised prompted him — following the lead of Yakovlev and other anti-communist-inclined advisors — to direct the anger of the people at the country's revolutionary past by means of a new deception. From 1988 — even before it had become possible to publicly criticize Gorbachev — a torrent of slander was poured on Lenin and the Bolsheviks in the Soviet press. In this way, the last ideological layer, which had survived for decades in the people's consciousness, was destroyed.

All these ideological factors were an important element of the destructive process which led to the disintegration of the USSR and the restoration of capitalism in its former republics. Under conditions of a growing national catastrophe, those who continued to call themselves communists proved capable of merely filling the new ideological vacuum with the rehabilitation of Stalinism. One of the ideologists of this movement was R. Kosolapov, who advanced the thesis of a "two-sided role, both purifying and prophylactic, and destructively injurious," played by the mass terror in the 1930s.[14] What precisely Kosolapov sees as "purifying prophylaxis" becomes clear from the tirade which he delivers immediately after citing Stalin's words about sabotage: "After all, wasn't the atomic explosion at Chernobyl the starting point in the chain reaction leading to the destruction of socialism?"[15] From this transparent reference to the hostile intent that supposedly provoked the Chernobyl catastrophe, it follows that, by cauterizing "sabotage," Stalin shielded Soviet society in the 1930s and in subsequent years from similar tragedies.

As for the "destructively-injurious" role of the terror, Kosolapov attributes it to "the new forms of class struggle which had already been fostered by Soviet reality." To these forms he assigns "the infiltration of the law enforcement bodies by foreign elements, who tried exactly to discredit and bleed white the Soviet authorities, often striking with the sword entrusted to them by the authorities even those who were devoted to Soviet power."[16] From these arguments it follows that the crimes during the period of the great purge were committed by Yezhov and his underlings with Stalin's knowledge; the latter, as Kosolapov explains, "was by no means always in control of the situation" which had developed in the "organs."

19. The Historical Fate of the Moscow Trials

In order to counterpose an adequate picture of the events of 1936-1938 to the new and old myths, it is appropriate to examine in succession the role of the main agents of the Great Terror, and after this — its influence on the basic social institutions and social groups of Soviet society.

Kalinin, Yezhov, Stalin, Mikoyan, Molotov, Kaganovich

Kaganovich, Stalin, Postyshev, Voroshilov

20. Stalin and His Intimate Circle

The complete renovation of the entire party and state apparatus left almost untouched its upper layers — people who from the beginning of the 1920s had grouped around Stalin, supported him in the struggle against all the oppositions, and had been tightly bound to him by many years of shared work and personal, everyday proximity. Their preservation at the helm of power was motivated by several reasons. First of all, Stalin had to give the impression that he based himself on the former Bolshevik Party. In order to do this, at the upper echelons of the party he had to preserve a group of Old Bolsheviks, for whom official propaganda had created the image of "true Leninists" and leading political figures.

Secondly, without these people, who possessed no small amount of political experience, Stalin could not have guaranteed the leadership of the country under conditions of the total destruction of party, state, economic and military cadres.

Thirdly, these people were needed by Stalin so that, while basing themselves on their own authority and the authority of "Lenin's Central Committee," they carried out reprisals with their own hands against the party leadership of the republics, territories and regions. After 1928, Stalin himself never once went on working trips about the country. As during the period of collectivization, to carry out punitive measures in the localities, he sent his closest stooges.

Fourthly, these people shared with Stalin not only political, but ideological, responsibility for the mass terror. After outlining, at the February-March Plenum in 1937, the starting points for "liquidating Trotskyist and other double-dealers," over the next two years Stalin never spoke publicly on these questions. On the contrary, in his infrequent articles and speeches of 1937-1938, he included statements about the value of every human life, and so forth. Thus, an article about a meeting between Stalin and the crew of the airplane *Motherland*, who had performed a record flight, states: "Comrade

Stalin warns about the necessity of being especially cautious and careful with the most valuable thing which we have, — with human lives... These lives are more valuable to us than any records, no matter how great and noteworthy these records may be."[1] Stalin "entrusted" the ideological justification of the mass repressions to his "closest comrades-in-arms."

All these considerations explain the fact that the percentage of victims in the Politburo was less than the percentage of victims among members and candidate-members of the Central Committee, apparatchiks of all levels, and rank-and-file members of the party.

In order to guarantee the absolute subordination of his "closest comrades-in-arms," Stalin gathered a dossier on each of them that contained information about their errors, blunders, and personal sins. This dossier would then be supplemented by testimony about the Kremlin leaders that had been obtained in the torture chambers of the NKVD. On 3 December 1938, Yezhov sent Stalin "a list of people (mostly members and candidate-members of the Politburo – V. R.) with a description of the material contained about them in the secretariat of the NKVD."[2] In Stalin's private archive one can also find dossiers with compromising material about Khrushchev, Malenkov, Beria, and Vyshinsky prepared by Yezhov's apparatus.

In addition, Stalin placed each member of the Politburo "whenever possible, in a position where he would have to betray his friends and co-thinkers of yesterday and deliver slanderous attacks against them."[3] Stalin also tested the submissiveness of his stooges by noting their reaction to the arrest of their relatives. Guided by the same Jesuitical goals, he sent people from his closest entourage to confront their recent comrades who had been arrested.

Not all members of the Politburo were privy to the more acute questions surrounding the Great Purge. As Molotov recalled, the Politburo always contained "a leading group. For instance, during Stalin's rule this group included neither Kalinin, nor Rudzutak, nor Kosior, nor Andreev."[4] Officially this extra-statutory "leading group" was constituted by a Politburo decree on 14 April 1937 in the form of a "permanent commission" of the Politburo which was entrusted with preparing "issues of a secret character" for the Politburo, and "in instances of special urgency,"[5] with resolving them itself.

Only members of this commission (Stalin, Molotov, Kaganovich, Voroshilov and Yezhov) developed the strategy and tactics of the Great Purge and had a full conception of its scale. This statement is confirmed by the journals that recorded the names of all the persons who were received by Stalin, and the duration of their stay in his office. Using the published versions of these records,[6] the historian O. Khlevniuk concluded that in 1937-1938, Molotov spent 1,070 hours in Stalin's office; Yezhov — 933; Voroshilov — 704; and Kaganovich — 607 hours.[7] These totals are several times greater than the total hours devoted to receiving the remaining members of the Politburo.

Stalin allowed Molotov, Kaganovich and Voroshilov (and much less frequently, other members of the Politburo) to read the reports sent to him by Yezhov. The *first* group of such reports consists of lists of people whose arrest required Stalin's personal approval. On one of these lists, which included the names of people who "are being verified for arrest," Stalin left the instruction: "You need to arrest them, not 'verify' them."

This group of reports also includes the transcripts of interrogations sent to Stalin with testimony from those arrested against people who still remained at liberty. On one of these transcripts Stalin wrote: "Cde. Yezhov. You should arrest the people I have marked in the text with the letters 'ar.', if they have not already been arrested."[8]

The *second* group of reports includes information about the course of investigations. On such documents Stalin, Molotov and Kaganovich left instructions of the following kind: "Beat, and beat some more."[9] When he received the testimony of the Old Bolshevik Beloborodov, Stalin sent the papers back to Yezhov with the instructions: "Isn't it time to put pressure on this gentleman and force him to tell of his filthy deeds? After all, where is he: in prison or in a hotel?"[10]

The *third* group includes lists of people whose sentences had to be approved by Stalin and his closest stooges. Several of these lists are called "albums." In these albums, which contain 100-200 names each, the cases against the indicted are briefly outlined on separate sheets. At the end of each case is printed the names of the members of the supreme "troika," — Yezhov, Ulrikh and Vyshinsky, as yet without their signatures. On these pages Stalin wrote the number "1," signifying execution, or the number "2," which meant "ten years of incarceration." The fate of those people for whom Stalin didn't assign a number fell to the disposition of the "troika," after which its members placed their signatures beneath each sentence.

In August 1938, Yezhov sent four lists for confirmation, which contained 313, 208, 208, and 15 names (the last list included the names of wives of "enemies of the people"). Yezhov sought approval for sentencing all of these people to be shot. On the same day, Stalin and Molotov placed the same laconic instruction on each list: "For."[11]

As Khrushchev announced at the Twentieth Congress, Yezhov alone sent 383 lists including thousands of names of people whose sentences required confirmation by members of the Politburo. Of these lists, Stalin signed 362; Molotov, — 373; Voroshilov, — 195; Kaganovich, — 191; and Zhdanov, — 177. Eleven volumes of lists, confirmed by members of the highest echelons of the party and state leadership, contain the names of 38,848 communists sentenced to be shot, and 5,449 sentenced to terms in prisons and camps.[12]

Thus, the fate of a significant number of victims was decided in advance by Stalin and his stooges; then, their decisions were formulated as the sentence of a "troika," Special Board, or Military Collegium.

A *fourth* group of reports and records sent to Stalin by Yezhov and Ulrikh contained the results of a precise bureaucratic enumeration of the number of victims. Thus, Ulrikh announced that from 1 October 1936 through 30 September 1938, the Military Collegium of the Supreme Court of the USSR and the regional sessions of the local military collegiums convicted 36,157 people, of whom 30,514 had been sentenced to be shot.[13]

Stalin often established direct personal contact with leaders of the local party organizations. Thus, when he received news about a fire at the Kansk Mill Combine, he sent a telegram to the Krasnoyarsk regional committee: "Fire at mill combine *must have* been organized by enemies. Take all measures to uncover arsonists. Swiftly try the guilty. Sentence to be shot. Publish news of shooting in local press" (my italics – V. R.).[14] It is understandable that when they received a telegram with such content in the heated atmosphere of 1937, the party secretaries and members of the local NKVD would do everything to confirm Stalin's "assumptions." In the case being cited, within two months the following people had been sentenced to be shot for arson at the combine: its former director, the chief mechanic and a group of rank-and-file workers — 16 altogether. Three months later, the local press announced that these people had received 80,000 rubles from foreign intelligence services for burning down the combine.[15]

Stalin sent similar telegrams in code to the district committees with the following warning: "Top secret. Copies are forbidden. Must be returned within 48 hours."

At first, some party secretaries did not believe in the more monstrous directives and turned to Stalin for clarification. Thus, after he had received a directive about establishing "troikas," Yerbanov, the first secretary of the Buriat district committee, sent Stalin a telegram: "I seek clarification, does the troika of Buriat-Mongolia, confirmed by the Central Committee, have the right to carry out sentence?" Stalin quickly replied: "According to established practice, the troikas carry out sentences which are final."[16]

In this way, only a narrow circle of highly placed party secretaries knew of Stalin's actual role in the organization of mass repressions, and the majority of these figures would soon perish in the flames of the Great Purge. For party activists in the localities, the role of supreme executioner was being played by "the closest comrades-in-arms" sent there by Stalin.

In 1938, Barmine wrote the following in characterizing the moral and political profile of Stalin's stooges:

> "They all allowed charges of espionage and treason, and then even murder, to be lodged against three or four of their deputies, one

after another, and their best coworkers, not only without trying to defend them, ... but while heaping cowardly praise on these murders, glorifying the executioners who carried them out, thereby preserving their own posts at the cost of this betrayal and degradation, and thus purchasing their own careers and positions as first people in the state... To our shame and disgrace, a number of Soviet people's commissars occupy such a position, or to be more exact, three or four of them who paid this price to secure their re-election to the new cabinet 'formed' by Molotov. Only in this way did they avoid the fate of 25 of their liquidated colleagues."[17]

Given all this, the people who organized and directed the Great Purge were not primordially bloodthirsty monsters. Even Yezhov, as many who knew him noted, gave the impression of an ingenuous and forgiving person right up until the mid-1930s. But they all lacked character and were noted for their subservience; these were traits that were not inherently part of their character, but were the inevitable consequence of being broken by the unceasing pressure of Stalin's merciless willpower.

In Stalin's relations with those closest to him, the psychological idiosyncrasies of the "boss," which were clearly described by Trotsky, had a telling effect: "Cunning, self-possession, caution, and the ability to play on the worst sides of the human soul were developed in him to a monstrous degree. In order to create such an apparatus, he needed a knowledge of man and his inner motives, a knowledge which was not universal, but a particular knowledge of man from the standpoint of his worst sides, and the ability to play on these worst sides. He had to have the desire to play on them, and a stubbornness, an untiring desire dictated by a strong will and by an uncontrolled, irrepressible ambition. He had to be completely free of principles and he had to lack historical imagination. Stalin is immeasurably more able to use the bad sides of people than their creative qualities. He is a cynic and he appeals to cynicism. He could be called the greatest agent of demoralization in history."[18]

These traits, which allowed Stalin to organize the greatest judicial frame-ups in history and mass killings, were, in Trotsky's opinion, an inherent part of his nature. But "years of uncontrolled totalitarian power were required to lend these criminal traits truly apocalyptic dimensions."[19]

Stalin played on the worst sides not only of those who belonged to his closest entourage, but of those whom he did not know personally, but who were becoming the executors of his sinister plans. During the years of the Great Purge, an atmosphere of permissiveness was created throughout the land when it came to searching for "enemies of the people," or to denunciations and provocations. Here everything could be used — slander, conjecture, public insults, settling of personal accounts, anything which indicated freedom from political principles and moral norms, the absence of moral restraints, and the loss of human traits. Stalin personally raised people capable of such behavior onto a pedestal. An example of this can be seen, for instance, in his attitude to the Kiev graduate student, Nikolaenko, whom he praised at the February-March 1937 Plenum as "a little person" who dauntlessly was able to "expose enemies."

Inspired by Stalin's words, Nikolaenko really let herself go. Thus, after a conversation with one of the Old Bolsheviks, she locked him in a room and called the NKVD: "An enemy of the people is in my office, send some people to arrest him."[20]

When he sent Khrushchev to the Ukraine, Stalin advised him to use Nikolaenko's help in the fight against enemies of the people. When he had become familiar this individual, Khrushchev came to the conclusion that she was mentally ill. When he told Stalin about this upon his return to Moscow, Stalin "flared up and kept repeating: '10 percent of the truth is already the truth, it already demands decisive measures on our part, and we will pay if we do not act accordingly.'" Only after Stalin had received new denunciations from Nikolaenko containing charges against Khrushchev as an "undisarmed Trotskyist," did he allow her to be transferred from the Ukraine to another place. But even then, Stalin "made jokes" as he listened to Khrushchev's stories about the fear which the Kiev communists felt when facing Nikolaenko.[21]

As can be seen from Stalin's correspondence with Molotov, even in personal, confidential communications between the Kremlin leaders an unspoken code of sorts was used. With unceasing certainty and a business-like attitude, the "leaders" told each other about the testimony received from the NKVD as if it were absolutely reliable and indisputable proof of the arrested persons' guilt.

1. Molotov

After enduring a brief period of Stalin's disfavor in 1936 (which can be seen from the absence of his name in the list of leaders against whom the defendants of the first Moscow Trial had allegedly prepared terrorist acts), Molotov soon again became Stalin's right hand, his most trusted confidant and his primary assistant in conducting the Great Purge.

In a number of instances, Stalin turned to Molotov for "advice" in reacting to one or another denunciation. Thus, he sent Molotov a statement in which Lomov, an Old Bolshevik and member of the October Central Committee, was accused simply of being in personal contact with Bukharin and Rykov. After he had read Stalin's note: "Cde. Molotov, what should we do?", Molotov added his own comment: "I am for the immediate arrest of this scum Lomov."[1]

20. Stalin and His Intimate Circle

Molotov and Stalin

In his memoirs Khrushchev mentions a note from Yezhov in which he proposed to exile from Moscow several wives of "enemies of the people." On this note Molotov wrote down next to one of the names: "Shoot."[2] This fact was noted in Suslov's report at the February Plenum of the Central Committee of the CPSU in 1964. The report also stated that Molotov changed a sentence of ten years in prison, given to the wife of a prominent party leader, to the death penalty.[3]

While in other instances Molotov could refer to his "confidence" in Yezhov's investigations, for this act alone he could be criminally indicted according to the laws of any civilized state. But herein lay the halfheartedness of Khrushchev's exposés — Khrushchev decided not to supplement the "party trial" of the closest participants in Stalin's crimes with the criminal trial that they definitely deserved. Such an open trial would have been dangerous for the survival of the post-Stalinist regime. In addition, the defendants at such a trial would have undoubtedly pointed to the participation of Khrushchev himself in the repressions, as well as to the participation of other party leaders who remained at the helm of power.

Decades later Molotov explained his ("military," to use his word) decision in the following way:

> "There was such an instance. By decision I had this list and corrected it. I made a correction."
>
> "And this woman, who was she?"
>
> "That has no significance."

"Why did the repressions spread to wives, to children?"

"What do you mean — why? They had to be isolated to a certain degree. Otherwise, of course, they would have made all sorts of complaints..."[4]

With such arguments Molotov justified the most monstrous crimes of the Stalinist regime, crimes in which he took an active part.

According to Chuyev, almost every time he met with Molotov the question of Stalinist repressions arose. Molotov did not avoid this topic, but, on the contrary, spoke in detail about the motives behind the victimization of various members of the party. What is striking in these conversations is the ease with which Stalin and his stooges decided the issue of annihilating their recent comrades-in-arms. For instance, Molotov recalled that at one of the plenums of the Central Committee he cited the testimony of Rukhimovich about his wrecking activity. "[Although] I knew him personally very well, and he was a very good man... It is possible that the testimony was false, but then not everybody went so far as to acknowledge their own guilt. Rudzutak — he didn't admit to (being guilty of) anything! They shot him."[5]

When it comes to the "guilt" of Rudzutak, who told Molotov face-to-face how they had tortured him in the chambers of the NKVD, Molotov reasoned in the following manner: "I think that he was not a conscious participant (in a conspiracy – V. R.)... A former prisoner, he had been at hard labor for four years... But toward the end of his life — I formed the impression when he was my deputy, he had begun to self-indulge a bit... He had somewhat of an inclination to relaxation, and to engage in things that were connected with relaxation... He enjoyed the life of a philistine — he would sit around, dine with his friends, spend time with companions — he wasn't a bad companion... It is difficult to say what brought his downfall, but I think that he shared the type of company where non-party elements were present, or god knows what other kinds."[6] From this set of empty phrases it is impossible to understand why Rudzutak's "inclination to relaxation" made him deserve arrest and execution.

The most shocking pages in Chuyev's book are those that deal with the fate of Arosev, Molotov's comrade in the underground whose letters Molotov retained throughout his life (two such personal letters are printed in the book). Referring to Arosev with unchanging warmth, Molotov explained his arrest and death in the following way:

"He disappeared in 1937. The most devoted person. It seems he was not discriminating in his acquaintances. It was impossible to mix him up in anti-Soviet affairs. But he had ties... That's a difficulty for the revolution..."

"And you couldn't rescue him?"
"It was impossible to rescue him."
"Why?"
"Testimony. What would I say, believe me, what would I do, conduct an interrogation?"
"And what were the charges against Arosev?"
"He could be charged with only one thing: somewhere he tossed off some kind of liberal remark."[7]

As happened with all of Molotov's other "closest comrades-in-arms," almost all of his assistants and colleagues were arrested. As this happened he understood that testimony would be wrung from these people against himself. In the 1970s he told Chuyev:

"They arrested my first secretary, then they arrested the second. I could see that around me..."
"And did they write things, report things about you?"
"I'll say! But no one told me."
"But Stalin didn't accept this?"
"What do you mean didn't accept it? They arrested my first assistant. A Ukrainian, also from the workers... it seems they put a lot of pressure on him, but he did not want to say a thing and threw himself down the elevator shaft at the NKVD. That's the way it was with all my staff."[8]

After Stalin's death, Molotov, much like Kaganovich, showed himself to be an insignificant political figure. Unlike Khrushchev, Malenkov, and even Beria, neither of them was capable of advancing a single serious idea about reform. With great stubbornness, Molotov opposed any attempts to disgrace Stalin and shed light on his most serious crimes.

In 1955, Molotov was appointed chairman of the commission to review the open trials and the closed trial of the military leaders.[9] At this post he did everything possible to prevent the rehabilitation of the victims. He also resisted in every way the return from exile of the relatives of former prominent oppositionists. In 1954, M. I. Yefremova, the widow of Tomsky, appealed to the Party Control Commission for her own rehabilitation. They received her warmly, promised to restore her party membership and provide her with an apartment in Moscow; and they gave her a trip to a sanatorium. However, after returning from the sanatorium she learned that Molotov had ordered that she be returned to exile. When Khrushchev found out about this, he sent Yefremova a telegram about the restoration of her party membership and permission to return to Moscow. This telegram did not find her among the living; her heart had not withstood the blow delivered by Molotov.[10]

At the June Plenum of the Central Committee in 1957, where documents were made public about Molotov's active role in the great terror, Molotov could not help but acknowledge his participation in "mistakes," as he called the crimes of the Stalinist clique. "I cannot deny my responsibility and I never have denied my political responsibility for those misdeeds and errors which have been condemned by the party," he declared. "I bear responsibility for this, as do other members of the Politburo."[11]

To justify himself, Molotov referred to his report which was devoted to the twentieth anniversary of the October Revolution, where he spoke of the moral and political unity of the Soviet people. In his words, this slogan was aimed at "shifting to moral methods, to methods of persuasion."[12] In reality, the formula that Molotov thought up sounded particularly blasphemous during the year of the great terror. And Molotov did not mention the fact that it was pronounced in the context of extolling Stalin even more: "The moral and political unity of the people in our land has its living incarnation," he declared. "There is a name among us which has become the symbol of the victory of socialism. In addition, this name is the symbol of the moral and political unity of the Soviet people. You know that this name is — Stalin!"[13]

For more than two decades after Molotov was expelled from the party, he appealed to the Central Committee and party congresses to be reinstated. In his appeals he always defended the policy of mass terror. And he repeatedly spoke about this topic in his conversations with Chuyev. Despite Chuyev's obvious admiration for Molotov, the conversations he records reflect Molotov's intellectual and moral degradation. The reasons for this do not stem from senility. As can be seen clearly from his statements recorded by Chuyev, Molotov retained a clear mind and outstanding memory almost until his death. But the ordeals which he experienced after the war (semi-disgrace in Stalin's eyes, the arrest of his wife) and particularly after Stalin's death (removal from high posts, and then expulsion from the party) evidently broke him as a politician, and removed whatever political qualities he had possessed in the 1920s-1940s. In his arguments and evaluations, what inevitably predominates are unconstructive, "defensive" reactions — the blind stubbornness of an inveterate Stalinist and a demonstrative moral deafness.

Until the day he died, Molotov never uttered a word about pangs of conscience for his participation in Stalin's crimes. Stressing that the policy of terror "was the only salvation for the people, for the revolution, and was the only policy which corresponded to Leninism and its basic principles,"[14] from year to year he repeated that he was prepared to bear responsibility for this policy. It should be noted that no one made him answer for the terror, if one does not count the punishment which was incommensurate to his guilt — expulsion from the party. However even this punishment seemed overly severe to Molotov. "They should have punished me, that is true, but expel me from the party?" he said. "I should have been punished, because, of course, we were forced to start chopping without always sorting things out. But I feel that we should have gone through a period of terror, I am not afraid of this word, because there wasn't time to sort things out, there was no chance to do so."[15] This idea about needing to "hurry," during which "you hardly get to know everyone," was often modified by Molotov in explaining even the "mistakes" he acknowledged in carrying out the purges. In excerpts which Chuyev cites from Molotov's manuscript "Before New Tasks (On Completing the Construction of Socialism)," he writes: "In the 1920s and even more so in the 1930s, the group of Trotskyists which was extremely hostile to Leninism threw aside all restraint and became insolent (further on he repeats all the accusations of the Moscow Trials – V. R.)... The party, and the Soviet state could not allow sluggishness or delay in carrying out the punitive measures which had become absolutely necessary."[16]

In Molotov's remarks one can discern the mechanism of the great terror and the atmosphere which reigned during those years in the staff headquarters of Stalinist totalitarianism. "I signed and sent on to Beria what Stalin had sent me with his signature. I also placed my signature both where the Central Committee could not investigate thoroughly, and where undoubtedly there were some honest, good and devoted people. ... In actual fact, of course, cases proceeded on the basis of trust in the [security] organs... Otherwise, you couldn't verify everyone yourself."[17]

In conversations about the open trials, Molotov never once repeated the ravings about how the oppositionists had tried to overthrow Soviet power and restore capitalism. As for the charges that the defendants made a "deal" with the governments of Germany and Japan over the dismemberment of the USSR, he said: "I do not allow that Rykov agreed, that Bukharin agreed to this, or even Trotsky — to give the Far East, and the Ukraine, and almost all the Caucasus — this I exclude, but some kind of discussions were held around these matters, and then the investigators oversimplified things."[18] By the way, on another occasion, in complete contradiction with these statements, Molotov declared that the charge that Trotsky and Bukharin had been negotiating with the imperialists "had been proven beyond any doubt. That's how it looked in reality. Perhaps what I was reading were forged documents, and I shouldn't have believed them, but there were no other documents refuting them!"[19]

Assuming that Yezhov and his underlings "messed things up" to such a degree that following generations would never be able to get to the truth, Molotov commented in the following way about the charges at the Moscow Trials: "Some things were true, and some things were not true. Of course, it was impossible to get to the bottom of things. I could say neither yes nor no, although I never accused anyone (here Molotov "forgot" about his many ferocious philippics against "traitors" – V. R.). The Chekists had the material, they made the investigations... There was obvious exaggeration. But there was something serious there, although it wasn't sufficiently investigated and it could have been much worse."[20]

Appealing to trial transcripts as documents deserving trust, Molotov noted that Bukharin, Rykov, Rozengolts, Krestinsky, Rakovsky and Yagoda confessed to charges that could not fail to seem absurd. He shamelessly called this circumstance "a method of prolonging their struggle against the party at an open trial — to slander oneself so much as to make the other charges implausible... They deliberately ascribed such things to themselves in order to show how absurd all these charges supposedly were."[21]

The comments from Molotov we have cited confirm the correctness of Khrushchev's thoughts: "Stalin's abuses of power.. during Stalin's lifetime were passed off as a display of wisdom... And even now there are numbskulls who defend the same positions, who pray to their idol, the murderer of the flower of the entire Soviet people. The person who most boldly reflected the viewpoint of Stalin's times was Molotov."[22] Molotov adhered to the same position, even in the 1980s, when he said: "Of course, there could have been, perhaps, fewer victims, if we had proceeded more cautiously, but Stalin insured the cause — by sparing no one, but by guaranteeing a hopeful situation during the war and after the war, for a prolonged period... Stalin, in my opinion, pursued a very correct line: let an extra head fly off someone's shoulders, but let there be no vacillation during the war or after."[23]

In these cannibalistic statements, one can almost hear the voice of Stalin himself, although he never spoke so openly with a detailed explanation of the causes behind the great purge. It follows from Molotov's words that the main motive for the mass terror was the fear of the ruling clique over the possible activation of oppositional forces during the war. Endlessly repeating that if there had not been a purge, then "arguments might have continued" in the leadership of the party, Molotov declared that the very presence of such debates was dangerous and unwanted. "I feel," he said, "that we acted correctly by committing a few inevitable, albeit serious, excesses in the repressions, but then, at that time, we had no other option. And if the opportunists (i.e., Stalin's opponents – V. R.) had prevailed, then they, of course, would not have gone this way (the way of mass terror – V. R.), but then during the war we would have faced such internal dissension that it would have had a telling effect on all our work, on the very existence of Soviet power."[24] Customarily identifying "us," i.e., the Stalinist clique, with Soviet power, Molotov implicitly acknowledged that the most serious threat for the clique was allowing "debates" and dissident thinkers in the party leadership who were capable of forming their own opinion. Molotov unintentionally blurted out the true motives of Stalin and his stooges even more clearly in the following statement: "Of course, the demands came from Stalin, and of course, we went too far, but I feel that all this was admissible for the sake of one fundamental thing: to somehow retain power!"[25]

The gradual rehabilitation of Stalin in the 1970s led to something of an artistic rehabilitation of Molotov, who was depicted with unconcealed sympathy in the "film epic" *Liberation* and in the hefty novels written by Chakovsky and Stadniuk. At the same time, the Brezhnev leadership did not dare to embark on Molotov's party rehabilitation — out of fear that this would provoke consternation in Soviet and foreign public opinion. However, from the bowels of the party apparatus "signals" were sent upwards indicating the desirability of such a rehabilitation. Kosolapov, one of the leading ideological apparatchiks of the "time of stagnation," still speaks with pride of his "contributions" to this cause. He recalls that, in 1977, the journal *Communist*, whose editorial board he then headed, received a "theoretical" letter from Molotov. After reading it, Kosolapov invited Molotov to meet him. They conducted a confidential conversation, during which Molotov complained about the "limited nature of his contacts and of the opportunities to exchange opinions about theoretical issues of the day in a competent manner." Sensing sympathy on the part of his interlocutor, Molotov returned to his favorite theme and "noted sternly: 'As before, I consider the policy of the 1930s to be correct. If not for this policy, we would have lost the war.'"

After this conversation, Kosolapov sent to the "higher echelons" a letter in which, "on my own initiative, I called attention... to the neglect of Molotov's intellect and experience and of the need to return him from political non-existence... Many of those with whom I worked and socialized in those years can confirm my unchanging point of view: Molotov, who, like any mortal, undoubtedly deserved criticism and even censure, nevertheless should not have been expelled from the CPSU... My resolve to assist the process of returning Molotov to the party, now that I have better looked into his interests, has only grown." Kosolapov adds with evident satisfaction that his wishes were granted a few years later when Chernenko, who had become general secretary, personally gave Molotov his party card. Kosolapov calls this event "an act of historical justice," insofar as "the matter involved the last knight of Lenin's guard (sic! – V. R.)."[26]

With even greater clarity, a similar point of view was recently expressed in the pages of *Pravda*, where Chuyev declared in commentaries to new excerpts from his conversations with Molotov: "No matter what people say, Molotov completed a heroic journey. And heroes are entitled to much. That is what I think."[27]

Lazar M. Kaganovich
(1893-1991)

2. Kaganovich

Even during the years preceding the great terror, Kaganovich showed himself to be one of the most devoted and flattering of Stalin's satraps, capable of the most ruthless cruelty. During the period of collectivization he and Molotov constantly traveled to restless regions of the country with extraordinary plenipotentiary powers to carry out punitive measures. Their ferocity was visited equally on the unruly masses and on party workers who had displayed inadequate resolve in carrying out repressions. At the June Plenum of the Central Committee in 1957, it was reported that in the Donbass people still remembered the arrival of Kaganovich. What his trip initiated was "the devastation and annihilation of cadres, and as a result the Donbass went into sharp decline."[1] Molotov and Kaganovich were also reminded "of what a slaughter they conducted in the Kuban and in the steppe regions of the Ukraine (in 1932-1933 – V. R.), when so-called sabotage had been organized. How many thousands of people perished there at that time! And then all the heads of the political departments who unleashed this filthy episode ... were victimized, and all traces were erased."[2]

Despite his extremely low level of education, Kaganovich frequently issued "theoretical justifications" of Stalin's actions on the "ideological front." Brazenly falsifying Marxism, he uttered the most ludicrous ideas. Thus, in a speech at the Institute of Soviet Construction and Law (in December 1929) he said: "We reject the concept of a state based on law... If a person who has pretensions of being called a Marxist speaks seriously about a state based on law, and then moreover applies the concept of the 'state based on law' to the *Soviet* state, then this means that he ... is departing from the Marxist-Leninist doctrine of the state."[3] In a speech "For a Bolshevik Study of Party History," delivered in 1931 at a session of the presidium of the Communist Academy, Kaganovich declared that the four-volume *History of the VKP(b)* which had been published under the editorship of Yaroslavsky was "history tinted in Trotskyist colors."

During the first few months of the great purge Kaganovich did not immediately overcome the moral barrier connected with the need to destroy his closest party comrades. At the end of 1936, Furer, a well-known party member, committed suicide. In Khrushchev's words, he had "given birth" to Stakhanov and Izotov by organizing a loud propaganda campaign about their records. Kaganovich highly valued Furer, with whom he had worked both in the Ukraine and in Moscow. In his farewell note, Furer wrote that he was ending his life because he was incapable of reconciling himself with the arrests and executions of innocent people. When Khrushchev, who had been given the note, showed it to Kaganovich, the latter cried; "he literally began to sob." Then the letter fell into Stalin's hands, and at the December Plenum of the Central Committee in 1936, he ironically declared with regard to Furer: "What a letter he left behind after his suicide. In reading it, you can break into tears." Stalin called the suicides of Furer and other party members "one of the very last, acute and easiest (sic – V. R.) means" which oppositionists used in order, "for the last time before their deaths, to deceive the party by means of suicide and to leave the party in a foolish position." After this, as Khrushchev recalled, Kaganovich never mentioned Furer; "evidently he simply feared that I might somehow let the cat out of the bag and tell Stalin how he had cried."[4]

Occupying three high posts at the same time in 1937-1938 (secretary of the Central Committee, People's Commissar of Transport and People's Commissar of Heavy Industry), Kaganovich directed his main efforts as an executioner at a merciless purge of the commissariats that were subordinate to him. Kaganovich sanctioned the arrest of all his deputies in the Commissariat of Transport, all the heads of the railways, and many other people whose efforts had lifted railway transport out of a state of breakdown in 1935-1936.

At a session of the bureau of the Moscow City Committee on 23 May 1962, where the question of expelling Kaganovich from the party was being examined, he was presented with a volume of photocopies of his letters to the NKVD with demands to arrest hundreds of railway workers. He was also shown denunciations which had been sent to Kaganovich on which he placed the comments: "I assume that this is a spy, arrest him"; "the factory is working poorly, I assume that everyone there is an enemy." In one of his letters

Kaganovich demanded the arrest of one communist as a German spy on the grounds that his father had been a major industrialist before the revolution and three of his brothers lived abroad. When asked why he sent such letters, Kaganovich replied, "I don't remember them, this was 25 years ago. If these letters exist, it means that they exist. It was, of course, a crude error."[5]

One of the participants in the session of the bureau of the Moscow City Committee related: "My father was an old railway worker, we lived next to the commissariat in a building where the communist members of railway transport lived... And how did Kaganovich settle accounts with all these people? ... Once I came home to find my father holding a group portrait and crying. Not a single person remained alive out of the people who were in this photograph."[6]

At the June Plenum of the Central Committee in 1957, Zhegalin spoke about the atmosphere which arose in the 1930s in railway transport: "I remember well the time when he (Kaganovich) took the law into his own hands and instigated lawlessness; I remember how all the railroad workers (I worked as an engine-driver) would tremble, and, as a result of these repressive measures, the best, most qualified engineers became frightened and simply drove by the control-arrows and semaphores, for which they received unjust punishment. So here you have a People's Commissar who created his cult of the iron Commissar on the blood of others."[7]

At the June Plenum of the Central Committee in 1957 and at the session of the bureau of the Moscow City Committee in 1962, Kaganovich was reminded of many concrete facts concerning his participation in the Great Purge: "Do you remember the former head of the Artem Coal Trust, Comrade Rudenko?... His wife curses you, Comrade Kaganovich."[8] "I recall how you reviewed the Ural Railway Car Factory, how you embraced the director of the factory, Comrade Pavlotsky, in the presence of the economists and builders who had gathered there. I recall how well they bid you farewell and what a good mood everyone was in. And that very night, everything was clouded over by the third arrest of almost all the leaders of the building site... I recall how, after your visit to Nizhnii Tagil, the head of the NKVD shot himself. His attempt at suicide was not successful, he lived for a few days more and gave the following explanation for his act: 'I cannot create any more enemies.'"[9]

Besides the victimization of workers in his "own" commissariats, Kaganovich signed countless lists containing names of party members to be shot. In the archives, for instance, a list was found with 114 names of people sentenced to be shot on which Kaganovich wrote: "I welcome [this decision]!"[10] Also found was one of Kaganovich's directives concerning special deportees who had completed their sentence and had returned to their former places of residence: "Arrest all returning special deportees and shoot them. Report the execution."[11]

20. Stalin and His Intimate Circle

In 1937-1938, Kaganovich participated in several punitive expeditions in local areas. After returning from Kiev he described how, at a meeting of party activists and economists, he "had literally called out: 'Well, come on up and report whatever anyone knows about enemies of the people.'"[12] At a meeting in the Donbass Kaganovich declared that among those in the audience there were many enemies of the people. That evening and night they arrested about 140 party and economic leaders.[13]

Particularly sinister was Kaganovich's trip to the Ivanovo region, a trip which the communists there would later call "the black tornado." Shreider, the deputy head of the NKVD for the Ivanovo region at that time, recalled that, on 7 August 1937, a special train arrived in Ivanovo with a group of Central Committee staff headed by Kaganovich and Shkiriatov, who were protected by a group of more than thirty men. All the leaders of the area NKVD came to the station to meet the Central Committee commission (the area committee and regional executive committee had not been told of Kaganovich's arrival). Kaganovich and Shkiriatov refused to stay at the dacha of the party's area committee where they were about to be lodged, but went straight to the dacha of the head of the area NKVD, Radzivilovsky. Almost the entire operative staff of the city police guarded the road leading to the dacha. Behind the dacha, in the forest, was stationed a squadron of mounted police who were placed in a state of combat readiness.[14]

On the day after arriving in Ivanovo, Kaganovich sent Stalin a telegram in which he said: even the "first acquaintance with material" had led him to conclude that it was necessary to arrest immediately two leading members of the area committee. After a few days, he sent a second telegram: "Acquaintance with the situation shows that the right-Trotskyist wrecking here has taken broad dimensions — in industry, agriculture, supply, trade, medicine, education and political work."[15]

After receiving plenipotentiary powers from Stalin to carry out arrests, Kaganovich did not deny himself the pleasure of turning the reprisals against party members into a kind of horrendous, but effective, spectacle. To do this, he convened a plenum of the area committee at which the majority of its members were arrested.

How this occurred is described in the novella *There Are No More Questions*, written by A. Vasiliev, son of the arrested secretary of the Ivanovo City Committee of the party. The main character of the novella, an apparatchik who miraculously survived the 1930s, recalls:

> "First onto the stage was a man with a beard (in actual fact, Kaganovich had replaced his beard, in imitation of Lenin, with a moustache, in imitation of Stalin, in 1933 – V. R.). Before this I had only seen him in portraits. At that time he held great power — he

was both narkom [people's commissar], and secretary of the Central Committee, one of among about seven people. In the hall there was silence. The narkom frowned, evidently he did not like how they had greeted him; he had grown used to triumphant receptions. Someone who was quick-witted guessed what was going on and began to clap. Others joined in and everything proceeded as it was supposed to...

Only then did the plenum learn about the agenda. The first item was the status of the agitational and propaganda work in connection with the upcoming harvest, and the second was organizational questions...

Kostiukov, head of the area agricultural directorate, was sent to the tribune ... to speak about the agitational-propaganda work...

Kostiukov raised his eyes from his report, and I felt terrified — they were as glassy as the eyes of a corpse...

Kostiukov nevertheless gathered his strength and we listened:

'Two days ago, I went with the chairman of the area executive committee, Comrade Kazakov, to visit the Budenny collective farm...'

The narkom stood up in a challenging pose and strangely, either with surprise or with sarcasm, asked the reporter:

'With whom? With whom did you visit the collective farm?'

'With Comrade Kazakov...'

The narkom continued in the same incredulous tone:

'Consequently, if I understand you correctly, you consider Kazakov a comrade? Answer me!'

Kostiukov turned white and began to babble...

'Of course... If it is so... Why not consider him a comrade...'

The narkom looked at his wristwatch, then glanced behind the curtains, and some kind of person, not one of ours, immediately rushed toward him. The narkom listened for a second and then declared...

'Enemy of the people Kazakov was arrested twenty minutes ago...'

And then something entirely unbelievable happened, if you measure things by today's standards: one of those sitting at the presidium began to applaud. At first people joined in timidly, then more energetically. Someone cried out in a bass voice:

'To our glorious NKVD — hurrah!...'

Kostiukov went completely limp, muttered a few more words, and left the tribune to the sound of his heels on the floor. No one ever saw him again — he went behind the curtains and disappeared forever.

> The narkom once again looked at his watch and with the same incredulous tone turned to the secretary for propaganda:
> 'Perhaps you can add something to the unsuccessful report?'
> The secretary went to the tribune as pale as could be, cleared his throat for order and began relatively boldly:
> 'The state of the agitational propaganda work in the village cannot fail to cause legitimate concern among us… It is true that Comrade Kostiukov did not note…'
> With these words the narkom once again stood up and asked snidely:
> 'Kostiukov is your comrade? Strange, very strange…' He once again looked at his watch and stunned the hall:
> 'The accomplice of enemy of the people Kazakov, his belated follower Kostiukov, was arrested five minutes ago…'
> The entire bureau of the area committee, and the entire presidium of the area executive committee, were swept away to the last man within forty minutes."[16]

Kaganovich continued to carry out arrests after the plenum as well. Several times a day he telephoned Stalin and reported to him about the course of the investigation. During one such telephone conversation, when Shreider was present, Kaganovich repeated several times: "I hear what you are saying, Comrade Stalin. I will put pressure on the NKVD leaders to stop being liberal and to increase to the maximum the discovery of enemies of the people."[17]

Kaganovich also revealed his sadistic proclivities in his "everyday leadership." As members of the Moscow City Committee would say in 1962, during committee sessions he would "feel no qualms about spitting in the face of a subordinate, tossing a chair at him," or hitting him in the face.[18]

Despite the weight of the crimes he had committed, during the first years after Stalin's death Kaganovich acted with great self-confidence. Much like other members of the "anti-party group," he assumed that the majority they held in the Presidium of the Central Committee would allow them to obtain an easy victory over Khrushchev. Kaganovich had grown accustomed to the fact that the actual all-powerful boss of the party and the land was the Politburo (the Presidium) of the Central Committee, and the plenum of the Central Committee acted as an obedient executor of its will. At first, Kaganovich conducted himself aggressively at the sessions of the June Plenum of 1957, and he even allowed himself to shout at its members. However, it soon became clear that the plenum of the Central Committee was seen by its participants as the highest organ of the party, as it should be according to its Statutes. Discussion of the case of Molotov, Kaganovich and others began to resemble, in its tone, the discussion of the Bukharin-Rykov case at the February-March Plenum of 1937 — with two important exceptions. First of all, the accused here were not oppositionists who had repeatedly been denounced earlier, but leaders of the party who had been members of the Politburo without interruption for more than thirty years. And secondly, Molotov and Kaganovich were charged not with imaginary, but with actual, crimes.

During the work of the plenum, Kaganovich "refreshed" his memory because he evidently feared new references to his crimes. Witness of this is the fact that his speech at the December Plenum of the Central Committee in 1936, which contained shameless slander against "Trotskyists" and "rightists," was sent in June 1957 from the party archive to Kaganovich's secretariat.[19]

During the last days of the plenum, when the mood of the overwhelming majority of its participants had taken final form, Kaganovich spoke with words of repentance. Five years later, during the investigation of his personal case at a session of the bureau of the Moscow City Committee, he once again behaved rather brazenly, declaring: "When people say here that I am a dishonest man, that I have committed crimes... you should be ashamed of yourselves." At that time he gave the following assessment of the Great Terror: "Mass shootings — yes, there were excesses."[20]

In evaluating the "lessons" of the struggle of his group against Khrushchev, Kaganovich, who had always denounced factionalism, declared to Chuyev: "Our mistake lay in the fact that we ... were not a faction... If we had been a faction, we could have taken power."[21]

During the last years of his life, Kaganovich was not inclined to hide his true sympathies. In conversations with Chuyev he repeatedly said of Stalin: "He was a great man, and we all bowed down before him."[22]

Kaganovich explained his own active participation in the Great Terror by the fact that "it was impossible to go against public opinion at that time"; "the situation was such in the country and in the Central Committee, the mood of the masses was such, that there was no thought of acting in any other way."[23]

However, Kaganovich once blurted out unexpectedly to Chuyev the true reasons for the bloody reprisals against former leaders of the opposition. To the question: "Was it worth shooting them? Perhaps they should have been removed from their posts, and sent somewhere in the provinces?", Kaganovich replied: "You see, my dear friend, under conditions in which we were surrounded by capitalism, how many governments were at liberty, for they all had been members of the government. There had been a Trotskyist government, there had been a Zinoviev government, and there had been a Rykov government. All this was very dangerous and inadmissible. Three governments could have arisen from among Stalin's opponents." From Kaganovich's further explanations, it is extremely clear how frightened the Stalinist clique was of the possibility that these people might unite, despite the fact that they had passed through a long period of capitulation and humiliation. "Bukharin met with Kamenev (in 1928 – V. R.), they talked, they discussed the policies of the Central Committee and other things," said Kaganovich. "How could we hold them at liberty? ... Trotsky, who was a good organizer, could have headed a rebellion... Who, after all, could believe that old, experienced conspirators, using all the experience of Bolshevik conspiratorial methods and Bolshevik organization, that these people would not establish ties among themselves and would not create an organization?" In actual fact, Kaganovich was explaining the use of torture against the oppositionists by their revolutionary past. This idea was expressed by him in the following rhetorical sentence: "It is possible that there was torture, but one must also assume that these were old and experienced Bolsheviks, and do you think that they would have given testimony of their own free will?"[24]

Unlike the correspondence between Stalin and Molotov, the correspondence between Stalin and Kaganovich has not yet been published. However, even by 1957, there were two volumes of this correspondence already assembled, "filled with sickly sweet language, groveling, and an obsequious tone" on Kaganovich's part.[25]

3. Voroshilov

Stalin placed the responsibility of conducting the purge in the army on Voroshilov. Trotsky evinced the opinion that, at a certain moment, Voroshilov "began to show signs of independence with regard to Stalin. It is highly probable that Voroshilov was being egged on by people close to him. The military apparatus is voracious and finds it hard to bear the limits placed on it by politicians, by civilians. Foreseeing possible friction and conflicts with the powerful military apparatus, Stalin decided to put Voroshilov in his place in a timely fashion. Through the GPU, i.e., through Yezhov, he prepared a noose for Voroshilov's closest colleagues behind his back and without his knowledge. At the last moment, he presented him with the necessity of choosing. It is clear that Voroshilov, who betrayed all his closest colleagues and the flower of the commanding staff, emerged after this as a demoralized figure, incapable of further resistance."[1]

This hypothesis, offered by Trotsky, is confirmed by the notes of a speech given by Voroshilov at the February-March 1937 Plenum of the Central Committee, where he stresses: "In the army at the present time, fortunately, not so many enemies have been discovered. I say 'fortunately' in hopes that there are few enemies in the Red Army as a whole."[2] A bit later, in a note he wrote for himself, Voroshilov confessed that, while opposing the dismissal from the army or the arrest of various commanders, he feared that "it is pos-

Kliment Voroshilov
(1881-1969)

sible to fall into an unpleasant situation: you defend someone and he turns out to be a genuine enemy, a fascist."³

At first, Voroshilov actually tried to defend several of his subordinates. Thus, he managed to prevent the expulsion from the party and dismissal from the army of Petrov, the head of the Tashkent military academy, who during the Second World War successfully commanded whole armies and fronts and finished the war with the title of General of the Army.

After the Tukhachevsky trial, Voroshilov as a rule began to approve without objection lists of commanders who were to be arrested; he often added comments of the following type: "You must arrest them," "I agree to their arrest," "Round up all these scoundrels," and so forth.⁴ On a report concerning a party meeting where the corps commissar, Savko, called the arrest of one of the military leaders a misunderstanding, Voroshilov wrote: "Arrest him!"⁵

Arrested commanders turned for help first of all to Voroshilov. The reception room alone of the People's Commissar of Defense throughout 1938 received more than 200,000 letters, and in 1939, more than 350,000 letters, among which no small number consisted of statements sent from prison.⁶ Some officers and generals sent Voroshilov dozens of such statements, telling of the torture and humiliation to which they were being subjected. A group of commanders who had been Voroshilov's comrades during the Civil War wrote: "Kliment Efremovich! You must check how the cases against the commanders of the Red Army are being handled. You will find that material is extracted from the arrested by means of violence, threats and by turning men into limp rags. They force one arrested person to write denunciations of another, and in this way they present charges, saying that whoever falls into the clutches of the NKVD will never return."[7] There is no evidence, however, that Voroshilov ever responded to any of these appeals.

After the arrest of all his deputies, the leaders of the army, navy and air force, and hundreds of other people who had worked with him for many years, Voroshilov felt sharply the blow which had been dealt the army. In notes made for himself, he writes with concern that "the authority of the army has been shaken throughout the land... This means that the methods of our work, the whole system of directing the army, and my work as narkom have suffered a devastating collapse."[8]

Apparently Voroshilov carried out the functions of executioner with less zeal than Molotov and Kaganovich. At the June Plenum of 1957, Khrushchev separated Voroshilov from the other "closest comrades-in-arms" and said that Voroshilov, "more than the others was upset by the abuse, particularly with regard to the military."[9] As is clear from Khrushchev's memoirs, he came to this conclusion on the basis of a conversation between Stalin and Voroshilov, at which he had occasion to be present. During the Finnish war, when Stalin was angrily criticizing Voroshilov, "the latter flew into a rage, turned red, stood up and, in reply to Stalin's criticism, hurled the accusation at him: 'You are to blame for this. You exterminated the military cadres.' Stalin also replied. Then Voroshilov seized the plate which held a roast piglet and slammed it against the table. This was the only time I saw such an incident."[10]

Unlike Molotov and Kaganovich, Voroshilov recalled the Great Purge with a feeling of sorrow and revulsion. At the June Plenum of 1957 he asked that its participants "stop telling about these horrors."[11] It seemed that Voroshilov was trying to erase from his memory the most shameful and terrible pages of those years. This, apparently, explains his stormy and indignant reaction to Kaganovich's confession that the members of the Politburo had signed a secret decree about using torture. "Not only did I never sign such a document," Voroshilov claimed heatedly, "but I declare that if something of the sort had been presented to me, I would have spit in their face. I was beaten in (tsarist) prisons when they demanded confessions, how could I sign a document of this kind? And you say that we all sat there (at a session of the Politburo where this decree was adopted – V. R.). You cannot do that, Lazar Moiseevich."[12]

Voroshilov differed from Molotov and Kaganovich also by the fact that, after Stalin's death, he never mentioned the guilt of the military leaders when it came to the crimes ascribed to them. Even in Stalin's time, as Snechkus, the first secretary of the Central Committee of the Lithuanian Communist Party, relates, he told the Lithuanian leaders that "Uborevich had been shot unjustly."[13]

In the last years of his life, Voroshilov tried to mitigate his own guilt over the generals who perished. In an order on June 12, 1937, he called Gamarnik "a traitor and a coward, who was afraid of facing trial before the Soviet people." Thirty years later, Voroshilov wrote a sketch of Gamarnik which ends with the words: "The entire, relatively short, life of Yan Borisovich Gamarnik — is a feat of labor and of arms... He was a genuine Bolshevik-Leninist. And so he will remain in the hearts of those who knew him personally, and in the memory of all workers."[14]

4. Mikoyan

Molotov, Kaganovich and Voroshilov joined Stalin and Yezhov in forming a virtual "little Politburo" which developed the strategy and tactics of the Great Purge and signed a majority of the blacklists. But Stalin also made other, less significant figures from his closest entourage co-participants in his crimes. In order to crush their political will and human conscience he used "dubious" moments in their biography. As a subject for blackmailing Mikoyan, Stalin chose the circumstance that he had managed to survive in 1918 during party work in Baku. As Mikoyan himself was to say in 1956, Stalin told him at the beginning of 1937: "The story of how the 26 Baku commissars were shot, and how only one of them — Mikoyan — remained among the living, is dark and tangled. And as for you, Anastas, don't make us untangle this story."[1]

After this statement, Mikoyan unquestioningly fulfilled all the actions as an executioner that were assigned to him, as well as the ideological actions that accompanied them. In December 1937, he delivered a speech devoted to the twentieth anniversary of the ChK-OGPU-NKVD. In this speech there are two "striking places" which deserve attention. First, Mikoyan declared: "Every worker in our land is a member of the People's Commissariat of Internal Affairs!" Secondly, in speaking about the results of the past year, he exclaimed: "The NKVD has worked gloriously during this time! ... We may wish that the workers of the NKVD in the future will work as gloriously as they have this year."[2]

With Mikoyan's national origin in mind, Stalin sent him along with Yezhov and Malenkov to Armenia, where they decimated the entire party leadership of the republic. Although at the time, the press underscored the leading role in these events of none other than Mikoyan, his name was not mentioned when they were recalled at the Twenty-Second Congress in 1961.[3]

After Stalin's death, Mikoyan revealed an ability to criticize Stalinism boldly and decisively. Among the members of the Politburo of 1937, he proved to be the only one who supported Khrushchev in the matter of exposing Stalin's crimes. During the strained days of the Twentieth Congress, when the question had still not been settled about the reading of Khrushchev's secret report, Mikoyan gave an impassioned speech which provoked an enor-

20. Stalin and His Intimate Circle

Anastas Mikoyan
(1895-1978)

mous response both in the Soviet Union and throughout the world. Without mentioning Stalin's name, he nevertheless gave an unequivocal assessment of the Stalinist regime by pointing out that "in the course of about twenty years we actually had no collective leadership. A personality cult flourished which had been condemned as early as Marx, and then by Lenin, and this, of course, could not help but have an extremely negative effect on the situation in the party and on its activity."[4]

Mikoyan's speech differed from the lackluster speeches of the remaining members of the Politburo, due to the abundance of facts cited and the clarity of his formulations. Special attention was devoted in it to a critique of the party's historical literature, including what was sacred for the Stalinists, *The Short Course of the History of the VKP(b)*. "If our historians," said Mikoyan, "genuinely and deeply began to study the facts and events of the history of our party during the Soviet period... then they would now be able to cast a better light, from the positions of Leninism, on the many facts and events described in the *Short Course*."[5]

Mikoyan chose the theme of historical falsification as a bridgehead in order to make a statement for the first time about the groundlessness of the charges against several party leaders who had been declared enemies of the people. "One Moscow historian," he said, "agreed even to the following: had Comrade Antonov-Ovseenko and Comrade Kosior not been among the Ukrainian party leaders, it is possible that there would have been no Makhno or Grigoriev movements; Petliura would not have had success during various periods; there would have been no great desire to spread the communes (by the way, not only a Ukrainian phenomenon, but a common phenomenon for the party at that time); and immediately, you see, the line would have been taken in the Ukraine which the entire party and country began to pursue as a result of the NEP."[6] Most stunning in this tirade was the use of the word "Comrade" in connection with the names of Bolsheviks who had been castigated a hundred times over.

After Mikoyan's speech, it was difficult for the inveterate Stalinists in the Politburo to oppose the delivery of Khrushchev's speech about Stalin.

5. Andreev

The secretary of the Central Committee, Andreev, was blackmailed by Stalin by a fact in his biography which was unprecedented among the "closest comrades-in-arms." During the debate over the trade unions in 1920-1921, Andreev, who was one of the youngest members of the Central Committee, voted for Trotsky's platform. Therefore, despite his unwavering defense of positions of the ruling faction during all subsequent discussions, he began to be followed by the reputation of "being an active Trotskyist in the past." Keeping Andreev in the Politburo was designed to serve as confirmation of the fact that Stalin did not punish "Trotskyists who had disarmed," and who were displaying ruthlessness with regard to their former co-thinkers. At a session of the Military Council which preceded the trial of the Tukhachevsky group, Stalin pointed to Andreev, who was sitting next to him, and declared that he "had been a very active Trotskyist in 1921," but then had abandoned Trotskyism and "is fighting against the Trotskyists very well."[1]

Khrushchev recalled that "Andrei Andreevich did very much that was bad during the repressions of 1937. It is possible that because of his past he feared that he would be suspected of being soft on former Trotskyists. Wherever he went, many people perished."[2]

Andreev's bloodiest expedition was his trip in the fall of 1937 to Uzbekistan. Its formal goal was "to explain" to the Central Committee of the Communist Party of the republic the letters written by Stalin and Molotov regarding the first secretary of the Central Committee of Uzbekistan, Ikramov, who remained at liberty. The explanation said that, on the basis of testimony obtained from arrested persons and in face-to-face confrontations, the Central Committee of the VKP(b) had established: "Comrade Ikramov has not only displayed political blindness and short-sightedness with regard to bourgeois nationalists and enemies of the Uzbek people, ... but he sometimes has even provided a cover for them"; "evidently" he had

20. Stalin and His Intimate Circle

Stalin, Andreev, Kaganovich

"ties with leaders of the Trotskyist-rightist group in Moscow." It was proposed that the plenum of the republic's Central Committee "discuss the question of Comrade Ikramov and inform the CC of the VKP(b) of its opinion."[3]

By the time of the plenum the majority of the members of the Uzbek Central Committee were already in prison. The plenum, which gathered in reduced numbers, expressed its opinion as demanded about Ikramov and opened a new wave of terror in the republic. The situation which arose during Andreev's stay in Tashkent was so terrifying that, immediately after the plenum, Ikramov told a female colleague who had been promoted to secretary of the area committee: "Do not accept the appointment under any circumstances. They will quickly arrest you. Fall ill, go away, do whatever you want. They have to fulfill a plan concerning the nomenklatura."[4] Ikramov himself was ordered to travel in the same train with Andreev to Moscow, where he was soon arrested.

After Yezhov was removed from the post of People's Commissar of Internal Affairs, Andreev was appointed chairman of the Politburo commission to investigate the activity of the NKVD. Thousands of letters in his name began to arrive with requests from arrested people to review their cases. Kedrov, a 62-year-old Bolshevik who knew Andreev well, wrote: "From a dismal cell in Lefortovo Prison, I appeal to you for help. Hear the cry of horror, do not pass by, intervene on my behalf, help destroy the nightmare of interrogations... I am convinced that if there is a calm, unbiased investigation, without repulsive obscenities, without malice, without outrageous humiliations, the groundlessness of the charges will easily be established."[5] The letter received no answer from Andreev. Although Kedrov's trial exonerated him, he was executed at the beginning of the Second World War on orders which came directly from Beria.

Kalinin walking alongside Stalin

6. Kalinin

Among the members of Stalin's Politburo, Kalinin was present longer than anyone else — he had been a member of the Politburo from the moment of its formation in March 1919. At that time, on Trotsky's recommendation, he was elected to the post of chairman of the VTsIK [All-Russian Central Executive Committee] (during this election Trotsky called Kalinin for the first time "the all-union village elder"). Whereas he had the courage in the 1920s to voice his own independent views, by the 1930s Kalinin had turned into a purely decorative figure. During the years of the Great Terror, he unquestioningly sanctioned the arrest of members of the country's supreme governmental organ. In just the second half of 1937, he sent the Prosecutor of the USSR fifteen lists with incriminating evidence against 181 members of the Central Executive Committee. After receiving the "conclusion" of the Prosecutor, Kalinin signed directives to expel these people from the Central Executive Committee and to transfer their cases to the NKVD.[1]

Kalinin turned out to be the first member of the Politburo to have his wife arrested (the wives of Molotov and Andreev would get their turn after the war). According to Bukharin's wife Larina, E. D. Kalinina was arrested in the summer of 1938 for describing Stalin in the following way during a conversation with an old friend: "He's a tyrant and a sadist who has destroyed Lenin's old guard and millions of innocent people."

Relatives of people who had been arrested often turned to Kalinin as the head of the government with requests to influence the resolution of their fate.

20. Stalin and His Intimate Circle

Zhdanov, Stalin, Voroshilov, Kalinin

When one Moscow professor asked him to help free his wife from a prison camp, Kalinin ingenuously replied: "My dear friend, I am in the exact same position. No matter how much I have tried, I have not been able to help my own wife. I have no chance of helping yours either."[2]

As a result of the insistent requests from the "all-union village elder," Stalin ordered the release of his wife only after the war.

7. Zhdanov

As secretary of the Central Committee and candidate-member of the Politburo, Zhdanov belonged to the cohorts of those Stalin personally promoted. He directed the purge in Leningrad which had begun immediately after Kirov's assassination and which was particularly broad in its scope, since the majority of members of the Leningrad party organization had supported the "new opposition" in 1925. Besides this, Zhdanov was ordered to travel to other areas to deal with local party cadres. In their cruelty, these trips are comparable to the punitive expeditions carried out by Kaganovich and Andreev.

In October 1937, Zhdanov directed the plenum of the Bashkir area committee of the VKP(b) at which he charged the leadership of the area committee with participating in a Trotsky-Bukharin and bourgeois-nationalist conspiracy. "From a political point of view, these are fascists and spies. From a social standpoint they are lousy, degenerate bureaucrats." Zhdanov described Bykin, the first secretary of the area committee, in the following way: "Bykin is an old wolf; *in my opinion, he will prove to be* an old spy with 8-10 years of service (my italics – V. R.)."¹

In his speech at the ceremony devoted to the fourteenth anniversary of Lenin's death, Zhdanov declared that "1937 will go down in history as the year that the enemies of the people were routed."²

Although he was one of the most cynical and ruthless of Stalin's satraps, Zhdanov was no stranger to a specific form of humor. Yakovlev, the aircraft designer, who was allowed into the circle of Kremlin leaders during those years, recalled a joke that Zhdanov had told him: "Stalin complains that his pipe has disappeared. He declares: 'I would give a lot to find it.' Within three days Beria has already found ten thieves, and each of them 'confesses' that he was the one who stole the pipe. A day later Stalin finds his pipe, which had simply fallen behind the couch in his room." "And Zhdanov laughed merrily at this terrible joke," added Yakovlev.³

8. Khrushchev

Promoted to a high post in the apparatus only in 1932, Khrushchev successfully continued his ascension in the party during the years of the Great Purge. He spent 1937 as first secretary of the Moscow Committee and the Moscow City Committee, and at the beginning of 1938 he was transferred to the post of first secretary of the Central Committee of the KP(b) of the Ukraine. Khrushchev was the only person during these years (not counting Yezhov) who was promoted as a candidate-member into the Politburo, the ranks of which had grown rather thin.

Khrushchev's behavior did not differ substantially from that of other republic and area secretaries who were obliged to sanction the arrest of staff members among the nomenklatura of their party committees. However, it is no accident that it was precisely Khrushchev who became the initiator of the exposures of Stalin's crimes. His memoirs show that the repressions of 1936-1938 left him truly bewildered; after Stalin's death this bewilderment turned into sharp indignation.

In his memoirs, Khrushchev did not conceal his awe before Stalin during the 1930s, or the torment he suffered in the process of shedding illusions about Stalin. He wrote that only after the investigation of Stalin's crimes did he fully realize: at their foundations lay "the carefully calculated steps of a despot who was able to instill the idea among very many people that Lenin did not understand people, that he had not been able to choose the right people, and that almost all of those who headed the country after his death had turned out to be enemies of the people."¹ In Khrushchev's words, the Great Purge had been unleashed by Stalin "with a goal of preventing the possibility that any people or groups would arise in the party who wished to return the party to Lenin's inner-party democracy, and to turn the country toward a democratic form of social construction... Stalin said that the people were manure, an amorphous mass that follows the strong. And it was he who demonstrated that strength. He destroyed everything that might have nourished in any way a truthful understanding of events, or reasoned judgements which might have contradicted his point of view. Herein lay the tragedy of the USSR."[2]

In describing the situation which had developed during the years of the Great Terror in the Ukraine, Khrushchev tried to justify himself by saying that the narkom of internal affairs for the republic, Uspensky, buried him with papers, "and no matter what the paper was, everywhere there were enemies, enemies and more enemies." In reviewing the lists of those arrested and condemned, Khrushchev thereby "exerted a type of party control (over the republic's NKVD)." However he knew all too well that at the same time these lists were being sent to Yezhov, who reported on them to Stalin. Thus any refusal by the local party leader to sanction the arrests would be immediately noticed by Stalin. In describing this mechanism of the Great Purge, Khrushchev justly remarked: "What kind of control was there here when the party organs themselves had fallen under the control of those whom they were supposed to be controlling? ... The Cheka had risen above the party."[3] Returning to a characterization of the relationship between the party organs and the organs of the NKVD, he wrote: "Strictly speaking, we weren't directing them, they were forcing their will on us, although superficially their subordination was fully maintained. In actual fact, with their material, documents and actions they sent us wherever and however they wanted. According to the practice that had developed, however, we were obliged to trust completely the documents which they sent to the party organs."[4]

It is understandable that Khrushchev paused in his memoirs to linger in great detail over the instances when he managed to prevent the arrest of various people. Thus, he saved the poet Maksim Rylsky from arrest by telling the People's Commissar of Internal Affairs that the song the poet had written about Stalin "was being sung by the whole Ukraine." Khrushchev also mentioned those episodes when of his own volition he dared to go to the NKVD for a discussion with arrested people whose guilt he doubted, or when he told Malenkov about his distrust of certain testimonies.[5]

In his memoirs Khrushchev vividly describes a campaign of repression which was prompted by widespread plague among horses in the border areas of the Ukraine. In order to investigate the causes for the deaths of the horses several commissions were formed, but their members were being arrested at the beginning of their work as participants in a conspiracy to commit sabotage. As he was trying to investigate this episode, Khrushchev learned that the professors and veterinarians were being accused of preparing and sprinkling

Khrushchev and Stalin

some kind of poison into the horse feed. After this, he asked Uspensky to obtain from the arrested people the chemical formula of this poison. When horse feed was prepared according to this recipe, the horses did not fall ill. Then Khrushchev personally tried to interrogate those arrested. They told him that they had actually poisoned the horses with a poisonous additive to the feed which had been received from Germany. Thus, the arrested did everything "to confirm their testimony and prove the correctness of their Chekist tormentors."[6] Meanwhile the plague continued among the horses. Then Khrushchev formed two new parallel working commissions, plus one more — of Moscow scientists. These commissions found the actual cause of the horses' destruction: it lay in the infectiousness of old feed which was being given to the horses, caused by a microscopic mushroom which was found in hay. After strict instructions were written about preparing the feed, the plague came to an end. Khrushchev's story was confirmed by a statement from the academician Sarkisov, who has survived until the present, and who, at the end of the 1930s, joined Ukrainian scientists in discovering the toxicity of the mushroom.[7] However, by the time the discovery had been made, many collective farm chairmen, agronomists, livestock specialists, and scientists had already been shot on charges of sabotage.

According to Khrushchev, even after these events he did not allow himself to think that false testimony had been beaten from victims by the organs of the NKVD, insofar as "these organs were considered to be beyond reproach."[8] Here Khrushchev was undoubtedly resorting to cunning. For he had often met with people who told him about the torture which they had endured. Thus, Lukashov, the former People's Commissar of Trade in the Ukraine, told Khrushchev after he had been freed from prison how they had turned him into an invalid when they demanded testimony that he had been sent abroad by Khrushchev to establish contact with foreign intelligence services. When Khrushchev told Stalin about this, the latter replied: "Yes, there have been such distortions. They are also gathering material about me. Yezhov collects it."[9]

Khrushchev also told Stalin how he received a young teacher who had just come from prison, where they tortured him while demanding testimony that Korotchenko, the chairman of the Council of People's Commissars in the Ukraine, was an agent of the Rumanian royal court. When he heard that Korotchenko had ties, according to the NKVD, with the Rumanian king, Stalin "began to joke": "'Or with the queen? How old is the queen?' Khrushchev answered in the same spirit: 'The king there is underage, but then there is the queen mother. It must be that he has ties with the queen mother.' This prompted even more jokes."[10]

This episode, as well as the joke told by Zhdanov cited earlier, clearly depicts the atmosphere which reigned among the Stalinist camarilla. It is true, however, that in this case, the "exchange of jokes" resulted in the shooting of the investigators who had cobbled together the "Korotchenko affair."

In this story Khrushchev is evidently referring to the case of the Moldavian teacher Sadaliuk, from whom they beat incriminating testimony not only about Korotchenko, but also about Khrushchev. Sadaliuk's appeal in December 1938 was reviewed at a session of the Politburo, which led to the adoption of the resolution: "Organize an open trial, shoot the guilty ones, and publish (about this) in the press (both central and local)."[11]

This episode characterizes the special trust which Khrushchev enjoyed under Stalin; after the Eighteenth Congress he was made a member of the Politburo.

9. Beria

Beria turned out to be one of only two secretaries of the communist parties in the republics who survived the Great Purge in good standing. The second was the secretary of the Azerbaidzhan Central Committee, Bagirov. They both had previously headed the organs of the Cheka-GPU in the republic, and, unlike other party secretaries, neither depended on the local NKVD, but fully subordinated it to themselves as they personally directed the terror in their respective republics.

Stalin did not hinder the creation of a Beria cult in Georgia, one that exceeded any other "local" cult in its scope. Georgian poets wrote celebratory

Lavrenty Beria (1899-1953)

verses and songs about Beria, and his stooge Merkulov published a pamphlet entitled *True Son of the Party of Lenin-Stalin*.

In his memoirs, Erenburg writes how he first saw Beria at a ceremony devoted to the birthday of Rustaveli. "Several speakers praised him, and then everyone stood there applauding. Beria applauded as well and gave a self-satisfied smile. I already understood that when Stalin was mentioned everyone would applaud, and if this was at the end of a speech, they would stand. But I was surprised — who was this Beria? I quietly asked a neighboring Georgian, and he abruptly replied: 'A big shot.'"[1]

Sensing Stalin's confidence and anticipating his wishes, Beria waged a provocative campaign against Ordzhonikidze, who stood immeasurably higher than he in the party hierarchy. He arrested Sergo's older brother, who together with his wife was sentenced to be shot in 1937 by one of Beria's "troikas." Earlier, in November 1936, the head of the secret political department of the Georgian NKVD, Kobulov, declared in a report to Beria that the arrested Gogoberidze had confessed to spreading "counter-revolutionary and slanderous fabrications about the past of Comrade Beria... on the basis of what he had heard from Comrade Ordzhonikidze."[2]

In 1937, on Beria's orders, the NKVD arrested and brought to Tbilisi the former leaders of Georgia who, in the last years before their arrest, had worked beyond the borders of the republic. One of them, the former chairman of the Georgian Sovnarkom, Orakhelashvili, said, among other things, during the investigation: "I learned that Sergo Ordzhonikidze had been joined by Levan Gogoberidze, Petr Aniashvili and Nestor Lakoba in waging the most active struggle against the secretary of the Central Committee of the

KP(b) of Georgia, Lavrenty Beria, deliberately spreading slanderous and disturbing fabrications about him." As Goglidze, the former narkom of internal affairs in Georgia, was to say in 1953, such testimony was wrung out in order to "send the transcript to I. V. Stalin and to compromise Ordzhonikidze even after his death."[3]

According to Kobulov, Beria took the initiative in conducting the repressions against Georgian party members, and "Goglidze was his errand-boy... If Beria gave orders to 'interrogate harshly,' then the investigators... were afraid of not carrying out these orders, since they themselves might fall into a similar situation."[4] Frequently Beria personally beat arrested people and ordered them to be beaten even more before they were shot.

During the investigation of Beria's case, twenty-six volumes were collected of his arrest orders, and more than 100 of his resolutions of the following kind: "Thrash him thoroughly," and "get to work on him and squeeze out everything." Beria directed a republic-level "troika" which reviewed the cases of thirty thousand people, of whom ten thousand were sentenced to be shot.[5]

In 1936, Beria destroyed with his own hands two prominent party members in the Transcaucasus. In the summer of that year, he shot in his office the first secretary of the Central Committee of the Armenian Communist Party, Khandzhian. In the press it was announced that Khandzhian had committed suicide. Several months later, Beria poisoned Lakoba, the chairman of the Central Executive Committee and the Sovnarkom of Abkhazia. An official announcement indicated that Lakoba had died from a heart attack. Lakoba was ceremoniously buried, and expressions of sympathy regarding his death were sent by Dimitrov, Budenny and other famous party members. But a few months later, a trial of the leaders of Abkhazia declared that Lakoba was the head of a local conspiracy. Beria gave orders to exhume his body and burn it, and then scatter his ashes to the wind. On Beria's orders all of Lakoba's colleagues were shot, as well as all members of his family, including a young son.[6]

10. Malenkov

In the 1920s, Malenkov worked in Stalin's secretariat, and during the sharpest period of the struggle against the Left Opposition headed the party organization at the MVTU [Moscow Higher Technical Institute], where the influence of the Trotskyists was particularly great. From 1934 to 1939 he headed the department of leading party organs in the Central Committee. At this post he became one of the organizers of reprisals against local party leaders.

In 1936, Malenkov and Yezhov created an account about the existence of an underground anti-Soviet network in Belorussia. This was the pretext for

Stalin and Georgy Malenkov

expelling from the party more than half of the communists in the republic. When, in 1937, Goloded, the chairman of the Council of People's Commissars of Belorussia, expressed doubts about these charges, Malenkov traveled to Belorussia. Almost all the leaders of the republic were arrested during his visit.[1] In September 1937, Malenkov joined Mikoyan and Beria in carrying out reprisals against the party and state leaders of Armenia. During this time he personally interrogated many of those arrested, resorting in a number of instances to having them beaten.[2]

Just as sinister were Malenkov's trips to the autonomous republics and areas of the Russian Federation. They led to the arrest of the first secretary of the Tula area committee, Soifer; the first secretary of the Yaroslavl area committee, Zimin; and the first secretary of the Tatar area committee, Lepa.[3]

After Yezhov's arrest, Beria interrogated him specifically about Malenkov. In 1955, when Malenkov received a transcript of this interrogation which evidently seriously compromised him, he destroyed the document.[4]

After the Great Purge, Malenkov's formal status was brought into alignment with his actual political role. In March 1939 he was chosen member and secretary of the Central Committee, and in February 1941, candidate-member of the Politburo.

11. Mekhlis

In 1937, Mekhlis was appointed head of the Main Directorate of Political Propaganda for the Red Army and Deputy People's Commissar of Defense. The *Bulletin of the Opposition* commented on this appointment in the following manner: "By appointing his horse a Senator, Caligula wanted to humiliate the Roman Senate. By appointing his lackey, Mekhlis, a leader of the Red Army, Stalin is pursuing much less platonic goals. Stalin's former

20. Stalin and His Intimate Circle

Lev Mekhlis
(1889-1953)

personal secretary, an untalented careerist, a specialist in behind-the-scenes intrigues, and the executor of his boss's most filthy affairs, Mekhlis is powerful only with Stalin's support. Mekhlis — deputy narkomvoen! Who would have believed this even half a year ago? The more 'enemies of the people' Stalin exterminates, rising upward on their corpses, the greater the void which forms around him. The reserves of the faithful are limited today to subjects like Mekhlis."[1]

At his new post, Mekhlis played a leading role in decimating the officer cadres. He repeatedly traveled into military districts where he carried out the arrests of mid-level commanders and sent Stalin coded messages asking him to sanction the arrest of more prominent military leaders.

In his memoirs B. Yefimov describes Mekhlis's Jesuitical zeal and the sadistic pleasure he experienced during the years of mass repressions. Here is a story told by Mikhail Koltsov about a conversation with Mekhlis: "We are sitting in my office and suddenly he says: 'You know what, Misha, you have to take a very careful look at Avgust Pototsky. Without any doubt, this is a camouflaged enemy.' I was stupefied. 'What are you saying, Lev,' I ask, 'Avgust?! This most honest and devoted Bolshevik? An old political prisoner?' 'Yes, yes, Misha,' Mekhlis replies impatiently and spitefully, 'precisely him, the most honest and devoted Bolshevik. It was precisely from these, as you say, "most honest" people that the tsarist Okhranka [secret police] recruited provocateurs!..' And at that moment into the office walked ... Avgust, with a newspaper column to be signed. You should have seen how instantaneously and outrageously Mekhlis's face changed, as he warmly and cordially started to speak: 'A-ahh!... Comrade Avgust! Am I glad to see you! How are you getting along, my friend, how is your health?' 'Thank you! We're getting old, Comrade Mekhlis, we're getting old...' 'What do you mean, Comrade Avgust! It's too soon for you to grow old! What a warrior you are. You still have to work a bit for *Pravda*, for the party!' ... And here, you see, Avgust was already a doomed man. It was only a question of days."²

12. Shkiriatov

Shkiriatov, who worked from 1934 as secretary of the party collegium of the Party Control Commission, became virtual head of this Commission after Yezhov was instructed in September 1936 "to devote nine-tenths of his time to work in the NKVD." The character of Shkiriatov's participation in the Great Purge was described at the June Plenum of the Central Committee in 1957: "Shkiriatov mechanically rubber-stamped all the illegal activities of the organs..., which without any grounds arrested many communists and informed Shkiriatov about this, but Shkiriatov, in his turn, made the individual decision: expel those arrested from the party as an enemy of the people... It turned out that the grounds for expelling an arrested person from the party was the notification ... of the fact of the arrest, and the grounds for charging the arrested with hostile activity was the ruling of the Party Control Commission about his expulsion from the party as an enemy of the people."¹

The following fact speaks of the power which Shkiriatov had acquired. In 1939, the party worker A. V. Snegov, who had been released from prison, was with several members of the Politburo, and he told them about what was going on in the torture chambers of the NKVD. Afterwards, only Mikoyan felt that it was necessary to ask Shkiriatov to expedite Snegov's party rehabilitation. When Snegov came to Shkiriatov at the Party Control Commission, he was arrested once again on the spot, after which he spent seventeen years in the camps.²

* * *

The conduct of the above-named people in 1936-1938 confirmed the correctness of Trotsky's comment that Stalin's closest entourage "consists of mediocre bureaucrats, intoxicated by the power they have extorted from the party."²²

Apparently, the majority of these people carried out their diabolical missions without much satisfaction. Left to themselves, they probably would have refused to conduct the Great Purge. A sign of this is the fact that literally the day after Stalin's death they put a stop to the new wave of terror which was threatening to surpass everything that had gone before. After this, they rather quickly and easily dealt with Beria and his satraps who had seized all the leading posts in the MVD, and then they proceeded to the mass rehabilitations of those who had been condemned earlier.

20. Stalin and His Intimate Circle 167

Shkiriatov, Yezhov and Frinovsky

These people, who had not dared while Stalin was alive to hint at their doubts over the correctness of the repressions, clearly acknowledged their groundlessness. When Khrushchev declared at the July Plenum of the Central Committee in 1953: "Let us examine the cases of 1937 and after 1937. Among them were many forged cases," someone cried out from the audience: "More than half of them were forged, you are right." Nor did another declaration made by Khrushchev meet with any objection: "A special board — now that's the most genuine terror."[23]

The facts provided in this chapter show that the members of Stalin's entourage who were closest to him did not fully coincide with the official party hierarchy. For instance, Malenkov, who was not even a candidate-member of the Central Committee, was closer to Stalin and wielded more real power than several members and candidate-members of the Politburo who were doomed to perish in the fires of the Great Purge.

21. In the Bowels of the Politburo

At the plenum of the Central Committee which took place on 10 February 1934, the Politburo was selected with a composition of ten members (Stalin, Molotov, Kaganovich, Voroshilov, Kalinin, Ordzhonikidze, Kuibyshev, Kirov, Andreev, Kosior) and five candidate-members (Mikoyan, Chubar, Petrovsky, Postyshev, Rudzutak). The list of names is presented here in the order in which they were listed in the informational bulletin describing the Central Committee's plenum. The order reflected the place that these people occupied in the party hierarchy and their popularity in the party and the nation (or to be more precise, the popularity which official propaganda was trying to assign them).

Before 1937, changes in the composition of the Politburo occurred only at the February Plenum of the Central Committee in 1935, where Mikoyan and Chubar were chosen members, and Zhdanov and Eikhe —candidate-members of the Politburo. By the time of the February-March Plenum of the Central Committee in 1937, there were nine members of the Politburo (because Kirov, Kuibyshev and Ordzhonikidze had died), and five candidate-members. Of the Politburo members during the Great Purge, two fell victim to repression, and the rest made it into the Politburo which was selected at the Eighteenth Congress [in March 1939]. Among the candidate-members of the Politburo, three fell to repression, one (Petrovsky) was removed from leadership duties, and one (Zhdanov) was transferred after the Eighteenth Congress to full membership in the Politburo.

In many foreign works about the Great Purge, the arrested members and candidate-members of the Politburo are placed in something of a "liberal group" that supposedly tried to resist the Stalinist terror. Avtorkhanov, for instance, asserts that Kosior, Chubar, Rudzutak and Postyshev joined Ordzhonikidze in speaking out against the trial of Rykov and Bukharin.[1] Sources which have become available in recent years prove the complete groundlessness of such versions. The "selection" made by Stalin was explained by other

Robert Eikhe (1890-1940)

Vlas Chubar (1891-1939)

Stanislav Kosior (1889-1939)

reasons, most likely his attitude of distrust toward "non-Russians." Of the five who were repressed, only Postyshev was Russian; Rudzutak and Eikhe were Latvians; Kosior was Polish; and Chubar, Ukrainian. None of these people ever entered into Stalin's closest circle or, with the exception of Rudzutak (and from 1934, Chubar as well), ever participated in the daily work of the Kremlin upper echelons, since they lived outside Moscow. In 1937-1938, Eikhe and Kosior were transferred to work in Moscow, and a few months after this transfer were arrested. As for their expulsion from the Central Committee and the party, not even the formal procedure of polling the members of the Central Committee was followed.

In October 1937, Eikhe was appointed People's Commissar of Agriculture for the USSR, and at the January Plenum of the Central Committee in 1938, he delivered a report which met with Stalin's approval. His arrest took place on 29 April 1938.

In January 1938, Kosior was appointed deputy chairman of the Council of People's Commissars of the USSR and chairman of the Soviet Control Commission under the Council of People's Commissars. In April 1938, he was removed from all the posts he occupied, and in May he was arrested. With regard to this act there was neither a resolution of the Politburo nor an exchange of opinion among its members.[2]

We can assume that one of the reasons for reprisals against Kosior was what Stalin would see as his impermissible "guilt": the attempt to intervene on behalf of his brother Vladimir, "an undisarmed" Trotskyist who had been in exile since 1928. At the beginning of 1936, after V. Kosior's wife had been arrested, Vladimir wrote an angry letter to his brother in which he demanded her release. S. Kosior forwarded this letter to Yezhov and asked him to look into the given case. When he learned of this, Stalin expressed his sharp indignation over the fact that "St. Kosior finds it possible to interfere in this case of blackmail."[3]

In January 1938, Chubar received a promotion, being appointed to the post of first deputy chairman of the Council of People's Commissars. On 16 June 1938, the Politburo passed a resolution which said: "In view of the fact that the testimony given by Kosior, Eikhe, Tr. Chubar (the brother of V. Ya. Chubar), as well as the testimony of Rudzutak and Antipov, cast a shadow on Comrade. V. Ya. Chubar, the Politburo of the Central Committee does not consider it possible to retain him as member of the Politburo of the CC and deputy chairman of the Council of People's Commissars of USSR and considers it possible to give him work only in the provinces for a trial period." On the next day, one more Politburo resolution was adopted — about the appointment of Chubar as head of construction of the Solikamsk cellulose combine.[4]

Khrushchev, who happened to be present during the last telephone conversation between Stalin and Chubar, recalled that after the call Stalin said to those around him: "'Chubar cries, is upset, and tries to prove that he is an honest man'; but Stalin's tone was sympathetic to Chubar. It seems that he understood what Vlas Yakovlevich was going through. And I was strongly surprised when literally the next day Chubar was arrested."[5]

The victimized members and candidate-members of the Politburo, who distinguished themselves before their arrest by unswerving obedience, stressed in court that they were always in complete agreement with Stalin's policies, which they were accustomed to calling the policies of the party. Rudzutak assured the court that "personally he never had entertained any thought against the policies of our party." Eikhe said that he would die "with the same faith in the correctness of the party's policy as he had held for the entire duration of his work."[6]

The only person in the Politburo who was not arrested, but was also not left in a leadership position, was Petrovsky. In January 1938, he was chosen deputy chairman of the Supreme Council of the USSR, and a month later was awarded the Order of Lenin in connection with his sixtieth birthday. The disgrace that befell Petrovsky soon after this was evidently related to the fact that his son and son-in-law were arrested, and a second son, the commander of a corps, was dismissed from the army. In 1939, Petrovsky was deprived of all his posts and remained without work for about a year, until his old comrade Samoilov, who worked as director of the Museum of the Revolution, proposed that he become his deputy.

Khrushchev explains that the reason that Petrovsky was not arrested was that "after the revolution he had not been considered an active organizer in the party. He filled, so to speak, the role of a party icon. Therefore Petrovsky was no danger to Stalin and it turned out to be enough to hide him away in the Museum of the Revolution."[7]

22. Liquidation of the Central Committee

Historians seeking the roots of the great terror in the decrees issued during the Leninist period of party life most often refer to the resolution adopted in 1921 at the Tenth Congress of the RKP(b) "On Party Unity." There is no question that this resolution, drafted during the extreme circumstances of the Kronstadt rebellion, led to significant limitations of inner-party democracy. This applies particularly to its seventh paragraph, which was not publicized, and which gave the Central Committee the right to apply to its members, "in cases of violations of discipline or the instigation or tolerance of factionalism, all measures of party censure up to expulsion from the party."[1]

In his concluding remarks at the Congress, Lenin said directly that this paragraph contradicted the party Statutes and the principle of democratic centralism. He expressed the hope that the extreme measure designated in it, prompted by the threat of the party splintering into several factions, would not be used.[2] And, of course, no one could envision that at some point, on the basis of this paragraph, the overwhelming majority of the Central Committee would not only be expelled, but annihilated.

In justifying the reprisals against the Central Committee in 1937-1938, Molotov stated that this process proceeded without any formal violations of the party Statutes or of democratic centralism. "The situation was not such that a minority expelled a majority," he said. "This gradually occurred. Seventy expelled 10-15 persons, then 60 expelled 15... In essence this led to a situation where a minority of this majority remained within the Central Committee... Such was the gradual but rather rapid process of clearing the way."[3]

Despite Molotov's sophistry, in the course of "clearing the way," i.e., exterminating the majority of the Central Committee, many formal violations were allowed. Most of all this concerned the procedure stipulated in the resolution of expulsion from the party: the discussion of a given case at a plenum of the CC. However, such an investigation into matters was conducted only with Bukharin and Rykov, whose case was reviewed at two such plenums.

After the February-March Plenum of 1937, decisions about expelling members of the Central Committee were made by polling members and then were confirmed by ballot. At three plenums (in June and October 1937, and in January 1938) seventy-five people were expelled by voting with ballots (thirty-six members and thirty-nine candidate-members), i.e., more than half the membership of the CC.[4] Many of these people had already been arrested by the time of the voting.

The June plenum confirmed the expulsion from the CC of eight people who had been arrested in April-May 1937. Besides these, on the first day of the plenum's work, twenty-six people were expelled, and on the following days, five more. Several of those expelled had been relieved of their posts long before the plenum (Chudov in June 1936, Kalmanovich in April 1937). Others had been arrested a few days before the plenum opened (Kubiak, Rumiantsev, Unshlikht) or during its work (Sulimov, Sedelnikov, Struppe). A small number of those expelled remained formally at their posts for some time after the plenum. Lavrentev was dismissed in July 1937; Liubimov in September; and Antipov in January 1938.

During the work of the next, October (1937) plenum, a new regimen of passes was instituted. Thus, Bubnov and Zatonsky were not allowed into the Kremlin on the strength of their Central Committee identification papers. An NKVD member on duty by the entrance told them that a new regimen had been established: in order to attend the plenum, besides identification papers one needed to have a special pass. Bubnov returned to his commissariat, where he learned from a radio announcement that he had been dismissed from his post as one who "had not measured up to his job"[5] (this formulation was used with regard to several other CC members). He was expelled from the party and arrested in December 1937. Zatonsky returned to the Ukraine, where he was arrested in 1938.

On 11 October, the plenum of the CC reviewed the question of the election campaign for the Supreme Council of the USSR. On the next day the second point on the agenda was discussed: "On Composition of the CC." This discussion amounted to a speech by Stalin, who announced that, in the period after the June plenum, eight members and sixteen candidate-members of the CC "had left the ranks and been arrested." "In examining all this material, in verifying the material, it has turned out that these people, they are enemies of the people," he declared. "If there are no questions, I would propose that this information be taken into consideration."

At the same time, during the October plenum, Stalin offered a "gift" to several candidate-members of the CC who had managed to survive that long. He proposed that ten of them be made full members of the CC. Insofar as

22. Liquidation of the Central Committee

the list of candidate-members of the CC chosen at the Seventeenth Congress (1934) had been put together according to who had received the most votes, Stalin proposed that the candidates who occupied the first ten places on this list be made full members of the CC.

After Stalin's speech, Khrushchev proposed that, in addition to the ten people named by Stalin, four more candidates who "are carrying out very big work" be transferred to full membership. Following a vote on the proposals from Stalin and Khrushchev, the question of the composition of the CC was declared to have been fully examined.[6]

The January Plenum of 1938 confirmed the expulsion of thirteen more members and candidate-members of the CC who had been arrested after the October Plenum. The majority of them had been expelled by referendum from 4 to 8 December 1937; on the referendum lists the Politburo gave information about their arrest and asked the CC members to "sanction" their removal from the CC and their arrest. In the minutes of the January Plenum this "sanction" was explained in the following manner: "On the basis of irrefutable evidence, the Plenum of the Central Committee of the VKP(b) recognizes the necessity of removing from membership in the CC VKP(b) and subjecting to arrest as enemies of the people: Bauman, Bubnov, Bulin, Mezhlauk V., Rukhimovich and Chernov, who proved to be German spies; Ivanov V. and Yakovlev Ya., who proved to be German spies and agents of the tsarist Okhranka; Mikhailov M., who was connected though counter-revolutionary work with Yakovlev; and Ryndin, who was connected through counter-revolutionary work with Rykov and Sulimov. Secretary of the CC, I. Stalin."[7] Of these nine people, two (Chernov and Ivanov) were included in the trial of the "Right-Trotskyist Bloc," and from the others, it seemed, it was impossible to obtain confessions. Bauman, who had been dismissed from his post in April 1937, was arrested on 12 October and died in Lefortovo Prison two days after his arrest. He was expelled from the CC posthumously.

During the December vote, A. I. Yegorov wrote the following on his referendum list: "Wipe all these scoundrels and bastards from the face of the earth as the most insidious vermin and repulsive monsters."[8] This, however, did not save Yegorov himself. With regard to him, on 28 February 1938 Stalin sent the following letter to members and candidate-members of the CC:

> "In view of the fact that, as shown by the face-to-face confrontation between Comrade Yegorov and the arrested conspirators Belov, Griaznov, Grinko and Sediakin, Comrade Yegorov turned out to be politically more tainted than could have been imagined before this confrontation, and taking into account that his wife, née Tseshkovskaya, with whom Comrade Yegorov has lived heart and soul, turned out to be a long-standing Polish spy, as is evident from her own tes-

timony — the CC VKP(b) and Sovnarkom have resolved to free Comrade Yegorov from his duties as commander of the Transcaucasian military district and dismiss him from the army. In connection with this the Politburo of the CC VKP(b) has recognized the need to expel Comrade Yegorov from candidate-membership of the CC VKP(b)."[9]

Within a few days, Yegorov was arrested. Among other charges, he was accused of establishing "criminal ties" with Trotsky in 1919 and of preparing a terrorist act against Stalin in 1920 (!).[10]

After the January Plenum and right up to the Eighteenth Congress of the VKP(b) (March 1939), no more plenums of the CC were convened. The expulsion of fourteen more members and eleven candidates in 1938 was done by referendum. With regard to seven people, there was not even the formal procedure of a referendum.

Of the 139 members and candidate-members of the CC elected at the Seventeenth Congress, 98 fell victim in 1936-1940, including 44 (of 71) members of the CC, and 55 (of 68) candidate-members of the CC. More than 80 percent of them were under 50 at the time of their arrest, i.e., at the full height of their powers.

In the period between the Seventeenth and Eighteenth Congresses, the composition of the Central Committee decreased by 108 people, or by 78 percent. During this time, five died natural deaths (Kuibyshev, Menzhinsky, Krupskaya, Tovstukha, and Shteingardt), and two died violent deaths (Kirov and Ordzhonikidze). As for Central Committee member I. V. Kosior, it was announced that he died in a sanatorium outside Moscow on 3 July 1937. However, the very fact of his sudden death only a few days after the June Plenum of the CC which had opened a new wave of repressions, and also the fact that he was not buried on Red Square (where even candidate-members of the CC were usually buried), suggests that he probably committed suicide. Three (Tomsky, Gamarnik and Liubchenko) shot themselves as they were about to be arrested, and the official announcements attributed their acts to the fact that they "had become tangled up in criminal ties."

By the time the Eighteenth Congress began its work, only thirty-one people remained in the Central Committee. Of these, seven were not re-elected to the CC at the Eighteenth Congress. Of these, five (Petrovsky, Krzhizhanovsky, Broido, Chuvyrin, Shvarts) were removed from leading positions or put on a pension, two (Iurkin and Zaveniagin) were returned to the CC at the Nineteenth and Twentieth Congresses.

Only twenty-four people elected to the CC at the Seventeenth Congress became members at the following congress. Of these, four subsequently died violent deaths. M. M. Kaganovich, accused of espionage, committed suicide on 1 July 1941. Lozovsky was shot in 1952, according to the sentence at the trial of the Jewish Anti-Fascist Committee. Beria and Bagirov were sentenced to death after Stalin died.

Of the remaining twenty people, eight died before Stalin — Nikolaeva (the only former member of an opposition who remained in the CC), Kalinin, Zhdanov, Litvinov, Mekhlis, Badaev, Veinberg and Makarov. After Stalin's death, the following people died: Manuilsky (1959), Poskrebyshev (1965), Voroshilov (1969), Shvernik (1970), Khrushchev (1971), Andreev (1971), Budenny (1973), Bulganin (1975), Mikoyan (1978), Molotov (1986), and Kaganovich (1991).

Of the members of the Central Committee at the Seventeenth Congress, fifteen were elected to the Central Committee at the Nineteenth Congress, eleven at the Twentieth Congress, four at the Twenty-Second Congress (Budenny, Mikoyan, Khrushchev, Shvernik), four at the Twenty-Third Congress (Budenny, Voroshilov, Mikoyan, Shvernik) and two at the Twenty-Fourth Congress (Budenny and Mikoyan).

The majority of the victimized members and candidate-members of the CC (89 people) were rehabilitated along legal and party lines in the period from 1954 to 1961. The rehabilitations of those years did not generally reach the victims of the Moscow Trials (Piatakov, Sokolnikov, Bukharin, Rykov, Rozengolts, Chernov). Their legal and party rehabilitation occurred only in 1988.

Two members of the Central Committee were sentenced to be shot at the trial of the "anti-Soviet Trotskyist Center" (1937), eight at the trial of the "right-Trotskyist Bloc" (1938), and three at the closed trial of the military leaders. News that two had been shot (Yenukidze and Sheboldaev) was announced in an official statement about a closed trial that supposedly was held in December 1937. In actuality, Yenukidze and Sheboldaev had been shot without a trial on 30 October of that year.

There was no official announcement about the arrest and subsequent fate of the remaining members and candidate-members of the Central Committee. Therefore, for many years in the West they were considered not to have been shot, but to "have disappeared." Public opinion could not imagine the gravity of the repressions which Stalin visited on the ruling elite.

More than half of the victimized members and candidate-members of the Central Committee were subjected to group executions. Twelve of them were shot on 30 October 1937, seven on 27 November 1937, five on 10 February 1938, nine on 28 July 1938, and seven on 25 and 26 February 1939.[11]

Other higher party organs were also subjected to a ruthless purge. In 1937-38, eighteen of twenty-two members of the Central Revision Commission were arrested and sentenced, and around half (twenty-nine of sixty-one) of the members of the Party Control Commission of the CC VKP(b).[12]

Given all these figures, the question remains: why was it that the members and candidate-members of the Central Committee, who possessed at least the formal opportunity to oppose the repressions, were not able to impede the reprisals even against themselves?

In general form, the reply to this question was given at the June Plenum of the Central Committee in 1957: "If the plenum (of the CC) had been taking an active part in leading the party, would its members have shot themselves?"[13]

The meaning of the existence of a party and its elected bodies lies in the collective working out of the most important political decisions. The form of this process is party-wide discussions, in the course of which alternative positions and platforms are freely discussed at party meetings. During the years of the Civil War, i.e., in the least propitious time for such discussions, they proceeded without interruption and covered the key questions of domestic and foreign politics. The existence of factions and groupings in the party was considered a normal phenomenon at that time. The Left Opposition, which arose in 1923, tried to re-establish such a position. In response to this attempt, the ruling group tried to make the ban on factions permanent, using Paragraph 7 of the resolution of the Tenth Congress "On Party Unity," which was first made public at the Thirteenth Party Conference (January 1924). From this time forward the struggle against all oppositions was waged under the flag of counterposing their "splitting" activity to the "monolithic" Central Committee.

All people capable of opposition activity were removed from the Central Committee in the 1920s and early 1930s. However, even by 1937, the Central Committee remained an institution with which Stalin had to reckon to a certain degree; at the very least he had to submit resolutions about the arrest of its members for ratification. In order to fully achieve Stalin's ideal of "monolithism," what was required was the virtual liquidation of the former Central Committee and its replacement with new people whose submission to Stalin's dictates would be guaranteed under all circumstances.

During the years of Stalin's totalitarianism, the pyramid of higher party organs was actually inverted in comparison with what it should have been according to the Party Statutes. Under Lenin the hierarchy of these organs was constructed in the following order: Party Congress, Plenum of the Central Committee, Politburo of the Central Committee, Orgburo of the Central Committee, and Secretariat of the Central Committee. The congresses and plenums of the CC discussed the most important questions of party policy, around which lively discussion developed that was then published in the press. In the course of polemics, which at times assumed a very sharp character, communists sharply criticized each other, but by no means did they insult each other. This situation changed immediately after Lenin's death, when the atmosphere at the congresses and plenums began to assume an outright hooligan character, and polemics completely lost the traits of party comradeship.

22. Liquidation of the Central Committee

Even by 1923-1924, the Politburo had turned into a hypertrophied metagovernment, simultaneously functioning as the supreme legislator in the land (such a situation was maintained right up until the last years of Gorbachev's "perestroika"). Thus, "party policy" was determined not by the party or its CC, but by a narrow ruling group.

In the middle of the 1930s, each session of the Politburo discussed tens, and sometimes hundreds of questions (the majority of these were actually decided by referendum). Insofar as the members of the Politburo were not able to investigate the content of these issues, the resolution of problems was prepared by the Central Committee's staff members, whose role grew steadily. The most important questions passed through Stalin's personal office.

Only a few of the decisions made by the Politburo, Orgburo, and secretariat of the Central Committee were published in the press. The majority of them remained strictly secret.

The plenums of the CC, in essence, merely confirmed the decisions prepared by the apparatus and approved by the Politburo. After 1929, there were no discussions at the plenums, and all decisions were made unanimously. Only the resolutions of the plenums were published, and sometimes the reports given at them, and on very rare occasions — speeches made during discussions. The transcripts of the congresses were published in their entirety, but the congresses themselves were ceremonial and decorative by nature, and the speeches at them amounted to bureaucratic accounts and official glorification of the "general line." Thus, the following law began to operate: the greater the real power of a party organ, the greater the degree that its work was wrapped in secrecy.

During the period of the Great Purge, the rights of the Central Committee and its members were restricted even more. In the first years after the Seventeenth Congress, "rank-and-file" members of the CC could attend sessions of the Politburo without taking part in the discussions of questions. At closed sessions of the Politburo, rank-and-file members of the CC were not allowed, but they were given the opportunity to become familiar with the secret decisions made at these sessions ("Special Files"). After the Great Purge and right up until the liquidation of the party in 1991, the overwhelming majority of Central Committee members never once attended sessions of the Politburo, although according to the Statutes, the Politburo continued to be an organ subordinate to the Central Committee. In addition, the sphere of information available to members of the CC was significantly reduced. The demand to "not stick your nose into matters that are not your own" became an unspoken commandment, an integral part of the disciplinary code which was obligatory for a highly-placed bureaucrat.

As Khrushchev recalled, "by 1938, the earlier democracy in the Central Committee had already been greatly undermined. For instance, as a candidate-member of the Politburo, I did not receive the material of our sessions. After the terrible year of 1937, I did not know, strictly speaking, to whom this material was sent in general. I received only the material which Stalin sent to me on his own orders."[14]

From all that has been said, one can understand the pitiful role and lack of rights of rank-and-file members and candidate-members of the CC; in their minds what often dominated, above all else, was fear for their own fate, and the dread of ending up on the next blacklist. The mood of these people is described in the memoirs of the writer Avdeenko, who worked in 1937 as a correspondent of *Pravda* in the Donbass. In a conversation with him, Sarkisov, a candidate-member of the CC and secretary of the Donets area committee, said: "In the Donbass, we don't have a single enterprise, collective farm, Soviet farm, or establishment where political bandits with party cards in their pockets are not active."

"Where did so many of them come from?"

"They are from Trotsky's club. Old descendants and today's protégés. Secret readers of the Trotskyist *Bulletin of the Opposition*."*[15]

Sarkisov had particularly good reasons to fear Stalinist reprisal: he was the only person in the Central Committee of the Seventeenth Congress (not counting Piatakov, who was shot in January 1937), who had been expelled from the party in 1927 for active participation in the "opposition bloc." But even Pramnek, the candidate-member of the CC who replaced Sarkisov in May 1937 and who had never participated in any of the oppositions, became maniacally suspicious and fearful no less than Sarkisov. Avdeenko described a conversation with him in the following way:

> "How is your work going in the Donbass?" I asked.
> He waved his hand hopelessly, in complete despair.
> "Who can I work with? All the first and second secretaries of the city committees and regional committees have turned out to be enemies of the people. Almost all the members of the bureau have been arrested. The directors of the enterprises have proved to be wreckers or spies. The main engineers, chief technicians, and even the main physicians at the polyclinics and hospitals, they, too, are a bunch of scum. You have to look far and wide for honest people. You have to be as wise as Solomon to know a decent man from a scoundrel and a fascist hireling."

---

* This passing comment testifies both to the Stalinist clique's sharp fear of Trotsky's publication, which appeared in distant France in a meager press run, and to the fact that this publication filtered through into the USSR even in 1937.

Drawn into the senseless hunt for "enemies of the people," Pramnek hastened to demonstrate his vigilance to his interlocutor, sharply sensing his own vulnerability, and his fear of paying for any incautious word.

Disclosing the rules of the game silently adopted in his conversation with Pramnek, Avdeenko wrote: "Pramnek and I were filled with fear of the repressions sweeping the land, but we carefully hid from each other this side of our worries, so that, god forbid, the dangerous thought would not arise: he's given the game away. We drowned our fear of 'Yezhov's iron rule' in high-flown and ultra-patriotic talk. And that's what we had to do. The instinct for self-preservation requires losing any trace of human conscience."[16]

The picture outlined by Avdeenko plunges us into the atmosphere of 1937. Even during confidential conversations, people conceal their actual thoughts and concerns from each other; they speak an artificial language consisting of a mixture of newspaper clichés and abusive language. The unspoken password of the Stalinist epoch lives in their souls: "that's the way it has to be." This means that you must subordinate yourself to the established demands and prohibitions, without questioning their rationality, even in your own mind. Both the journalist and the secretary of the area committee are in a state of fear for their own fate and camouflage this fear with curses hurled at "enemies of the people." They understand that if they do not conceal their own fear, then the person they are talking with might suspect that *this one* has something to fear. A candidate-member of the CC endures not less, but more fear than simple mortals. Without fully realizing it, he senses that the hunt is primarily for party activists on the same level as himself. He sees that the main factor in his survival is a continuous demonstration of his personal devotion to Stalin.

The concentration of all efforts on the search for enemies of the people created a kind of vicious circle. It shifted the attention of party leaders away from the direction of the economy. As a result, the neglected economy witnessed new disorder, including accidents and catastrophes, for which new scapegoats were sought. "Industry in the Donbass fails to fulfill the government plan in iron, steel, coal, chemicals, and machine-building," Avdeenko said in completing his story about the conversation with Pramnek. "In this year, the enormous region is working more poorly than in '36. The productivity of labor has sharply fallen. But the new secretary is much less concerned with a breakthrough on the labor front than on the cadre, or ideological, front. The first matter is to root out enemies of the people, to replace them with people of a Stalinist tempering, and all the rest will follow."[17]

What was the actual frame of mind of Central Committee members before and after their arrest? Unfortunately, almost no evidence has been preserved about this. Apparently these people were kept in conditions of greater isolation than other prisoners, or were among other condemned figures much like themselves (among the arrested members and candidate-members of the CC, *not a single* person was saved from being shot).

One of the few eye-witness accounts belongs to M. Shreider, who worked in 1938 as Deputy People's Commissar of Internal Affairs in Kazakhstan. He recalls that, at the May First demonstration in 1938, many columns bore enormous portraits of the first secretary of the Central Committee of the republic's Communist Party, Mirzoyan. After a day or two, Stalin's directive arrived in Alma-Ata to relieve Mirzoyan of his duties and to place him at the disposal of the CC. While on the way to Moscow, Mirzoyan was arrested.

According to Shreider, who was kept in the same cell as Mirzoyan, the latter endured particularly savage torture, as they broke all his ribs. Beria was present at several interrogation sessions and personally beat Mirzoyan. At one interrogation, Molotov, Kaganovich and Malenkov entered the room where Mirzoyan was being questioned. Mirzoyan told them that he had been brutally tortured, after which he could not keep speaking and began sobbing. "And what did you expect, with a scum like you, that they would kiss you?" Kaganovich tossed at Mirzoyan, and everyone present smiled at this "witticism."

Even in October 1954, the party functionary Moskatov, who worked in 1937 as a plenipotentiary in the Alma-Ata Party Control Commission, declared to Shreider that Mirzoyan was "a dangerous enemy of the people." When, in reply to this comment, Shreider told how testimony against Moskatov had also been beaten from Mirzoyan, Moskatov was visibly shaken.[18]

In his memoirs, Avtorkhanov tells of his meeting in a cell at the Butyrki Prison with a group of former members of the Central Committee, including Postyshev and Vareikis. According to Avtorkhanov, Postyshev had not signed any confession, and therefore was being relentlessly tortured. Before Postyshev appeared in their cell, the prisoners had charged careerists in the NKVD with terror; they claimed that the NKVD had devised a monstrous plan in an inner-party conspiracy to destroy the old revolutionaries, and then destroy Stalin himself and establish a fascist dictatorship in the land. Such views were held, for instance, by Vareikis, who argued for "a conspiracy of Yezhov against Stalin." When he had heard these arguments, Postyshev told Vareikis: "Your formula would be correct if you turned it around: 'a conspiracy of Stalin against Yezhov.' Yezhov is a hunting dog on Stalin's leash, but a faithful dog and a wise one who, at his master's discretion, is destroying the party and terrorizing the people. As soon as the dog finishes the hunt (and we will no longer be among the living), Stalin will declare that it is mad, and destroy it."

Even more principled in character were the objections voiced by Postyshev when Vareikis said: "If the price of saving socialism in the land is our death, then a Bolshevik must be ready to make this sacrifice." In reply to this statement Postyshev declared: "If the price of saving socialism is the execution of the party which guided its construction, and imprisonment for mil-

22. Liquidation of the Central Committee

lions who built it, then I spit on such socialism. In addition, we still have not constructed socialism... Yes, Ilich said that we have all that is necessary to build socialism, but Stalin has proved that we also had, it turns out, everything necessary to create a one-person tyranny which depends on executioners from the NKVD, prostitutes from the party, and criminals from society... And Vareikis should not worry about this 'triumphant socialism' which we left at liberty. It will go nowhere; not only will it remain, but in its interests Stalin will justify both the present Inquisition and all of his future crimes."[19]

Avtorkhanov's memoirs can hardly be considered a fully reliable source — and not only because in many other instances he presented his own fabrications as dependable facts. It is hardly the case that a large number of arrested Central Committee members would have been held in a single cell. And the transition is too sharp from the Postyshev as he was before his arrest, to the same Postyshev as he is presented by Avtorkhanov. At the same time, the arguments which Avtorkhanov put in Postyshev's mouth could have found their way into the minds of many CC members in prison (and perhaps, even before prison). They are very close to the arguments of imprisoned Trotskyists (see Chapter 33) and the "non-returners" of 1937-1938 (see Chapters 39-40).

Delegates to the Eighth Extraordinary Congress of Soviets in December 1936. Seated, from left to right: Chubar, Andreev, Yezhov, Khrushchev, Zhdanov, and Kaganovich. Mikoyan is standing behind Andreev, and Malenkov is seated behind Zhdanov and Kaganovich.

23. The Party Apparatus

On many pages of his memoirs, Khrushchev paints a picture of how "they literally seized people and carried them away to be cut up." This concerned, first of all, party leaders at all levels who were arrested, as Khrushchev put it, in three generations: "those who had earlier been in the leadership; second, those who had been promoted; and third, those who had also been promoted."[1] Almost all the apparatchiks who worked with Khrushchev in Moscow in 1937 were killed. The same picture met Khrushchev in the Ukraine, where by the time of his arrival there at the beginning of 1938, "as for cadres, it was what they called 'clean': not a single secretary of an area committee, not a single chairman of an area executive committee was left; there was not a single chairman of the Council of People's Commissars, nor any of his deputies."[2]

The apparatchiks who remained at liberty felt doomed; they felt like people on the edge of an abyss. "Among party members there was hardly a person without testimony against him."[3] "Today a representative of some party organization speaks out to expose people who have been arrested earlier, and tomorrow he himself has disappeared, which also finds its explanation. They say that he zealously spoke out because he, too, was mixed up, and he wanted to hide the truth... The party organs have been absolutely reduced to nothing. The leadership has been paralyzed, and no one can be promoted without approval from the NKVD. ... What has been formed is a closed chain of faulty practices by the leadership, which thereby starts down the road toward its own apparent self-destruction."[4]

The books of R. Medvedev, R. Conquest, and other authors contain impressive lists of the names of leaders who perished in 1937-1938. I will not provide such lists. It is sufficient to say that, from the repressions in those years, there was hardly a single party secretary (of a regional, city, or area committee, of the Central Committee of the national communist parties) saved, nor a single chairman of an executive committee at any level, nor a single director of a major factory, nor a single all-union or republic-level people's commissar. In this milieu, what reigned was a situation characterized in one of Trotsky's diary entries: "With the aid of systematic slander which embraces everything: political ideas, service duties, family relations and personal ties, people are led to suicide, insanity, prostration, and treachery. In the realm of slander and defamation, the apparatuses of the VKP, GPU and Comintern work hand in hand. The center of this system is Stalin's office."[5]

One of the most fundamental contradictions that gave birth to the Great Purge was the contradiction between the Bonapartist aspirations of Stalin, who was prepared to realize them even at the price of betraying the interests of socialism and the country, and the attitudes of the majority of apparatchiks, who remained devoted to these interests. Of course, even before 1937, Stalin had involved many of these people as collaborators in his crimes. They tried to justify this collaboration, at least in their own eyes, by saying that the extermination campaigns against the peasantry or oppositionists were dictated by certain higher interests. But even the most sophisticated casuistic moves could not explain how the cause of socialism could be served by the complete decapitation of the party, state, army, economy, and culture. "When Stalin accuses one or another part of the apparatus of losing 'vigilance,'" wrote Trotsky, "by this he is saying: you are worrying about the interests of the economy, of science, or of the army, but you are not looking out for my interests! Each of Stalin's agents, in all areas of the country and in all the tiers of the bureaucratic tower, is in the same situation. The bureaucracy can support its own power in no other way than by undermining all the foundations of economic and cultural progress. Thus, on new historical soil is reborn unexpectedly the ages-old Russian antagonism between the oprichnina [the old administrative elite under Ivan IV] and the zemshchina [the domains of the boyars]. The struggle between them is turned into the extermination of the best people in the country by the most corrupt dregs of society."[6] While indicating that in the Great Purge the contradiction between the October Revolution and the Thermidorian bureaucracy had found its most dramatic expression, Trotsky wrote: "In the struggle for power and income, the bureaucracy is forced to chop off and crush those groups who are connected with the past, who know and remember the program of the October Revolution, who are sincerely devoted to the tasks of socialism. The extermination of the Old Bolsheviks and of the socialist elements of the middle and younger generations is a necessary link in the anti-October reaction."[7]

Hypocrisy and duplicity became a way of life and permeated the mentality of the Stalinist bureaucracy long before 1937. Even the best people from this milieu were condemned to hiding their true thoughts and publicly repeating official lies. For a characterization of the psychology and behavior of such people, Stalin used the word "double-dealer." According to Stalin's canons, a double-dealer was one who, in his public statements, duplicated the statements of official propaganda and in his behavior subordinated himself to party rituals, but in his soul maintained his own convictions and internal disagreements with Stalin's policies. The higher the post an apparatchik occupied, the better he was informed about the situation in the country, the more deeply he had to strangle his own doubts and hide his vacillations under a thick layer of ritualistic lies.

A double standard ruled in the daily personal behavior, too, of a significant part of the bureaucracy, which had proceeded far down the road of degeneration in everyday life. Many bureaucrats, who kept repeating the traditional formulas about the modesty of a Bolshevik, were proving to be infected with arrogance, lordliness, and the idiosyncrasies of grandees. The bureaucratic elite, headed by Stalin himself, gave an example of this. "From the time that Stalin declared: 'Life has become better, comrades! Life has become more joyful!'," wrote Orlov, "the Soviet ruling elite turned away from the practice of secret parties with drinking, dancing and card-playing, and began to organize such forms of entertainment openly, without any shyness."[8]

Up to a certain time the displays of vulgar conduct, self-indulgence, and petty tyrannical behavior on the part of the apparatchiks did not serve as an object of public denunciation. In the transition to the Great Terror, Stalin built a new amalgam. In the pages of the press and at broad meetings with the participation of people who did not belong to the party, they began to publicize the mores and relations that are now considered typical only of the period of stagnation [Brezhnev's time]. Thus, *Pravda* wrote in an article about Surnin, the secretary of a village regional committee: "On his direct orders Soviet trade in the region has been stopped. Commodities are reserved and lie for weeks under the counter. The director himself of the regional department of internal trade carries items to the homes of high-ranking people, and others are served by the director of the regional department store. Nor does Surnin forget about the collective farm storehouses. At the collective farm "The Way to Communism," he took five poods* of white flour and 116 kilograms of pork. The chairman of the collective farm obtained the products for him and was soon after promoted to chairman of the regional union of consumers' cooperatives."[9]

At first, criticism of this kind seemed even to perceptive people to be an attempt to cleanse the social atmosphere. Thus, M. Prishvin turned his attention to the article, "Banality," which ridiculed the secretary of the party committee at the factory "Hammer and Sickle." He had organized a two-day party meeting at which he proposed that those attending were to decide by open vote who at the factory should be considered bootlickers.[10] "How long this policy of 'bashing noses' will continue is hard to say," wrote Prishvin in his

---

* A pood is about 36 pounds.

diary. "Evidently, behind it lies a sincere desire to put an end to the regimes of toadyism and to lend a voice to patriots and generally honest people, on the one hand, and on the other, to create a more reliable party apparatus."[11]

Of course, such intentions were not the true goal of the campaign of extermination launched by Stalin against the apparatchiks. The Great Purge was not "an anti-bureaucratic revolution," as some domestic and foreign researchers are inclined to think. Among the generation that perished in 1937-1938, there were many more unselfish people who were untouched by the corrosive influence of corruption and bureaucratic arrogance than among those who replaced them. The exposure of the moral and social defects from which many bureaucrats of the 1930s did indeed suffer was a means of frightening the apparatchiks, of setting them against each other in order to prevent their consolidation in view of the blows which were being dealt to the entire ruling layer.

In characterizing the processes which led the first generation of Soviet bureaucrats to their tragic end, Trotsky wrote: "The more that the masses lost their ardor and grew tired under the knout of historical difficulties, the higher the bureaucratic apparatus raised itself above them. At the same time it completely transformed its inner character. By its very essence the revolution means the application of violence by the masses. The bureaucracy, which came to power thanks to the revolution, decided that violence is the only factor in history... At the same time the bureaucracy came ever more frequently to the conclusion that, once the masses had given it power, they had fulfilled their mission. Thus the Marxist philosophy of history was replaced by a policeman's philosophy... When the bureaucracy crowned the revolution with itself in an isolated and backward country, it almost automatically raised on its shoulders Stalin, who fully responded to its policeman's philosophy and was more capable, i.e., more ruthless than all others, of defending its power and privileges." However, to the extent that the Stalinist leadership retreated from the principles of the October Revolution, the remaining devotion to these principles by the best part of the bureaucracy became a threat to Stalin's omnipotence. "Fearing the masses more than at any other time, he sets the bureaucratic apparatus against them. But this very apparatus never achieves the necessary 'monolithism.' The old traditions and new spiritual needs of society give birth to discord and criticism within the apparatus. Hence the ever-present need for a 'purge'... And since for a caste of upstarts what is most dangerous of all are the representatives of the revolutionary generation who at least partially have retained their loyalty to the old banner, the GPU proves that the Old Bolsheviks are all spies, traitors and renegades."[12]

The political and moral degeneration of the bureaucracy was expressed most clearly in its rejection of the principles of social equality, in whose name the October Revolution had been carried out. Accepting the privileges they had been given as something they were due, the apparatchiks lost the qualities of revolutionaries and communists, distanced themselves from the masses and became guided most of all by the interests of their own social layer.

Trotsky often stressed that the dividing line between the Stalinists and the Left Opposition was connected primarily to the attitude toward social inequality. "The bureaucracy," he noted, "arrived at the judicial frame-ups not immediately, but gradually, in the process of fighting for its domination. Lying and forgery were inherent in the very situation of the Soviet bureaucracy. In words, it fights for communism. In actual fact, it fights for its own income, its privileges, and its power. With the fear and malice of a social parvenu, it exterminates all oppositionists. In order to justify this ferocious terror in the eyes of the people, it is forced to ascribe to its victims ever more monstrous and fantastic crimes."[13]

Noting that the bureaucracy was raised for years on shameless slander directed against the Left Opposition, Trotsky wrote: "Tens of thousands of newspaper articles in tens of millions of copies, the transcripts of innumerable indictment speeches, popular pamphlets in press runs in the millions, and thick books have spread and continue to spread from day to day the most repulsive lies which the thousands of hired writers, without conscience, without ideas and without imagination, are capable of preparing."[14] The repetition of these lies was a necessary condition for any apparatchik to be able to remain at his post and obtain promotions in his work.

Initially the strengthening of the social positions of the bureaucracy and the growth of Stalin's Bonapartist might were two processes running in parallel. But gradually the basic contradiction on which the Bonapartist regime arose, the contradiction between the bureaucracy and the people, was supplemented ever more by the contradiction between the revolutionary and Thermidorian elements within the bureaucracy itself. Leaning on the bureaucracy against the people and on the Thermidorians against the revolutionaries, Stalin unswervingly moved toward a Thermidorian "monolithism," i.e., to the crushing of all vestiges of the revolutionary spirit and of the slightest displays of political independence.

Such a "monolithism" could be fully achieved only by physically exterminating the representatives of the bureaucracy who remained devoted to Bolshevik ideas and traditions, and therefore who opposed from within the interests of their own social layer. And as soon as the repressions against their recent comrades aroused confusion and protest among even the Stalinist-inclined section of the apparatus, Stalin made the decision to liquidate the entire ruling stratum in the form in which it had developed by 1937, and to replace it with a new generation of people without a revolutionary past, without links to the traditions of Bolshevism. Hence arose the fundamental contradiction of the Great Purge: almost all the former representatives of the ruling layer were exterminated, but the positions of this very layer, which became politically homogenous and fully subordinated to the will of the "leader," became reinforced.

The scale of the extermination of the apparatchiks assumed unprecedented proportions during the period of the elections to the Supreme Council of the USSR, which Stalin called "the freest and truly most democratic elections, unknown before in history." In an article entitled, "The Supreme Council of Praetorians," the *Bulletin of the Opposition* analyzed the official data about the nominated candidates and the deputies who were elected. This analysis showed that during the two or three weeks before the elections, 54 candidates disappeared, including Mezhlauk, who had just been appointed chairman of Gosplan, many people's commissars, military leaders, secretaries of area committees, and so forth. Among those who disappeared were those who had not long before been called "the organizers of the rout of the Trotsky-Bukharinist counter-revolutionaries," or "steadfast Bolsheviks, sent by Comrade Stalin to liquidate the Trotsky-Bukharinist degenerates."

Among the deputies chosen, workers engaged in production and collective farmers comprised 14 percent. More than three quarters of the deputies were apparatchiks of various levels, including 68 people (6 percent of the deputies altogether) who were high-ranking members of the NKVD. Twenty-five percent of the party secretaries and chairmen of executive committees who were elected deputies, were listed as "acting," i.e., they had occupied these posts only recently. These figures gave the authors of the article good reason to conclude that the Supreme Council was a "gathering of Praetorians, ... 'elected' under siege conditions."[15]

The results of the next stage of the "cadre revolution" were described in an article, "The Loyalty of Stalin's Cadres," which was devoted to a comparison of the composition of the party committees elected in the spring of 1937 and the summer of 1938. During this period the party committees in all the republics, regions, areas and major cities saw no less than 85 percent of their members replaced. From the secretaries of area committees elected in 1937, no one was re-elected the following year except Zhdanov, Khrushchev, and the secretary of the Gorky area committee, Yu. M. Kaganovich, the brother of the "iron people's commissar."[16] Moreover, as the article stressed, in the majority of instances the fate of those who had "disappeared" was unknown — had they been arrested, shot, or only removed from their posts?

Today, we can fill in the blank spots of the analysis made by the *Bulletin of the Opposition*. Thus, from the 1,996 delegates to the Seventeenth Congress of the VKP(b) with deciding or advisory votes (the overwhelming majority of them were apparatchiks), 1,108 were arrested, of whom 848 were shot.[17]

It would be naive to think that all the apparatchiks of the 1930s shared the fetishistic attitude toward Stalin that was characteristic, for example, of

Khrushchev, who confessed thirty years later: "When Stalin unmasked enemies, I thought that he was insightful: look how he sees enemies, whereas what do I do? It turns out that around me there were so many enemies, so many arrested people with whom I was in daily contact, and here I never noticed that they were enemies."[18] Khrushchev was not an Old Bolshevik, he did not have to his credit revolutionary service in the years of the Tsarist underground and Civil War. He had been suddenly promoted at the beginning of the 1930s to leadership positions by Stalin and Kaganovich. He knew little about Stalin's past and had a poor understanding of the issues of the innerparty struggle. In their frame of mind, a majority of the party leaders of the 1930s were closer not to Khrushchev's views, but to those of the Bolshevik "non-returners" who decided to break with Stalinism.

By the beginning of 1938, four men had dared to make such a break. Only one of them — an envoy to Rumania, Butenko — announced his break with Bolshevism. Unlike the other non-returners, Butenko was neither a professional diplomat nor an espionage agent. As a staff worker among Soviet personnel at the world exhibition in Paris in 1937, like many other rapidly promoted figures, he soon leapt over several stages in his career and became within a few months advisor to the embassy, and then ambassador. After his sudden disappearance, the Soviet government hastened to announce that he had been murdered by Trotskyists. However, a few days after this announcement, Butenko surfaced in Rome, where he declared that he had never been a communist by conviction and that in his political views he was close to Ukrainian fascism.

In commenting on Butenko's unexpected defection, Trotsky wrote: "Did he have to renounce much? Did he have to destroy much within himself? We do not think so. A very significant and growing part of the Stalinist apparatus consists of fascists who have not recognized themselves. To identify the Soviet regime as a whole with fascism is a vulgar political mistake into which ultra-left dilettantes are inclined to fall who ignore the difference in the social foundations. But the symmetry of the political superstructures, the similarity of the totalitarian methods and psychological types is striking. Butenko is a symptom of enormous importance: he shows us the careerists of the Stalinist school in their natural form."[19]

Trotsky considered an even more important symptom of the political divisions within the "monolithic" party to be the emigration of three communists who broke with Stalin, but not with Bolshevik principles. Trotsky expressed certainty that the moods of the most consistent among them — Reiss — were shared by many people who belonged to the Soviet bureaucracy. Of course, he emphasized, the majority of the apparatchiks were not capable of such a bold act. "They despise their surroundings. They hate Stalin. And at the same time they engage in endless drudgery. The reason for such adaptation is rooted in the very character of Thermidor, as a slow, creeping, all-embracing reaction. The revolutionary is steadily and unnoticeably drawn into a conspiracy against the revolution. Every new year reinforces his ties to the apparatus and deepens his isolation from the working masses. The bureaucracy, especially the bureaucracy of the GPU, lives in an artificial atmosphere which it creates for itself. Each deal with revolutionary conscience prepares an even more serious deal tomorrow, thereby making a break more difficult. In addition, the illusion still remains that the issue is service to the 'revolution.' People hope for a miracle which tomorrow will return the policy of the ruling clique to the old course, — they hope, and continue to engage in drudgery."[20]

In disclosing the social heterogeneity of the Soviet bureaucracy, Trotsky noted the hidden formation of various political types within it. "If it were possible to politically X-ray the entire Soviet apparatus, we would find within it: concealed Bolsheviks; bewildered, but honest revolutionaries; bourgeois democrats; and finally, candidates for fascism." As often happened with Trotsky's analyses, this analysis, which correctly predicted the tendencies of development, was somewhat outstripped by the course of historical events. The first group he named was basically exterminated during the years of the Great Purge. The second, ideologically estranged group, remained throughout the entire duration of the party's existence. The formation and consolidation of the last two groups required several decades more. Only the years of Gorbachev's "perestroika" and Yeltsin's "reforms" revealed with full clarity the correctness of Trotsky's thoughts that "the ranks of the Soviet apparatus are filled with bureaucrats of a bourgeois frame of mind. When they cast off the uniform of Stalinism, they will simply unveil their true political nature."[21] It was precisely bureaucrats of this type — Gorbachev and members of his Politburo such as Yakovlev, Yeltsin, and Shevardnadze — who became the people most to blame at the beginning of the 1990s for the collapse of the USSR and the shifting of its former republics to a capitalist path of development.

Only by taking into account the destruction of party cadres that occurred during the years of the Great Purge and that broke the thread to Bolshevik continuity; only by taking into account the subsequent decay of the Stalinist and post-Stalinist regimes, can one correctly assess the striking fact that the ban on the many-millioned CPSU in 1991 was met with not even a semblance of resistance. Most apparatchiks found comfortable niches in the new structures of power; the former leaders of the communist parties of the republics became heads of the majority of states that were formed on the ruins of the USSR. Loud declamations from these people about their sudden "recovery of sight" were just as false and hypocritical as their apologetic speeches the day before about "developed socialism."

Therefore, despite the radical nature of the social turn-about that occurred at the end of the 1980s and beginning of the 1990s, in order to carry it out there was no need to smash the state machinery and replenish the personnel of the entire state apparatus from top to bottom, as usually happens during such social cataclysms. For the ruling bureaucracy, the "painlessness" of this upper-echelon overturn ("counter-revolution from above") was paid for by the suffering of tens of millions of people who became its victims.

Top: Voroshilov and Stalin

Middle: The five marshals, Tukhachevsky, Voroshilov, Yegorov (sitting), Budenny, and Bliukher (standing)

Left: Lev Mekhlis, from December 1937 head of the Political Directorate of the Red Army; responsible for "turning the army upside down" (see page 201)

24. The Army

Trotsky considered the extermination of the flower of the commanding staff of the Red Army on the threshold of war to be "a fact unprecedented in human history,"[1] and the clearest example that Stalin "has inexorably sacrificed the interests of the whole," i.e., of the nation, when these interests had come into conflict with his personal interests.[2] Trotsky saw the main reason for the annihilation of the best military leaders in the fact that "Stalin flirts in every way with the army, but he has a mortal fear of it."[3]

During the time of the party purges of 1933-1936, the Soviet press praised the trustworthiness and purity of the communist cadres in the army. As proof, figures were given about the extremely low percentage of army communists who were purged. In the period of the Great Purge, the blow fell mainly on the commanders who were members of the party. As a result, by the end of 1937, the number of communists in the Red Army had fallen by a factor of two in comparison with 1932 — to 150,000 men.[4]

In commenting on the results of the first year of the purge, Barmine wrote: "Knowing well the command staff of the Red Army, I can count only about ten truly talented and independent officers who are capable of creatively guiding operations and directing masses of troops in the conditions of extreme stress of modern war. Stalin can boast that with one act of reprisal in June (the trial of the military leaders – V. R.) he destroyed seven of them. ... Only two major military officers are left — Marshals Bliukher and Yegorov. They remain ... But for how long?"[5]

The trial of June 1937 became a signal for unleashing a campaign of extermination against the military cadres. In just the nine days after the defendants had been shot, 980 commanders and political advisors had been arrested.[6]

On 21 June, Voroshilov and Yezhov signed a secret order calling upon all military personnel "mixed up in the activity of counter-revolutionary fascist and sabotage organizations, or knowing about their existence," to appear with an acknowledgment of guilt; for this confession they were promised an amnesty. The fact that no one appeared with a confession only heightened Stalin's fury after he had demanded an increase of repression in the army. At a meeting of the NKVD in the summer of 1937, Yezhov announced that Stalin thought "the military-fascist conspiracy must have a number of branches."[7]

A significant number of the arrests of higher-ranking military leaders were carried out under Stalin's direct orders. Thus, in August 1937, after he had read the transcript of the interrogation of Aleksandrovsky, the deputy head of counter-intelligence of the Red Army, Stalin sent it to Yezhov after adding the comments, "seize," or "arrest," next to 30 names mentioned by the man under investigation.[8]

An atmosphere was created in all military units resembling a hysterical witch hunt for enemies of the people, an epithet assigned to former members of the oppositions, of course, before anyone else. In all military units and military academies a thorough count of all former oppositionists was made. For example, the military commissar of the Military Electro-Technical Academy sent to PUR [the military political directorate] a list of 269 communists at the Academy "who participated in oppositions and anti-party groups, who vacillated, who spoke in defense of oppositionists, or who had ties with them."[9]

Another category of people subject to a total purge included representatives of nationalities that had state formations outside the borders of the USSR. On 10 March 1938, Malenkov instructed Mekhlis to present lists of army communists who were Poles, Germans, Latvians, Estonians, Finns, Lithuanians, Bulgarians, Greeks, Koreans and representatives of a number of other nationalities. In June 1938, Voroshilov signed a directive about dismissing from the Red Army commanders and political advisors who belonged to these nationalities or who were foreign nationals.[10] This revealed Stalin's opinion that all "non-Russians" were unreliable and capable of betraying socialist principles, even in those instances when they had devoted all their previous lives to defending them.

The People's Commissariat of Defense [NKO] kept a careful count of the repressed commanders. As Shchadenko, the head of the directorate of the NKO for command personnel, announced in a report to Stalin, Molotov, Voroshilov, and Andreev, from 1 March 1937 through 1 March 1938, 21,300 people were dismissed from the Red Army, including 17,400 for political reasons, of whom 5,329 were arrested. The repressions involved mainly the higher command personnel, but the lower and middle commanding ranks were also seriously weakened. From 1 January through 1 November 1937, more than 14,500 captains and lieutenants were dismissed from the Red Army.[11] Parallel to the bacchanalia of repression in the army, there was an epidemic of suicides. Those who committed suicide were primarily those who had been subjected to vilification and who were expecting an imminent arrest. For instance, the head of one of the directorates of the People's Commissariat of Defense, Levenzon, shot himself after he had been charged with showing sympathy for Trotsky twelve years before. In all, the Red Army recorded 728 suicides or attempted suicides in 1937; and in 1938, — 832 incidents.[12]

Many commanders who had passed though the first stages of repression (expulsion from the party or dismissal from the army) chose the only available method of fighting for their salvation by sending complaints and appeals to higher organs. The flood of appeals was so great that the bureaucratic apparatus could not manage to look into them. At the beginning of 1938, Shchadenko composed a list which indicated that in the defense commissariat there were 20,000 complaints that had not been examined and 34,000 complaints on which no final decision had been made.[13]

Only in August 1938, when the consequences of the pogrom that had been unleashed in the army began to threaten the ability to direct it, was a special commission created to investigate the complaints of dismissed commanders. It reviewed about 30,000 declarations and returned about 12,500 commanders and political advisors to the Red Army.[14]

Several commanders publicly pointed to the destructive effects of the army purge on the defense capability of the country. Thus, the head of the Chemical Directorate of the Red Army, Stepanov, declared at a meeting of the party activists: "Look what they are doing with our cadres. 40-45 percent of the heads of the chemical departments of the districts have been arrested, 60-65 percent of the heads of the chemical departments at the corps and divisional level have also been arrested... We are now so weak and demoralized that we are absolutely incapable of fighting."[15] While speaking at a session of the Military Council of the People's Commissariat of Defense, the commander of the Transcaucasian Military District, N. V. Kuibyshev, called the combat preparation of the troops unsatisfactory. "The basic reason for this lies," he declared, "in the fact that the district has had its cadres severely weakened." Voroshilov offered a "consoling" reply when he said: "No more so than others."[16]

The results of the army purge were summarized by Voroshilov at a session of the Military Council on 29 November 1938. "When, in the last year, the group of despicable traitors of our Motherland and of the Red Army, headed by Tukhachevsky, was discovered and destroyed by a revolutionary court," he declared, "none of us could or did imagine, unfortunately, that this baseness, this rot, this treachery had so widely and deeply penetrated the ranks of our army. Throughout the rest of 1937 and 1938, we have been compelled to ruthlessly purge our ranks, mercilessly cutting out the infected parts of the organism from the living, healthy tissue, cleansed of the loathsome and treacherous decay ... The purge has been conducted in a radical and wide-ranging manner ... from the very top ranks to the lowest ... Therefore the quantity of those purged has proven to be very, very impressive. It is sufficient to say that in this entire period we have purged more than forty thousand people."[17]

From May 1937 through September 1938, about half of the regimental commanders were purged, almost all the commanders of brigades and divisions, all the corps commanders and the troop commanders of the military districts.[18] With few exceptions, all the heads of the directorates and other senior members of the Commissariat of Defense and the General Staff were arrested, as well as all the heads of the military academies and institutes, all the leaders of the Navy and the commanders of the fleet. Following Tukhachevsky, all the remaining deputy People's Commissars of Defense — Yegorov, Alksnis, Fedko and Orlov — were arrested and shot.

The higher the level in the military hierarchy, the greater the number of those facing repression. Out of 837 people who had been given military titles in November 1935 (from colonel to marshal), 720 were arrested.[19] Of the sixteen people who received the title of commander or marshal, only Voroshilov, Budenny and Shaposhnikov survived the Great Purge.

The reason for Stalin's special good will toward Shaposhnikov, a former colonel in the Tsarist army who joined the Communist Party only in 1930, apparently lies in the fact that, during the Soviet-Polish war of 1920, Shaposhnikov published a chauvinist article in a military journal about "the naturally Jesuitical Poles," to which he contrasted the "honest and open spirit of Great Russians." For the publication of this article, the journal was closed down by special directives coming from Trotsky, and Shaposhnikov was dismissed from work in the General Staff.[20] In 1937, Stalin undoubtedly recalled this incident and not only protected Shaposhnikov from repression, but appointed him head of the General Staff and Deputy People's Commissar of Defense.

Of the nine military figures elected to the Central Committee of the VKP(b) at the Seventeenth Congress, only Voroshilov and Budenny survived.

It must be noted that the military leaders who were shot were at the very height of their physical and mental powers. Among those tried at the June trial in 1937, the oldest (Kork) was 49, and the youngest (Putna) was 39. Tukhachevsky was only three years older than Zhukov and Rokossovsky, who assumed the posts of division commander in 1937.

The corps of political advisors to the Red Army and Fleet was devastated. In 1938 alone, 3,176 political advisors were dismissed, including those dismissed "in connection with arrest" — 265 people; those expelled from the VKP(b) — 982 people; former participants of inner-party groupings — 187 people; and "non-Russians" released according to the directive of the People's Commissar of Defense — 863 people.[21] All the political advisors who in 1935 received the upper-level rank of army commissar (sixteen people) were shot.

The majority of military theoreticians and historians were repressed, and their works were removed from circulation.

The higher the rank of those subjected to repression, the greater the number of those shot. Out of 408 members of the leading and commanding staff of the Red Army condemned by the Military Collegium, 401 were sentenced to be shot, and only seven were sentenced to various lengths of imprisonment.[22] Of the brigade, division and corps commanders who were victimized, 643 were shot, sixty-three died under arrest, eight committed suicide and eighty-five served long prison terms.[23] As a result of the pre-war repressions, the Red Army lost more military leaders of high rank than during all the years of the Second World War.

In 1935, the Military Council of the People's Commissariat of Defense was formed, containing eighty-five high-ranking leaders of the army and navy. The fate of these people unfolded in the following way. One (S. S. Kamenev) died in 1936, two committed suicide in anticipation of arrest, seventy-six were subjected to repression in 1937-38. Of those repressed, sixty-eight were shot, one (Bliukher) was beaten to death during interrogation in Lefortovo Prison, one died in prison camp, and three emerged from the camps after Stalin's death.[24] Only nine remained untouched by the Great Purge, out of whom three suffered repression in subsequent years: Shtern was shot in 1941, Kulik in 1950, and Meretskov was arrested in 1941. After several months, Meretskov was freed from prison and returned to the army. Thus, only six people escaped repression (Voroshilov, Budenny, Timoshenko, Shaposhnikov, Apanasenko and Gorodovikov). All of them, apart from Shaposhnikov, had served in the First Cavalry during the Civil War.

Commenting on the (far from complete) information which he had received about the purge in the Red Army, Trotsky recalled that, during the First World War, the tsarist government had arrested the defense minister on charges of state treason. In this regard foreign diplomats said to Prime-Minister Sazonov: you have a strong government if it decides during a war to arrest its own defense minister. "In actual fact, the strong government was on the verge of collapse," wrote Trotsky. "The Soviet government has not only arrested the person who is virtually a defense minister, Tukhachevsky, but it has also exterminated the entire commanding staff of the army, navy and air force."[25]

Among the high-ranking commanders who survived, there was not a single one against whom the NKVD organs did not gather compromising material in 1937-1938. Such "material" was prepared on Zhukov, Konev, Malinovsky, Bagramian, Sokolovsky and other future marshals and military leaders of the Second World War. They were all forced to endure many trials and humiliations during the period of the Great Purge. For instance, Zhukov was compelled to add the following passage to his autobiography on 9 February 1938: "I have never had ties with enemies of the people and I do not have them now. I have never been at their homes, nor have I ever invited them to my own. My wife has also had no ties to enemies of the people and has never been to their homes. Ties with Uborevich, Mezis and other enemies of the people from the commanding staff of the district were connected purely with military service."[26]

In 1937, a denunciation was received against Konev which indicated that at a party conference of the Belorussian military district "he alone spoke in defense of Uborevich (before the latter was arrested – V. R.) and began to praise him as a good man and member of the party."[27] As a result of this denunciation, Konev sent a letter to the Central Committee of the VKP(b) in which he stated that "pursuant to my duty in the service I had business relations with enemies of the people Uborevich and Feldman, but never considered them Bolsheviks." In addition, Konev acknowledged that he was guilty in that he "never officially raised the question of the hostile activity of these people."

Another test for Konev was his speech at a meeting of one of the regiments in his division, where he said: "We must remember that two to three times more spies and saboteurs — on Comrade Stalin's orders — will be sent into our country than into the capitalist countries." Immediately after this speech, Konev was told of his involuntary slip of the tongue, and he spoke for a second time, "correcting his mistake" (he should have said: "as Comrade Stalin has indicated"). Despite the correction, he sent a letter to the CC of the VKP(b) expressing repentance for the "mistake" he had committed.[28]

By the end of the Great Purge, very few people survived who, like Zhukov and Konev, occupied the position of divisional commander in 1937. In the new general staff of the Red Army, hastily promoted people predominated who, by their military training and experience in the service, clearly did not measure up to their new duties. That is how matters stood at all other levels of the military hierarchy. A report presented to Stalin about the composition of the commanding cadres indicated that in 1939 about 85 percent of the commanders at all levels were younger than 35 years of age.[29]

The following data attest to the level of training among the upper- and middle-ranking commanders on the eve of war. Even among the army commanders there were people who did not have higher military education. Out of 225 people assembled at a gathering of regimental commanders in the summer of 1940, only twenty-five had finished a military institute, and 200 had completed only the courses for junior lieutenants.[30] Only 7 percent of the commanders had received a higher military education, and 37 percent had not even completed a full course of study at a mid-level military school.[31]

The tragic consequences of the reprisals against the military cadres quickly became clear during the period of the Finnish War. Apparently, its woeful experience prompted Stalin to give orders to release and return to the army some of the commanders who remained in prisons and in the camps.

24. The Army

Of the 9,579 commanders arrested in 1937-1938, 1,457 were freed and reinstated into the army in 1938-1939.[32] On the eve of World War Two and during its first months, about a quarter of the arrested officers and generals who remained alive at the time were rehabilitated and returned to the ranks.[33] Among the freed prisoners was the future marshal Rokossovsky, who had been held in an internal prison of the NKVD two and a half years.

However, this "reverse tide" could not influence decisively the combat readiness of the Red Army, insofar as less than 10 percent of the dismissed and arrested members of the higher command staff were returned to their positions.[34]

The decimation of the generals' and officers' corps not only drained the lifeblood of the Red Army, but also undermined military discipline and order within it. Under these conditions, the re-establishment of the institution of commissars, which produced a state of dual power in the army units, weakened the leadership of the military even more. In describing the situation that arose as a result of these measures, Trotsky wrote: "The historical film is being rewound, and what was a progressive measure of the revolution (the introduction of Military Councils and the institution of commissars – V. R.), returns as a repulsive and Thermidorian caricature... At the head of the army stands Voroshilov, a people's commissar, marshal, holder of medals, and so forth and so on. But the actual power is concentrated in Mekhlis's hands, and he, on Stalin's direct orders, is turning the army upside down. The same thing is occurring in every military district, in every division, in each regiment. Every place has its own Mekhlis, an agent of Stalin and Yezhov, who instills "vigilance" instead of knowledge, order and discipline. All relations in the army have become unsteady, shaky and fluid. No one knows where patriotism ends and treason begins. No one is sure what may be done and what may not. When contradictions arise between the orders of a commander and commissar, everyone is forced to guess which of the two paths leads to a decoration, and which leads to prison. Everyone is biding his time and looking from side to side. Honest people are losing heart. Swindlers, thieves and careerists look after themselves, while taking refuge behind patriotic denunciations. The foundations of the army are being shaken. Neglect reigns in things large and small. Weapons are not cleaned or inspected. Barracks are filthy and look uninhabitable. The roofs leak, there are not enough bathhouses, the Red Army troops are clothed in unclean garments. Food is becoming ever poorer in quality and is not served at appointed hours. In response to complaints, the commander refers to the commissar, and the commissar accuses the commander. Those who are actually guilty cover themselves with denunciations of saboteurs. Drunkenness is growing among the commanders, and in this regard the commissars compete with them. A regime of anarchy cloaked in police despotism now undermines all sides of Soviet life; but it is particularly fatal in the army, which can live only under conditions of a correct regime and full transparency in all relations."[35]

The degree to which the picture of the internal life of the army (created, apparently, by means of generalizing from articles in the Soviet press) corresponded to reality can be seen in the most honest memoirs of Soviet military leaders. In a conversation with Konstantin Simonov, Zhukov said that the weak sides of the Red Army that revealed themselves in the course of the Soviet-Finnish War were "the result of 1937-1938, and a most severe result at that. If you compared the preparation of our cadres before the events of these years, in 1936, and after these events, in 1939, then you would have to say that the level of military training of the troops had fallen sharply. A terrifying decline in discipline could be seen, and matters often reached the point of troops going absent without leave, of deserting. Many commanders felt bewildered, and incapable of establishing order."[36]

Repressions against the officer cadres were accompanied with the creation of an atmosphere in which those in the military service at all levels, beginning with simple soldiers, were called upon to "expose" their commanders. During the first period of the war, such conditions had a negative effect on the state of military discipline.

German military intelligence intently followed the purge in the Red Army. On 28 January 1938, the General Staff of the Wehrmacht prepared a "Short Review of the Soviet Armed Forces," which stated: "At the present time, many positions must be considered vacant as a result of the many arrests. Attempts are made to overcome the lack of officers by shortening the length of officer training courses and by means of promoting junior commanders of long standing to the rank of junior lieutenant. ... After Tukhachevsky and a number of generals had been shot in the summer of 1937, only a few people remain from the military leaders. According to all available data at the present time, the middle and senior commanders appear to be the weakest link. Independence and initiative are absent. In battle, this category of commanders adapt with difficulty to the conditions of changing circumstances and crisis situations."[37] The events of 1941-1942 confirmed this prognosis made by German military analysts.

Toward the end of the Great Purge, the official journal of German military circles, *Deutsche Wehr*, published an article, "Is the Soviet Union on the Road to Bonapartism?" Here the reasons for eliminating almost the entirety of the command staff of the Red Army were seen to lie in the ruling clique's "feeling of self-preservation." "The Kremlin does not trust the commanders and constantly changes people in command posts so that they not solidify their positions and win the sympathy of the mass of soldiers," the article says. "Despite the views that are widespread in Europe, what is involved is by no means people who came from the ranks of the intelligentsia. The reverse is more likely — in a majority of cases they are all 'true proletarians' and Old Bolsheviks." With unconcealed pleasure the journal noted that only two marshals remained alive out of five, and these two were "typical marshals for Soviet parades."[38]

The main role in Hitler's decisions to conclude a Soviet-German Pact was played by his assessment of the state of the Red Army which had been drained by the purges. Certain that the decimated Soviet command cadres would be replaced by men of equal caliber only after several years, Hitler had grounds to assume that in the East his hands would not be bound, and that this would allow him to win the war in the West. In order to prevent a military alliance between England, France, and the USSR, he ordered his special agents to vigorously spread information about the extreme weakness of the Red Army after the purges. As Leopold Trepper, a leading Soviet intelligence officer, correctly noted, "the French and English general staffs did not try to form a military alliance with the Soviet Union precisely because the weakness of the Red Army had become obvious to them. It was then that the way was opened for signing a pact between Stalin and Hitler."[39]

Marshal Vasilevsky, who before the war occupied the post of deputy head of the General Staff of the USSR, later was inclined to conclude: if Stalin had not exterminated the general staff of the Red Army, then not only would the whole course of the war have developed in a different way, but the war itself might never have taken place. "The fact that Hitler decided to begin the war in 1941," he said, "was largely influenced by the assessment of the degree to which our military cadres had been destroyed."[40]

This view was confirmed in a number of statements made by Hitler and leaders of the Wehrmacht. It is known that many German generals warned Hitler against invading the Soviet Union, pointing to such unfavorable factors for Germany as the enormous territory of the USSR, its huge population, and natural resources, etc. While not denying any of this, Hitler offered one counter-argument — the weakness of the Red Army as a result of the destruction of its officer corps. In Keitel's words, Hitler "always proceeded from the fact that... Stalin had destroyed the whole first echelon of high-ranking military leaders in 1937, and for the time being, there were no capable minds among those who had replaced them."[41]

While speaking on 23 November 1939 at a secret meeting of Wehrmacht leaders, Hitler characterized the USSR as a state that had been weakened by many internal trials and that did not present a serious military threat to Germany. "It remains a fact," he declared, "that at the present moment the fighting capacity of the Russian armed forces is insignificant. For the next year or two, the present situation will remain."[42]

Similar conclusions were drawn by Halder, the head of the German general staff, who, after hearing in May 1941 the report of Krebs, military attaché in the USSR, wrote in his diary: "The Russian officer corps is exceedingly poor. It gives a pitiful impression. It is much worse than in 1933. Russia will need 20 years in order for its officer corps to reach its former level."[43]

Although Halder inflated the time it would take to reestablish the former fighting capacity of the Red Army, his ideas were largely confirmed by the course of military actions, especially during the first years of the war, when the Red Army lost many times more soldiers and officers than the army of its opponents — primarily because of the weakness of the command cadres.

The consequences of the Great Purge influenced in the most tragic way the course of the military operations in 1941-1942, when the majority of the cadres of the Red Army were destroyed or taken prisoner. In 1941, due not so much to the material or technical superiority of the German troops as to the gross mistakes and miscalculations of the Soviet military command at the time, 67 percent of the small arms were lost, 91 percent of the tanks and self-propelled artillery, 90 percent of the fighter planes, and 90 percent of the artillery and mortars which belonged to the arsenal of the Red Army at the beginning of the war.[44]

In speaking about the sacrifices of the Soviet people during the Second World War, Khrushchev noted: "If the cadres who had been taught and raised by the party and who passed through the school of the Civil War had remained alive, ... then matters would have gone much differently when Hitler invaded the Soviet Union... There had probably been two, three, and sometimes even four changes of the commanding staff. I know people of even a fifth round of changes. Many of them made their way forward courageously. These were capable and honest people, devoted to the motherland. But they needed experience, and they gained such experience in the course of the war at the cost of soldiers' blood and material losses of the resources of the motherland. Such lessons cost an enormous number of lives and the destruction of our land. In the end, we survived, we were victorious, we learned from our own mistakes how to command correctly, and we smashed the enemy. But what did this cost? If what Stalin did had not occurred, when he dreamt up 'enemies of the people' and destroyed honest people, I am convinced that victory would have come at a much cheaper cost, if, of course, this word is morally admissible when talking about the amount of blood and human lives we were forced to sacrifice during the war. The outcome would have been achieved at a much cheaper cost and much more easily for our people."[45]

25. The NKVD

One of the first steps Yezhov took as People's Commissar of Internal Affairs was to issue a directive that the NKVD must unleash a much wider purge, starting with itself. On 18 March 1937, Yezhov delivered a report at a meeting of the leading members of the people's commissariat, in which he declared that spies had occupied key posts within this institution. He demanded that people "firmly understand that even Feliks Edmundovich Dzerzhinsky had displayed vacillation on his own part in 1925-1926. And he sometimes conducted policies that vacillated."[1] These words served as an impulse for the arrest of all of Dzerzhinsky's former colleagues, especially if they were Poles.

The first wave of repression against the Chekists touched not only veterans of the Cheka, but people promoted by Yagoda, who knew too much about the provocations and investigatory frame-ups of the preceding years. One who was arrested at the beginning of 1937 was the head of the secret-political department of the Main Directorate of State Security of the NKVD, Molchanov, who had been the immediate director of persecution of the Trotskyists and other oppositionists from the start of the 1930s. When he informed Trotsky about his conversations with Krivitsky, Sedov wrote: the charges that Molchanov showed indulgence toward Trotskyists "had been served up in such a way that my informer kept asking me: And is it really true that you had no ties with Molchanov?"[2]

Soon after the February-March Plenum of the Central Committee, almost all the heads of departments in the NKVD and their deputies were arrested. Among them was the head of the operative department, Pauker, who had supervised Stalin's personal bodyguards. As Orlov said, "Lenin's personal bodyguards numbered two people. After Kaplan wounded him, the number of bodyguards was doubled. When Stalin came to power, however, he created a group of bodyguards for himself which included several thousand secret operatives, not counting the special military units which were always nearby in a state of full combat readiness."[3] The creation of such a powerful armada (which after Stalin's death was reduced many times over, only to be resurrected during Yeltsin's regime) was the work of Pauker's hands, and he directed it for almost a decade.

For faithful service Stalin gave Pauker two imported automobiles and awarded him six medals. By May 1937, however, Pauker had already been removed from his position, arrested, and declared a German spy. At the same time, the entire leadership of the Kremlin bodyguards was replaced.[4]

The regime established in the central apparatus of the NKVD after Yezhov's arrival was described by his closest assistants who had been arrested at the end of 1938 and the beginning of 1939. Thus, Radzivilovsky stated at his investigation that Yezhov had declared at the banquet devoted to decorating a large group of NKVD members: "We must now train Chekists so that they form a closely knit and secretive sect, unquestioningly carrying out my orders." Frinovsky, a former deputy people's commissar, said at trial that Yezhov demanded that "we choose investigators who either were completely linked to us, or who had certain sins behind them; knowing that they had these sins behind them, and on the basis of these sins, we could keep them in our hands."[5]

Replacing the former cadres were young, shameless careerists who simply lacked any moral restraints. In his report to the Twentieth Congress and in his memoirs, Khrushchev told of the impression he received from Rodos, the former deputy head of the investigatory part of the NKVD for particularly important cases, who had been called in 1956 to a session of the Presidium of the Central Committee. Among other things, Rodos had conducted the investigation in the cases of Kosior, Chubar, and Kosarev. From his explanations it was clearly evident that this was "an insignificant person, with a chicken's range of interests, and literally a moral degenerate." When they asked Rodos how he managed to extract confessions from those under investigation, he replied in plain terms: "They told me that Kosior and Chubar were enemies of the people. Therefore I, as investigator, must extract a confession from them that they were enemies." Rodos said that he received detailed instructions about how he must interrogate these people, and in particular, he received a direct order with regard to Chubar: "Beat him until he confesses."[6]

Prior to the June Plenum of the Central Committee in 1937, which gave the NKVD extraordinary powers, the use of torture during interrogations was officially forbidden. Shreider, the former head of the police department of the NKVD of the Ivanovo area, recalled that he and his comrades did not at first believe the rumors that investigator Feldman had beaten Molchanov: "At that time we all regarded with distrust the tales and rumors about beatings, and we naively thought that Feldman had gone too far on his own initiative, for which he received the punishment he deserved."[7]

The situation changed in July 1937 after a secret directive was sent out from the Politburo on the use of physical methods of coercion during interro-

25. The NKVD

Yezhov strangling a multi-headed, swastika-tailed snake labelled "Trotsky-Bukharin-Rykov spies, wreckers, and saboteurs."
Cartoon by Boris Yefimov

gation. However, even toward the end of the Great Terror, some party leaders who had just taken their posts assumed that torture was used on the initiative of local officials of the NKVD (relevant directives were returned to the CC immediately after people became familiar with them and were unknown to new party cadres). When enquiries about this issue arrived at the CC, Stalin sent out an encoded telegram on 10 January 1939 to the secretaries of the republic and area party organizations and leaders of the people's commissars and directorates of the NKVD. The telegram said: "The CC of the VKP(b) explains that the application of physical coercion in the practice of the NKVD was allowed from 1937 with permission of the CC VKP(b)… As you know, all bourgeois intelligence services apply physical coercion with regard to representatives of the socialist proletariat; moreover, they use it in the most monstrous forms. One might ask why the socialist intelligence service must be more humane with regard to the inveterate agents of the bourgeoisie, sworn enemies of the working class and collective farmers. The CC VKP(b) feels that the method of physical coercion must certainly be used in the future, as an exception, with regard to clear and undisarmed enemies of the people, as an absolutely correct and expedient method."[8] In this way, the "explanation" of the "expediency" of "the most monstrous forms" of physical torture was given by Stalin on behalf of the Central Committee, 80 percent of whose members by this time were themselves experiencing this "absolutely correct method." Stalin knew very well, of course, that torture was being used only in fascist torture chambers, but by no means by all "bourgeois intelligence services." In addition, no person thinking as a Marxist could harbor the thought that Soviet intelligence should "compete" with its capitalist counterparts in using inhuman methods. However, by this time Stalin had stopped being shy about informing the apparatus about his most barbaric and fiendish directives.

Ten days after sending this telegram, Stalin supplemented it with a new secret message in which he indicated that "the use of the method of physical pressure, which the NKVD employs, was allowed in 1937 on the basis of agreement from the Central Committees of the Communist Parties of all the republics."[9] This "clarification" was a brazen lie. As is clear from explanations given by Molotov and Kaganovich at the June Plenum of the Central Committee in 1957, the directive about the use of torture was signed by Stalin and a narrow circle of his stooges, apparently without even the participation or knowledge of the remaining members and candidate-members of the Politburo, let alone of the Central Committees of the union republics.

Even during the first months of the Great Purge, the NKVD apparatus in the center and in the localities was increased several times over. As Khrushchev recalled, "Stalin ... decided to put to work there people directly from production, from the work-bench. These were inexperienced people, sometimes completely underdeveloped politically. It was enough to give them some kind of order and say: 'The main thing is to make the arrest and demand a confession.'"[10] Finding themselves face to face at interrogations with people of a completely different social milieu, and sensing their unlimited power over them, many of these "novices" quickly mastered the devices of an executioner and turned into complete sadists. Among the new crop of Chekists were also no small number of those who, stunned by the atmosphere reigning in the "organs," went mad or committed suicide.

For the sake of creating a special caste in the NKVD which valued its privileges, the pay of its members in 1937 was raised significantly and began to exceed even the pay of party members. Besides, built into the NKVD system was a special network of stores which sold at extremely low prices the confiscated property of those who had been victimized. According to Goglidze, the former people's commissar of internal affairs in Georgia, such a regime had been established well before 1937, "but who established it, I do not know... And it was this way not only in Georgia, but everywhere."[11]

Corrupted by absolute power and material privileges, the most zealous leaders of the "organs" in the localities excelled in surpassing each other in the number of those arrested and convicted. For instance, in Kirgizia, a "socialist competition" was established between departments of the NKVD. The republic's commissar of internal affairs issued an order, "On the Results of the Socialist Competition Between the Third and Fourth Departments of the UGB [Directorate of State Security] of the NKVD of the Republic for February 1938," which stated: "The fourth department exceeded by one and a half times the number of arrests by the third department during the month, and it exposed thirteen more spies and participants in counter-revolutionary organizations than the third department. However, the third department sent twenty cases to the Military Collegium and eleven cases to the special collegium, which the fourth department does not have, yet the fourth department exceeded the number of cases completed by its apparatus (not counting the outlying districts), and reviewed by a troika, by almost one hundred people."[12]

The bacchanalia of arrests was helped along when the union-wide NKVD established quotas and control figures; these figures in turn were allotted by local satraps to the departments of the NKVD and its directorates. As the Chekist Postel testified at his investigation, in Moscow "mass arrests, which had been set beforehand according to control figures for the arrest in each department and each month of 1,000-1,200 men, turned into a literal hunt... and the annihilation of the adult section of the male population... If you analyze the transcripts and 'albums' of convicted terrorists, ... then you get the following absolutely wild and unbelievable picture: during the holidays of 1 May and 7 November, in the columns of demonstrators on Red Square, there were marching tens, if not hundreds, of 'terrorists.'"[13]

"Distribution papers" sent to the localities often were targeted at specific people and were orientated primarily at persecuting Old Bolsheviks and party activists. The former chairman of the Sovnarkom of Belorussia recalled how the republic's NKVD commissar declared: "So what am I to do? ... It's beyond me. Yezhov has sent another directive regarding old communists. And where am I to find them? There aren't any left."[14]

Similar documents were sent by the leaders of the republic and area organs of the NKVD to regional departments. The chairman of one of the regional executive committees, Ilyasov, told how he and the first secretary of the regional committee were summoned by the head of the regional department of the NKVD. He read them a coded message he had received from his area superiors that said: "You must prepare twenty bulls." He then explained that by "bulls" they had in mind leading staff members in the region, and noted that he himself had chosen some of the "bulls" for arrest. As for the rest, he proposed that the people he was talking with choose victims from the members of the apparatus of the regional committee and regional executive committee. After they had received several such coded messages, all the party and Soviet cadres had been arrested in the region, as well as almost all the collective farm chairmen, the directors of the state farms, and the bosses of the machine tractor stations. Ilyasov himself was saved from arrest only because he had a nervous breakdown and ended up in a psychiatric hospital.[15]

Although in word the organs of the NKVD were under party control, in actual fact matters were just the opposite: every party leader was an object of undying control and manipulation on the part of these organs. Then the practice was codified that made it mandatory for the party organs to receive information from the NKVD on all leading officials being appointed. All the material of the investigation was located exclusively in the hands of the NKVD, and all that remained for the party secretaries to do was to review papers for arrest and sentencing. In Khrushchev's words, "leaders who were even, like me, of a rather high rank ... were completely under the power of documents presented by NKVD officials."[16]

In order to more firmly link party functionaries to participation in the repressions, Stalin, as Khrushchev recalled, "proposed that the secretaries of party area committees should go into the prisons and verify the correctness of the actions of the Chekists... This was not control, but a fiction, a smokescreen which covered their activity... Now it is clear that Stalin did this deliberately. He thought up the whole thing so that, when it was necessary, he could say: 'There's a party organization there. They are monitoring things, they are obliged to monitor things'... In actual fact, it was not the party organization that was monitoring the Chekists, but the Chekists who were monitoring the party organization, and all the party leaders."[17]

In order to make the terror ever more savage and to carry it out on "legitimate foundations," Stalin and his stooges widened the "legal safeguards" of the repressions. For instance, a decree of the Central Executive Committee of the USSR on 2 October 1937 raised the maximum sentence for espionage and treason from ten to twenty-five years.[18] On 14 September 1937, the simplified procedures for reviewing cases concerning terror, established in 1934 (hearings without the participation of prosecutor or lawyer, a ban on appeals of sentences and appeals for clemency, the execution of sentence immediately after being pronounced), were extended to cases of sabotage and wrecking.[19] Such procedures, in essence, copied Stolypin's laws regarding courts martial.

In 1937, the sphere of extrajudicial reprisals was significantly widened. Here also the traditions of tsarist Russia were used, with the wide use of what had been established under Alexander II, administrative exile without trial — by edict from a Special Board of the Ministry of Internal Affairs. At the beginning of the twentieth century, the number of administrative exiles in Siberia stretched into the hundreds of thousands.

On 8 April 1937, the Politburo confirmed the status of the Special Board under the NKVD, which was granted the right to exile "people considered to be socially dangerous," under overt supervision, or to imprison them in corrective labor camps for a period of five years. The Special Board was also invested with the right to imprison for a term of five to eight years "people *suspected* of espionage, wrecking, sabotage and terrorist activity" (my italics – V. R.).[20] After a few months, the measures of punishment carried out by the Special Board were expanded to twenty-five years of imprisonment and execution. The adoption of these extraordinary laws raised extrajudicial repressions to the level of juridical norms.

Conditions for unrestrained repressive measures were established also in sub-judicial acts and orders from the people's commissar of internal affairs. Thus, in an order from Yezhov on 30 July 1937, confirmed by the Politburo, "troikas" were created in the republics, territories, and areas. They were invested with the right to review cases in the absence of the accused and to carry out sentences, up to the highest measure of punishment. The "troika" usually did not even meet, but papers were simply brought to its members to sign from its chairman, a high-ranking NKVD official. By Yezhov's orders on 11 August and 20 September 1937, extrajudicial review of cases was also granted to "dvoikas" [two-person teams], consisting of local NKVD leaders and prosecutors.[21]

These orders were supported by directives coming from the general prosecutor of the USSR, Vyshinsky. Thus, in the summer of 1937, Vyshinsky instructed prosecutors to hand over to "troikas" cases about state crimes "which have still not been reviewed by the courts." On 27 December 1937, he distributed a circular that contained instructions to present to Special Boards for review criminal cases in those instances when "the character of the evidence of the accused's guilt does not allow it to be used in a courtroom session."[22] Such "evidence" included denunciations by secret informers, testimony from false witnesses and provocateurs, etc.

Everything was done countrywide to raise the authority of the higher officials of the NKVD. In elections to the Supreme Council of the USSR, all the people's commissars from the union and autonomous republics were chosen as deputies, as well as all the heads of area and territory departments of the NKVD. In elections to republic Supreme Councils, all their deputies were elected.

Of course, many members of the NKVD could not have helped but ask themselves why they were facing demands for open falsifications and forgeries. We can form an opinion about the type of answer given to this question in the central apparatus of the NKVD from the memoirs of the former general secretary of the Central Committee of the VLKSM, Milchakov. At his interrogation, the investigator Lieutenant Meshik (who later rose under Beria to the rank of general and the post of people's commissar of internal affairs of the Ukrainian SSR) cynically declared:

> "People like you have outlived their time, even though you are not old. You hang on to the pitiful trinkets of Soviet and party democracy, of self-criticism. Who in hell needs them? You have not grasped the changing circumstances. We need a rejuvenated, new regime, and most of all firm authorities headed by a strong 'master.' The epoch of Stalin has arrived, and with it — new people who occupy all the positions in the apparatus. In the vanguard goes Stalin's guard, the Chekists... We, the Chekists, are a party within the party. We will

purge from the ranks of the party half of any kind of trash like the so-called 'old guard' and persons connected with the old men, with the views of yesterday. We have probably already shaken loose about a million people who were in the party... And the rest will be re-educated. They will follow us, they will follow Stalin like little darlings. They will take your places in all the apparatuses and will appreciate the trust they have been given."[23]

It is highly unlikely that a young satrap invented such ideas by himself. Apparently they had been voiced by Yezhov at conferences and instructional meetings of the apparatus.

The most cynical members of the NKVD did not feel compelled to conceal the mechanism of fabricating cases from those under investigation who had been slated for participation in the open trials. After he returned from prison, Rozenblium, who had been a party member since 1906, recounted how the head of the Leningrad UNKVD, Zakovsky, had shown him several variants of the outlines of the "Leningrad center" that were being prepared from the upcoming open trial. After he had acquainted Rozenblium with these schemes, Zakovsky declared: "you will not have to make up anything on your own. The NKVD will prepare for you an outline of every branch. Your job is to learn it by heart, and to remember well all the questions and answers which might be given at the trial. The case will be prepared over a period of four to five months, perhaps even half a year. During all this time you will prepare so that you will not put the investigation or yourself in a bad position. Your subsequent fate will depend on the course and outcome of the trial."[24]

Many of the people in the NKVD who carried out the Great Purge were themselves to perish in the meat grinder of those years. From 1934 to 1939, 21,800 members of this people's commissariat were arrested on charges of "counter-revolutionary crimes."[25] Behind this figure stand three basic groups: 1) Chekists who tried to resist the repressions; 2) those who knew too much, for instance, about the Kirov affair or about the mechanics of fabricating the open trials; and 3) organizers of "false" cases, who were arrested at the end of 1938 and the beginning of 1939.

26. The Komsomol

The Komsomol organizations were subjected to local purges from the beginning of the 1930s. Thus, in November 1932, the Central Committee of the VLKSM (Komsomol) adopted a resolution about purging the village Komsomol organizations of the Northern Caucasus, where dissatisfaction with forced collectivization had been particularly strong. As a result of this purge, in the Kuban alone, 56.3 percent of the Komsomol members were expelled. During this purge whole cells with all their members were often expelled.[1]

A number of the founders of the Komsomol belonged to the inner-party oppositions. One of them, for instance, was Shatskin, who had been chosen at the Sixth and Seventh Congresses of the VLKSM as an honorary Komsomol member. In 1929 Shatskin was sharply criticized for his article in *Komsomolskaia Pravda* in which he condemned the position of the "party philistine" who is ready, without thinking, to approve any directive coming from above, and to act as a "voting machine."[2] At the Ninth Congress of the VLKSM, Kosarev, the general secretary of the Central Committee of the VLKSM, declared that Shatskin, who had participated in the activity of the Syrtsov-Lominadze group, "had chosen the path of openly betraying the party."[3]

Despite the reprisals of the preceding years, by 1937 the leadership of the Komsomol was dominated as before by people who had begun their political activity during the first years of Soviet power. The young people in the Komsomol were a danger to Stalin's regime since they represented a part of society distinguished by their sensitivity toward injustice and by their personal lack of fear. Not burdened, like many of the Old Bolsheviks, by self-imprecations and humiliating repentance for their "mistakes," they could emerge as a force of social protest against arbitrary rule and the repressions.

For this reason Stalin kept the purge of the Komsomol under his strict control and directly guided it. In this work he depended primarily on Kosarev, who had become general secretary of the Central Committee of the VLKSM at the age of 26. Throughout the land a "little cult" was created around Kosarev, and his name adorned the Central Aeronautics Club of Osoaviakhim, a mining institute, a tank of the newest construction, border outposts and military detachments.[4]

As one of the most devoted Stalinists, Kosarev obediently repeated directives about combatting enemies. In 1935, in a report to the plenum of the Central Committee of the VLKSM, he said: "The enemy will not voluntarily yield his place. He can be eliminated only with force, with methods of economic coercion or methods of organizational and political isolation, and when the need arises — with methods of physical extermination."[5]

In 1937, the scale of the repressions in the Komsomol no longer satisfied Stalin. At a meeting with three secretaries of the CC of the VLKSM, he demanded that they "review their positions and lead the fight against enemies of the people."[6] After this discussion, Kosarev told his comrades: "I simply cannot understand where so many enemies came from." He repeated this same thought in a conversation with his wife: "What can I do? Stalin demands people. He demands heads... Who can I name? Where are the enemies?"[7]

However, very soon Kosarev was able to overcome his doubts and join the hunt for "enemies of the people." At one session he wrote in the outlines to his speech: "Put an end to the liberal attitude toward enemies and hostile elements. Fully implement the campaign to root them out."[8] This directive found expression in the work of the Fourth Plenum of the Central Committee of the VLKSM (21-28 August 1937), where one question was raised: "On the Work of Enemies of the People Within the Komsomol." Before the plenum opened, 35 members and candidate-members of the Central Committee of the VLKSM were arrested, including the secretaries of the CC, Lukyanov, Fainberg and Saltanov; the representative of the delegation of the VLKSM to the Communist Youth International, Chemodanov; and the editor of *Komsomolskaia Pravda*, Bubiakin.

Stalin sent Kaganovich, Andreev, Zhdanov, and Malenkov to participate in the work of the plenum. These four joined the commission that prepared a resolution speaking about the inadmissible tardiness in exposing a "united Trotskyist-rightists organization" that had been acting within the Komsomol. The day after the plenum closed, *Pravda* published a lead article that said: "The inveterate enemies of the people Saltanov, Lukyanov, Fainberg, Bubiakin, Andreev and others, taking advantage of the idiotic illness of political blindness which infected a number of leading members of the Bureau of the Central Committee of the VLKSM, including Comrade Kosarev most of all, carried out their wretched, filthy work."[9] Mention of being infected with an "idiotic illness" did not augur well for Kosarev and other surviving members of the Komsomol leadership.

26. The Komsomol

Aleksandr Kosarev, shot on 23 February 1939

Dozens more members of the Central Committee and hundreds of members of local Komsomol committees were arrested soon after the plenum. Before the end of 1937, in just the apparatuses of the regional committees and area committees, 561 people were removed from work as "enemies of the people" and 830 for ties with "enemies of the people."[10]

All Komsomol literature published in the 1920s and early 1930s was declared "politically harmful." In December 1937, the bureau of the Central Committee of the VLKSM adopted a resolution banning and removing from libraries sixty books on the history of the VLKSM and the KIM (Communist Youth International).[11]

After the August plenum, Kosarev's activity became more frenzied. "We still are not able, as we must be," he declared, "as the party demands of us, to uncover enemies, to seek them out and expose them... And some of our comrades look for Trotskyists and enemies of the people in any organization except their own, not in the Komsomol, and because of this, they fail to wage the battle sharply enough."[12]

In March 1938, Kosarev met with a former secretary of the Leningrad area committee of the VLKSM, Utkin, who had recently been released from prison. After meeting with him, Kosarev sent a letter to Yezhov in which he said: "In great secrecy Utkin told me that the testimony which he had given at the NKVD supposedly did not correspond to reality, was forced, and that he considers himself an honest person. In response to these statements, he received the appropriate rebuff from me. I told him that his behavior was a hostile slander against the NKVD, and that such behavior shows once again that he, Utkin, is an enemy, and an enemy that has not laid down his arms."[13]

With this denunciation, Kosarev directly provoked Utkin's new arrest, after which the latter spent sixteen years in the camps, only to emerge in the mid-1950s as an invalid.

At the same time, in a number of instances Kosarev tried to prevent or to mitigate the most outrageous forms of reprisal. One such attempt, which ended tragically for himself and for the leadership of the Komsomol at that time, was the "Mishakova affair." In September 1937, Mishakova, an instructor from the Central Committee of the VLKSM, was sent to a Komsomol conference being held to hear reports and elect new officials in Chuvashia. There, she declared that not only the entire Komsomol leadership of the republic, but also the first secretary of the party's area committee, were enemies of the people. The Bureau of the Central Committee of the VLKSM dismissed Mishakova for slander. In the fall of 1938, Mishakova sent Stalin a letter in which she complained that she was being persecuted for fighting against enemies of the people. This letter served as a signal for Stalin that the time had come to deal with the leadership of the Komsomol.

These reprisals were delayed for a while because of the ceremonial celebrations devoted to the twentieth anniversary of the Komsomol. On 29 October 1938, a jubilee plenum of the Central Committee of the VLKSM was convened, and its opening was described in *Komsomolskaia Pravda* in the following words: "Five, ten, fifteen minutes of thunderous applause. From all sides of the hall people were shouting greetings: 'Long live the leader of peoples, Comrade Stalin!', 'For dear Stalin, a Komsomol hurrah!'... With inspiration and exhilaration the jubilee plenum accepts the impassioned, heart-felt greetings for Comrade Stalin."[14]

During the work of the plenum, Kosarev was on the presidium next to Stalin; he gave the introductory remarks and then the main report. On the same day, *Pravda* published his article, "A Young Man in the Land of Socialism." Thus nothing foretold the impending reprisals against him and other members of the Central Committee of the VLKSM.

Three weeks later, a new plenum of the CC of the VLKSM was called that lasted from 19 to 22 November. All the big guns of the Great Purge appeared at it: Stalin, Molotov, Kaganovich, Andreev, Zhdanov, Malenkov and Shkiriatov. The transcript of the plenum records several dozen of their questions and interjections during Kosarev's report. Besides the reports of the Komsomol leaders, the plenum heard Shkiriatov's report on the situation in the Komsomol.

In his speech at the plenum, Kosarev took credit for the fact that the Central Committee of the VLKSM "often went ahead of the NKVD." He gave many examples of the arrest of Komsomol members "on the basis of our material" and "after our investigation." During Kosarev's report, however, Stalin clearly let it be known that the scale of the reprisals against the Komsomol cadres did not satisfy him. When Kosarev spoke about mistakes in the work of the Komsomol, Stalin tossed out an interjection filled with meaning: "And, perhaps, this is a system and not a question of mistakes? After all that has happened, there are too many mistakes. For two years sabotage has been liquidated, but there still are very many mistakes. Isn't this a system here?" In a following speech, Zhdanov developed this idea by citing the testimony of arrested Komsomol members about Kosarev's "hostile work." [15]

Just as ominous was the speech given by Andreev, who reproached Kosarev for the fact that "many times we were forced to hear from him, ... that in the Komsomol, he says, there are no enemies... This position has been a lie, and Comrade Kosarev repeatedly received warnings from the Central Committee of the VKP(b), as well as at plenums of the Central Committee of the Komsomol, that there could not be a situation in which there were neither enemies nor double-dealers of every kind in the Komsomol."[16]

The plenum dismissed Kosarev and four more secretaries of the CC of the VLKSM for "a soullessly bureaucratic and hostile attitude toward honest members of the Komsomol who have tried to reveal shortcomings in the work of the CC of the VLKSM, and for persecuting one of the best Komsomol members (the case of Comrade Mishakova)."[17]

Out of ninety-three participants in the plenum, seventy-seven were arrested, and of these, forty-eight were shot. Altogether, in 1937-1938, ninety-six out of 128 members and candidate members were arrested from the Central Committee of the VLKSM that had been elected at the Tenth Congress of the Komsomol in 1936.[18]

Vladimir Vernadsky (1863-1945)

Ilya Erenburg (1891-1967)

Boris Pilniak, shot on 21 April 1938

27. The Non-Party Intelligentsia

From the beginning of the 1930s, the layer of upper-echelon intelligentsia, which included the most famous scientists, engineers, writers, and artists, turned into a privileged group whose social position differed little from the position of the ruling bureaucracy. Even during the most difficult years of the first Five-Year Plan, Stalin steadily raised the living standards of this layer — by means of increasing their salary, giving them access to closed retail establishments, granting them spacious government apartments, etc.

During these years, the concept of "fellow-traveler," which distinguished the non-party representatives of culture from the communists, went out of usage in literary and artistic life. Generous sops, such as the writers' home on Lavrushinsky Lane or the community of cottage-homes in Peredelkino, were given to the regime's favorites, regardless of their party membership.

In 1936, another category disappeared: the "disenfranchised," i.e., those from the former ruling classes who had been deprived of the right to vote. All this led to a situation where many members of the intelligentsia, who had condemned the October Revolution, began to support and praise the Stalinist regime. The ideology and practice of social inequality and privileges initiated by Stalin appealed more to them than the egalitarian regime of the first years of Soviet power.

Even in private documents of this period — personal diaries — an impassioned glorification of Stalin replaced previous invectives against the Bolsheviks. In this regard, the diary of Kornei Chukovsky is instructive, since it reflects the moods of not only the author himself, but other famous writers who belonged to his circle.

In describing in his diary one of his conversations with Tynianov, Chukovsky records the thoughts of his interlocutor in the following way: "I am a historian. And as a historian I admire Stalin. From the historical point of view, as the author of the collective farms, Stalin is the greatest of the geniuses who have transformed the world. If he were to do nothing besides create the

Boris Pasternak and Kornei Chukovsky

collective farms, even then he would be worthy of being called the most brilliant man of the epoch. But please, do not speak about this to anyone. — Why? — Well, you know, so many toadies praise him now in self-defense, that if we begin to praise him too loudly, then people will include us among this unscrupulous group."[1]

No less expressive are the pages of the diary where Chukovsky himself lavishes panegyrics on Stalin which, in their servility and thralldom, surpassed even the official publications of the time, and today are regarded as parodies. The genuine ecstasy of the writer found particularly clear expression in the anxious description of the impressions made by Stalin's appearance at the congress of the Komsomol in April 1936: "What had happened to the audience! Here HE was standing, a bit weary, pensive and majestic. One sensed his enormous strength, the fact that he was accustomed to power, and at the same time, something feminine and soft. I looked around: everyone had the same tender, enraptured, inspired, and smiling face. To see him — simply to see — was a joy for all of us. Demchenko kept turning to him with comments of some kind. And everyone was jealous, envious of her, — how lucky she was! We noted every one of his gestures with reverence. I had never even imagined that I was capable of such feelings. When they applauded him, he took out his watch (silver) and showed it to the auditorium with a charming smile — and we all started whispering: 'His watch, his watch, he showed his watch' — and then, as we were leaving, when we had reached the cloakrooms, we again recalled this watch. Pasternak kept whispering enthusiastic words about him to me, and I to him, and we both said in unison: 'Ah, that Demchenko shielded him from view!' (for a moment). I went home with Pasternak, and we were both intoxicated with joy."[2]

Of course, during the years of the Great Terror, moods of this type were bound to fade somewhat. Nevertheless, as they subordinated themselves to the laws of Stalinist totalitarianism, cultural figures seemed to vie with each other after each trial in finding the most furious invectives for the condemned. In one week alone, *Literaturnaia gazeta** published about thirty articles by famous writers. Among them were Yuri Olesha's article, "Fascists Before the Court of the People"; Isaak Babel's "Lies, Treachery and Smerdyakovism"; Marietta Shaginian's "Monstrous Mongrels"; "Path to the Gestapo," by M. Ilyin and S. Marshak; Andrei Platonov's "Overcoming Villainies"; Yuri Tynianov's "The Court's Verdict Is the Country's Verdict"; and D. Bergelson's "The People's Vengeful Sword."[3]

There was no shortage of attempts to lend "artistic formulation" to versions of the perfidious activities of enemies of the people. Such attempts did not give birth to, and could not give birth to, a single work that was worthy of being called art. This confirmed once more the law of art, according to which a false idea foisted upon someone from without cannot create anything but a caricature of creativity. The disgraceful verses that appeared during the Moscow Trials on the pages of *Pravda* are examples of such caricatures. V. Lugovskoy's "Poetic Response" reads as follows:

> ... But the hour approaches, and the evil gangs
> In the silence of their dens and flats
> Betray our beautiful, and gigantic land
> To traitor and thief...
> They vilely reek of graveyard rot:
> The conversation of beasts in a typhoid fever.
> And behind them — Trotsky in his doctor's pince-nez,
> Like a bloodthirsty ghoul.
> He divides valleys and bays,
> Dashes about our maps like a sparrow.
> May you be damned, thievish degenerate,
> You Oslo-Mexican Bonaparte![4]

A. Bezymensky tried to dilute the flood of vulgar abuse with certain poetic refinements, leading to poems which appeared even more wretched, and at times, completely nonsensical:

> Little Judas Trotsky sits at a table,
> Shaking his goatlike beard.

---

* *Literaturnaia gazeta* [Literary Gazette]: official weekly newspaper of the Union of Soviet Writers.

> He's all hunched over. Fate has been heavy
> And time is filled with misfortune...
> But long the pitiful buffoon haggles
> O'er the list of other's goods,
> Bargaining with Serebriakov's piece of silver
> And Piatakov's well-worn coin...
> Just try, show your pig's face here!
> We'll argue with you about prices.
> And with good conscience we'll explain to you fast
> With Soviet weapons of steel
> How much the Ukraine and Far East shores are worth.[5]

Only a few of the most farsighted and perceptive writers were courageous enough to remind themselves at least of the unsightly nature of their servile behavior. M. Prishvin recorded in his diary the words he had spoken in conversation with Stavsky, the secretary of the Union of Soviet Writers: "Now we must hold fast to the state's line ... to Stalin's line." He then added: "At home I began to think about what I had said, and what everyone thinks: 'Along one line they send you into exile or shoot you, along the other, the state line or Stalin's, everything is fine. Which means that, instead of 'Stalin's' line, I could have simply said that we have to hold fast to the line where everything is fine. It was probably in such a state that Peter renounced Christ. Most likely so."[6]

As the Great Terror unfolded, an ever more desperate fear settled in among cultural figures. In his memoirs, I. Erenburg told vividly about the atmosphere which reigned in such circles. When he returned from Spain at the end of 1937, he was struck by a sign hanging on the elevator in his apartment building: "Flushing books down the toilet is forbidden. Those guilty of doing so will be found and punished."[7] As if continuing this story, Nadezhda Mandelshtam recalled: "With every new arrest, everyone looked over their books, and into the stove flew the works of leaders now in disgrace. But the new homes had neither stoves, nor burners, nor even air-vents, so forbidden books, writers' diaries, letters and other seditious literature were cut up with scissors and flushed down the toilet."[8]

The same theme found further expression in V. Kaverin's story about Leningrad in the fall of 1937, when the city was seized with "some kind of feverish sense of inevitability, of expectation. Some were afraid, but pretended that they were not; others referred to the fact that everyone was afraid; others pretended that they were more courageous than other people; still more tried to prove that it was useful and even necessary to be afraid. I went to see an old friend, a profound scholar who studied the history of Russian life in the last century. He was calm but embittered.

27. The Non-Party Intelligentsia

'Look,' he said, leading me to the window which looked out as usual onto the wall of the neighboring building. 'Do you see?' ...

And I saw, not the courtyard, but the air in the courtyard, and a scattered, fine, barely-visible, ashen dust which lay motionless on the narrow stone well.

'What is it?'

He smiled.

'They are burning memory,' he said. 'They've been doing it a long time, and every night...'

'I go mad,' he said, 'when I think that every night thousands of people are throwing their diaries into the fire.'"[9]

In the chapter of his memoirs which depicted Moscow in 1937-1938, Erenburg expressed the following reservation: he could describe only what he observed personally — the everyday life and intellectual state of people in his own circle, chiefly writers and artists. In characterizing the mood of these people, he noted: "We thought (probably because we felt like thinking this way) that Stalin did not know about the senseless persecution of communists and of the Soviet intelligentsia." As confirmation, the writer described an episode which occurred in circumstances that definitely excluded any insincerity: "At night, as I was walking with Chuka, I met Pasternak on Lavrushinsky Lane; he waved his arms among the snowdrifts: 'If only someone would tell Stalin about all this!'"[10]

In the last pages of his book, as he recalled his promise to readers to disclose the "reasons for our errors," Erenburg confessed that he was in no position to do so, for he knew too little to draw any conclusions, and among what he did know, there was much, as before, that he did not understand. In returning to a description of his moods in the years of the Great Purge, he wrote: "I did not love Stalin, but for a long time I believed in him, and I feared him... I did not immediately guess the role of the 'one most wise'. ... Like many others, I tried to whitewash Stalin for myself, attributing the mass persecutions to the inner-party struggle, to Yezhov's sadism, to disinformation, and to social mores." As he listed his closest friends who perished at the end of the 1930s (the writer referred to them only by their first name and patronymic, thereby avoiding mention of Bukharin's last name), Erenburg stressed: "Yes, I knew about many crimes, but it was not within my powers to stop them," he said as he summarized his conclusions. "But what am I talking about: the crimes could not be stopped by people who were far more influential than I, and far better informed."[11] In confirmation of this statement, the writer referred to the decree of the Central Committee of the CPSU, "On Overcoming the Personality Cult and Its Consequences," written by co-participants in Stalin's crimes. This decree states that "the Leninist core of the Central Committee" (that is what Molotov and people like him called themselves) did not act against Stalin and remove him from power because "it would not have been understood by the people."[12]

In characterizing the frame of mind of his milieu, Erenburg wrote: "Not only I, but many others thought that the evil was emanating from the little man they called 'Stalin's narkom.'* For we saw how they were arresting people who had never belonged to any opposition, who were loyal followers of Stalin or honest non-party specialists."[13] This acknowledgment, which slipped out unintentionally from the writer, is noteworthy. It tells how confusion was caused in his milieu only by repressions against non-party people or "loyal supporters," but by no means when they were against party oppositionists.

As other sources demonstrate, the illusions described by Erenburg were hardly shared by all members of the Soviet intelligentsia. At the beginning of 1938, the academician Vernadsky recorded in his diary: "It now seems as if people have begun to think, and now they believe less than before... Dissatisfaction is growing and you hear its expression, despite the fear. Earlier this was not so."[14]

Vernadsky expressed these thoughts even more explicitly in his diary entry devoted to the trial of the "Right-Trotskyist Bloc":

> "Madmen. They themselves are destroying the major things they have begun to create, and what will fundamentally never disappear. But it is they who are undermining the strength of the state, in which the interests of the masses — in all their real meaning (apart from freedom of thought and religious freedom) — serve as the basis of the state.
>
> Everyone has an enormous impression of alarm — for various reasons — but *no* feelings of the strength of the ruling group. Stupid motives are described in the newspapers (leading articles)... Who will believe them? And if part of the crowd does believe them, then this part is the kind that will believe everything and on which you cannot depend... (This) might have fatal significance for the entire future. A feeling of instability and chagrin that the destruction proceeds not from without, but due to the arbitrary whims of the authorities themselves."[15]

Isaak Babel understood even more profoundly the meaning of the events taking place, which can be seen vividly in the denunciations contained in his investigatory dossier. In November 1938, a "source" reported Babel's statements regarding the trial of the "Right-Trotskyist Bloc": "A monstrous trial. It is monstrous in its terribly limited nature, and in the belittling of all problems.

---

* Yezhov.

27. The Non-Party Intelligentsia

Isaak Babel, shot on 27 January 1940

Bukharin was trying, apparently, to raise the trial to theoretical heights, but they did not allow him. For Bukharin, Rykov, Rakovsky, and Rozengolts they have deliberately selected criminals, bodyguards and spies like Sharangovich, about whose activity in Belorussia I was told horrible things: he expelled people, provoked them and so forth (unable to investigate Stalin's amalgams, Babel allowed that the zeal of "deviationists" like Sharangovich might arise from their work for foreign intelligence services – V. R.)... They will die, convinced of the death of the tendency they represent, and along with it the death of the communist revolution — for Trotsky convinced them that Stalin's victory would signify the death of the revolution (and here Babel took on faith the Stalinist amalgam which presented Bukharin and Rykov as Trotsky's "pupils" – V. R.)... People are becoming accustomed to arrests as they do to the weather. What is terrible is the submissiveness of party members and intellectuals to the thought of ending up behind bars. All this is characteristic of the state regime. Given the experience of the January Plenum of the Central Committee, we see that what is happening is different from what is said in the resolutions. What we need is several people of a historical scale who could head the country. But, where are they to be found, since there is nobody left? We need people who have solid experience in international politics. There are none. There was Rakovsky — a man of great breadth..."

According to the "source," Babel expressed these thoughts in February 1939. "The existing leadership of the VKP(b)," he said, "knows very well, only doesn't say so openly, what kind of people Rakovsky, Sokolnikov, Radek, Koltsov and others are. These are people marked by great talent, and they rise many heads above the surrounding mediocrity of today's leaders. But as soon as the issue arises that these people have even the slightest contact with power, then the leadership begins to demand ruthlessly: 'Arrest them, shoot them.'"[16]

Both the style of the arguments cited, and the boldness of the ideas contained in them, suggest that Babel's genuine secret thoughts are reported here, and that the "source" was a person who enjoyed the writer's absolute trust.

When he was in prison, Babel gave detailed written testimony. If one clears these records, much like the transcripts of his interrogations, of epithets inserted by the investigator such as "slanderous," "counter-revolutionary," and so forth, it is possible to understand the reasons for the writer's perceptive abilities.

Like many other non-party writers, from the beginning of the 1920s Babel felt the ideological influence of the major literary critic and active participant in the Left Opposition, A. Voronsky. At first they were united by common views on literary problems, but with time Babel began to share Voronsky's views on political issues and the situation in the land. In 1924 or 1925, Voronsky organized in his apartment a recital by Bagritsky of his "Thoughts About Opanas." Trotsky attended this gathering, and he questioned the writers there about their biographies and creative plans.

From Voronsky, Babel (as well as V. Ivanov, Pilniak, Seifullina, Leonov and other "fellow-travelers") heard criticism of the inner-party regime and "attacks against the existing party leadership and personally against Stalin." Voronsky acquainted the writers grouped around him with other famous oppositionists — Lashevich, Zorin and V. M. Smirnov — and "constantly referred to them as the best representatives of the party." When he learned in 1928 about Lashevich's suicide, Babel wrote to L. Nikulin: "I read today about the death of Lashevich and am very sad. He nevertheless was a man — if only there were more like him!"[17]

Babel was also close to the group of commanders in the corps of the red Cossacks — Primakov, Kuzmichev, Okhotnikov, Shmidt, and Ziuk. They all belonged to the Left Opposition and were the first to be arrested among the Red Army officers. According to Babel, he "was close to their milieu, enjoyed their love, and dedicated his stories to them... He studied them with interest, and felt that their biographies and the paths of their unusual lives were priceless material for literature."[18] Babel dedicated one of the stories in *Red Army Cavalry* to the glorious horseman, Shmidt, who received a second Order of the Red Banner during the Civil War; Bagritsky dedicated the libretto of the opera, *Thoughts About Opanas*, to him as well.

As the evidence gathered by agents shows, Babel kept company with such famous oppositionists as Dreitser, Serebriakov, Rakovsky, Mdivani and Yevdokimov.

Babel's friends, Gaevsky and Okhotnikov, were involved in 1932-1933 in the case of the opposition group led by I. N. Smirnov. According to Gaevsky

27. The Non-Party Intelligentsia

Aleksandr Voronsky,
shot on 13 August 1937

Vitaly Primakov,
shot on 12 June 1937

(from the transcript of his interrogation, which is kept in Babel's dossier), the members of this group "set as their goal ... to surround the leadership of the party with a wall of hostility, distrust and derision."[19]

"Being under the constant influence of Trotskyists," Babel wrote in his testimony, "after the arrests of Voronsky, Lashevich, Yakir and Radek (I was also close to the latter for a number of years), I repeatedly expressed my doubts about their guilt in conversations." As he tried to understand the falsified nature of the Moscow Trials, he noted the incongruities between the text of the court transcripts and the records of the people who were at the trial. In conversations with Olesha, Kataev, Mikhoels and other people close to him, Babel said that what was happening in the country was "not a change of people, but a change of generations, ... those arrested are the best and most talented political and military figures." Apparently, his discussions with Eisenstein were particularly sincere; Babel told him that "there is no place for talented people on Soviet soil, that party policy in the realm of art excludes creative experimentation, the independence of the artist, and the display of genuine mastery." He associated the possibility that Soviet culture might flourish with "the establishment of a democratic regime in the land, based on the political views which the Trotskyists have been defending."[20]

During his trips abroad, Babel spoke candidly with foreign left activists who held anti-Stalinist views, primarily with Souvarine, who showed particular interest in the fate of the persecuted oppositionists. Babel told him all that he knew about the life of Rakovsky, Zorin and others in exile, "trying to portray their situations in tones that were sympathetic to them."[21] These statements are confirmed in Souvarine's memoirs, in which he recalls how

Babel told him that about ten thousand Trotskyists had been arrested and sent into exile.[22]

No less dangerous themes were touched upon in Babel's correspondence with André Malraux. In responding to Malraux's questions about the reaction of the Soviet people to the Moscow Trials, Babel wrote that, from what he could observe, the trials "appeared convincing to the working layers of the population, but provoked bewilderment and a negative reaction among part of the intelligentsia." In this regard he cited "concrete facts which he had at his disposal about the moods of people from various professions, and, without providing names, quoted two negative responses to the trial — from a professor of mathematics and a woman physician."[23]

Like Babel, Boris Pilniak, another famous writer who was victimized, was on friendly terms with many oppositionists who actively influenced his political views. When he told the investigator of his conversations with Victor Serge, Pilniak said: "We came to one conclusion, that the political situation was extremely difficult, that the invisible knout of the state was felt on the individual, that we lacked the minimal rights to express our opinion, and that we were now living under siege conditions. There is no socialism, since socialism suggests an improvement of relations between people, yet in our country wolfish relations are being cultivated."[24]

The political moods among the workers and peasants were just as complex as among the milieu of the intelligentsia.

28. The People

In his book, *People, Years, Life*, when he was speaking of the cult around Stalin, Erenburg noted that "by the beginning of 1938, it would be more correct to simply use the word 'cult' in its original, religious meaning. In the minds of millions of people, Stalin had turned into a mythological demigod; *everyone* trembled when repeating his name, and believed that he alone might save the Soviet state from invasion and collapse (my italics – V. R.)." In support of these statements, however, the writer provided only one episode: at a session of the Supreme Council of the USSR, when the oldest deputy, academician Bakh, finished his introductory remarks with a toast in Stalin's honor, "thunderous applause resounded... I was sitting up high, and around me were ordinary Muscovites — workers and white-collar workers — and they applauded wildly."[1]

Of course, it was precisely such a cult, which approaches idol-worship, that Stalin and his clique propagated. There are no grounds to doubt the picture which Erenburg paints. But the writer did not mention that the people "applauding wildly" were carefully chosen for the political forum by the apparatus. If any people were insufficiently zealous during ovations, even at forums that were not so important, it would immediately be noted by the undercover agents liberally scattered throughout the audience, and lead to extremely unpleasant consequences for anyone insufficiently "displaying their zeal."

Far from everyone shared the feeling described by Erenburg. The moods and behavior of common people during these terrible years were described more objectively in the memoirs of N. Ya. Mandelshtam, who observed workers not at ceremonial meetings, but in everyday work and routine. Since she received a "minus" after exile, i.e., a ban on living closer than 100 kilometers to Moscow and other major cities, Mandelshtam settled in Kalinin, and rented a room in the home of a metal-worker. Here Nadezhda Yakovlevna became convinced that "in workers' families during those severe times people spoke much more directly and openly than in families of the intelligentsia." "Both the fathers and children of our hosts had worked in the factories," she recalled. "Tatiana Vasilievna explained, not without pride: 'We are hereditary proletarians'... Both completely condemned the trials: 'What things are being done in our name,' and the head of the household would toss the newspaper aside with disgust. 'It's their struggle for power' — that is how he understood what was taking place. That all this was called the dictatorship of the working class led both of them into a frenzy: 'They're pulling the wool over your eyes with our class.' Or: 'The authorities, they say, are for our class, but you go and have a look — they'll show you your class' ... They both defended the concept of proletarian conscience, which they did not want to renounce."

After the arrest of her husband, Mandelshtam settled in a small village called Strunino, where she worked at a textile factory. "They treated me well, especially the older men," she recalled about this time in her life. "... At every step I noted friendly concern — not toward me, but toward a 'hundred-fiver.'"*

Once, at night (the factory worked in three shifts) two young men appeared in the workshop and ordered Nadezhda Yakovlevna to follow them to the department of cadres. The path there led through several shops. As Mandelshtam and the NKVD men moved through the shops, the workers shut down their machines and followed: they knew that people were frequently taken straight from the personnel department to the NKVD. "What they wanted from me," Mandelshtam wrote, "I did not understand, but that night they let me go, perhaps because the workers had gathered in a crowd in the courtyard... When the night shift ended, one after another, workers began to come to our window. They told me: 'Leave,' and placed money on the window sill. The wife packed my things, and her husband and two neighbors put me on one of the first trains. Hence, I slipped away from a catastrophe thanks to people who had still not learned to be indifferent. If the personnel department had not been ready to arrest me at first, then after the 'send-offs' that people had given me, I, of course, would not have survived."[2]

The attitude of workers toward people being persecuted can also be discerned in Mandelshtam's story about how, in the mornings, workers would walk along the railway tracks looking closely at their feet: they were looking for notes that prisoners would often throw from the trains that usually passed through Strunino at night. If someone found a note, he would place it in an envelope, write the address and drop the envelope into a mail box. We find evidence of this type in many other memoirs: thousands of people received bits of news from their relatives by means of similar voluntary mailings.

Works devoted to Stalin's repressions usually treat the peasants and intelligentsia as their victims. Much less attention is paid to repressions which

---

* "Hundred-fiver": the wife of a political prisoner not allowed to live within 100 kilometers of a major city, but allowed to live within the 105-kilometer zone.

befell the working class. But during the years of the Great Purge, tens of thousands of people were torn from its ranks, mainly the most active and conscious part: the communists and Stakhanovites. Almost all the workers, engineers and technicians who spent time abroad in foreign factories were arrested. These arrests were guided by conceptions which became established in the "organs": a Soviet citizen who spent time abroad could not help but respond to recruitment by foreign intelligence services.

As the author of this book was told by Professor D. I. Galperin, who worked in 1937 as the chief engineer at a Tambov defense factory, from September 1937 through February 1938 that factory saw the arrests of two factory directors, all their deputies, all the heads of departments, three sets of the party committee, two groups of deputies of the party committees, and more than one hundred Stakhanovites. A similar picture could be observed at all the military factories. The percentage of those who were shot among the arrested depended on the degree of sadism in the local leadership of the NKVD. In February 1938, all the leaders of the NKVD in Tambov were shot. After this, about one third of the people who had been arrested were set free, and the rest were sent to the camps. Galperin himself spent five years in a "sharashka,"* where he participated in creating the "Katiusha," for which he was amnestied and received the title of Stalin Prize laureate. As he recalled, when the members of a "sharashka" had their convictions rescinded, being a party member was an aggravating circumstance.

D. B. Dobrushkin, an engineer at the Moscow factory "Kauchuk," told how several dozens of workers at his workplace were arrested, primarily those who were Stakhanovites or winners of decorations.[3]

In the countryside, the victims of the Great Purge were mainly communists and members of the collective farm intelligentsia. In many rural areas there were open trials at which the defendants were chairmen of collective farms, leaders of the region's party and Soviet organizations, agronomists, veterinarians and others. Their hostile activity was used to explain the actual disorder and misfortunes that the countryside was enduring: cattle plague; feed shortages; harvests that came too early, or, on the contrary, too late; low wage levels in the collective farms, etc. All of this, as the many spectators of the trials were learning, was being done in order to make the peasants bitter against the Soviet authorities. These provocative methods frequently caused the collective farmers to perceive the arrests and shootings as punishment that the "wreckers" deserved and as a prelude to "the good life" which Stalin had promised and whose arrival was ostensibly being hampered by the enemies of the people being "liquidated."

---

* "Sharashka": a prison with better food and working conditions where the prisoners worked on government projects.

During the time of forced collectivization and after it, the village communists, as well as many from the cities who were mobilized to participate in the official campaigns to extort grain from the countryside, were forced — under threat of losing their party cards or even of being arrested — to resort to repressive measures against the peasants. On this wave, the cruelest and most unscrupulous people were promoted, many of whom a few years later were themselves to fall into the meat grinder of the Great Purge. News of reprisals against them caused a feeling of satisfaction among many peasants; they felt that justice, which had been trampled upon, had been restored.

1937 witnessed the first public statements about many events that had previously been passed over in silence, including the massive starvation of recent times. Thus, in the novel *Bruski* [Bars], F. Panferov sketched nightmarish scenes which equaled in their expressiveness the depiction of starvation in the works of art in the 1960s-1980s:

> "On both sides of the road they would often see the corpses of horses with bones picked bare, but somewhere they saw something even more terrible, more monstrous, which Kirill could not look at without shuddering. Not far from the road, a peasant with a reddish beard was sitting on his haunches... Instead of a cap, his head was covered with a layer of ice. The ice went from his head down his neck and stretched along his back.
>
> "Should we go up to him?" asked the driver.
>
> "He's dead," answered Kirill, concealing his fear...
>
> "From an alley a man emerged on a sledge. He was traveling along the street and shouting, as if he was trying to corner the market:
>
> "Hey! Who has corpses? Give them up!"
>
> At a bend in the street he was leaning over Nikita Gurianov.
>
> "What, are you dying?" he asked, nudging Nikita with his foot.
>
> "I'm dying," he whispered hoarsely.
>
> "So get into the sledge... we'll take you away."
>
> "With the corpses?"
>
> "With who else?"[4]

Panferov needed these terrible scenes, however, only to proclaim through the mouth of one of his "exemplary" heroes:

> "Who put several of these villages ... on a starvation ration? Who? The enemy! Many do not see the enemy, many plod along behind the enemy, and say yes to the enemy.... But we have to beat the enemy. Beat him like lice. The enemy has settled down in agricultural organs, in planning bodies, in organs of the commissariat of educa-

28. The People

Olga Adamova-Sliozberg
(1902-1991)

tion, in scientific institutes, in the Academy... Burn them ruthlessly, without tears, without mercy, don't slobber over them... otherwise they will burn you, they will burn your children."[5]

Six years of collectivization had produced a deep antagonism between the peasantry and upper-echelon layers in the city, for whom collectivization turned out to be, in part, the chance to hire for miserable wages a housemaid from among the women who were fleeing the starving villages or the anti-kulak campaign. The issue of how difficult it was for representatives from these opposed layers to understand each other was addressed in O. Adamova-Sliozberg's memoirs, which open with a conversation between the author and her housemaid, a woman who had miraculously escaped the anti-kulak campaign and who had received a letter about the fate of her closest relatives. "For three months there has been nothing from your old man, I heard that he is digging a canal," wrote her neighbor. "Your children were living with grannie (in Siberia), they all fell sick. The land is damp, and there's little food... Scarlet fever had just started to mow down the children when mine also got sick. I barely nursed them through it, but God has taken yours. Your mother has just about lost her mind, she won't eat, won't sleep, moans all the time, probably she too will soon die."

When Adamova told her husband, a university lecturer, about this letter, he said to her: "You see, a revolution is not done in white gloves. The process of annihilating the kulaks is bloody and harsh, but it's a necessary process. In Marusya's tragedy, far from everything is as simple as it seems to you. What did her husband end up in a camp for? It is difficult to believe that he is not guilty of something. They don't put people into camps for no reason."[6]

Is it surprising that the Great Purge, which did not touch the majority of the rural population, was greeted with relative tolerance in the countryside that had begun to emerge in those years from the consequences of forced collectivization? And it was then that the situation of those who had been victims of the anti-kulak campaign was improved somewhat. In 1938, the Politburo confirmed a draft decree of the Sovnarkom allowing the children of those who had been re-settled or exiled, upon reaching the age of 16, to receive regular passports; in addition, the decree said not to impede their travel to study or to work.[7] On 22 December 1938, a decree of the Sovnarkom transferred special settlements to the regime of normal village artels. By the beginning of the war, less than a million victims of the anti-kulak campaign and members of their families remained in the special settlements.

In 1937-1938, the Politburo adopted several resolutions about the work of area committees, in which the hostile activity of local apparatchiks was given as the reason for arbitrary decisions with regard to collective farmers and individual farmers, for the diminished size of personal plots on the collective farms, etc. In order to correct this "wrecking," decrees were passed to remove the many arrears from the collective and individual farmers, and to allow them to graze their livestock without hindrance in the forests; several other privileges were granted.[8]

Of course, all of these measures were palliatives and could not fundamentally change the atmosphere of Soviet society, which, as Trotsky put it, was "seething with hatred for the privileged upper layers."[9] One of the functions of the Great Purge was to shift this hatred from the regime and its masters, the Stalinist clique, onto local functionaries with whom the population was in direct contact.

As for the reasons why the tales of mass terrorist and sabotage activity were believed by a significant part of the population, it is important to consider the following circumstances. Sabotage and terror frequently have served in history as a means of legitimate self-defense on the part of the people against their oppressors, or as a weapon of partisan activity which has accompanied civil war or wars of national liberation. These means were widely employed during the years of the Second World War not only by the partisan movement in the USSR, but by the resistance movement in all the countries occupied by Hitler's forces. These powerful means have also been used by reactionary forces (death squads, "soldiers of fortune") right up to the present (the Chechen war).

In 1937-1938, millions of Soviet people remembered well the acts of sabotage and terror which, in spontaneous, elemental, singular and scattered forms, had occurred among the Cossacks as a response by the peasants to forced collectivization. Stalinist propaganda greatly exaggerated the scale of this activity, appealing not only to the conscious but also the unconscious elements of the human psyche. The writer Fazil Iskander skillfully captured this psychological mainspring of the Great Terror when he noted that Stalin "understood well one important side of human psychology. He knew that people have a burning curiosity about the other world. The idea that alongside the usual, normal life, there is a secret life, a demonic one, brings particular delight to people. Man cannot reconcile himself to the idea that the world is simply material. He seems to say to fate: 'If you have deprived me of god, then at least do not deprive me of the devil.'"[10] Stalin cleverly played on these hidden strings of the human psyche as he stoked the fires of medieval hysteria and obscurantism.

A rational understanding of the Great Terror was hindered by the total ban on expressing any doubts whatsoever, or of even posing the questions which inevitably arose during the years of the Great Purge: Why, in the land of "triumphant socialism," did there prove to be so many spies, traitors and saboteurs, more than had ever been seen in history? Why was almost every Soviet citizen who went abroad such easy prey for foreign intelligence services? Why had the majority of foreign communists who had come to the "fatherland of all workers" turned out to be its most vicious enemies?

The show trials that took place, not only in Moscow but in the majority of the other regions of the country, served to stupefy the people with the gigantic scale of the hostile activity. They were also constructed according to the principle of the amalgam. Their defendants, for example, were often traders who were accused of artificially creating shortages and lines in order to provoke dissatisfaction among the population toward the government. Often those put on trial were genuine embezzlers, con-men, and looters, whose activity was explained not by personal greed, but by the desire to damage the Soviet authorities.

In order to better understand the psychological atmosphere which accompanied the Great Purge, let us examine the way it was perceived by diametrically opposed social and political strata in society.

29. The Great Purge as Seen by Enemies of Soviet Power

In dozens of memoirs which describe prison cells, the movement of prisoner convoys, their arrival in the camps, and so forth, we meet one and the same picture: the overwhelming majority of those arrested in 1936-1938 were communists. N. A. Ioffe recalls that the entire "party geography" met at camp transfer points. When various convoys met, the prisoners would call out to each other: "'Hey, friends, is there anyone from Novocherkassk — your party secretary is here'; 'Anyone from the Chelyabinsk area committee of the Komsomol, cry out.'"[1] Adamova-Sliozberg, who was arrested twice, reports that in 1949 the prisoners in her cell were about 10 percent party members, whereas in 1936 this proportion was the reverse: communists made up about 90 percent of the prisoners.[2]

Meanwhile, there was neither social nor political homogeneity among the victims of the repressions of those years. The orientation of the Great Purge toward the extermination of primarily communists (including hundreds of thousands of people who had been thrown out of the party during the official party purges) did not exclude the deliberate annihilation of several other categories of the population. After deciding to secure himself from any opposition and from any unwanted excesses in a future war, Stalin gave instructions for reprisals against members of former socialist parties, former members of the White armies, re-emigrants* (for instance, from the ranks of the Cossacks), etc. Therefore, the composition of prisoners was highly varied, and clashes on ideological and political grounds often arose among them.

There are many accounts of the malicious delight with which "former people" greeted communists in prisons and the camps. A. M. Larina's cellmate told her: "At least I know why I am here. My father was a major mer-

---

* *Re-emigrant*: a person who has returned to the country from which he/she emigrated.

chant... He was a counter-revolutionary, not a revolutionary, and I, too, hate your revolution. I can only gloat because your leader has slaughtered all the prominent Bolsheviks."[3]

Many anti-Soviet prisoners saw the Great Purge as the revenge they longed for against the Bolsheviks and the realization of what they themselves had not managed to accomplish during the years of the Civil War. In the camps, a former White-Guard officer told the Old Bolshevik Nemtsova: "What is happening now is the fulfillment of our slogan: All power to the Soviets, but without communists!... You can be certain: all (the Old Bolsheviks – V. R.) will end up in the camps."[4]

Similar feelings were felt by many of the victims of the anti-kulak campaign who, by 1937, had ended up in "leading" positions in the camps. O. Adamova-Sliozberg recalled how a norm setter, who decided how the work would be distributed among the prisoners, learned that her brigade consisted entirely of former party members, and then said: "When these party members persecuted me as a kulak in 1929 and drove me out of my home with six children, I told them: 'And what are the children guilty of?' They replied: 'That's the way Soviet law is.' So, observe Soviet law and dig nine cubic meters of soil each."[5]

During those same years, outside the camps, significant shifts in the social structure of society occurred. The assault on the Bolsheviks was combined with the restoration of civil rights and the growing possibility of social mobility for recently disenfranchised elements, i.e., representatives of the former ruling classes.

In the cycle of historical novels written by Anatoly Rybakov, one of the most vivid and memorable images is that of Sharok, who came from a petty-bourgeois family that secretly hated Soviet power. "Having stewed in a workers' cauldron," i.e., having worked for a year at a factory, Sharok was promoted to work in the NKVD, where he found rapid advancement in his new-found career. After becoming one of Yezhov's chief investigators, he felt profound satisfaction from the fact that he had received the chance to destroy "those whom I hated from childhood, those who have destroyed Russia — Old Bolsheviks, the so-called 'Leninist guard,' as well as all kinds of Jews, Latvians, and Poles who made the October Revolution. Of course, he was destroying these revolutionaries, communists and Bolsheviks in the name of the revolution and of the Communist Party, but this was not the most essential thing, it was important that he was destroying precisely these people."[6]

It was precisely people like Sharok — who were capable of social mimicry and adaptation, free from any ideas and moral restraints, guided only by careerist considerations, and cynical to the marrow of their bones — who had the greatest chance of survival during the years of the Great Purge.

The social and political consequences of this process became evident during the Second World War. As Zemskov, a researcher into the statistics

29. The Great Purge as Seen by Enemies of Soviet Power

of Stalin's repressions, correctly notes, it was then "that it became clear: tens of thousands of people who hated the Soviet social and state structure and dreamed of carrying out a mass slaughter of communists ... had avoided arrest in 1937-1938 because they had not aroused any particular suspicion among the NKVD organs due to their ostensible 'allegiance' (it was precisely such people in the occupied territories who became Vlasovites,* policemen, executioners, village-elders, burgomasters and so forth – V. R.)... At the same time the GULAG was filled with people devoted to the communist party and to the Soviet regime, and who... in their letters to various authorities asked for only one favor — to send them to the front and allow them to defend with weapons in hand the Motherland and the ideals of Great October and socialism."[7]

Not only did the Great Purge not liquidate a "fifth column," as Stalinist propaganda proclaimed in every key, but, on the contrary, it filled the ranks of potential collaborators and future stooges of Hitler with people who were embittered by the Stalinist terror.

The moods of people who had been called "internal émigrés" in the 1920s found ideological expression in the circles of foreign émigrés, who were close to them in spirit.

---

* Vlasovites: Soviet prisoners of war during the Second World War who joined General A. Vlasov in fighting on the side of the Nazis against the Soviet forces. After the war, most were returned by the Allies to the Soviet Union, where they faced execution or lengthy sentences in the camps.

Georgy Fedotov
(1886-1951)

Fyodor Dan
(1871-1947)

Rafail Abramovich
(1880-1963)

30. The Great Purge as Seen by Russian Émigrés

The social and political meaning of the Great Purge was correctly captured both by the left and right wings of the emigration, although the assessment of this process by various emigrant tendencies was often diametrically opposed.

At one of the extreme wings of the emigration stood pro-Stalinist elements, whose organizational center was the "Union of Return to the Motherland." In the Union's report about the Moscow Trials, they were called "the last link in the long chain of struggle by the Bolsheviks against their inveterate enemy — Trotskyism... Only a brilliant leader like Stalin could foresee what Trotsky would turn into, along with Trotskyism and all its stooges." Seeming to outdo the Moscow ideologues in apologetics for the Stalinist regime, the reporter asserted that "in the USSR there is greater freedom of conscience than in any other country, and no one is put on trial for his convictions if he does not begin to propagate views hostile to the interests of socialism."[1]

In the extreme right wing of emigration, the events in the USSR were also viewed with satisfaction, although, of course, for quite other reasons. The White-Guard General Lampe, who actively participated in preparing and sending to Moscow provocative documents about the "treachery" of Old Bolsheviks, wrote in June 1937 to Kusonsky, the deputy chairman of the Russian General Military Union (the militarized organization of former White officers): in the USSR "the victims are now those whom we ourselves would have hanged without any hesitation... For twenty years they (the Bolsheviks – V. R.) lived without doing in their *own* people, but in the second twenty years, that is exactly what they are starting to do. Mutual slaughter and executions in *their own* milieu is the normal *end* of every revolution... Let Stalin do the dirty work as much as he can... Of course, all talk about 'betrayals,' or 'espionage on behalf of one of the superpowers' is arrant nonsense."[2]

Similar views were expressed in the pages of the White émigré press. In 1936, the author of the journal *Tret'ia Rossiia* [Third Russia] stressed that "all of Stalin's power today has grown in the belittling and from the belittling of the communist party," and that Lenin, fortunately for him, "died in good time, otherwise he would have received the same fate as Trotsky... if he, of course, had remained the same Lenin as before."³

As the Great Purge developed, the pages of *Third Russia* ever more clearly showed its unconcealed and malicious delight over the anti-Bolshevik coup that Stalin had unleashed. "If the authors of the mass reprisals that are now taking place," wrote one of the journal's contributors, "hand over the Marxist-Trotskyist dogs to be morally and physically torn to pieces, then, in their own way, they know what they are doing."⁴

The centrist part of the emigration conducted itself in a different way. It did not share the mocking judgments of the White-Guardists and did not express a sense of triumph at the destruction of the communists in the Soviet Union. The pages of the newspaper *Poslednie novosti* [Latest News], edited by P. N. Miliukov, regularly published death lists — reprints of articles from the Soviet central and provincial newspapers about all the new trials and executions (from such material it was possible to get an idea of the scale of the mass terror).

Latest News reprinted excerpts from an article in the influential French newspaper *Le Temps*, whose positions the editors of Miliukov's paper clearly endorsed. This article, dedicated to the twentieth anniversary of the October Revolution, said: "What is the Soviet government celebrating? The anniversary of communism? But communism in Russia long ago turned into a hollow sound... The liquidation of tsarist despotism? But its place has been taken by a new despotism that is even more onerous and bloody. A break with the past? Textbooks once again contain praise for the history of holy Russia. The liberation of the working class? But in Russia the workers are stripped of all rights. No, the ceremonies are organized not for praising the regime, but for glorifying one man — Stalin."⁵

Perceptive statements about the essence of the Great Purge came from G. Fedotov, who wrote that it created the impression of "a complete replacement of the ruling class — of that layer of 'aristocrats' created by Stalin, which included the party, specialists and commanders of the Red Army." In Fedotov's opinion, the elite of the non-party intelligentsia, which during the years of Soviet power had merged into one layer with the party intelligentsia, belonged to this "aristocracy." "Bukharin, Rykov, and every Soviet high official have dragged along behind themselves dozens of specialists, professors, and colleagues, without whom it would be unthinkable to run the state. And now the entire intelligentsia is paying for these compromising links."

Stressing that the blow was being directed mainly at the associates and friends of Lenin, Fedotov explained the direction of this main blow by the fact that Stalin was trying to replace the communist elite with declassed elements who "hate the intelligentsia, or at least the Leninist intelligentsia, with a bitter hatred. Thus Stalin himself hates Trotsky and Bukharin, the blue bloods of Leninism."[6]

Condemning the joyful response which the murders of Bolsheviks found in the right-wing circles of the emigration, Fedotov noted that these murders were causing colossal damage not only to the Bolshevik Party, but to Russia as well. "If one could imagine, even as a historical play of fantasy," he wrote, "that Hitler managed to place his own trusted agent at the head of Russia and its Communist Party, he could not act better than Stalin."[7]

The left wing of the emigration, primarily the Mensheviks, perceived the Great Purge with growing horror. Commenting on articles in the Soviet newspapers about "restructuring" and the "democratization" of political life, one author in *Sotsialisticheskii vestnik* [Socialist Herald] directed attention to the true meaning of this campaign: the denunciation of bureaucratism and the bureaucrats was needed by Stalin in order to destroy the entire former apparatus, and to replace it with people of a new make-up, free from the Bolshevik mentality. In pursuit of this goal, true examples of the Pompadourism* of bureaucrats who had gone too far were brought to light. "Now with malice, and often without any caution," the article states, "they brand with the latest epithets members of executive committees and party members who yesterday were all-powerful... The sluices of discontent have been opened. At every meeting the listeners are treated to horrific tales, one after another, like in a talking motion picture, of how the Soviet citizen takes evasive action in order to survive, struggles along, gets around, and wins over the soulless bureaucrat or predatory person on the make."[8]

The *Socialist Herald* published an interview with a non-party Soviet engineer on a work assignment abroad, who called himself a sworn enemy of communism and who declared that it was precisely for that reason that he was applauding Stalin with all his heart. The latter was leading, "under the flag of the struggle against Trotskyism and Trotsky... the struggle which was actually *against communism,* both as a theory and as a world outlook... Stalin is conducting a purge in the country of outmoded ideas nobody any longer needs, and of the people who cling to them."[9]

Meanwhile, the Menshevik analysis of the social and political processes during the time of the Great Purge suffered from serious inner contradictions

---

* Pompadourism: in the Soviet Union by the 1930s, the term had come to mean a despotic (and often extravagant) bureaucrat, a tyrannical administrator. Although originating in reference to the Marquise de Pompadour from the reign of Louis XV, the term became popular in Russia after M. E. Saltykov-Shchedrin's *Pompadury i pompadurshi* [The Pompadours : A Satire on the Art of Government, 1863].

and misunderstandings. On the one hand, the ideologists of Menshevism clearly exaggerated the social gains which had been made in the USSR, closing their eyes to the humiliating position of a Soviet working class deprived of its rights. "The working class," wrote O. Domanevskaia, "is the ruling class in the land, and the masses, which have borne on their shoulders the entire weight of the radical reconstruction of the country, have thereby laid a firm foundation under their rule. The exceptional privileges and rights which the working class enjoys in Soviet Russia are unthinkable in any capitalist country."[10]

On the other hand, the Mensheviks, who retained their former assessments of Bolshevism, viewed the inner-party struggle in the USSR as a falling out between "Bolshevik cliques," the outcome of which in any case would lead to the triumph of bureaucratic absolutism. "'Stalinism' and 'anti-Stalinism,' wrote F. Dan, "are only two doors which lead equally to a counter-revolutionary Bonapartist (or, expressing it with the same degree of approximation in more modern terms — to a fascist) completion of the Russian Revolution."[11]

Crying contradictions were frequently found within the framework of a single article in *Socialist Herald*. Thus, an article devoted to the results of the second Moscow trial states: "The goal and meaning of the *trial* consists in a truly summary persecution of any communist opposition, in the moral and physical annihilation of 'Old Bolshevism,' which is becoming ever more a dire necessity for Stalin's autocracy in his struggle for survival." In the article, these just comments were neighbor to diametrically opposed arguments, which identified the executioners and their victims. When citing the exultant article in *Pravda*, "The Death Sentence against Trotskyism Is Carried Out," the author stated: "No, this sentence has been carried out not against Trotskyism, but against *Bolshevism* with all its factions, shades, branches and deviations! ... What is there to say, then, about Bolshevism, which was able to lead the great revolution it headed into such a bloody and filthy quagmire... No matter how one approaches the question, the stench of moral decay comes not from 'Trotskyism' alone, but from all Bolshevism as a whole."[12]

With the further development of Stalin's terror, the assessments of the Menshevik leaders became more objective and circumspect. In a response to the trial of the "Right-Trotskyist Bloc," Dan wrote: "In committing the moral and physical murder of 'Old Bolshevism,' Stalin is killing the revolution itself, and is doing the work of the counter-revolution."[13]

An article by R. Abramovich, "The International Significance of the Moscow Trial," stresses that Stalinism is striking crushing blows against the cause of world revolution. Abramovich points out that the Bolshevik revolution, "by the very fact of its existence — the fact that in a gigantic country a party came to power which came from the proletariat and was permeated with proletarian ideology — has been an unusual stimulus to the revolutionary expectations, hopes, and moods for a significant portion of the world proletariat... The revolutionary enthusiasm of the Western European masses aroused by the war and by the post-war revolutions spontaneously pushed them to the side of Bolshevism and communism. What began was the triumphant procession of communism throughout all the countries of Europe and America." However in this period, when the prestige of the Bolshevik revolution reached its high point, when it could have become "an inexhaustible reservoir of forces for the world revolutionary socialism," the Stalinized Comintern set against itself the broad masses of the organized proletariat in the West, through its tactics of splits, demagogy and the corruption of the leaders of the foreign communist parties. As a result, these parties lost many of their members. Thus arrived the first stage in the weakening and demoralization of the revolutionary proletariat, which brought about its defeat in a number of countries. A new wave of revolutionary enthusiasm arose as a result of the world capitalist crisis, the disillusionment of the masses with bourgeois democracy and the victories of fascism. "The star of Bolshevism once again rose high above the horizon of the world proletariat; the prestige of the Soviet revolution grew to an unprecedented degree. The proletarian state... began to become a prototype of socialism; this state was forgiven all its defects, shortcomings and even crimes, just as a young titan is forgiven childhood illnesses and the sins of youth." Austrian Schutzbundists, prisoners in Hitler's camps, and other victims of fascism yearned for Soviet Russia, which represented for them the genuine "fatherland of all workers," a radiant vision of a socialist society under construction, a hope and base of support in the struggle for democracy and socialism. And at precisely this moment, when the ideological influence of the Bolshevik revolution had once again reached its apogee, "inexplicably and beyond the comprehension of all, what began was a paroxysm of the most horrific and cruel terrorism, and what began was a prolonged period of mass shootings and 'trials.' With confused fear, and then ever more with a feeling of revulsion and horror, the world proletariat observed the monstrous, incomprehensible, and inexplicable spectacle."[14]

Members of the Austrian "Schutzbund" participating in a May Day demonstration in Moscow. After fighting from 12 to 17 February 1934 against the rise of Fascism in Austria, many surviving Schutzbundists found refuge in the Soviet Union, only to be executed by the NKVD during the Great Terror (see also page 313).

31. The Great Purge as Seen by Communists

In the party milieu, the Great Purge was met not only with horror, but with confusion. Thousands of Soviet communists could find no explanation for the fact that people who had shed their blood for the revolution during times when it was hanging by a thread, had betrayed it when the Soviet regime seemed more stable than ever before, and when they themselves enjoyed honor and recognition.

Today, the question stands before us in another light: why was it that many, many Bolsheviks, who during the underground and Civil War had not experienced fear even when facing death, submissively followed Stalin during the time of the Great Terror, despite the increasingly arbitrary rule that was taking the lives, one after the other, of the Bolshevik cohorts?

Today there is no shortage of memoirs that reveal how the communists of that time perceived the Great Purge. As a whole, they create an extremely contradictory portrait of a confused mass consciousness, reflecting the profound ideological, social, and psychological heterogeneity of the party: the presence in it of different generations, possessing different political experience; the varied attitudes toward Stalin — from identifying him with Soviet power and believing in his greatness to seeing him as the grave-digger of the revolution; the existence of two opposed tendencies instilled by the Stalinist regime: tendencies toward conformism, a herd-mentality, and mass psychosis; and tendencies toward the separation and atomization of people, toward their mutual distrust.

One must, therefore, not take on faith the attempts of some memoirists to extend their own moods to "everyone." A careful comparison of memoirs, as well as other historical sources, reveals the existence within the party of highly varied social and psychological layers, i.e., layers united by common perceptions and attitudes toward the tragic events of their time.

Olga Berggolts
(1910-1975)

The first layer consisted of young communists who retained their belief that the repressions were well-founded — until the moment when they themselves ended up in prison cells, and often even after this. In speaking about the difference between the inmates of Stalinist prisons in 1936 and 1949, O. Adamova-Sliozberg noted that, after the war, whether in prison or at liberty, she did not meet "a single person with an unshaken faith in justice," whereas at the time of her first arrest "everyone, including myself, had faith in the infallibility of the Soviet authorities, of the Soviet courts and especially of Stalin... whose name was synonymous with the revolution, socialism, truth and justice."[1]

People of this kind included the poet Olga Berggolts, who, in 1935, recorded in her diary: "How... proud and glad I am that I am a Soviet person, that I live in these years. I am simply seized from time to time with some kind of inhibition because of my pride and joy, I don't feel like saying this out loud, just as sometimes you are ashamed to praise aloud with words the beauty of nature, because you fear insulting her by doing so and destroying the ineffable and pure which has arisen within you."

During the half year Berggolts spent in prison, these feelings were tragically shattered. One of her first diary entries after leaving prison reads: "Comrades, my dear ones, my beautiful comrades, everyone that I know and that I do not know, all who are languishing for no good reason in prisons in our Soviet land, oh, if I knew that my words might help you, I would give you my whole life! ... Before prison, everything, or almost everything, seemed clear: everything was arranged in a well-structured system, and now everything has been re-bored, many things have changed places, much has been re-evaluated. ... Perhaps everything has been shattered because the system was too well-structured, the fetishes were too inviolable, and the system itself was a system of fetishes?"

In preparing for a meeting at which she was to be reinstated in the party, Berggolts made the following diary entry: "Oh, how passionately I feel like saying: 'Dear comrades! I saw, heard, and experienced in prison this, and this, and this... everything that was revealed to me aches and burns in me like poison. I do not understand this and this, I am repulsed by this and this. Such things seem wrong to me. Here I stand before you, with all my pain, with all my confusion.' But I cannot do that. It would be idealism! What would these things explain? There would be expulsion and condemnation... And, most likely, prison once again."[2]

In their perceptions of the Great Purge, many low-level party officials were close to the layer of rank-and-file communists; they found painful the forced collectivization and other actions of Stalinism in which they were forced to take part as they subordinated themselves to party discipline. The breakthrough for these people is described in a book by I. I. Yefimov, who stressed that "we learned to think only in prison. Before prison, it was as if we all had curtains over our eyes, or we saw only one side of the coin, and heard only one truth."[3] Yefimov recalled how the regional party officials who took part in prison discussions arrived at a reassessment of the inner-party struggle and the role played by Stalin. "Whoever raised him to the throne was condemned to ruination," one of them reflected. "Those who surrounded Stalin and held onto his coat tails. To be next to power or to hold power was significantly more beneficial than to criticize its mistakes. And we, the young communists lent our support, not knowing the whole background to the inner-party struggle. We didn't think about anything, and we weren't supposed to do any thinking: we ... could only vote, without looking into who was right and who was wrong."[4]

Sharp clashes frequently arose in prison cells when prisoners were exchanging opinions about what was taking place. E. Ginzburg recalled how she communicated by means of tapping on the walls with Garei Sagidullin, a political figure from Tataria who was located in the neighboring cell and who had been arrested in 1933 on charges of "bourgeois nationalism." Like many other oppositionists, he had been brought for re-investigation, in order to "translate his case into the language of 1937," i.e., replace a previous sentence with one more severe. Sagidullin tapped out the following message to Ginzburg: "Speak openly about your disagreement with Stalin's line, name as many names as possible of people who also disagree. They will not arrest the entire party. And if there are thousands of such transcripts, then the idea will emerge of convening an extraordinary party congress, and hope will arise for 'his' overthrow. Believe me, inside the Central Committee they hate him no less than in our cells. Perhaps such a line will be fatal for us personally, but it is the only way to save the party."

Ginzburg confessed that at the time she had not matured enough to agree with such thoughts. "To declare my disagreement with the line — I could not do. It would have been a lie. For I so passionately and sincerely supported both the industrialization of the country and the collectivization of agriculture."[5]

This kind of fetishism with regard to the "general line of the party" and to the "Stalinist leadership" was characteristic, too, of several old party members who for a prolonged period had taken an active part in the "fight against Trotskyism." The testimony of such people about their perception of the Great Purge is extremely contradictory. Thus, as Lazurkina, a member of the party from 1902, was making the proposal at the Twenty-Second Congress of the CPSU to remove Stalin's body from the mausoleum, she said: "Not for one minute — either when I spent two and a half years in prison, or when they sent me to a camp, or after that when they sent me into exile (I spent 17 years there) — did I ever hold Stalin guilty at that time. I always fought for Stalin, who was cursed by prisoners, exiles and camp inmates. I always said: 'No, it could not be that Stalin allowed what is going on in the party. It cannot be!'" However, at the same time Lazurkina stressed that, in 1937, "fear dominated, which we, Leninists, were not used to. We slandered each other, we did not believe each other, we slandered even ourselves." And nevertheless she declared: "We did not believe that in our party of Lenin there could be such arbitrary rule," and "we fought to the end." This fight, in her words, was expressed after her arrest by the fact that "we wrote and wrote without end. If you look at the archive of my letters, then you could find a whole volume of letters to Stalin."[6]

A vivid example of the inner turmoil of a devoted Stalinist is the world outlook and behavior of Mikhail Koltsov during the years of the Great Purge. Before his arrest, Koltsov was one of the editors of *Pravda*, a leader of a newspaper and magazine publishing house ("Zhurgiz"), an editor of the journals *Ogonek*, *Krokodil*, and *Za rubezhom*. In 1938, he was awarded the Order of the Red Banner and elected deputy of the Supreme Council of the USSR and corresponding member of the Academy of Sciences. Besides this, he occupied many public posts and managed the international contacts of the Union of Soviet Writers. A month before his arrest, the first book of his *Spanish Diary* was published in a mass press run and bestowed with an exultant review by A. Tolstoi and Fadeev in *Pravda*.

Typical of Koltsov's statements were his words in the holiday issue of *Pravda*: "Damn, what an interesting and wonderful time! Never have our people stood so strong and peaceful before the entire world as now, as today, as this moment!"[7]

It would be wrong to see in these words only the repetition of mandatory official rapture. According to Koltsov's brother, the artist Boris Yefimov, Koltsov "sincerely, deeply, and, I am not afraid to say, fanatically believed in Stalin's wisdom. How many times after meetings with the 'master' did my brother tell me in the minutest detail about his manner of speaking, about

31. The Great Purge as Seen by Communists

Mikhail Koltsov in Spain

various comments he had made, about words he used, and the jokes he told. Everything about Stalin appealed to him."[8]

At the same time, Koltsov could not help but feel confusion in the face of news about ever newer repressions. In one of his frank discussions with his brother, he said: "I feel that I am going mad. After all, because of my position — as a member of *Pravda's* editorial board, a famous journalist, and a deputy — I should be able, it would seem, to explain to others the meaning of what is happening, the reasons for such a large number of exposures and arrests. But in actual fact, like the lowest, terrified philistine, I myself know nothing, I understand nothing, I am bewildered, confused, and in the dark."

As he wondered about whether Yezhov was feeding Stalin's suspicions, or, on the contrary, whether Stalin "carefully and insistently was egging Yezhov on," Koltsov told of an episode which explained much for him about the mechanics of the Great Purge. Dropping in once on Mekhlis, he found him reading a thick notebook which contained the testimony of Tal, the main editor of *Izvestiia*. Mekhlis said that he had no right to familiarize Koltsov with this testimony, but he could show him *his* resolution: "Comrades Yezhov and Mekhlis. Read this together and arrest all the bastards mentioned here." "Do you understand?" Koltsov said excitedly. "The people he was talking about are still at liberty, they are working, perhaps publishing articles in newspapers, visiting people with their wives or going to the theater, getting ready to go for a vacation somewhere in the South. And they do not suspect that they are already 'bastards,' that they are already convicted and, in essence, destroyed by one stroke of this red pencil. Purely technical details remain for Yezhov — to formulate the 'cases' and write out the orders for arrest."

"I listened to my brother," recalls B. Yefimov, "and my heart contracted with ominous feelings. I could not refrain from thinking that his fate, perhaps, had been decided in the same way... with a red pencil on someone's forced or fabricated testimony. I sensed that he was thinking the same thing, but we decided not to voice these thoughts aloud, although we read them in each other's eyes."9

Koltsov and Yefimov belonged to the circle of the party and near-party intelligentsia which found itself under the knout of constant tension and obsessive fear for their own fate and the fate of those close to them. The atmosphere in which these people lived was conveyed with penetrating exactitude in Yefimov's memoirs: "How can I describe the state of thousands and thousands of people, knowing no guilt, but each (each!) night listening with a sinking heart whether that fateful ring would come at their door, then breathing a sigh of relief and falling into a heavy sleep sometime near dawn, in order to think with horror during the daytime about the night that lay ahead?... These people passionately would like to find out something from someone, to ask questions, they would like to explain something to somebody, to justify themselves with regard to something, to refute something else. But they could not do this because no one asks them any questions, no one seeks any explanations, no one makes any claims or lodges any charges. A person feels like he is in some kind of horrible, delirious vacuum, but he must pretend that he has no reason to worry, he must look absolutely calm and cheerful, he must maintain his full ability to work, and carry out his duties as usual."10

After each arrest of a relative, coworker or close comrade, a person would feverishly recall whether he could have said something "forbidden" at some time in a private conversation with him. For even from the newspaper articles it was clear that even the slightest critical comments about Stalin or any aspect of his politics would be enough for someone to be accused at the very least of "counter-revolutionary agitation."

Of course, there were many people who understood the whimsical and fantastic nature of the "confessions" which the press and the radio were continuously reporting. As I. Reiss would say, "in Moscow people openly joked about the 'confessions.' Particularly popular were tales like the one which said that after Aleksei Tolstoi was arrested and interrogated, he confessed that he wrote 'Hamlet,' etc."11

But it may be that there were just as many people who believed not only that Stalin knew nothing about the provocations and savageries being committed in the prison torture chambers, but who also believed the widely propagated formula, "the NKVD does not make mistakes." Such people sincerely renounced even their closest friends or relatives as soon as they learned of their arrest. K. Ikramov recalled how his mother told a close friend when she learned about the arrest of her husband: "If they took him away, that means he's scum." When she heard these words, the other woman fainted — not because she was shocked by their cruelty, but because she remembered that, not long before, her husband had reacted to the arrest of his comrade in literally the same terms.[12]

Of course, far from all communists were guided only by concerns of self-preservation; not all lived under the power of an ostrich mentality, willfully or involuntarily striving not to burden their consciousness and conscience with reflections on the meaning of what was occurring. Much more tragic was the attitude of those who knew the criminal role being played by Stalin, and yet sharply felt their helplessness and inability to act in opposition to the wave of repressions. A psychologically convincing portrayal of this is given in G. Baklanov's novella *July 1941*. Here he describes how, at the end of the summer of 1937, when "events had reached a grand scale," Colonel Shcherbatov was visited by his friend and distant relative, Emelyanov. The latter had been of such "high rank," that Shcherbatov "never reminded him of his family ties, and almost never traveled to see him except perhaps on birthdays, when it would have been awkward not to go" (this detail speaks eloquently of the clear hierarchy that had become established by that time, which divided even "high-ranking communists" into invisible strata). Emelyanov emerges in the novella as a genuinely popular character, a man promoted to leading roles by the revolution and who was wholeheartedly devoted to its cause. "Of powerful build, strapping, with a clear and sober mind, he was one of those figures who always exist in great number among the people, but become visible only in crucial, transitional moments in history. During such decisive moments they arrive on the scene with masterful skills, confident, knowing what they should do, and without asking, they place their broad shoulder under that part of the burden which is the heaviest."

In a nighttime conversation with a friend, this courageous and powerful man clearly and distinctly characterizes the atmosphere of hopelessness in which people such as he lived in those days. "You are waiting for news?" asked Emelyanov point blank. "People now wait more for news than for the truth," he grinned. "So we sit in our corners and wait: 'Maybe they will pass me by.'... Well, go on out, talk out loud... Then tomorrow, whoever knew you will fear your name... If you think about it deeply, you begin to distrust yourself! We are two communists, and whatever they say there, nothing is dearer to us than Soviet power, even though we now find ourselves fearing our own words and thoughts."

Emelyanov, who lived in expectation of the inevitable arrest that was hanging over him, understood that, in an atmosphere of totalitarian hysteria, if the truth were expressed publicly it would only contribute to beliefs in the vast number "enemies" so insistently trumpeted by official propaganda. "It's terrible," he said "that we ourselves have helped strengthen the people's blind faith, and now we are powerless before it. The sacred truth looks like a terrible lie if it does not correspond to the ideas that people now share. Can you imagine what would happen if a person were found who would tell the whole country over the radio, for instance, what is actually going on, and would talk about Stalin? You know what would happen? From that moment on, even someone who had doubts would begin to believe. And then any act of cruelty would be justified."[13]

These thoughts are remarkable not only because of their understanding of the tragic guilt of those who during the years of the legal inner-party struggle helped Stalin gain absolute power. People of Emelyanov's intellectual level and moral quality also realized the vicious circle which confronted anyone who was capable of having the courage to publicly expose Stalin's crimes, let alone to commit a terrorist act against Stalin. If one of the Bolsheviks, perhaps even Emelyanov, had decided on such an act, then his contemporaries and descendants would hardly have believed in the arbitrary nature of the repressions against thousands of others charged with terrorist plans and actions. By fabricating the "anti-terrorist" cases and trials, Stalin removed the hand of vengeance from himself. Moreover, any public mention of the illegality of the repressions would have been understood in the circumstances of 1937 as "a Trotskyist outburst" and thereby would have worked in Stalin's favor.

Trotsky thought that it was possible that "the regime, which is exterminating the best minds of the nation under the pretense of a struggle against terrorism, will, in the end, provoke a genuine terror against itself. One could say more. It would be against the laws of history if the ruling gangsters did not raise terrorists of despair and revenge against themselves."[14]

We know that, already by the beginning of the 1930s, terrorist moods against Stalin actually appeared among several youth groups. A major factor in preventing such moods from developing into action was the understanding of a real alternative that consisted of the following during the period of the Great Purge.

If Stalin had died a natural death during these years, it seems that the repressions would have immediately stopped, as actually happened in 1953. If he had died from a terrorist act, however, all the preceding reprisals would have looked justified, and the machine of state terror would have begun working with ever more terrible force. In this case, Stalin would have remained, in the consciousness of those to follow, surrounded by the aureole of a hero and martyr who had fallen victim to a sinister plot.

Trotsky was apparently guided by similar conceptions when he wrote in 1937: "In the most severe criminal codes of mankind, one will not find sufficient punishment for the ruling Moscow clique, and most of all for its leader. If, nevertheless, in our appeals to the Soviet youth we have continuously raised a warning voice against individual terrorism, which so easily is born on Russian soil, permeated as it is with arbitrary rule and violence, then it has not been for moral, but for political reasons. Acts of desperation change nothing in the system, but simply make it easier for the usurpers to carry out bloody reprisals against their opponents."[15]

The success of Stalin's extermination campaign was determined also by the fact that all the charges against the victims of the mass terror were assembled with an eye toward the socialist spirit and patriotic qualities of the majority of Soviet people. They saw the Soviet Union as the mainstay of socialism and the world communist movement, as a fatherland threatened by hostile invasion, and as a powerful counterweight to fascism on the world arena. Correspondingly, the "enemies of the people" were charged with the desire to restore capitalism, to prepare the defeat of the USSR in the impending war, and to conspire with German fascism.

These charges, which were confirmed by the defendants at the Moscow Trials, created the impression that if people who had occupied extremely high posts confess their participation in such terrible crimes (and after all, even before these confessions, they had repeatedly repented their "objectively criminal" oppositional activity), then ridding the country of the many terrorists and wreckers who had multiplied and penetrated all the pores of the party and state mechanism is an undeniable blessing. One could only complain that "when you chop wood, the chips will fly."

The credulity of people who did not notice the many inconsistencies of the Moscow Trials, and who believed in the false testimony of the defendants, appears both blind and strange to us today. This credulity can largely be explained by the impact of the all-pervasive propaganda under conditions of a rather restricted flow of information. After all, in those years, there was no foreign radio which informed the USSR. Only after the Second World War did it become a canal and a source of counter-information for millions of Soviet people, destroying the Stalinist myths and falsifications. Trotsky's statements, which could have radically changed people's perceptions of the Great Terror, hardly penetrated the iron curtain which separated the Soviet Union from the rest of the world.

The history of the twentieth century has shown that a collective myth circulated by the mass media can attain enormous power over people's minds. And what is central here is not the backwardness of the Soviet Union or some special characteristics of the "Russian soul." No less powerful during those years were the fiendish myths about the superiority of a "higher race" for the German people, who had passed through the school of bourgeois democracy. And, in our days, haven't the minds of many Soviet people fallen under the sway of malicious myths about the primordial defects of the Bolshevik "utopian experiment" or of the worldwide "Masonic-Zionist conspiracy?" And didn't the upper-echelon intelligentsia, strutting its intellectual superiority over the broad masses, believe in Gorbachev's rhetoric about "crucial transformations" or in Yeltsin's democratic yearnings and the beneficence of "market reforms" for the country?

For many years, the main myths of 1937 — about Stalin's greatness and about vicious Trotskyist intentions, which were inextricably linked to each other — had steadily been driven into the consciousness of the masses. They could only be confirmed by a river of blood. For the Stalin cult was not a spontaneous expression of popular feelings. It strikingly contradicted the mass feelings during the first years of the revolution that are clearly conveyed by Mayakovsky in the poem, "Vladimir Ilyich Lenin":

> *If he had been*
> > *tsar-like and divine,*
> *I would not*
> > *have guarded myself*
> > > *from frenzy,*
> *I would have*
> > *stood*
> > > *in defiance of the processions*
> *opposed to the acts of worship*
> > *and the crowds.*
> *I would*
> > *have found*
> > > *words*
> > > > *of thunderous damnation*
> *and while I*
> > *and my cry*
> > > *might be trampled,*
> *I would hurl*
> > *blasphemies*
> > > *into the sky*
> *and toss*
> > *bombs*
> > > *about the Kremlin:*
> > > > *Down with him!*[16]

(From 1937 through 1953, the second, "terrorist" stanza was removed from all editions of Mayakovsky's works).

In order to instill the Stalin cult — a variety of secular religion — the totalitarian regime had to eliminate such feelings and annihilate those who were capable of standing "opposed to the acts of worship and the crowds." Such people included primarily the Trotskyists, whose influence had spread to many Soviet people. And if the twenty-year-old Sasha Pankratov, the hero of A. Rybakov's novel *Fear,* understood the actual essence of the Moscow Trials, then it was only because he met with Trotskyists in Siberian exile who opened his eyes to many things. As he read the court transcripts, Sasha recalled the unbroken oppositionist Zviaguro who "understood everything. Yet he argued with her when she said that Stalin was worse than a criminal who will gladly kill if the need arises. Her predictions were coming true."[17]

In a certain sense, it was easier for Sasha to understand the truth than for older members of the party who since 1923 had been led through a lengthy sequence of "anti-Trotskyist" campaigns by the ruling faction. Even a person as experienced in politics as Raskolnikov, who found the strength to break with Stalin, expressed reservations in his foreign statements that he was distant from Trotskyism. Meanwhile, like the hero in Molière who didn't know he was speaking prose, he essentially repeated the "Trotskyist" criticism of Stalinism.

Many thousands of people absorbed the lie about Trotskyism as an anti-party and anti-Soviet current, a lie which had been pounded into their heads for decades. It was not a big step from here to an acceptance of the thesis "confirmed" by the Moscow Trials: every Trotskyist is a criminal who is capable of treason, espionage and sabotage. Despite all their absurdity, these feelings dominated at party conferences in 1937, where each communist was invested with a duty to take an active part in the search for Trotskyists. One of these conferences was vividly described by G. Baklanov in the novella *July 1941,* — through the eyes of its main hero, Shcherbatov:

> "At that time, meetings were frequently held... And at one such meeting, a captain, one of his company commanders, a quiet, unassuming man, suddenly asked for the floor... He spoke in a somewhat muffled voice; in rank he was junior to many, but as he spoke at the tribune, he seemed to rise up above everybody. And everyone listened intently, understanding that something was about to happen.
>
> 'Let us ask ourselves, as communist to communist, let us ask with hand on our hearts: Have we always been sincere before the party?.. No, comrades! Not always! For here among us sits a colonel...'
>
> Here he raised his head for the first time and looked at the audience. And Shcherbatov saw his eyes, the eyes of his subordinate which so many times had been lowered before him. Now, they were the eyes of a man for whom nothing was forbidden, who had crossed a boundary and who would not stop at anything. Their gaze, as he looked up, passed through the rows.
>
> 'There, over in the corner, sits Colonel Masenko.'
>
> The whole audience turned in the direction that the finger was pointing from the tribune, and everyone who knew Masenko, or

who didn't know him by sight, immediately saw him: he sat there pale, rooted to the spot, and something invisible immediately separated him from all the rest.

'After all, you've been insincere before the party, comrade Masenko! ... In twenty-seven, do you remember, did you attend a meeting of Trotskyists? Why conceal from us such a fact in your own biography?'

The middle-aged Colonel Masenko was already walking, almost running, along the aisle, he reached for the tribune with his hand, and made indignant and menacing gestures... What everyone else was feeling, Shcherbatov now felt within himself. Imagine, Masenko. A pleasant, modest fellow with a record of combat. A Trotskyist! ... It would have been impossible to have imagined it...

Masenko was standing at the tribune irreconcilably, threateningly shaking his jowls, and gradually, because of the general commotion of the people who were startled by what had just been revealed, his voice nevertheless became audible:

'Yes, I was. I was sent... I was sent on a party assignment (in 1927, provocateurs and informers were indeed sent to factional meetings of the opposition – V. R.)... And you, my friend... What's with you? Why was it you saw me there: Why were you there? I'll say more. I myself wanted to speak ... to take the floor. I will name names...' The audience fell silent. 'There, there, if you will. Captain Gorodnitsky was there at that time... he attended. Colonel Fomin.'

There was full silence. And above the silence, above everyone's head, Masenko's trembling finger was raised even higher. Frowning because he could not see clearly, he was looking for someone else:

'There... Now... There...'

And suddenly his finger stopped at Shcherbatov. In that fraction of a second, when the audience was turning toward him, Shcherbatov managed to experience everything. He, who had been involved in nothing, who was guilty of nothing, suddenly felt with a terrible sharpness how his entire life might be obliterated if the finger stopped at him. He should have stood up, and spoken, but he sat before what was approaching, frozen to the spot. And then he joined everyone else in turning toward the person that Masenko's trembling finger was now pointing at."[18]

Today, everything in this scene is amazing and astounding — the inordinate significance of participating in a factional meeting ten years before; the loss of human dignity and worthiness when confronted with such charges by commanders who had often looked death in the face; the readiness to sacri-

31. The Great Purge as Seen by Communists

fice anyone whose slightest participation in the former opposition would be discovered; the mortal fear of those who knew this fateful guilt; the frenzy of the audience given news about the slightest suspicion of belonging to the Trotskyists; and the helplessness before false denunciations, even if they were voiced openly at a meeting.

But that is precisely how the "struggle against Trotskyism" was waged in 1937.

The gigantic separation of people who were poisoned by mutual suspicions and trained on lies and slander favored a situation in which people became active who, to use Khrushchev's words, "were simply charlatans, choosing for themselves the profession of exposing enemies of the people." In this regard, Khrushchev told of an incident which became a "joke that was passed from mouth to mouth throughout the whole Ukraine." At one meeting, a woman of some kind pointed a finger at the communist Medved and began shouting: "I don't know this man, but from his eyes I see that he is an enemy of the people." Medved, who remained calm, found the only appropriate response: "I don't know this woman who has just spoken against me, but from her eyes I see that she is a prostitute" (Khrushchev added that Medved "used a more expressive term"). What is most terrible is that Khrushchev thought: only such "quick-wittedness" saved Medved; "if Medved had started to prove that he was not an enemy of the people, but an honest person, then he would have aroused suspicion against himself."[19]

The belief that belonging, even in the distant past, to an opposition was an indisputable fault for which a person deserved persecution, determined the logic of the behavior of even those who dared to intervene on behalf of those expelled or arrested. The basic argument of people defending their comrades was the vow that they had never participated in any oppositions, but on the contrary, had always fought against them.

Even in private conversations between people who were close, doubts about the guilt of those arrested was frequently interpreted as "Trotskyist slander." When Erenburg, who had returned from Moscow to Spain, said to his friend Savich: "It is difficult to understand why every day they round up people who aren't guilty of anything," the latter responded with a question: "What have you done, turned into a Trotskyist?"[20]

The worldwide historical delusion, connected with a belief in the justice of Stalinist characterizations of "Trotskyism," was maintained by many "orthodox" party members even after many years spent in the camps. When P. V. Aksenov, a delegate to the Sixteenth and Seventeenth party congresses and chairman of the Kazan city committee, returned to freedom, Beilin, the former secretary of the party collegium of the Tatar Party Control Commission, who had taken an active part in his expulsion from the party and who also spent about twenty years in the camps, wrote to him: "I am sincerely happy that you have returned alive." In a reply letter to Beilin, Aksenov wrote: "In actual fact, you were one of the most fervent witch-hunters. Your zeal was so great, than when real witches were not found, you caught *everyone* who fell into your hands, branded them with labels and anathematized them. I myself and my family were victims of your inexhaustible activity... Yet you and Lepa (in 1937 the first secretary of the Tatar party area committee) knew me well enough not to include me among the Trotskyists... In this entire story, what occupies me is not so much my personal fate, as the explanation of the causes — why did our party prove to be defenseless? The question interests me: how was it that experienced fighters in the party — Lepa, Beilin, Volfovich and many, many others — suddenly lost their Bolshevik instincts and, without thinking, started to mow down communists?"[21]

Aksenov could not find an answer to these tragic questions, because, in the very way they were asked, he was guided by Stalinist logic. He reproached Beilin and others not for including him among spies, saboteurs or terrorists, but only and exclusively among Trotskyists ("the real witches"). As is evident from the letter's content, even a quarter of a century after 1937, Aksenov felt that "Bolshevik instincts" would not have been lost among "witch-hunters" if only they had been directed at persecuting genuine Trotskyists; such people, in Aksenov's mind, could and should have been "mown down."

Similar logic forced even people who recognized the criminal nature of the Stalinist regime to spin in a vicious circle when they reflected on the tragedy experienced by the party and the people. In Solzhenitsyn's novel *Cancer Ward* the Old Bolshevik Shulubin shares the questions which are tormenting him: "Tell me, what is the reason for the alternation of these periods in History? In one and the same people, within ten years all social energy falls, and the impulses of courage change their sign and become the impulses of cowardice... After all, how boldly I chased away the SR and Menshevik Duma in Tambov, although all we had going for us was I could put two fingers in my mouth and whistle. I took part in the Civil War. And we didn't spare our lives at all! We were simply happy to give our lives for the world revolution! What happened to us? How could we give in?... Well, all right, I'm just a little person, but Nadezhda Konstantinovna Krupskaya? Could it have been that she didn't understand, that she didn't see? Why didn't *she* raise her voice? How much would just one word from her have been worth for all of us, even if it cost her her life? Perhaps we had all changed, we had dug in our heels and wouldn't go any further? But Ordzhonikidze? Now there was an eagle! They didn't break him either with Schlusselburg or with hard labor — what prevented him from once, just once, speaking out publicly against Stalin?"[22]

Despite all the sincerity of the pain Shulubin felt, his arguments contain no small measure of craftiness — and even self-deception. It's as if he did not know that both he and the people he mentions gradually lost their courage and principles long before 1937 — in the course of the inner-party struggle, where, from the very beginning, among the weapons of the majority were a lack of principles and scruples with regard to their comrades of not long ago.

Often, it was only in the camps, where people were torn away from the usual atmosphere of official hypocrisy, and where whatever was deeply hidden in the recesses of the consciousness burst to the surface, that many communists renounced the judgements which for long years had seemed to be axiomatic. In this sense, we find interesting the reminiscences of I. Filshtinsky about an encounter in a camp with "one of the old hard-labor prisoners from the arrests of the thirties" — Voronin (the last name of this man, as the author indicates, was changed). During the twenties, Voronin had been party organizer at a large Leningrad factory, and then, secretary of one of the Leningrad regional committees, where he conducted a ruthless struggle against the opposition (as he put it, he had a special assignment from the area committee in 1928: to gather and destroy literature distributed by Trotskyists). He finished his party career in Arkhangelsk, where he was sent to "root out the remnants of the Trotsky-Bukharin opposition." When asked about the reasons for his own arrest, Voronin answered: "A replacement of bases of support... Stalin had to remove all of us and install everywhere people who were devoted to him. This is a law of the revolutionary process. For people say: 'The revolution is conceived by dreamers, carried out by heroes, and its fruits are enjoyed by scoundrels.' Our revolution is no exception."[23]

Voronin's abstract arguments about the "law of the revolutionary process" are just as unconvincing as the excited exclamations from Shulubin. Much more convincing are his arguments in a debate with a younger prisoner, Sh., whom Filshtinsky calls a "state loafer of a new form, alien and even hostile to the revolutionary ideas of general egalitarianism." Sh., who became in 1938 "a rising star on the party Olympus," acted as the main accuser of Voronin as a person having "ties with Trotskyists." Political debates often arose between Voronin and Sh., arrested in 1949 as part of the "Leningrad affair."

"You have given birth to a whole generation of money-grubbers and thieves, and retreated from our party ideals," shouted Voronin, who was usually restrained when political questions were being discussed. "You helped Stalin rout the old party guard, and you became philistine functionaries. You are driven only by mercenary interests, for their sake you are ready to commit any lowdown trick; you destroyed hundreds of thousands of people devoted to Lenin's cause, you accused anyone you could of Trotskyism."

"And what about you, were you acting like a saint, did you spare your opponents?" Sh. shouted in reply. "Didn't you persecute the same Trotskyists and other deviationists? ... You turned the party and the people into a submissive herd, and now you shout about our cynicism... You say that you acted selflessly. But didn't you live like boyars with your privileged stores, when the country was starving because of your experiments? And we followed your example and tried to live a bit more sweetly."[24]

Of course, there is much that is justified in Voronin's reproaches. His generation indeed was not infected with the virus of cynicism and self-interest to the same degree as the generation which came to replace it. But in the arguments of Sh. there was also no small amount of truth. The ruthlessness of people like Voronin with regard to their party comrades, and their use of "natural" privileges paved the way for the following generation of apparatchiks, in whose consciousness there was nothing left resembling Bolshevism. And Voronin himself thought that the guilt of his executioners lay in the fact that they "charged anyone they could with Trotskyism." Obviously, like Aksenov, he felt that genuine Trotskyists deserved their fate.

A critical attitude toward their own conduct during the years of the Great Purge appeared among many Stalinists only after many years in prisons and in the camps. E. A. Gnedin, who censored the articles of foreign correspondents at the Moscow Trials, noted that, among the people he knew, "who were undoubtedly honest, and among them there were also extremely perceptive people, — I did not know a single one who dared to bear the burden of the worst logical conclusions drawn from an analysis of the political events of that time, and of the trials in particular."[25]

It is understandable that, among the bureaucrats implicated in the "secrets" of the Moscow Trials, there could not be people who, as Gnedin wrote, "dared to bear this burden." However, reference to the conduct of those around him could not serve as a self-justification. Gnedin himself came close to such a conclusion when he wrote about his own behavior: "I acted in accordance with my duties and placed the interests of the state, and the prestige of its foreign policy, above the truth. It would be naive to blame myself for this today, but how can I not remember that during those same days in the neighboring building NKVD investigators, in their own turn, in the name of the interests of the state — as they understood them — were disregarding the truth and forcing testimony from innocent people?"[26] In this way, Gnedin correctly placed the committing of a conscious outrage on truth in the name of "fulfilling one's duties" on a par with the conduct of sadistic investigators.

I have tried to review the accounts of the most varied people in order to sketch a picture of the extreme psychological and moral heterogeneity of the party during the years of the Great Purge. This heterogeneity "was overcome" as the bearers of Bolshevik consciousness were annihilated. Such an evolution of mass political inclinations — from devotion to Bolshevik ideals to complete ideological desolation — was captured by the writer N. Narokov, who emigrated to the West in 1944. Some of the judgments in his novel *Imaginary Quantities* appear today to be perceptive historical prognoses. This includes, for instance, the words which the head of the area directorate of the NKVD shares with his deputy in a state of inebriation and a moment of frankness: "Only have no doubt: if they order our communist party tomorrow to throw Lenin's corpse out of the mausoleum, to damn Karl Marx and spit on communism, then it will throw him out, curse and spit."[27] These words, which are hardly applicable to the circumstances of 1937, characterize better than anything else the behavior of many party bigwigs of a later period, who raised a real uproar at the end of the 1980s and beginning of the 1990s over the names of Marx and Lenin, as well as over the very idea of communism.

Even in the 1950s, many Bolsheviks who emerged from the camps had sadly become convinced that the party, to which they had given their entire lives, remained the party it had once been in name only. In this regard, Adamova-Sliozberg tells a remarkable story about an old Bolshevik whose sons are visited by their factory comrade, a member of the party committee. When he learns that their mother had joined the party in 1916, he tries to persuade her to rejoin the party by enticing her with a personal pension of union significance and other privileges. "Masha was silent for a bit, and then replied: 'No, I was never in your party, I was in quite another party.'"[28]

For Bolsheviks, even those who passed unscathed through the dark years of the 1930s, the truth of the Great Purge was not a revelation. Three months after Stalin's death, the Old Bolshevik Linde wrote to G. I. Petrovsky: "Isn't it time to grant a quiet old age to the victims of 1937-1938? ... On the other hand: the children of these victims have grown up... and they all must pretend that their fathers and mothers were enemies of the people. Isn't this an unbearable lie?"[29]

After becoming familiar with Khrushchev's report at the Twentieth Congress, Linde sent Petrovsky a letter in which he made broad generalizations concerning not only Stalin's crimes, but also the political regime which had developed in the land as a whole: "How much that is new in recent times," he wrote. "True, not for you and me. But now it has become known for the broad party masses as well.... Just think more deeply about all the external manifestations: blue police jackets, police in the uniform of old city police, gold epaulets, which not even our enemies have any longer, the striking uniform of the bureaucrats, generosity for the elite, for the higher-ups of the organs of security, and all the other tinsel. Is this only tinsel or an attempt to return to the past? ... A horrible evil has been done. I feel sorry not only for people who perished at the height of their powers and talent, but I feel bad for the party, for our honest and beloved party, to which we gave both our youth and mature life, and which was so foully assaulted! I have many dossiers on the rehabilitation of comrades who died, and sometimes it seems as if I am the only living witness to a human life which was snuffed out for no reason. How long this rehabilitation will take!"[30]

Petrovsky's archives contain many such letters from party comrades, including those who were arrested but who, prior to the Twentieth Congress, did not dare to even ask for protection. I. G. Rogachevsky wrote from Magadan in January 1956: "If you are unable or you do not want to help me for some reason, I have a great favor to ask: do not send this letter anywhere else, but destroy it."[31]

Behind all this remains one of the cardinal questions which inevitably arise when thinking about the Great Purge: did there exist in the party and the land any genuine resistance to Stalinism? Were there people among the victims of the Great Purge who were actually "guilty" of criminal intent and actions against the Stalinist regime?

32. Was Anyone Guilty?

In almost all the works about the Great Purge, belonging to authors of the most varied political orientation, the absolutely arbitrary nature of Stalin's repressions is accepted as axiomatic. Paradoxically, both anti-communists and official Soviet critics of the "personality cult" share the idea that in the USSR in the 1930s there were neither enemies of the Soviet regime nor communist opponents of Stalin's totalitarianism.

An element of truth does exist in this view: in the 1930s there were no forces of capitalist restoration in the Soviet Union that took organized form. If the monarchists and White-Guardists had conducted any political struggle inside the country, place would have been found, of course, for a depiction of their "exploits" in the pages of the émigré press and in the works of western Sovietologists. However, up until now, no such accounts have been published.

The hatred borne by enemies of the October Revolution and the Soviet regime who lived in the USSR was deeply hidden. It came to the surface openly only during the Second World War, found expression in open collaboration with the fascist invaders, and then took ideological form in the writings of the right wing of the dissident movement in the 1960s to 1980s. Finally, it burst forth in the period of "perestroika" and "reforms," when the corresponding forces were given a chance to voice their political views.

However, in the 1930s, Soviet society was by no means completely paralyzed by Stalin's repressions. There existed various levels of resistance to Stalinism. We know of many cases when Soviet people risked their own lives in defending the good name of their slandered comrades. This was, so to speak, the first level of resistance to Stalinism and its repressive machinery. But there were other, higher levels of such resistance which arose mainly in the Bolshevik milieu. It came not only from the genuine Trotskyists. Unbeknownst to themselves, many other party members, who maintained a Bolshevik type of social consciousness and who were appalled by the profanation of the principles of the October Revolution, arrived at Trotskyist conclusions.

Newly available memoirs of eye-witnesses and participants of the events of those years, as well as published material from investigatory dossiers, overturn the conception of Solzhenitsyn's book *Gulag Archipelago* which suggests that the entire population of the USSR consisted of "rabbits" who dared not resist the violence and arbitrary rule, and that all arrests were made without any grounds. In forcing conceptions of this kind, Solzhenitsyn offers many examples of cruel sentences for absurd and insignificant reasons: a tailor sticks a needle into a newspaper and it pierces the eye in a portrait of Kaganovich; a watchman carrying a heavy bust of Stalin into a club wraps a strap around it which catches Stalin around the neck; a sailor sells a cigarette lighter to an Englishman; some older students who are fighting in a collective farm club accidentally tear some posters from the wall, and so forth.[1]

In Solzhenitsyn's opinion, "the trickle of political young people" began to flow only "it seems, in 1943 or 1944, when the first political circles in the schools distributed anti-Stalinist leaflets."*[2]

When it comes to the 1930s, Solzhenitsyn makes an exception only for the Trotskyists, who, as he put it, were "purely political — that you cannot take away from them." He calls all the remaining communists "orthodox"; supposedly even in prisons and the camps they retained their devotion to Stalin and Stalinism. In this milieu he finds only a few exceptions, which he knows from personal observation and from stories by prisoners who passed through the torture chambers of the NKVD in 1937-1938. He mentions communists who "spit on money, and everything personal," and for whom, despite all the ordeals which they experienced, "the communist faith was intrinsic, and sometimes the only meaning of the life they had left." One of these people was the Belorussian censor Yashkevich who "wheezed in the corner of the prison cell that Stalin was never Lenin's right hand, but a dog, and until he croaked there would be no good." Solzhenitsyn cites a story he heard about a Hungarian emigrant, Sabo, the commander of a partisan detachment during the Civil War, who told his cell-mates: "If I was at liberty now, I would round up my partisans, raise Siberia, march on Moscow and drive out all the scum."

Given all this, Solzhenitsyn states that the breakthrough, even for communists of this kind, came only in prison cells and "not one of them tried to fight ... if only the day before his arrest."[3] The following circumstances helped reinforce the idea that all Bolsheviks blindly believed in Stalin and Stalinist socialism. The most active oppositionists were sifted in the prisons and camps through a thick filter of secret informers. The acknowledgment — even in a

---

* M. Baitalsky, who, unlike Solzhenitsyn, was familiar with the events of the 1930s firsthand, recalls how, in May 1936, he had met in prison "many boys from circles that had gathered for the reading and discussion of works by Marx and Lenin. They received five years in the camps." (Baitalskii M., *Tetradi dlia vnukov* [manuscript], p. 150).

private conversation — that one remained faithful to his Trotskyist convictions threatened immediate execution. Even after Stalin's death, to say something about one's former oppositional activity meant to doom oneself, in the best case, to the preservation of any prior conviction. Therefore, in the memoirs of surviving Trotskyists, there is meager information about their oppositional work (legal or illegal).

The investigatory dossiers of 1937-1938 provide a completely different picture of political moods than the one given by Solzhenitsyn. There would be incomparably more such accounts if the "free" and "independent," "democratic" press did not use the opening of the Russian archives in order to shift attention from evidence of resistance to Stalinism to the sterile search for documents compromising Lenin and the Bolsheviks from the revolutionary period.

However, even a relatively few publications of recent times allow us to make significant adjustments to the traditional interpretation of the Great Purge. In this regard, let us dwell for a moment on the investigatory and trial material of the prominent Soviet physicist L. D. Landau.

It would seem that a young, non-party scientist who was completely devoted to his work should have been distant from politics, and that his arrest might serve as an example of the absolutely capricious nature of the political repressions. However, from Landau's investigatory dossier we learn that he confessed to participating in the preparation of an anti-Stalinist leaflet. Landau's colleague, the communist Korets, who was tried in the same case and who spent two decades in prisons and camps, recounted later that he wrote the text of the leaflet that they intended to distribute to the columns of demonstrators on 1 May 1938.

The contents of the leaflet are no less radical than the documents of the Trotskyists and Riutin supporters, and deserve to be cited in full.

> Proletarians of all lands, unite!
> Comrades!
> The great cause of the October Revolution has been foully betrayed. The nation is drowning in rivers of blood and filth. Millions of innocent people have been thrown into prison, and no one can know when his turn will come. The economy is collapsing. Hunger is approaching.
> Can you not see, comrades, that the Stalinist clique has carried out a fascist coup? Socialism remains only on the pages of newspapers which tell nothing but lies. In his diabolical hatred of genuine socialism, Stalin has equaled Hitler and Mussolini. Devastating the country for the sake of maintaining his own power, Stalin is turning it into easy prey for bestial German fascism.

Lev Landau as a student and in prison

The only escape for the working class and all the toilers of our country — is a decisive struggle against the fascism of Hitler and Stalin, the struggle for socialism.

Comrades, organize! Do not be afraid of the executioners from the NKVD. They are only capable of beating defenseless prisoners, capturing unsuspecting and innocent people, stealing the national wealth, and thinking up absurd trials about nonexistent conspiracies. Comrades, join the Anti-Fascist Workers' Party. Establish contact with its Moscow Committee. Organize groups of the AWP in the factories. Set up underground equipment. Prepare a mass movement for socialism through agitation and propaganda.

Stalin's fascism survives because of our lack of organization.

The proletariat of our country, which overthrew the power of the tsar and the capitalists, will be able to overthrow the fascist dictator and his clique.[4]

Even according to today's existing Russian legislation, this leaflet could not help but be classified as a call for the violent overthrow of power (or, to be more precise, of the ruling elite).

For all the charges made against him (to his actual deeds was added the charge of wrecking, which was dreamt up by the investigator), Landau was sentenced by a Special Board to eight years in prison. The very fact that he received such a relatively light sentence by the standards of the time indirectly shows that the preparation of a leaflet with an open call to overthrow Stalin's clique was not seen by the "organs" to be an exceptional event.

Many other leaflets have been found in the archives of the NKVD with no less merciless assessments of Stalin's regime than the leaflet of Korets-Landau:

> Esteemed comrade! For you, probably, like for all thinking people, it has become insanely difficult to live. A medieval terror, hundreds of thousands of innocent people tortured and shot by the NKVD, the best and most devoted members of the Soviet regime — this is only part of what lies ahead!!! The leaders of the Politburo are either mentally ill, or hirelings of fascism, trying to arouse the entire population against socialism. They do not listen and do not know that over the last years millions have abandoned the Soviet regime because of these methods of rule, and friends have become sworn enemies.
>
> Eternal memory to the legendary heroes of the Red Army who died from the bloody hand of the NKVD, Comrades Bliukher, Bubnov, Tukhachevsky, Yegorov and others.
>
> By the hundreds of thousands, our regime ... in violation of the Constitution, is arresting Soviet citizens, the great majority of whom are guilty of nothing; it is exiling and shooting them... Everyone is afraid of saying a word, everyone fears one another. Our regime is Stalin and his bureaucrats, toadies and scoundrels without honor or conscience.
>
> Comrades by birth. Remove your caps and get on your knees before the suffering of the people and your comrades in struggle... Before you are rivers of blood and seas of tears. There is but one directive of the extraordinary congress: Stalin and the Stalinists must be destroyed.[5]

More accurate words to characterize Stalin's crimes could hardly be found today. In leaflets written by various people or groups of people, we inevitably detect not only their angry protest against the arbitrary rule, but also a clearly formulated juxtaposition of the degenerated Stalinist clique to millions of honest supporters of Soviet power and socialism. We are also struck by the fact that the authors of the leaflets signed them on behalf of either an extraordinary party congress, or an "anti-fascist workers' party," trying to create an impression of the existence in the country of an organized communist underground.

The content of these leaflets shows that their authors, like the Korets-Landau group, argued and acted in the spirit of Trotsky's appeals for a political revolution aimed at the liquidation of Stalin's regime while preserving the social gains of the Soviet regime.

Returning to the Landau case, let us note that his fate unfolded in a unique way compared to the fate of others who tried to fight against the Stalinist regime. After the academician Kapitsa and the famous Danish physicist Niels Bohr turned to Stalin with an appeal to free Landau, the latter was released under the personal guarantee of Kapitsa. However, the charge that Landau engaged in anti-Soviet activity remained in force right up until 1990, when he was rehabilitated.

If we cleanse the many investigatory dossiers of expressions such as "anti-party," "anti-Soviet," "counter-revolutionary," "slanderous," and so forth, usually written into the interrogation transcript by the investigators, then what emerges is a picture of widespread oppositional moods, shared even by prominent party figures. Thus, Orakhelashvili, one of the oldest Georgian Bolsheviks and former chairman of the Georgian Sovnarkom, said during interrogation: "I referred slanderously to Stalin as dictator of the party, and I considered his politics to be excessively cruel... Being closely tied to Sergo Ordzhonikidze, I witnessed his protective and conciliatory attitude toward bearers of anti-party and counter-revolutionary moods... In particular, I was a witness when Budu Mdivani, in a conversation with Sergo Ordzhonikidze, expressed his dissatisfaction with the party leadership."[6]

As one becomes acquainted with material from investigatory dossiers, it is possible to arrive at the following conclusions. Whereas at the open trials Stalin forbade any talk of the actual political motives of the oppositionists, from the investigations he demanded a thorough exposure of these motives. Upon receiving the testimony of those under investigation, he would learn what many Bolsheviks thought of his "socialism." This in turn gave an impulse to unleashing more of the Great Terror.

A comparison of many testimonies with the statements of "non-returners" (cf. chapters 39-40) shows convincingly that the Old Bolsheviks for the most part were neither blinded nor deceived. Much of what was said nationwide after the Twentieth Congress was clear to them even in the 1930s.

By no means everything in the testimony of the accused was, to use the expression of the 1930s, a "novel" placed in their mouths by investigators. Of course, there was no shortage of invented testimony of the lowest sort in the activity of the investigators, especially in the provinces. However, the investigators conducting the cases of prominent party members, Chekists, and others had assignments to obtain information about the actual political moods of these people and those around them. At the disposal of the investigators were agents' reports collected over many years, reflecting the true opinions of Stalin's political opponents.

In this regard, the case of L. M. Subotsky is extremely interesting; in the 1930s he occupied two seemingly incompatible posts: assistant to the main military prosecutor and editor of the *Literary Gazette*. But even this person, who was called upon to be the legal and ideological custodian of the regime, shared oppositional moods to a certain degree. Testimony given against him states that he "made a hostile assessment of the inner-party regime; slanderously accused the party leaders of bureaucratism, red tape, and inactivity; charged them with suppressing the activity of the masses and forbidding the free expression of political views," and spoke about "the savagery of the GPU, whose functionaries are above the law." In Subotsky's dossier the following statement is recorded: famine in the Ukraine and the Northern Caucasus had been prompted "by the cruel policies of party leaders who, in carrying out the forced collectivization of agriculture, are exterminating the most cultured peasants."[7] All of this, it would seem, would be sufficient grounds to be viciously persecuted for "anti-Soviet agitation," at the very least. However, soon after Subotsky was sentenced to six years in the camps, his case was closed and he was set free. In the future, he worked as deputy main editor of the journals *Krasnaia nov'* [Red Virgin Soil] and *Novyi mir* [New World], and during the war, as deputy prosecutor on several fronts.

Of course, leniency of this kind was not extended to the Old Bolsheviks who occupied higher positions than Subotsky. In this regard, let us consider the case of A. Kh. Artuzov, one of Dzerzhinsky's closest associates. In the 1920s, he headed the operations "Trust" and "Syndicate"; lured Savinkov and Sidney Reilly to the USSR; and in the 1930s, supervised the recruitment of the group of graduates from Cambridge University who for several decades passed valuable information to Soviet intelligence.

Artuzov was accused of having worked for German intelligence since 1925, for the French since 1919, and for the English even earlier from 1913. But even in this thoroughly falsified case, there is testimony given by the defendant which Yezhov's investigators would be incapable of inventing. Artuzov declared that the political program which Bukharin, Rykov, Tomsky and Tukhachevsky shared consisted in restoring foreign concessions; achieving the entry of Soviet currency onto the world market; cancelling the limits on foreigners entering and leaving the USSR; allowing a free choice in the forms of agriculture — from collective farms to single farms; introducing a broad amnesty of political prisoners and free democratic elections; and establishing freedom of speech, press, trade unions and assembly. As we can see, he is talking about an entirely realistic political program, aimed not at destroying, but reinforcing, the principles of socialism.

In recounting his conversations with Yagoda, Artuzov said: Yagoda told him that, in the country as a whole and in the party, what dominates is dissatisfaction with the leadership, "whose despotism stands in crying contradiction to declarations of Soviet democracy."[8]

Even at the very height of the Great Terror, such political discontent appeared in the behavior of communists and people not in the party who remained at liberty. This can be seen in part from documents obtained from the party archives of Zaporozhe. Thus, in a statement sent to the area control commission, the communist Teleshko wrote about the "absolute power of the apparatus" and of the "unbelievable inner-party Stalinist clamp-down." At a meeting dedicated to a discussion of the draft of the constitution, Yakhno, a student at the medical training college, declared: "In the USSR we have no democracy, and there will be none, since everything has been done and is being done as the dictator Stalin dictates." Anti-Stalinist leaflets were distributed at factories in Zaporozhe, and a sign appeared on the wall of a steel mill: "Comrades, beware, Russia is dying. Stalin is exterminating the people. CC VKP(b)."[9]

One more source for characterizing the genuine moods of the Soviet people during the years of the Great Purge is their letters to influential people in the land, to deputies of the Supreme Council and others. Thus, the theme of repressions is addressed in 400 letters located in the deputy's archive of A. N. Tolstoi. It is curious that Tolstoi saved these letters until the end, in spite of their dangerous content and the unflattering assessments of his own behavior found within them. These letters to the deputy can be divided into three groups.

The first group consists of letters not only signed by their authors, but containing their return addresses. In one of these letters, V. V. Kalinin tells of the fate of his arrested brother and notes: "I know beforehand that you can do nothing, that you can help in no way. You receive hundreds of letters with similar content. I ask you not on behalf of my brother, I have another reason for turning to you." Knowing from the press that Tolstoi was working on a book about Stalin, Kalinin sent him the following words: "Can it really be that there is no defense from careerists, toadies, and cowards who earn their bread on each slogan, yesterday for collectivization, today for vigilance... Can it really be that you, a deputy, are created only in order to shout hurrah for Stalin and to applaud Yezhov?" Asking the writer to send his letter to Stalin, Kalinin wrote: "Do not fear, I am not mad, I am a living person, I have a family, I have a son, I have work which I love, I am not a careerist, I am not a toady... A coward? — Perhaps, but no more so than others. But right now the feeling of truth is stronger to me than the fear of ten years in the camps."[10]

A. V. Filippchenko, the wife of a famous scientist sentenced to ten years without right of correspondence,* also risked her own freedom when she wrote that she had learned from one of her husband's cell-mates who had been set free, that his confessions were obtained by using "extremely cruel coercive measures, those which a man cannot bear."[11]

---

* A sentence of "ten years without right of correspondence" usually meant that the victim had been executed.

The second group of letters was also signed, but without any indication of the return address. This group includes the letter from Kozub, who stressed that no acknowledgment by the people would be forthcoming for authors who "write lies, who act as toadies in the existing structure and who praise only the name of Stalin, who has caused people to weep and who created an artificial famine in which *millions* died."[12]

Soloviev from Tashkent reproached the writer for remaining silent about the status of millions of Soviet prisoners. "Do you know that prisoners live in nightmarish conditions, that they are not considered human beings... and that therefore they are dying a slow and torturous death?" Soloviev wrote that during the Civil War he had served in the Red Army, but that after he had been sent into exile in 1931 "as a prophylactic measure," he had shifted into an illegal status.[13]

The third group of letters, containing the boldest and most denunciatory statements, were sent without a signature. In one such letter, an unnamed woman refers to a speech Tolstoi had given about Jewish pogroms in Germany and notes that the fate of prisoners in the torture chambers of the NKVD was by no means easier. After citing many examples of the jailers' sadism, she wrote: "Horror is generally in the air from stories about Astrakhan. There they have spared neither young nor old, and one woman who was led to despair by interrogations threw herself from the third story and smashed to the ground before people passing by. Can it be that the affairs in Astrakhan do not cry out?... Can it be that you will remain silent?"[14]

In response to the same speech, another correspondent wrote that the German Jews "can cry and wail, and the whole civilized world, including you, my esteemed writer, can protest and be indignant." As opposed to this, innocent women who were living in Soviet camps and "who have already lost their minds from fear, ... do not have the right to send a letter asking: why? why? why?!"[15]

One anonymous letter serves as an impassioned invective against the Stalinist regime. It reads: "People who call themselves fathers of the homeland, people who have become the leaders of the nation, — suddenly bring down upon our heads the foulest, most savage and senseless terror! Across the entire face of suffering Russia one hears the wail and moan of victims of sadists who call themselves 'the vigilant eye of the revolution.' Two years of savage, open mockery. You know... about this cynical outburst... and you remain silent. Where, then, is the truth for a writer of the Russian land?" Noting that the "bloody affair has passed, and that the gracious citizens have satisfied themselves by muttering something about the end of the Yezhov period," the author writes that those who were released from prison had turned into "moral and physical cripples."[16]

It seems to me that the strongest letter is from a woman who tells how she tore up a portrait of Tolstoi after reading an article which outlined the content of his novel *Grain*. "You appeared to me to be an instrument which would never, under any circumstances, be able to emit a false note," she writes in her letter. "And suddenly I hear, instead of a beautiful melody, the squeal of a fattened pig, transported from delight at the sound of slops being dumped into his trough... For in *Grain* you work in the claim that the revolution triumphed thanks only to Stalin. In your book, even Lenin is Stalin's pupil... That is of course a device used by cheats... You show Trotsky to be a traitor. You are a wretch after this! A pygmy standing next to this most honest giant of thought! For it sounds like a joke that he and thousands of the noblest people, real Bolsheviks who have now been arrested, were trying to restore capitalism in our land... No one believes this!"

The author of the letter arrives at profound generalizations about the fate of a country in which "a wave of reaction has spread," and millions of people are suffocating in poverty and a stifling intellectual atmosphere. "The best people, who are devoted to Lenin's idea, and who are honest and incapable of being bought, are sitting behind bars, they are being arrested by the thousands, they are being shot. They cannot bear the grandiose Baseness which is triumphing throughout the land, and they are leaving this life, committing suicide... Arbitrary rule and violence are leaving bloody marks on Soviet soil. The dictatorship of the proletariat has turned into the dictatorship of Stalin. Fear — is the dominant feeling which seizes citizens of the USSR... The party has abandoned the masses, and has turned into a dictatorial party... Lenin's shining idea has been replaced by Stalin's convulsive efforts to hold on to power. Where is the majestic pathos which in October moved millions to mortal combat? Overcome by the fetid breath of Stalin and yes-men like you, the age-old idea of socialism has wilted like a wildflower in the sweaty hands of a bastard!"[17]

In all these letters there is not a single anti-Soviet statement, they are all written from the position of people who are in pain over the destruction of the edifice erected by Bolshevism.

33. Oppositionists in the Camps

Information about the thoughts and behavior of the oppositionists must have disturbed Stalin particularly. While the majority of the opposition leaders had issued statements of capitulation after moving from comfortable conditions of existence to the difficult conditions of exile, thousands of rank-and-file Trotskyists remained unbroken even in places of confinement.

Until 1936, the majority of persecuted oppositionists were in exile and in political isolators — prisons for political prisoners, where the regime was relatively soft. In 1936, their mass transfer from places of exile to the concentration camps began. Parallel to this, the regime in the political isolators became much harsher. Just as they did in response to the first Moscow Trials, the oppositionists answered this with indignant letters to the party and secret police, which only increased the repressions against them. In February 1937, Yezhov signed an order demanding a trial for "those held in prisons of the Main Directorate of State Security, who have been sentenced to various terms of imprisonment, and who have sent me insulting declarations with regard to the introduction of the new prison regime." Among the people who were subject to new repressions because of this directive, we find the names of many Trotskyists, as well as the leader of the group of "Democratic Centralists," V. M. Smirnov, and one of the most irreconcilable "rightists," V. V. Kuzmin.[1]

At the February-March Plenum of the Central Committee, Stalin announced his plans regarding the Trotskyists and Zinovievists. Stating that they numbered about thirty thousand, he declared that of this number about eighteen thousand had already been arrested. Thus, "somewhere around twelve thousand, perhaps, remain from the old cadres, ... whom we will soon shoot."[2] Of course, these cannibalistic statements did not enter into the published text of his speeches.

Meanwhile, in the camps the oppositionists resorted to collective acts of protest. For instance, in August 1936, the Trotskyists who were in Kolyma declared a hunger strike, after sending statements to the Central Executive

Solomon Serbsky (1907-1937)   Evgeniia Zakharian (1901-1937)

Committee and the NKVD demanding that they be placed under a regime for political prisoners. On the thirteenth day of the hunger strike, the administration resorted to forced artificial feedings, as a result of which the condition of many hunger-strikers sharply deteriorated. After a while, the demands of the participants in the hunger strike were granted, the Trotskyists began to be held as a group, and husbands and wives were allowed to live together (if they had children — then they too could join them).³

In one of the camps which held 190 Trotskyists, the center of their personal contact became the barracks room in which the couple Serbsky and Zakharian lived with their child. In a guard's report, they were charged with the following "crime": "Their son of four to five years perks up when he hears the names of leaders of the working class of the USSR from children of the free employees, but his mother categorically and threateningly forbids him to accept them and pronounce them... He is being raised, cut off from the joys of our Soviet reality and the happy life of children, and is being forged as a future Trotskyist."

Serbsky and Zakharian turned out to be among the first for whom a new "camp" case was fabricated (before this, they had already been arrested five times). In September 1937, they both were sentenced to the death penalty, and shot a month later.⁴

At about the same time, T. I. Miagkova was subjected to investigation and trial. At the end of the 1920s, she was a member of the All-Ukrainian underground center of the opposition. In 1928, she was sent into exile for three years in Astrakhan, where she worked as Rakovsky's secretary and participated in making leaflets demanding Trotsky's return from exile and the release of oppositionists from prison. In 1929, after submitting a declaration

33. Oppositionists in the Camps

Tatiana Miagkova in 1929

Tatiana Miagkova (1898-1937)

about breaking with the opposition, she was released ahead of schedule. In 1932, together with other participants of the group led by I. N. Smirnov, she returned to illegal oppositional activity and was arrested for a second time. From 1933, she was held in the Verkhneuralsk political isolator, and then in exile in Kazakhstan. In June 1936, she was arrested in Alma-Ata, and sent to Kolyma camps for five years.[5] Here she worked at first as an economic planner, lived in a comfortable barracks for employees, received the same pay as free employees, and enjoyed the right to conduct unlimited correspondence.

As Miagkova's friend, M. Varshavskaia, recalls, Miagkova told Mosevich, the head of the secret political department of the Magadan UNKVD, who had been convicted in the trial of the Leningrad Chekists in 1935: "They will destroy not just us. They will destroy you, too, because you know that we (Trotskyists – V. R.) did not kill Kirov."[6]

In the fall of 1937, Miagkova was arrested because she started a conversation with her old comrade, Poliakov, who was passing by her barracks among a prison convoy of Trotskyists. In response to a guard's demand that she step away from the column, she shouted: "Fascists, fascist hirelings, I know neither women nor children are spared under this regime. Soon there will be an end to your arbitrary rule."[7]

In the 1950s, the former oppositionist S. Smirnova, told how, in the summer of 1937, Miagkova, as well as other Trotskyists, were brought to Magadan from the distant camps in order to face new charges. They put the prisoners in a large barracks with two-tiered bunks. At night, a team of guards would appear in the barracks and read a list of those sentenced. On one of those nights, they called out Miagkova's name.

The last letter from Miagkova to her relatives is dated the eighteenth of September. A month later she was sentenced to death on the following charges: while in prison camp, she systematically established contact with imprisoned Trotskyists; she maintained a hunger strike for six months; and she expressed counter-revolutionary, defeatist ideas.

At the end of 1937, massive measures began to be taken to liquidate "the organizers and instigators of delays (i.e., strikes – V. R.) among the Trotskyists." In the 1950s and 1960s, the relatives of the victims of these extermination operations were refused a party rehabilitation of their loved ones. The majority of Trotskyists were fully rehabilitated along legal and party lines only at the end of the 1980s.

The situation of Trotskyists in the camps was complicated by the fact that prisoners who were among the most unquestioning or most frightened Stalinists continued to nourish and display a sincere hatred of them. In memoirs written in the 1960s, one of these "orthodox" Stalinists told of his first prison-camp encounter with Trotskyists. In Magadan, where, in his words, "they met us (who had been arrested) as workers and people required for major construction and for mining gold, which the nation needed greatly," one of the old imprisoned Trotskyists walked up to the newly arrived convoy and said: "Well, comrade Stalinists, have you received thanks from your wise father for your loyalty and devotion?" "I write about this detail," the author of the memoirs added to this story, "because the current opinion that 100 percent of those arrested in those years were innocent, is untrue. There were at that time real enemies of our socialist construction. Even in the camps they conducted anti-party work, and tried to weaken our Leninist convictions."[8]

An episode described in K. Simonov's novel *The Living and the Dead*, tells much about the relationship between Stalinists and Trotskyists in the camps. With obvious approval, Simonov tells how the main hero of the novel, brigade commander Serpilin, while a prisoner, "without long explanations beat to a bloody pulp one of his former colleagues in the Civil War, a Trotskyist who mistakenly chose him as his confidant and shared thoughts with him that the party had degenerated and the revolution had perished."[9]

By leading each party member from 1923 through a series of pogrom-like campaigns, where an unchanging condition for survival was the expression of bitter hatred for "Trotskyism," Stalin introduced profound dissension in the party which did not die down even under camp conditions. Among people who were assigned to them "by mistake," increased cruelty against "Trotskyists" was only intensified by the thought that those to blame for their misfortunes were genuine Trotskyists, who for them were indeed a danger to the state.

Historians will still have to determine who among those convicted under the article of KRTD (counter-revolutionary Trotskyist activity) actually be-

33. Oppositionists in the Camps

longed to the Trotskyists. Such a count might be facilitated by the fact that oppositionists who never issued declarations of capitulation were arrested in the first wave of the Great Terror and were held in the camps, as a rule, in compact groups. A comparison of several accounts about the number of genuine Trotskyists allows one to conclude that, in the Kolyma and Vorkuta camps alone, the number reaches into the thousands, and perhaps tens of thousands.

The camp administration was given an assignment: to create a particularly harsh regime for the Trotskyists. Insofar as the Trotskyists did not conceal their convictions and carried out collective acts of protest, they were subjected to savage extermination on orders from Moscow.

Meanwhile, the countless Stalinist amalgams gave birth to a serious paradox. The overwhelming majority of genuine Trotskyists were sent into the camps in 1936, when the Special Boards did not have the right to give more than five years of imprisonment. The majority of those who arrived in the camps in 1937-1938, when sentences of ten to twenty-five years were being given according to the article for "KRTD," never belonged to any opposition. The unquestioning Stalinist jailers were incapable of separating real Trotskyists from those who were placed under that article in the heat of the Great Terror. Therefore, among the thousands of Trotskyists there remained tens, and perhaps hundreds, who were not shot in the camps. Several of these made it to freedom after serving their sentences and took part in the Second World War.

One of those who survived, for instance, was A. R. Pergament, first arrested for oppositional activity in 1927 and sent into exile to the Viatka area for two years. After returning from exile, and right up until January 1935, he worked in Moscow as an assistant to the chairman of Gosplan. On 26 August 1936, he was sentenced by a Special Board to five years of prison. In the camps, he signed a group declaration to the CC of the VKP(b) and the Executive Committee of the Comintern with a demand to review the cases of Trotskyists. On 17 July 1938 he was sentenced to be executed; this sentence was changed by the Supreme Court of the RSFSR to ten years of prison.[10]

At the end of the 1940s, all former Trotskyists who remained at liberty became "repeaters" who were sent to the camps once again, without any new charges.

34. The Tragedy at Vorkuta

The most wide-scale operation directed at the mass annihilation of Trotskyists has been called the "Vorkuta tragedy."* News of it reached the West soon after the war — from former camp inmates who had wound up among the "displaced persons." Accounts by Suzanne Leonhard of Trotskyists who were victims of camp shootings at Vorkuta appeared at the beginning of the 1950s in Trotskyist publications of various countries.[1]

In 1961, the *Socialist Herald* published an article "Trotskyists at Vorkuta," written by a former Vorkuta prisoner who remained concealed behind the initials M. B. The article tells how, by 1937, several thousand oppositionists were located in the Vorkuta camps; since the end of the 1920s they had been held in exile and "to the end remained faithful to their platform and leaders." In the one camp alone where the author of the article was living, there were about a thousand "veteran" Trotskyists. Besides this, according to the author, in the camps of the Pechora territory there were several thousand prisoners who, "as former communists or Komsomol members, had belonged to the Trotskyist opposition, and then at various times and for various reasons... had been forced to repent of their 'mistakes' and leave the opposition."[2]

A large number of memoirs about the fate of Trotskyists in the Vorkuta camps was collected by B. I. Nicolaevsky. In 1952, he sent N. I. Sedova a letter with accounts from several former Vorkuta prisoners about the fate of Sergei Sedov. They recounted how in the summer of 1936, many Trotskyists arrived among the new convoys at the Vorkuta mines. This included both Trotskyists who had been recently arrested, and those who had been transferred from

---

* Insofar as this event was unprecedented in the history of Stalin's camps, A. Solzhenitsyn felt that it was necessary to devote several pages to it in his book *Gulag Archipelago* ("Novyi mir," 1990, № 11, pp. 83-86). However, he uses dubious sources in his description, to which he added, as usual, no small amount of ad-libbing, departing from the actual facts and reliable evidence.

Sergei Sedov's photos at time of arrest in 1935 by NKVD

other camps, political isolators, and places of exile. They were put in canvas tents, each of which was designated for 250 people. The group of Trotskyists containing Sedov was the largest and most highly organized at the mine.[3]

The Nicolaevsky collection contains a list compiled by one of the former prisoners of more than 100 active Trotskyists who arrived at Vorkuta in 1936 and were shot in March-April 1938. The list includes, in particular: the secretary of the party organization at FON (the department of social sciences) at Moscow State University and member of the Moscow Trotskyist center, the "organizer for higher education" Sokrat Gevorkian; one of the active participants of the Sapronov "Group of 15," Minkov, and his wife; Lado Yenukidze (the nephew of A. S. Yenukidze); the Moscow worker Krivtsov; the secretary of the Donbass group of "Zaboi" writers, Bagliuk; the secretary of the party organization of the Lugansk pedagogical institute, Deineka; member of the Moscow Center of Trotskyists, Magid; and others.[4]

The article, "Blood in the Tundra (from the memoirs of a Vorkuta prisoner)," states that Trotskyists in Vorkuta were "the only significant group of prisoners which offered resistance to the Stalinist dictatorship in an organized and stubborn way until the end, characterizing the regime as fascist."[5]

The most detailed portrayal of the events of 1936-1938 at Vorkuta is contained in the memoirs of Balashov, "The Vorkuta Tragedy." He tells how the

34. The Tragedy at Vorkuta

camp was organized in 1931 at the Vorkuta mines, and how in 1936 more than three thousand prisoners arrived, the largest group among them being "genuine, convinced Trotskyists." Their leaders were S. Gevorkian, Vladimir Ivanov, V. V. Kosior, Melnais (a major economist and former member of the Central Committee of the Komsomol), and Trotsky's former secretary, Poznansky.

In the fall of 1936, this group of Trotskyists declared a hunger strike, which had been preceded by collecting signatures beneath a declaration of "Bolshevik-Leninists," containing the following demands:

1. To cancel the illegal decision of the NKVD to transfer all Trotskyists from administrative exile to the camps. The cases of political opponents of the regime must be reviewed not by a Special Board, but at open court sessions;

2. The working day in the camp should not exceed eight hours;

3. The food for the prisoners should not depend on work quotas; performance should be stimulated not by bread rations, but by monetary awards;

4. To place the political prisoners in the barracks and the work sectors separately from the criminal elements;

5. To move the invalid political prisoners, women and old men from the arctic camps to places located in more temperate climatic conditions.

"In the conditions of the Soviet camps, this was an unprecedented mass hunger strike and protest by political prisoners," wrote Balashov. "About a thousand people participated in it, half of whom were living at the mine. Beginning on the 27th of October 1936, the hunger strike lasted 132 days and ended only in March 1937."

The forced artificial feeding of the starving saved many prisoners from death, but the number of those who were dying grew with every day. Many prisoners from neighboring camps joined the hunger strike, which threatened all the production plans and assignments. One of the hunger strikers told his wife about the strike through a local inhabitant. The wife was English by birth and citizenship, and she soon left the Soviet Union for her homeland. There, a number of newspapers published her letter about the hunger strike in the Soviet arctic region. The House of Commons made an enquiry about this matter for the English government.[6]

The hunger strike by the Trotskyists ended with their complete victory. In March 1937, they were sent a wireless message from Moscow: "Tell the starving prisoners of the Vorkuta Pechlag that all their demands will be met." Only after this message was the hunger strike halted. Almost all its participants who remained alive had to be hospitalized because they were so weak.

After a while, the Trotskyists returned to work. They were not sent into the mine shaft. They worked exclusively at surface locations, and several even in the office of the mine administration as accountants, bookkeepers, economists, etc. Their working day did not exceed eight hours, and their food did not depend on the completion of work quotas.[7]

Meanwhile, preparations were being made for reprisals against the Trotskyists that were to be carried out in the strictest secrecy with regard to the other prisoners. To this end, an old brick factory was chosen that was located 20 kilometers from the Vorkuta mine, far from any settlement. In the fall of 1937, large tents were set up there, surrounded by a thick network of barbed wire.

At the beginning of the winter of 1937-1938, around 1,200 prisoners were gathered at the brick factory. With the exception of seven or eight "religious prisoners," they were all communists who had joined the party before the revolution or during its early years.[8]

E. I. Kashketin arrived at Vorkuta at the beginning of 1938. He had been granted extraordinary powers according to NKVD order № 00409. The significance of the order can be judged by the two zeroes, which were used only in cases when the order was undertaken on Stalin's personal initiative.

Several details in the biography of Kashketin are worth noting. In September 1936, a medical commission declared him a group III invalid with a diagnosis of schizoid psychoneurosis. After this he was dismissed from the NKVD and sent to work in the Moscow Committee of the VKP(b). In January 1938, he was once again enlisted for service in the NKVD and sent to Vorkuta to lead the operational group for the struggle against Trotskyists.[9]

As M. M. Ioffe recalls, during an interrogation Kashketin assured her that "all the area committees, city committees and republic central committees have been infected with your Trotskyist heresy."[10]

One of the first to be interrogated was the Old Bolshevik and former member of the Central Committee of the Communist Party of Armenia Virab Virabov. As Balashov recounts, "returning from the interrogation accompanied by two guards, Virabov was shouting angrily and gesticulating: 'I will show you how to beat someone... To beat me, an old revolutionary, in the face... Stalinist scum, fascist executioners!..' His disheveled grey hair was blowing in the wind; distorted with malice and hatred, and with eyes blazing, his face was terrifying. The guards, clutching their sub-machine-guns in their hands, shuddered with every sharp outcry or gesture and slowed their steps."[11]

I. M. Poznansky was tortured with particular savagery during interrogation: "They tortured him, demanding some kind of special confessions. Stalin wanted to obtain as much material as possible that would discredit Trotsky."[12]

The interrogations, which had begun even before Kashketin's arrival, were replaced in March with group shootings. Almost daily, tens of prisoners were sent into the tundra, where they were met by a detachment of marksmen equipped with light and heavy machine-guns and "fastened," according to Kashketin's report, "at the place of carrying out the operation."

They shot not only the Trotskyists themselves, but any members of their families who were with them. "When a husband was shot, his imprisoned

34. The Tragedy at Vorkuta

wife was automatically sent to be shot; with the most significant oppositionists, their children who had reached the age of twelve were also subject to shooting."[13] The slaughter continued until slightly more than one hundred people remained alive.

In covering the traces of its crime, the camp administration ordered the removal of all structures in the vicinity of the old brick factory and the complete destruction of the factory itself. For two weeks in the summer, explosions of dynamite shook the tundra: they blasted the frozen earth at the "place of the operation" into order to at least somehow cover the corpses of those killed.

Today, documents signed by Kashketin have been published which concern the execution of sentences pronounced by the troika of the NKVD for the Arkhangelsk area "for newly committed crimes in the camp." The first document records the shooting of 173 prisoners on 1 March 1938. Among the names of those shot we find such "veteran" Trotskyists as Gevorkian, Yakovin, V. B. Eltsin and Brover. In a note accompanying the document, Kashketin states that the "operation" lasted ten hours. The next document recounts the shooting in March 1938 of 351 people, including V. V. Kosior, Poznansky, Dingelshtedt, and Radomyslskaia (Zinoviev's sister). Altogether, Kashketin and his command shot 2,901 prisoners.[14]

In recent years in Russia, memoirs of former prisoners in Stalin's camps have been published which contain stories about the Vorkuta tragedy.[15]

In the book *Tracing the Fate of My Generation*, A. Voitolovskaia tells of the Vorkuta tragedy and notes: "We know little about the last minutes of individual comrades, but as a whole they died just as they lived — without fear, steadfastly, heroically, preferring death to the betrayal of their youth and themselves. Their life and death should leave an indelible imprint in the consciousness of their contemporaries and of future generations."[16]

Isaac Deutscher's book cites an account by a prisoner of Stalin's camps, the Polish journalist Zinger, about how the thousands of prisoners from the Baltics, Western Ukraine and Western Belorussia who showed up in the camps in 1939-1940 did not meet any Trotskyists or Zinovievists among the old prisoners. "The older prisoners told about their execution in a whisper or by hints, because there was nothing more dangerous, even for an unfortunate prisoner, than to arouse the suspicion that he felt sympathy or pity for the Trotskyists." In this regard, Deutscher correctly notes that the mass slaughter of Trotskyists in 1937-1938 was the main reason that "during the remaining fifteen years of Stalin's rule no group was left in Soviet society, not even in the prisons and camps, capable of challenging him... A tremendous gap had been torn in the nation's consciousness. Its collective memory was shattered; the continuity of its revolutionary traditions was broken; and its capacity to form and crystallize any non-conformist notions was destroyed. The Soviet Union was finally left, not merely in its practical politics, but even in its hidden mental processes, without any alternative to Stalinism."[17]

35. Who Benefited from the Great Purge?

While at one pole of Soviet society there were the opponents of Stalin's regime who were doomed to die, at the other pole there were those who were living a good life indeed in 1937.

Such a broad-scale phenomenon as the Great Purge cannot fail to have its own social base — in the form of groups in the population who are vitally interested in the mass repressions. Stalin placed his bets on such groups, and official propaganda was primarily oriented toward them.

The Great Purge was a gigantic redistribution of positions in the social structure of society and the regime. Such a redistribution was determined most of all by the fact that the arrest of any highly placed person immediately resulted in the upward movement of not one, but several people. Following the replacement of such a person, what occurred was a rapid movement up the rungs of the career ladder by a number of people who consequently occupied the evacuated posts. And, insofar as people were being removed in "layers," this process occurred somewhat spontaneously, and many instantly jumped across several rungs, a movement which would have taken years under normal social conditions. As a result, the people promoted in 1937-1938 ended up in posts which could not have appeared in their dreams only a few years before. And, since most often they were young and politically inexperienced people who were not inclined to deep thoughts, they could not help but approve of everything which was taking place in the country; they sincerely praised Stalin, who had truly secured for them a better and more joyful life.

Shifts in the distribution of personal property were just as significant as those in the structure of the distribution of power. This process began earlier, in the years of collectivization, when the struggle against the kulaks amounted, not to the reduction of kulak accumulation by means of tax policy and other economic measures as the Left Opposition proposed, but to the ruthless expropriation of the property of families who were driven into the category of "kulak" or "near-kulak" and deported to remote regions of the country. In this process, the productive property of those who fell victim to dekulakization was handed over to the collective farms (precisely for this reason the official formulation referred to "rapid collectivization on the basis of liquidating the kulaks as a class"), and their everyday property (homes, clothing, domestic inventory, etc.) was given to fellow-villagers.

During the years of the Great Purge, the process of forced redistribution of property proceeded along far more devious paths. As a rule, a sentence according to Article 58 ended with reference to the confiscation of all property belonging to the convicted prisoner. Such mass confiscations affected primarily those layers who had been granted status and material privileges and who had managed to accumulate impressive wealth.

In citing the list of the property confiscated from his father, A. V. Antonov-Ovseenko writes that many things are missing from it which were evidently pocketed by the people carrying out the confiscation. "I can testify," he stresses with a kind of pride, "that my father's apartment did not resemble in the least the shop of a poor junk-dealer described in the document." The list did not include "original engravings by famous artists, a typewriter, a radio phonograph player with eight albums of records, his wife's jewelry, her squirrel coat, expensive French perfume... and much, much more."[1] In the 1930s, such things were available to only a very narrow, privileged layer.

The tragedy of families who were thrown from the ranks of the privileged into the ranks of society's outcasts was accompanied by the entry onto the road to success by the new "servants of the people." In place of the party, Soviet, economic, military and Komsomol cadres (who were being removed "in layers") came younger cohorts who, along with power, were given the attendant material privileges — from high pay and personal automobiles to spacious apartments and government dachas. It is superfluous to say what all this meant for people who had recently shared the poverty and deprivation that the majority of the country's population was enduring.

The confiscated property of people who had been arrested was handed over to the State, and a certain portion of it was redistributed "legally" (through "special trading centers") to the benefit of NKVD officials, apparently raising their interest in the bacchanalia of the Great Terror. A significant number of the apartments of the victims were also handed over to NKVD personnel. Besides this legalized looting, illegal looting was also widely practiced — the appropriation of things and valuables by agents who were on their toes during searches.

Mercenary gains from the repressions were derived not only by open and secret agents of the NKVD, but by volunteer informants, who used the circumstances of the hunt for "enemies of the people" to settle personal scores, to remove competitors at work, and sometimes to openly extort material benefits. The Eighteenth Congress of the VKP(b) heard the story of the Kiev school teacher Mogilevskaia, who not only slandered honest people, but, by intimidation and blackmail, extorted money and trips to resorts from various organizations. When those in charge refused to lend her such "assistance," she would write denunciations declaring them enemies of the people.[2]

To use Engels's words, more qualified "scoundrels who knew how to coin profit from the terror"[3] shamelessly unleashed their criminal instincts in other ways. For example, the article "Marx," which had been prepared by the famous philosopher Sten for the *Great Soviet Encyclopedia*, was published after Sten's arrest under the name of Mitin, the man Stalin had promoted "on the philosophical front." When this plagiarism was disclosed at the beginning of the 1960s, Mitin escaped with a small scare and retained his positions at the academic Olympus right up until his death in 1987.

The type of crafty agent who significantly raised his social status in 1937 is described in A. Solzhenitsyn's novel *Cancer Ward* under the name of Rusanov. In the first years after Stalin's death, Rusanov feared the return from the camps of his former co-worker and neighbor Rodichev, whom he had slandered. Rusanov recalled: "Kapa (Rusanov's wife) planned the following: as soon as they arrested Rodichev, then they would immediately evict Katka Rodicheva and seize the entire apartment, and the balcony then would be all theirs... The operation with the room was all agreed upon, and they came to evict Katka, but she pulled a fast one — she declared that she was pregnant. They demanded verification — and she produced a certificate. And by law a pregnant woman could not be evicted. It took until the next winter to evict her, and for long months they had to put up with her, and live side by side — while she bore her child, gave birth, and then completed her maternity leave."

Rusanov recalled 1937 and 1938 as a "wonderful and honorable time," when "the social atmosphere was noticeably cleansed, ... and people of principle who were steady and devoted, both he and his friends, walked in dignity with their heads held high."[4]

It was precisely people like Rusanov, who had entered the circle of the new Soviet elite, who comprised the social base of the Great Purge. Their swift climb upwards had been even easier because the occupation of posts in the apparatus in those years did not demand past accomplishments, special knowledge or professional preparation (besides taking, in some cases, party courses of short duration, where the newly promoted "studied" an uncomplicated selection of Stalinist dogmas and falsification). It was to just such people, "awaiting their promotion," that Stalin issued his call at the February-March Plenum of the Central Committee in 1937, and they understood all too well the meaning of such a call.

Stalin's directive was widely seized upon by the entire propaganda machine, which tirelessly repeated that enemies of the people were preventing the promotion "of young and remarkable cadres," and keeping down the "new, fresh forces." The newspapers printed appeals to "more boldly promote into the party organs our talented Soviet youths, educated by the Stalinist epoch," those who were "merciless toward enemies" and "experienced in the struggle against enemies of the people." Mikhail Koltsov exultantly wrote that thousands of people who considered themselves "small and modest cogs" were being promoted "to ever greater, yes, ever and ever greater and more responsible work."[5] At the height of the massacre of the commanding staff in the army, Voroshilov declared at a meeting of lieutenants: "Each one of you is potentially a marshal."[6]

Party bosses speaking at the Eighteenth Congress eagerly cited figures of those promoted in their eparchies. It was stated that, in 1938 alone, 2,942 people were promoted to party work in Kiev, and to Soviet and economic work — 11,700 "party and non-party Bolsheviks."[7]

It is not true that all Soviet people lived in 1937-1938 in constant fear and nightly expectation of arrest. The representatives of the latest layer of "promotees" were completely free of such fears since, up until then, they had possessed neither a political biography nor dangerous ties. Much to their own surprise, they had completed in just a few months the ascension from a modest engineer or petty office worker to secretary of an area committee or chairman of the executive committee of a city council. They had moved into the vacated apartments that had been built for the party and governmental elite; received at their disposal private chauffeurs and other "services"; visited plush sanatoriums and other closed, "perquisite" social establishments that they had never seen before. The majority of these people happily made it through the war, since, located as they were at their bureaucratic posts, they were not subject to being called into the army.

It was precisely because it had been undermining the positions of this social layer, which had managed to become firmly accustomed to their bureaucratic omnipotence and to their privileges, that the policy of de-Stalinization was conducted so halfheartedly and inconsistently under Khrushchev, and was so quickly overturned after he was deposed.

In order to more clearly envision the social profile of the "new recruits of 1937," it would be appropriate to provide at least a brief description of their composition.

36. The New Recruits of 1937

The age composition of the apparatchiks at the end of the "cadre revolution" can be seen by examining statistics from the mandate commissions of the Eighteenth Congress of the VKP(b) (March 1939) and the Eighteenth All-Union Party Conference (February 1941). About half the delegates to the Eighteenth Congress with deciding votes were no older than 35 years; 81.5 percent were no older than forty.[1] Among the delegates to the Eighteenth Party Conference, 35.6 percent were people up to 35 years of age; 42.8 percent were from 36 to 40.[2]

No less significant is the composition of delegates to the Eighteenth Party Conference according to length of party membership. Forty-five percent of them joined the party in 1927-1928, 35 percent in 1929 or later. Thus, the overwhelming majority of those who ran the country in 1941 were children or adolescents during the years of the October Revolution and civil war; they became communists at a time when the existence of party discussions and legal oppositions was no longer possible.

Of the 71 members and 68 candidate-members of the Central Committee elected at the Eighteenth Congress, 44 and 66 respectively were elected to this body for the first time. Among the new members and candidate-members there were only six people who had been in the party before the revolution, and four who had been party members since 1917. By comparison, at the Seventeenth Congress, out of 71 members of the Central Committee only ten were elected for the first time, passing over the candidate's stage for the CC; and of the candidate-members, more than half had belonged to Central Committee bodies elected at previous party congresses. Among those who entered the CC for the first time, the majority had joined the party no later than 1917.[3]

In April 1917 the party had more than 100,000 members and, by August 1917, its membership grew to 240,000.[4] Tens of thousands more people joined the party in the last months of 1917. In 1973, 702 people remained in the

Aleksei Kosygin as a student at a textile institute in 1935

Andrei Gromyko as a student in 1931

CPSU who had been in the party since before February 1917, and 3,340 people who joined the party in 1917.[5] A significant number of these people had spent many years in Stalin's prisons and camps, and some had been preserved by Stalin as "party icons" to illustrate the continuity of the party of Lenin and Stalin.

The scale of the "cadre revolution" carried out between the Seventeenth and Eighteenth Congresses can be seen in the figures cited by Stalin himself, which, in his opinion, served to illustrate the success of his cadre policy. Stalin announced that during this period "more than 500,000 young Bolsheviks, in the party and close to it,"[6] had been promoted to leading party and governmental posts.

As he was describing how the fourth or fifth layer of apparatchiks occupied leading posts after the Great Purge (the previous layers had been almost entirely exterminated), Khrushchev noted that these were people "without any revolutionary past, without kith or kin you might say, if you were talking about revolutionary activity."[7]

In place of several generations of Bolsheviks (sixty-, fifty-, and forty-year-olds), almost entirely consumed by the fires of the Great Purge, came a generation of people who only recently had crossed the thirty-year threshold. From them, Stalin could expect unreserved conformism and unquestioning, unthinking obedience during any shifts in his political course.

To illustrate the rapidity with which the promotions of these people occurred, let us cite several biographical facts about those who later ran the party and the nation.

Brezhnev was born in 1906, became a party member in 1931, and in 1936 worked as the director of a technical school. In 1937, he was promoted to the post of deputy chairman of the executive committee of the Dneprodzerzhinsk city committee and, in 1939, to the post of secretary of the Dnepropetrovsk party area committee.

Kosygin was born in 1902, and was a party member from 1927. In 1937 he held the post of engineer, and from there he was promoted to director of a small Leningrad factory. In 1938 he occupied ever more responsible posts in the Leningrad area committee and the area executive committee. In 1939 he was appointed People's Commissar of Textile Production in the USSR and elected member of the Central Committee of the VKP(b). In 1940, he became deputy chairman of the Sovnarkom of the USSR.

Gromyko was born in 1909, and was in the party from 1931. Until 1939, he worked as a researcher at the Institute of Economics, and then suddenly was transferred to diplomatic work. In 1943, he occupied the post of ambassador from the USSR to the United States.

One can see how such people were selected for responsible positions from Molotov's story about searching for a candidate for the vacated post of People's Commissar of Finances of the USSR. After asking that he be presented with a list of party members who had finished the finance institute, Molotov looked at their personal dossiers and decided on the candidacy of Zverev, who at that time was secretary of one of the Moscow regional committees.[8]

Many people who were promoted filled the vacuum of leading figures at the same enterprises where they had been sent after finishing the institute. Thus, V. A. Malyshev, who finished a technical school in 1937, was sent to the Kolomenskoe machine-building factory, where he was immediately appointed chief engineer. There were no other candidates for this position, since all the engineers who had worked at this major enterprise had been arrested.[9] In 1939, Malyshev was elected to the Central Committee and appointed People's Commissar of Heavy Machine-Building, and a year later — deputy chairman of the Sovnarkom of the USSR.

Several promotees who could not cope with their new duties, not only because of their lack of experience, but also because of the disorganization of production as a result of the innumerable arrests, fell under the steamroller of repressions themselves. Shreider recalled meeting with a young man in a prison cell who told him that, while studying in his last year at the aviation institute, he was suddenly summoned to the People's Commissar of the Aviation Industry, M. M. Kaganovich. There he learned of his appointment as head of the Central Aerodynamic Institute, where the entire management staff had by that time been arrested. Soon, the young head of the enormous institute was confirmed as chairman of a government commission created to monitor quality control of a new military airplane. During tests, the plane crashed, and the famous pilot who was flying it, Chkalov, was killed. The chairman of the commission, along with all the other people having anything to do with testing the plane, were arrested.[10]

In many instances, worker-Stakhanovites who had no idea of management techniques were promoted to leading positions. Khrushchev recalled how the engineers who were placed under the famous Stakhanovite Diukanov complained about the "methods of leadership" used by the latter: "If something wasn't right or something wasn't done, then he had one argument: 'Watch out, or I'll spank your ass.' And twice a day, each one of us, the engineers, went to see him to be spanked."[11]

At the end of the Great Purge, even those whose closest relatives were enemies of Soviet power made their way into leading bodies — provided that they had no ties with the old Bolshevik milieu. In the 1970s, a member of the Politburo of the CPSU and first secretary of the Central Committee of the Communist Party of Kazakhstan, Kunaev, who had begun his climb up the career ladder at the end of the 1930s, erected a pompous monument on the grave of his father-in-law — the former merchant Yalymov, who had occupied a high post in Kolchak's administration in the city of Akmolinsk during the years of the Civil War. Kunaev was not embarrassed even by the fact that Yalymov's participation in the persecution of Bolsheviks had been described in a novel by the famous Kazakh writer Saken Seifullin who perished in 1937.[12]

The "recruits of 1937" were incomparably less competent and ideological than the people they replaced. With them, the devotion to Bolshevik ideals was replaced with a truly unlimited personal devotion to the leader and a readiness to zealously execute any directives coming from his office. The writer Chuyev, who was raised in this milieu, provides a remarkable story from the former secretary of the Central Committee of the Communist Party of Georgia, Mgeladze, about his conversation with Suslov, who enthusiastically said, "Understand, it is only thanks to Stalin that we have all risen so high. Everything we have is thanks only to Stalin."[13]

Right up until their last days, such people were inclined to glorify Stalin and acknowledge the "benefit" of Stalin's repressions. Thus, in the 1980s, Benediktov, a former minister of agriculture, stressed in an interview: "I think that Stalin used Beria, as well as Mekhlis, as a kind of 'truncheon of fear.' He used it to beat out of the leaders of all ranks, slovenliness, scatter-brained behavior, carelessness and the other ills we share... And, I have to say, such a method, even though not very attractive, worked effectively."[14]

Being sterile and "pure" in the sense of being free from any kind of political doubts, let alone dissenting thoughts, the "recruits of 1937" worried much less about moral purity in their everyday personal behavior. Many of them very quickly displayed a susceptibility to forms of corruption which were known to be impossible before the Great Purge. An example of this is the behavior of Usman Yusupov, who applied himself to the destruction of the first generations of Uzbek communists and was promoted in 1937 to the post of first secretary of the Central Committee of the Communist Party of Uzbekistan. During the war years it was discovered that Yusupov was the owner of his own cattle-breeding farm, a herd of racehorses, and an underground

36. The New Recruits of 1937

Suslov and Stalin

artel which had been producing wine sold through secret channels in cities throughout the Urals. When an inspector from the Central Committee of the CPSU related these facts to Malenkov, he received the following directive from the latter: "close the investigation, return immediately."[15]

Such facts were astounding for any unbiased person. In 1941, the academician Vernadsky recorded in his diary: "He (Stalin) made one basic mistake: under the influence of revenge or fear, by destroying the flower of the people of his party, he caused losses which are irreparable, since the real conditions of life lead to an enormous influx of the many thieves who continue to crawl into the party. The level of such people in the milieu in which I work, is clearly lower than non-party people."[16]

At the moment of Stalin's death, the "recruits of 1937" were, on the average, 50 years old. Having come to power when they were very young and then being schooled in Stalinist methods of leadership, these people were neither capable of, nor inclined to, restructuring their way of life or way of thinking. But they were sufficiently energetic to achieve the lifelong reinforcement of their positions of power and of their material privileges. They did not like the systematic rejuvenation of party cadres at all levels as stipulated by the new Statutes of the CPSU; nor did they like the growing desire in the party and non-party masses to expose the crimes of the past more boldly, and to democratize social and political life.

The interests and psychology of this irremovable layer, which had grown firmly accustomed to its bureaucratic omnipotence and to its privileges, corresponded fully to the political course established in the period of stagnation:

a refusal to undergo any serious changes, whether in the economic, social, and political structures which had developed, and in the personal composition of the leading cadres.

The ruling elite which had been promoted during the years of the Great Purge continued in power for half a century. As it became older and more feeble, the economic, social, and political system of Soviet society stagnated more and more. The social growth of the generation which had been formed intellectually under the influence of the Twentieth Congress of the CPSU was artificially held back.

Having removed Khrushchev, the Brezhnev clique not only placed an unconditional taboo on the further illumination and interpretation of the tragic lessons of Stalinism, but also took steps toward Stalin's gradual rehabilitation. Works of art were commissioned with this goal in mind, and carefully edited memoirs of Stalinists were published, restoring Stalin's prestige as a stern, but wise, governmental figure and great military leader. This meant a retreat even from the halfhearted and inconsistent thaw under Khrushchev.

The last prominent representatives of the generation of the "recruits of 1937" either died in the first half of the 1980s (Brezhnev, Kosygin, Suslov, Ustinov, Andropov, Chernenko), or went into retirement in the first years of "perestroika" (Gromyko, Tikhonov, Zimianin, Ponomarev and others). In their stead came a new generation of bureaucrats who had grown up under their aegis. They had paved the way to power through long years of service in the apparatus, gradual advancement up the steps of the party hierarchy, and obsequiousness or servility before those above them. Bureaucratic impunity and balancing in the world of bureaucratic games and intrigues turned the majority of the representatives of this generation into cynical and corrupted people, concerned exclusively with their own careers. When they received the freedom to act, they proved capable only of carrying out the dismantling of the socialist foundations of Soviet society, covering their activity with the deceptive slogans of "revolutionary perestroika" and "the rejuvenation and rebirth of socialism." Continually changing their slogans, these "heirs of the heirs" of Stalin led the nation with blindfolded eyes toward collapse, economic chaos, and political catastrophe. Thus the Great Purge redounded on the fate of our country a half century later.

37. Who Was Punished, and in What Way, After Stalin's Death?

The most glaring indicator of inconsistency in the exposure of Stalin's crimes was the leniency shown toward the people who most immediately carried them out.

In the 1950s, criminal proceedings were brought against only several hundred of Yezhov's and Beria's executioners. In the majority of cases, even when the victims who survived the terror provided direct information about their inquisitors, this did not lead to the latter's punishment. Thus, in 1955, the Old Bolshevik Lazurkina sent the Central Committee a statement which said that the former NKVD investigators Galkin and I. P. Karpov had used brutal torture against her and the former secretary of Leningrad area committee of the VLKSM, Utkin. After verifying these facts, the Special Inspection of the NKVD adopted a resolution which stated: "Karpov denies the use of coercive measures against Utkin. It is impossible to confirm Utkin's statement by means of other evidence." Having thereby shown that they trusted an executioner more than his victims, the officials of the Special Inspection limited themselves to telling Karpov that he "had received from Utkin testimony which does not correspond to reality." With regard to Galkin, it was noted that he "is judged favorably according to his work," and therefore his punishment must be limited to a demotion.[11]

Even when an investigation established indisputable proof of the guilt of former investigators, they were subjected to extremely mild forms of punishment. One of the examples of this is when the Party Control Committee looked into the crimes of G. G. Karpov, who had worked at the end of the 1950s as chairman of the Council on Affairs of the Russian Orthodox Church under the Council of Ministers of the USSR. As indicated in the Committee's report, Karpov, who in the 1930s had occupied high posts in the Leningrad directorate and the Pskov district department of the NKVD, "conducted mass arrests, applied unnatural methods of investigation, and falsified interrogation transcripts." These facts had been established in 1941 by a military collegium of NKVD troops in the Leningrad military district, which issued a determination about initiating criminal proceedings against Karpov. However, by this time Karpov was working in the central apparatus of the NKVD, where this decision was relegated to the archives.

When they had become familiar with all these facts, the party investigators of the 1950s made the following decision, worthy of Solomon: "For violations of socialist legality in 1937-1938, Comrade Karpov G. G. deserved expulsion from the CPSU, but, taking into account that the misdemeanors he committed occurred long ago, and that he has performed positive work in recent years, the Party Control Committee has limited itself with regard to Comrade Karpov to issuing a strong reprimand to be duly registered."[22]

A "party trial" also awaited the former officials of the UNKVD in the Ivanovo area, Volkov, Serebriakov, and Kozlov. It was established that they participated in fabricating several major cases. After they received testimony from the arrested secretary of the area committee, Yepanechnikov, against 63 leading area officials, they fabricated a group case in which a large number of people were convicted. Many of those convicted, including two area committee secretaries, the chairman of the area executive committee, the secretary of the Komsomol area committee, and the secretary of the Party Collegium of the Party Control Committee for the Ivanovo area, were shot. After these area leaders had been replaced, the same NKVD members arrested one more area committee secretary and obtained testimony from him about the existence of a "reserve Right-Trotskyist Center" in the area. Three area committee secretaries who had replaced the former leadership had supposedly joined this center, as well as the chairman of the area executive committee, the area prosecutor, and the chairman of the area court. For all these crimes, the executioners escaped with expulsion from the party.[33]

Punishment that was just as "harsh" was applied to Gorodnichenko and Boyarsky, who had worked in 1937 in the NKVD in the Northern-Osetian ASSR. The Party Control Committee established that they had fabricated a case about the existence of a bourgeois-nationalist organization in the republic; more than 600 people were arrested in connection with this case. These executioners, too, remained at liberty after the exposure of their crimes. They were simply expelled from the CPSU.[44]

While many people who were convicted of the most severe malfeasance in office got off with a light scare, and at worst with punishment along party lines, the "party investigators" reacted much more severely to those who committed acts in the 1920s and 1930s for which the "justice system" in the times of Khrushchev and Brezhnev did not observe a statute of limitations.

37. Who Was Punished, and in What Way, After Stalin's Death?

Juridical rehabilitation in the 1950s did not cover those few surviving communists who participated actively in the work of the oppositions. This included, for example, S. N. Ravich, who in the past had been the wife of the Old Bolshevik V. A. Karpinsky. Lenin's complete collected works contain dozens of letters addressed to Karpinsky and Ravich. In 1935, Ravich was arrested as an active participant in the "new" or "Leningrad" opposition of the 1920s. She spent about twenty years in the camps and exile and died in 1957, after being refused rehabilitation despite the requisite appeals by G. I. Petrovsky and E. D. Stasova.[55]

Well ensconced in the party and judicial organs, even after the Twentieth Congress of the CPSU the Stalinists did much to impede rehabilitations, or to prevent those rehabilitated from returning to work. On 28 June 1956, G. I. Petrovsky, who had appealed for the rehabilitation of his party comrades, wrote in his diary: "The liquidation of Stalinism is going slowly. Those who return are not trusted. They are restored to membership and rehabilitated very slowly. Old people are not accepted at work."[66]

Often, statements made many years ago, which were not completely "orthodox" from the standpoint of the Stalinists, were declared to be "crimes," or at least misdemeanors that prevented reinstatement into the party. Thus, during consideration of an appeal from former party member Yefimov, they reminded him about a "mistake" he had committed during a lecture delivered in 1935. His "mistake" amounted to the following: in response to the question as to why Zinoviev had not been sentenced to be shot at his first trial, Yefimov answered: Zinoviev was an old revolutionary and theoretician who had worked at Lenin's side in emigration; he was a member of the Central Committee from 1907 through 1927, and after the revolution, a member of the Politburo and chairman of the Executive Committee of the Comintern. Therefore his execution would have been "a moral blow to the world communist movement, and would have undermined its moral authority in the party masses abroad." After he had read this reply, for which a denunciation was contained in the party archive, the first secretary of the Leningrad area committee, Spiridonov, reproached Yefimov for the fact that, twenty years before, he had answered the question "incorrectly, not in a party way." This fact, along with other similar "mistakes" Yefimov had committed in the 1930s, served as grounds for refusing to reinstate him into the party.[77]

The "re-investigators" of the 1950s and 1960s reacted even more cautiously to participants in former oppositions, whose fate after being released from the camps was far more difficult than the fate of other prisoners of Stalinism. The very fact of participation in the legal Left Opposition of the 1920s (not to mention its underground formations in later years) was considered sufficient to preclude party rehabilitation.

Reflecting this situation, a directive from the Party Control Committee indicated: "In reviewing cases it sometimes happens that among those rehabilitated in court and appealing for reinstatement in the CPSU, there have been people who, during the period of sharp struggle against Trotskyists, Zinovievists and right opportunists, actively spoke out against the party in defense of the opposition. There were no grounds to put these people on trial, but at one time they had been expelled from the party correctly. Therefore, the Party Control Committee has refused to readmit such people into the CPSU."[88]

The memoirs of E. Osipov relate how the appeals of former oppositionists were handled. When his case was being heard in 1958 at the bureau of the Leningrad area committee, he discovered that the party organs in the 1930s had used different material than the NKVD. After pulling Osipov's personnel file, located in the party archive, the reporter "enumerated many examples of my 'apostasy,' far more than the NKVD had been aware of. In any case, several of them had never been mentioned at a single interrogation connected with my case — neither in 1935 nor later." Thus, the party investigator announced that during the celebration of the tenth anniversary of the October Revolution, when an alternative oppositional demonstration had been held in Leningrad, Osipov, who was then serving in the military, was guarding machine-guns at the Petropavlovsk fortress. "If the NKVD had known all this at that time," notes Osipov, "not that I had done anything there, but that I had simply had some kind of connection with arms during those demonstrations, ... then they would have shot me on the spot."

The party investigator outlined in detail the year in which Osipov defended the opposition and read its platform, when he attended oppositional meetings, and so forth. After this presentation, the reporter was not asked a single question, and the session's chairman, Spiridonov, declared: "I recommend that Osipov not be reinstated in the party in view of the fact that he was too active in the opposition, and also... in view of the fact that he has been outside the ranks of the party for too long."

The same session reviewed the appeal of a former worker from the Izhora factory, who had led five hundred Red Guards from Kolpino in storming the Winter Palace. Having supported, like the majority of the Leningrad communists, the "new opposition" in 1925-1927, this man nevertheless worked as deputy chairman of the Leningrad Council under Kirov. He then lived in exile from 1935. After the arrests began there he went on his own to the local branch of the NKVD and declared: "Why are you rounding up all my comrades, but not me?" He was told in reply: "Go on, walk around for a while, and don't worry. Your turn will come too. Why are you so upset?" Soon he was arrested on false charges of trying to escape from exile and received ten years in the camps. The Leningrad bureaucrats refused to reinstate this man, too, using the cynical formulation of "being cut off from the party (during his years of exile and the camps! – V. R.)."⁹⁹

In reviewing appeals for rehabilitation, the same veil of secrecy was preserved as before. Neither the people seeking their own rehabilitation, nor the relatives of those convicted (if it was an issue of posthumous rehabilitation) were given the chance of familiarizing themselves with the material in their dossiers, particularly "agents' material," i.e., denunciations and surveillance reports. Nor were they granted confrontations with their investigators or with those who had denounced them. The rehabilitation proceeded by means of a bureaucratic investigation of cases in the inner recesses of party or secret police offices. The "re-investigators" (the same "dvoikas," "troikas," and Special Boards as before) simply leafed through the investigatory and trial documents. If they found obvious absurdities in them, they decided on rehabilitation, but if they discovered information about genuine oppositional activity, they decided against it. That such activity had occurred thirty years before was not considered a mitigating circumstance, insofar as the issue at hand was the most dangerous form of "guilt," from the standpoint of party bureaucrats, the infamous charge of being "anti-party." For everything in Stalin's policies, with the exception of overtly illegal repressions, continued to be seen as an expression of the correctness of "the party's general line."

Gustav Klinger, Hugo Eberlein, Vladimir Lenin, and Fritz Platten during the First Congress of the Communist International in 1919. Klinger, Eberlein, and Platten were shot or they died in the camps.

38. Terror against Foreign Communists

Until now we have been dealing with mass repression against Soviet citizens. With no less fury, however, the purge was directed against revolutionary emigrants, members of the international communist movement.

In the mid-1930s, several tens of thousands of foreign communists were living in the Soviet Union. Some of them worked in the Comintern, the Profintern, the Communist Youth International and other international organizations. Others worked in Soviet enterprises and establishments. Significant, too, was the number of non-party emigrants who had used the right of asylum; according to the Constitution of the USSR, this right was extended to "foreign citizens persecuted for defending the interests of workers, or for their scientific activity, or for participating in national-liberation struggles."[1] As the famous Soviet intelligence officer L. Trepper believed, 80 percent of these people were repressed during the years of the Great Purge.[2]

Among the first to be arrested in the USSR were the founders of foreign communist parties, participants in the first congresses of the Comintern, and past members of the left wing of the Second International. There is a famous photograph of the Presidium of the First Congress of the Comintern where, next to Lenin, sit the foreign delegates Klinger, Eberlein, and Platten. They all perished in Stalin's prisons and camps.

One of the oldest revolutionary-internationalists was Edmondo Peluso, who, during various years of his life, was a member of the social-democratic and communist parties of France, Spain, Portugal, Austria, Switzerland, Bavaria and Italy. While being investigated, Peluso was accused of having ties with Zinoviev, Bukharin, Radek, and others. To this he replied that he might just as well be accused of having ties with Lenin and Rosa Luxemburg. As he wrote in a complaint sent to the prosecutor, "four men, armed with various instruments, beat me for forty minutes after hanging me upside down." In

1940, Peluso was sentenced by a Special Board to five years in exile, and, in 1942, he was shot on charges of belonging to a "counter-revolutionary insurgent organization."³

As I. Reiss would recount, at the beginning of 1937 the NKVD prepared a memorandum which stated that all prisoners of war remaining in Russia after the Brest Treaty had actually stayed in order to engage in espionage. This memorandum, wrote Reiss, "evidently was supposed to give grounds for persecuting foreign communist-emigrants who now are being slaughtered to a man in the USSR." Reiss stressed that "the situation is especially desperate for those whose homelands are ruled by fascism: Germans, Poles, Hungarians and others. No one was going to defend them, and therefore they were dealt with unceremoniously. As a rule, they were all charged with espionage. Very soon arrests began of Russians married to foreign women, i.e., to 'spies.'"⁴

The repressions fell with particular cruelty on the apparatus of the Comintern. In 1937-1938, a Comintern trial was prepared in Moscow. Malenkov and Poskrebyshev came several times to the prison where Comintern officials were held in order to find out how the "Comintern case" was proceeding. On the sixth day after his arrest, Jan Anvelt died during interrogation; he had been the executive secretary of the International Control Commission of the Comintern, and chairman of the Estonian Workers Commune in 1918-1919. After being sentenced to death, Melnikov, the director of the communications between the Comintern and its foreign centers, continued to run the foreign network for eight more months from his cell in the internal prison of the NKVD, after which he was shot.⁵

Georgii Damianov, the head of the cadre department of the Comintern who worked under the pseudonym of Belov, took an active part in reprisals against the revolutionary emigrants. Before Damianov was appointed to this post, he had been ferocious in Spain as the inspector of the International Brigades. Without the sanction of Manuilsky and "Belov," the NKVD did not have the right to arrest foreign communists. Damianov prepared hundreds of reports and recommendations for the NKVD with comments like the following: "He does not enjoy our political trust," "dubious from the standpoint of his acquaintances," and so forth.⁶ From 1946, Damianov was at the post of Minister of Defense, and, after Dimitrov's death, became Chairman of the Presidium of the People's Council of Bulgaria.

Given the mass persecution of Comintern cadres, the majority of high-ranking leaders, however, survived — members of the Presidium and secretariat of the Executive Committee of the Comintern [ECCI]. These people loyally recommended themselves as the obedient executors of Stalin's will, as participants in the struggle against all oppositions and "deviations" in the international communist movement. Supported for many years by Moscow and enjoying privileges on a par with the highest Soviet bureaucrats, these people step by step lost the qualities of a communist. Having in mind this "leading core," Trotsky wrote in 1937: "The apparatus of the Comintern consists of people who are diametrically opposed to the revolutionary type. A genuine revolutionary has his own opinion which he has established, and in whose name he is prepared to make sacrifices, up to sacrificing his life. A revolutionary prepares the future and therefore in the present reconciles himself easily to any difficulties, deprivations and persecution. In contrast to this, the bureaucrats of the Comintern are complete careerists. They have no opinions and subordinate themselves to the order to the bosses who pay them. Since they are agents of the all-powerful Kremlin, each one of them feels like a small 'superman.' They can do anything. They easily denigrate the honor of others since they have no honor of their own. This completely degenerated and thoroughly demoralized organization maintains itself in radical public opinion, including in the minds of the workers, as the 'builder' of socialist society only through the authority of the Kremlin."[7]

Of course, these words of Trotsky's should not be taken as absolute. Many leaders of the Comintern had a significant revolutionary past and subjectively were devoted to the cause of communism. In a number of cases they tried to oppose the terror which was descending on their parties and the communist movement as a whole, although the majority limited themselves to appeals to Stalin and his assistants. On 28 March 1938, E. Varga wrote to Stalin: "As a result of the mass arrests, the cadres who are at liberty in the Soviet Union are profoundly demoralized and dismayed. This demoralization seizes the majority of Comintern officials and is spreading even to individual members of the secretariat of the ECCI. The main reason for this demoralization is the feeling of complete impotence in matters concerning the arrests of political emigrants... Many foreigners gather their things every evening in expectation of a possible arrest. Because of the constant fear, many have become half-mad and are incapable of work."[8]

In a number of cases, G. Dimitrov, who was sent investigatory material concerning foreign communists, provided the secretaries of the CC VKP(b), the leaders of the NKVD and the procuracy with positive characterizations of those arrested, which sometimes aided in their release. However his influence was not very great. L. Trepper tells of a meeting between Dimitrov and Bulgarian communists who said to him:

"If you don't do everything necessary to stop the repressions, then we will kill Yezhov, this counter-revolutionary."

Dimitrov left them no illusions: "I have no chance of doing anything, all this remains exclusively in the hands of the NKVD."

In telling this story, Trepper added that "the Bulgarians did not manage to remove Yezhov. He shot them all like rabbits. Yugoslavs, Poles, Lithuanians, Czechs — all disappeared. In 1937, besides Wilhelm Pieck and Walter Ulbricht, not a single one of the main leaders of the Communist Party of Germany remained. The repressive madness knew no limits."[9]

Stalin put constant pressure on the leaders of the Comintern, trying to draw them further into the execution and ideological justification of the political terror. On 11 February 1937, he received Dimitrov for a discussion of the draft of a decree by the ECCI with regard to the Radek-Piatakov trial. As can be seen from Dimitrov's notes, Stalin declared to him: "The European workers think that this is all because of the falling-out between myself and Trotsky, because of Stalin's poor character." In order to repudiate such opinions, Stalin demanded that the decree state that Trotsky and his supporters "fought against Lenin and against the party even during Lenin's lifetime." At the close of the discussion, Stalin uttered the ominous phrase: "All of you there, in the Comintern, are working to the advantage of the enemy."[10]

In November 1937, when he had become familiar with the official draft of the ECCI's decree on the struggle against Trotskyism, Stalin gave Dimitrov an even more fanatical directive: "Trotskyists must be driven out, shot, and destroyed. They are world-wide provocateurs, and the most vicious agents of fascism."[11]

Foreign communists presented a particular threat to Stalin because, while they traveled in their countries, they had access to Trotskyist sources. Their familiarity with "Trotskyist literature" often served as the basis for the arrest of political emigrants. In this regard, the fate of D. Gachev is noteworthy. He was a member of the Bulgarian Communist Party from 1921 to 1926 and a member of the VKP(b) from 1926-1938 (frequently, after arriving in the USSR, revolutionary emigrants changed membership in their native parties into membership in the VKP(b)). In a statement to the general prosecutor of the USSR, Gachev, who was sentenced to eight years in the camps for "counter-revolutionary Trotskyist activity," wrote that the sole "crime" imputed to him was reading, in 1934, an article by Trotsky which he had discovered accidentally in a French newspaper used to wrap some produce belonging to his comrade who had arrived from Bulgaria. In a private conversation, he had referred to this article as "a new example of the degeneration of Trotskyism into the most undisguised fascism." Despite these words, the investigators described this conversation as evidence that Gachev, "while subjectively not a Trotskyist, objectively propagated counter-revolutionary Trotskyist ideas."[12]

In many instances the very fact that a foreign communist had been arrested was seen as evidence that he was a spy or a Trotskyist. On 31 August 1937, Belevsky, the chairman of the Communist Party of Poland in the ECCI, wrote to Moskvin (pseudonym of the former Chekist Trilisser), the secretary of the ECCI: "The fact that the NKVD organs have arrested a number of members of the CPP, and members of the Central Committee of the CPP in particular, points to the existence in the ranks of the CPP and its CC of agents belonging to the class enemy, namely supporters of Pilsudski and Trotsky."[13]

In such an atmosphere, to use the words of the German emigrant and poet Johannes Becher, what inevitably arises is "a jungle atmosphere, where no one believes anyone else, where hunter becomes prey and prey becomes hunter, and all political activity is reduced to 'giving away' one's closest associates." In describing the contradictory feelings which gripped him and other foreign communists, Becher recalled: "To the degree that I respected and loved Stalin, I was shaken by several things which were happening in the Soviet Union… My very being was shattered… 'People don't talk about that' — this unwritten, general rule was simply a sign of our general hypocrisy."[14]

The ferocity of the persecution of the foreign communists was explained to a significant degree by Stalin's fear that socialist revolutions in other lands might arise outside his control. As a result, the center of the revolutionary movement might shift from Moscow, and the movement itself might end up under the leadership of the Fourth International. In order to maintain his unlimited control over the communist movement, Stalin ruthlessly annihilated foreign communists, with the exception of those who showed their personal devotion and "reliability" through joint participation in his criminal actions.

In talking about the annihilation of the internationalists, Trotsky recalled that the murder of Jean Jaurès had been committed by an ignorant, petty-bourgeois chauvinist, and the murder of Karl Liebknecht and Rosa Luxemburg by counter-revolutionary officers. Now, however, "imperialism need no longer rely on 'good fortune': in Stalin's mafia it had a ready international group of agents for the systematic extermination of revolutionaries."[15]

Communists from countries with fascist or semi-fascist regimes, where communist parties worked in the underground (in the 1930s, dictatorial, totalitarian and authoritarian regimes existed in more than half the nations of Europe), turned out to be in the most difficult of straits. If they were living in the USSR, members of the communist parties of Germany, Austria, Hungary, Italy, Rumania, Bulgaria, Yugoslavia, and Finland were subjected to particularly cruel annihilation.

In July 1937, Milan Gorkic, the general secretary of the Central Committee of the Communist Party of *Yugoslavia*, was summoned to Moscow. After a few months, officials of the political secretariat of the Communist Party of Yugoslavia (CPY), located in Paris, were told that Gorkic had been arrested as "an English spy," the remaining leadership of the CPY was being disbanded, and the party's monetary assistance from the Comintern was being halted until the "Comintern decides otherwise."[16]

After Gorkic's arrest, Tito was ordered to fulfill the duties of senior secretary of the Central Committee of the CPY. In March 1938, he arrived in Yugoslavia from Paris in order to form a provisional leadership of the CPY, which would have to fulfill the role of the Central Committee until the resolution of the ""question of the CPY" by the leadership of the Comintern. In May, Tito created such a provisional leadership, which included A. Rankovic, M. Djilas, and I. L. Ribar.[17]

While he was still in Paris, Tito published three articles expressing enthusiasm for the "merciless purges" in the USSR. In the article "Trotskyism and its Accomplices" he revealed an understanding of the Stalinist interpretation of "Trotskyism" when he declared: "From hidden Trotskyists you often hear: 'I am not a Trotskyist, but neither am I a Stalinist.' Whoever speaks this way is surely a Trotskyist."[18]

In August 1938, Tito came to Moscow, where by this time 800 Yugoslav communists had already been arrested. Here, before anything else, he had to write an extensive explanation in connection with the arrest of his wife, the German communist L. Bauer. In it Tito said that he had asked his wife "not to have any ties with emigrants from Germany, since he feared that someone would use her for hostile goals in relation to the USSR." Nevertheless he confessed that "he had been insufficiently vigilant," and declared that his ties with Bauer were "a great stain" on his party life.[19]

Afterwards, Tito called his trip to Moscow the most difficult period in his life. He said that at that time "almost every Yugoslav was suspected of Trotskyism. In such an atmosphere, one after another the Yugoslav communists disappeared, people who had left their homeland because of police terror, ... volunteers who had returned from Spain, who had survived in battles for the republic, as well as those who remained in Soviet Russia after the world war in order to build the first socialist state in the world."[20]

During his stay in Moscow, Tito was accused of "Trotskyist distortions" allowed in his translation into Serbo-Croatian of the fourth chapter of *The Short Course of the History of the VKP(b)*. This charge was removed only after his personal case had been reviewed by the Comintern's Control Commission.[21]

As archival documents show, in Moscow Tito participated as much as he could in the persecution of his party comrades. Thus, he wrote a fifty-page memorandum regarding the activity of the former secretary of the Serbian territory committee of the CPY, P. Miletic, in which he called the latter "an inveterate factionalist." In the fall of 1939, Miletic, who had finished many years of a prison sentence in Yugoslavia, arrived in Moscow, whereupon he was arrested.[22]

At a session of the secretariat of the ECCI which reviewed the "question of the CPY," Tito gave a report which said: "The new leadership stands before the task of purging the party of various factionalists and Trotskyist elements both abroad, and in our nation... Our party... will gladly accept any decision which the Comintern makes." However, the leaders of the Comintern considered such a declaration insufficient for them to completely pass the leadership of the Yugoslavian Communist Party into Tito's hands. On 30 December, Dimitrov declared that Tito did not deserve "the complete trust of the ECCI" and that to win such trust he must "show in deed that he is carrying out the directives of the ECCI in good conscience." In response, Tito assured Dimitrov that he would see to it that the CPY wiped "the mud from its name before the Comintern."[23]

After this, the secretariat of the ECCI gave Tito full powers to form a new Central Committee. Before leaving Moscow, Tito told Dimitrov that he thought the leadership of the CPY should be located in Yugoslavia. "What leadership?" Dimitrov asked in surprise. "You are the only one left, Walter (Tito's party name – V. R.). It's a good thing that at least you are left, otherwise we would have to disband the CPY."[24]

In March 1939, Tito returned to Yugoslavia, where he held a session of the "provisional leadership," at which the decision was made to expel from the party the communists arrested in Moscow, as well as several members of the CPY living in Yugoslavia and France, — on charges of Trotskyism. He entrusted the investigation of the "actions of Trotskyists" to Djilas and Kardel.[25]

Persecution of the Yugoslav "Trotskyists" continued also during the war. One of its victims became Gorkic's closest comrade, Zh. Pavlovic, who had been expelled in 1937 from the CPY. In 1940 he published the book *The Balance of the Soviet Thermidor* in which he describes the repressions against Yugoslav Trotskyists and "Gorkichists." This book, which was banned by the authorities of royal Yugoslavia, could see the light only at the end of the 1980s. In 1941, Pavlovic surfaced in the territory of the partisan "Uzhitskaia Republic," where he was arrested. Djilas recalled that Tito told him: Pavlovic is a police informer. "He categorically denied this even though they beat him horribly." Not long before the fall of the "partisan republic," Pavlovic was shot.[26]

Thus, the sole ruling communist party which cast off the yoke of Stalinist hegemonism in the 1940s was headed by people who had tainted themselves with active participation in a whole series of ruthless purges. Even though, after Tito's break with Stalin, the Soviet press called the Yugoslav leaders Trotskyists, they had not the slightest relationship to Trotskyism. In the past they had been, on the contrary, inveterate Stalinists who had exterminated Trotskyists.

Total repression reached the Communist Party of *Poland*, for whom Stalin had nursed a special distrust since 1923-1924, when its leadership spoke in support of the Left Opposition in the RKP(b). The repressions against the Polish communists started at the end of the 1920s, when the party split into a "right' and "left" faction. As noted in the *Bulletin of the Opposition*, even in 1929 "the Comintern with the aid of the GPU 'arbitrated' the debate between the right group of the Central Committee of the Polish Communist Party (Warski, Kostrzewa and others) and the left (the Lenski group), by sending into exile the majority of the rights."[27] At the end of the 1920s the repressions began against the activists in the communist parties of Western Belorussia and Western Ukraine, which then were part of Poland. In 1933, the "rights" were arrested and declared agents of the Polish dictator Pilsudski. In 1933-1934, several members of the Central Committee of the Communist Party of Poland (CPP) and communist delegates to the Polish Sejm were shot, as well as the poet Wandurski, who headed the Polish theater in Kiev.

After these repressions, the Lenski group declared the "destruction of provocateurs" and the "cleansing of the atmosphere" in the CPP. On Stalin's orders, the Central Committee of the CPP conducted an ultra-left, adventuristic policy, and then just as submissively shifted to the diametrically opposed policy of the "popular front." In 1937, it became this group's turn. Almost all the Polish communists who were located in the USSR were arrested. The leaders of the CPP, including its general secretary, Lenski, and the 70-year-old Warski — one of the founders of the social-democratic and communist parties of Poland — were shot.

This campaign was completed with the ECCI's decree disbanding the Polish Communist Party. After reading the draft of the decree, Stalin told Dimitrov: "You were late in disbanding them by two years. They must be disbanded, but in my opinion it is not necessary to make an announcement in the press."[28]

In the "Appeal of Polish Bolshevik-Leninists regarding the Disbanding of the Polish Communist Party," it states: "The destruction of the CPP is the last link in the chain of Stalinist crimes, it is the furthest step in the victorious movement of the Thermidorian counter-revolution which is annihilating the old revolutionary generation — and not only the Russian — with fire and sword."[29]

The arrests and executions of the *German* emigrants in the USSR started in 1934. During the years of the Great Purge the following people were arrested: member of the Central Committee of the Communist Party of Germany (CPG), Remmele; Thälmann's former secretary, Hirsch; one of the leaders of the Red Front, Kupferstein; the writers Otwald and Günther; as well as leading journalists of the German communist press.

In January 1937, Krinitsky, the first secretary of the Saratov area committee of the VKP(b), told Stalin that in the republic of Germans of the Povolzhe, "a counter-revolutionary Trotskyist organization had been uncovered, the leading core of which were former members of the Communist Party of Germany."[30] The head of this organization was declared to be W. Leow-Hofmann, the former leader of the Union of Red Front Fighters — the milita-

38. Terror against Foreign Communists

Willi Münzenberg
(1889-1940)

rized organization of the CPG, created in 1925 to defend workers' meetings and demonstrations.

One of the victimized leaders of the CPG was Heinz Neumann, who in 1936 had been assigned the translation of the transcript of the first Moscow trial. As his wife, M. Buber-Neumann, later recalled, after completing this work he said: "I assure you that if they put me on public trial, then I will find the strength to shout: 'Down with Stalin!' No one will prevent me then." "After a long silence he added: 'Only what can these dogs do to people!?'... After this night-time confession he began to talk for the first time about suicide."[31]

At the beginning of 1937, the Neumanns received from their friend in Spain a letter which at first seemed strange. It contained the text of a song which supposedly all Europe was singing at that time. In the text there was a nonsensical proposal: "Therefore take a hot iron and put it to the paper." Realizing what was going on, Neumann "developed" the secret text and read: "Maybe you will lose everything, but you must try to leave the Soviet Union before it is too late. But never, under any circumstances, should you come to Spain, for there also the NKVD is in a frenzy."[32] Two months after receiving this letter, Neumann was arrested.

The fate of another prominent member of the CPG, Willi Münzenberg, unfolded in a different way. He had become famous throughout the world after he had organized a counter-trial in Paris and London with regard to the burning of the Reichstag. In October 1936, Münzenberg arrived in Moscow on a summons from the leadership of the Comintern. Recounting her Moscow meetings with him, Buber-Neumann wrote: "The trial against Zinoviev raised doubts in Münzenberg's mind, at the same time as the beginning of the civil war in Spain became a source of hope for him." Soon after he arrived, Münzenberg was called to the ECCI for interrogations. "After the first interrogations Münzenberg was seized with a feeling that he had already fallen into the hands of the NKVD. It was enough to spend only a few days in Moscow for Münzenberg and Babette (Buber-Neumann's sister and Münzenberg's closest collaborator – V. R.) to feel the same panic-stricken fear which held in its talons many thousands of people in this land... Immediately a vacuum formed around him. People avoided him like a leper. His small number of friends slipped into his hotel only under the cover of darkness."[33]

Münzenberg was saved only by the fact that Stalin had issued a secret directive to send Soviet arms and specialists to Spain. Togliatti declared that Münzenberg was indispensable for carrying out such an assignment, since he had more of the necessary contacts in Europe than any other communist functionary. After returning to Paris, Münzenberg broke with the Comintern and published a series of anti-Stalinist articles.

The scale of the repressions against the German political emigrants can be seen by the memorandum from the head of the service for counting, registering, and verifying the cadres of the representatives from the CPG to the ECCI, Isaak Dietrich, who reported to the leadership of the delegation. It said that on 28 April 1938, the representative body had registered 842 arrested Germans. "In actual fact the number of arrested is of course higher... In the provinces, for instance, in Engels, not a single German (emigrant) remained at liberty. In Leningrad, at the beginning of 1937, the group of German communists stood at 103, and in February 1938, of these only twelve comrades remained... One could say that more than 70 percent of the members of the CPG have been arrested. If the arrests continue at the same rate as in March 1938, then in three months not a single German member of the party will remain."

In describing the atmosphere which reigned among the German emigrants, Dietrich noted: "The mood of a certain portion of the comrades is exceedingly agitated. They are shaken and depressed by the many arrests. If they meet one another, then they ask: 'Are you still alive?'"

"Several wives of those arrested have committed suicide," reported Dietrich. "Some of the wives and children of those arrested are starving in the literal sense of the word... After some of the comrades had been sent on assignment to Spain, several of their wives came and said that they had been visited by agents of the NKVD who had come to arrest their husbands."[34]

The Ninth Congress of the SED [Sozialistische Einheitspartei Deutschlands, the governing party of the German Democratic Republic] (January 1989) reported that at least 242 prominent members of the German Communist Party had perished in the Soviet Union.[35]

By the beginning of 1937, the majority of *Austrian* Schutzbundists had already been arrested. They were members of the socialist military organization "Schutzbund" who, after the defeat of the anti-fascist uprising in 1934, had emigrated to the USSR and had been received there as heroes.

Out of more than three thousand *Bulgarian* emigrants, one third were persecuted. Six hundred Bulgarian communists, comprising the most active cadres of the Bulgarian Communist Party, perished in Stalinist prisons and camps.[36]

After the wave of repressions had subsided, G. Dimitrov and V. Kolarov, the leader of the Bulgarian Communist Party, made considerable effort to help out their party comrades. In February 1941, Dimitrov sent Andreev, the secretary of the Central Committee of the VKP(b), a list of 132 arrested Bulgarian emigrants whose cases, in his opinion, should be reviewed, insofar as, "according to the information we have about these people, it would simply be impossible to consider them capable of committing anti-Soviet and anti-party acts." Dimitrov mentioned also that many cases, which the Prosecutor's office had long ago unequivocally established to be groundless, remained on the books, and the people sentenced according to them continued to be held in the camps. He asked Andreev to facilitate "the closing of at least those cases concerning political emigrants which, according to officials from the prosecutor's office, were clearly 'frame-ups.'" According to Dimitrov, the cases of many Germans, Austrians, and others under arrest were also frame-ups. "The question arises," he stressed in his letter, "not only about the rehabilitation and salvation of innocent people who are suffering, but of the return to useful work and to militant activity against our class enemies in the capitalist countries by loyal cadres belonging to our fraternal communist parties."[37]

After the war, Dimitrov turned to Stalin with a request to free 29 Bulgarian communists "for extremely necessary work in the interests of the party." The given question was handed over for review to the Minster of State Security, Abakumov, who said in a memorandum sent to the Council of Ministers of the USSR: "In connection with the methods of physical coercion used during investigation against the majority of those arrested, it would be inexpedient to release them abroad at the present time."[38]

Meanwhile Dimitrov and Kolarov did nothing to save Bulgarian oppositionists (the Iskrov group) who had criticized the policies of the Central Committee of the Bulgarian Communist Party.

In 1937, Popov and Tanev, Dimitrov's co-defendants in the Leipzig frame-up trial, were arrested. Between them, only Tanev was released, on Dimitrov's request. In a memo about Popov, Dimitrov wrote that "in 1927, after expressing solidarity with the famous Trotskyist Iskrov, Popov insisted on a broad and prolonged discussion, and did not agree with the methods

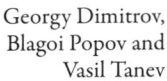
Georgy Dimitrov, Blagoi Popov and Vasil Tanev

of fighting against the Trotskyists."³⁹ Popov was sent to a prison camp, from which he was sent into exile after the war. He was released only in 1953.

At the beginning of the 1920s and 1930s, about twenty-five to thirty thousand *Hungarians* were living in the Soviet Union, the largest portion of whom were political emigrants. The majority of them became victims of persecution. Ten of sixteen members of the first Central Committee of the Hungarian Communist Party were killed, as well as eleven out of twenty people's commissars of the Hungarian Soviet Republic of 1919.⁴⁰

From the beginning of 1937, the threat of arrest hung over the head of Bela Kun, the former chairman of the Council of People's Commissars in Hungary. As his wife later recalled, for several months before his arrest, Kun would return from work, "talk with nobody, and moreover, wouldn't even read anything... He would sit, staring at one spot. When people spoke to him, he wouldn't answer." At times Kun tried to shrug off the idea of his inevitable arrest. A few days before his arrest he said to his relatives: "Just think what people are saying. I met Enö Varga on the street and asked him: 'How are things?' 'I'm still free,' he answered. Even such an intelligent person as Varga, and he is talking nonsense."

In June 1937, Stalin phoned Kun and merrily said: "Foreign newspapers write that you have been arrested in Moscow. Please, talk to a French journalist, let him be persuaded that the opposite is true."⁴¹ After this meeting, the French newspapers published refutations of the news about Kun's arrest. But a few days later, Kun was arrested. In 1938 they arrested his wife, Irina, and his brother-in-law, the famous Hungarian writer, Antal Gidazs. Then in 1941, they took his daughter Agnessa.

38. Terror against Foreign Communists

Bela Kun, shot on August 29, 1938

In the arrests of the Hungarian and other political emigrants, an active role belonged to the future Prime Minister of Hungary, Imre Nagy. Although documents of his activity as an agent were hidden in the inner recesses of the NKVD, rumors about him as a provocateur circulated even in the 1940s. In his memoirs, Khrushchev mentions that, although Rakosi accused Nagy of a "right deviation" after the war, "Stalin did not arrest Nagy. People said that it was because in the USSR Nagy had helped him decimate the Comintern cadres."[42]

Only at the end of the 1980s were documents found showing that Nagy, who emigrated in 1929 to the USSR, had been a secret informer for the NKVD since 1933. His denunciations led to the arrest of dozens of Hungarian, German, and Polish communists. Even in 1941, as it states in an NKVD report sent to Malenkov, Nagy "dug up a group of anti-Soviet Hungarian political emigrants."[43]

Communists from the *Baltic countries* who were living in the USSR were subjected to total persecution. The scale of the devastation caused in these parties by Stalinist repression can be seen from Dimitrov's letter to Andreev on 3 January 1939: "After the arrest of the former leaders of the communist parties of Lithuania, Latvia and Estonia in Moscow as enemies of the people, the honest communists in these countries remained disoriented and without ties to the Comintern. We do not have now in Moscow a single comrade from these parties whom we can fully rely on, for establishing ties or eventually to be sent into that country."[44]

At the June Plenum of the Central Committee of 1957, Snechkus, the secretary of the Central Committee of the Communist Party of Lithuania, announced that the most active part of the Lithuanian communists, who were living in the Soviet Union in the 1930s, had perished. The only ones to survive had been engaged in underground work or had been in Lithuanian prisons. One of the leaders of the Lithuanian Communist Party, Aleksa-Agnaretis, was shot in 1940, literally three weeks before Lithuania was liberated. Snechkus reported that, after the death in 1935 of one of the oldest Lithuanian communists, Mitskiavichus-Kapsukas, a commission was formed to study his archives. "Several months ago we received from the Central Committee of the CPSU the archival materials of this commission. How shocked I was when I saw that of this commission, I alone remained alive! And I remained alive because I had been carrying out underground work in fascist Lithuania."[45]

Altogether, more communists from Eastern European countries were killed in the Soviet Union than died at home in their own countries during Hitler's occupation.

Many foreign communists, who were not touched by the Stalinist repressions, were forced to reconcile themselves to persecution of members of their families, without even daring to ask about the fate of the latter. Paolo Robotti — the son-in-law of Togliatti — was arrested in 1938 and tortured in prison. Kuusinen's wife spent 17 years in exile in Siberia, and his son was arrested.

In 1936, Kalnberzin, one of the leaders of the Latvian Communist Party, was sent from Moscow to Latvia in order to direct the party underground. In 1939, he was seized by the Latvian police and given a death sentence, which was then commuted to many years in prison. During his absence from the Soviet Union, his wife was arrested and their three children were sent to orphanages. After the Sovietization of Latvia in 1940, Kalnberzin was elected the first secretary of the Communist Party of Latvia. The only thing that he managed to do with regard to his family was to get his children out of an orphanage. Several years later, Kalnberzin told his daughter: "I asked nothing about your mother. It would have been senseless. Nor did they ever tell me anything."[46]

In *Mongolia*, which was a satellite of the USSR in the 1930s, mass repressions touched every tenth inhabitant of the republic. The persecution was directed by Marshal Choibalsan; Frinovsky, the deputy People's Commissar of Internal Affairs, had been sent to instruct him. Out of 11 members of the Politburo of the Central Committee of the Mongolian People's Revolutionary Party, 10 were killed — all except Choibalsan.[47]

The purge encompassed all the Communist Parties, including those with small memberships, which were deprived of the most experienced and educated people, capable in the future of heading mass revolutionary movements in their lands. The section of Korean communists which was located in the USSR was completely liquidated. The leaders of the Communist Party of

Iran, Sultan-Zade, and of Mexico, Gomez, were shot. Among the victimized Indian communists was Professor Mukardji, a member of the Indian Revolutionary Party since 1905, a historian with a European education and the author of many books. So, too, was Chattopadiaia, about whom in 1920 the English intelligence agent wrote to his superiors: "Chatto hopes to make all Indians Bolsheviks and hopes to get started with this together with Rabindranath Tagore,... whose latest statements reinforce Chatto's hopes."[48]

During the years of the Great Purge, the leaders of the Communist Parties who survived were primarily those who took a hand in destroying their party comrades. Among these is, for instance, Nosaka, who for many years headed the Japanese Communist Party. In 1992 a group of experts of the CPJ was sent to Moscow, where it discovered letters from Nosaka to Dimitrov which served as the grounds for arresting and shooting many Japanese communists. Only after this discovery was the 100-year-old Nosaka stripped of his post as honorary chairman of the Communist Party of Japan.[49]

In the torture chambers of the NKVD, incriminating testimony was coerced from those under arrest against almost all the leaders of the Comintern and "fraternal parties." The archives have disclosed such testimony against Togliatti, Pollitt, Duclos, Mao Tse-Tung, Zhu De, Pieck, Ulbricht, Gottwald, Šmeral, and Zapotocki. Some of them avoided persecution because they were outside the jurisdiction of the NKVD (for instance, the Chinese leaders), others, because Stalin personally favored them. And those who displayed special zeal in destroying revolutionaries in Spain also survived and retained their posts. This includes W. Ulbricht, who directed the persecution of German, Swiss, and Austrian Trotskyists, and A. Marty, who received the nickname of "the executioner of Albacete" (the Spanish town where the headquarters of the emissaries from the Comintern was located).

The leaders of the Communist Parties of bourgeois-democratic lands, who did not have to participate in persecuting the members of their own parties (the latter were protected from repression by public opinion in their countries), fulfilled the shameful mission of justifying the Great Purge. L. Trepper tells about a mass meeting in Paris, where Marcel Cachin and Paul Vaillant-Couturier, who had attended the first Moscow trial, spoke of Stalin's far-sightedness "in exposing and disarming the terrorist group."

"We heard with our own ears how Zinoviev and Kamenev confessed to committing the most heinous crimes," exclaimed Vaillant-Couturier. "What do you think, would these people have begun to confess if they were innocent?"

Trepper reasonably notes that, even if the leaders of foreign Communist Parties sincerely believed in the justice of the trials of the Soviet communists, they could not help but understand the falseness of the charges made against Comintern members with whom they had worked hand in hand for many years. "After the Twentieth Congress they pretended to be completely bewildered. To hear them, it turned out that Khrushchev's report was a revelation for them. But in reality they were knowing participants in the liquidation of true communists, even when this involved their own party comrades."[50]

In 1961, the leaders of the "fraternal communist parties," who for long years had tried to persuade their parties of the authenticity of the Moscow Trials, intervened in the internal affairs of the CPSU when they convinced Khrushchev not to release material about these trials at the Twenty-Second Congress. Unnerved by the consequences which the exposure of the judicial frame-ups might bring to their authority in their own parties, they tried in every way to prevent the exposure of Stalin's crimes.

Only a few foreign communists decided in 1937-1938 to break with the Comintern and join the Fourth International. This included, for instance, a group of Palestinian Communist Party members, who sent a letter in November 1938 to the editors of the *Bulletin of the Opposition*, stating: "We are not writers, nor the usual journalists, but simple workers, armed, thanks to relatively many years of political activity, with certain experience and having used years of prison and unemployment for the most through study of Marxism we could manage." *The Bulletin of the Opposition* published a declaration from this group which stressed:

> "Can anyone imagine a thinking person who believes in the power and significance of socialism, and who is capable at the same time of believing in this entire exhibition... of fantastic, insane treachery which Stalin's Moscow trials are offering us? Can it really be that in the land of the greatest revolution the moral power of fascism is so great, and the influence of socialism is so insignificant, that all the acknowledged leaders and genuine revolutionaries, and along with them the broad masses, hundreds of thousands of communists, have turned out to be traitors to communism and are selling themselves to fascism? ... If all this were true, if people believed in this — then socialism would be disgraced for all time, and it would be dealt a mortal blow as an idea and a movement."

The authors of the letter declared:

> "In our best, politically conscious years, we followed Stalin. Not because we actually considered him our 'father.' In our self-deception we believed that devotion to Stalin was the same as devotion to the cause of the Soviet Union and the world revolution. We hoped that these (Stalinist) methods were accidental and transitory. But Stalin exploited our devotion in order to continue his dark deeds without

end or limit... The relentless war which Stalin has been waging against party, economic, and military cadres, is liquidating the gains of the revolution and is destroying the foundations of the Soviet state... If bourgeois reaction had managed to place a provocateur at the head of the worker's movement and socialist construction, it could not have caused more harm than Stalin with his evil deeds."[51]

The annihilation of thousands of foreign communists, as well as the political and moral degeneration of many of those who remained at liberty, was one of the main reasons that, in the majority of countries which became "socialist" after the Second World War, no forces emerged which were capable of resisting the installation of regimes patterned after the regime which existed in the USSR. At the end of the 1940s and beginning of the 1950s, many of the former leaders of the Comintern (Gottwald, Rakosi, and others) instigated in their own countries purges and trials like those which had occurred earlier in the Soviet Union. Even those political figures in the "countries of people's democracy" who dared to oppose Soviet hegemonism were deeply infected by the virus of Stalinism and were tainted by active participation in the purges of the 1930s.

It is characteristic that in the majority of Eastern European countries, the rehabilitation of the victims of political repression proceeded in a more half-hearted and inconsistent manner than even in the USSR. Only at the very end of their reign did the leaders of the communist parties of these nations decide to provide statistics about how many of the members of their parties were persecuted in the Soviet Union.

Ignatii Reiss (Natan Markovich Poretsky), murdered near Lausanne on 4 September 1937

The killers:

Left: Viktor Pravdin (also known as Roland Abbiate and Francois Rossi)

Right: Boris Afanasiev

Left: Sergei Spiegelglas, according to Sudoplatov the main organizer of the murder

Right: Renata Steiner rented the car used by Reiss's killers

39. Non-Returners of 1937

1. Ignatii Reiss

Despite the mass persecutions which were taking the lives of ever newer cohorts of Soviet and foreign communists, beyond the borders of the Soviet Union a broad, anti-Stalinist movement continued to be active. At the crest of the Great Purge, it was joined by several "non-returners," i.e., Soviet citizens who were living abroad and who refused to return to the USSR for political reasons.

The first Bolshevik non-returner was Ignatii Reiss, one of the most important Soviet intelligence agents. Being a consistent revolutionary internationalist, Reiss took an active part from the beginning of the 1920s in the communist movement in a number of European countries, where he was often arrested and put in prison. During the revolutionary crisis of 1923 in Germany, he was there with Radek, Piatakov, and Larisa Reisner.

Later Reiss worked in the fourth department of the General Staff of the Red Army — the main organ of Soviet military intelligence — hand in hand with such people as Sorge, Manevich, and Rado, whose names became legendary after the Second World War.

Observing the degeneration of the VKP(b) and Comintern, Reiss continued to see the moral justification of his work in the defense of the USSR. "He clings to this goal," Reiss's wife, Elisabeth Poretsky, would write in her memoirs. "But he withdraws ever more into himself and suffers endlessly over what was occurring in the Soviet Union. Trotsky's expulsion from the party is a heavy blow for him. However, when they exiled Trotsky from the Soviet Union, Ludwig (Reiss's conspiratorial name – V. R.) said: 'Now, at least, Stalin has made one contribution that will remain, he has saved the head of the revolution.'"[1]

After staying in Moscow in 1930-1932, Reiss returned for intelligence work abroad. "His ability to socialize with people, his level of culture, and his directness, even in years of disillusionment, helped recruit intellectuals, professors and journalists for the Soviet Union."[2]

From 1935, Reiss and his long-time comrade in intelligence work, Krivitsky, came to the conclusion that the Comintern had lost the revolutionary orientation in which they saw the meaning of their activity. Among themselves they ever more frequently said: "The Stalinists need us, but they can't trust us. We are international communists, our time is over. They will replace us with men... to whom the revolutionary movement means nothing."[3]

After the second trial of Zinoviev and Kamenev, Reiss and Krivitsky began to discuss the necessity of breaking with Stalin. The main thing which held them back from making this step was the idea that, by remaining at their posts, they might be able to help the Spanish revolution, whose victory would facilitate the destruction of Stalin's domination over the USSR and the Comintern.

If they broke with Stalin, Reiss and Krivitsky felt that the only move possible for them was to join the movement of the Fourth International. But they feared that Trotsky would regard them with distrust, since they were people he did not know.

Meanwhile Reiss ever more frequently received directives from Moscow which strikingly contradicted his convictions. A letter sent at the end of 1936 from Slutsky, the head of the foreign department of the NKVD, stated: "All of our attention should be concentrated on Catalonia (the Spanish province in which the independent Marxist party, POUM, enjoyed overwhelming influence – V. R.) and on a merciless fight against the Trotskyite bandits." In this regard, Reiss was ordered to Moscow for "personal consultations."[4]

Reiss made the decision to sabotage this assignment and not to return to the USSR. In his place, Elsa Poretsky left for Moscow. In her stay of two months there she became convinced that what reigned among her comrades — intelligence agents and political emigrants — was bewilderment, horror, and the expectation of inevitable arrest. One of Reiss's close friends told her: "If you ever get out of here, tell Ludwig never to come back... Never, not under any circumstances, never, never. I know that they (Stalinists – V. R.) can kill him abroad, and Ludwig knows it, too, but both he and I know that it is better for the likes of us than a Soviet prison."[5]

The atmosphere in the milieu that surrounded Reiss abroad also changed radically. As he writes in his notes, after the first Moscow trials, "Officials of the GPU abroad were forced to spend night after night 'agitating' among their foreign subordinates — the trials had spread demoralization even into this milieu."[6] The circles of Soviet agents contained ever fewer people with whom it was possible to speak candidly. "You wouldn't recognize them, our former friends," recalled Poretsky. "Those who not long ago had been in despair and agreed with us, are now justifying everything... They are ecstatic that they have managed to set some government or other against Trotsky, or to cut through a wire in order to deprive him of the chance to give a speech (this incident occurred during an attempt to organize a live broadcast of Trotsky's speech to a mass meeting in New York – V. R.)."[7]

Once he had made the final decision to break with Stalin, Reiss tried to establish contact with Sedov. Not knowing him personally, he turned to Sneevliet, the deputy of the Dutch Parliament who headed a group close to Trotsky in its political views. Sneevliet told Sedov about Reiss's action, but did not agree to arrange their meeting in Paris, since he felt that a provocateur was in Sedov's surroundings. Reiss and his family settled in a small Swiss village. Recalling the few days they spent there, Poretsky wrote: "We were free, but this was a break with everything that we felt dear: with our youth, with the past, with our comrades. Within a short time Ludwig aged greatly, and his hair turned white... His soul was in the cellars of the Lubianka. If he managed to fall asleep, then he would see in his dreams either executions or suicides."[8]

From Switzerland, Reiss sent letters to several of his comrades, calling upon them to follow his example. This call was answered by Reiss's long-time colleague, Gertrude Schildbach, who had just returned from Moscow and told of the shock she had felt during the Zinoviev-Kamenev trial.

However, Stalin's agents had been able to turn Schildbach into an informer who pointed the way for the assassins. With this in mind, Spiegelglas introduced her to Abbiate, Reiss's future killer, who pretended that he was in love with this young and homely woman tormented by her unsettled personal life.

Active participation in organizing Reiss's murder came from a group of White emigrants headed by S. Ya. Efron, one of the leaders of the "Union of Return to the Motherland," a pro-Soviet organization supported by the NKVD. When the participation of this group in Reiss's murder became known, Sedov gave Trotsky information about Efron which he had gleaned from conversations with emigrants close to the latter: "Efron officially declared everywhere that he was a Stalinist, a Marxist of the Stalin school... In a candid moment he once said about himself to V. A. (Sedov's informer – V. R.): "There are two Efrons. One — the crystal pure, honest man whom everyone knows, and the other — a Jesuit, a callous man, etc." He is married to Marina Tsvetaeva. They have two children: a daughter of 20, who lives in Russia, she traveled there two years ago and writes ecstatic letters... Marina Tsvetaeva has right-wing views, but is unbalanced and changes her views very often. She even supposedly wrote some kind of poem not long ago where she speaks enthusiastically about (Tsar) Nikolai; Efron asked her not to publish it, since it might do him great harm. They lived in very great poverty, and only two years ago did their situation improve somewhat as soon as Efron began to receive a salary in the Union of Return. People who know him say that he worked for the GPU for ideological reasons, and not for money."[9]

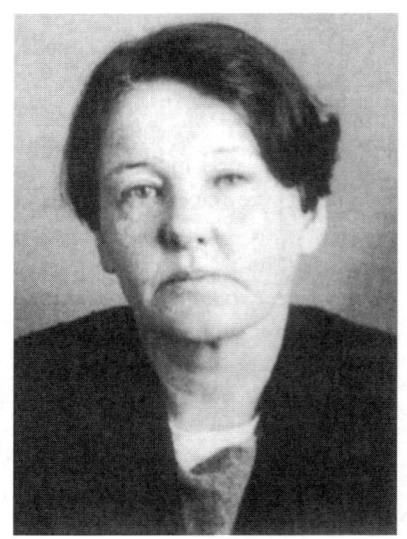

Sergei Efron in Paris, 1937   Nina Klepinina

Later, during interrogations at the NKVD, Efron gave twenty-four names of people he had recruited, including such an experienced and crafty spy as Vera Suvchinskaia (Trail), daughter of the famous White emigrant, Guchkov.[10] In 1936-1937, after marrying the English communist R. Trail, she spent more than a year in Moscow, where she met several times with Yezhov.

The people closest to Efron were the Klepinin couple. On assignment from the Soviet special services, N. Klepinina went to Norway in February 1936, in order to verify information that Trotsky was living there. She even managed to have a brief conversation with Trotsky.[11]

Transferred to the USSR after Reiss's murder, Efron was arrested in 1939. During interrogation he named several participants in Reiss's murder, including the émigré Renata Steiner, who had been trying to return to the USSR. People from Efron's team promised to obtain a repatriation visa for her if she "performed services for the Soviet Union."[12] Not suspecting that they were talking about murder, Steiner followed Reiss in Switzerland, and then rented a car that the murderers used.

The decision to commit the murder was made after a provocation organized by Stalin's agents did not achieve its goal: they sent the police of various countries anonymous letters in which the Czechoslovak businessman, Hans Eberhard (Reiss worked under this name abroad), was declared to be an international adventurer and weapons smuggler.[13]

The group hunting Reiss was joined by Etienne Charles Martignat, Pierre Louis Ducomet, Kondratiev, Smirensky, Shtrange, and others. The French and Swiss police were able to arrest only three participants in the murder. The immediate killers managed to slip away. Material from the investigation of Reiss's murder established that one of these was Roland Abbiate (also known as Francois Rossi and Vladimir Pravdin) — a Frenchman of Russian origin who had lived in Petrograd until 1923. Immediately after Reiss's murder, Abbiate's sister left Paris for Moscow.[14] Abbiate himself received a solid post in the administration of Soviet intelligence, worked during the war as a TASS correspondent in New York, and died in the USSR in 1970.

At the end of September, Abbiate's mother received in the mail a transfer of ten thousand francs, supposedly sent on behalf of her son by a famous French modiste. Madame Abbiate, who had no news from her son, went to the modiste with the intention of returning the money, but to her surprise she learned that the modiste had not sent the money. Then she went to the police, who soon arrested one of the clients of the modiste, Vera Trail, whose handwriting on the transfer form was identified. Trail confessed that she had used the name of the modiste for sending money to Abbiate's mother, allegedly at the request of a "non-returner" she knew, who by this time was living in Spain.[15]

Shtrange, who was considered the "coordinator" of Reiss's murder, returned to the USSR and lived there safely until his death in 1967.[16]

Efron was secretly brought with a group of his colleagues to Moscow in 1937. Until her arrival in the USSR in 1939, Tsvetaeva maintained ties with him through the NKVD, which paid her the wages being earned by her husband.

Reiss's murder occurred on the eve of the day when he was supposed to meet in the French city of Rheims with Sneevliet and Sedov. Before this trip he scheduled a meeting with Schildbach — in a restaurant located close to the Swiss city of Lausanne. As they were leaving the restaurant, a car drove up to them; several cutthroats jumped out and riddled Reiss's body with bullets.

Having carried out her assignment, Schildbach did not, however, carry out another order from Spiegelglas, the deputy head of the foreign department of the NKVD, who was directing the "operation": to give Elsa Reiss a box of poisoned chocolates. Because of this, Reiss's wife and child were saved.

Immediately after the murder, one more provocation was attempted — in order to send the police in the wrong direction. In an anonymous letter sent to Swiss authorities, Reiss was declared an agent of the Gestapo who had broken with the Nazis; the latter supposedly killed him in revenge for his act. However, an abandoned car discovered by the police with traces of blood led the investigation to Renata Steiner, who named the true killers. After a five-month investigation, the Swiss authorities published an official statement that the murder had been committed by agents of the NKVD.

Soon the Soviet intelligence agent Bruesse, who was Krivitsky's subordinate, received an assignment to break into Sneevliet's home and steal Reiss's notes which were kept there, not hesitating to kill if necessary.[17] Krivitsky, whom Bruesse had despairingly told about this assignment, suggested how he should sabotage it. Soon Reiss's notes, which exposed Stalin's crimes, appeared in the pages of the *Bulletin of the Opposition*.

Reiss's murder showed the whole world that the Stalinists who charged innocent people in the USSR with terrorist murders and poisonings were resorting to the most brutal forms of these crimes beyond the borders of the Soviet Union.

In an article published on the anniversary of Reiss's death, Trotsky stressed that the break with Stalin's clique did not mean for "Ludwig" a retreat into private life as had occurred with several other non-returners. Having prepared to continue his revolutionary activity in the ranks of the Fourth International, Reiss "died at the very beginning of this new chapter in his life. All of us feel his death as one of the heaviest blows, and there have been no small number of them. It would be an inadmissible mistake, however, to think that the sacrifice he made was fruitless. By the courageous nature of his turn — from Thermidor to revolution — Reiss made a much greater contribution to the proletarian struggle than all the 'disillusioned' (with communism – V. R.) people who have exposed Stalin taken together."[18]

2. Walter Krivitsky

After Reiss, the next person to announce his break with Stalin was W. Krivitsky, one of the organizers of Soviet espionage in Europe. In 1931, he was one of five members of Soviet military intelligence awarded the Order of the Red Banner.

Krivitsky's last trip to Moscow took place in the spring of 1937. When he returned to Europe, he told Reiss and his wife about his meetings with Yezhov. As Poretsky recalled, Krivitsky "was convinced that Yezhov was mad. In the middle of an important and confidential conversation, Yezhov might suddenly burst into ridiculous laughter and tell a story from his own life using the most obscene language."[1]

After Reiss's death, Krivitsky went underground and lived for more than a month in the south of France. On 9 November 1937, he arrived in Paris and contacted Sedov, who in turn appealed to the Menshevik Dan for help; Krivitsky was hiding from NKVD agents in Dan's apartment.

In recounting to Trotsky the content of his conversations with Krivitsky, Sedov wrote that Yezhov told Slutsky as the latter was offering some advice to Krivitsky before sending him abroad: "You have to teach him to hate our enemy Trotsky." Krivitsky told Sedov facts which showed behind-the-scenes negotiations between Stalin's emissaries and high-ranking officials of the

39. Non-Returners of 1937

Walter Krivitsky
(1899-1941)

Third Reich, and Stalin's efforts "to do everything to reach an agreement with Hitler."²

In a statement sent to the European left-wing press, Krivitsky wrote that for a number of years he had followed the activities of the Soviet government with growing concern, but that he had subordinated his doubts to the thought of the necessity of defending the interests of the Soviet Union and socialism. However, under the influence of recent events he had become convinced that the policies of Stalin's leadership were ever more at variance with the interests of the USSR and the world workers' movement. In the Soviet Union, not only the most outstanding figures of the old party guard were being persecuted, but also "the best the Soviet Union had among the October and post-October generations — those who had built the Soviet regime in the fires of the civil war, in famine, and in cold ."³

In an interview given to Sedov, Krivitsky confirmed that he fully preserved his loyalty to the "October Revolution, which was and remains the starting point of my political development." He explained his desire to get into contact with Trotskyists by the fact that "in my mind and convictions, Trotsky is indissolubly linked with the October Revolution."⁴

Krivitsky stressed: he had taken his risky step in possession of much evidence that "my head has a price on it... that Yezhov and his assistants will not stop at anything to kill me and thereby force me into silence; that dozens of Yezhov's people who are prepared to do anything are following my tracks to do so."⁵ Confirmation of this was information received by the French police that an attack on Krivitsky was being prepared in Marseilles, from where he planned to leave for the USA. This action was prevented when Krivitsky was accompanied to the harbor by the police inspector.[6]

In the United States, Krivitsky published a series of articles which were then compiled in the book *In Stalin's Secret Service*. The American journalist F. Lewis, who studied Krivitsky's activity, wrote that while working on these articles, Krivitsky was torn "between a desire to expose Stalin's intrigues and conspiracies, and the desire to defend old comrades, old ideals, old affections... For he wanted to pass a death sentence on Stalinism, but not on socialism."[7]

In the foreword to his book, Krivitsky wrote: "I forced my mind to know that, whether there was any other hope in the world or not, I was serving a totalitarian despot who differed from Hitler only in the socialist phrases, the relic of his Marxist training — socialist phrases to which he hypocritically clung... If these last tragic years have taught us anything, it is that the march of totalitarian barbarism cannot be halted by strategic retreats to positions of half-truth and falsehood."[8]

In the USA, Krivitsky spoke before the House Committee on Un-American Activities. The next session was scheduled for 10 February 1941. On the morning of that day, Krivitsky was found dead in his hotel room, shot in the head. The American police were inclined to accept the version of suicide. N. I. Sedova felt that Krivitsky had become a victim of political murder. Evidence from Krivitsky's lawyer serves as confirmation of this version. Krivitsky had told him many times: "If they find me dead sometime, and it looks like an unfortunate accident or suicide, do not believe it! I am being hunted..."[9]

3. Alexander Barmine

At nearly the same time as Krivitsky, Alexander Barmine, the chargé d'affaires for the USSR in Greece, announced his break with Stalin.

At the beginning of 1937, Barmine spent several months in Moscow, where he learned much about the mechanism of fabricating the show trials. A meeting with a friend who had worked in *Pravda* made a particularly strong impression on him. His friend told him about how the Stalinist justice system and propaganda had misfired. At the trial of Zinoviev-Kamenev, the defendants denied that they had a political program which differed from Stalin's. Following them, both the prosecutor, the court, and the press all stated that the defendants had no political disagreements with Stalin. "But if they... were fighting only for power," said the journalist, "then this means that Stalin himself had no political disagreements with them and ... was ready to send Lenin's friends to their deaths simply for the sake of consolidating his personal position... When he learned about this maneuver by the defendants from telegrams and newspapers, Stalin flew into a rage. He vented his rage on the court, the GPU, Yagoda, and on us — the journalists, because we had fallen into this trap."[1]

After returning to Greece, Barmine learned about the reprisals against Tukhachevsky and other military leaders with whom he had been close. Shaken by this, he shared with several of his comrades from the embassy his concern over the fate of the USSR after the decapitation of the Red Army. In these conversations, he condemned the way those executed were being covered with mud and slander in the entire Soviet press. Soon, from several indications, he began to feel that in Moscow the content of his conversations had become known, and from this the corresponding conclusions had been drawn. He stopped receiving news from his friends at the People's Commissariat of Foreign Affairs who had previously sent him cordial letters with every diplomatic pouch.

The officials at the embassy became ever more wary about entering into open conversation with Barmine. Several times he observed that some of his subordinates were searching his desk or looking into his briefcase. Several facts showed that they were preparing his kidnapping and forced return to the Soviet Union. Barmine telegraphed the People's Commissariat of Foreign Affairs that he was taking a vacation, and immediately left for France. Both the telegram and his departure came as a complete surprise for Moscow.

In recounting his moods and feelings at that time, Barmine wrote: "Contradictory feelings had gripped me... It seemed that, despite the crimes of renegades who had betrayed the revolution, behind them still stood the as yet undestroyed, but severely damaged and disfigured edifice of socialism... Along with apathy was a readiness to put an end to this strained situation and moral isolation — to go back home and hear the charges... and accept the punishment that I deserved for my 'guilt' (i.e., being upset by Stalin's purges – V. R.)... This seemed much clearer and simpler than a tortuous break, a catastrophe, and the destruction of the meaning of your entire conscious life. But events developed and accumulated with monstrous rapidity, ruthlessly brushing aside these ideas."

As the scale of the bloody slaughter grew, what in the beginning had appeared as inexplicable cruelty and madness began to find its social and political meaning. It became ever clearer that what was occurring was the deliberate extermination of thousands of people who belonged to the revolutionary generation. "In carrying out a counter-revolutionary shift in the politics of the nation, a reactionary dictatorship has destroyed that entire layer which could not serve the new goals. It was impossible to be deceived any more... The thoughts about submissively giving myself to be slaughtered now disappeared, for any inner meaning of such a step had been lost; it would have only become a moral justification of renegades and executioners... The murderers of Reiss miscalculated. His death neither stopped nor frightened me. It only urged me on."[2]

Alexander Barmine
(1899-1987)

After arriving in Paris, Barmine immediately got in touch with the editors of the *Bulletin of the Opposition*. In one of her letters to Trotsky, L. Estrine wrote: "Barmine knows very much about a number of people mentioned in the trials. He had close personal ties to Goltsman, Romm, Pushin, and was with Redhead (Piatakov – V. R.) in Berlin."[3]

Barmine sent a statement to the Paris Commission to Investigate the Moscow Trials, in which he announced his break with the Stalinist regime. Noting that, more than any other time, he remained true to the ideals to which he had devoted his entire life, Barmine stressed that "remaining further in the service of the Stalinist government would signify for me the worst demoralization, and would make me an accomplice in the crimes which are being committed every day against my people... May my voice assist public opinion in understanding that this regime has renounced socialism and anything humanitarian."[4]

Getting down to work on his memoirs, in which he was aided by Sedov, Barmine asked that he tell Trotsky that he wanted to know his opinion of his articles before he began working on the book he had conceived.[5] The Harvard archive contains several dozen pages of Barmine's memoirs which he had sent to Trotsky.

"When I turn to my reminiscences," wrote Barmine, "I cannot look back at a single period in the past without a feeling of great pain, I cannot summon in my memory a given month or day in my life without shuddering... The people whom I respected and loved, with whom I worked for many years, give rise in my mind to images of them, murdered and shot, lying on a concrete floor, with lifeless and bloody bodies."[6]

Barmine's memoirs contain a number of profound reflections explaining the political meaning of Stalin's purge. He stressed that during the change of governments and regimes, when the social structure of the country does not change, the basic cadres of the army and diplomatic corps usually remain at their posts. That is what occurred, for instance, after the coming to power of the fascists in Germany and Italy. When, however, the social base of the regime changes, as happened during the Russian Revolution of 1917 and in the initial period of the Spanish Revolution of 1936, this is accompanied by the complete replacement of the military and diplomatic corps. The extermination of the flower of the Soviet military and diplomatic cadres serves as an expression of the radical shifts in the social structure of society and the powers that be. "Preserving people who are connected by their ideology and traditions with a revolutionary past, with the workers' movement and the Bolshevik Party, who expressed — even weakly — the interests of the working class, is impossible for a counter-revolutionary regime which is changing its social base... The new regime needs new servants with a 'dubious' past, without international traditions, without any principles or any conception of revolutionary Marxism, people who owe everything to the 'brilliant leader alone.'"[7]

Barmine labelled as fruits of ignorance and literary fantasy "all European conversations about the special psychology of the Russian people, about its specific attraction to a dictatorial regime. The establishment of fascism in various countries of Europe shows that there is nothing specifically Russian in that."[8]

When he learned that Barmine was working as a laborer at a Paris factory and writing his book at night, Trotsky wrote to L. Estrine on 15 May 1938: "Please tell Comrade Barmine that I would be very glad to enter into direct correspondence with him."[9] However, by this time Zborowski (see Chapter 46) had done much to push Barmine away from the editorial board of the *Bulletin* and away from Trotsky. In a letter from Estrine to Trotsky on 28 June 1938, she states that Barmine "is moving ever further away from us politically." Later the following assessment of Barmine's views was sent on: "B. says that he is very disillusioned, that he has to review everything (i.e., Bolshevism and Lenin's methods). We cite his words: 'If it was necessary to start from the beginning (i.e., October), then I would think seriously, keeping in mind what it has led to.'"[10]

Evidently, these words were not thought up by Zborowski. Receiving ever newer and more terrible news from the USSR, and being deprived of immediate contact with Trotsky, Barmine drifted ever more to the right. Soon he left for America, where in 1945 he published the book *One Who Survived*. In it, along with an objective portrayal of events in Soviet history, one finds passages which show that Barmine had gone over to positions of bourgeois democracy, arguments about the superiority of private enterprise over a planned economy, and so forth. In the future, Barmine was to work for the American special services.

40. Non-Returners of 1938

1. Alexander Orlov

In July 1938, Alexander Orlov, one of the leaders of Soviet intelligence services abroad who had been sent to Spain to direct the operations of the NKVD there, became a non-returner.

Following the course of the Great Purge, Orlov had no doubt that his turn would soon come. He understood the first signal of the danger hanging over him to be a telegram from the "Center" about their intention to send twelve men to guard him. As a pretext, they said that, according to captured documents, the general staff of Franco's army was preparing to kidnap him. As Orlov told the Senate Sub-Committee of the USA on National Security, he decided that these people would be assigned to liquidate him. Therefore, he instructed his assistant, Eitingon, who worked in Spain under the name of "Kotov," to select ten German members of the International Brigade for his bodyguards. According to Orlov, these people would have considered anyone who ordered them to liquidate him as a traitor, since they "did not believe anyone except Stalin."[1]

On 10 July 1938, Orlov received a telegram from the "Center" with instructions to go to Antwerp and board a Soviet steamer, supposedly for a meeting with an NKVD emissary who had come from Moscow. Realizing that they were preparing a trap for him, he quickly gathered his wife and daughter, who were living in France, and flew together with them to Canada. There he used his diplomatic passport to receive an entrance visa for the USA from the American embassy. Then he turned for help to the Lawyer John Finerty, who had served in 1937 as legal advisor to the Dewey Commission. Having learned that, out of fear of persecution, Orlov wanted to keep his presence in the United States a secret, Finerty arranged that the permission given to

Orlov for permanent residence in this country would not be officially registered.[2]

After this, Orlov asked his cousin Kurnik, who lived in the USA, to go to Paris and put in the mailbox of the Soviet embassy there two letters addressed to Yezhov. In them, he indicated that he had fled from Spain because he was afraid that he would share the fate of the foreign resident agents of the NKVD who had already been destroyed. As confirmation that these people had not been spies, he wrote: "If P., for example, was a spy, why did he keep working with such a man as 'Tulip,' whom he recruited?... Or, if 'M.' had been a spy, why did he not betray Weise or Söhnchen or any of the others who are still operational sources?"[3]

P. signified "Peter" — the code-name for the Paris resident agent, S. M. Glinsky, who operated in Paris under the name Smirnov, and "M." signified the nickname "Mann," under which the Soviet spy Teodor Mally worked. The nickname "Tulip" meant Zborowski, and "Weise" and "Söhnchen" were members of the so-called Cambridge group, Maclean and Philby, in whose recruitment Orlov took an active part.

Enclosed in the letter was a list of the most important foreign operations of the NKVD, designated by their code names, and of sixty-two nicknames of Soviet agents. As Orlov warned, in the event of his murder, information about these agents would be made public by his lawyer. If, however, they left him in peace and did not touch his elderly mother, Orlov added unequivocally, then he never would "embark on anything harmful to the party or the Soviet Union."[4]

The warnings about the possible exposure of secret agents' networks, in the event that Orlov met the same fate as Reiss, found their mark. After he received Orlov's letter, Yezhov cancelled the order which had already been prepared to hunt him down and liquidate him. Spiegelglas reported this during interrogation by the NKVD. This information became known from articles by Petrov, an official in the Soviet embassy in Australia who fled to the West after the war. He recounted that, in 1938, when he worked as an encoder in the Center, a telegram arrived from Paris which said: Orlov has warned that in the event of his murder, his lawyer will make public information "about all his agents and contacts in Spain, and also a description of his important and highly secretive work carried out on orders of the Soviet government."[5]

Despite the fact that Orlov understood the full significance of his threats, he feared persecution on the part of Soviet agents. Therefore, he and his family often changed cities and hotels. In the safe of a Boston bank he placed rolls of film which evidently contained not a list of Stalin's crimes (as he told the American senators), but negatives of his letter to Yezhov and the attached list of secret operations and agents.

Only in the beginning of 1953, literally a month before Stalin's death, did Orlov decide to take steps connected with the legalization of his residency in

40. Non-Returners of 1938

Alexander Orlov
(1895-1973)

the USA. He gave the American magazine *Life* a series of articles later making up the book *The Secret History of Stalin's Crimes*. This book, one of the few reliable memoir sources about the background of the tragic events which occurred in the 1930s in the USSR, was soon translated into many foreign languages. Its Russian text appeared for the first time in 1983; for thirty years not a single emigrant publishing house had undertaken the publication of a book written from the position of Bolshevism that did not contain the traditional anti-communist passages.

The appearance of Orlov's articles came as a shock to J. Edgar Hoover, the director of the FBI, who learned only from them that a general of the NKVD had been living in his country for fifteen years. Hoover ordered a thorough investigation of Orlov's activity. As a result of many years of interrogations by the FBI and special hearings of the Senate Sub-Committee on National Security, the American authorities remained convinced that Orlov had told them everything he knew about the activity of Soviet intelligence. A book published by the Senate Sub-Committee in 1973, *The Legacy of Alexander Orlov*, opened with his biography, written by Senator Eastland, who had chaired the hearings of 1955. This biography, filled with profound respect for Orlov, was written in warm, and at times even emotional, tones.

In the 1950s and 1960s, investigations into the "Orlov case" were also made by the KGB. They concluded that Orlov had not given away any of the foreign agents and had not told about operations carried out with his participation. The "Cambridge boys" he had recruited, as well as Abel, who worked at one time as a radio operator in a group organized by Orlov, continued to obtain extremely valuable intelligence information.

As the authors of the detailed investigation into Orlov's activity correctly note, "If Orlov had broken faith with Lenin's revolution and had given the secret list of underground Soviet agents to the FBI, ... he might have single-handedly changed the course of history, ... he would have deprived Stalin of vital information from such agents as Philby and the *Rote Kapelle* ... If he had exposed these Soviet underground networks, Stalin's agents might never have stolen the secrets of the atomic bomb."[6]

In 1969 and 1971, Orlov was visited by the KGB agent Feoktistov, who said that in the USSR they did not consider Orlov a traitor, but, on the contrary, they highly valued his activity in the 1930s in recruiting people abroad with communist convictions. Orlov told the Americans that he did not enter into any conversations with Feoktistov. However, as can be seen from Feoktistov's reports, Orlov told him which facts he had concealed from the FBI and on what issues he had given American intelligence disinformation. When Feoktistov handed him an invitation to return to the USSR, Orlov replied that he had maintained loyalty to his communist convictions, but he did not want to return to the USSR, since the Soviet state was run by former minions of Stalin and by a younger generation of party apparatchiks who had played an auxiliary role in the crimes, due to which the revolution had been betrayed.[7]

One of the professors at the University of Michigan, where Orlov worked during the last years of his life, told the FBI that Orlov had remained a communist at heart and a "strong Leninist." The professor mentioned that Orlov "violently objected" to his comment that Lenin and Stalin were of the same breed, and when he had heard arguments about the financial support supposedly given to the Bolsheviks in 1917 by Germany, he declared that this was slander which was "defaming the revolution and Lenin's integrity."[8]

Orlov died on 7 April 1973, having long outlived the other non-returners.

2. Fyodor Raskolnikov

The name of Raskolnikov was more famous than the names of the other non-returners who belonged to the second generation of Bolsheviks joining the party during the years of the Civil War. Raskolnikov was one of the most active figures among the old party guard, the organizers of the October Revolution, and was well acquainted with Lenin and Trotsky.

In 1923, in the journal *Proletarian Revolution*, Raskolnikov published his reminiscences of the events preceding the October Revolution. He wrote that after Trotsky returned to Russia in 1917, "all of us, the old Leninists,

40. Non-Returners of 1938

Fyodor Raskolnikov
(1892-1939)

felt that he was ours."[1] It seems that in order to repudiate this account from an Old Bolshevik, the Stalinist editors in 1931 added to Gorky's memoirs about Lenin a sentence with diametrically opposed content which had not been there earlier. Lenin supposedly says: "But nevertheless (Trotsky) is not ours! He is with us, but he is not ours!"[2]

In citing these and several other similar accounts from Raskolnikov that were discarded from subsequent editions of his works, Trotsky wrote: "Raskolnikov met with me during our work very often during the summer months of 1917; he drove me to Kronstadt, turned to me more than once for advice, talked with me a lot in prison (where they were being held after the July days – V. R.), and so forth. In this sense, his memoirs are a valuable testimony, since his later 'corrections' are nothing other than a product of the work of falsification carried out under orders."[3]

After the end of the Civil War, Raskolnikov was mainly engaged in diplomatic work — in Afghanistan, Estonia, Denmark, and Belgium. In 1936, he was appointed ambassador to Bulgaria, where he spent almost the entire period of the Great Purge. During this time, he repeatedly received summonses to Moscow — supposedly for negotiations about an appointment to more responsible work. Knowing the fate that had befallen the majority of Soviet diplomats, Raskolnikov delayed his trip from Bulgaria in every way he could. He, of course, did not know that the NKVD had already fabricated testimony about his belonging to an "anti-Soviet Trotskyist organization." However, according to many indications, he felt that distrust toward him was growing and that even in the embassy he was under surveillance by agents.

When he received the next categorical instructions to immediately come to Moscow, Raskolnikov set off, in April 1938, from Sofia. Before crossing the Soviet border, he learned from foreign newspapers that the Stalinist clique had been in a hurry and had announced his removal from his post as ambassador. From this news it became absolutely clear: all the proposals to return to Moscow were an attempt to lure him to the Soviet Union for liquidation. Raskolnikov halted his journey and headed for France. In later explaining this move, he wrote: "Above the portal to the Church of the Paris Virgin, among other sculptures there stands the statue of Saint Denis, who humbly carries his own head in his hands. But I prefer to live on bread and water in freedom, than to innocently languish and die in a prison without having a chance to clear myself of the monstrous charges made against me."[4]

For several months Raskolnikov lived in Paris, without engaging in any political activity or speaking out in the press. On 12 December, he was invited to a reception by the ambassador of the USSR in France, Surits, who assured him that the Soviet government had no complaints against him besides "unauthorized residency abroad," and therefore he could travel to the USSR without any fear. However, Raskolnikov knew very well that even according to the official statute "On Declaring Citizens of the USSR Abroad... Refusing to Return to the USSR to Be in Violation of the Law," "unauthorized residency abroad" was equal to betrayal of the Motherland.

Nevertheless, Raskolnikov continued to vacillate over the question of returning to the Soviet Union, and on 18 December 1938, he even sent Stalin an abject and flattering letter in which, among other things, he said the following: "Dear Iosif Vissarionovich! After the death of Comrade Lenin, it became clear to me that the only person capable of continuing his cause was you. I immediately and unerringly followed you, sincerely believing in your qualities as a political leader, sharing and supporting your party line not out of fear, but in good conscience."[5]

In July 1939, Raskolnikov learned that the Supreme Court of the USSR had declared him to be above the law for "passing into the camp of enemies of the people." On 26 July, he sent an article to the foreign press, "How They Made Me an Enemy of the People," in which he wrote: "Declaring me a criminal is dictated by a blind fury toward a man who refused to submissively place his head on the chopping block and who dared to defend his life, freedom and honor."[6]

In August 1939, Raskolnikov's open letter was published. At the end of August, Raskolnikov, who was living in Nice, fell ill with pneumonia and on 12 September he died.

Unlike other non-returners, Raskolnikov was posthumously rehabilitated — during the second wave of exposures of Stalin's crimes which arose after the Twenty-Second Congress of the CPSU. On 10 July 1963, the plenum of the Supreme Court of the USSR reversed the ruling in his case "for the absence in his actions of a corpus delicti [the facts constituting a crime]." Soon, Raskolnikov was reinstated in the party.

In December 1963, the journal *Voprosy istorii* [Questions of History] published an article by V. S. Zaitsev, "Hero of October and the Civil War," which states that until the last days of his life, Raskolnikov "remained a Bolshevik, a Leninist, and a citizen of the Soviet Union."[7] This article was followed by an anthology of reminiscences and stories by Raskolnikov, *At Battle Stations*. Raskolnikov's wife and daughter were cordially received in the Soviet Union. The question was discussed of returning Raskolnikov's remains to his homeland and giving him a new burial at Kronstadt.

However, the campaign of re-Stalinization which began in 1965 could not pass by Raskolnikov. For Stalinists, the very precedent of restoring the good name of a "non-returner" was unacceptable. Trapeznikov, the head of the Central Committee's department of science and learning institutes, assumed the initiative in defaming Raskolnikov for a second time. In September 1965, at an imposing conference, he used unbridled Stalinist vocabulary when he declared: "When it comes to ideology, Raskolnikov was always an active Trotskyist. Having fraternized with White-Guardists and fascist scum, this renegade started to spit on everything that had been achieved and then secured by the sweat and blood of the Soviet peoples; he began to blacken the great banner of Leninism and praise Trotskyism. Only irresponsible people could consider Raskolnikov's desertion, his fleeing from the Soviet Union, a heroic deed."[8]

Similar opinions were contained in an article by five semi-official historians, "For Leninist Party-Mindedness in Studying the History of the CPSU," which signaled a retreat even from those modest exposures of Stalin's crimes that had appeared in the first decade after Stalin's death. In this article, the following instructive paragraph was devoted to Raskolnikov: "In no way can one include among the true Leninists, as some historians are now doing, those who in actual fact spoke out against Leninism and participated in factional fighting, ... for instance, those like F. F. Raskolnikov, who fled to the enemy camp and slandered both the party and the Soviet state."[9]

"Non-returning" and emigration for Bolsheviks of the 1930s were a much more difficult problem than for Soviet dissidents of the 1970s and 1980s — not only because in the 1930s each non-returner clearly understood that he was threatened with death at the hands of foreign blood-hounds of the NKVD, and not only because of the system of hostage-taking, which had received the status of the law at that time in the Soviet Union. Whereas dissidents of the recent past renounced the entire Soviet system and were openly oriented toward the West, the overwhelming majority of Bolsheviks retained their hostility to the capitalist structure and their loyalty to communist ideals. Therefore, they could not expect a warm welcome in the West.

In characterizing the difference between non-returners of 1937 from those of earlier years, the journal *Socialist Herald* wrote: "At that time, those who 'did not return' were mainly non-party 'specialists,' prepared in conditions unfavorable to them to serve for the time being the Bolshevik government, but inwardly remaining absolutely foreign not only to this government, but to the revolution in general. Or, the non-returners were 'political' figures of the type like Besedovsky, Dmitrievsky and Agabekov, whose further adventuristic 'career' shows all too clearly the absence in them of any kind of intimate ties not only with Bolshevism, but with the workers' movement and socialism in general... Now, on the contrary, people have begun to run from Stalin, ... people in whom doubts have for many years battled with the old faith. These are people who have forced themselves to continue, ... sometimes gritting their teeth, to do the work assigned to them by the Stalinist dictatorship 'in the name of the revolution,' — until the time has come when no more room remains for any doubts or illusions, and they have been forced to say, willy-nilly: I cannot go one step further!... Their 'flight' is therefore one of the clearest symptoms of the ever growing and ever sharper gap between 'Stalinism' and the world of the revolution, the proletariat, and socialism."

Noting that these people had the chance to cast off Stalin's yoke because they were serving abroad, the journal stressed: "Can one doubt that their moods reflect the moods of hundreds of their comrades..., who have passed through the same school of revolution as they, but who, under the threat of a revolver placed to their head by the Stalinist dictatorship, are forced even now not only to sing its praises, but, on its orders, to exterminate their friends and co-thinkers."[10]

Out of five non-returners, four (all except Raskolnikov) looked to Trotsky, although in the circumstances of those years, this was far from the most "convenient" way out for emigrants from the USSR.

All these people gave a profound and clear analysis of events in the USSR. Judging from their books and articles, one can imagine the gigantic intellectual potential of the Soviet people which was squandered during the years of the Great Purge.

From the actions of the non-returners, Stalin received ever newer confirmation that the Old Bolsheviks were deeply hostile both to him and his "socialism." This reinforced his thoughts that, as long as the first generations of Bolsheviks were alive, there still remained a threat that he would lose his absolute power. An even greater fear was generated in Stalin by the energetic activity of Trotsky, who was effectively repulsing the Moscow falsifications and frame-ups.

41. The Verdict of the Dewey Commission

When he arrived in Mexico, Trotsky actively joined in the work of preparing an investigation into the Moscow Trials. His moods at this time can be discerned from a letter sent on 2 February 1937 to Angelica Balabanova: "What does pessimism mean? A passive and whining sense of resentment toward history. Can one really be offended by history? One must take her as she is, and when she delivers extraordinarily swinish tricks, one must knead her with one's fists! Only in that way can one survive in this world."[1]

After a month, Trotsky wrote to Francis Heisler, the author of the book *The First Two Moscow Trials:* "I sincerely congratulate you on this work! By the carefulness and veracity of the analysis, in which jurisprudence is happily combined with politics, this book should make a great impression on any serious and thoughtful reader... With all my heart I wish your book the widest distribution. I would also like to wish you a serious critique from your opponents. But such a wish, unfortunately, is utopian. To the arguments of reason, the Stalinists are capable of answering only with abusive language. This does not prevent the truth, however, from finding its way."[2]

Trotsky directed all his efforts at preparing material for the Commission to Investigate the Moscow Trials, working under the chairmanship of the famous American philosopher John Dewey. For nine months this commission worked in New York, Mexico, Paris, and other cities. It assiduously studied thousands of documents, letters, books, and articles, as well as the oral and written testimony of hundreds of witnesses. By the beginning of April [1937] alone, Trotsky was sent 80 statements from witnesses that had been gathered for the commission in France, England, Belgium, Denmark, Holland, and other countries.[3]

During the preliminary hearings of the commission, which took place in Trotsky's home, he outlined a number of ideas which could be seen as drafts of unwritten philosophical and sociological works. When Finerty, the legal advisor to the commission, asked the question, Does a revolutionary government have the right to carry out executions against its enemies, Trotsky answered: "This is not an abstract right. I hope that after one or two victories in other countries, revolutions will become absolutely friendly revolutions." "Bloodless revolutions?" asked Finerty. "Yes, bloodless revolutions," answered Trotsky. "But pioneers everywhere have been severe people. I think that Americans know about this better than myself."[4]

In reply to the question whether, after the world socialist revolution, all countries could live in peace, Trotsky answered that he thought this was "absolutely possible." Concretizing this thought, he said: "...The scientists, engineers and the leaders of the trade unions will in a conference, in a world conference, establish what we have, what we need, the productive forces, the natural resources, and the creative forces of humanity... Then they will begin cautiously, ... by a plan, not by war..."[5]

Speaking about the fact that mankind still had not achieved significant success in rationalizing its history, Trotsky said that, in his opinion, the main question was, can people move far ahead in perfecting their own nature, because "after every great step forward mankind makes a small detour, even a great step backward. I regret it very much, but I am not responsible for it (Laughter)."[6]

Dewey asked about the acceptability of the conclusion that privileges in the USSR had reached such a level that it was possible to talk about the class division of society, i.e., its division into exploited and exploiters. In response, Trotsky answered that, for a characterization of today's stage of development in the USSR, it was difficult to find a strict sociological formula, because "we are meeting with such a social structure for the first time in history. We must develop our own terminology, and new social categories. But I am inclined to think that this is not a genuine (traditional) class division."[7]

In explaining his position on the question of the state, Trotsky declared that the socialist state is a transitional form, necessary for the construction of a classless and stateless society. This state would exist until people have the chance to freely satisfy their needs, much like at a "smorgasbord." "There is no need for a dictatorship when you have a 'smorgasbord.' On the contrary, each can take from the table what he needs, with ladies first. But when the table is very poor, people already forget where the ladies or the men are. Each grabs whatever possible. Then a dictatorship is necessary. The reason for the existence of gendarmes is the poverty of the people."[8]

Stressing the limited nature of conceptions according to which the presence of a democratic constitution acts as a guarantee against the rise of totalitarian regimes, Trotsky pointed out that "Hitler did not touch the Weimar Constitution, the democratic Constitution. It was an astonishment for every-

41. The Verdict of the Dewey Commission

Special Broadsheet by Pioneer Publishers Exposes Moscow Trials, April 1937

body. Everybody believed that Hitler would change the Constitution, but the Constitution remains. But he broke the backbone of the Constitution. That is all he did, and even the secret vote gave him the majority."[9]

On 21 September 1937, all the members of the Dewey commission signed a verdict, the full text of which, filling 422 typeset pages, was published in New York under the title *Not Guilty*. This book, wrote Trotsky, "will remain forever a monument to ideological honesty, legal and political insight, and inexhaustible industriousness... All doubts have been dispelled, and what has been established is unshakable facts, from which unshakable conclusions have been made."[10]

On the basis of a careful comparison of the official transcripts of the Moscow Trials with many documents and testimony by witnesses, the commission felt that it was thoroughly proven that the basic factual aspects of the charges and the confessions of the defendants were the purest fabrication. Trotsky never gave terrorist instructions to any of the defendants, nor did he meet with any of them in the 1930s; he did not order anyone to organize sabotage and wrecking, or to make any treasonous agreements with foreign powers. The commission also indicated that the prosecutor monstrously falsified Trotsky's role before, during, and after the revolution.

The verdict stated that the confessions of the defendants — independent of the manner in which they were obtained — contained so many improbable things, that this would convince an unbiased person that they did not correspond to reality. The concluding paragraphs of the verdict state: on the basis of the investigation, the commission came to the conclusion that "the Moscow trials are frame-ups, ... Trotsky and Sedov are not guilty."[11]

A short text of the verdict was made public by Dewey on 12 December at a meeting in New York before 2,500 people. The next day, Trotsky released a statement to journalists in which he emphasized: "All the members of the commission have dozens of years of active political, party or literary work. They all have irreproachable names. If there had been even one among them who could be bought, he would have been bought long ago. My enemies have millions at their disposal for such purposes, and they are not miserly when it comes to such expenditures. As for me and my son, we have not had at our disposal even the necessary means to cover the technical expenses of the investigation. The modest cash-box of the Commission has been filled by collections among workers and by individual donations."

Trotsky pointed out that "the Commission looked for an authoritative Stalinist or someone sympathetic to Stalinism, who would not limit himself to... the slander and insinuations contained in irresponsible or worthless publications, but would have the courage to openly make the Moscow charges under the control of criticism." Indicating that not a single Stalinist responded to the proposal to participate in the work of the commission, Trotsky warned that in the future it would be in vain to wait for some kind of "articulate reply from the falsifiers. The only response which remains for them and which they use so often, is the shot from a revolver or the blow from a dagger. With such an argument, one can kill an opponent, but one can never kill the voice of the world's conscience."

Trotsky noted that, in essence, the verdict dealt not only with him and his son, and not only with the honor and good name of those sentenced to be shot at the Moscow Trials. "What was at stake is something incomparably larger, namely the basic principles of the workers' movement and of the liberation struggle of mankind. First and foremost, it dealt with the eradication of the demoralization and infection which the apparatus of the Comintern, combined with the apparatus of the GPU, spread everywhere."[12]

In responding to the journalists' questions about how Stalin and his assistants could allow so many contradictions and absurdities as they conducted the Moscow Trials, Trotsky said: "All these people, starting with Stalin, have been corrupted by their immunity from control or punishment. In the articles and speeches of Stalin himself, one meets at every step not only political contradictions, but the crudest factual distortions, not to mention grammatical mistakes. Since no one dares to criticize him, Stalin gradually has grown unaccustomed to controlling himself. The same applies to all the other bureaucrats. They do not study, or think, they only give orders. The totalitarian regime guarantees the surface success of the confessions. The chairman of the courtroom, the prosecutor, the accused, the defense lawyers and the witnesses — all carry out the lesson they have been assigned. The newspapers subordinate themselves to a telephone call. There is no discussion, there is no criticism. The people have the right to express only their thanks. Under such conditions, the stimulus to good work disappears, even in the realm of frame-ups."

If the Stalinist bureaucracy had tried to do its work better, continued Trotsky, then things still would have ended unsuccessfully. The problem of sitting in a political office and creating the scheme of a false conspiracy without crude contradictions is in principle without a solution. Even more so when we are speaking about a "conspiracy" of people who are known to the whole world, with complex political and personal ties and relations. "Of course, if one were to assign this problem to dozens of people like Shakespeare, Cervantes, Goethe, and Freud, then they would do a much better job than Stalin, Vyshinsky, and Yezhov. But people of genius, as a general rule, do not engage in frame-ups."

The journalists asked what would be the fate of Troyanovsky, the Soviet ambassador to the USA who had been assigned to disrupt the work of the Dewey Commission. Trotsky replied by referring to the words of Diego Rivera: "Troyanovsky's career has perished, and along with his career, he has probably lost his head." However, noted Trotsky, if the journalists were to publish this answer, they would do Troyanovsky a great favor, since in such a case, "it will not be easy for Stalin to act in strict correspondence with Diego Rivera's predictions." It seems that these words, which circulated throughout the world, were instrumental in guaranteeing that Troyanovsky did not share the fate of the majority of Soviet diplomats.

With regard to the political consequences which the reading of the verdict might bring, Trotsky said: "I do not expect, it goes without saying, that a sound of the trumpet, even if it is the trumpet of truth, will immediately topple the walls of Jericho." At the same time he expressed certainty that "the opponents who have been slandered and killed by Stalin will be rehabilitated by world public opinion. For Stalin there will be no rehabilitation... Stalin will leave the scene, covered with infamy."

When asked if pessimistic conclusions about the perspectives of socialism could be drawn from the Moscow Trials, Trotsky replied: "No, I do not see any grounds for pessimism. One must take history as she is. Mankind moves like some pilgrims: two steps forward, one step back. During the movement back, it seems to skeptics and pessimists that all is lost. But this is a mistake in historical vision. Nothing is lost. Mankind has risen from the ape to the Comintern. It will rise from the Comintern to genuine socialism. The sentence of the commission shows once again that a correct idea is stronger than the most powerful police. In this conviction lies the indestructible foundation of revolutionary optimism."[13]

The ideas advanced by Trotsky during the work of the Dewey Commission were developed in a number of his theoretical and historical works written in 1937-1938. These works become particularly valuable in light of today's discussions about the relationship of Bolshevism to Stalinism.

French edition of Trotsky's *Revolution Betrayed*, translated by Victor Serge

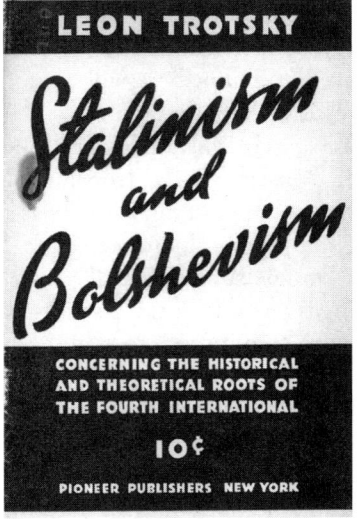

English edition of Trotsky's *Stalinism and Bolshevism*, published in 1937 by Pioneer Publishers

42. Bolshevism, Stalinism, Trotskyism

In reading today's philippics against Bolshevism, one is involuntarily struck by the laziness and lack of independent thought displayed by their authors. Indeed, over the last fifty years, they have not come up with a single new argument, or advanced a single new demonstration of proof! One and the same myths pass from one work to another. They play one and the same "trump cards." Of course, repeating a lie one thousand times does not make it true. However, a lie transmitted by today's means of mass communication has the power to affect actively the consciousness of the masses. This effect is reinforced when a one-way flood of information arises after long years of banning the discussion of certain historical questions. That is what happened during the years of "perestroika" and "reform," when hackneyed arguments in the West, expressing the incorrigibility and epigonism of reactionary thought, were transplanted to Soviet soil.

The difficulty in refuting anti-communist falsifications is connected with the fact that, despite an abundance of works crammed with Marxist phraseology, the development of the Marxist tradition was interrupted in the USSR from the beginning of the 1930s. A genuinely Marxist criticism of anti-communism was also cut short. And given the existence of the "iron curtain," Trotsky's arguments were simply unknown to several generations of Soviet people.

Even after Stalin's death, the attacks on "Trotskyism" continued to come from two directions. On the one hand, from semi-official Soviet historical literature, which interpreted "Trotskyism" as an anti-Leninist and anti-party current. On the other hand, from "tamizdat," which was penetrating the USSR ever more widely. These were products of the reactionary wing of Western Sovietology (the so-called "totalitarian school"), proceeding from the idea of the USSR's "unbroken" historical development, from the idea that

Trotsky and Lenin had paved the way for Stalinism. The thinking of Soviet intellectuals became hopelessly entangled in these untrue postulates, all the more so since in the Soviet Union, as before, the strictest ban on becoming familiar with the works of Trotsky and "Trotskyists" was still in effect.

Driven only by conservative incentives aimed at self-preservation, and ignorant in the area of Marxism (which did not exclude a search for "appropriate" quotations from the "classics" to "lay a foundation" for each new zigzag in their politics), the ruling clique in the USSR retained the Stalinist version of the inner-party struggle, although in a slightly more proper form. They displayed cowardice when it came to making public even the purely factual side of these pages of history.

Foreseeing the complex ways that the process would take of cleansing Marxist thought from the layers deposited by the Stalinist school of falsification, Trotsky wrote in 1937: "Reactionary epochs lower the general ideological level of the movement, throwing political thought backwards to stages which have already been passed long ago. The task of the avant-garde in these conditions consists primarily in not allowing oneself to be carried along by the general reverse current — one must be able to swim against the stream. If an unfavorable relationship of forces does not allow one to hold on to political positions seized earlier, then one must at least hold on to ideological positions, for in them is expressed the experience of the past which has been dearly paid for."[1]

In a polemic against the many critics of Bolshevism, Trotsky noted that their favorite device was the method of making historical analogies and juxtapositions. Much like the Stalinists called fascism and social-democracy twins, the liberals declared fascism and Bolshevism to be twins. On the opposite political wing, similar devices were used by Hitler and Mussolini, who declared that liberalism, social-democracy, and Bolshevism are only different variations of one and the same evil.

The "method of twins" found its base of support in identifying the forms of activity associated with reaction and revolution, which was always characteristic of moralizing philistines. This device lived as a parasite on several actual historical facts. "Certain common features among the tendencies grouped together above are beyond doubt," wrote Trotsky. "... Fighting armies are always more or less symmetrical, and if there was nothing in common in their methods of fighting, then they could not inflict blows upon one another."[2]

An even more complex task was explaining why the thesis of Stalinism as the legitimate product of Bolshevism had received such wide circulation. In defense of this thesis there was unanimity between Stalinists, fascists, liberals, Mensheviks, anarchists, and several left-wing doctrinaires calling themselves Marxists.

If one were to set aside the Stalinists, then it would not be difficult to become convinced that, for all the remaining adherents to the "method of twins," a shared trait was the approximation, or even the identification, of Stalinism and Trotskyism. Agreement existed on this question for political tendencies which had major differences on other questions, such as conservatives, liberals, social-democrats, and fascists. "If the Stalinists cannot join this 'Popular Front,'" Trotsky noted sarcastically, "then it is only because they happen to be occupied with exterminating Trotskyists."[3]

In developing this thought, Trotsky turned to the defenders of the "theory of twins" with the following questions: "You say that Marxism is inherently flawed, and that Stalinism is its legitimate offspring? But why is it that we, revolutionary Marxists, are locked in mortal combat with Stalinism throughout the world? Why does the Stalinist gang see in Trotskyism its main enemy? Why is it that whenever anyone draws close to our views or our system of activity (Durruti, Andrés Nin, Landau and others), this forces the gangsters of Stalinism to resort to bloody reprisals?"[4]

Trotsky stressed that, not very long before, a significant part of the capitalist press had not identified but counterposed Trotskyism and Stalinism, seeing the first as "revolutionary romanticism," and the second as "realistic politics." By means of this juxtaposition, bourgeois philistines justified the alliance of their governments with a Stalinist regime which had broken with the doctrine of world revolution. "The French League of the Rights of Man, which fulminated against the amoralism of Lenin and Trotsky in 1917 when they severed the military alliance with France, rushed to conceal the crimes of Stalin in 1936 in the interests of a French-Soviet pact... Only a year ago, these gentlemen... were by no means saying that Stalinism and Trotskyism are one and the same thing. They openly stood for Stalin, for his realism, for his justice system and for his Yagoda... Until the moment Tukhachevsky, Yakir and others were executed, the grand bourgeoisie of the democratic countries observed the extermination of revolutionaries in the USSR not without pleasure, although it was concealed beneath a certain squeamishness."[5] Only the execution of the generals alarmed these political circles by forcing them to realize that the far-going degeneration of the political regime in the Soviet Union objectively strengthened the positions of Germany and Japan on the world arena.

Only after this, the bourgeois philistines returned to arguments that the struggle between Stalinism and Trotskyism was only the clash of personal ambitions, or in the best case, the struggle of two "shadings" within Bolshevism. Such an interpretation was connected with the reaction to Stalin's crimes on the part of liberals and social-democrats, whom the October Revolution had almost forced to lose faith in their ideas. "The moral gangrene of the Soviet bureaucracy seems to them to be the rehabilitation of liberalism. Hackneyed commandments are dragged out into the light; 'Every dictatorship contains within itself the seeds of its own decomposition'; 'only democracy guarantees the development of the individual,' and so forth." Such a juxtaposition of democracy and dictatorship served to condemn socialism in the name of the bourgeois regime. The theoretical bankruptcy of such arguments is revealed in the fact that "the loathsomeness of Stalinism as a historical reality is juxtaposed to democracy as an ahistorical abstraction. But democracy has also had its history, in which there has been no shortfall of loathsomeness. To characterize the Soviet bureaucracy, we borrow the terms 'Thermidor' and 'Bonapartism' from the history of bourgeois democracy, for — let this become known to belated liberal doctrinaires — *democracy appeared on this earth by no means in a democratic way.*"[6]

More concrete were the arguments of those doctrinaires who considered themselves Marxists but who counterposed their positions in a hostile way to Bolshevism. "'We always predicted this,' they say. 'Beginning with the ban on other socialist parties, with the crushing of the anarchists, with the establishment of the dictatorship of the Bolsheviks in the Soviets, the October Revolution could not help but arrive at a dictatorship of the bureaucracy. Stalinism is the continuation and, at the same time, the bankruptcy of Leninism.'"[7]

In such statements, Trotsky emphasized, there is a virtual identification of three closely connected, but independent, historical phenomena — Bolshevism, the October Revolution, and the Soviet Union. As a result of such an identification, a complex and contradictory social reality is replaced by one of its elements, logically abstracted — "pure" Bolshevism.

Meanwhile, Bolshevism itself "saw itself as one of the factors of history, its 'conscious' factor — very important, but not decisive."[8] The conquest of power did not turn the Bolshevik Party into an omnipotent master and demiurge of the historical process. Having received the chance to influence the development of society with a power that had not been available before, the party at the same time was itself subjected to the heightened influence from all of its other elements. Under the direct blows of hostile forces, it could be stripped of power. Having held on to power, it might degenerate internally. In repeatedly pointing to both of these dangers, Lenin stressed that the bureaucratization of the Soviet regime was capable of leading to the degeneration of the workers' state which had emerged from the October Revolution. This dialectic of the historical process was not understood by those who tried to find in the decay of the Stalinist bureaucracy an overwhelming argument against Bolshevism. From the fact that the October Revolution, at a definite stage of its development, led to the triumph of the bureaucracy with its system of the knout, predation, and falsifications, they drew a false conclusion: one cannot fight against Stalinism without rejecting Bolshevism.

Of course, Trotsky said in reply to such arguments, Stalinism in a formal sense grew out of Bolshevism. The Moscow bureaucracy lived as a parasite on such circumstances, and for the sake of deceiving the masses, continued to call itself the Bolshevik Party and used old Bolshevik symbols. These methods of camouflage were taken seriously by those apostates of Bolshevism who replaced essence with appearance and thereby rendered the greatest service to the Stalinist regime.

In actuality, as Trotsky underscored, Stalinism "grew" out of Bolshevism "not logically, but dialectically: not as a revolutionary confirmation, but as a Thermidorian negation... Today's 'purge' draws between Bolshevism and Stalinism not simply a bloody line, but a whole river of blood. The extermination of the entire older generation of Bolsheviks, a significant part of the middle generation which participated in the civil war, and that part of the youth which seriously accepted the Bolshevik traditions, shows not only the political, but the literally physical incompatibility of Stalinism and Bolshevism. How can one not see this?"[9]

Trotsky considered the derivation of Stalinism from Bolshevism or from Marxism a particular case of deriving counter-revolution from revolution, which is characteristic of liberal-conservative and reformist thought. This method has speculated on the fact that revolutions in which the class divisions of society are maintained have always given birth to counter-revolution. "Does this not show, asks the moralizer, that there is some kind of inherent flaw in the revolutionary method? So far, neither liberals nor reformists have been able, however, to invent more 'economical' methods. But if it is not easy to rationalize *in deed* the living historical process, it is, however, not hard at all to rationalistically *interpret* the succession of its waves, logically deriving Stalinism from 'state socialism,' fascism from Marxism, reaction from revolution, in short, antithesis from thesis."[10]

Some of the rationalists, as Trotsky emphasized, used more concrete arguments, deriving Stalinism not from Bolshevism as a whole, but from the political methods used by the latter in extreme historical conditions: from the ban on other political parties, supplemented by the ban on factions within the ruling party itself. The use of these forced measures, which did not flow from the theory of Bolshevism, signaled the greatest danger, as was clear to the Bolsheviks from the very beginning. Keeping well in mind the temporary character of these measures, the Bolsheviks used them in a historical situation that was characterized by the weakness of the Soviet state, which had been established in a backward and exhausted country, and was surrounded on all sides by enemies. "If the revolution had been victorious, if only in Germany, the necessity of banning other Soviet parties (i.e., which until 1921 were part of the Soviets – V. R.) would have immediately fallen away."[11]

As soon as the domestic and international situation of the USSR became stabilized and stronger, the Left Opposition demanded the widening of party and Soviet democracy. It was precisely for this sake that it entered into irreconcilable battle with the ruling faction headed by Stalin. Emerging victorious in this struggle, the Bonapartist clique crushed all democratic elements and institutions, replaced the dictatorship of the proletariat with the dictatorship of the bureaucracy, and virtually strangled the Bolshevik Party itself.

The question of the fate of democracy was closely linked with the question of the fate of the state, around which the anarchists constructed their arguments. Seeing in Stalinism the organic product, not only of Bolshevism and Marxism, but mainly of "state socialism," they pointed to indisputable historical facts: one branch of "state socialism" — social-democracy — came to power in a number of countries and preserved the capitalist organization of society; another branch, which was in power in the USSR, not only preserved a strictly centralized state, but gave birth to a new caste of privileged people.

Trotsky felt that in the arguments of the anarchists, seen from a broad historical point of view, one could discover a grain of truth. Marxists are completely in agreement with anarchists that the removal of the state as an apparatus of compulsion is the final goal of the communist transformation of society. It is precisely Marxism which points to the ways and methods which will allow mankind to free itself from the straightjacket of the state. To attain this goal, mankind must rise to an immeasurably higher cultural level than now.

During the heroic epoch of the Russian Revolution, the Bolsheviks fought hand in hand with the revolutionary anarchists. The Bolshevik Party included many of them in its ranks. Trotsky recalled that he had often discussed with Lenin the question of granting anarchists opportunities for conducting their stateless experiments — in various regions of the country and with the agreement of the local population. But the circumstances of the Civil War, of the economic and military blockade, and of economic ruination left little room for social experiments of this kind. The same circumstances caused the Bolsheviks to use force, frequently in the harshest forms. However, given all this, one cannot help but see a radical difference between the Bolshevik regime and the regime of Stalinism which replaced it. The Bolshevik regime acted as a weapon in the overthrow of social relations, which served the interests of the broadest popular masses. The Thermidorian overthrow which was made by Stalinism led to the restructuring of these new and still unstable social relations, in the interests of a privileged minority. It was precisely this that explained the monopolization of the system of compulsion by the Stalinist bureaucracy, which used it in such forms and on a scale that surpassed by far the excesses of the Civil War of 1918-1920. If Bolshevism had tried to establish a state without a bureaucracy, or a state of the "Commune type," then Stalin "had created a state of the self-enriching bureaucracy, of the 'GPU type.'"[12]

Correspondingly, the social types of the objects of repression differed radically at various stages of the development of the Soviet state. Whereas in the first post-revolutionary years, they were open enemies of the October Revolution which had stripped them of their class and property privileges, in the years of the Great Terror, the spearhead of the repressions was aimed at the communist opponents of Stalin's regime.

Trotsky also thought that the identification of Stalinism with Bolshevism and Marxism was wrong because the Stalinist bureaucracy did not possess a fully formulated political doctrine and a strict ideological system. "Its 'ideology' is fully permeated with police subjectivism, its practice is the empiricism of naked violence... Stalin revises Marx and Lenin not with the pen of his theoreticians, but with the jackboots of the GPU."[13] The hostility of Stalinism to any serious theory flowed from the existence of the social interests of the caste of usurpers, and this caste could give neither themselves nor others an account of their actual social role.

The contradictory nature of the social position of the ruling layer in the USSR consisted in the following: having broken with Marxist doctrine, it was forced at the same time to adapt to the social heritage of the October Revolution which had not been fully liquidated. Meanwhile the confrontation between the Bonapartist bureaucracy and the adherents of Bolshevism assumed ever more the character of class warfare. These hostile political forces spoke as the bearers of opposed social interests. The victory of the defenders of Bolshevik principles over the caste of thugs would have brought a moral and political renaissance to the Soviet regime. For this not to happen, the ruling clique carried out the mass extermination of those who were dissatisfied on a scale which virtually signified a new civil war.

Western liberals, who were repeating assurances that the Bolshevik Party was a new version of Tsarism, did not want to see this dialectic of the social struggle. In adopting this position, they were closing their eyes to such "minor details" as the elimination of the monarchy, nobility, and gentry, the expropriation of capital, etc. "If the Stalinist bureaucracy even manages to destroy the economic foundations of the new society," wrote Trotsky with foresight, "the experience of a planned economy conducted under the leadership of the Bolshevik Party will enter forever into history as the greatest school for all mankind."[14]

The correctness of Trotsky's views on the relationship between Bolshevism and Stalinism becomes strikingly clear if one compares his writings with a work which the anti-communists of all stripes have studied for many decades — Arthur Koestler's book *Darkness at Noon*. Its author, who had renounced communism at the end of the 1930s, seemed to be justifying his own renegacy when he tried to persuade the reader (through the words of his main hero, Rubashov) that "the whole activity of the so-called opposition had been senile chatter, because the whole generation of the old guard was just as worn out as he himself... , that an active, organized opposition to No. 1 (Stalin) had never existed; that it had all only been talk, impotent playing with fire."[15]

Giving a highly approximate history of the inner party struggle in the VKP(b) (as can be seen from the quote above), Koestler, who had been an inveterate Stalinist in the past, nevertheless had a certain conception of the ideological positions of the oppositionists. His Rubashov was keenly aware of the radical difference between the Stalinist and Bolshevik regimes; under the latter "discussions in the Central Committee and at the congresses had been on a level never before attained in history by a political body."[16] He condemned many aspects of Stalin's politics — the omnipotence of the dictator, mass terror, and forced collectivization, in which "we sent about ten million people to do forced labor in the Arctic regions and the jungles of the East (the number of people victimized in the anti-kulak campaign is exaggerated by Koestler at least two times over, but in the given instance, this does not have major significance – V. R.)."[17]

During the investigation, Rubashov was placed in a face-to-face confrontation with the son of his old friend, Kiefer, during which the son, according to Rubashov, conveyed his thoughts with unusual precision. "My father considered that, one day, the cup would overflow and the Party would depose him or force him to resign; and that the opposition must propagate this idea... Rubashov laughed at my father, and repeated that he was a fool and a Don Quixote... One could hope for nothing from the Party either, for No. 1 held all the threads in his hand, and had made the Party bureaucracy his accomplice who would stand and fall with him, and he knew it."[18]

This dialogue marvelously mixes together the views of true Trotskyists and the renegade arguments of capitulators (to whom Rubashov belonged; before his arrest he repeatedly renounced his oppositional views).

Rubashov's answer to the question asked by the investigator Gletkin was clearly "Trotskyist" in character:

"If you think sabotage is a mere fiction, what, in your opinion, are the real causes of the unsatisfactory state of our industry?"

"Too low piece-work rates, slave-driving, and barbaric disciplinary measures..."

In virtual agreement with this conclusion, Gletkin unfolded a chain of sophistries before Rubashov, trying to prove that the way out of this enchanted circle might be in finding scapegoats. "Experience teaches," said Gletkin, "that the masses must be given a simple, easily grasped explanation for all difficult and complicated processes... If one told the people in my village that they were still slow and backward in spite of the revolution and the factories, it would have no effect on them. If one tells them that they are heroes of labor, more efficient than the Americans, and that the only evil comes from devils and saboteurs, that at least has some effect."[19]

Somewhat surprisingly, these arguments were persuasive to Rubashov, who had earlier muttered to himself that Gletkin was a "Neanderthaler." "Rubashov continually reminded himself that the Gletkins were continuing the cause begun by the old intelligentsia. That their earlier ideas had not degenerated, although they sounded absolutely inhuman in the mouths of the Neanderthalers."[20] He also virtually endorsed Gletkin's views that "any day now international capitalism may start a war against our country, and the slightest vacillation among the toiling masses will lead to innumerable catastrophes. The party... must become a united monolith, which is welded together by iron discipline and selfless devotion to the Leadership."[21] Such arguments were typical of Molotov, who found in them the justification for his criminal activity during the years of the Great Purge (see Chapter 20). But they were profoundly alien to genuine Bolsheviks, as one can judge from the statements made not only by Trotskyists, but from those made by the non-returners who did not belong to them, but expressed the ideological positions of their own social and political milieu.

While he was in prison, Rubashov created a "law of the relative maturity of the masses." Proceeding from this "law," he convinced himself that "a simplified and endlessly repeated idea makes its way more easily into the popular consciousness — what is today declared correct, must shine with blinding whiteness; what is today declared wrong, must be as black as pitch; right now the masses needed cartoon-like literature."[22] This disparaging conception of the masses led Rubashov to acknowledge the correctness of Stalin's propaganda methods; the latter's speeches "consisted of questions and answers, in which events were presented in the simplest logic that the masses found irrefutable."[23]

In these sophistries Koestler completely ignored the difference between leading the masses and enslaving them or crushing them. The theory which he ascribed to the Bolsheviks was based on a condescending attitude toward the masses, whereas genuine Bolshevik theory was based on trusting the masses and finding support among them. The Bolshevik view of the relationship between the party and the masses was most fully outlined in Trotsky's work "Their Morals and Ours." "The liberation of the workers can only be the cause of the workers themselves," Trotsky stated here. "There is therefore no greater crime than to deceive the masses, to pass off defeats as victories, and friends as enemies, to buy leaders, to fabricate legends, and to stage frame-up trials, — in short, to do what the Stalinists are doing. These means can serve only one end: to prolong the domination of a clique which has already been condemned by history."[24]

Stating that the minority of the population acts as the active force in the revolution, Trotsky added that the success of the revolution becomes possible only when this minority "finds more or less support, or at least friendly neutrality, on the part of the majority. The succession of various stages of the revolution, much like the transition from revolution to counter-revolution, is determined immediately by the changing political relationship between the minority and the majority, between the avant-garde and the class."[25]

Noting that idealizing the masses was always foreign to the Bolsheviks, Trotsky wrote: "The masses, of course, are by no means without sin... We have seen them in various conditions, at various stages, and in the greatest historical shocks. We have observed their strong and weak sides. The strong sides — decisiveness, selflessness and heroism — always found the clearest expression when the revolution was on the upswing. During this period the Bolsheviks stood at the head of the masses. Then another historical chapter approached, when the weak sides of the oppressed were revealed: heterogeneity, insufficient culture, narrowness of vision. The masses became tired of the tension, became disillusioned, lost faith in themselves and — cleared the way for a new aristocracy. In this period, the Bolsheviks ("Trotskyists") ended up isolated from the masses."

"With these great events," continued Trotsky, "the 'Trotskyists' studied the rhythm of history, i.e., the dialectic of the class struggle. They studied and, it seems, to a certain degree learned to subordinate their subjective plans and programs to this objective rhythm. They learned not to fall into despair because the laws of history do not depend on our individual tastes or bow down to our moral criteria... They learned not to fear the most powerful enemies, if their might contradicts the demands of historical development. They are able to swim against the current with profound assurance that a new historical flood of powerful force will carry them to that shore. Not all will arrive there, many will drown. But to participate in this movement with open eyes and with tense will — only this can give the highest moral satisfaction to a thinking human being!"[26]

Trotsky concretized these theoretical ideas in a critical analysis of the historical legends created around various episodes in the revolution. Among these legends being widely circulated in the 1930s, the legend of the Kronstadt rebellion of 1921 occupied a leading place.

43. "Hue and Cry over Kronstadt"

In 1938, a campaign about events that had happened sixteen years before was opened simultaneously in Miliukov's *Latest News*, in the Menshevik *Socialist Herald*, and in publications of the anarchists. Trotsky found particularly painful the participation in this campaign of his former supporters Serge, Eastman, Souvarine, and Ciliga. Shaken by the scale of Stalin's savagery, these people tried to find its source in some kind of "original sin of Bolshevism," and that is what they declared the crushing of the Kronstadt rebellion to be. Isaac Deutscher correctly called their contributions on this theme an example of those "recurrent processes of political conversion by which the radicals and revolutionaries of one era turn into the middle-of-the-roaders or conservatives and reactionaries of the next."[1]

The question of the Kronstadt rebellion was raised in a letter to Trotsky from Wendelin Thomas, a member of the Commission to Investigate the Moscow Trials. In replying to this letter, Trotsky wrote: "Your assessment of the Kronstadt rebellion in 1921 is fundamentally wrong... The best and most self-sacrificing sailors were completely removed from Kronstadt and played an important role on the fronts and in the local Soviets throughout the land. What remained was a grey mass with great pretensions ('we, the Kronstadters!'), but without political education and without a readiness to make revolutionary sacrifices. The country was starving. The Kronstadters demanded privileges. The rebellion was dictated by a desire to receive a privileged ration. The sailors had cannons and ships. Then reactionary elements both in Russia and abroad latched onto the rebellion. The White emigration demanded that aid be sent to the rebels. The victory of the uprising could bring nothing but the victory of the counter-revolution, completely independent of what ideas were in the heads of the sailors. But even these ideas were profoundly reactionary. They reflected the hostility of the backward peasant toward the worker, the condescension of the soldier or sailor toward 'civilian' Petrograd, and the hatred of the petty bourgeois toward revolutionary discipline. The movement had, therefore, a counter-revolutionary nature, and since the rebels were in control of the arms inside the fortress, they could be crushed only by using arms."[2]

These issues were treated in greater detail in Trotsky's article "Hue and Cry over Kronstadt," where he set out to explain why such highly varied political forces — from open counter-revolutionaries and liberals to anarchists and several Trotskyists of yesterday — had seized precisely on Kronstadt. Trotsky noted that during the years of the revolution, the Bolsheviks frequently clashed with Cossacks, peasants, and even with several groups of workers. The basic cause of these clashes was the antagonism between the workers, as consumers, and the peasants, as the producers and traders of grain. In order to provide the army and the starving cities with at least the minimum amount of produce, the Bolsheviks were compelled to resort to extraordinary measures of food requisitioning (measures, by the way, to which both the tsarist and provisional governments had resorted before them). At first, the majority of the peasants reconciled themselves to the requisition of grain as a temporary evil. But the Civil War stretched on for three years, during which the city gave almost nothing to the countryside and took almost everything from it, mainly for the war effort. A result of this was a change in the moods of the peasants, whereupon the Whites often managed to win them over to their side. Manifestations of ferment among the peasantry were the Makhno movement, the activities of the "Greens," and the Tambov uprising, which occurred under SR slogans. "Kronstadt differed" from all these petty-bourgeois movements, Trotsky noted, "only in that it was superficially more successful."[3]

The idealization of the Kronstadt rebellion, presented as an act of the worker and peasant masses against the "Bolshevik dictatorship," was explained most of all by the fact that Kronstadt was surrounded by a revolutionary halo. The authors of the Kronstadt legend depicted matters as if the Bolsheviks, in March 1921, had aimed their weapons against the same sailors who, in 1917, were in the vanguard of the October Revolution.

In reality, detachments of Kronstadt sailors from the first months of the Civil War formed the skeleton of the first units of the Red Army. These detachments participated actively in military operations, food requisitioning, and the organization of the Soviet regime in many provinces. "At first it seemed that Kronstadt was inexhaustible," wrote Trotsky. "From various fronts I had to send dozens of telegrams about mobilizing more and more 'reliable' detachments of Petrograd workers and Baltic sailors." As a result of these mobilizations, the social composition of the Kronstadt garrison changed radically. "Those sailors who remained in 'peaceful' Kronstadt until the beginning of 1921, without finding any use for themselves on one of the fronts of the Civil War, were, as a general rule, significantly below the average level of the Red

Army, and included in their ranks a large percent of absolutely demoralized elements in bell-bottomed trousers wearing their hair like pimps."[4]

This account by Trotsky was confirmed in a report sent to him on 7 March 1921 by an official in the special department of the VChK [the political police]. This document states: one of the main reasons for the Kronstadt events was that a large number of sailors who had not participated in military activities for more than three years had turned into an isolated, caste-like group, which, under the influence of inactivity, had degenerated into a "parasitic element," unconsciously replacing revolutionary ideology with "an unshakable certainty that they were the 'glory, pride and vanguard of the revolution.'"[5]

By the beginning of 1921, communists made up a relatively modest minority at Kronstadt. Out of 26,687 men at the Kronstadt base, only 1,650 were members and candidate-members of the party. Altogether, the Bolshevik cells in the military and civilian establishments at Kronstadt added up to 2,680 people at that time.[6] Among these people, only a few individuals had been in the party before 1917, and more than half were peasants who had entered the party during the Party week which had occurred in September 1920.

During the Kronstadt events, about 900 people left the RKP(b).[7] The rest were subjected to cruel persecution by the rebels in charge of the fortress. On 10 March, the commandant of Kronstadt published an order requiring all communists to turn in all arms belonging to them within a two-day period. Despite many appeals to free the communists who were in the hospital at the time of the uprising, the decision was made "not to free anyone for the time being." Communists remaining at liberty were threatened with arrest if "statements begin to be received indicating their hostile activity."[8]

The revolutionary committee which had been established in the first days of the rebellion set up troikas, which were given the exclusive task of removing former commissars and senior communists from the posts they occupied. The hastily formed troikas appealed in turn to the revolutionary committee for an emergency decree to "conduct a general search of all commissars, communists, and party officials, without regard to previous searches, and to remove all weapons in their possession."[9]

After the start of the rebellion, 500 communists were arrested and imprisoned in the Kronstadt investigatory prison, where they organized the publication of a newspaper explaining the meaning of the events taking place. Kuzmin, the commissar of the Baltic Fleet who had been sentenced to be shot, was freed by Red units who arrived in time only minutes before the sentence was to be carried out.[10] In addition, 165 communists left the fortress with arms in hand; 135 went underground and, risking their lives, conducted propaganda among the deceived sailors.[11]

A general meeting of imprisoned communists appealed to the provisional revolutionary committee for permission to allow Zosimov, the former commissar of the battleship subdivision, to go to Moscow for a session of the All-Russian Central Executive Committee (VTsIK) in order to clarify there the true position of matters at Kronstadt. In reply to this appeal, the revolutionary committee ruled: "Permission for a trip to Moscow for Comrade Zosimov is denied, ... since ... the release of Zosimov might be interpreted by the government of the RSFSR as weakness on the part of the Provisional Revolutionary Committee and as its desire to compromise with the Soviet government, of which there can be no talk, in view of the firmly expressed desire of the popular masses at Kronstadt to free Russia forever from the power of the communists."[12]

The rebels used the radio to broadcast a call "to the proletariat of all lands," in which they said that White-Guard generals were not directing the uprisings and that the rebels had no ties whatsoever with people abroad. Meanwhile, in the garrison, ever more power was being seized by the head of the artillery, the former tsarist general Kozlovsky. The absence of food in the fortress forced the revolutionary committee to start negotiations about obtaining food from American warehouses of the Red Cross in Finland (by the time the uprising had been crushed, 400 poods of produce had arrived in Kronstadt). The message contained an appeal for "aid in rations, medicine, and, primarily, military aid." "Our main appeal," the broadcast said, "is to Russian people who have found themselves on foreign soil (i.e., White emigrants – V. R.). We know that they will come to our aid."[13]

Keeping in mind the changes in the social composition of the Kronstadt sailors and the practical activities of the revolutionary committee, Trotsky noted that one must not take on faith the appeals of the rebels, which seemed on the surface to be revolutionary. Recalling Marx's famous idea that parties, like people, cannot be judged by what they say about themselves, Trotsky wrote: "The characteristics of a party are determined much more by its social composition, its past, and its relationship to different classes and strata, than its oral and printed declarations, particularly at a critical moment in a civil war."[14]

The actions of the Kronstadters who were protesting against the continuation of the methods of war communism, coincided in time with the announcement of the shift to the New Economic Policy by the Tenth Congress of the RKP(b). Later Lenin often confessed that the party's delay in this shift had been a crude political mistake. From this, as Trotsky stressed, one cannot conclude that to pacify the Kronstadters it would have been enough to announce to them the decrees about introducing the NEP. "The regime of the NEP could only gradually appease the peasantry, and after them, the dissatisfied sections of the army and navy. But for this, both experience and time were needed."[15]

The authors of the Kronstadt legend advanced one more argument: the sailors were threatening no one, they "only" had seized the fortress and combat ships; therefore the Bolsheviks should have confined themselves to delaying tactics with regard to the rebels, and applied such tactics to themselves by not rushing to crush the rebellion. From such an assessment of the Kronstadt events, Trotsky noted, it followed that "the Bolsheviks advanced across the ice with bared chests against the fortress only because of their poor character, their desire to artificially provoke conflicts, and their hatred for the Kronstadt sailors or for the doctrine of anarchism."[16] In reality, the need for food supplies alone would have made the fortress directly dependent on the foreign bourgeoisie and White emigrants. All the necessary preparations for such "aid" had already been made.

These retrospective comments by Trotsky have also been confirmed by recently published documents about the Kronstadt events. On 10 March 1921, Trotsky sent the members of the Politburo a letter in which he said: "We can seize Kronstadt only before the ice thaws. As soon as the gulf becomes clear for sailing, contact will be established between Kronstadt and abroad. At the same time, the island will become inaccessible for us. Hopes for surrender because of insufficient food supplies are absolutely groundless, since, up to the point navigation becomes possible, the rebels have enough food."[17]

The "peace-loving" nature of the rebellion's leaders can be seen from their testimony during interrogation. Koslovsky declared that, "burning with a flaming desire to save Russia, and to restore its power by preserving the old traditions of a one and indivisible country," he felt that it was necessary to overthrow Soviet power by armed force. In pursuit of these goals, he used the parties of the SRs and Mensheviks, as well as the slogan "of a just Soviet power, keeping in mind that upon receiving help from abroad he would throw this superfluous ballast overboard."[18]

Petrichenko, the chairman of the revolutionary committee, stated during interrogation that Makhno's organization, which had been defeated in open combat with the Soviet regime, felt that it was necessary to send its forces into underground organizations in the northern parts of the country, where it would be possible to utilize food and heating difficulties for anti-Soviet purposes.

An agent of the Entente stole across Finland and reached Kronstadt. He had served among Denikin's troops and after their defeat had turned up in emigration, where the proposal was made for him to go to Russia for underground work. The French consulate in Sweden gave him gold, documents, and instructions for the trip to Kronstadt.

Even before the rebellion began, its organizers established contact with émigré circles in Western Europe, primarily with the leader of the Party of SRs, Chernov, who sent his own representative to Kronstadt and intended soon to go there himself. On the eve of his arrival, Chernov declared: "The Soviet regime is so strong that one cannot overthrow it immediately... One must act with caution. Open action should be taken only against communists, but not against Soviet power." Another famous SR leader, Savinkov, wrote instructions about how one must act in order to overthrow the Soviet regime.[19]

Several weeks before the uprising, articles appeared in the foreign press about how a rebellion was occurring in Kronstadt. From the early days of the uprising, the rebels by no means limited themselves to waiting tactics, but used artillery fire from ships to shell troops loyal to the Soviet regime who were located close to the fortress. They also shelled military targets in the city of Oranienbaum. Red soldiers captured an order to advance on Petrograd. This order was not carried out only because the insurgents did not have large enough forces to attack.

The bitterness of the resistance by the rebels can by seen by the fact that the Tenth Congress of the RKP(b) had to mobilize a quarter of its members to crush the rebellion as quickly as possible. During the fighting for Kronstadt, the Red Army units lost up to 1,200 killed.

Recalling several of these facts, Trotsky wrote that "the Bolsheviks felt that it was their duty to put out the fire at the very beginning and, consequently, with the smallest number of casualties."[20] Thanks to this belief, the Kronstadt rebellion did not open a new chapter in the Civil War, but became its concluding episode.

The "Hue and Cry over Kronstadt" included one more important aspect — Trotsky's personal responsibility for supposedly heading the crushing of the rebellion. Several former Trotskyists acknowledged the counter-revolutionary nature of the uprising but declared that Trotsky should not have carried out merciless reprisals against its participants after the rebellion was put down. Claiming that Trotsky was deliberately silent in his autobiography about his role in pacifying Kronstadt, Souvarine ironically noted: "There are exploits which people are not proud of."

After citing the most odious statements of this type, Trotsky wrote that in previous articles about Kronstadt he had not touched upon his role in these events "not because I had something to conceal, but just the opposite, because I had nothing to say." He stressed that he was not removing responsibility from himself for suppressing Kronstadt, insofar as he and other members of the Central Committee voted to put down the rebellion forcefully, if they did not manage to convince the fortress to surrender by means of peaceful negotiations. But when critics started to charge him personally with excessive cruelty that had not been warranted by the circumstances, Trotsky continued, he considered that he was justified in saying: "Mr. Moralists, you are exaggerating a bit."[21]

On 14 November 1938, in a letter to his Paris correspondents, Trotsky noted that on 5 March [1921], as chairman of the Revolutionary Military

43. "Hue and Cry over Kronstadt" 363

Funeral procession in Petrograd for Red Army soldiers who died during the storming of Kronstadt

Council, he had signed an order to crush the rebellion.²² In this order, which outlined a series of operational measures, there was a warning to the rebels: if in the next 24 hours the rebellion did not stop, military activities by regular Red Army units would begin against the fortress. On the same day, Trotsky published an appeal, "To the Garrison and Inhabitants of Kronstadt and the Rebellious Forts," in which he proposed that "all who have raised their hand against the Socialist Fatherland immediately lay down their arms." In the appeal Trotsky also announced: "at the same time I am issuing orders to prepare everything in order to crush the rebellion and the rebels with arms in hand."²³

As he recalled these events, Trotsky suggested that, after the publication of these documents in Petrograd, rumors were deliberately circulated that he was leading the actions of the Red Army — in order to frighten the rebels. However, both the first, unsuccessful assault on Kronstadt, which began on 8 March, and the new attack, which began during the night before 17 March, proceeded without his slightest participation. As a result of the second attack, the fortress ended up in the hands of the Red Army the next day.²⁴

In speaking about his complete and demonstrative absence from direct or indirect participation in the military operations and subsequent repressions, Trotsky indicated that the reasons for his behavior were political. Several weeks before the uprising he had visited Petrograd and Kronstadt, where he spoke at party meetings to outline his positions in the trade union discussion. The overwhelming majority of the communists at Kronstadt then voted for the platform defended by Zinoviev, which was counterposed to Trotsky's platform. After receiving news about the rebellion, Trotsky declared at a session of the Politburo that his participation in the military actions might be interpreted by the Kronstadters as his attempt to get revenge against them because they had voted against him in the recently concluded discussions. Therefore, he proposed that negotiations with the rebels, and if necessary, their suppression, be carried out by party leaders who not long before had enjoyed the confidence of the sailors. None of the Politburo members objected to these considerations. As for the repressions of the insurgents, Dzerzhinsky was ordered to direct them.[25]

On 17 March, the "leaders" of the rebellion abandoned the sailors and escaped to Finland. They were joined by a significant part of the rank-and-file rebels, but after a few days, sailors began to come back from Finland to Soviet Russia. By the middle of May, several hundred people had returned to their homeland. Half a year after the rout of the rebellion, the Presidium of the VTsIK marked the fourth anniversary of the October Revolution by declaring a full amnesty for all rank-and-file participants in the uprising and gave them the opportunity to return to Soviet Russia.

Of course, after the rebellion was crushed, there were repressions directed against its active participants. From 20 March through 15 April 1921, three thousand people were arrested, of whom 40 percent were sentenced to be executed, 25 percent were sentenced to five years of hard labor, and 35 percent were set free.[26]

"Were there too many victims? I do not know," wrote Trotsky. "I believe Dzerzhinsky in this sphere more than his belated critics. To decide now, *a posteriori*, who should have been punished, and how, I will not undertake, because I lack the facts... But I am prepared to acknowledge that civil war is not a school of humanism. Idealists and pacifists have always charged the revolution with 'excesses.' But the essence is such that these 'excesses' flow from the very nature of the revolution, which itself is an 'excess' of history. On this basis, let whoever it pleases condemn (in little articles) revolution in general. I do not condemn it. In this sense, I bear full and complete responsibility for the suppression of the Kronstadt rebellion."[27]

44. "Their Morals and Ours"

In works of the 1930s devoted to the Kronstadt rebellion and other events of the first post-revolutionary years, no small amount of space is occupied by "exposés" of the Bolsheviks for their supposed amorality. This line of attack on Bolshevism is also a component part of the ideological campaign directed at identifying Stalin's savagery with the politics and ideology of Bolshevism. This prompted Trotsky to write a number of works about the principles of revolutionary, Bolshevik morality, the most important of which was the article "Their Morals and Ours." Under "our" morals he had in mind the morals of the Bolsheviks, and under "their" morals — both bourgeois morality and the morals of the Stalinists.

We know that Stalin himself never spoke publicly on questions of morality. In his works, of course, the direct preaching of moral nihilism is absent. However, there is a historical source which illustrates his true attitude toward moral and ethical principles. We are talking about the extensive notes that he left on the cover of his copy of Lenin's book *Materialism and Empiriocriticism*. These notes, made by Stalin for himself, contained an affirmation of the cult of force as the only effective political principle, before which all moral flaws and defects prove to be insignificant (it was precisely such a "moral physiognomy" which Koestler unjustly attributed to all Bolsheviks). Insofar as the given notes can be seen as the only instance where Stalin sincerely expressed the foundations of his behavioral credo, it would be appropriate to quote them fully:

"1) weakness
2) laziness
3) stupidity -
the only things that can be called defects.
All the rest — given the absence of the above-mentioned defects are undoubtedly virtue!

Iosif Stalin

NB! If a man is
1) strong (spiritually)
2) energetic
3) intelligent (or capable), then he is good, independent of any other "defects"!
(1) and (3) give (2)."[1]

The 1920s saw many works by Bolshevik ideologists which were devoted to questions of ethics and morality. Many of them contain a nihilistic and relativistic explanation of moral principles which was bound up with the vulgarization of Marxist doctrine coming from the works of Preobrazhensky and Bukharin. In the pamphlet "Morality and Class Norms," while categorically rejecting "eternal norms" of morality, Preobrazhensky insisted on the relativity of all moral principles and defended the pragmatic assumption according to which, in any society (including socialist society), only that which is beneficial to the ruling group or class is considered moral. A similar understanding of morality is presented in the works of Bukharin, who was Preobrazhensky's co-author of *The ABCs of Communism*. In the book *The Theory of Historical Materialism* he is inclined to interpret morality (identifying it with ethics) as the fetishistic form of social consciousness which should disappear under communism. "The very essence of ethics," he wrote, "consists in the fact that there are norms which are wrapped in a fetishistic casing. Fetishism is the *essence* of ethics... Ethics ... presupposes a fetishistic fog in which many lose their way." The proletariat, however, in Bukharin's opinion, needs simple and comprehensible norms of conduct, bearing the character "of the same technical rules as for a joiner who is making a footstool... If the proletariat wants to

44. "Their Morals and Ours"

Evgeny Preobrazhensky

Nikolai Bukharin

achieve communism, then it must do so-and-so, and so-and-so, just as a joiner who is making a footstool. And everything that is expedient from this point of view, must be done."[2]

It is not difficult to discover here the influence on Bukharin of Alexander Bogdanov's "organizational science," in which morality is seen as one of the means of organizing the collective strivings of a class.

Of course, in the literature of the 1920s and 1930s, one meets more correct views on morality and its relationship to politics.[*] However, not a single one of the works of those times (or, for that matter, earlier or later) contained an elaboration of the Marxist ethical conception which was as profound and as consistent as Trotsky's work "Their Morals and Ours."

The many anti-communist authors demonstrating the "amorality" of the Bolsheviks usually pass by this classic Marxist work and reduce the entire content of revolutionary Bolshevik morality and ethics to Lenin's thesis: "Our morality is subordinated fully to the interests of the proletariat's class struggle."[3] In doing so, they ignore the circumstance that these words were spoken by Lenin in a speech to the Third Congress of the Komsomol, i.e., in a conversation with fifteen to twenty-year-old boys and girls, and not presented in a theoretical treatise. They were, therefore, based on journalistic arguments which were accessible to the consciousness of the masses, and not on a system of scientific proofs. They also do not pay attention to the further elaboration

---

[*] For more detail about this, see the article: Rogovin, V. Z., "Diskusii po problemam byta i kul'tury v Sovetskoi Rossii 20-x godov [Discussions about the Problems of Everyday Life and Culture in Soviet Russia during the 1920s]," *Sotsial'nye issledovaniia*, Issue 7, M., 1971.

of this formula in Lenin's speech, which reveals its humanistic, and in the final analysis, universally human content: "morality serves the purpose of helping human society to rise higher..."; communist morality is opposed to "the psychology and those mores which say: I am trying to obtain my own profit, all the rest means nothing."[4]

In Trotsky's article, there are no direct references to Lenin's speech. But the denial "of morality taken apart from human society" brings it close to this speech. So does the removal of morals and morality from "God's commandments," and "from the idealistic or semi-idealistic phrases which always amounted to something very similar to God's commandments."[5] As we shall see a bit further, the same thoughts are essentially repeated in Trotsky's article, although they are presented in a stricter, more consistent, and more polished form — in accordance with the difference between a theoretical work and a popular speech.

In his work "Their Morals and Ours" Trotsky seems to be making Lenin's ideas more concrete, by showing *what* actually serves the cause of the revolutionary proletariat, and *what* detracts from its great class, and at the same time, universally human, world-historical tasks.

In his scientific analysis, Trotsky relied upon both the positive and negative experience accumulated during the years of socialist construction in the USSR, material which was not at Lenin's disposal. He criticized the moral and ideological illusions which were characteristic of the first stages of this construction; he ruthlessly uncovered the mistakes and angrily denounced the crimes which emerged in the course of the first great struggles for social equality, i.e., for the liberation of mankind from all forms of class and national oppression.

Least of all was Trotsky (or Lenin) inclined to claim that revolutionary politics renders morality unnecessary, or "frees" itself from moral obligations. In the same way, he by no means gave any indulgences to all the mistakes and excesses which might be encountered in the course of revolutionary practice.

In describing the real state of moral relations in class-antagonistic societies, Trotsky investigated the question: in what historical conditions does the need arise to use such political means as murder or lies? In this investigation, he was just as strictly objective as a Marxist economist or a sociologist who is showing the inevitability of unemployment or of social differentiation in a society based on market relations.

This objectivity did not prevent Trotsky from using the concept of the "court of morality" — for turning to this court to discover the differences in social meaning between political acts that were outwardly similar, or for differentiating between the various forms of social violence.

Trotsky proceeded from the position that morality, more than any other form of ideology, has a class character. This position is not contradicted by the existence of elementary norms of morality, worked out during the development of mankind as a whole and necessary for the existence of any human collective. These norms express the fact that man in his individual behavior must subordinate himself to certain rules which are derived from his membership in society. But these generally acknowledged rules of morality (taking the form of commandments in religion) are abstract in nature. The limited and unstable character of their activity can be traced in the fate of the most "categorical" moral rule or moral ban. "In 'normal' conditions a 'normal' person observes the commandment, 'Thou shalt not kill,'" wrote Trotsky. "But if he kills under exceptional circumstances of self-defense, then a jury will acquit him. If, on the other hand, he falls victim to a murderer, then the court will kill the murderer… As for the state, in peaceful times it is limited to the legalized murder of only a few people, so that in times of war it can turn the 'universally obligatory' commandment, 'Thou shalt not kill,' into its opposite. The most humane governments, which in peacetime 'hate war,' proclaim in times of war that the highest duty of their armies is to exterminate as great a part of humanity as possible."[6]

Nor, from a purely moral point of view, is it possible to answer the question about the admissibility or inadmissibility of individual terror. The uselessness of moral absolutes in this acute issue can be seen by the fact that even "conservative Swiss burghers heap official praise on the terrorist William Tell." Progressive public opinion has been on the side of Irish, Russian, Polish, or Hindu terrorists who have fought against political or national oppression. During a civil or national-liberation war, the murders of individual aggressors cease to be acts of individual terrorism. "If, let us say, a revolutionary blew up General Franco and his staff, this would hardly evoke moral indignation even among democratic eunuchs."[7] Today we may add to this that in Germany they honor the memory of participants in the conspiracy which carried out an unsuccessful attempt on Hitler's life in July 1944.

Trotsky indicated that the elementary rules of morality, along with the principles of democracy and the mores of the social world, are in force during an epoch of the relatively crisis-free development of society. Under these conditions, "in order to guarantee the triumph of their interests in big questions, the ruling classes are forced to make concessions in lesser questions, of course, only as long as these concessions reconcile themselves with bookkeeping. During the epoch of a capitalist upswing, particularly during the last decades before the war, these concessions … were indeed real. … The relations between classes softened, at least superficially. … One received the impression of an ever freer, just and humane society. From the standpoint of 'common sense,' the rising line of progress appeared to be never-ending."

However, instead of a further movement along these lines, the First World War broke out, bringing mankind a mass of shocks, crises and catastrophes. "The safety mechanisms of democracy began to explode one after another. The elementary rule of morality proved to be even more fragile than the institutions of democracy and the illusions of reformism. Lies, slander, corruption, bribery, violence, and murders reached an unprecedented scale."[8]

The assessment of the moral status of mankind which the Marxist Trotsky gave coincides with the assessments made by several authoritative liberal scholars investigating the middle and second half of the twentieth century. Among them, for instance, is the Nobel Prize laureate Albert Schweitzer, whose humanism was confirmed by his selfless way of life. "The ethical sun of our generation has been covered by heavy clouds," he wrote in the 1950s. "... In an absolutely incomprehensible manner, society is beginning to look favorably... on ideas of anti-humanism." Schweitzer saw the reasons for this, in part, in that "we have grown accustomed to a situation where the high hopes of preceding generations are subjected to derision... We are afraid to admit to ourselves that, for many decades, our souls have been corroded by the rust of pessimism." According to Schweitzer, modern philosophers find "refuge in ethical ruins," insofar as they do not control their degree of engagement, and do not notice that they are building their world view according to a self-interested, egotistical and supra-moral attitude toward life.[9]

Such a coincidence of views shows that the "class approach" not only does not hinder an adequate vision of ethical reality, but even helps anticipate its future condition.

The elementary rules of morality are closely bound up with "universally human" common sense, which Trotsky called the lowest form of intellect. "The basic capital of common sense consists of the elementary conclusions of general human experience: don't put your fingers in the fire, follow the path of least resistance, let sleeping dogs lie, ... and so on. When the social milieu is stable, common sense proves to be sufficient in order to trade, cure ills, write verse, lead a trade union, vote in parliament, form a family and give birth to children. But when this same common sense tries to go beyond its legitimate confines into the arena of more complex generalizations, it finds itself to be merely the accumulation of prejudices of a given class and a given epoch." Such limitations of common sense are prompted by the fact that it "rests on unchanging quantities in a world where only mutability is unchanging."[10] Common sense, therefore, proves to be useful only in epochs of evolutionary development, which are characterized by their relatively slow tempos of social change. To comprehend the catastrophic violations of the "normal" course of things, such as economic crises, revolutions, counter-revolutions, and wars, higher intellectual qualities are needed, for which dialectical materialism gives philosophical expression.

From the positions of dialectical materialism, Trotsky reviewed the problem of ends and means, the solution of which anti-communists have al-

44. "Their Morals and Ours"

Arthur Koestler
(1905-1983)

ways thought was the main moral defect of Bolshevism. This point of view is expressed most clearly in A. Koestler's novel *Darkness at Noon* where the movement of the principle of "the end justifies the means" is declared to be the point at which, during the years of the Great Terror, "the difference was erased between interrogator and interrogated, executioner and victim."[11] The investigator who is extorting false confessions from Rubashov declares: "The law of 'the end justifies the means' is and will remain for ages to come the sole law of political ethics; all the rest is the chatter of dilettantes."[12] Before his death, Rubashov makes the following amendment to this thesis: "It is possible that the mistake (of the Bolsheviks – V. R.) was rooted ... in the axiom that the end justifies the means. It killed revolutionary brotherhood and turned the warriors of the Revolution into madmen."[13] Finally, Koestler himself reinforced this thesis with the following expressions in the afterword to his book: "Their (the Bolsheviks') true guilt lies in the fact that they placed the interests of mankind higher than the interests of a man, morality was sacrificed to expediency, and means — to the end. And so they must die, for, from the standpoint of History, their death is expedient, they should die from the hand of people who think just like them."[14]

As for how much all this sophistry has to do with the truth, one can see from Trotsky's investigation of the "most popular and most impressive charge made against Bolshevik 'amorality,'" which was advanced long before Koestler. In responding to questions from Wendelin Thomas, Trotsky wrote: "Like many others, you see the source of evil in the principle 'the end justifies the means.' By itself, this principle is very abstract and rationalistic. It allows the most varied interpretations. But I am prepared to take upon myself the defense of this formula — from a materialist and dialectical point of view. Yes, I think that there is no means which would be good or bad in itself, or in dependence on some kind of absolute, super-historical principle."

This does not mean, Trotsky stressed, that venality and treachery are admissible and justified, if they lead to an "end." The very choice of means depends on the character of the goal. "If the goal is the liberation of mankind, then lies, falsification, and betrayal can in no way be expedient means. The opponents of the Epicureans accused them of the following: while 'preaching happiness' they descended to the ideal of a swine. The Epicureans responded, not without grounds, that their opponents understood happiness... in a swinish way."[15]

One cannot help but note that, for several decades, it is precisely this problem — the indissoluble link between ends and means, assuming the moral foundations primarily of the end — that has been viewed as central in the most fundamental Soviet works on ethics. One of the leading specialists in this realm, O. G. Drobnitsky, emphasized that even Kant's categorical imperative is not universal, insofar as "from a purely formal principle, it is impossible to deduce any concrete moral content... With its aid, one still cannot make a choice... The ability of a man to present his maxim (i.e., his goal and chosen means – V. R.) as universal does not exclude morally arbitrary behavior."[16] Therefore, it is not "universally human values" and not a "moral sense," but a rational, moral *grounding* of one's *goals* that is the core of the morality of man and of society. As Jean-Paul Sartre correctly noted, when man chooses an act or a principle of action, then he chooses along with himself all mankind as it should be.[17] If one agrees with this, then one must acknowledge that the political (i.e., class) choice — is the fundamental element in the moral position not only of society, but of every man.

The question of the relationship between ends and means in revolutionary practice was widely discussed in party debates of the 1920s. This problem stood, for instance, at the center of an article by the Old Bolshevik Lepeshinsky, in which the author was replying to a question that was often raised during those years at party and Komsomol meetings: "How do you see the Jesuitical morality of the end justifying the means?" "From the class standpoint, it could be nothing but the adaptation of all means to the achievement of the ends which a class sets for itself," wrote Lepeshinsky. "The entire secret lies in correctly recognizing this means. If a means only apparently leads to an end, but in actual fact moves away from it, then the means is poor, and if in this process it can become the object of moral evaluation, then you may boldly call it immoral." Among these means Lepeshinsky included, first and foremost, mass reprisals which are dictated by a blind feeling of revenge and which do not distinguish between the innocent and guilty.

The inseparability of the criteria of expediency and moral permissibility lay also at the heart of Lepeshinsky's reply to a more concrete question:

44. "Their Morals and Ours"

Panteleimon Lepeshinsky
(1868-1944)

"How do you see torture? Does communist conscience justify torture if some secret police unit begins to resort to it?" "I reply without hesitation," wrote Lepeshinsky. "Torture belongs among the most inexpedient methods of uncovering conspiracies, crimes or military secrets. Even tsarist generals or officers did not resort to torturing spies, and, in any case, this was not due to their love of fellow-men. Therefore, methods of this type cannot be justified by any reasoning — either from the standpoint of the interests of the class struggle, even though it may be very sharp, or from the standpoint of common, everyday morality." The same approach to the problem of ends and means in the revolution guided Lepeshinsky's answer to the question: "Does a communist have the moral right to intervene on behalf of a person sitting in the Lubianka in Moscow?" "Well, of course, he has the right and should even do so," wrote Lepeshinsky, "if he is certain that his intervention in the 'Lubianka's' realm of competence not only will not hinder the struggle of communists against their class enemies, but will even aid in the correction of a mistake that has been committed or in the elimination of unnecessary, pointless cruelty."

Lepeshinsky stressed that magnanimity and humanism belong among the norms of Bolshevik ethics. "Wherever considerations of simple humanism... do not contradict the interests of the proletariat's class struggle, this 'humanism' is not simply 'allowed' by the ethics of the proletariat, but is included in such ethics as a component part," he wrote. "The proletariat, for instance, does not refuse, when the need arises, to kill the class enemy, but he is magnanimous (and elevates this magnanimity to the level of an ethical principle) toward an enemy who has been defeated and disarmed."[18]

Sharing views of this type, Trotsky examined the problem of ends and means in a wide philosophical context. "If we want to take the gentlemen unmaskers seriously," he wrote, "then we will have to ask them, first of all, what are their own moral principles... Let us allow that, indeed, neither personal nor social goals can justify the means. Then we must, obviously, search for other criteria, beyond historical society, and the goals which are presented by its development. Where are they? If not on earth, then in the heavens... The theory of eternal morals simply cannot manage without god."

In examining the views of those philosophers who have tried to found eternal principles of morality without appealing to religion, Trotsky stressed that their arguments inevitably have led "to recognition of a special substance, of a 'moral sense,' or of 'conscience' as some kind of absolute, which is nothing other than a philosophically cowardly pseudonym of god."[19]

The social necessity of developing "morality transcending class" arises because a regime which is establishing and defending privileges for a minority of the population "could not hold out for even a week on force alone. It needs the cement of morality. Developing this cement is the profession of petty-bourgeois theoreticians and moralists."[20]

In this regard, Trotsky recalled that, at the end of the nineteenth century, a whole school of philosophers arose who tried to supplement the "limited" class approach of Marx with a self-sufficient, i.e., supra-class moral principle. Beginning with Kant and his categorical imperative, all these theoreticians and social activists ended by turning into fervent anti-communists and defenders of religion. "Struve is now a retired minister of the Crimean Baron Wrangel, and a faithful son of the church; Bulgakov is an orthodox priest; Berdyaev explains the apocalypse in various languages. What is, at first glance, such an unexpected metamorphosis can by no means be explained by a 'Slavic soul' — Struve has a German soul — but by the scale of the social struggle in Russia. The basic tendency of this metamorphosis is essentially international."

The authors who reproached the Bolsheviks for following the principle of "the end justifies the means" usually called this principle Jesuitical, insofar as it was first advanced in the epoch of the Reformation, when the social struggle assumed theological form — as the struggle between Jesuits and the adherents of other religious doctrines. "Such an internally contradictory and psychologically inconceivable doctrine," wrote Trotsky, "was maliciously ascribed to the Jesuits by their Protestant, and sometimes Catholic opponents, who were not shy in choosing the means to achieve their own goals." In reality, the Jesuit theologians, who, like the theologians of other schools, raised the question of personal responsibility, taught that, by itself, the means is indifferent in a moral sense and that its moral justification or condemnation flows from the goal which its serves. "Thus, a gunshot by itself is indifferent; a shot aimed at a mad dog which is threatening a child is good; a shot whose goal is violence and murder is a crime. The order's theologians wanted to say nothing more than these general statements."

In accordance with the character and interests of the classes upon which they rested, the Jesuits represented reaction, and the Protestants — progress. However the limited nature of this progress found reflection in Protestant morality. "Thus, the doctrine of Christ which they had 'purified' by no means prevented the urban bourgeois, Luther, from calling for the extermination of rebellious peasants as mad dogs."[21]

In passing to an analysis of the dialectical interrelationship between ends and means, Trotsky emphasized that their dualistic interpretation is alien to Marxism. In practical life and in a historical movement, ends and means continually change places. The nearest goal becomes a means for achieving a more distant goal.

Recognition that the means must be organically subordinated to the goal leads to the conclusion that the goal, in turn, must be justified. From the standpoint of Marxism, "the goal is justified if it leads to increasing man's power over nature and to destroying the power of man over man." These general and truly universal human criteria, however, do not give a ready answer to the question of what is allowed and what is inadmissible in each concrete instance. The correct answer to such questions can be given only by the living experience of a political movement which is guided by theory. In this sense, revolutionary morality merges with revolutionary strategy and tactics. In a more general, summary form, the answer will say: for a revolutionary, all is allowed which *truly* leads to the liberation of mankind. "Precisely from this it follows that *not* all means are permissible. When we say that the end justifies the means, then the conclusion follows for us that a great revolutionary goal rejects as means all those base devices and methods which ... try to make the masses happy without their participation; or which lower the confidence of the masses in themselves and in their organization, replacing it with bowing down before 'leaders.'"[22]

Qualities of will, necessary for victory in political struggle, are by themselves neutral in a moral sense. Their moral or amoral content depends on what historical goals they serve. "The morality of each party," wrote Trotsky, "derives in the final analysis from the historical interests which it represents. The morality of Bolshevism, which includes self-sacrifice, disinterestedness, courage, and contempt for all that is false and tawdry — the best qualities of human nature! — flowed from revolutionary irreconcilability in serving the oppressed. In this area, too, the Stalinist bureaucracy imitates the words and gestures of Bolshevism. But when 'irreconcilability' and 'inflexibility' are realized through a police apparatus which serves a privileged minority, they become the source of demoralization and gangsterism."[23]

Trotsky was guided by these criteria when he evaluated the superficially similar concrete political measures employed by the Bolsheviks and Stalinists, in particular, the use of hostages. "Stalin arrests and shoots the children

Lev Trotsky

of his political opponents after these opponents have already been shot on false charges. With the aid of family hostages, Stalin forces those Soviet diplomats to return from abroad who have allowed themselves to express doubts about the irreproachable nature of Yagoda or Yezhov." In this regard, several "moralists" pointed out that in 1919, Trotsky "also" introduced a law about taking hostages, i.e., about holding relatives of officers in the Red Army who went over to the side of the enemy. "We will not insist upon the fact," Trotsky wrote in this regard, "that the decree of 1919 hardly even once led to the shooting of the relatives of officers whose betrayal not only caused innumerable human losses, but directly threatened the doom of the revolution.* In the end, the main point lies elsewhere. If the revolution had displayed less excess magnanimity from the very beginning, hundreds of thousands of lives would have been saved. One way or another, I bear full responsibility for the decree of 1919. It was a necessary measure in the struggle against the oppressors."

According to Trotsky, the difference in the moral content of identical measures applied by opposed political forces in the name of opposite histori-

---

* Today's "democrats," who have gained access to all the Russian archives, have not been able to find a single document in them testifying to the shooting of relatives of officers who betrayed during the years of the Civil War.

cal goals has been seen in all civil wars. "Let us propose to some Emil Ludwig or those like him," he noted, "that they write a portrait of Abraham Lincoln with little pink wings on his shoulders. The significance of Lincoln lies in the fact that to achieve a great historical goal, posed by the development of a young people, he did not stop before the most severe measures, once they proved to be necessary. The question is not even which of the warring camps caused or endured the greatest number of victims. History has different standards for the cruelties of the Northerners and the cruelties of the Southerners in the Civil War. A slave-holder who, with the aid of deception and force, puts a slave in chains, and a slave, who with the aid of deception and force, breaks the chains, — let despicable eunuchs not tell us that they are equal before the court of morality!"[24]

Every war is accompanied not only by "necessary," but by "excessive," so to speak, cruelty: pillaging, violence against the civilian population, etc. Under conditions of war, the warring sides simply forget about the Kantian imperative, for the "enemies," the "hostile nation," are seen as people of a different sort, for whom moral prohibitions cease to function. In this regard, it is appropriate to stress, the critics of Bolshevism ignore the fact that it was precisely the Bolsheviks, and Trotsky most of all, as leader of the Red Army, who used a merciless hand in stopping the excesses of the Civil War. Thus, in the theses "Guiding Principles of Impending Policy in the Don" published soon after a Cossack uprising, Trotsky wrote: "We will explain to the Cossacks in word and show them in deed that our policy is not the policy of revenge for the past... We will see to it as strictly as possible that the Red Army, as it moves forward, does not engage in theft, assaults, and so forth."[25]

In his work "Their Morals and Ours" Trotsky expressed the firm conviction that future generations would show a fundamentally different attitude toward the cruelty of the Bolsheviks and the crimes of the Stalinists. "Mankind's memory is magnanimous when severe measures are used in the service of great historical goals. But history does not forgive even a single drop of blood shed in sacrifice to a new Moloch of arbitrary rule and privileges. Moral sense finds its highest satisfaction in the indestructible certainty that historical vengeance will respond to the scale of the crimes."[26]

The historical content of the social and political struggle forms and determines the moral profile of its agents. Proceeding from this, Trotsky wrote about the charges of Lenin's "amorality," which were widely circulated by the enemies of Bolshevism: "Lenin's 'amorality,' i.e., his rejection of class-transcendent morals, did not prevent him from remaining faithful his whole life to one and the same ideal; from giving his whole life to the cause of the oppressed; from displaying the highest conscientiousness in the sphere of ideas and the highest courage in the sphere of activity; from acting without a hint of superiority toward the 'simple' worker, the defenseless woman, or the child.

Does it not seem that 'amorality' in the given instance is only a synonym for a higher human morality?"[27]

All the moral qualities named by Trotsky as those which Lenin possessed were simply absent from the camp of the Stalinists. The culmination of their true amorality — the judicial frame-ups — by no means flowed from the Bolsheviks' rejection of class-transcendent morality. Just like other important events in history, these frame-ups emerged as the product of a concrete social struggle, which in the given case assumed the most perfidious and savage character of the struggle of a new aristocracy against the masses which had raised it to power. "In order to adapt the ruling party to the tasks of reaction, the bureaucracy 'renewed' its composition by means of exterminating the revolutionaries and recruiting careerists."

In this process, Stalinism, like every social reaction, was forced to mask its actual goals. "The sharper the transition from revolution to reaction, the more that reaction depends on the traditions of the revolution," wrote Trotsky, "i.e., the more it fears the masses, the more it is forced to resort to lies and falsification in the struggle against representatives of the revolution." Every reaction fosters and reinforces those elements of the pre-revolutionary past which were dealt a blow by the revolution, but with which it has not been able or has not managed to fully contend. This applies particularly to Stalinism, whose methods "perfect, induce the greatest tension in, and reduce to the absurd all the devices of lies, cruelty and baseness which comprise the governing mechanism in any class society, including democracy. Stalinism is the accumulation of all the monstrosities of the historical state, its sinister caricature, and repulsive grimace."[28]

In connection with this, it is appropriate to emphasize one more aspect of the problem regarding the relationship of ends and means. Repeatedly in history, the secret intentions of reactionary political figures have differed radically from the public statement of their goals, and the means they have chosen have differed from those which they have declared. Thus, Stalin never declared that he planned to annihilate physically the majority of the party and its Central Committee. Stressing that the true goals and means of Stalin were deeply hidden and concealed by his declarations of an opposite character, M. Baitalsky wrote in his memoirs: "In actions, which in the end will nevertheless come to light, one can find the essence of the hidden intent. The means expose the end."[29]

Not only was Stalin's conduct amoral; so too was the conduct of the foreign "friends of the USSR," who ignored the warnings of future judicial frame-ups being prepared in view of the entire world. The Moscow trials were the true offspring of the official cult of lies, servility, hypocrisy, venality, and other forms of corruption which began to flourish in Moscow in the mid-1920s. When, however, the Moscow trials forced the whole world to be amazed, among the "friends of the USSR," "only the most stupid believed them. The rest did not want to trouble themselves with verification... In addition, oh, they did not forget about this! — incautious truth might harm the prestige of the USSR. These people covered the crimes with utilitarian considerations, i.e., they openly applied the principle of 'the end justifies the means.'" Only after the commission headed by John Dewey had announced its verdict, "for any even slightly intelligent person it became clear that a further open defense of the GPU would contain the risk of political and moral death. Only from this moment on did the 'friends' decide to drag into the light god's eternal moral truths, i.e., to occupy a second line of trenches."

Among the petty-bourgeois moralists and sycophants, Trotsky paid particular attention to former "Stalinists and semi-Stalinists" who were frightened by the Great Purge. "Having thrown overboard their own Stalinism, people of this kind — and there are many — cannot help but seek, in the arguments of abstract morality, compensation for the disillusionment or the ideological humiliation they have experienced."[30] These words apply fully to such people as Arthur Koestler or, in more recent times, to Milovan Djilas and Howard Fast.

In uncovering the ideological decline which revealed itself in the arguments and recipes of the "moralists," Trotsky stressed that they were right in that history often chooses cruel paths. "But what conclusion must then be drawn for practical activity?" he noted sarcastically. "Lev Tolstoy recommended that one must live more simply and perfect oneself... Tolstoy recommended at the same time that one must free oneself from the sins of the flesh. However, statistics do not confirm the success of his preaching. Our centrist homunculi managed to rise to the level of class-transcendent morality while living in class society. But almost 2000 years have passed since it was said: 'Love thine enemies,' 'Turn the other cheek'. ... However, even the Holy Father in Rome has not 'freed himself' as yet from hatred of his enemies. The devil, enemy of the human race, is truly strong!"[31]

Trotsky concluded "Their Morals and Ours" with the following words: "I wrote these pages during days when my son, unbeknownst to me, was struggling with death. I dedicate to his memory this small work, which, I hope, would have met with his approval: Lev Sedov was a true revolutionary and he despised Pharisees."[32]

Lev Sedov and Trotsky in France, 1933

45. "The Old Man Would Find It Hard Without Sonny"

Although he lived only thirty-two years, Lev Sedov had an outstanding and heroic biography. While he was still a teenager, he accompanied his father several times on trips to the front during the Civil War. At the beginning of the 1920s, he moved by choice from his Kremlin apartment to a student dormitory, so that he would not differ from other Komsomol members in his life style. "He refused to sit with us in an automobile, so that he would not use this privilege of the bureaucrats," Trotsky recalled. "However he eagerly took part in all the voluntary Saturdays and other 'labor mobilizations.' He cleared snow from the Moscow streets, 'liquidated' illiteracy, unloaded grain and firewood from railway cars, and later, as a polytechnic student, repaired locomotives." Noting the articles in French newspapers about the extremely modest conditions in which Sedov lived in emigration, Trotsky added: "In the years when his father and mother occupied high posts, he lived no better than during the recent period in Paris, but worse. Was this the rule among children of bureaucrats? No, even then it was an exception... His political orientation was determined by the same instinct which compelled him to prefer crowded streetcars to Moscow limousines."[1]

According to Trotsky, between him and his son "there lived and burned a mutual affection, based on something immeasurably greater than common blood: on the solidarity of views and values, sympathies and hatred, on joys and suffering which had been mutually experienced, on shared great hopes."[2] This affection became particularly strong during the exile in Alma-Ata, where Sedov conducted correspondence with hundreds of oppositionists scattered throughout the land, and helped his father in selecting material for literary work.

In emigration, Sedov became the actual publisher of the *Bulletin of the Opposition*. He continued to conduct a wide correspondence with Soviet op-

Lev (Leon) Sedov

positionists and met with supporters of the Left Opposition from various countries. After 1932, when the GPU severed Trotsky's main ties with his co-thinkers in the USSR, Sedov "had to search for fresh information by indirect paths. Lev was always on his toes as he eagerly sought out threads from Russia, intercepting returning tourists, Soviet students on foreign assignments or sympathetic functionaries at the foreign consulates. He would run around Berlin for hours, and later around Paris, in order to escape from the spies of the GPU who were tailing him, and not compromise his informers. During all these years there was not a single instance when someone suffered as a consequence of his lack of caution, lack of attention or rashness."[3]

Stalin's intelligence services were well informed of the role which Sedov played in the movement of the Fourth International. In describing to his father his conversation with Krivitsky, Sedov passed on the latter's words: "L. L. (Lev Lvovich) has the nickname 'Sonny' in the GPU. He says that they value him highly there. He works well, without him it would be bad for Trotsky... I'm only telling you what I heard; forgive me for this involuntary lack of modesty."[4]

Meetings with Sedov were sought, and his opinion and advice were valued, by revolutionaries from many countries, including Bolshevik non-returners arriving from the USSR who did not dare to trust anyone else. These contacts helped Sedov in publishing the *Bulletin of the Opposition*, which was, for him, both a living link to his homeland, and a tribune, called upon to reflect the thoughts, feelings and hopes of thousands of Soviet oppositionists who were in the underground or who were languishing in Stalinist solitary confinement. Many Soviet and foreign communists who had managed to escape from the USSR were attracted to collaborate on the *Bulletin* thanks to Sedov's efforts.

Despite his youth, Sedov was a fully developed and mature revolutionary, an experienced politician and a talented journalist. "How many times we rejoiced," recalled Trotsky, "when we found in his newly printed writings the same considerations and conclusions which I had called to his attention the day before."[5]

After the second trial of Zinoviev and Kamenev, when Trotsky did not have the opportunity to reply to the unbridled slander because he was interned by the Norwegian government, Sedov issued a crushing rebuke to the falsifiers by publishing *The Red Book on the Moscow Trial*. As they expressed high admiration for the merits of this work, many foreign journalists felt that, despite the strict conditions of his internment, Trotsky had somehow managed to participate in its composition. They declared that "Trotsky's pen is felt" in the *Red Book*. In this regard Trotsky noted: "The book contains not a single one of my lines. Many comrades who have been inclined to regard Sedov only as 'Trotsky's son,' — just as they saw Karl Liebknecht for a long time as merely the son of Wilhelm Liebknecht! — have now had the chance to become convinced on the basis of this book alone that he is not only an independent, but a major figure."[6]

An article in the *Bulletin of the Opposition* dedicated to the first anniversary of Sedov's death states: "This was a genuine Bolshevik, in the best sense of the word, and his eyes would shine joyfully when people told him that he was a real Bolshevik. For him there was no higher praise. Not the Bolshevism defiled by Stalin and the Moscow trials, but heroic Bolshevism, and all that was good in it — honesty, firmness, devotion to ideals, energy, vitality and modesty — that is what was characteristic of Sedov."[7]

Courageously inflicting ideological blows as he exposed many of Stalin's sinister intentions, Sedov, however, proved to be defenseless before the insidious activity of the Stalinists that was directed primarily against himself. Although he was an experienced and capable conspirator, he nevertheless overlooked a provocateur who had been planted by Stalinist agents among those who were in his closest circle.

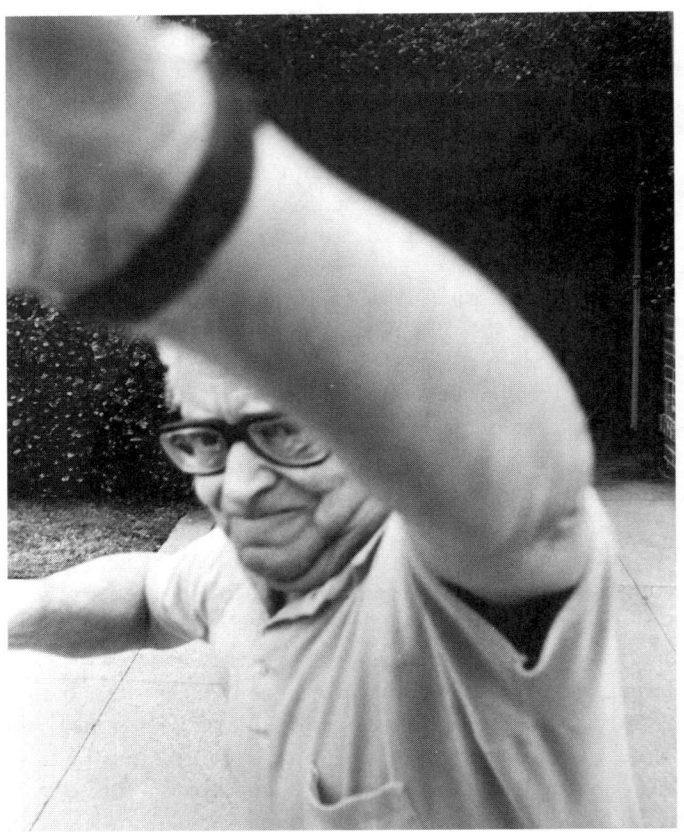

Mark Zborowski in San Francisco in August 1975. Photo by David North

46. An Agent Known as "Tulip"

Mark Zborowski, who was the same age as Sedov, proved to be such a provocateur. He was born in Uman, in a well-to-do family which emigrated in 1920 to Poland. At the start of the 1930s, he moved to France, where he began his studies in Grenoble. In 1933, Zborowski met a man who proposed that he emigrate to the USSR; he promised that Zborowski would find much more favorable material conditions than in France. After a while, the same man put him in contact with an official at the Soviet embassy, who passed on his request to receive a visa for entry into the USSR. The agent to whom Zborowski was "handed over" told him that this request would be granted if he showed in deed his devotion to the Soviet Union.

Thus began Zborowski's recruitment. He filled out a detailed questionnaire and wrote his autobiography, where, in particular, he included information about his relatives — a sister and two brothers who were living in the USSR. After a thorough verification of the facts he had provided, he was enrolled as a secret agent of the NKVD and given the nicknames "Mac" and "Tulip."

In 1935, Zborowski was given his first assignment — to get in touch with a group of French Trotskyists and provide information about their work. Soon Zborowski was introduced to Sedov — through the latter's wife, Jeanne Molinier. A few months after this, Zborowski's Paris chief told Moscow: "The source 'Mac' has begun working in the 'International Secretariat' of Trotskyists... At the present time the source meets with the son almost every day. Therefore, we consider that your directive to move the source into Trotsky's surroundings has been fulfilled."[1]

At first, Sedov had certain suspicions with regard to Zborowski. According to Glinsky, the head of the Paris network of agents, in 1936 Sedov "excused himself before 'Mac' and almost with tears in his eyes asked his forgiveness because, at the beginning of their acquaintance, he had suspected that he was an agent of the GPU."[2] Zborowski, who was called "Etienne" in

Mark Zborowski
(1908-1990)

Trotskyist circles, obtained access to Sedov's documents and was able to regularly inform the agent with whom he was in contact about all the activities and intentions of Trotsky and Sedov.

In one of his reports to Yezhov, Slutsky indicated that, during the first Moscow trial, Sedov had proposed that "Mac" travel to the USSR for illegal work, and had said the following: "We will give you instructions, money and a passport. You will travel for two or three months, go to several places according to addresses which I will give you. The work is not easy. There, unfortunately, there is no center where you could go. Our people are isolated and you will have to search for them."[3]

Even greater concern must have been aroused in Stalin by Zborowski's report that, after a conversation about the second Moscow trial, Sedov said to him: "Now there is no need to waver any more. Stalin must be killed" [see page 389]. Zborowski filed a similar report in February 1938, a few days before Sedov's death, when he informed the Center about the latter's words: "The entire regime in the USSR depends on Stalin, and it would be enough to kill him in order for everything to come crashing down."[4]

Although the *Bulletin of the Opposition* was published in a press run that was thousands of times smaller than the press runs of Stalinist publications, this single Trotskyist publication in the Russian language prompted Stalin's deep anxiety. In order to diminish the strength and influence of the exposures published in this organ, a coded message was sent from Moscow to the Paris NKVD agents which aimed at introducing provocative changes in articles being prepared for publication in the *Bulletin*. Two variants were proposed: the first — "to place our articles under the name of L. D.", and the second — "to dilute articles" in the *Bulletin* "with our paragraphs, our inserts." In pursuit of these goals the assignment was made "to recruit without fail the *Bulletin*'s typesetter."[5] However, neither Zborowski nor the other NKVD agents managed to carry out this task.

One of Zborowski's first acts of provocation was connected with the theft of Trotsky's archive. At the end of 1936, Trotsky instructed Sedov to divide the archives in his possession into three parts, and to hand one of them over to the Paris branch of the Dutch Institute of Social History, which was headed by the Menshevik, Nicolaevsky. Zborowski, who took part in taking the archive there, immediately told the Soviet resident agent about it. A few days later, a nighttime break-in was made at the institute, and all the material which had been taken there was stolen and soon redirected to Moscow.

The police investigation of the theft of the archives did not yield any results. According to the report of the Paris NKVD agent, even after the theft of the archives, the transfer of which had been known, besides Zborowski, only to Sedov, Nicolaevsky and Lola Estrine (Sedov's closest assistant), Sedov said that "he had absolute trust in Mac."

In 1937, Sedov wrote to his father that he suspected the presence of an "alien" in his surroundings. However, despite all this, he stubbornly rejected suspicions of people close to him with regard to "Etienne." When he went on a brief vacation in August 1937, he told Trotsky that he "would be replaced by Etienne, who is in the closest contact with me... Etienne deserves absolute trust in all matters."[6] During his absence in Paris, Sedov entrusted Zborowski to conduct all current correspondence, including the sending of mail and documents to Trotsky. To carry this out, he gave Zborowski his notebook with all the addresses. "As you know," the "Center" was informed in this regard, "we have dreamed about this notebook and its contents for more than a year, but we never managed to get hold of it because 'Sonny' never handed it over to anyone, and always kept it on his person. We are sending you a photo of these addresses with this mail. In the next few days we will study them in detail and send the information. There are a whole number of interesting addresses."[7]

At first glance, Sedov's behavior seems inexplicable. As an experienced conspirator, he was able to hide from the GPU all traces of his ties with oppositionists in the USSR, but he overlooked a provocateur who had wormed his way into his confidence and become his closest assistant. Evidently, Zborowski had unusual abilities when it came to mimicry and chameleon-like behavior; in addition he was sufficiently trained by experienced agents as to how he should conduct himself in order not to arouse suspicion. For Sedov, who had no close ideological ties in the emigrant milieu, the presence of Zborowski seemed to fill the vacuum of "Russian-speaking" people. Depicting himself as a Stalinist who had seen the light and become completely devoted to the cause of the Fourth International, Zborowski skillfully dispelled all suspicions that Sedov or Estrine might have had.

From the very beginning, the French Trotskyists suspected that Zborowski was an agent of the NKVD. Sneevliet shared the same opinion. His serious disagreement with Sedov was prompted by the fact that he feared the presence of a spy in Sedov's surroundings and did not immediately agree to set up a meeting between the latter and Reiss.

Despite the certainty expressed by Krivitsky that there was a provocateur in Sedov's milieu, the latter instructed Zborowski to accompany Krivitsky in his movements around Paris. At a hearing before the Senate subcommittee, Zborowski announced that he had reported about Krivitsky to the resident NKVD agent, but had not told him about the place where Krivitsky was hiding.[8]

Suspicions about the presence of a provocateur in Sedov's surroundings grew when it became known that Stalin's agents had learned of Sneevliet's contacts with Reiss. However, even after this, Sedov continued to maintain his unconditional confidence in Zborowski, who all the while was rendering the NKVD ever greater services. In his reports he described in detail the discussions which were held in the international secretariat of the Fourth International, and he photographed many documents from Trotsky's archives in order to send them to Moscow. With Zborowski as intermediary, the manuscript of *Revolution Betrayed*, or its separate fragments, appeared on Stalin's desk before the book was published in Paris in the summer of 1937. Stalin also received reports about the preparation of editions of *Revolution Betrayed* in other countries, and who was engaged in its translation into foreign languages.

Knowing that Stalin was interested in literally everything that had to do with Trotsky, Yezhov regularly sent him documents he received from his agents, including letters from Sedov to Trotsky, as well as 103 letters taken from Trotsky's archives, including the correspondence with Eastman and his wife Ye. V. Krylenko (the sister of N. V. Krylenko, the People's Commissar of Justice). Besides this, Yezhov systematically sent Stalin detailed lists of all the Trotskyist newspapers, journals and other editions being published in various countries around the world, as well as summaries outlining their content.[9]

Zborowski's activity as an agent became known at hearings of the Senate Subcommittee of the USA on National Security which took place in 1955. Before he gave his testimony, Zborowski was told that the Subcommittee had received evidence of his activity as an agent of the GPU from "a very reliable and highly placed agent in the Soviet espionage network (Orlov – V. R.)."[10]

Zborowski acknowledged that, in his youth, he had been a member of a Polish student organization headed by communists, but he had never been a member of the Communist Party. When asked why, then, if this were so, he

46. An Agent Known as "Tulip"

A report by Mark Zborowski sent to Moscow detailing alleged conversations with Sedov in January 1937

Translation of the report: *"On January [22], during our discussion at his apartment concerning the second Moscow trial and the role in it of individual defendants (Radek, Piatakov and others), L. Sedov declared: 'Now there is no need to waver any more, Stalin must be killed.' For me this declaration was so unexpected that I didn't have time to react to it. L. Sedov immediately shifted our conversation to other issues.*

On January 23, L. Sedov, in my presence, as well as L. Estrine's, blurted out a sentence of the same content as on the 22nd. In response to his statement, L. Estrine said, 'Hold your tongue.' They did not return to this question again.

M. Zborowski"

had told Estrine that he had been in the Polish Communist Party and had been arrested as a communist, Zborowski replied that "this was in the interests of his work."[11]

In answering the senators' questions, Zborowski was very evasive and declared that he could not recall many events that had occurred twenty years before. Meanwhile, he said that he knew from Soviet agents that Stalin was directly informed about his infiltration of Sedov's surroundings, and viewed his work as extremely important. Zborowski also admitted that he regularly provided information about the activity of Trotskyists and that he received payment for this, although supposedly "I tried to avoid receiving money from these people."[12]

At the hearings Zborowski declared that, after the Moscow Trials, he had changed his attitude toward the NKVD and the Stalinists, insofar as he knew very well that the trials were frame-ups: Trotsky and Sedov had not collaborated with the Nazis, and were not preparing a conspiracy against the USSR. Therefore, as he put it, he frequently gave the resident agents distorted information, deliberately delayed reports and sabotaged various orders. Thus, he did not carry out the assignment to lure Sedov to a place where they intended to kidnap him for a forced and secret return to the USSR.[13]

Meanwhile, the investigations conducted in the 1950s in the USA did not provide an exhaustive answer to the question of Zborowski's role in the main crime in which he was a suspect — his participation in the poisoning of Lev Sedov.

47. The Death of Leon Sedov

In 1937, Sedov's life was particularly intense. He carried out enormous work in gathering material for the Dewey Commission, answered hundreds of letters and met with many oppositionists from various countries. He managed to do much to uncover the murderers of Reiss, and to save Krivitsky from persecution at the hands of Stalin's agents. In the last months of his life, Sedov was gathering material to assemble a card file of foreign agents of the GPU.

In letters to his father, Sedov often said that he felt that he was being followed unremittingly. This surveillance became particularly intense after 1935. It was conducted by members of Efron's group, who followed literally in Sedov's footsteps. Efron's assistant, Smirensky, settled into a place neighboring Sedov's apartment, from which he kept a constant watch over him.

When he was later being interrogated by the NKVD, Efron declared that he had entrusted the surveillance of Sedov to an agent he had recruited. After this agent had been noticed by Sedov, the latter turned to the French police, who detained the "observer," questioned him, and then released him after interrogation, but placed him under strict surveillance. Therefore, for a certain time, any contact between Efron's group and Smirensky was stopped.[1]

When Sedov traveled for two weeks to the seaside town of Antibes (this was his only vacation in many years), Renata Steiner settled into the same pension, from where she sent daily reports to Efron and Smirensky, who were staying in the same town. She was told that Sedov was a speculator who was supplying arms to Franco's forces.[2]

Members of Efron's group waited for Sedov at the train station in Mulhouse, where he was preparing to go in order to meet with a Swiss lawyer participating in the investigation of the Moscow Trials. Sedov avoided this deathtrap only because he fell ill on the eve of the scheduled trip and could not leave Paris. In the summer of 1937, the hunt for Sedov was halted for a while because the terrorists were reassigned to organize Reiss's murder, which Moscow considered to be a more pressing matter.

Sedov's friends repeatedly wrote Trotsky that his son was in serious danger in Paris, and insisted that he move to Mexico. Recognizing that such danger was beyond any doubt, Sedov felt more strongly that Paris was a post that was too important for him to abandon.[3]

At the beginning of 1937, Sedov published an article in the French magazine *Confession*, in which he declared that he was in excellent health and that he was not inclined toward depression or suicide. He warned that, in the case of his sudden death, one would have to look for those to blame in the camp of the Stalinists.[4]

In November 1937, Zborowski reported that Sedov, who feared a sudden attempt on his life, had written a will in which he indicated where his archive was kept.[5]

In his last letter to Trotsky on February 4, 1938, Sedov did not mention any symptoms of illness, and spoke of his intense activity in connection with the impending trial in the case of Reiss's murder.[6]

Sedov's illness began on 10 February. In order to protect his security, he was not placed in a French hospital, where he would have been forced to present his passport and thereby disclose his real name. He was placed under the name of the French engineer Martin in a private clinic belonging to a Russian emigrant.

Jeanne Molinier insisted that not even his closest comrades be told of Sedov's illness and location. However, as people soon learned, Zborowski, who visited the patient, "confidentially" reported his visits to several French Trotskyists.[7]

Immediately after entering the clinic, Sedov was operated on for appendicitis, after which his health improved noticeably for four days. However, on the fifth night, Sedov became delirious and wandered about unsupervised through the corridors of the clinic. A day later he was dead.

In describing his condition, after receiving the news about his son's death, Trotsky noted: "February 16 has been the darkest day in our personal life... Along with our child, everything has died that was still young within us."[8]

The first weeks after Sedov's death coincided with news about a new Moscow trial. "My wife and I live these days just as we have always lived, only under the weight of the greatest loss which we have been forced to endure," wrote Trotsky. "... The mail brings to us each morning many letters of sympathy from every end of the earth... We read telegrams from Moscow, clarify details in articles... Respite comes from remembering about a son whose life was so inseparably bound with our life for the last three decades. Night is followed by day. We are sustained by the thought that we continue to serve the cause that we have served our entire lives."[9]

In the first response to his son's death, Trotsky wrote: "The wound is too fresh, and I still find it difficult to talk about Lev Sedov as one who has died.

47. The Death of Leon Sedov

Photograph of Lev Sedov from the *Bulletin of the Opposition*

He was not only my son, but my best friend. But there is still one question about which I am obliged to respond immediately: this is the question of the causes of his death."[10]

Considering that it was highly probable that Sedov was poisoned, Trotsky emphasized that the GPU had at its disposal extraordinary scientific and technical resources which could render extremely difficult the work of a medical autopsy. The secrets of the art of poisoning, which had been perfected in connection with the development of military chemistry, "are inaccessible, it is true, to simple mortals. But everything is accessible to the poisoners of the GPU."[11]

Trotsky's ideas about Sedov's poisoning were reinforced by information from the third Moscow trial that a special laboratory for testing the latest poisons was at Yagoda's disposal, and that the luminaries of Moscow medicine had hastened the death of patients by using methods which do not yield to control or are difficult to control. "From the standpoint of the issue which interests us," Trotsky wrote, "it is almost the same whether in the given concrete instances the testimony of the defendants is true or false. It is sufficient to note that secret methods of poisoning, infecting, influencing illness and generally expediting death are officially included in the arsenal of the GPU."[12]

On 19 July 1938, Trotsky sent a letter to the French official who was in charge of investigating the causes of Sedov's death. In it he stated that the investigation's version about the natural cause of death (infection acted upon an organism weakened by an operation) raised doubts because "for a long time, especially in the last two years, Sedov lived under a relentless blockade on the part of a gang from the GPU which enjoys almost as much freedom on the territory of Paris as it enjoys in Moscow." Therefore, the death of Sedov must be seen not as a typical case, but as the death, unexpected even by the doctors, "of a lone exile after prolonged single combat between him and a powerful state apparatus armed with inexhaustible material, technical and scientific resources... We are dealing with an absolutely determined international gang which has committed not its first crime on the territory of France, while enjoying and covering itself with friendly diplomatic relations (between the USSR and France – V. R.)."[13] For Trotsky this relationship explained why the investigation into the causes of Sedov's death had not led to any results in five months, much like the investigation into the theft of his archives or the attempt to kill Sedov in Mulhouse.

Trotsky saw one indication of the enigmatic nature of Sedov's death when he learned that the operating surgeon had asked J. Molinier if Sedov had tried to attempt suicide before. "The turn for the worse in the condition of the patient," Trotsky wrote in commenting on this fact, "was so sharp and sudden that the surgeon, who knew neither the personality of the patient nor the condition of his life, felt compelled to resort to a hypothesis of suicide."[14] After he had received new information about the course of the investigation, Trotsky sent an additional statement on 24 August to the investigator. Pointing to the obvious oversights allowed by the investigation, he recalled that the investigation of Reiss's murder had firmly established: "Among the enemies of the GPU and the victims they had marked, Lev Sedov occupied first place, along with me. The GPU never let him out of their sight. For at least two years, the GPU bandits hunted for Sedov in France as one hunts after wild prey.... Can it be allowed for a minute that the GPU lost sight of Sedov when he was placed in the clinic and let slip an extraordinarily opportune moment? The investigatory bodies have no right to allow this."[15]

Trotsky named a number of facts established by the investigation which confirmed suspicions about the violent character of Sedov's death. According to information from the French police, the director of the clinic where the patient was located "sympathized with the Bolsheviks." Sedov's real name had been revealed only to Simkov, the clinic's owner, who spoke with the patient in Russian even though Sedov had been placed in the clinic under a French name. The surgeon who performed the operation refused to provide explanations to the investigator in the name of professional secrecy. "If Sedov's death naturally and inevitably flowed from the character of his illness,"

Trotsky wrote in this regard, "then the surgeon could have not the slightest interest in refusing, or psychological reason to refuse, to provide the necessary explanations."[16]

The investigation was complicated by the fact that soon after Sedov's death, Simkov lost two sons who fell victim to an accidental cave-in. In the period when the fate of the missing boys remained unknown, Simkov said in an interview with a French newspaper that, if his sons had been kidnapped, this could have been done only by Trotskyists who were trying to get revenge for the death of Sedov. "I must candidly say," wrote Trotsky, "that such an idea could only arise in the mind of a man whose conscience was not entirely clear, or who moved in political circles which are mortally hostile to Sedov and me, where agents of the GPU could directly implant the fantastic and outrageous idea in the mind of a distraught father."[17] Trotsky was also very suspicious about the fact that the French communist press, which had earlier written much about Sedov (of course, in a hostile vein), had not written a single line about his death. "'Caution' of this kind," Trotsky indicated, "becomes particularly significant if one calls to mind that in issues which are sensitive for Moscow, the French press of the Comintern receives direct instructions from the GPU through the old agent of the GPU, Jacques Duclos and others."[18]

At the end of his "Supplementary Declaration," Trotsky stated that the French police were not trying to uncover the truth insofar as "the GPU has powerful accomplices in the French police and above it. Millions of gold rubles are expended annually in order to secure the impunity of Stalin's mafia in France. To this must be added considerations of a 'patriotic' and 'diplomatic' order, which are conveniently used by the murderers who serve Stalin and act as freely in Paris as they do at home. That is why the investigation into the case regarding Sedov's death has been and continues to be a fiction."[19]

Of course, Trotsky possessed only partial information about the circumstances of his son's death. Letters from Estrine and Zborowski about this matter could only disorient him, insofar as they provided a version of Sedov's death ascribing it to natural causes, and discounted Jeanne Molinier's opinion that Sedov had been poisoned.[20]

New facts connected with the circumstances of Sedov's death emerged in 1955, during Zborowski's interrogation before the Senate Subcommittee in the USA. Here Zborowski was forced to acknowledge that he had given the resident GPU agent information about Sedov's illness and about the clinic to which he had been taken.[21] The version of Sedov's death as a camouflaged murder finds confirmation in the fact that it occurred on the eve of the third Moscow trial, at which Sedov was charged with new crimes which without doubt he would have thoroughly refuted had he been alive.

After studying Zborowski's reports, which are preserved in Moscow's archives, Volkogonov came to the conclusion that there remains little doubt about the participation of the NKVD in Sedov's death. It is true that he did not manage to find direct orders to kill Sedov. Volkogonov explained this by the fact that such orders were given orally in order to leave behind no compromising material. Besides, after completing "operations" of this kind, a significant portion of the documents connected with them would be destroyed.[22]

In the Spiegelglas dossier, the latter mentions that Yezhov said after receiving news about Sedov's death: "A good operation. We did a good job on him, didn't we?"[23] Although at his interrogation Spiegelglas called these words groundless boasting and claimed that the NKVD had no part in Sedov's death, these statements cannot be accepted on faith. Stalin's special services abroad had so many branches that the given operation could have been carried out without Spiegelglas's participation, or even his knowledge.

B. A. Bronstein, arrested 17 June 1937 and shot soon after. (See next page)

48. Trotsky in Mexico

It is natural that Stalin's agents fixed their attention not only on Sedov, but also on Trotsky. Immediately after his arrival in Mexico, these agents set about organizing provocations in order to limit Trotsky's access to the world press. At the beginning of 1937, a certain Lieber refused to collaborate with Trotsky; earlier he had arranged the publication of Trotsky's articles in the most popular American magazines and had concluded contracts with major American publishing houses for the publication of his books. Later Lieber was exposed as an agent of the NKVD.[1]

In Mexico, Trotsky was surrounded by a solid ring of surveillance. Besides the actual agents of the NKVD, the embassies of the USSR in the USA and in Mexico regularly provided information about his activity. They sent reports to members of the Politburo about Trotsky's statements and responses to them in the world press. In this process, Trotsky's statements were often quoted in the reports in falsified form to please the people reading them.[2]

D. Volkogonov, who received access to material in Stalin's personal archive, discovered that Stalin read each issue of the *Bulletin of the Opposition*, paying particular attention to articles about himself.[3]

When he arrived in Mexico City, Trotsky learned about the persecution of all his close relatives. As was established by V. B. Bronstein, one of Trotsky's few relatives who survived, in 1937-1938 the following people were shot: Trotsky's son, S. Sedov; Trotsky's older brother, A. D. Bronstein; the latter's son B. A. Bronstein (a Bolshevik from 1912, and an active participant in the Civil War); Trotsky's first wife, A. L. Sokolovskaya; the husbands of Trotsky's daughters, P. Volkov and M. Nevelson. These executions were followed by the arrest of Trotsky's sister, O. D. Kameneva; the wife of B. A. Bronstein; the second son and daughter of A. D. Bronstein; the first wife of L. Sedov; the wife of S. Sedov; and several more distant relatives of Trotsky.[4]

From the very beginning of Trotsky's stay in Mexico, pro-Stalinist elements directed their unrelenting efforts at denying his right to asylum. Pres-

Natalia Sedova, Frida Kahlo, Trotsky, and Max Shachtman in Mexico

sure on the Mexican government aimed at Trotsky's deportation from the country was so great that President Cárdenas, who felt a profound respect for Trotsky, never dared to meet with him.

In the middle of 1937, the streets of Mexico City were covered with leaflets which claimed that Trotsky had formed an alliance with Mexican reactionary generals to prepare a reactionary coup in the country.

Such actions were organized by the leader of the Federation of Mexican Trade Unions, the Stalinist Lombardo Toledano. In an article, "The Totalitarian Right to Asylum," Trotsky wrote: "Toledano is still not the boss in Mexico. He cannot, following the example of his teacher and patron, shoot or poison unarmed emigrants. The means which remain at his disposal are slander and defamation. And he uses them as widely as possible."[5]

Trotsky noted that, by the right to asylum, Toledano understood "the right for agents of the GPU to enter Mexico." This remark was based on real facts. Material in the archives of the NKVD and recollections by its agent Sudoplatov show that already by the start of 1937, experienced underground agents had been sent to Mexico to observe Trotsky and prepare a terrorist act.[6] During the investigation of Reiss's murder, it was found that the immediate murderers, Roland Abbiate and Martigny, had spent some time in Mexico in February 1937, along with other cutthroats. During a search of Abbiate's apartment, police found a map of Mexico, plans of Mexico City and its environs, and a copy of a statement about providing an entry visa into Mexico.[7]

The resident NKVD agents in Mexico were not squeamish about crude attempts to organize a terrorist act. Thus, at the beginning of 1938, a suspicious person who pretended to be a messenger bringing a gift tried to gain entrance to Trotsky's house. After the guards refused to allow him into the house, he disappeared, leaving nearby a package with explosive material.[8]

The dispatch of a new group of agents began in the spring of 1938, when a representative of the Center came to Paris with orders to "promote" Zborowski into Trotsky's surroundings and, if this plan failed, to send to Mexico "two or three German Trotskyists" who "might prove to be extremely valuable in the future."[9]

In April 1938, the French press contained an article which reported that a GPU agent named George Mink had been sent to Mexico in order to organize an attempt on Trotsky's life.[10] This man, who according to Krivitsky had worked in the intelligence directorate of the Red Army, headed an espionage group in Denmark until 1935, when he was arrested in Copenhagen and sentenced to 18 months of prison. After leaving prison, Mink headed for Spain, where his name was linked to the disappearance, arrest and murders of Erwin Wolf, Mark Rein and other anti-Stalinist revolutionaries.

Attempts to recruit murderers occurred in Mexico itself. As Valentin Campo, one of the former leaders of the Mexican Communist Party, announced in 1978, a Comintern emissary proposed that he organize a terrorist attack against Trotsky. When Campo flatly refused to carry out this assignment, he was driven from the party.[11]

The Mexican agents of the GPU acted so successfully that they seized important information intended for Trotsky from Europe. On 19 November 1937, Sedov told Trotsky: "In my last letter I wrote that probably part of your mail, if not all, is monitored. This is based on the following. One of the GPU-ers* working in this area (Spiegelglas – V. R.) told my informer (Krivitsky – V. R.) this summer: we already have a telegram from Mexico stating that Trotsky knows that Ludwig has surfaced. This was before the matter became officially known."[12]

Jean van Heijenoort, one of Trotsky's former secretaries, relates in his memoirs that Trotsky had no doubt about the intentions of the NKVD to infiltrate their agents into his entourage, but that, nevertheless, he did not show the necessary caution in a number of cases. In the spring of 1938, Trotsky's secretaries appealed to Trotskyists in Europe to recommend a Russian typist. Soon a reply arrived that a Czech girl who was completely fluent in Russian was ready to come to Mexico, but that there were suspicions that she was a Stalinist. When van Heijenoort told Trotsky about this, the latter said: "We shall invite her! We will win her over to our side."

On 14 May, Trotsky wrote his former secretary, Jan Frankel: "She is still a very young woman, she is only eighteen years old. I do not believe that she can

---

* Trotsky and Sedov used this term in their articles and correspondence to designate members of the GPU-NKVD.

be a horrible agent of the GPU. Even if she harbors sympathy for the Stalinists and bad intentions toward us ... we feel strong enough to watch her, monitor and re-educate her." A month later, once again informing Frankel of his readiness to immediately accept this girl, Trotsky added: "An eighteen-year-old girl will not be able to form conspiracies in our home: we are stronger. In two or three months she will be completely assimilated."

Trotsky was guided by similar considerations with regard to Zborowski. Trusting the opinion of the late Sedov and of Lola Estrine, he replied to the suspicions of one of the French Trotskyists with regard to "Etienne": "You want to deprive me of my collaborators."[13]

At hearings of the Senate Subcommittee which took place in 1955, Orlov said that, in 1936, he had already learned about the presence of an NKVD agent in Sedov's circle who "was valued so highly that even Stalin knew about him." At that time Orlov, who happened to be abroad, made the decision to tell Trotsky about this agent.

While he was in Spain and France, Orlov made no small effort to learn in greater detail about this provocateur. This endeavor was facilitated by the fact that the agents in Paris valued Orlov highly and trusted him completely. Orlov was told about the existence of an agent named Mark by Alekseev — an agent who was in direct contact with Zborowski. After telling Orlov: "If this man disappears, my head will roll," Alekseev took Orlov to one of his meetings with Zborowski which occurred in a Parisian park. Sitting down on a neighboring bench, Orlov observed as "Mark" gave Alekseev some papers.[14]

In 1965, during questioning by the CIA, Orlov stated that he had made his first attempt in 1937 to warn Trotsky about Zborowski's activity as a provocateur, but that he had not managed to find out whether his letter had reached Trotsky at that time.[15]

On 27 December 1938, Orlov sent Trotsky a registered letter, written in Russian words on a Latin typewriter, insofar as he did not have a typewriter with Russian letters. Fearing that Stalin's agents might seize a letter addressed personally to Trotsky, Orlov sent a copy in the name of Sedova.

Assuming that Trotsky's circle might contain spies who would learn about the letter's contents, Orlov made one more conspiratorial maneuver. He presented himself in the letter as a long-time Russian emigrant and relative of the NKVD official, Liushkov, who had fled from the USSR. In order to increase Trotsky's trust in the information being sent, he wrote that not long before he had been in Japan, where he learned from Liushkov about "the presence in the center of your organization of a dangerous provocateur who for a long time had been an assistant to your son, Sedov, in publishing The Bulletin of the Opposition." Then he provided such detailed and precise information about the provocateur, which he supposedly had received from Liushkov (his name, height, nationality, origin, family situation, external looks), that there could be no doubt about whom he was describing. Orlov wrote that the provocateur had taken an active part in stealing Trotsky's archives and that he "had reported about every step Sedov took, about his activities and his correspondence with you."

Declaring that Liushkov had related the fear that the NKVD would try to send murderers to Trotsky through this provocateur or through Spanish agents sent to Mexico under the guise of being Trotskyists, Orlov wrote: "Most importantly, Lev Davidovich, protect yourself. Do not trust a single person, either man or woman, who comes to you with a recommendation from this provocateur."

Having said that the provocateur met regularly with Soviet agents, Orlov begged Trotsky to instruct "reliable comrades in Paris to check out Mark's biography and see with whom he meets. There is no doubt that your comrades will see him with officials from the Soviet embassy."

After signing the letter with the words, "Your friend," Orlov asked Trotsky not to tell anyone about this letter and particularly about the fact that it had been received from the USA.[16]

Documents contained in Orlov's Moscow dossier show that he knew much more about operations directed against Trotsky and Trotskyists than he related in his letter. In 1937, he had directed the surveillance of contacts between Trotskyists in Paris and Spain. In one of his reports to the "Center," he told of infiltrating an agent into the Spanish Trotskyist group, and about establishing control over the "secret channel of communication between this group and the Trotskyist center in Paris." When he listed in a letter to Yezhov the secret operations about which he was well informed, Orlov mentioned "all the work done by 'Tulip' and 'Gamma' (the secret nickname of the NKVD agent Afanasiev, Zborowski's Paris handler). Two pages from one of Zborowski's reports even ended up in Orlov's hands.[17]

One can assume that, if Orlov had possessed a reliable and secure channel of communications with Trotsky, he would have told him about these facts as well. He was silent about them, evidently out of conspiratorial considerations, since any possible interception by Stalin's agents of a more detailed letter would have easily established his authorship.

Nor is the following supposition lacking foundation: if Orlov had been able to establish systematic contact with Trotsky, then the assassination in Coyoacan would have been prevented. For Orlov had met in Spain with Mercader's mother, and had recruited Mercader himself, who was sent along with other Spanish agents by the Center to Mexico.

Both Orlov and Trotsky took steps to establish regular contact. In his letter, Orlov asked Trotsky to place an ad in the American Trotskyist newspaper, *Socialist Appeal*, indicating that he had received a letter from "Stein" (a code name with which the letter was signed). Soon an announcement appeared in this newspaper addressed to "Stein": "I insist that you immediately go to the editorial office of *Socialist Appeal* and talk with Comrade Martin."[18]

At the same time Trotsky sent a letter to his co-thinkers in Paris which began with the words: "Extremely confidential, very important and very urgent." In it he said that he had received very important information from a source who did not identify himself, but who claimed that he had been meeting with major officials in the GPU. After outlining Orlov's information about "Mark," Trotsky stressed: "The source (the informer) is certain that it will not be difficult to trace the provocateur's ties to the Soviet embassy." Trotsky advanced two possible versions, as far as he was concerned, about the "source": 1. He is a "timid friend"; 2. "He is acting on behalf of the GPU, which wishes to spread demoralization in our ranks." Feeling that it was necessary to verify the information he had received about the provocateur, Trotsky proposed the formation in Paris of a commission made up of three reliable people, joined by two or three young people, who would begin a secret surveillance of "Mark's" contacts. "If the information is confirmed," wrote Trotsky, "you must tell the French police about him as a participant in the theft of the archives and make sure that he is not allowed to disappear."[19]

After this Trotsky sent a letter to Wright, a member of the Socialist Workers Party in the USA, in which he relayed the message he had placed in the newspaper, and added: "If you receive a reply, then you must personally meet with this man. This question may turn out to be very important."

However, contact between Orlov and the American Trotskyists did not work out. Orlov visited the editorial office of the *Socialist Appeal* and asked them to show him "Comrade Martin," but he did not dare speak to him since he suspected that he was an agent of the NKVD.[20]

In the spring of 1939, Trotsky discussed the letter from "Stein" with Lola Estrine, who had come to visit him, and he questioned her at length about Zborowski. Estrine declared that she was sure of "Etienne's" unconditional honesty, and felt that the letter was the work of the GPU, which was trying to tear away from Trotsky one of his most devoted collaborators.[21] After this, Trotsky sent his friend a letter in which he called "Stein's" warning "seventy-five percent provocation, aimed at sowing suspicion with regard to a loyal comrade."[22]

Upon returning to Paris, Estrine told Zborowski about her conversation with Trotsky. In June 1939, Zborowski informed the Center that the "'Old Man' did not believe the denunciation and feels that the letter is a GPU provocation."[23]

49. Murders Abroad

Meanwhile, events confirmed the timeliness of Orlov's warnings. At a time when the Stalinist justice system was accusing Trotskyists of preparing terrorist acts in the USSR, foreign countries were to witness a series of such acts against Trotsky's supporters and other revolutionaries hostile to the Stalinist regime. After D. Volkogonov studied the NKVD archives, he came to the conclusion that agents of the secret political and foreign departments of the NKVD clandestinely murdered hundreds of people beyond the borders of the Soviet Union.[1]

The foremost area of political murders in 1937 was Spain, where the following people died at the hands of the Stalinists: Andrés Nin, the leader of the POUM; Erwin Wolf, Trotsky's former secretary; the Austrian revolutionary Kurt Landau; Mark Rein, the son of the Russian emigrant and Menshevik Abramovich; and many others.

In other countries of Europe, the NKVD also committed several political murders by using the services of the emigrant groups they financed.

At the beginning of 1938, Stalin launched a new provocation of a diplomatic nature, directed against foreign Trotskyists and most of all against Trotsky himself. The Soviet ambassador in France turned to the French Ministry of Foreign Affairs with a protest on behalf of the Supreme Council of the USSR regarding the granting of political asylum to "terrorists," and "to foreigners of Russian origin." Simultaneously, the Soviet government proposed to create a tribunal against terrorists under the League of Nations. The goal of this action was to have Trotsky handed over to Soviet authorities. However, in the given instance, Trotsky seized the political initiative once again and sent a statement to the judicial section of the secretariat of the League of Nations. In this statement, directed essentially at world public opinion, he said: "In the last half year the world has been witness to a number of *genuine* terrorist acts, committed in various countries according to a common plan and with an undoubtedly common goal. I have in mind not the judicial and

Erwin Wolf
(1902-1937)

extrajudicial murders in the USSR, where this involves, one way or another, the legalized actions of the state apparatus, but acts of open banditry on the international arena." Enumerating a number of instances of kidnapping and murder committed by the Stalinists abroad, Trotsky wrote: "Even the portion of the judicial and extrajudicial investigations which has become available to public opinion is sufficient to warrant intervention of the International Tribunal against the centralized mafia of terrorists acting on the territory of various states."

Trotsky expressed his readiness to provide eye-witness testimony, documents and irrefutable political arguments "to show ... that the head of this criminal gang is Joseph Stalin, general secretary of the All-Union Communist Party of the USSR." In conclusion, he sarcastically expressed the hope that Litvinov, who had been insisting on the acceptance of the mutual obligation of governments to hand over terrorists, "will not refuse to exert his influence in order that the above-named Joseph Stalin, as head of an international terrorist gang, be placed at the disposal of the tribunal under the League of Nations."[2]

In the given instance, the duel between the powerful Stalinist governmental apparatus and a solitary political exile was essentially won by the latter. The creation of an international tribunal ground to a halt.

At the same time, in the bourgeois-democratic countries the secret kidnappings and murders continued. In the spring of 1937, Juliet Stuart Poyntz, a former activist in the Communist Party of the USA, disappeared without a trace. From 1934, she had worked in Soviet intelligence, and at the end of

49. Murders Abroad

Rudolf Klement
(1908-1938)

1936, she broke with the Communist party and began to write her memoirs. Suspects in her kidnapping were George Mink and another NKVD agent, Shakhno Epstein, editor of a Communist newspaper and in the past a close friend of Poyntz.[3]

In 1938 there was one more insidious political murder, accompanied by a crude provocation. On 13 July of that year, the German emigrant Rudolf Klement mysteriously disappeared in Paris. In 1933-1935 he had worked as Trotsky's secretary, and then had become the secretary of the Bureau of the Fourth International. Klement actively participated in the collection of material for the investigation into the Moscow Trials and in preparing the founding conference of the Fourth International. Five days before his disappearance, a briefcase containing papers had been stolen from him on the metro. Klement immediately notified all sections of the Fourth International about this theft, and proposed that they stop sending letters to the old addresses.

When on 15 July, French Trotskyists who had received a letter from Klement visited his apartment, they discovered in the empty room a breakfast which had been prepared but which remained untouched; everything was in its proper place, and there were no signs of preparations for a trip.

Soon, several European Trotskyists, and then Trotsky himself, received similar letters signed by "Frederick." Klement had indeed used this nickname, but only until 1936, when he suspected that the name had become known to the NKVD or the Gestapo. The letters spoke of Klement's break with the movement of the Fourth International, and in justification named other people who supposedly had left this movement. Among the names were those who were genuine renegades, as well as Nin (who had been murdered in Spain), and exposed agents of the NKVD such as the Sobolevicius brothers (Senin and Roman Well) and Jan Frank. The author of the letter mentioned imaginary conversations between Trotsky and Klement about the admissibility of "temporary concessions to Fascist leaders in the name of the proletarian revolution."

Victor Serge, who knew Klement well, thought that even if this letter, which was typewritten, had not been a complete forgery by the Stalinists, then it had been dictated to Klement at the point of a gun.[4] Evidence that the letter was a forgery could be seen from the way the address was written on the envelope, which was done as only Russians write such addresses: first comes the name of the city, then the name of the street (Klement, like every European, usually wrote these names in the reverse order).

In his first response to Klement's disappearance, Trotsky expressed certainty that he had been killed, and that the letter was fabricated by agents of the GPU. "It is very easy," wrote Trotsky, "to refute this one acceptable hypothesis: 'Frederick' should emerge from his place of refuge and issue open accusations."[5]

Soon, Trotsky received a letter from Klement's aunt. She stated that Rudolf's mother, who lived in Germany, was in despair over the absence of any news about her missing son. As Trotsky stressed, this letter "is extra proof of the GPU's crime. If Rudolf had indeed left Paris voluntarily, as the GPU wants to force us to believe with the help of agents of various categories, then he would not, it goes without saying, have left his own mother in the dark."[6]

Several months after Klement's disappearance, his brutally dismembered body was found in the Seine. Final light was shed on this crime by the memoirs of Sudoplatov, who named the agents of the NKVD who had killed Klement, and told how this murder had been carried out.[7]

Klement was the sixth of Trotsky's secretaries to die a violent death. Four of them perished in the USSR, two of them beyond its borders.

50. Paris Intrigues

Besides organizing murders, the GPU relentlessly provoked conflicts and intrigues among Trotsky's supporters, particularly in the circle of Paris Trotskyists, where they had arisen while Sedov was still alive. The intrigues were given a new impulse by events connected with the entry of Reiss, and then Krivitsky, into the Paris circle. Reiss first met with Sneevliet on 11 June 1937. A few days later Krivitsky learned from Spiegelglas: on either 13 or 14 June, Moscow had already received information that "one of the senior agents" had been meeting with Sneevliet (ten days later the "Center" learned that this agent was Reiss).[1]

When Krivitsky told Sedov about all this, the latter once again came to the conclusion that a provocateur existed among his closest associates. But even then Sedov did not stop trusting Zborowski, who in turn expressed his suspicions that Sneevliet and Serge were to blame for the information leak. Under the influence of these intrigues, Sedov sent Trotsky a letter with sharp accusations against Sneevliet for the fact that the latter had been delaying Sedov's meeting with Reiss and had not been displaying the necessary concern about Reiss's security.[2]

A new web of intrigue arose after Sedov's death. Sedov had left a will in which he entrusted his archive exclusively to Jeanne Molinier and no one else.[3] When they informed Trotsky about this, Estrine and Zborowski complained that, by placing the archive at Jeanne's disposal, Sedov "had deprived the organization of any control over the fate of these documents." In the same letter, they said that, besides the main archive which Jeanne had in her possession, a significant part of the archives was in their hands.[4]

Moscow was greatly interested in the fate of the archive. A report sent by one of the Paris NKVD agents indicated that J. Molinier did not trust Zborowski and therefore did not agree that he could participate in examining the archive.[5]

On 1 March 1938, Trotsky appointed a commission to receive the archive. But even after this, Jeanne declared that she objected to the composition of the commission.[6]

After Sedov's death, the publication of the *Bulletin of the Opposition* passed entirely into the hands of Estrine and Zborowski. It was in their name that Trotsky sent his articles, copies of which Zborowski gave to the resident NKVD agent. As a result, they often appeared in Moscow even before they were published.

In the spring of 1938, the "Center" sent Zborowski an order "to assume control of further contact with the 'International Secretariat.'"[7] He managed to carry out this order since Trotsky, who knew the unlimited confidence which his son had placed in "Etienne," gave Zborowski the most responsible assignments. Soon Zborowski reported to the "Center": "The Old Man has ordered that I be added to the secretariat and be invited to all sessions of the International Secretariat."[8] In another report Zborowski noted: the French Trotskyists had proposed that he "assume responsibility for all the work of the Russian group" and had declared that they would consider him alone to be "the representative of the Russian group."[9]

In September 1938, at the founding conference of the Fourth International, Zborowski was the only person to represent the delegation from the USSR. He informed the Center in detail about the participants of the congress and the resolutions passed at it.

Zborowski did everything possible to prevent non-returners from going over to the side of the Trotskyists. He proposed that the "Center" spread rumors about Krivitsky's participation in the murder of Reiss.[10] Although this provocation failed, Zborowski and Estrine told Trotsky that Krivitsky was "unreliable." Their letters gave one-sided information about Krivitsky's collaboration with the Mensheviks, and expressed doubts about his truthfulness. Krivitsky supposedly "talks only about what corresponds to his interests, and remains silent about things that are not to his benefit."[11] The next letter concluded: "We must be done with W. (Walter)."[12]

Similar intrigues unfolded around Barmine, who openly expressed his distrust of the editors of the *Bulletin* and declared that he did not consider them Trotsky's representatives.[13] In a letter to Trotsky, Estrine announced: "E. (Etienne) met with Barmine. Things won't work out with him."[14]

A conflict also arose between the publishers of the *Bulletin of the Opposition* and the worker-oppositionist Tarov, who had fled the USSR in 1936 and published articles in the *Bulletin* while Sedov was still alive.* Estrine told Trotsky that "Tarov has broken off relations with us."[15]

While stirring up an atmosphere of squabbles and intrigues among the people who might have become Trotsky's loyal collaborators, Zborowski made a special effort to compromise Sneevliet and Serge (whom he called

---

* Tarov's fate was tragic: during the war he joined an Armenian resistance group in France and was killed by Hitler's forces in 1942.

50. Paris Intrigues

"Manager" and "Writer" in his correspondence with Trotsky). Hoping to preempt warnings from these two figures about suspicions which they had against the publishers of the *Bulletin*, Estrine and Zborowski wrote to Trotsky that "manager" considered Etienne a provocateur and was voicing suspicions about the means on which he lived.[16] Another letter said that "writer" suspected "Paulsen" (Estrine's nickname) of working for the NKVD. Offering assurances that this was being done in order to compromise Estrine and thereby sever the publication of the *Bulletin*, Estrine and Zborowski wrote that they were sending this information "under the strictest secrecy, and on the condition that in no instance would any part of this information be used until the appropriate letter has been received from us (one rash step might ruin everything, and excessive haste might place all of us in a very difficult position)."[17]

Many of the letters from the publishers of the *Bulletin* to Trotsky were filled with hints at Serge's collaboration with the GPU. In describing a conversation with Reiss's widow in which Serge participated, Zborowski wrote: "During our entire conversation V. Serge asked Elsa Reiss questions of various kinds about the activity of the GPU; moreover he showed a familiarity with several agents of this 'institution.'"[18]

In their next letter, Estrine and Zborowski wrote of Krivitsky's suspicions with regard to Serge. Krivitsky actually harbored such suspicions (as did Reiss), insofar as Serge was the only famous oppositionist whom Stalin allowed to be freed from exile and sent abroad.*[19] Estrine and Zborowski exaggerated Krivitsky's suspicions when they wrote: "In the opinion of W., 'writer' was sent with the special goal of sowing dissension in the ranks of the Fourth International. W. even said that 'writer' was probably given special instructions to write sharply against Stalin in order to win people's trust in this way."[20]

In another letter, the authors of this correspondence added slanders of an everyday character which were supposed to create the impression that Serge was being financed by the NKVD: "The reputation of 'writer' is the following — he is always whining that he has no money... Meanwhile he lives quite well. He keeps his wife at a boarding-house (pension), his young daughter at another boarding-house, and he lives with his son in conditions where they know no needs." Stating that "Liova always displayed great distrust toward 'writer,'" whose biography contained "very many dark episodes," Estrine and Zborowski did not refrain from casting a shadow on Serge's conduct in the USSR: "We learned, for instance, that 'writer' wrote mournful letters from

---

* The release of Serge, a Belgian citizen, was the result of the untiring efforts of Romain Rolland, who, starting in 1933, in almost every letter to Gorky asked the latter to facilitate Serge being sent to Belgium; in 1935, Rolland raised this question in a conversation with Stalin.

exile, stating that he was living very badly, and asking for help. Here, however, his wife tells us that they lived very well in exile, that they always ate chicken and generally had never lived so well."[21]

Zborowski's intrigues were apparently inspired by the Paris agents of the NKVD. We can assume that, from time to time, Stalin's agents consciously gave him and Estrine information about the situation in the USSR which was supposed to disorient Trotsky, and prompt him to give assessments and prognoses that did not correspond to reality. Thus, in a letter from 14 February 1938, they told of a conversation with a "foreign journalist, sent from Russia at midnight." Using the words of this person they passed on a whole cluster of fabrications: "There is no Trotskyism in Russia, not to speak of in the party… it is primarily right deviations which are being persecuted… The whole gang is lined up against Stalin: in the party, the Politburo, in particular, Kalinin, Molotov, Voroshilov and Kaganovich are so strongly opposed to Stalin that he dares not introduce a single proposal. He makes decisions autocratically, resting on Yezhov and his apparatus, and lets the Politburo know that he has done this and that, i.e., post factum." Just as disorienting were the prognoses made by the "story-teller": "If a war breaks out, Russia will be seized with peasant rebellions. There, in the countryside, there is a ferocious war going on between single farmers and the collective farmers; these are two clans who are constantly at war with one another." The story-teller was also used to pass on "disinformation" of a more personal character. He stated, for instance, that Natalia Sats, "Ordzhonikidze's intimate friend," had been shot.[22]

If, with the information he received about the situation in the USSR, Trotsky, as a rule, sifted out all that was dubious, matters were different with information concerning the Paris circle of Trotskyists. Preventative letters about suspicions harbored by Serge and Sneevliet toward Zborowski accomplished their goal: Trotsky stood on the side of the provocateur. On 2 December 1938, he sent Estrine and Zborowski a letter containing the following: "Comrade E. (Etienne) must, in my opinion, immediately demand that Sn. and V. S. present their accusations to a competent commission… Here you must show the greatest initiative, in order to force the accusers as quickly as possible into a corner."[23]

Feeling that Sneevliet was guilty of irresponsible behavior in failing to guarantee Reiss's security, Trotsky wrote an article "Once More on Comrades Sneevliet and Vereeken," which contained many unfair and overly critical words about Sneevliet and his conduct in the "Reiss affair." It also gave unequivocal support to the positions of Estrine and Zborowski, who, according to Trotsky, "have shed light on the true history of this matter."[24]

Thus, an enormous role in Trotsky's break with the non-returners who were at first attracted to him and Sedov, and with major foreign political figures who were close to him in their views, was played by tendentious and

50. Paris Intrigues

Victor Serge
(1890-1947)

false information which came from people who were immediately responsible for the publication of his main creation — the *Bulletin of the Opposition*. Attempts to sow discord between Trotsky and his most prominent foreign supporters produced results. Trotsky trusted people he should not have trusted, but who continually declared their devotion to his cause, and broke with those who, although they entered into polemics with him and made several wrong theoretical and political conclusions, might have remained his close collaborators.

Trotsky's break with Soviet non-returners and foreign friends cannot be explained simply by Zborowski's provocations. People such as Krivitsky and Barmine, who experienced a difficult inner drama and who were forced to change their way of life drastically, might have maintained a clear ideological orientation if they had been in direct communication with Trotsky. In an atmosphere of the constant and vital communication and creative dialogue which politicians and revolutionaries need, the differences between Trotsky and such leading social activists as Sneevliet and Serge might also have been smoothed over.

So too, the absence of a lively exchange with people whose views were close to his, which could not be replaced by the most intensive correspondence, had a painful effect on the activity of Trotsky himself.

To this must be added several peculiarities of Trotsky's personality, to which the famous saying is applicable: "Our shortcomings are an extension of our virtues." While retaining an immutable faith in the power of great political ideas, Trotsky simultaneously was disgusted by the replacement of principled ideological arguments with personal squabbles, slander, and intrigue. Incapable of petty political intrigue, he was, in a certain sense, helpless before these phenomena when they inevitably intervened in political relationships. Hence flowed his strength in periods of revolutionary upheaval, when such political intrigues were compelled to retreat into the background. Hence, too, flowed his famous weakness in periods of revolutionary decline, when intrigues palpably influenced the disposition of political forces. This weakness surfaced in 1923-1925, when Trotsky stood alone against all the remaining members of the Politburo, who were united on unprincipled grounds in fighting against his influence in the party and the country. This weakness also let itself be known in the second half of the 1930s, when dark intrigues unfolded among the small circle of his co-thinkers.

In over-emphasizing the possibility of persuading people through the force of great political ideas, Trotsky often let slip from view the "human, all-too-human" (Nietzsche), i.e., the purely psychological factors, including base ones, which are capable of influencing the political struggle. Clarity and perceptivity, which were ever-present in evaluating great historical events and the political profile of major historical figures, often betrayed him in evaluating concrete human relationships, particularly when they were poisoned by provocation. Hence his famous susceptibility to the unprincipled and biased assessments coming from Zborowski and Estrine, and the equally unjustified sharpness toward the people they slandered, people who might have become his loyal supporters in constructing the Fourth International.

51. The End of the "Yezhov Period"

In the fall of 1938, it became clear to Stalin how much the Great Purge had weakened the Soviet Union and what fateful consequences might ensue if it continued. It was then that he evidently came to the conclusion that Yezhov must be sacrificed. This was the person the majority of the population associated with the nightmare of the purges. Stalin dealt with the "iron narkom" gradually, preparing public opinion by degrees for his elimination. On 9 April 1938, Yezhov was appointed People's Commissar of Water Transportation in addition to the three posts he already occupied. Four months after this, Beria was transferred to Moscow and appointed First Deputy People's Commissar of Internal Affairs and head of the Main Directorate of State Security — the structure of the NKVD that was responsible for conducting political repressions.

By this time, according to Khrushchev, Yezhov "had literally lost his human form, he had simply taken to drink." After his transfer to Moscow, Beria openly told Stalin and other members of the Politburo that innocent people were being arrested, and he "complained, where will the limit be? For we have to stop somewhere, we have to do something."[1]

Similar signals arrived from various localities, from young party members who dared to express their doubts about the correctness of continuing the mass repressions. Thus, on 23 October 1938, Chuyanov, the first secretary of the Stalingrad area committee, sent Stalin a letter in which he listed incidents of provocation, torture and falsification committed by the NKVD. Since, like all other party secretaries, he was not invested with the authority to control the activity of the "organs," Chuyanov asked Stalin to create a commission to monitor the activity of the area directorate of the NKVD.[2]

Many letters about the tyrannical acts being committed throughout the land arrived at the Central Committee from ordinary citizens. For in-

Nikolai Yezhov, shot 4 February 1940

stance, V. Chernousov wrote from Odessa: "Right now in our country there is hardly a single home which does not have someone in prison. The picture that emerges in the end is that the entire country is against the Soviet regime... Given our extremely low wages, with an absence of commodities of primary necessity, moreover, no one is certain that he will not end up in prison tomorrow. After this, it is difficult to imagine what moods exist among the masses."

In Leningrad, V. Antipov described "incredible scenes at the train stations of large and small cities," where thousands of families were living who had been evicted from their native homes because their families had people who had been arrested or who were serving time. "You are given 24 hours to leave — people in panic sell their things for nothing and go wherever they can." The letter's author explained these evictions by the fact that "the members of several NKVD directorates had lost all restraint and were acting at their own whim."³

The first sign of changes in the policy of repression appeared on 17 November 1938, when a secret resolution of the Council of People's Commissars and the Central Committee was adopted: "On Arrests, The Directorate of Public Prosecutions and the Conduct of Investigations." The resolution praised the work done by the organs of the NKVD in "cleansing the USSR of many spies, terrorists, saboteurs and harmful cadres," including "Poles, Rumanians, Finns, Germans, Latvians, Estonians, Kharbintsy, and others who had come to the USSR in great numbers from beyond the borders under the guise of being so-called political emigrants and asylum-seekers." The resolution indicated that the "purge" should continue, but it should use "more perfected and reliable methods."

After this preamble, the resolution listed "the greatest shortcomings and distortions in the work of the organs of the NKVD and the Prosecutor's office": mass arrests which were unwarranted, over-simplified conduct of investigations and trials, crude violations of procedural norms, and so forth. When it came to concretizing these charges, what was uncovered in the legal system was an atmosphere dominated by arbitrary rule and the trampling of the rights of those arrested: "the investigatory dossiers are sloppily put together, they contain rough drafts of testimony corrected by unknown persons, with sections crossed out; they contain transcripts of interrogations which are neither signed by those being questioned nor corrected by the investigator; unsigned and unverified indictments are included."

The blame for all this — in a truly Stalinist spirit — was placed on "enemies of the people and spies of foreign intelligence services who forced their way into the NKVD organs." They had deliberately falsified investigation documents, created provocative cases against innocent people and, at the same time, "had saved their accomplices from destruction, especially those who had settled into the NKVD organs." Thus the decree indicated the need for one more purge and the construction of a new series of amalgams leading to an identification of the falsifiers and investigators with spies and conspirators.

The decree of the Central Committee banned the conduct of new mass operations involving arrests and exile, liquidated the judicial troikas and even pointed to the need to "secure for the accused the procedural rights guaranteed him according to the law."[4]

Immediately after the adoption of this decree, Stalin went directly after Yezhov. He was prompted to do this when Orlov and Liushkov fled abroad, and also when Uspensky, the People's Commissar of Internal Affairs for the Ukraine, disappeared. As Khrushchev recalled, Stalin told him about the impending arrest of Uspensky. However the latter was not arrested since he disappeared. After a while Stalin told Khrushchev that Yezhov had apparently listened to their telephone conversation and warned Uspensky.[5]

On 17 November, Yezhov sent Stalin a statement in which he confessed that "he had given Liushkov the opportunity to hide in Japan and Uspensky the chance to hide at an as yet unknown location." Yezhov saw another of his "major blunders" to be the fact that he had not unmasked "the conspirators from the NKVD" and "in many instances, while not politically verifying an employee, he had delayed the question of his arrest and waited until they picked a replacement." In justifying himself, Yezhov referred to the fact that "conspirators from the NKVD and foreign intelligence services connected with them had for ten years at least (until his arrival at the commissariat – V. R.) managed to recruit not only the upper echelons of the Cheka, but the middle layers as well, and often even the low-ranking employees." In trying once again to indicate the gigantic scale of the hostile activity, Yezhov announced that "in essence we must create our foreign intelligence service from scratch," insofar as the entire foreign department of the NKVD had turned out to be saturated with spies. In conclusion, Yezhov stressed that, despite the "major shortcomings and blunders" in his work, "in the everyday leadership of the Central Committee and NKVD he had done a good job in routing enemies."[6]

On 19 November, the Politburo granted Yezhov's request to relieve him of his duties as People's Commissar of Internal Affairs. However, in the decree which was adopted, there was no indication that Yezhov would remain at liberty only briefly. It said that Yezhov was being relieved of his duties as Commissar of Internal Affairs because of "his state of ill health, which does not allow him to direct simultaneously two large People's Commissariats."[7] He still retained the posts of secretary of the Central Committee, chairman of the Party Control Commission and People's Commissar of Water Transport.

On 25 November, an announcement appeared about Yezhov's replacement by Beria at the post of People's Commissar of Internal Affairs. During the first few months of his presence at this post, Beria arrested the majority of the leaders of the NKVD apparatus both in the center and in the localities. The years 1939-1940 saw the trial and execution of such executioners and falsifiers as Frinovsky, Zakovsky, Nikolaev-Zhurid, B. Berman, M. Berman, Ushakov-Ushimirsky, and many others. As Khrushchev recalled, Beria showed particular zeal in "completing the purge of Jewish cadres in the Cheka already begun by Yezhov."[8] To prepare replacements for the arrested personnel, "the best Komsomol members" were called upon to join the NKVD; after completing short-term courses, they occupied the vacant posts.

After Yezhov's removal from the post of People's Commissar of Internal Affairs, the Soviet people began more boldly to call the terrible years that had just passed the "Yezhov period." We may assume that this very term, which is supposed to lay all responsibility for the Great Terror on Yezhov, came from Stalin's office. In any case, Stalin often spoke in the circle of those close to him about Yezhov's blame for reprisals against innocent people, clearly hoping that these words would receive wide circulation. The aviation engineer Yakovlev, who was one of few people enjoying Stalin's trust, recalled how, at an evening meal, Stalin began to speak of the widespread shortage of good personnel, adding: "Yezhov is a bastard! He destroyed our best cadres. He was a degenerate. You would call him at the commissariat and they would say: he went to the Central Committee. You would call him at the Central Committee, and they would say: he went to work. You would send for him at home, and it turns out that he would be lying on his bed, dead drunk. He killed many innocent people. We shot him for this."[9]

51. The End of the "Yezhov Period"

Stalin and Yezhov

Konstantin Simonov's novel *Soldiers Are Not Born* contains a psychologically realistic scene depicting a conversation in 1943 between Stalin and General Serpilin, who had been arrested in 1937, only to return to the army on the eve of the war. When Stalin expressed his surprise that Serpilin had only learned during the war about the T-34 tank, which had been released in 1940, Serpilin "unexpectedly for himself said what he absolutely need not have said:

'In 1940, Comrade Stalin, I was still Nikolai Ivanovich's guest.'

'Which Nikolai Ivanovich?' asked Stalin with certain, even bemused, interest that was prompted by the unexpected reply.

'When we soldiers were in prison, that's what we called Yezhov among ourselves,' said Serpilin; it was too late to retreat, once the words had escaped his lips, he had to continue.

Stalin burst out laughing. Then he stopped laughing and ... looked past Serpilin, noisily fidgeting with his pipe, 'We punished Yezhov.'

After Serpilin had left, Stalin thought to himself: 'It turns out that these soldiers, when they were in the camps, called this Yezhov by his first name and patronymic — Nikolai Ivanovich. They gave significance that was too great to a man that was too little. From a political standpoint that's not so bad, but it is amusing!'"[10]

In November 1938, Yezhov's wife, Khayutina, died in mysterious circumstances. According to the testimony of her first husband, A. F. Gladun, the director of the Kharkov Instrument Factory who was arrested in the spring of 1939, in the mid-1920s she "went into raptures over Trotskyists." Babel, who knew Khayutina well, said during his own investigation that she "kept company with Trotskyists — Lashevich, Serebriakov, Piatakov, and Voronsky."[11]

In the 1930s, Khayutina virtually ran the editorial board of the journal *USSR Under Construction*, the main editor of which was Piatakov.

Yezhov's dossier contains letters by Khayutina in which she begged him "to check up on my entire life, and on me entirely... I cannot reconcile myself with the thought that I am suspected of double-dealing and of some crimes that never happened."[12] In October 1938, Khayutina was sent for treatment of a neuro-psychological disorder to a sanatorium, where she died a month later.

Yezhov appeared in public for the last time at a formal observance of the fifteenth anniversary of Lenin's death. He did not attend the Eighteenth Congress and was not elected to the Central Committee. On 10 April 1939, he was arrested. People conducting the search of his office were surprised not only by the many bottles of vodka hidden on shelves behind books, but by spent cartridges they found in his desk. They were wrapped in paper on which was written: "Zinoviev," "Kamenev," "Smirnov."[13] Apparently, Yezhov kept these "souvenirs" in order to remember the first Moscow trial.

It was only three months after Yezhov's arrest that a decree was signed about indicting him on criminal charges. The decree reproduced the standard selection of charges: "traitorous espionage ties with circles in Poland, Germany, England and Japan," placing conspiratorial cadres and leading an anti-Soviet conspiracy within the NKVD, preparing a coup d'état and terrorist acts against Stalin, Molotov and Beria. Added to this list was the purely criminal charge of sodomy.

The official indictment a few months later presented a more complex amalgam. Here, his imaginary crimes were joined by true crimes, for instance, Yezhov's creation "for careerist and adventuristic reasons" of the case about being poisoned by mercury, which was mentioned at the trial of the "Right-Trotskyist Bloc." Yezhov was also charged with organizing the murders of "a whole number of unwelcome people," who were trying "to unmask his treacherous work."

On 2 February 1940, Yezhov's case, which comprised eleven volumes, was tried at a closed session of the Military Collegium under the chairmanship of the irreplaceable Ulrikh. At the trial Yezhov declared that he had confessed to crimes as a result of the most severe beatings. When it came to the charge of terror, he said quite reasonably: "If I had wanted to commit a terrorist act against anyone in the government, I would not have recruited anybody for this assignment, but using the technology at hand, I could have carried out this foul deed at any moment." In rejecting the charge of working for Polish intelligence, he said that he had started his work in the NKVD with "the destruction of Polish spies who had crawled into all departments of the Cheka. Soviet intelligence was in their hands."

51. The End of the "Yezhov Period"

Meanwhile, Yezhov confessed that he was guilty of "no less heinous crimes," for which he "could be shot." In his last remarks he said that his "enormous guilt" lay in the fact that, having purged fourteen thousand Chekists, he had not finished the job. "All around me were enemies of the people, my enemies," he said. "I purged Chekists everywhere. I did not purge them, however, in Moscow, Leningrad, and in the Northern Caucasus. I considered them honest, but in fact it turned out that I was hiding under my own roof saboteurs, wreckers, spies, and other varieties of enemies of the people." Yezhov ended his final remarks with a request to tell Stalin that he would die with Stalin's name on his lips.[14]

The day after the trial, Yezhov was shot. There was no official announcement of his arrest or execution. His name did not figure in the lists of "enemies of the people"; it simply disappeared from the pages of the press.

After Yezhov had been removed from the post of People's Commissar of Internal Affairs, several tens of thousands of people who were being investigated were freed and their cases were closed. The camps witnessed a certain decrease in their population. In 1939, an unprecedented number of prisoners were freed from the GULAG — 327,400 people.[15] Of course, common criminals were among them, but no small portion of those released were political prisoners whose cases had been reviewed.

From the beginning of 1939, articles began to appear in the press about the expulsion from the party and lodging of criminal charges against slanderers whose denunciations had led to the arrest of innocent people. In many cities there were open trials of slanderers and investigators who falsified cases. Avtorkhanov states that he was present as a witness at the trial of the leaders of the Checheno-Ingush NKVD which occurred in 1942.[16]

The exposure of judicial falsifications prompted many arrested people and their relatives to submit statements requesting the review of their cases. These appeals proved to be so numerous that special commissions were created in area and regional centers to look into them. Gorev, the secretary of the Starorussky regional committee who headed one of these commissions, said that it was allowed to investigate only the cases of those who were being investigated at the time; "our authority did not extend" to those who disappeared in 1937. As a result of three months' work, the commission compiled five volumes of documents which exposed the former head of the regional department of the NKVD, Beldyagin, who occupied at that time the post of head of the Pskov area directorate of the NKVD. It also exposed three investigators; all were arrested and tried.[17]

The "post-Yezhov" rehabilitations, however, involved hardly any of the prominent party members and state figures whose cases had not been fully investigated by the end of 1938. Throughout 1939-1940, all of these people were tried and the overwhelming majority were shot.

Yezhov's fall is illustrated in a retouched photograph published after his arrest and execution

The end of the "Yezhov period" did not signify any review of the historical falsifications which had been put into circulation after the Great Purge. On the contrary, all the falsifications which existed at the end of 1938 were reproduced in a book which would serve as the source of historical knowledge for several generations of Soviet people.

52. The Falsification of History

After the third Moscow trial, Stalin's stooges realized that from now on, there were no limits to the fabrication of new falsifications, particularly concerning Trotsky. Their zeal increased so much that even Stalin had to restrain it from time to time. Thus, at the end of 1938, Yezhov and Beria presented Stalin with a report about the results of "measures undertaken to search for documents confirming Trotsky's activity as a provocateur." The first such "document" to be named was the book of memoirs by the chairman of the Petrograd Soviet in 1905, Khrustalev-Nosar, who supposedly spoke of Trotsky as a member of the Okhranka [the tsarist secret police]. To this, the NKVD chiefs added the following: they "learned" that Khrustalev-Nosar, whose role as a provocateur had been exposed during the first months after the October Revolution, had been shot on an order coming from Trotsky which had been issued by the latter in order to eliminate a witness to his service in the tsar's secret police. The second "document" was a forgery from British intelligence which stated that during the First World War, Trotsky's literary activity in the USA had been funded "by Germans and people sympathetic to them." The third "document" said that Trotsky had joined Khrustalev-Nosar and Lunacharsky in working for the former police directorate. Unlike the "book" written by Khrustalev-Nosar, the existence of which has never been confirmed, the last document was not a simple fabrication concocted by Yezhov and Beria; it had been discovered in 1917 and at that time had been sent both to Kerensky and to Burtsev, who was the most skilled specialist in exposing provocateurs in the Russian revolutionary movement. They both acknowledged that this document was an obvious forgery — one of many which were circulating at the time.[1]

E. Yaroslavsky, the ardent falsifier of the Stalinist school, made just as unpardonable an attempt to compromise Trotsky's pre-revolutionary past. On 25 September 1938, he sent Stalin a letter in which he spoke about joining Shkiriatov in "studying" the testimony of Vatsetis, the former Commander-in-Chief of the Red Army. He writes that they found the testimony to be a "shocking document," which was a "deadly indictment of Trotsky." The testimony confirmed his growing "conviction" that Trotsky had been recruited before 1917 by the German general staff and the tsarist Okhranka. Proposing to launch an investigation to verify these allegations, Yaroslavsky justified his proposal by referring to the "hypothesis" that had arisen in his mind: "If Trotsky could resort to such monstrous treachery with regard to Lenin, Stalin and the Soviet republic (he had in mind the interpretation at that time in Soviet historiography that Trotsky's conduct in 1918 had been "treasonous" – V. R.), then *why not allow* that his conduct during the formation and activity of the August bloc and before had been dictated by the Trotskyist 'slogan': each makes the revolution for himself (my italics – V. R.)?"[2]

Of course, Stalin could not help but find it tempting to put into circulation allegations and "documents" concocted by his obliging stooges. However, in the end, he did not allow these documents to go beyond the confines of his office: too fresh was the memory of the devastating blows Trotsky had delivered against even more "modest" historical forgeries. Besides, Stalin knew that Trotsky was working on his biography. It was natural to expect that, in response to a new and light-minded slander, Trotsky would hasten the publication of the material he had at his disposal about dubious moments in the pre-revolutionary biography of Stalin himself.

It was apparently for the same reasons that Stalin rejected the obsequious proposals to "erase" several unpleasant statements made by Lenin. Thus, he did not approve the initiative from Stasova and Sorin, who proposed to him in May 1938 that they make "corrections" to the transcript of Lenin's speeches containing criticism of Stalin's position on the question of the Brest-Litovsk Treaty.[3]

In a number of instances, Stalin banned the publication of books where flattery directed at him exceeded all imaginable bounds. On 16 February 1938, he sent a letter to Detizdat [Children's Publishing House] in which he proposed to "burn" the manuscript sent to him for review of a book by a certain Smirnova, *Tales of Stalin's Childhood*. Indicating that this book "is filled with a mass of factual errors, distortions, exaggerations and undeserved praise," dreamt up by "fairy-tale seekers," "liars," and toadies, Stalin saw particular harm in the fact that it "has a tendency to embed in the consciousness of Soviet children (and people in general) a cult of individuals, leaders, and perfect heroes."[4] This letter from Stalin, which became known in literary and publishing circles, was not published. It first saw the light at the end of 1953, when Stalin's successors, who had begun the first round of criticizing the "cult

---

* This absurd slogan was, it goes without saying, a complete fabrication by Yaroslavsky himself.

52. The Falsification of History

of the individual," found it necessary to depend on Stalin's authority to find support for this criticism.

During the years of the Great Purge, Stalin found time to keep under his unrelenting control the publication of memoirs and fictional works on historical and party themes. For the twentieth anniversary of the October Revolution, he gave his blessings to the publication of works which were immediately declared the "high points" of Soviet art: A. Tolstoi's novella *Grain* and M. Romm's film *Lenin in October*. Those works which deviated even slightly from the dominant canons were banned. Such a ban was placed, in particular, on the further publication of M. Shaginian's novella *A History Question*, the first part of which was printed by the publisher "Young Guard." This work about Lenin's childhood and teenage years was called "politically harmful" and "ideologically hostile" in a Politburo decree.[5]

Toward the end of the Great Purge, Stalin decided to give the party, the people, and the foreign communist movement a new ideological guidebook, which he called "an encyclopedia of basic knowledge in the realm of Marxism-Leninism." He felt that it was not questions of Marxist theory which should be key in this "encyclopedia," but questions of history, which were more accessible to the masses. With these goals in mind, he formed a commission of old and young falsifiers who were instructed to write a textbook on party history.

In May 1937, Stalin published a letter to the textbook's authors, in which he proposed a schema for the periodization of the history of the VKP(b) and demanded that they place special emphasis on "the struggle of the Bolsheviks against anti-Bolshevik currents and factions."[6] In this endeavor, the overcoming of "inner-party contradictions and disagreements" was explained as a ruthless struggle against oppositions that were presented as nests of snakes which had been exposed and destroyed thanks to Stalin's farsightedness.

The commission brought together all the previous falsifications of party history which had accumulated since 1923, and supplemented them with historical forgeries which had been made public at the three Moscow trials. Stalin subjected the manuscript he received to careful editing and wrote the chapter, "On Dialectical and Historical Materialism." Here he included a selection of primitive dogmas from which several generations of Soviet people were forced to draw their conceptions of the content of Marxist philosophy.

In places where the falsifiers hesitated, not daring independently to insert in the textbook a particularly filthy slander, Stalin resolutely corrected their "omissions." Thus, he wrote into the *Short Course* that the Left SR uprising was begun in 1918 not only with Bukharin's knowledge, but with Trotsky's as well.

When Samoilov, the director of the Museum of the Revolution, asked Stalin to send for an exhibition in the museum a few pages written or corrected by him from the manuscript of the *Short Course*, Stalin replied with an angry note: "I did not think that in your old age you would busy yourself with such trifles. If the book is already published in millions of copies, why do you need the manuscript? In order to set your mind at rest, I burned all the manuscripts."[7]

In 1947 Stalin was presented with a dummy of his "Short Biography," which repeated the official version that the *Short Course* had been written "by a commission under the leadership of Comrade Stalin and with his active personal participation." Stalin crossed out this customary phrase and in its place inserted a new one, repeated in thousands of books, pamphlets and articles: "In 1938, a book appeared called *The History of the VKP(b). A Short Course*, written by Comrade Stalin and approved by the commission of the Central Committee of the VKP(b)."[8]

Immediately before the publication of the *Short Course*, Stalin ordered the convocation of a meeting of propagandists from Moscow and Leningrad, who were joined by all members of the Politburo. He delivered a speech at the meeting where he said, for the first time, that the new textbook was "the only guide" which "the Central Committee officially recommends as an expression of the ideas and the views of the party." Unlike all previous textbooks and study guides on party history, which did not have "the agreement (and approval) of the CC," the given "guide" should not, in his words, cause "any doubts."[9]

Stalin stubbornly kept repeating these thoughts, interrupting the speeches of other orators. After declaring that earlier in the study of theory and history there had been "very much that was local, personal and individual," he stressed that after the appearance of a "uniform textbook," it would be necessary to introduce "uniformity ... through the press."

Interrupting the propagandist Shvarev, Stalin expressed interest in whether discussion and debates between students arose during study sessions. Shvarev replied that "earlier this had occurred in our practice. There were discussions on a number of questions, but now we have no longer been engaged in this." After this reply, there was an exchange of comments between the propagandist and the Kremlin leaders:

Molotov: Do they ask questions at seminars? Are there debates on these grounds?
Shvarev: Of course, there are.
Stalin: Do you run into Trotskyists during such debates?
Shvarev: No, Comrade Stalin, we haven't had any.[10]

The statements about "uniformity" were reinforced in the Central Committee Decree of 14 November 1938, "On the State of Party Propaganda

52. The Falsification of History

in Connection with the Publication of the *Short Course of the History of the VKP(b).*" The contents of this decree were so odious that it was published for the last time in 1954 in the anthology, *The CPSU in Resolutions and Decisions*; later editions of the anthology omitted this decree.

In the Central Committee decree, the *Short Course* was called "the official interpretation, verified by the CC of the VKP(b), of the basic questions of the history of the VKP(b) and of Marxism-Leninism, which does not allow any arbitrary interpretations." Leaving no doubt that the usual criteria for developing scientific knowledge should be cast aside when applied to this book, the decree stated: "The publication of the *Course of the History of the VKP(b)*, approved by the CC of the VKP(b), puts an end to arbitrariness and confusion in explaining party history; it puts an end to the abundance of differing points of view and arbitrary interpretations of the most important questions of party theory and party history."[11]

The codification of ideological and historical myths in the *Short Course* — this encyclopedia of Stalinist dogmatism and falsification — was intended to completely eradicate the people's historical memory and bureaucratically deform their political consciousness.

The Central Committee's decree virtually established the indisputable nature of not only each sentence, but each phrase and each letter of this canonical edition. This directive was obeyed so consistently that even appeals by famous historians in the Central Committee, who pointed to factual errors contained in the book that had resulted from authorial oversights, did not lead to the correction of a single one of these errors.

The Central Committee decree founded a new methodology in explaining history. The *Short Course* was counterposed to earlier textbooks which had described the history of the VKP(b) "primarily around historical figures and which had in mind the education of cadres on the basis of these historical figures and their biographies."[12]

This juxtaposition was needed because the names of the majority of people who had truly created party history and had vanished without trace in the Great Purge were excluded from the *Short Course*. This exclusion determined the long tradition of "blank spots" and "forgotten names" in historical and party literature. An exception was made for only two groups of Bolsheviks. The first included victims of the open trials, whose entire activity was declared to be "treacherous" or "treasonous." The style of the corresponding passages is so specific, that it reveals the indubitable authorship of Stalin. "These White-Guard gnats," the book states when mentioning the defendants at the Moscow Trials, "forgot that the master of the Soviet nation is the Soviet people, whereas Messrs. Rykov, Bukharin, Zinoviev and Kamenev are only temporary figures at the service of the state, and at any moment the state can toss them out of their offices like useless rubbish. These insignificant lackeys of Fascism forgot that the Soviet people simply have to shake their finger and not a trace will be left of them. The Soviet courts sentenced the Bukharin-Trotskyist degenerates to be shot. The NKVD carried out the sentence. The Soviet people approved the smashing of the Bukharin-Trotskyist gang and moved on to other matters."[13]

The second group of "mentionables" included several Bolsheviks who "were lucky enough" to die from natural causes, and a ring of "closest comrades-in-arms," the very presence of whom showed that Stalin had made a final decision to leave them at liberty. Evidently it is no accident that the publication of the *Short Course* coincided with the conclusion of the arrests of Old Bolsheviks. On the pages of the textbook, the places of the heroes of the October Revolution and the Civil War, who were exterminated almost to a man, were taken by people who took no part in these events or who had played an insignificant role in them. "The new history," Trotsky wrote in this regard, "turns all the leaders of the Bolshevik Party into traitors, and appoints Stalin's current adjutants as participants in the civil war and victorious uprising." An extreme expression of these historical manipulations was the phrase that "in Belorussia, Comrade Yezhov prepared the uprising of the masses of soldiers." In reference to this, Trotsky recalled that "when Yezhov first appeared on the arena of big politics in 1935, no one knew his name."[14] By the way, the name of Yezhov, whose fate Stalin had still not finally decided at the moment the *Short Course* was published, figured only in the book's first edition. The removal of two references to Yezhov became the only instance of "excisions" from the *Short Course*.

Of course, Stalin would not have been Stalin if he had not combined a dogmatic and canonical approach to the *Short Course* with an appeal to put an end to dogmatism, pedantry and scholasticism in the social sciences. The Central Committee decree of 14 November condemned "the fear of boldly raising theoretical questions," as well as "over-simplification and vulgarization," as a result of which "the question of the role of the individual in history has been explained by certain pseudo-theoreticians and propagandists from semi-SR positions."[15] In this way Stalin, who had approved a book which is thoroughly saturated with the spirit of a cult, criticized the very same cult of the individual in a decree about the book. It should be noted that soon this concept was removed from the party lexicon — right up until 1953-1956, when Stalin's successors began to use it to characterize the entire sum of Stalin's errors and crimes.

Along the way, the Central Committee decree included one more important subject which was not directly related to the questions of history it was examining. It demanded an end to the "disdainful attitude" toward the Soviet intelligentsia; such an attitude was declared in an unquestioning, imperative, and threatening tone to be "savage, delinquent, and dangerous to the Soviet state."[16] These sentiments served as the theoretical foundation for the final shift of social support for the Stalinist regime from the working-class and peasant masses to the upper layer of the intelligentsia, which turned thereby into the second — following the ruling bureaucracy — privileged group in Soviet society.

During the Great Purge, all historical and party literature which had been published before was placed in special closed depositories in libraries. It was replaced by innumerable compilations which consisted of Stalin's quotes and formulations from the *Short Course*, provided with or without attribution.

After the official ban on "various points of view" in interpreting questions of theory and party history, several generations of Soviet sociologists, teachers of social sciences in the schools and places of higher learning, propagandists, and agitators were condemned to repeat mechanically all the absurdities and falsifications contained in the *Short Course*.

The intellectual crippling of the Soviet people continued even after the denunciation of the *Short Course* at the Twentieth Congress of the CPSU. A significant portion of the historical and party literature of the 1920s and 1930s remained hidden away in the special depositories. An unconditional taboo was maintained when it came to any positive mention of, or even a neutral reference to, members of the former oppositions. In the new textbooks, books, and articles on party history, what remained, as before, was largely a history without names.

It was precisely for this reason that Soviet historians proved to be unprepared ideologically to resist the wave of anti-communist literature published in the 1950s-1980s in the West, which burst forth from the end of the 1980s in a sudden flood onto the pages of the Soviet press.

Under conditions in which the permitted versions of the history of Bolshevism were falsified, writers and journalists who were trying to understand historical truth were forced to develop their own version of this history in isolation, or to use the versions spread by "samizdat" and "tamizdat."* This explains the fact that even such an outstanding Soviet writer as Vasily Grossman set out to blacken Lenin and Leninism in his books *Life and Fate* and *Forever Flowing*.

The Great Purge and the historical falsifications accompanying it profoundly deformed the social consciousness of the Soviet people, and drove millions of people away from the communist movement abroad. As a result of this, Stalin was unimpeded in concluding the pact with Hitler which served as the prologue to the Second World War. I intend to tell about the events preceding this bloodiest war in human history in my next book, *World Revolution and World War*.

---

* "Samizdat": material published unofficially in the Soviet Union; "tamizdat": material published abroad.

Appendix I

From the History of the Exposure of Stalin's Crimes

Immediately after Stalin's death, people who had been persecuted during Stalin's regime began to be set free and rehabilitated. It is curious that the initiative in this matter, as Khrushchev would later acknowledge, initially belonged to Beria, who "raised this question at that time, developed it, introduced relevant proposals, and we (i.e., members of the CC's Presidium – V. R.) agreed with him."[1] These actions concerned primarily people who had been persecuted in the last years of Stalin's life, when Beria did not manage the affairs of the MGB [Ministry of State Security]. As for the victims of the repressive measures of the 1930s, the members of "the collective leadership" began a review of their cases only on the eve of the Twentieth Congress of the CPSU.

In the first post-Stalinist years, as Khrushchev remembers, "we ourselves were bound by our activity under Stalin's leadership, and we still had not freed ourselves from his posthumous pressure, although we could not imagine that all these executions could turn out to be without foundation, that this was, to use legal language, a patent crime."[2]

Khrushchev states that he first felt the incorrectness of this position when he traveled to Yugoslavia in the summer of 1955 for a reconciliation with Tito. When he was explaining, in a conversation with Yugoslav leaders, that the mass repressions were a result of Beria's intrigues, he noted that the Yugoslavs "began to smile and make ironic replies. This upset us, and, as we defended Stalin, we got into a major argument, which even reached the level of a scandal." Under the influence of this argument, Khrushchev soon publicly spoke against the Yugoslavs in defense of Stalin. "Now it is clear to everyone that this was wrong," Khrushchev confessed. "I had adopted the position of a person who has not recognized the need to go all the way in exposing Stalin's crimes..."[3]

By 1954, the general prosecutor of the USSR, Rudenko, had presented the Central Committee of the CPSU with information about the number of victims from 1921 through 1954, as well as several other items concerning Stalin's reprisals. After this, Khrushchev asked Rudenko a question: how well founded were the charges made against prominent party figures at the open trials? Rudenko answered that "from the standpoint of juridical norms, no evidence existed for the conviction of these people. Everything had been based exclusively on personal confessions, and personal confessions obtained by means of physical and moral torture cannot serve as the basis for convicting people." When Khrushchev declared that he had himself heard the defendants confessing to their crimes, Rudenko smiled: "Here we are dealing with the art of those who conducted the investigation and who directed the trial. Evidently they reduced people to such a state that the only way they had to put an end to their suffering and humiliation was to confess, and the next step was death."[4]

After this, according to Khrushchev, he felt "the need to raise the curtain and find out, nevertheless, exactly how the investigations were conducted ... what initial material existed for arrests, and what the investigation then proved by these arrests?"[5] Khrushchev raised these questions at a session of the Presidium of the Central Committee, where a decision was made to create a commission to thoroughly investigate all these questions. On 31 December 1955, the composition of this commission was established (CC secretaries Pospelov and Aristov, chairman of the Party Control Commission, Shvernik, and his deputy Komarov). The commission's report, presented to the Presidium of the Central Committee of the CPSU on 9 February 1956, stated that from 1935-1940, 1,920,635 people were arrested on charges of anti-Soviet activity, of whom 688,503 people were shot.[6] Khrushchev explained that the Presidium of the CC decided to keep these numbers secret because "after the long hysteria of hunting for 'enemies of the people,' we simply could not psychologically cast off the burden of the past."[7]

As Khrushchev would stress, "the note from Pospelov's commission gnawed away at my brain." Even before receiving this information, he had begun — unbeknownst to other members of the Central Committee's Presidium — to prepare his secret report to the Twentieth Party Congress. Aside from trusted apparatchiks, he turned for help in writing it to several former party members who had spent about twenty years in Stalin's prisons and camps.

Khrushchev told other members of the Presidium about his decision to deliver this report only during one of the breaks between sessions of the Twentieth Congress. As soon as Khrushchev had finished speaking, the remaining members of the Presidium made sharp objections. Voroshilov was particularly nervous in his reaction. "Can we really tell all this to the congress? How will it reflect on the authority of our party, of our country? After all, you won't be able to keep this secret. What will we say about our personal role?... People will hold us responsible."

In response, Khrushchev offered carefully considered ideas, implicitly indicating that his personal guilt was less than the guilt of other members of the Presidium of the CC who stood closer to Stalin during the 1930s than he did. "I, yes and many others," he said, "were in a position where, of course, we did not know much, because the regime that had been established was such that you were supposed to know only what you had been ordered and they did not tell you the rest; when they said, don't poke your nose into things any further, then we didn't do so. But not everyone was in such a position. Several of us knew, and several even took part in deciding these questions. Therefore, the degree of responsibility here is different. As a member of the party's Central Committee from the Seventeenth Congress and as a member of its Politburo from the Eighteenth Congress, I am prepared to bear my own share of responsibility, if the party finds that it is necessary to call to account those who were in the leadership during the times of Stalin, when arbitrary rule was allowed." A noisy reaction again followed these arguments, particularly on the part of Voroshilov, Kaganovich and Molotov: "'But do you understand what will happen?' Voroshilov declared that, in general, the question of mass repressions should not be raised. 'But who is it that is asking us?' he kept repeating." Khrushchev's opponents referred to the fact that, in the Central Committee's main report which had already been delivered at the congress, nothing had been said about Stalin's crimes; meanwhile Khrushchev was proposing to give what was essentially a second report, in many ways refuting the CC's main report.

The situation changed only after Khrushchev appealed to the party's statutory norms and presented the remaining members of the Presidium with an ultimatum: if there would be no resolution on this question by the Presidium, then he would speak before the congress in his own name. "A congress of the party is in session," he declared. "During the congress, the internal discipline which demands leadership unity among the members of the CC and members of the CC's Presidium no longer operates, for the congress is higher in significance. The main report has been given, now every member of the CC's Presidium and every CC member has the right to speak at the congress and outline his own point of view, even if it does not coincide with the point of view of the main report." Khrushchev added a serious moral argument: "Even for people who have committed a crime, there comes a time, once in their lives, when they can confess, and this brings them, if not vindication, then leniency."[8] Only after this statement did he receive permission to read the report in the name of the Presidium of the Central Committee.

At the beginning of the 1990s, Khrushchev's statement received de facto confirmation when Kaganovich told Chuyev: "Khrushchev ... said: I will give

Khrushchev speaking at the Twentieth Party Congress in 1956

a report. We objected. I objected, so did Molotov, and Voroshilov. I will not say that we spoke actively against... That was impossible. There had been facts, there were facts, the congress was waiting... Perhaps this was our mistake. We did not want to split the congress."[9]

Having made the decision about the closed-session report hastily and in confusion, the members of the Presidium initially agreed that the report would be secret. As Khrushchev told the delegates of the Italian Communist Party in the summer of 1956, "we felt that the report would not be published, otherwise we would have constructed it differently. Moreover, the decision to raise this question was adopted not during preparations for the congress, but as it was taking place. Therefore we were denied the possibility of consulting with our fraternal parties and of balancing to a sufficient degree the positive and negative sides with regard to Stalin."[10] The facts and generalizations contained in the report were so stunning for the leaders of the "fraternal parties" that, for instance, Togliatti revealed its contents only to members of the secretariat of his Central Committee; the rest of the leaders of the Italian Communist Party "were informed only about the political aspects of the report."[11]

The Twentieth Congress adopted only a brief resolution on the report. Nothing was reported about this resolution or about the closed-session report given by Khrushchev in the published material of the congress. Nevertheless, several days after the congress was finished, the report began to be read not only in party organizations, but at mass meetings attended by Komsomol members and people not in the party.

It is natural that, under these conditions, the leaking of information abroad was inevitable. A few weeks after it had been delivered, Khrushchev's "secret" report was published in full abroad (in the USSR it was published only in 1989). Very soon foreign journalists asked Khrushchev about the authenticity of the document published in the West. With his reply, Khrushchev placed himself in an awkward position. He declared that he did not know such a document, "and let US intelligence answer this question." "And how should I have replied, since the subject under discussion was a secret?" — Khrushchev commented on his statement in his memoirs.[12]

Immediately after the Twentieth Congress, resolutions were passed proposing massive reviews of political cases from previous years and releasing innocent people who remained in camps and in exile. On 19 March 1956, the Presidium of the Central Committee of the CPSU adopted a decree creating ninety-seven commissions of the Presidium of the Supreme Council for "verifying in places of imprisonment the foundation for the conviction of each person accused of committing crimes of a political nature," as well as economic crimes or malfeasance in office. A central commission chaired by Aristov was created to monitor the activity of these smaller commissions. According to a report by Aristov sent on 17 October 1956 to the Central Committee of the CPSU, the given commissions reviewed the cases of 176,325 people, of whom 100,139 were freed, and 42,016 had their sentences reduced. Of those convicted of political crimes, 50,944 people were released.[13]

During discussions of the report submitted by Aristov's commission at a session of the CC's Presidium, Molotov "was upset that so many had been released."[14] A year before this, in discussing the review of a number of falsified cases, Kaganovich challenged Rudenko: "You now are calling to account those who earlier had been doing the arresting, but we will call you to account for the fact that you are releasing people."[15]

On 13 April 1956, the Presidium of the Central Committee adopted a decree "On Studying Material of the Open Trials." A new commission was created for this headed by Molotov, and whose members included Kaganovich, Voroshilov, Aristov, Furtseva, Shvernik, Suslov, Pospelov and Rudenko. According to Aristov, at sessions of this commission "the sharpest arguments took place. The positions of Molotov and Kaganovich were absolutely rigid and clearly defined from the very first session. They said that the trials had been correct, that they were in the interests of the party, and that is the way things should have been."[16]

After reviewing documents presented by Serov and Rudenko about the use of investigation methods banned by law, the crude falsification of cases, and the illegal execution of many thousands of people, Molotov and Kaganovich began to admit a few things. However, as before, they said that the repressions had been dictated "by political expediency." According to Khrushchev, Molotov "did everything to not allow a serious investigation of these cases."[17] In summation, the Commission presented the Central Committee with "conclusions concerning the material under review." This document stated that "mass repressions along state lines were the result of the abuse of power by I. V. Stalin, as well as by careerists and provocateurs who had infiltrated the organs of the NKVD and falsified cases against honest Soviet citizens." Appended to these conclusions, which in fact did not go further than the formulations given in Khrushchev's report at the Twentieth Congress, was a "conclusion" clearly tacked on by Molotov, Kaganovich and Voroshilov, that "there are no grounds... for reviewing the cases regarding Bukharin, Rykov, Zinoviev, and Kamenev, insofar as they had headed for many years an anti-Soviet struggle directed against the construction of socialism in the USSR."[18]

Meanwhile, the facts that Khrushchev had revealed at the Twentieth Congress which were connected with the mass repressions caused legitimate bewilderment among rank-and-file communists over how Stalin's closest stooges, who shared with him responsibility for these repressions, could remain in the Presidium of the Central Committee. As the apparatchiks declared at the June Plenum of 1957, they had to resist "the pressure of communists in order to justify Malenkov, Kaganovich and Molotov"; "everywhere, at all meetings, without any organized effort, people are demanding the personal accountability of Kaganovich, Molotov and Malenkov for violating revolutionary legality. We slowed things down as an insurance measure, and only reported about these moods in informational bulletins of the Central Committee."[19]

Meanwhile, with the help of his supporters in the party apparatus and in the leadership of the MGB, Khrushchev was accumulating material on the participation of Molotov, Kaganovich and Voroshilov in the repressions. At sessions of the Presidium, more documents began to be circulated which contained their sanctions of arrests and executions. In this regard, the main Stalinists declared: "Such were the times, what could we have done when we ourselves should have been sitting in prison?"[20]

Khrushchev repeatedly raised the question of returning to an investigation of the open trials. A few days before the last clash in the presidium, he declared that "Zinoviev had been shot for nothing." In reply to this "Kaganovich and Molotov raised a storm: if you please, the Zinovievists were our enemies. But, in saying this, they did not explain the reasons for which they were declared enemies of the people and shot."[21]

At that time, Khrushchev declared openly that Stalin's "closest comrades-in-arms" had been responsible for the mass repressions. "Here, comrades, we are reviewing material, we are rehabilitating posthumously innocent communists who were shot," he said. "What shall we do with those guilty of these executions, will we return to this question or will we continue to remain silent about it before the party?"[22]

Molotov, Kaganovich and Voroshilov were especially angered by Khrushchev's declaration before the scheduled departure of members of the Presidium of the Central Committee to celebrate the 250th anniversary of Leningrad. Khrushchev said that the leaders of the party were traveling for the first time to Leningrad to bring happiness to the inhabitants of the city, whereas earlier they had only brought them tears and blood. In saying this, he mainly had in mind the trip to Leningrad in 1934 by Stalin, Molotov and Voroshilov to investigate Kirov's assassination; after their trip tens of thousands of people were deported from Leningrad, and hundreds of former Leningrad oppositionists were sent into exile or into the camps.

In light of all that has been said, Khrushchev's statement at the June Plenum of the Central Committee in 1957 does not seem groundless. He declared that Molotov, Kaganovich, Voroshilov, and Malenkov were planning to remove him from his post as first secretary of the Central Committee, and Serov from the post of chairman of the KGB, in order to "seize the organs of state security, seize the archives both there and in the party's Central Committee. Then, you would find none of their signatures on documents. For indeed, there, on the last letters of innocent people condemned to death, they wrote their inscriptions which make one's blood run cold, and their monstrous greetings."[23]

In the middle of June, Molotov, Kaganovich, Voroshilov, and Malenkov enlisted the support of three more members of the Presidium of the CC and thereby achieved an "arithmetical majority." They then raised the issue of removing Khrushchev from the post of first secretary of the Central Committee. Along with dogmatic arguments and absurd charges, they blamed Khrushchev for his qualities and actions which later would be declared signs of "subjectivism and voluntarism." In reply, Khrushchev and his supporters placed special emphasis on the crimes of their opponents during the years of Stalinism. At sessions of the Presidium, Zhukov and other supporters of Khrushchev divulged a number of documents which exposed Molotov, Kaganovich and Voroshilov for committing "reprisals against cadres." This provoked the indignation of the latter, who declared that making public the truth about the mass repressions would lead to the destruction of the revolutionary movement, irreparable damage to the party, and even to its disintegration.[24]

Soon, in response to demands from "rank-and-file" members of the Central Committee, an extraordinary plenum of the CC was convened to review the question of keeping Khrushchev at the post of first secretary. This plenum spilled over into the trial of the "anti-party group." But even after colliding with the unanimity of the Central Committee, the group's members continued to try to prove the "harm" in returning to the subject of Stalin and the repressions. Kaganovich conducted himself very aggressively; he shouted at the plenum's participants and even attempted to give a "theoretical" explanation of the "damage" the party would suffer, in his opinion, as a result of exposing Stalin's crimes any more. When Zhukov demanded: "Let's talk about responsibility for crimes, for the executions, this is the most important issue," Kaganovich replied: "The issue which has been raised — is a policy issue (*Zhukov*:

And a criminal one). It must be viewed not from the vantage point of 1957, but from the point of view of 1937-1938. That is what is demanded by Marxist dialectics." Guided by a similar understanding of "dialectics," Kaganovich stubbornly insisted: "We have dethroned Stalin and, unbeknownst to ourselves, we are debunking thirty years of our work, without wanting to, before the entire world... When you, comrades, stir up this matter, once again we are starting this wave, this campaign, which had somewhat subsided, which the party suffered through... We should not raise this matter again... I approach this issue politically, not legally. It is politically harmful to raise the question this way for the party, for the state, for our defense, for foreign policy. I cannot agree with this."[25]

Kaganovich declared that he had listened to Khrushchev's report about Stalin "with great pain. I loved Stalin, and there was good reason to love him — he was a great Marxist."[26] In reference to the documents read at the plenum which testified to his active role in organizing the terror, Kaganovich said: "There were exaggerations, excesses — as they say, in a brawl you don't count the fists that are flying..."[27] When it came to his policy of repression in railway transport, Kaganovich stated that he "defended hundreds of thousands (! – V. R.) of people, railway workers, and we arrested some of the people, who, on paper, seemed to be enemies."[28]

Molotov spoke in a somewhat more restrained manner, but essentially in the same spirit. He declared that, on the issue of Stalin, "we have been allowing a certain injustice, which we must correct." Praising Stalin's services as before, Molotov complained that in recent times the Soviet press "has modestly remained silent about Stalin, as if for these 30 years Stalin did not play a leading role in the history of our party and of the Soviet state."

In defending himself, Molotov read out casuistic formulations from the Central Committee's decree of 30 June 1956, according to which any attack on Stalin "would not be understood by the people, and what was at stake was by no means a lack of personal courage. It is clear that anyone who spoke out in these conditions against Stalin would not receive support among the people." In response someone called out from the audience: "You wrote (this) in order to cover your own crimes."[29]

Shepilov dotted the i's more clearly. Not personally disgraced by participation in the repressions, he nevertheless spoke in agitated tones about what it meant, in essence, when the crimes of Stalin's clique were made public: "You propose that we now say to the communist parties and to our own people: for a number of years people stood in the leadership of our party who were murderers, and who should be placed on the defendants' bench. They will say: what kind of a Marxist party is this? ... I said to Comrade Zhukov: the facts that he cites are facts, but why do this now, who will benefit from this?"[30]

Participants in the "anti-party group" unequivocally let their main opponents know that they also shared the guilt for repressions in 1937-1938. The one who spoke the most aggressively on this subject was Kaganovich, who accused Zhukov of a "factional maneuver," insofar as he "dragged out the names of two or three people who signed documents, but he doesn't name the others... He ruins those who are to his liking, but remains silent about others." Counting on distributing the blame for the misdeeds of the Stalinist clique evenly, so to speak, on all the leaders who lived through the Great Terror, Kaganovich reminded people that directives about reprisals were signed by all who were Politburo members at the time, and in all the republics and areas, troikas were operating which were headed by the first secretaries of party committees. After he had turned to Khrushchev with the question: "And could it be that you signed no papers about executions in the Ukraine?", Kaganovich then shifted the focus to Zhukov. The following noteworthy exchange took place between them:

Kaganovich: And what are you saying, Comrade Zhukov, as commander of a division, you didn't sign any papers?
Zhukov: I did not send a single person to be shot.
Kaganovich: This is difficult to verify... But then again, didn't you approve the policies of the Central Committee, the policy of fighting against enemies?
Zhukov: Of fighting against enemies, but not of shooting people.
Kaganovich: We did not know all these subtleties (sic! – V. R.).

The going was harder for Khrushchev, who in 1937-1938 occupied significantly higher posts than Zhukov. "We all gave our approval," confessed Khrushchev. "I voted many times and branded people as a traitor, for instance, Yakir... After the trial (of the generals), I also spoke at meetings, and stirred up the anger of the people against them." Khrushchev explained his behavior by saying that he believed in the correctness of the charges, "since I felt that you had investigated things, that he was an enemy, but you betrayed our trust. And yet you were a Politburo member at that time, you should have known."[31]

During the work of the plenum, its participants characterized the actions of Molotov, Kaganovich, and Malenkov, particularly during the Great Terror, not as "mistakes," but as heinous crimes which deserved criminal punishment. "You should face severe punishment and, as a bloodstained person," Zhegalin said to Malenkov, "you should not only be expelled from the party, but put on trial."[32] Similar conclusions with regard to Kaganovich were made in Poliansky's speech, when he declared: "Comrade Kaganovich busied himself with everything: metallurgy, coal, agriculture, transport, and I must say that he remained at these posts at the expense of repressions and savage methods of directing the economy... The blood of honest people is dripping from his hands. You shot tens of thousands of innocent people — and yet you have the moral right to sit in the Presidium of the Central Committee!"

Zhukov: He should be sitting behind bars!

Poliansky: Yes, he should be sitting behind bars, or for the crimes that he committed, he should be punished more severely."[33]

When the discussion turned to evaluating Stalin and the repressions as a whole, the formulations of the speakers noticeably softened. Thus, Kuusinen said that "as a result of *certain* crude errors committed by Stalin, we *temporarily* faced a *partial deviation* from the regime, which, according to Lenin's doctrine, should exist under the dictatorship of the proletariat" (my italics – V. R.).[34]

Zhukov explained the softness of the sanctions which should be applied to Molotov, Kaganovich, and Malenkov by the fact that it was not necessary "to give any advantage to our enemies." "In order to avoid compromising our leading organs, I do not propose that we put this trio on trial or expel them from the party. This should belong only to the party and must be kept within the confines of the party. Here, at the Plenum, we must say everything and hide nothing, and then we will see what to do with them." Zhukov acknowledged that "other comrades, too, are guilty, former members of the Politburo," but he declared that "these comrades (Khrushchev and Mikoyan – V. R.), because of their honest work and directness, deserve the trust of the Central Committee and of our entire party, and I am certain that we will be recognizing them as leaders in the future because of their candid and heartfelt confessions."[35]

At times the mutual recriminations and words of self-justification "of the leaders" assumed tragicomic tones. Both Khrushchev and his opponents essentially confessed that their participation in the repressions had been due to fear for their own hides. When Khrushchev hurled the highly significant rejoinder at Voroshilov: "And you don't have to say that you did not fear Stalin. Everyone who was not afraid was destroyed, they have already vanished, they no longer exist," Voroshilov found nothing better to say than: "It was by accident that I did not vanish."[36]

Going on in his criticism of Stalin's crimes to a more painful subject for the Stalinists, Kirov's assassination, Khrushchev said: "Even now I do not believe that Zinoviev had anything to do with this matter... After Kirov's murder, hundreds of thousands of people went to the executioner's block. Why was this necessary? Even today this is a mystery, and it should have been investigated. But do you think that Molotov will look into it? No. He trembles at the thought, he fears even a hint with regard to this issue; Kaganovich is in the same position."[37] Turning to Molotov, Khrushchev declared that "we must return to this matter (investigation of the Moscow Trials and the mass repressions of the 1930s – V. R.)... You must shed light on the history of this period and show your true face."[38]

Appendix I

However, in subsequent years, having rid himself of his main opponents, Khrushchev did not dare to expose Stalin's crimes completely. The facts which were cited at the June Plenum were not made public. Members of the "anti-party group" not only were not put on trial, but they were even left in the party and received third-tier but nevertheless leading positions.

To be sure, a new commission was created to investigate Stalin's crimes. An appeal that the indefatigable Molotov made to the Central Committee on the eve of the Twenty-Second Congress of the CPSU (1961) served as an impulse to make public some of its conclusions. Molotov accused the authors of the draft of a new program for the CPSU of writing a "non-Marxist" draft. Angered by this, Khrushchev gave the green light to publicizing at the congress several facts which had been cited at the June Plenum of the CC in 1957. However, he did not dare to publicize at the congress either the circumstances connected with Kirov's murder, or the facts which testified to the real nature of the Moscow Trials.

Only in his memoirs, written at the end of the 1960s, did Khrushchev admit that Rykov, Bukharin, and other prominent defendants at the Moscow Trials "deserved to be called leaders." He gave two explanations for the fact that, during his tenure as first secretary of the CC, he had not led matters to a review of the open trials of the 1930s: "the ambivalence of our behavior" and pressure coming from the leaders of "fraternal communist parties." "Once again we feared going all the way in what we said, although there was no doubt that these people were innocent, and that they had been victims of arbitrary rule. The open trials were attended by the leaders of fraternal communist parties who then testified in their own countries to the just nature of the sentences. We did not want to discredit their statements, and therefore we postponed the rehabilitation of Bukharin, Zinoviev, Rykov, and other comrades for an indefinite period. I think that it would have been more correct to reveal everything. The truth will out!"[39]

The half-hearted and inconsistent nature of the exposure of the crimes committed by Stalin's clique was one of the main factors in the decay of the post-Stalinist political regime which led to its fall at the beginning of the 1990s.

Isaak Babel, shot 27 January 1940

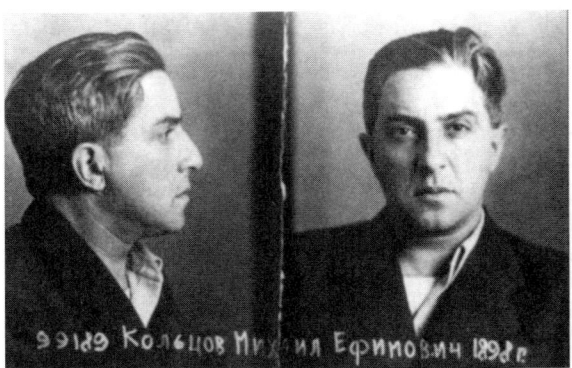

Mikhail Koltsov, shot 2 February 1940

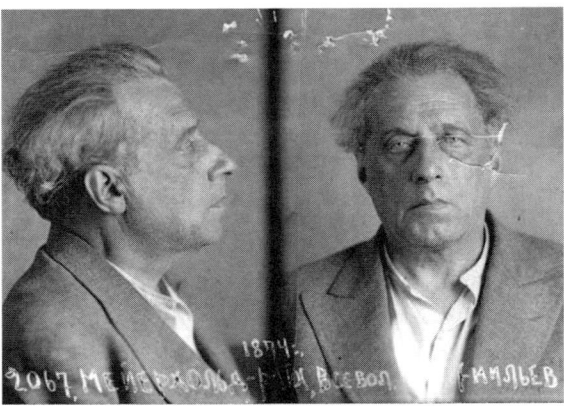

Vsevolod Meyerhold, shot 2 February 1940

Appendix II

Statistics about the Victims of Mass Repressions

1. *Myths*. For several decades, Soviet and Western societies have remained under the influence of statistical computations in which the number of those repressed for political reasons in the USSR has been exaggerated, as a rule, by an order of magnitude. In this process, the statistical data wandering from one work to another belonged not to specialists — statisticians or demographers — but to dilettantes in this area, who remained silent about the sources and methods which guided them in making their calculations.

Overestimating the number of victims of political repression is a phenomenon which has been encountered earlier in history. In the novel, *The Priest from Tours*, Balzac wrote: "People of an ironic frame of mind would probably receive no small pleasure from the strange statements made by abbé Birotteau and Mademoiselle Gamard... Who would not laugh upon hearing them claim, while relying on truly curious evidence, ... that more than one million, three hundred thousand people perished on the scaffold during the revolution."[1] Balzac's characters, however, were content to discuss their "evidence" in private conversations; they did not circulate them in print throughout the entire world.

That has not been the case with contemporaries of Stalin's repressions. Staggered by their unprecedented scale, they published figures they invented and presented them as reliable. Thus, in 1945, Alexander Barmine stated that twelve million people were in the concentration camps of the USSR.[2]

Similarly fantastic numbers figure in the "samizdat" or "tamizdat" works which were written in the 1950s and 1960s by Soviet authors, particularly by those who passed through the camps themselves. Thus, in the novel, *The Department of Useless Things,* Yuri Dombrovsky writes as if it were obvious and beyond any need of proof that, in 1937-1938, "according to the most modest estimates, the number of prisoners exceeded ten million."[3]

In his novel *The First Circle,* Alexander Solzhenitsyn discussed the political reasons for the frequent exaggeration of the number of camp inhabitants by the prisoners themselves. He noted with a certain amount of irony: "The prisoners were sure that no men remained at liberty besides the authorities and the MVD." These personal conceptions of people who were repeatedly being sent from one transfer prison or camp to another, and who met there an enormous number of ever newer faces, gave rise to the myths that circulated among the prisoners. Solzhenitsyn wrote that "in the prisons people were generally inclined to exaggerate the number of prisoners, and when in actual fact there were only twelve to fifteen million behind bars, the prisoners were certain that there were twenty, and even thirty, million."[4] This last sentence was a "slight deception" on Solzhenitsyn's part. It was intended to create the impression that the "objective" author, who was pointing out the exaggerations of the prisoners, was himself providing an absolutely reliable figure. However, if the prisoners were naming a figure only one and a half to two times greater than the figure given by Solzhenitsyn, the latter increased his number by a factor of five to six times over the true number of prisoners.

A significant contribution to the circulation of falsified statistics was made by A. V. Antonov-Ovseenko, who displays in his works on Stalinism an unusual glibness when dealing with facts. In his book, *Portrait of a Tyrant*, which came out in 1994, he claims that the peak of the repressions was in 1938, when sixteen million prisoners were in the camps. A bit later he indicates that the same number of camp inmates existed in 1933.[5] His book repeatedly asserts that, from 1935 through 1940, 19,840,000 people were arrested, of whom seven million were shot. In order to increase the believability of these figures, Antonov-Ovseenko declares, without a shade of hesitation, that they are contained in a report from the KGB presented after the Twentieth Congress to the Central Committee of the CPSU.[6]

Figures that are closer to the truth, but also inflated, are contained in recent publications by D. Volkogonov and R. Medvedev. Thus, Medvedev writes that no less than five million people were arrested for political reasons in 1936-1938 alone. Even stranger is his assertion that "the general number of prisoners in the USSR in 1941-1942 was approximately equal to the number of soldiers in the active army. And the losses of people at that time in the East (i.e., in the camps – V. R.) and in the West (i.e., at the front – V. R.) were also approximately equal."[7]

Khrushchev also made a contribution to misinforming the public about the scale of Stalin's repressions when he asserted in his memoirs that, at the time of Stalin's death, the camps held about ten million people.[8] He needed to raise the true figure four times over, apparently in order to make his role in freeing political prisoners seem more significant (a role which would have

Appendix II 443

been judged in the manner it deserved by his contemporaries and successors even without this exaggeration).

In order to refute such "miscalculations," it would be necessary to cite statistics which were at the disposal of the authorities, for the organs of the OGPU-NKVD-MGB kept a careful bureaucratic count of the number of people arrested, shot, and located in the camps. However, the lying, sluggish, and cowardly ruling bureaucracy did not remove the seal of secrecy from the statistics of repression even in the first years of the unfolding offensive in the USSR of anti-communist forces who relied on fantastic figures of tens of millions of victims of the "Bolshevik terror." The Gorbachev leadership decided to counterpose true figures to these fabrications only at the end of its reign.

Despite the appearance in the 1990s of many publications disclosing the true number of those arrested for political motives, the "democratic" journalists continue to operate with arbitrary numbers, pursuing transparent political goals as they do so. Thus, the journalist Yu. Feofanov, in "surpassing" all the falsifiers who preceded him, announced on the eve of the presidential elections of 1996 that, in the 1930s alone, sixteen to twenty million people died from repressions, and "God alone knows how many souls were squandered by the Soviet communist regime."[9]

2. *The number of those convicted for political reasons*. Soon after Stalin's death, the Presidium of the Central Committee of the CPSU demanded that the law-enforcement agencies provide data about the number of people convicted for "counter-revolutionary crimes." The report presented in February 1954 by the General Prosecutor of the USSR Rudenko, the Minister of Internal Affairs Kruglov, and the Minister of Justice Gorshenin, states that, from 1921 through 1 February 1954, 3,777,380 people were convicted on charges of counter-revolutionary crimes, which includes 642,980 people who were sentenced to death; 2,369,220 who were confined in camps and prisons; and 765,180 who were sentenced to exile or deportation. Of this number, approximately 2.9 million people were convicted by extrajudicial organs (by a collegium of the OGPU, by "troikas" and by Special Boards), and about 900,000 people were convicted by courts, military tribunals, the Special Collegium and the Military Collegium of the Supreme Court.[10] Numbers close to this (3,778,234 arrested, including 786,098 shot) were first made public at the beginning of the 1990s by leading members of the KGB.[11]

We should note that in these figures some people, but by no means the majority, are counted more than once, insofar as many political prisoners, primarily from among the oppositionists, were convicted during this period from two to five times.

In 1992, the head of the department of registration and archival forms at the Ministry of Security for the Russian Federation released data covering all the years of the Soviet regime. According to these figures, for the years

1917-1990, 3,853,900 people were convicted on charges of state crimes and other similar articles in the Criminal Code; out of these 827,995 people were sentenced to death.[12] These figures also tend to confirm the veracity of the data contained in the report of 1954. Differences in the number of people sentenced to death can be explained by the fact that, in the last instance, the concept of "political prisoners" is interpreted more widely ("those convicted according to several other similar articles of the Criminal Code"), and also by the fact that some of the death sentences were not carried out. Upon review, they were replaced by sentences of long periods of incarceration.

The dynamics of political repression were reflected in the table compiled in 1954 by officials of the MVD, which presents the number of those convicted in cases falling under the jurisdiction of the VChK-OGPU-NKVD in the period 1921-1940. These figures raise slightly the number of those convicted in political cases in the 1920s, since the organs of the VChK-OGPU conducted investigations during this period into several other types of crimes, for instance, economic ones.

According to the table's data, in 1921, when part of Soviet territory was still embroiled in military activity and there were many White-Guard bands, the number of convictions reached 35,800 people. It sharply fell over the next two years (6,000 in 1922 and 4,800 in 1923), and then began to rise, reaching 17,800 in 1926, and 33,800 in 1928. The next, more significant growth reflects the increased repressions with regard to oppositionists, non-party specialists and peasants, in particular, who fought back with arms in hand against the extraordinary measures and forced collectivization. In comparison with 1929 (56,200 people), the number of victims of political repressions increased almost fourfold in 1930, reaching 209,000 people. Over the next three years, the number of people arrested was measured in six-digit figures (180,700; 141,900; and 239,700 people). After decreasing in 1934 three times over in comparison with 1933, in the wake of Kirov's assassination, the number exceeded the indicators of the period of forced collectivization (267,100 in 1935, and 274,700 in 1936).[13]

In 1937-1938, there was a qualitative leap, which we will address in section 6.

3. *The number of people located in places of confinement and in special settlements*. The first sources of statistical data concerning this issue are the results of the census of 1937 (declared to be falsified and the work of saboteurs because it reflected the unpleasant picture of the demographic development of the USSR during the 1930s) and the census of 1939. According to the figures from these censuses, the prisons, camps and special settlements contained on 1 January 1937 no less than 1.8 million people, and on 21 February 1939 no less than 2.6 million people.[14] Of this number, about a million people lived in special settlements, i.e., they were former kulaks who had been subjected

to deportation. At the end of the 1930s, this category had its civil rights restored, as a result of which the living standards in the special settlements approached the general standards throughout the nation.

More detailed statistics are contained in the statistical reports of the GULAG, in reports from the directors of the GULAG to the People's Commissars of Internal Affairs, and in the reports of the latter to Stalin. These figures of the statistical counts made with bureaucratic accuracy in the bowels of the very machinery of repression can be considered reliable for good reason. After all, the leaders of the NKVD were not interested in underestimating the number of prisoners if for no other reason than the fact that production plans in the camps were calculated according to the number of prisoners located there.

In 1940, the centralized card index of the GULAG contained statistics for almost eight million people, including 1) people who were then in prison; 2) people who had finished their sentences and had been released; and 3) those who had died in the camps.[15] Taken together, as follows from the archival material of the GULAG, from 1921-1953 about ten million people passed through the camps.

The dynamics of the movement of prisoners can be seen from data about their total number which were compiled on 1 January of each year. On this date in 1930, the camps held 175,000, in 1933 — 334,300 people. The number of prisoners in the camps and corrective-labor colonies in 1934 reached 510,300 people, in 1935 — 965,700, in 1936 — 1,296,000, in 1937 — 1,196,000, in 1938 — 1,882,000, in 1939 — 1,672,000, and in 1940 — 1,660,000.[16]

Therefore, even in the years of the Great Purge, the number of prisoners did not exceed one percent of the country's population. This portion is two to three times greater than the corresponding indicator in 1994, when the prisons, corrective-labor and education colonies in the Russian Federation contain more than 600,000 prisoners.

Before the start of Stalin's repressions, the number of prisoners was much lower. In September 1923, the RSFSR counted 79,947 prisoners, of whom 4.8 percent (i.e., around four thousand people) had been convicted of state crimes.[17] These figures testify to the onset of civil peace and a sharp reduction of general criminal activity in the nation, which had just emerged from a seven-year period of wars.

In 1926 the places of incarceration in the Russian Federation held 97,300 convicted prisoners, which comprised a bit more than 0.1 percent of the total population of the RSFSR (92.8 million people).[18] This proportion is about five times lower than the corresponding figure in the USA today.

By the beginning of the war, the number of prisoners in the camps and colonies of the GULAG stood at 2.3 million people (the growth in 1940-1941 occurred as a result of the repression on territories added in 1939-1940 to the USSR, and as a result of the introduction of criminal penalties for absenteeism and other violations of labor discipline).

From the beginning of the war through December 1944, 2,550,000 people came into the camps, and 3,440,000 left the camps.[19] The decrease in the number of prisoners is explained primarily by the fact that hundreds of thousands of men were freed before completing their sentences (mainly among those convicted of absenteeism, common and petty economic crimes and crimes of malfeasance) and sent to bring the Red Army up to full strength. Just according to the Decrees of the Presidium of the Supreme Council of the USSR on 12 June and 24 October 1941, 600,000 men were freed from places of imprisonment, of whom 175,000 were mobilized into the Red Army.[20] At the same time, during the war years a halt was put to releasing Trotskyists and others convicted of "especially serious state crimes," even if they had finished their sentences.

After the end of the war, the number of prisoners began to climb once again. For the entire time that the GULAG existed, the maximum number of prisoners was reached in 1950 (2,561,000 people).[21] The same year witnessed the greatest number of people who were located in places of partial confinement — around three million people. This contingent, which included people in special settlements, exile settlements, exile and deportation, was largely made up of nationalities deported during the war years.

The average monthly number of prisoners in jails fluctuated from 350,500 in January 1939 (the maximum figure) to 155,200 in January 1944 (the minimum figure).[22]

4. *The death rate among prisoners.* In the period from 1 January 1934 through 31 December 1947, 962,100 people died in the camps. In 1937-1938, the number who died reached 5.5-5.7 percent, and in 1939 — 3.29 percent of the yearly contingent of prisoners. In absolute figures, the number of those who died reached 25,400 people in 1937; in 1938 — 90,500; in 1939 — 50,500; and in 1940 — 46,700 people. The mortality rate was particularly high in 1941-1943, when 516,000 people died. The peak of mortality (248,900 people) came in 1942.[23]

5. *The number of political prisoners in the camps.* The previous sections have cited figures about the entire number of prisoners, including those convicted of violent, mercenary, work-place, economic, and other crimes. The number of prisoners who were convicted on charges of counter-revolutionary (state, political) crimes comprised (according to the figure on January 1 of each year) in 1934 — 135,200 people; in 1935 — 118,300; in 1936 — 105,900; in 1937 — 104,800; in 1938 — 185,300; and in 1939 — 454,400 people. For the duration of 1940-1941, it remained approximately on the same level as in 1939, then fell to 268,900 in 1944 and rose once again to 579,000 in 1950.[24]

Some of those arrested for political reasons were convicted under criminal statutes. At the same time, criminals were often convicted under article 58,

Appendix II   447

when their criminal activities were classified as wrecking, sabotage, and so forth. In view of these circumstances, V. N. Zemskov, the most serious researcher of statistics on Stalin's repressions, thinks that the "relationship between political prisoners and criminals is highly relative, but in principle it corresponds to the real composition of the prisoners in the GULAG."[25]

One of the foulest Stalinist amalgams consisted of the fact that, after the war, those who fought against Stalinism and those innocently convicted were united in one category of state criminals along with Vlasovites, Polizei, members of punitive detachments, and other stooges of the forces of occupation, i.e., with collaborationists who were severely punished not only in the USSR, but in other countries liberated from Fascism.

6. *Number of those repressed during the years of the Great Purge*. Data about the number of people repressed in 1937-1938 were not declassified until the beginning of the 1990s. The only thing that Khrushchev dared to do on this plane was to announce at the Twentieth Congress that the number of people arrested on charges of counter-revolutionary crimes increased in 1937 by ten times in comparison with 1936.[26]

The first data about the number of victims of the Great Terror were cited at the June Plenum of the Central Committee in 1957, where it was announced that in 1937-1938, more than one and a half million people were arrested, of whom 681,692 people were shot.[27] More exact data about the number of people arrested (1,372,329) were contained in the report from Shvernik, the chairman of the Commission of the Presidium of the CC, which was compiled at the beginning of 1963.[28]

Thus, about a third of the acts of political repression committed during all the years of Soviet power were carried out in these two terrible years.

What appears even more striking is the dynamics of those sentenced to be shot (in cases involving the VChK-OGPU-NKVD). In the seven years of the New Economic Policy (1922-1928), their number reached 11,271 people. In 1930, the number of people shot rose to 20,201, and then began to decrease, reaching 10,651 people in 1931 and 9,285 people in the next five years (1932-1936). In 1936, 1,118 people were shot on political charges. In 1937, the number of people shot was three hundred fifteen times (!) greater than the previous year, reaching 353,074 victims. Almost the same number were shot (328,618 people) in 1938, after which this indicator sharply fell, reaching 4,201 people for 1939 and 1940 combined.[29]

The number of people shot in 1937-1938 exceeds by more than seven times the number shot in the remaining 22 years of Stalin's reign (from 1930-1936 and 1939-1953, 94,390 people were executed[30]). The scale of state terror during the years of the Great Purge has no equal in human history.

7. *Statistics about rehabilitation*. By 1954, in the prisons and camps there were 467,946 and in exile 62,462 people convicted of counter-revolutionary

crimes.³¹ As a result of the early release and rehabilitation of people belonging to this category, by the beginning of 1959, 11,000 people who had been convicted of political offenses remained in places of incarceration.³²

Over the course of 1954-1961, 737,182 people were rehabilitated (including those posthumously), and 208,448 people who had been convicted were refused rehabilitation upon review of their cases.³³ Rehabilitation continued in the 1960s-1980s, although at a slower pace.

A new stage of rehabilitation began in the third year of "perestroika." From 1987 to 1989, 838,630 people were rehabilitated, and 21,333 were denied rehabilitation. The last group included traitors to the fatherland and members of punitive detachments from the time of the Second World War; participants in and accomplices of nationalist bands; and former officials of administrative organs who had been caught falsifying criminal cases. At the time the Soviet Union disintegrated, about 1.5 million cases remained unreviewed in its republics.³⁴

Thus, the statistics of rehabilitation coincide with the figures cited in section 5.

8. *The number of party members repressed.* In 1991, Katkov, the senior official of the Party Control Commission of the CC CPSU, announced that among the people repressed in 1937-1938 there were 116,885 communists.³⁵ This figure is clearly an underestimation for at least two reasons.

First of all, a significant portion of those repressed during those years were expelled from the party before their arrest. The picture portrayed by A. Milchakov was typical: in the prelude to the arrest of a communist, members of his party organization would be called into the regional committee and told: "You have to expel him from the party, otherwise he will be arrested with a party card."³⁶ Therefore, while these people underwent investigation or were being sentenced, they figured as non-party persons.

Secondly, among those repressed were hundreds of thousands of people who had been expelled from the party during previous party purges. At the February-March Plenum of the Central Committee in 1937, Stalin announced that there were 1.5 million people who had been expelled from the party nationwide since 1922. Moreover, in several regions and at many factories the number of those expelled exceeded the number of party members. For instance, at the Kolomenskoe engine-building works there were two thousand former communists compared to the 1,400 party members.³⁷ It is natural that special attention of the NKVD organs was directed at this category of people, and especially at those expelled for participation in opposition groups.

The figures presented by A. D. Sakharov in his article, "Reflections on Progress, Peaceful Coexistence and Intellectual Freedom," are close to the truth. Here he notes that in 1936-1939, more than 1.2 million communists, who made up half the general number of party members, were arrested. Of these, according to Sakharov's figures, 50,000 were eventually released, and the rest were either shot (600,000) or perished in the camps.[38]

A more detailed picture of the number of repressed communists can be given by a comparison of these figures with party statistics. At the time of the Seventeenth Congress (February 1934) the party had 1,872,488 members and 935,298 candidate-members; at the time of the Eighteenth Congress (March 1939) there were 1,588,852 members and 888,814 candidate-members.[39] If, in 1934-1938, there had not been mass party purges and repressions, and all candidates had been promoted to full members of the party, then by the time of the Eighteenth Congress the party would have had around 2.8 million members (adjustments for natural deaths would not be significant, since in 1934 approximately 90 percent of party members and almost 100 percent of candidate-members were people less than 50 years of age). Besides this, acceptance into the party, which had been closed in 1933, had been renewed starting 1 November 1936. From this time until March 1939, hundreds of thousands of people became party members who had not been candidate-members at the Seventeenth Congress. Since most of the people expelled from the party in 1933-1938 were subjected to political repression, it is not hard to come to the conclusion that communists made up, according to the most conservative calculations, more than half of the victims of the Great Terror.

In several regions, the losses of communists as a percentage were greater than in the country as a whole. Thus, in the Communist Party of Ukraine, the number of party members shrank from 456,000 in 1934 to 286,000 in 1938, i.e., by almost 40 percent.[40]

The figures cited show the justice of Trotsky's observation: "To establish the regime which is correctly called Stalinist, what was needed was not the Bolshevik Party, but the extermination of the Bolshevik Party."[41]

This idea is confirmed in the fate of those communists who managed to survive in Stalin's prisons and camps. As A. D. Sakharov notes, "only a handful of those rehabilitated were allowed to work at responsible posts, and even fewer were able to participate in investigating the crimes of which they had been witnesses and victims."[42] Meanwhile, at the time of their rehabilitation, many communists who had occupied responsible positions in the past were no older than the current party bosses. For instance, the former general secretary of the Central Committee of the VLKSM, A. Milchakov, who was rehabilitated in 1955, was one year younger than Suslov and four years younger than Pelshe. It would have been natural to expect that this man, who had great political experience, would have been offered responsible work in the party or state apparatus. However, after his rehabilitation, Milchakov was put on a pension, whereas Suslov and Pelshe stayed in power for twenty-five years more. The "recruits of 1937" who occupied key posts in the apparatus in the

1950s were not inclined to waive even a tiny portion of their power to the benefit of Bolsheviks who had been released from prisons and the camps.

Glossary

Cheka: acronym for the Extraordinary Commission for Combatting Counterrevolution, Sabotage and Speculation (1918-1922). Political police in the early Soviet regime, succeeded by the GPU, OGPU and NKVD.

Comintern: The Communist International, or Third International, founded in 1919 to build proletarian revolutionary parties throughout the world. Disbanded by Stalin in 1943.

Dashnaks: members of the Armenian Revolutionary Federation, a nationalist political party opposed to Bolshevik rule in Armenia. Exiled in 1920.

GPU: State Political Directorate, one of the names of the Soviet political police, predecessor of the NKVD.

Great Soviet Encyclopedia: begun in 1926 and completed in 1947, the sixty-five volumes of this work were the first attempt to produce a major encyclopedia from a Marxist standpoint. Several of its editors, including Bukharin, Kritsman, Osinsky, Preobrazhensky, and Radek, fell victim to Stalin's terror.

Gulag: acronym for "**G**lavnoe **u**pravlenie **lag**erei" [Main Administration of the Camps], the body in charge of the prison camp system.

Komsomol: also VLKSM; acronym for "**Kom**munisticheskii **so**iuz **mol**odezhi [Communist Union of Youth], the youth organization of the Communist Party.

KP(b): Communist Party (Bolshevik), often follows the initials or names of the consitutuent republics of the Soviet Union, e.g., "UKP(b)" for Ukrainian Communist Party (Bolshevik).

MGB: Ministry of State Security.

Mussavatists: members of the "Mussavat," a nationalist party in Azerbaidzhan which opposed the early Bolshevik regime.

MVD: Ministry of Internal Affairs.

narkom: acronym for "**Na**rodnyi **kom**issar," or People's Commissar. Officially subordinate to the Central Executive Committee of the USSR, People's Commissars were similar to ministers in Western governments.

NKO: People's Commissariat of Defense.

NKVD: The People's Commissariat of Internal Affairs; the political police of the USSR during the time period covered in this book.

nomenklatura: members of the ruling party elite in the Soviet Union. Officials throughout the party and state apparatus were appointed by lists of candidates drawn up by leading party bodies.

OGPU: United State Political Directorate, successor to the Cheka and GPU as the Soviet regime's secret police.

perestroika: [rebuilding], the name given to reform policies launched by Mikhail Gorbachev in 1985 which ended in the collapse of the Soviet Union.

pood: A Russian measure of weight, about thirty-six pounds [16.38 kilograms].

Profintern: The Red International of Trade Unions, formed in 1921 to coordinate trade union activities by Communist Party members and sympathizers. Challenged the International Federation of Trade Unions (IFTU), led by the Second International. Disbanded by Stalin in 1937.

RKKA: Workers' and Peasants' Red Army. The name of the army in the early Soviet Union.

RSFSR: the Russian Soviet Federated Socialist Republic, largest of the fifteen republics of the former Soviet Union. Moscow is its capital.

samizdat: material published unofficially in the Soviet Union.

Sovnarkom: Council of People's Commissars; subordinate to the Central Executive Committee, performed ministerial functions in the Soviet government.

SRs: Members of the Party of Socialist Revolutionaries, a populist, peasant-based party, founded in 1902 and disbanded in 1922. For a few months in 1917-1918, the Left SRs supported the Bolshevik regime.

tamizdat: material published unofficially beyond the borders of the Soviet Union.

troika: a group of three; in this book, a three-person panel, initially comprised of a local party secretary, a local executive committee member, and a member of the secret police. Troikas often charged and convicted people of counter-revolutionary crimes. In 1937-38, the troikas frequently consisted solely of secret police officials.

TsIK: Central Executive Committee

VChK: *see* Cheka.

VKP(b): All-Union Communist Party (Bolshevik). Earlier name of the Communist Party of the Soviet Union.

VLKSM: All-Union Communist Youth League; *see* Komsomol.

Dates of Party Congresses, Comintern Congresses and Trials

Party Congresses

10th Congress of the Russian Communist Party (Bolsheviks) [RKP(b)] – March 8-16, 1921
11th Congress of the RKP(b) – March 27-April 2, 1922
12th Congress of the RKP(b) – April 17-25, 1923
13th Congress of the RKP(b) – May 23-31, 1924
14th Congress of the All-Union Communist Party (Bolsheviks) [VKP(b)] – December 18-31, 1925
15th Congress of the VKP(b) – December 2-19, 1927
16th Congress of the VKP(b) – June 26-July 13, 1930
17th Congress of the VKP(b) ["Congress of Victors"] – January 26-February 10, 1934
18th Congress of the VKP(b) – March 10-21, 1939
19th Congress of the Communist Party of the Soviet Union [KPSS/CPSU] – October 5-14, 1952
20th Congress of the CPSU – February 14-25, 1956
21st Congress of the CPSU – January 27-February 5, 1959
22nd Congress of the CPSU – October 17-31, 1961
23rd Congress of the CPSU – March 29-April 8, 1966
24th Congress of the CPSU – March 30- April 9, 1971

Congresses of the Third Communist International (Comintern)

1st Congress – March 2-7, 1919
2nd Congress – July 21- August 6, 1920

3rd Congress – June 22-July 12, 1921
4th Congress – November 4- December 5, 1922
5th Congress – June 17-July 8, 1924
6th Congress – July 17-September 1, 1928
7th Congress – July 25-August 20, 1935

Moscow Trials

There were three "open" or "show" trials held in Moscow during the Great Terror. In addition, there was one closed, secret trial of military officers:

1st Moscow Trial [Trial of the Sixteen; Kamenev, Zinoviev, Ter-Vaganian, et al.] – August 19-24, 1936
2nd Moscow Trial [Trial of the Seventeen; Radek, Piatakov, Sokolnikov, et al.] – January 23-30, 1937
Closed Trial of Military Officers [Tukhachevsky, Eideman, Yakir, Uborevich, et al.] – June 1937
3rd Moscow Trial [Trial of the Twenty-One; Bukharin, Rykov, Rakovsky, Krestinsky, et al.] – March 2-13, 1938

Main Participants in the Third Moscow Trial

State Prosecutor: Andrei Vyshinsky

President of the Military Collegium of the Supreme Court of the USSR: Vasily Ulrikh

Defendants:

Right Oppositionists: N. Bukharin & A. Rykov;

Former Left Oppositionists: Kh. Rakovsky (capitulated 1934); N. Krestinsky & A. Rozengolts (broke from Left Opposition in 1926-7);

G. Yagoda, former head of the NKVD; Medical "murderers": Dr. D. Pletnev, Dr. L. Levin, Dr. I. Kazakov; P. Kriuchkov (Gorky's secretary), V. Maksimov-Dikovsky (Kuibyshev's secretary);

Eleven other leading members of the bureaucracy, including People's Commissars, secretaries of republic party organizations, etc: S. Bessonov, P. Bulanov, M. Chernov, G. Grinko, A. Ikramov, V. Ivanov, F. Khodzhaev, V. Sharangovich, I. Zelensky, P. Zubarev.

Endnotes

Note from the editors: *Full translations of several of the articles written by Trotsky that are cited below can be found at the World Socialist Web Site:* http://www.wsws.org/category/feature/archive.shtml

Introduction
1. Tvardovskii A. Poemy, M., 1988, p. 327-330.
2. "Pravda," 17 May 1995.
3. "Pravda," 24 May 1995.
4. Gete, I. V. [Goethe], Izbrannye sochineniia po estestvoznaniiu [Selected Works on Natural Science], 1957, p. 393.
5. "Biulleten' oppozitsii," 1931, № 23, p. 9. [L. D. Trotsky, "Answers to Questions from a Representative of Associated Press America," 14 July 1931].

1. "Mass Operations"
1. "Istoricheskii arkhiv," 1994, № 2, pp. 49-50.
2. "Trud," 4 June 1992.
3. "Istoricheskii arkhiv," 1993, № 4, p. 81.
4. "Trud," 4 June 1992; Reabilitatsiia, p. 13.
5. Soprotivlenie v GULAGe. Vospominaniia. Pis'ma. Dokumenty [Resistance in the GULAG. Memoirs, Letters, Documents], M., 1992, pp. 115, 120, 127.
6. Ibid., p. 119.
7. Khlevniuk O. V. Politburo. Mekhanizmy politicheskoi vlasti v 30-e gody [Politburo. Mechanisms of Political Power in the 1930s], M., 1996, pp.189-191.
8. "Moskovskie novosti," 21 June 1992, p. 19.
9. Kislitsyn S. A. Skazavshie "Net" (Epizody iz istorii politicheskoi bor'by

v sovetskom obshchestve v kontse 20-kh pervoi polovine 30-kh gg.) [Those Who Said "No" (Episodes from the History of Political Struggle in Soviet Society at the End of the 1920s and During the First Half of the 1930s], Rostov-on-the-Don, 1992, p. 62.
10. Soprotivlenie v GULAGe, p. 118.
11. Ibid., p. 119.
12. Tak eto bylo [And So It Was], V. l, M., 1993, p. 86.
13. "Voprosy istorii," 1994, № 4, p. 65.
14. "Daugava," 1989, № 12, pp. 118-119.
15. "Daugava," 1989, № 4-12.
16. Tak eto bylo, V. III, p. 283.
17. Belaia kniga o deportatsii koreiskogo naseleniia v 30-40-e gody [White Book on the Deportation of the Korean Population in the 1930s and 1940s], Book 1, M., 1992, pp. 32-36.
18. "Voprosy istorii," 1994, № 5, p. 141.
19. "Pravda," 23 April 1937.
20. Belaia kniga o deportatsii koreiskogo naseleniia v 30-40-e gody, Book 1, p. 64.
21. "Izvestiia," 10 June 1992.
22. "Voprosy istorii," 1994, № 5, p. 144; Tak eto bylo, V. Ш, p. 277.
23. Так eto bylo, V. I, pp. 87, 96-97.

2. The January Plenum of the Central Committee: "On the Errors of Party Organizations"
1. "Biulleten' oppozitsii," 1938, № 62-63, p. 21 [M. P. T., "Supreme Council of Praetorians"].
2. RTsKhIDNI, 17, op. 2, d. 633, 1. 3-4.
3. Ibid., 1. 32-37.
4. RTsKhIDNI, f. 17, op. 2, d. 634,1. 21-23.
5. KPSS v resoliutsiiakh i resheniiakh..., V. 5, M., 1971, p. 306.
6. RTsKhIDNI, f. 17, op. 2, d. 633,1. 125-126, 132-133.
7. Ibid., 1. 42, 62.
8. Ibid., 1. 65-68.
9. Ibid., 1. 165-166, 184.
10. RTsKhIDNI, f. 17, op. 2, d. 634,1. 166.
11. Ibid., 1. 183.
12. RTsKhIDNI, f. 17, op. 2, d. 636,1. 98-100.
13. RTsKhIDNI, f. 17, op. 2, d. 782,1. 78, 98.
14. KPSS v resoliutsiiakh i resheniiakh..., V. 5, M., 1971, pp. 304-312.

3. The January Plenum of the Central Committee: The Postyshev Affair
1. "Biulleten' oppozitsii," 1937, № 56-57, p. 2 [L. D. Trotsky, "Decapitation

of the Red Army, 17 June 1937].
2. Stalinskoe Politburo v 30-e gody, M., 1995, p. 164.
3. RTsKhIDNI, f. 17, op. 2, d. 640,1. 1-3.
4. "Izvestiia," 10 June 1994.
5. Stalinskoe Politburo v 30-e gody, p. 162.
6. RTsKhIDNI, f. 17, op. 3, d. 994,1. 55.
7. Stalinskoe Politburo v 30-e gody, M., 1995, pp. 160-162.
8. Ibid., p. 164.
9. RTsKhIDNI, f. 17, op. 2, d. 633,1. 171-172, 186.
10. Stalinskoe Politburo v 30-e gody, M., 1995, pp. 166-167.
11. RTsKhIDNI, f. 17, op. 3, d. 995,1. 4.
12. RTsKhIDNI, f. 17, op. 2, d. 640,1. 1-3.

4. Preparation for the Third Show Trial
1. Avtorkhanov A. Tekhnologiia vlasti, M., 1991, p. 310.
2. Orlov A. Tainaia istoriia stalinskikh prestuplenii [The Secret History of Stalin's Crimes], SPb., 1991, p. 282.
3. "Biulleten' oppozitsii," 1939, № 73, p. 15 [L. D. Trotsky, "Behind the Kremlin Walls," 8 January 1938].
4. "Zaria Vostoka [Dawn of the East]," 27 May 1937; "Pravda," 5 June 1937.
5. "Biulleten' oppozitsii," 1937, № 56-57, p. 9 [N. Markin, "The Case of Mdivani-Okudzhava, 1922-1937"].
6. "Pravda," 7 October 1988.
7. Kislitsyn S. A. Skazavshie "Net," pp. 45-56.
8. The Trotsky Archives, Houghton Library, Harvard University (henceforth: Trotsky Archives), № 15865, p. 39.
9. Arkhivy raskryvaiut tainy... [The Archives Reveal Their Secrets...], M., 1991, pp. 240-241.
10. "Istochnik [The Source]," 1994, № 6, p. 95.
11. Rakovskii Kh. "Ne dolzhno byt' nikakoi poshchady!", "Pravda," 21 August 1936.
12. Cherniavskii G. I., Stanchev M. G. V bor'be protiv samovlastiia. Kh. G. Rakovskii v 1927-1941 gg. [In Struggle Against Despotism. Kh. G. Rakovsky in 1927-1941], Khar'kov, 1993, p. 275.
13. Sudebnyi otchet po delu "antisovetskogo pravo-trotskistskogo bloka" [Court Transcript of the Case of the "Anti-Soviet Right-Trotskyist Bloc"], (henceforth: Protsess pravo-trotskistskogo bloka), M., 1938, pp. 282-283.
14. Reabilitatsiia. Politicheskie protsessy 30-50-x godov [Rehabilitation. Political Trials of the 1930s-1950s], M., 1991, p. 239.
15. "Biulleten' oppozitsii," 1938, № 62-63, p. 14 ["Trotsky on Trips Abroad

by Bukharin and Rakovsky"].
16. Protsess pravo-trotskistskogo bloka, pp. 379-380.
17. "Sotsialisticheskii vestnik," 1938, № 5, p. 12.
18. "Biulleten' oppozitsii," 1938, № 65, pp. 11-12 [L. D. Trotsky, "The Defendants Zelensky and Ivanov," 11 March 1938].
19. RTsIKhlDNI, f. 17, op. 3, d. 989, point 39.
20. Protsess pravo-trotskistskogo bloka, p. 687.
21. Bukharin N. I. Tiuremnye tetradi [Prison Notebooks], Vol. I, M., 1996.
22. Bukharin N. I. Vremena [Times], M., 1994.
23. Bukharin N. I. Tiuremnye tetradi [Prison Notebooks], Vol. II, M., 1996.
24. Several of the poems are published in the second volume of *Tiuremnye tetradi*.
25. "Istochnik," 1993, № 0, pp. 23-25.
26. Bukharin N. I. Tiuremnye tetradi, Vol. I, p. 5.

5. The Episode with Krestinsky
1. Protsess pravo-trotskistskogo bloka, pp. 166, 170, 351.
2. Ibid., pp. 37-38.
3. Ibid., pp. 51-52.
4. Ibid., pp. 50, 54, 58.
5. Ibid., p. 53.
6. Ibid., pp. 70, 72.
7. Ibid., pp. 143-144.
8. "Biulleten' oppozitsii," 1938, № 65, p. 13 [L. D. Trotsky, "Corrections and Comments on the Defendants' Testimony," 4 March 1938].
9. Protsess pravo-trotskistskogo bloka, pp. 146.
10. Ibid., pp. 261, 270, 275.
11. Ibid., pp. 268, 277.
12. "Poslednie novosti," 12 March 1938.

6. Bukharin and Vyshinsky
1. Protsess pravo-trotskistskogo bloka, p. 331.
2. Ibid., pp. 334, 335, 358, 369, 374-376.
3. Ibid., pp. 377-378.
4. Ibid., pp. 110-113, 117-118.
5. Ibid., p. 343.
6. Ibid., pp. 342-344, 384.
7. Ibid., pp. 173, 332, 361, 365, 385.
8. Ibid., p. 367.
9. Ibid., p. 124.
10. Ibid., pp. 344-346.
11. Ibid., pp. 340-341.

12. Ibid., pp. 341-342.
13. Ibid., p. 348.
14. Ibid., pp. 74, 81, 163-164, 373, 503, 504.
15. Ibid., pp. 153-154, 355-357.
16. Chuev F. Tak govoril Kaganovich. Ispoved' stalinskogo apostola [Thus Spoke Kaganovich. Confessions of a Stalinist Apostle], M., 1992, p. 138.

7. The "Conspiracy" of 1918
1. "Pravda," 3 January 1924.
2. Stalin I. V. Sochineniia [Works], Vol. 12, pp. 100-101.
3. Trotskii L. D. Prestupleniia Stalina [Stalin's Crimes], M., 1994, p. 270.
4. Trotskii L. D. Portrety revoliutsionerov [Portraits of Revolutionaries], M., 1991, p. 76.
5. Protsess pravo-trotskistskogo bloka, p. 404.
6. Ibid., p. 414.
7. Ibid., pp. 398, 420.
8. Ibid., pp. 338, 421, 685.
9. Ibid., pp. 418, 420, 421.
10. Ibid., p. 429.
11. Ibid., p. 393.
12. Ibid., pp. 393-395, 409-410.
13. Ibid., pp. 404, 684.
14. Ibid., pp. 433-439.
15. Ibid., p. 440.
16. Ibid., pp. 442-445.
17. Ibid., pp. 446, 447.

8. The Mystery of Bukharin
1. Protsess pravo-trotskistskogo bloka, p. 577.
2. Ibid., p. 688.
3. Ibid., p. 681.
4. Ibid., p. 682.
5. Ibid., p. 680.
6. Fedotov G. P. Polnoe sobranie statei v shesti tomakh [Complete Collection of Articles in Six Volumes], Vol. IV, Paris, 1988, pp. 181-182.
7. "Poslednie novosti," 12 March 1938.
8. Sedova N. I. & V. Serge. *The Life and Death of Leon Trotsky*, pp. 238-239.
9. Fedotov G. P. Polnoe sobranie statei, Vol. IV, p. 182.
10. "Ivestiia," 2 September 1992.

9. Yagoda's Orbit
1. "Biulleten' oppozitsii," 1938, № 65, p. 9 [L. D. Trotsky, "The Role of

Genrikh Yagoda," 7 March 1938].
2. "Biulleten' oppozitsii," 1937, № 56-57, pp. 2-3 [L. D. Trotsky, "Decapitation of the Red Army, 17 June 1937].
3. "Biulleten' oppozitsii," 1938, № 65, p. 9 [L. D. Trotsky, "The Role of Genrikh Yagoda," 7 March 1938].
4. Protsess pravo-trotskistskogo bloka, p. 610.
5. Orlov A, Tainaia istoriia stalinskikh prestuplenii, pp. 121-122.
6. Trotskii L. D. Portrety revoliutsionerov, p. 74.
7. "Pravda," 4 April 1937.
8. "Biulleten' oppozitsii," 1938, № 65, p. 9 [L. D. Trotsky, "The Role of Genrikh Yagoda," 7 March 1938].
9. Ibid., p. 10.
10. Trotskii L. D. Portrety revoliutsionerov, pp. 73-74.
11. "Biulleten' oppozitsii," 1938, № 65, p. 12 [L. D. Trotsky, "Stalin and Hitler," 12 March 1938].
12. Protsess pravo-trotskistskogo bloka, pp. 466-469.
13. Ibid., p. 509.

10. Poisonings and Poisoners
1. Trotskii L. D. Prestupleniia Stalina, p. 254.
2. "Biulleten' oppozitsii," 1938, № 65, pp. 10-11 [L. D. Trotsky, "The Incident with Prof. Pletnev," 10 March 1938].
3. Reabilitatsiia, pp. 239-240.
4. "Biulleten' oppozitsii," 1938, № 66-67, p. 29 [Br., "Around the Trial of the Twenty-one"].
5. "Biulleten' oppozitsii," 1938, № 65, pp. 4-5 [L. D. Trotsky, "Results of the Trial," 10 March 1938].
6. Trotskii L. D. Portrety revoliutsionerov, p. 74.
7. Trotskii L. D. Prestupleniia Stalina, p. 306.
8. Povartsov S. Prichina smerti – rasstrel: Khronika poslednikh dnei Isaaka Babelia [Cause of Death – Shooting: The Chronicle of the Last Days of Isaak Babel], M., 1996, p. 109.
9. Trotskii L. D. Portrety revoliutsionerov, p. 75.
10. Protsess pravo-trotskistskogo bloka, pp. 62-63.
11. Ibid., pp. 470, 484, 496, 507, 513.
12. Trotskii L. D. Portrety revoliutsionerov, p. 75.
13. Ibid., pp. 74-75.
14. Trotskii L. D. Prestupleniia Stalina, p. 307.
15. Trotskii L. D. Portrety revoliutsionerov, p. 76.

11. What Was True at the Trial?
1. Protsess pravo-trotskistskogo bloka, pp. 294, 309.

2. Ibid., p. 189.
3. "Poslednie novosti," 12 March 1938.
4. Protsess pravo-trotskistskogo bloka, p. 204.
5. "Biulleten' oppozitsii," 1938, № 65, p. 13 [L. D. Trotsky, "Corrections and Comments on the Defendants' Testimony," 4 March 1938].
6. Trotskii L. D. Prestupleniia Stalina, p. 259.
7. Protsess pravo-trotskistskogo bloka, p. 516.
8. Ibid., p. 455.
9. Ibid., p. 494.
10. Reabilitatsiia, p. 238.
11. Protsess pravo-trotskistskogo bloka, pp. 546-547.
12. Ibid., pp. 85-86.
13. Ibid., p. 147.
14. Ibid., pp. 129-130.
15. Ibid., p. 484.
16. Fedotov G. P. Polnoe sobranie statei, Vol. IV, pp. 182-183.
17. Sedova N. & V. Serge. *The Life and Death of Leon Trotsky,* pp. 233-235.
18. Protsess pravo-trotskistskogo bloka, pp. 310, 315.
19. Ibid., pp. 47,61.
20. Broué P. "Party Opposition to Stalin (1930-1932) and the First Moscow Trial," In: *Essays on Revolutionary Culture and Stalinism*, Slavica Publishers, 1986, p. 108.

12. The Main Defendant
1. Orlov A. Tainaia istoriia stalinskikh prestuplenii, SPb., 1991, pp. 264-265.
2. "Sotsialisticheskii vestnik," 1937, № 3, p. 3.
3. Trotskii L. D. Prestupleniia Stalina, p. 248.
4. "Biulleten' oppozitsii," 1938, № 65, p. 4 [L. D. Trotsky, "Results of the Trial," 10 March 1938].
5. Protsess pravo-trotskistskogo bloka, p. 276.
6. Ibid., p. 238.
7. Ibid., p. 240.
8. Ibid., pp.234-235.
9. Ibid., p. 56.
10. Ibid., pp. 501, 506.
11. Sedova N. & V. Serge. *The Life and Death of Leon Trotsky*, p. 232.
12. Protsess pravo-trotskistskogo bloka, p. 61.
13. Ibid., p. 250.
14. Ibid., p. 63.

13. The Trial's Domestic Political Goals

1. "Biulleten' oppozitsii," 1938, № 66-67, p. 19 [L. D. Trotsky, "Does the Soviet Government Still Follow the Principles Adopted Twenty Years Ago?"].
2. Protsess pravo-trotskistskogo bloka, p. 116.
3. Ibid., p. 97.
4. Ibid., pp. 188-189.
5. Ibid., pp. 295, 298-299.
6. Orlov A. Tainaia istoriia stalinskikh prestuplenii, p. 270.
7. Protsess pravo-trotskistskogo bloka, pp. 296-298.
8. Ibid., p. 595.
9. "Izvestiia," 9 March 1938.

14. Foreign Policy Goals of the Moscow Trials
1. Cited in: Trotskii L. D. Portrety revoliutsionerov, p. 158.
2. "Pravda," 2 June 1931.
3. "Izvestiia," 4 March 1933.
4. "Biulleten' oppozitsii," 1938, № 65, p. 5 [L. D. Trotsky, "Moscow's Diplomatic Plans in the Mirror of the Trial," 8 March 1938].
5. Protsess pravo-trotskistskogo bloka, pp. 59-60, 63.
6. "Biulleten' oppozitsii," 1938, № 65, pp. 6-7 [L. D. Trotsky, "Moscow's Diplomatic Plans in the Mirror of the Trial," 8 March 1938].

15. The General Prosecutor
1. Orlov A. Tainaia istoriia stalinskikh prestuplenii, p. 300.
2. Ibid., p. 297.
3. Strogovich M. S. Ugolovnyi protsess [The Criminal Trial], M., 1936, p. 44.
4. Bol'shaia Sovetskaia Entsiklopediia, Vol. 23, M., 1931, column 31.
5. Ibid., Vol. 47, M., 1940, column 13.
6. Protsess pravo-trotskistskogo bloka, p. 612.
7. "Biulleten' oppozitsii," 1937, № 54-55, p. 4 ["Trotsky on the Trial (Speech to American Workers)" 9 February 1937].*
8. "Biulleten' oppozitsii," 1938, № 65, p. 3 [L. D. Trotsky, "Results of the Trial," 10 March 1938].
9. Orlov A. Tainaia istoriia stalinskikhprestuplenii, pp. 295-296.
10. Protsess pravo-trotskistskogo bloka, p. 269.
11. Orlov A. Tainaia istoriia stalinskikh prestuplenii, p. 294.
12. Ibid., p. 300.
13. Trifonov Iu. Sobranie sochinenii, Vol. 4, M., 1987, pp. 23-24.
14. Reabilitirovan posmertno [Posthumously Rehabilitated], M., 1988, pp.

---

* Later published as a pamphlet with the title "I Stake My Life."

23-24.
15. Trifonov Iu. Sobranie sochinenii, Vol. 4, M., 1987, p. 24.
16. Vaksberg A. Tsaritsa dokazatel'stv. Vyshinskii i ego zhertvy, M., 1992, pp. 100-105.

16. The Sentence
1. Gnedin E. Vykhod iz labirinta [Escape from the Labyrinth], M., 1994, pp. 36-37.
2. Avdeenko A. Nakazanie bez prestupleniia [Punishment Without a Crime], M., 1991, pp. 189-190.
3. "Pravda," 3 March 1938.
4. "Pravda," 6 March 1938.
5. Protsess pravo-trotskistskogo bloka, p. 551.
6. Ibid., p. 654.
7. Ibid., p. 642.
8. Ibid., pp. 674-676.
9. Ibid., pp. 671,674.
10. Reabilitatsiia, p. 240.

17. International Response to the Trial
1. Ponomarev B. N. The Plot Against the Soviet Union and World Peace, M., 1938 (this pamphlet was also published in German, French, and Spanish).
2. Cf. Buber-Neiman, M. Mirovaia revoliutsiia i stalinskii rezhim, M., 1995, pp. 246-247.
3. "Literaturnaia gazeta," 14 September 1988.
4. Cf. "Inostrannaia literatura," 1988, № 4, p. 166.
5. Cherniavskii G. I., Stanchev M. G. V bor'be protiv samovlastiia, Khar'kov, 1993, pp. 304-305.
6. "Sotsialisticheskii vestnik," 1938, № 5, p. 9.
7. Ibid., pp. 9-10.
8. Ibid., p. 11.
9. Ibid., pp. 10-11.
10. Ibid., p. 8.
11. "Biulleten' oppozitsii," 1938, № 65, p. 3 [L. D. Trotsky, "Results of the Trial," 10 March 1938].
12. "Sotsialisticheskii vestnik," 1938, № 5, p. 9.
13. Ibid., pp. 6-7.
14. Dan F. "Novaia boinia v Moskve. U poslednei cherty," "Sotsialisticheskii vestnik," 1938, № 5, p. 4.
15. Fedotov G. P. Polnoe sobranie statei v shesti tomakh, vol. IV, p. 185.
16. Ibid., p. 180.

17. Cf.: Cherniavskii G. I., Stanchev M. G. V bor'be protiv samovlastiia, p. 286.
18. Cf.: "Biulleten' oppozitsii," 1938, № 65, p. 7 [L. D. Trotsky, "Stalin's Article on World Revolution and the Current Trial," 9 March 1938].
19. "Biulleten' oppozitsii," 1937, № 58-59, pp. 1-2 [(Unsigned), "Beginning of the End"].

18. Trotsky on the Moscow Trials
1. Trotskii L. D. Prestupleniia Stalina, p. 249.
2. "Biulleten' oppozitsii," 1938, № 65, p. 1 [L. D. Trotsky, "Cain-Dzhugashvili Goes All the Way"].
3. "Biulleten' oppozitsii," 1938, № 64, p. 14 [L. D. Trotsky, "Moscow Trial of the Twenty-One. New Reprisals," 28 February 1938].
4. "Biulleten' oppozitsii," 1938, № 65, p. 3 [L. D. Trotsky, "Results of the Trial," 10 March 1938].
5. Ibid., p. 4.
6. Trotskii L. D. Prestupleniia Stalina, p. 255.
7. Trotskii L. D. Stalin, vol. II, M., 1990, p. 268.
8. "Biulleten' oppozitsii," 1938, № 65, p. 12 [L. D. Trotsky, "Stalin and Hitler," 12 March 1938].
9. Trotskii L. D. Stalin, vol. II, p. 203.
10. "Biulleten' oppozitsii," 1938, № 65, p. 8 [L. D. Trotsky, "Stalin's Article on World Revolution and the Current Trial," 9 March 1938].
11. Ibid., p. 12.
12. "Biulleten' oppozitsii," 1938, № 68-69, p. 3 [(Unsigned), "Totalitarian Defeatists"].
13. Trotskii L. D. Stalin, vol. II, p. 274.
14. "Biulleten' oppozitsii," 1937, № 58-59, p. 1 ["Beginning of the End"].
15. Ibid.
16. "Biulleten' oppozitsii," 1938, № 65, p. 5 [L. D. Trotsky, "Results of the Trial," 10 March 1938].

19. Historical Fate of the Moscow Trials
1. Reabilitatsiia, p. 27.
2. Ibid., p. 24.
3. "Istoricheskii arkhiv," 1994, № 2, p. 41.
4. Shelestov D. Vremia Alekseia Rykova [The Time of Aleksei Rykov], M., 1990, p. 296.
5. "Voprosy istorii," 1990, № 5, pp. 56-57.
6. Ibid., p. 56.
7. "Voprosy istorii," 1991, № 12, pp. 63.
8. Datt R. Palm. Problemy sovremennoi istorii [Problems of Modern

History], M., 1965, p. 46.
9. Vsesoiuznoe soveshchanie o merakh uluchsheniia podgotovki nauchno-pedagogicheskikh kadrov po istoricheskim naukam. Moskva. 1962 [All-Union Conference on Measures to Improve the Preparation of Research and Teaching Cadres in the Historical Sciences. Moscow. 1962], M., 1964, p. 298.
10. Pospelov P. "Bor'ba Bukharina i Rykova protiv Lenina i partii (Istoricheskii obzor) [The Struggle of Bukharin and Rykov against Lenin and the Party (A Historical Overview)]," "Pravda," 13 March 1937.
11. "Biulleten' oppozitsii," 1937, № 58-59, p. 4 ["Beginning of the End"].
12. "Biulleten' oppozitsii," 1938, № 65, p. 2 [L. D. Trotsky, "Cain-Dzhugashvili Goes All the Way"].
13. "Biulleten' oppozitsii," 1937, № 58-59, p. 4 ["Beginning of the End"].
14. Kosolapov R. Slovo tovarishchu Stalinu [Comrade Stalin Has the Floor], M., 1995, p. 313.
15. Ibid., p. 311.
16. Kosolapov R. "'Ottepel'' dala rasputitsu [The Thaw Made the Roads Impassable]," "Pravda Rossii," 15 February 1996.

20. Stalin and His Intimate Circle
1. "Pravda," 28 October 1938.
2. "Izvestiia," 10 June 1992.
3. Trotskii L. D. Stalin, vol. II, p. 265.
4. Chuev F. Sto sorok besed s Molotovym. M., 1991, p. 424.
5. Stalinskoe Politburo v 1930-e gody, p. 55.
6. "Istoricheskii arkhiv," 1994, № 6; 1995, № 2-6.
7. Khlevniuk O. V. Politburo. Mekhanizmy politicheskoi vlasti v 30-e gody, p. 291.
8. "Voprosy istorii KPSS," 1964, № 2, p. 19.
9. "Istoricheskii arkhiv," 1993, № 3, p. 88.
10. Reabilitatsiia, p. 258.
11. XXII s"ezd Kommunisticheskoi partii Sovetskogo Soiuza. Stenograficheskii otchet, M., 1962, vol III, p. 152.
12. Reabilitatsiia, pp. 13, 39; "Istochnik," 1995, №1, p. 124.
13. Volkogonov D. A. Triumf i tragediia, Book I, M., 1991, p. 522.
14. "Izvestiia," 10 June 1992.
15. "Krasnoiarskii rabochii," 8-10 September, 20 December 1937.
16. "Izvestiia," 10 June 1992.
17. Barmin A. "Otryvki iz vospominanii," Trotsky Archive, № 15865, p. 53.
18. Trotskii L. D. Stalin, vol. II, pp. 203-204.
19. Ibid., p. 201.
20. "Istoricheskii arkhiv," 1993, №6, p. 50.

21. "Voprosy istorii," 1990, № 4, pp. 70-71.

20.1 Molotov
1. XXII s"ezd Kommunisticheskoi partii Sovetskogo Soiuza, vol. II, p. 404.
2. "Voprosy istorii," 1992, № 2-3, p. 82.
3. Plenum TsKKPSS 10-15 fevralia 1964 g. Stenograficheskii otchet, M., 1964, p. 548.
4. Chuev F. Sto sorok besed s Molotovym, p. 415.
5. Ibid., p. 410.
6. Ibid., pp. 410-411.
7. Ibid., 422-423.
8. Ibid., pp. 414-415.
9. "Istoricheskii arkhiv," 1994, № 1, p. 67.
10. Larina A. M. Nezabyvaemoe, M., 1989, p. 300.
11. "Istoricheskii arkhiv," 1993, № 3, p. 85.
12. Ibid., p. 87.
13. Molotov V. M. K dvadtsaliletiiu Oktiabr'skoi revoliutsii. Doklad na torzhestvennom zasedanii v Bol'shom teatre 6 noiabria 1937 goda, M, 1937, p. 38.
14. Chuev F. Sto sorok besed s Molotovym, p. 428.
15. Ibid., p. 356.
16. Ibid., pp. 428-430.
17. Ibid., p. 400.
18. Ibid., p. 401.
19. Ibid., pp. 206-207.
20. Ibid., pp. 301-302.
21. Ibid., p. 401.
22. "Voprosy istorii," 1993, № 8, p. 80.
23. Chuev F. Sto sorok besed s Molotovym, p. 416.
24. Ibid., p. 407.
25. Ibid., p. 402.
26. "Marksist," 1994, № 2, pp. 113-115.
27. "Pravda," 1995, № 12, p. 9.

20.2 Kaganovich
1. "Istoricheskii arkhiv," 1993, № 3, p. 77.
2. "Istoricheskii arkhiv," 1994, № 1, pp. 20-21.
3. "Sovetskoe gosudarstvo i revoliutsiia prava," 1930, № 1, p. 9.
4. "Voprosy istorii," 1990, № 5, pp. 53-54; 1995, № 1, p. 11.
5. "Voprosy istorii KPSS," 1989, № 5, pp. 99-101.
6. Ibid., p. 99.
7. "Istoricheskii arkhiv," 1994, № 1, p. 10.

Endnotes

8. Ibid., p. 8.
9. "Moskovskaia pravda," 10 January 1989.
10. "Istoricheskii arkhiv," 1993, № 4, p. 51.
11. "Moskovskaia pravda," 10 January 1989.
12. "Voprosy istorii," 1990, № 4, p. 70.
13. Medvedev R. Oni okruzhali Stalina, M., 1990, p. 140.
14. Shreider M. B. NKVD iznutri [The NKVD from Within], pp. 64-65.
15. XXII s"ezd Kommunisticheskoi partii Sovetskogo Soiuza, vol. Ш, p.153.
16. "Moskva," 1964, № 6, pp. 49-50.
17. Shreider M. B. NKVD iznutri, pp. 68-69.
18. "Moskovskaia pravda," 10 January 1989.
19. "Voprosy istorii," 1995, № 1, pp. 8-9.
20. "Voprosy istorii KPSS," 1989, № 5, p. 102.
21. Chuev F. Так govoril Kaganovich, p. 193.
22. Ibid., p. 27.
23. Ibid., pp. 89, 105.
24. Ibid., pp. 138- 139.
25. "Istoricheskii arkhiv," 1994, № 1, p. 68.

20.3 Voroshilov
1. Trotskii L. D. Stalin, vol. II, p. 276.
2. "Voprosy istorii," 1991, № 6, p. 28.
3. Oni ne molchali, M., 1991, p. 377.
4. Reabilitatsiia, p. 299; "Voprosy istorii," 1991, № 6, pp. 28-29.
5. "Kommunist," 1990, № 17, p. 70.
6. Ibid.
7. Oni ne molchali, p. 380.
8. "Voprosy istorii," 1991, № 6, p. 29.
9. "Istoricheskii arkhiv," 1993, № 3, p. 87.
10. "Voprosy istorii," 1990, № 7, p. 104.
11. "Istoricheskii arkhiv," 1994, № 1, p. 18.
12. "Istoricheskii arkhiv," 1993, № 3, p. 88.
13. "Istoricheskii arkhiv," 1993, № 6, p. 71.
14. Yan Gamarnik, M., 1978, p. 130.

20.4 Mikoyan
1. Medvedev R. A. Oni okruzhali Stalina, p. 183.
2. "Pravda," 21 December 1937.
3. XXII s"ezd Kommunisticheskoi partii Sovetskogo Soiuza, vol. II, p. 213.
4. XX s"ezd Kommunisticheskoi partii Sovetskogo Soiuza, M., 1956, vol. I, p. 302.
5. Ibid., p. 325.

6. Ibid., p. 326.

20.5 Andreev
1. "Istochnik," 1994, № 3, p. 74.
2. "Voprosy istorii," 1990, № 4, p. 78.
3. "Znamia," 1989, №6, p. 95.
4. Ibid., p. 75.
5. Reabilitatsiia, pp. 55-56.

20.6 Kalinin
1. Nekrasov V. F. Trinadtsadt' "zheleznykh" narkomov, M., 1995, pp. 200-201.
2. Larina A. M. Nezabyvaemoe, pp. 224-225.

20.7 Zhdanov
1. "Voprosy istorii," 1988, № 9, p. 126.
2. "Pravda," 22 January 1938.
3. Yakovlev A. Tsel' zhizni, M., 1969, p. 509.

20.8 Khrushchev
1. "Voprosy istorii," 1993, № 8, p. 80.
2. "Voprosy istorii," 1991, № 12, pp. 62-63.
3. "Voprosy istorii," № 5, p. 64.
4. Ibid., p. 58.
5. Ibid., pp. 47,51.
6. Ibid., p. 61.
7. "Pravda-5," 1995, № 25, p. 11.
8. "Voprosy istorii," 1990, № 5, p. 63.
9. "Voprosy istorii," 1992, № 2-3, pp. 86-87.
10. "Voprosy istorii," 1990, № 5, pp. 48-49.
11. Khlevniuk O. V. 1937-i. Stalin, NKVD i sovetskoe obshchestvo, M., 1992, p.225.

20.9 Beria
1. Erenburg I. Sobranie sochinenii v deviati tomakh, vol 9, M., 1967, p. 183.
2. Beriia: konets kar'ery, M., 1991, p. 367.
3. Ibid., pp. 378-379.
4. Ibid., p.374.
5. Ibid., p. 316.
6. "Voprosy istorii," 1990, № 6, p. 86.

20.10 Malenkov

1. XXII s"ezd Kommunisticheskoi partii Sovetskogo Soiuza, vol. I, p. 291.
2. Ibid., vol. II, p. 214.
3. "Istoricheskii arkhiv," 1993, № 3, p. 23.
4. Ibid., p. 22.

20.11 Mekhlis
1. "Biulleten' oppozitsii," 1938, № 62-63, p. 23 [S., "Voroshilov is Next in Line"].
2. Mikhail Kol'tsov kakim on byl [Mikhail Koltsov as He Was], M., 1989, pp. 100-102.

20.12 Shkiriatov
1. "Istoricheskii arkhiv," 1993, № 6, p. 13.
2. Medvedev R. A. Oni okruzhali Stalina, p. 187.

* * *

22. "Biulleten' oppozitsii," 1933, № 33, p. 2 [L. D. Trotsky, "Alarm Signal," 3 March 1933].
23. "Izvestiia TsK KPSS," 1991, № 1, pp. 150, 154.

21. In the Bowels of the Politburo
1. "Oktiabr'," 1992, № 8, pp. 158-159.
2. Reabilitatsiia, p. 39.
3. Khlevniuk O. V, Politburo. Mekhanizmy politicheskoi vlasti v 30-e gody, p. 240.
4. Stalinskoe Politburo v 30-e gody, pp. 167-168.
5. "Voprosy istorii," 1992, № 2-3, p. 86.
6. Reabilitatsiia, pp. 36, 37.
7. "Voprosy istorii," 1990, № 3, p. 79.

22. Liquidation of the Central Committee
1. KPSS v rezoliutsiiakh i resheniiakh, vol. 2, M., 1970, pp. 220-221.
2. Lenin V. I. Poln. sobr. soch., vol. 43, p. 108.
3. Chuev F. Sto sorok besed s Molotovym, p. 463.
4. "Izvestiia TsK KPSS," 1989, № 12, p. 87.
5. Binevich A., Serebrianskii Z. Andrei Bubnov, M., 1964, pp. 78-79.
6. Stalinskoe Politburo v 30-e gody, pp. 157-158.
7. RTsKhIDNI, f. 17, op. 2, d. 630, 1.4.
8. Ibid., 1.51.
9. RTsKhIDNI, f. 17, op. 2, d. 640, 1.104.
10. "Voprosy istorii," 1995, № 4, p. 144.
11. "Izvestiia TsK KPSS," 1989, № 12, p. 86.

12. Reabilitatsiia, p. 83.
13. "Istoricheskii arkhiv," 1993, № 4, p. 70.
14. "Voprosy istorii," 1990, № 3, p. 70.
15. Avdeenko A. Nakazanie bez prestupleniia, pp. 171-172.
16. Ibid., pp. 182-183.
17. Ibid., p. 183.
18. Shreider M. B. NKVD iznutri, pp. 109-110, 172-174.
19. "Oktiabr'," 1992, № 8, pp. 158-159.

23. The Party Apparatus
1. "Voprosy istorii," 1990, № 4, pp. 65-66.
2. "Voprosy istorii," 1992, № 2-3, p. 86.
3. "Voprosy istorii," 1990, № 6, p. 81.
4. "Voprosy istorii," 1990, № 5, p. 52.
5. Trotskii L. D. Dnevniki i pis'ma, M., 1994, p. 154.
6. "Biulleten' oppozitsii," 1938, № 68-69, p. 4 [(Unsigned), "Totalitarian Defeatists"].
7. "Biulleten' oppozitsii," 1938, № 66-67, p. 21 [L. D. Trotsky, "Does the Soviet Government Still Follow the Principles Adopted Twenty Years Ago?"].
8. Orlov A. Tainaia istoriia stalinskikh prestuplenii, pp. 140-141.
9. "Kazennyi optimizm," "Pravda," 5 January 1937.
10. "Pravda," 29 March 1937.
11. "Oktiabr'," 1994, № 11, p. 159.
12. Trotskii L. D. Prestupleniia Stalina, pp. 251-252.
13. "Biulleten' oppozitsii," 1938, № 62-63, p. 5 [L. D. Trotsky, "Replies to Journalists' Questions About the Verdict of the International Commission," 13 December 1937].
14. Trotskii, L. D. Dnevniki i pis'ma, p. 154.
15. "Biulleten' oppozitsii," 1938, № 62-63, pp. 20-21 [M. P. T., "Supreme Council of Praetorians"].
16. "Biulleten' oppozitsii," 1938, № 70, pp. 11-13 [P. T., "The Loyalty of Stalin's Cadres"].
17. "Istoricheskii arkhiv," 1994, № 2, p. 40.
18. "Ogonek," 1989, № 28, p. 31.
19. "Biulleten' oppozitsii," 1938, № 65, p. 2 ["New Non-Returners"].
20. "Biulleten' oppozitsii," 1937, № 60-61, p. 5 [L. D. Trotsky, "A Tragic Lesson," 21 September 1937].
21. "Biulleten' oppozitsii," 1938, № 65, p. 2 ["New Non-Returners"].

24. The Army
1. Trotskii, L. D, Stalin, vol. II, p. 211.

2. Ibid., p. 250.
3. Ibid., p. 210.
4. Petrov, Iu. Partiinoe stroitel'stvo v Sovetskoi Armii i Flote, M., 1964, p. 312.
5. Trotsky Archive, № 15865, p. 12.
6. Reabilitatsiia, p. 299.
7. "Voprosy istorii," 1991, № 6, pp. 29, 30.
8. Reabilitatsiia, p. 299.
9. "Voprosy istorii KPSS," 1991, № 6, p. 23.
10. "Izvestiia TsK KPSS," 1990, № 1, p. 188.
11. "Voprosy istorii," № 6, p. 30.
12. "Kommunist," 1990, № 17, p. 73.
13. "Znamia,"1989, № 10, p. 41.
14. "Kommunist," 1990, № 17, p. 75.
15. Oni ne molchali, p. 379.
16. Samsonov A. M. Znat' i pomnit', M., 1988, pp. 281-282.
17. Reabilitatsiia, pp. 300-301.
18. Velikaia Otechestvennaia voina. 1941-1945. Kratkaia istoriia, M., 1965, pp. 39-40.
19. Samsonov A. M. Znat' i pomnit', p. 316.
20. Trotskii L. D. Stalin, Vol. II, p. 273.
21. "Izvestiia TsK KPSS," 1990, № 3, p. 193.
22. Reabilitatsiia, p. 302.
23. "Argumenty i fakty," 1995, № 41.
24. "Izvestiia TsK KPSS," 1989, № 4, p. 80.
25. Trotskii L. D. Stalin, Vol. II, p. 278.
26. "Izvestiia," 8 May 1992.
27. Oni ne molchali, p. 377.
28. "Izvestiia," 8 May 1992.
29. "Pravda," 20 June 1988.
30. "Znamia," 1989, № 10, p. 41.
31. Velikaia Otechestvennaia voina. 1941-1945. Kratkaia istoriia, p. 40.
32. "Argumenty i fakty," 1995, № 41.
33. Velikaia Otechestvennaia voina. 1941-1945. Kratkaia istoriia, p. 40.
34. "Voprosy istorii KPSS," 1990, № 5, p. 31.
35. "Biulleten' oppozitsii," 1938, № 68-69, p. 4 ["Totalitarian Defeatists"].
36. "Voenno-istoricheskii zhurnal," 1987, № 9, p.50.
37. Cited in: "Komsomol'skaia pravda," 22 June 1990.
38. Cited in: "Novaia Rosiia," Paris, 1938, № 57, pp. 13-14.
39. Trepper L. "Bol'shaia igra," M., 1990, p. 69.
40. "Kommunist," 1988, № 9, p. 88.
41. Otkroveniia i priznaniia. Natsistskaia verkhushka o voine «tret'ego

reikha» protiv SSSR, M., 1996, p. 306.
42. Ibid., p. 101.
43. Gal'der F, Voennyi dnevnik, Vol. II, M., 1969, p. 504.
44. "Izvestiia," 8 May 1990.
45. "Voprosy istorii," 1991, № 9-10, p. 72.

25. The NKVD
1. Oni ne molchali, p. 217.
2. Trotsky Archives, № 17106.
3. Orlov A, Tainaia istoriia stalinskikh prestuplenii, p. 306.
4. Ibid., p. 309.
5. "Pravda," 29 April 1988.
6. Reabilitatsiia, p. 41; "Voprosy istorii," 1990, № 4, p. 72.
7. Shreider M. B. NKVD iznutri, p. 37.
8. Reabilitatsiia, pp. 40-41.
9. Inogo ne dano, M., 1989, pp. 561-562.
10. "Voprosy istorii," 1990, № 6, p. 81.
11. Beriia: konets kar'ery, p. 317.
12. Reabilitatsiia, p. 249.
13. Soprotivlenie v GULAGe, pp. 119-120.
14. "Voprosy filosofii," 1988, № 12, p. 93.
15. "Sotsialisticheskaia industriia," 22 March 1989.
16. "Voprosy istorii," 1990, № 6, p. 91.
17. "Voprosy istorii," 1990, № 2, p. 104.
18. Sobranie zakonov i postanovlenii Pravitel'stva SSSR, 1937, № 66, p. 297.
19. Oni ne molchali, p. 216.
20. RTsKhIDNI, f.17, op. 3, d. 986,1. 24.
21. "Izvestiia TsK KPSS," 1989, № 10, pp. 81-82.
22. "Kommunist," 1990, № 10, p. 107.
23. Reabilitirovan posmertno, M., 1988, pp. 415-416.
24. Reabilitatsiia, pp. 37-38.
25. "Nedelia," 1990, № 20, p. 11.

26. The Komsomol
1. "Obshchestvennye nauki," 1989, № 6, p. 146.
2. "Komsomol'skaia pravda," 18 July 1929.
3. Kosarev A. Za bol'shevistskie tempy plius kachestvo. Doklad i zakliuchitel'noe slovo na IX Vsesoiuznom s"ezde VLKSM., M., 1931, p. 21.
4. Trushchenko N. Kosarev, M., 1988, p. 366.
5. Kosarev A. O perestroike raboty komsomola, M., 1935, pp. 23-24.
6. Oni ne molchali, p. 324.
7. "Ogonek," 1987, № 7, p. 27.

Endnotes

8. "Komsomol'skaia pravda," 16 June 1989.
9. "Pravda," 29 August 1937.
10. "Voprosy istorii," 1990, № 11, p. 139.
11. "Obshchestvennye nauki," 1989, № 6, p. 144.
12. "Izvestiia TsK VLKSM," 1937, № 10, p. 10.
13. "Molodoi kommunist," 1990, № 6, p. 66.
14. "Komsomol'skaia pravda," 30 October 1938.
15. "Obshchestvennye nauki," 1989, № 6, pp. 146-147; "Komsomol'skaia pravda," 16 June 1989.
16. Reabilitirovan posmertno, p. 251.
17. "Istoricheskii arkhiv," 1993, № 5, p. 77.
18. "Voprosy istorii KPSS," 1989, № 5, p. 101; Reabilitatsiia, p. 84.

27. The Non-Party Intelligentsia
1. Chukovskii, K. Dnevnik. 1930-1969, M., 1994, p. 9.
2. Ibid., p. 141.
3. "Literaturnaia gazeta," 26 January, 1 February 1937.
4. "Pravda," 28 January 1937.
5. "Pravda," 25 January 1937.
6. "Oktiabr'," 1994, № 11, p. 162.
7. Erenburg I. Sobranie sochinenii, Vol. 9, p. 182.
8. "Iunost'," 1989, № 8, p. 40.
9. Kaverin V. Sobranie sochinenii, Vol. 6, M., 1966, p. 269.
10. Erenburg I. Sobranie sochinenii, Vol. 9, p. 189.
11. Ibid., pp. 732, 735, 737.
12. KPSS v rezoliutsiiakh i resheniiahh...., Vol. 9, M., 1986, p. 120.
13. Erenburg I. Sobranie sochinenii, Vol. 9, p. 189.
14. "Sovershenno sekretno," 1990, № 8, pp. 11-12.
15. Tragicheskie sud'by: repressirovannye uchenye Akademii Nauk SSSR, M., 1995, p. 38.
16. Povartsov S. Prichina smerti – rasstrel, pp. 85-86.
17. Ibid., pp. 52, 60.
18. Ibid., p. 69.
19. Ibid., p. 82.
20. Ibid., pp. 97-98, 102.
21. Ibid., p. 145.
22. Suvarin B. "Poslednie ragovory s Babelem," "Kontinent," 1980, № 23, p. 352.
23. Povartsov S. Prichina smerti – rasstrel, pp. 128, 157.
24. Shentalinskii V. Raby svobody: V literaturnykh arkhivakh KGB, M., 1995, p. 200.

28. The People
1. Erenburg I. Sobranie sochinenii, Vol. 9, p. 189.
2. "Iunost'," 1989, № 8, pp. 37-39.
3. Told to the author by D. B. Dobrushkin.
4. Panferov F. Bruski, Vol. IV, M., 1937, pp. 110, 114.
5. Ibid., p. 124.
6. "Druzhba narodov," 1989, № 7, pp. 60-61.
7. RTsKhIDNI, f. 17, op. 3, d. 1002, l. 57.
8. RTsKhIDNI, f. 17, op. 3, d. 977, l. 49-50; d. 933, l. 88-90; d. 944, l. 11; d. 995, l. 32.
9. "Biulleten' oppozitsii," 1937, № 58-59, p. 3 ["Beginning of the End"].
10. Iskander F. "Staryi dom pod kiparisom," "Znamia," 1987, № 7, pp. 71-72.

29. The Great Purge as Seen by Enemies of Soviet Power
1. Ioffe N. A. Vremia nazad, M., 1992, p. 160.
2. Adamova-Sliozberg O. Put', M., 1993, p. 175.
3. Larina A. M. Nezabyvaemoe, p. 142.
4. "Ogonek," 1988, № 27, p. 6.
5. Adamova-Sliozberg O. Put', p. 82.
6. Rybakov A. Strakh (Tridtsat' piatyi i drugie gody), Book 2, M., 1991, p. 279.
7. Zemskov V. N. "GULAG. Istoriko-sotsiologicheskii aspekt," "Sotsiologicheskie issledovaniia," 1991, № 6, p. 20.

30. The Great Purge as Seen by Russian Émigrés
1. "Nash soiuz," Paris, 1937, № 3-4, p. 17.
2. Rezhim lichnoi vlasti Stalina. K istorii formirovaniia, M., 1989, p. 88.
3. "Tret'ia Rossiia," Paris, 1936, № 7, p. 35.
4. "Tret'ia Rossiia," Paris, 1938, № 8, p. 44.
5. "Poslednie novosti," 9 November 1937.
6. Fedotov G. P. Polnoe sobranie statei, Vol. IV, pp. 188-189.
7. Ibid., p. 178.
8. "Po Rossii," "Sotsialisticheskii vestnik," 1937, № 7-8, pp. 21-22.
9. "Sotsialisticheskii vestnik," 1937, № 11, p. 14.
10. "Sotsialisticheskii vestnik," 1937, № 1-2, p. 16.
11. "Sotsialisticheskii vestnik," 1937, № 4, p. 5.
12. "Sotsialisticheskii vestnik," 1937, № 3, pp. 2-3.
13. "Sotsialisticheskii vestnik," 1938, № 5, p. 13.
14. Ibid., pp. 7-8.

31. The Great Purge as Seen by Communists
1. Adamova-Sliozberg O. Put', p. 183.

2. "Neva," 1990, № 5, pp. 173-176.
3. Efimov I. I. Ne sotvori sebe kumira, L., 1990, p. 161.
4. Ibid., pp. 117-118.
5. Ginzburg E. Krutoi marshrut, M., 1990, p. 50.
6. XXII s"ezd Kommunisticheskoi partii Sovetskogo Soiuza, Vol. III, p. 120.
7. "Pravda," 7 November 1938.
8. Mikhail Kol'tsov kakim on byl, p. 103.
9. Ibid., p. 104.
10. Ibid., p. 100.
11. "Biulleten' oppozitsii," 1937, № 60-61, p. 21 [].
12. "Znamia," 1989, № 5, p. 55.
13. Baklanov G. Voennye povesti, M., 1986, pp. 258-260.
14. "Biulleten' oppozitsii," 1938, № 65, p. 2 [].
15. "Biulleten' oppozitsii," 1937, № 58-59, p. 3 [].
16. Maiakovskii V. V. Polnoe sobranie sochinenii, Vol. 6, M., 1934, p. 19.
17. Rybakov A. Strakh, Book 2, M., 1991, p. 235.
18. Baklanov G. Voennye povesti, pp. 201-203.
19. "Voprosy istorii," 1990, № 5, p. 50.
20. Erenburg I. Sobranie sochinenii, Vol. 9, p. 194.
21. "Ogonek," 1991, № 2, p. 21.
22. "Novyi mir," 1990, № 8, pp. 56-57.
23. Fil'shtinskii I. My shagaem pod konvoem, M., 1994, pp. 122-123.
24. Ibid., pp. 128-130.
25. Cited from: Medvedev R. A. O Staline i stalinizme, M., 1990, p. 339.
26. Gnedin E. A. Katastrofa i votoroe rozhdenie, Amsterdam, 1977, p. 104.
27. "Druzhba narodov," 1990, № 2, p. 35.
28. Adamova-Sliozberg O. Put', p. 117.
29. Golosa istorii, Issue 22, Book 1, M., 1990, p. 219.
30. Ibid., pp. 220-221.
31. Ibid., p. 222.

32. Was Anyone Guilty?

1. "Daugava," 1989, № 10, p. 78.
2. Ibid., p. 88.
3. Ibid., pp. 91-94.
4. "Izvestiia TsK KPSS," 1991, № 3, pp. 140-147.
5. Beriia: konets kar'ery, pp. 389-390.
6. Ibid., pp. 378-379.
7. Vaksberg A. Neraskrytye tainy, M., 1993, pp. 192-193.
8. "Rodina," 1995, № 2, p. 87.
9. "Kommunist," 1990, № 17, pp. 80-82.

10. Zven'ia. Istoricheskii almanakh, Book I, M., 1991, p. 509.
11. Ibid., p. 515.
12. Ibid., p. 508.
13. Ibid., pp. 517-520.
14. Ibid., pp. 510-511.
15. Ibid., pp. 523-524.
16. Ibid., p. 524.
17. Ibid., pp. 521-523.

33. Oppositionists in the Camps
1. Nekrasov V. F. Trinadtsat' "zheleznykh" narkomov, pp. 194-195.
2. "Voprosy istorii," 1995, № 11-12, p. 21.
3. Soprotivlenie v GULAGe, pp. 148-149.
4. Ibid., pp. 150-154.
5. Excerpts from T. I. Miagkova's Investigatory Dossiers, contained in the personal archive of R. M. Miagkova-Poloz.
6. Varshavskaia M. I. Vospominaniia (manuscript), contained in the personal archive of R. M. Miagkova-Poloz.
7. Soprotivlenie v GULAGe, pp. 126-127.
8. Reabilitirovan posmertno, p. 322.
9. Simonov K. Zhivye i mertvye, M., 1960, p. 160.
10. "V nedrakh Ukhpechlaga," Issue II, Ukhta, 1994, p. 20.

34. The Tragedy at Vorkuta
1. "Quatrième Internationale," 1951, Vol. 9, № 1; "The Militant," 1951, Vol. 15, № 3; "Proletarian Action," 1951, № 3, 4-5.
2. "Sotsialisticheskii vestnik," 1961, № 10-11, p. 201.
3. Hoover Institution Archives. Nicolaevsky Collection, Box 626, Folder 13.
4. Nicolaevsky Collection, Box 237, Folder 14.
5. Ibid., Box 236, Folder 4.
6. Ibid., Box 233, Folder 23.
7. Ibid., Box 237, Folder 14.
8. Baital'skii D. Tetradi dlia vnukov. Rukopis' (In the personal archive of R. A. Medvedev), p. 181.
9. "Zapoliar'e," Vorkuta, 18 September 1991.
10. Ioffe M. Odna noch', New York, 1978, p. 99.
11. Nicolaevsky Collection, Box 233, Folder 23, p. 12.
12. Baital'skii D. Tetradi dlia vnukov, p. 185.
13. "Sotsialisticheskii vestnik," 1961, № 10-11, p. 204.
14. "Zapoliar'e," Vorkuta, 18 September 1991; 15 January 1992.
15. Nil'skii M., Vorkuta, Syktyvkar, 1991, pp. 79-100; Pechal'naia pristan',

Syktyvkar, 1991, pp. 328-344.
16. Voitolovskaia M., Po sledam sud'by moego pokoleniia, Syktyvkar, 1991, p. 240.
17. Doicher I. Trotskii v izgnanii, pp. 451-452 [Deutscher I. *The Prophet Outcast. Trotsky: 1929-1940*, New York: Oxford University Press, 1963, pp. 418-419].

35. Who Benefited from the Great Purge?
1. Antonov-Ovseenko A. V. Portret tirana, M., 1994, p. 187.
2. XVIII s"ezd Vsesoiuznoi Kommunisticheskoi partii (bol'shevikov). Stenograficheskii otchet,, M., 1939, p. 596.
3. Marks K., Engel's F. Sochineniia, Vol. 33, p. 45. [See: Karl Marx & Frederick Engels, Collected Works, Vol. 44, p. 63.]
4. "Novyi mir," 1988, № 6, p. 105.
5. "Krasnaia zvezda," 23 February 1938.
6. "Krasnaia zvezda," 21 February 1938.
7. XVIII s"ezd Vsesoiuznoi Kommunisticheskoi partii (bol'shevikov). Stenograficheskii otchet,, p. 596.

36. The New Recruits of 1937
1. XVIII s"ezd Vsesoiuznoi Kommunisticheskoi partii (bol'shevikov), p. 149.
2. "Kommunist," 1988, № 1, p. 32.
3. Sovetskaia istoricheskaia entsiklopediia, Vol. 7, M., 1965, p. 707.
4. Sovetskaia istoricheskaia entsiklopediia, Vol. 7, p. 702.
5. "Pravda," 17 July 1917.
6. XVIII s"ezd Vsesoiuznoi Kommunisticheskoi partii (bol'shevikov), p. 30.
7. "Voprosy istorii," 1990, № 5, p. 51.
8. Chuev F. Sto sorok besed s Molotovym, p. 291.
9. "Znamia," 1990, № 12, p. 38.
10. Shreider M. B. NKVD iznutri, pp. 176-177.
11. "Voprosy istorii," 1990, № 6, p. 91.
12. "Kazakhstanskaia pravda," 7 June 1988.
13. "Pravda-5," 1995, № 12, p. 8.
14. "Molodaia gvardiia," 1989, № 4, p. 62.
15. "Znamia," 1989, № 6, p. 78.
16. "Literaturnaia gazeta," 16 March 1988.

37. Who Was Punished and In What Way after Stalin's Death?
1. "Istochnik," 1993, № 5-6, pp. 157-161.
2. Reabilitatsiia, p. 80.
3. Ibid., pp. 77-78.

4. Ibid., pp. 76-77.
5. Golosa istorii. Sb. nauchnykh trudov, Issue 22, Book 1, M., 1990, p. 226.
6. Ibid., p. 228.
7. Efimov I. I. Ne sotvori sebe kumira, p. 407.
8. Reabilitatsiia, p. 88.
9. Pamiat'. Istoricheskii sbornik, Issue I, Paris, 1978, pp. 348-350.

38. Terror against Foreign Communists
1. Konstitutsiia SSSR, M., 1937, p. 17.
2. Trepper L. Bol'shaia igra, p. 56.
3. Soprotivlenie v GULAGe, pp. 107-110.
4. "Biulleten' oppozitsii," 1937, № 60-61, pp. 13, 20 ["Notes by Ignaty Reiss"; "In the GPU" (Told by Comrade Reiss)].
5. Vaksberg A. Neraskrytye tainy, pp. 141-142.
6. Vaksberg A. "Komintern. Bolgarskii sled," "LG-Dos'e," 1994, № 8, p. 24.
7. "Biulleten' oppozitsii," 1937, № 62-63, p. 5 [L. D. Trotsky, "Replies to Journalists' Questions About the Verdict of the International Commission," 13 December 1937].
8. Istoriia i stalinizm, M., 1991, p. 192.
9. Trepper L. Bol'shaia igra, p. 59.
10. "Kommunist," 1991, № 7, pp. 94-95.
11. "Pravda," 7 April 1989.
12. "Druzhba narodov," 1989, № 7, pp. 178-179.
13. "Voprosy istorii KPSS," 1988, № 12, p. 50.
14. "Literaturnaia gazeta," 27 July 1988.
15. "Biulleten' oppozitsii," 1939, № 71, p. 11 [L. D. Trotsky, "A Fresh Lesson," 10 October 1938].
16. Girenko Yu. S. Stalin-Tito, M., 1991, p. 55.
17. Ibid., p. 59.
18. "Vercherniaia Moskva," 15 February 1990.
19. Girenko Yu. S. Stalin-Tito, p. 78.
20. Ibid., p. 70.
21. Ibid., p. 77.
22. Ibid., p. 79.
23. Ibid., pp. 63-65.
24. Arkhivy raskryvaiut tainy... Mezhdunarodnye voprosy: sobytiia i liudi, M., 1991, p. 362.
25. Ibid., p. 363.
26. Ibid., pp. 355-356.
27. "Biulleten' oppozitsii," 1938, № 66-67, p. 30 ["Results of the Destruction of 'Fraternal' Communist Parties"].
28. "Voprosy istorii KPSS," 1988, № 12, p. 52.

29. "Biulleten' oppozitsii," 1938, № 68-69, p. 32 ["Appeal of Polish Bolshevik-Leninists," July 1938].
30. "Istoricheskii arkhiv," 1993, № 3, p. 214.
31. Buber-Neiman M. Mirovaia revoliutsiia i stalinskii rezhim, M., 1995, p. 238.
32. Ibid., p. 242-243.
33. Ibid., p. 251.
34. "Istoricheskii arkhiv," 1992, № 1, pp. 118-122.
35. "Argumenty i fakty," 1989, № 36.
36. Komintern i vtoraia mirovaia voina, Part I, M., 1994, p. 503.
37. Ibid., pp. 501-502.
38. "LG-Dos'e," 1994, № 8, p. 24.
39. Ibid.
40. "Komsomol'skaia pravda," 14 November 1988.
41. "Ogonek," 1988, №45, p. 27.
42. "Voprosy istorii," 1994, № 5, p. 74.
43. "Istochnik," 1993, № 1, pp. 71-73; "Izvestiia," 19 June 1990.
44. "Kommunist," 1991, № 7, p. 95.
45. "Istoricheskii arkhiv," 1993, № 6, p. 71.
46. "Znamia," 1988, № 7, p. 91.
47. Otkryvaia novye stranitsy... Mezhdunarodnye voprosy: sobytiia i liudi, M., 1989, p. 409.
48. Arkhivy raskryvaiut tainy..., p. 369.
49. "Pravda," 17 October 1992.
50. Trepper L. Bol'shaia igra, pp. 56, 58.
51. Trotsky Archive, № 14714.

39. Non-Returners of 1937

39.1 Ignatii Reiss
1. "Biulleten' oppozitsii," 1938, № 68-69, p. 23 [Elsa Reiss, "Ludwig"].
2. Ibid.
3. Poretsky E. K. *Our Own People*, Ann Arbor, 1970, p. 219.
4. Ibid., p. 211.
5. Ibid., p. 174.
6. "Biulleten' oppozitsii," 1937, № 60-61, p. 21 ["In the GPU"].
7. "Biulleten' oppozitsii," 1938, № 68-69, p. 23 [Elsa Reiss, "Ludwig"].
8. Ibid.
9. Trotsky archive, № 17228.
10. Kudrova I. Gibel' Mariny Tsvetaevoi, M., 1995, p. 147.
11. Ibid., p. 54.
12. Poretsky E. K. *Our Own People*, pp. 237-238.

13. Ibid., p. 236.
14. Trotsky Archive, № 868.
15. "Poslednie novosti," 19 November 1938.
16. Kudrova I. Gibel' Mariny Tsvetaevoi, p. 143.
17. Poretsky E. K. *Our Own People*, p. 253; Nicolaevsky Collection, box 628, folder 10.
18. "Biulleten' oppozitsii," 1938, № 68-69, p. 24 [L. D. Trotsky, "On the Anniversary of Reiss's Death," 17 July 1938].

39.2 Walter Krivitsky
1. Poretsky E. K. *Our Own People*, p. 219.
2. Trotsky Archive, № 17106.
3. "Biulleten' oppozitsii," 1937, № 60-61, p. 8 [Walter Krivitsky, "Letter to the Workers' Press," 5 December 1937].
4. Ibid., p. 9.
5. Ibid., pp. 8-9.
6. Nicolaevsky Collection, box 628, folder 10.
7. Krivitskii V. Ia byl agentom Stalina, p. 322.
8. Ibid., p. 69, 71.
9. Ibid., p. 316.

39.3 Alexander Barmine
1. Barmine A. *One Who Survived*, N.Y., 1945, p. 295.
2. "Biulleten' oppozitsii," 1937, № 60-61, p. 11 ["Comrade A. Barmine's Reply to Two Questions"].
3. Trotsky Archive, № 860.
4. "Biulleten' oppozitsii," 1937, № 60-61, p. 8 [Alexander Barmine, "To the Committee to Investigate the Moscow Trials, 1 December 1937].
5. Trotsky Archive, № 860.
6. Trotsky Archive, № 15865, p. 25.
7. Ibid., pp. 41-42.
8. Ibid., p. 54.
9. Ibid., № 873.
10. Nicolaevsky Collection, box 92, folder 3.

40. Non-Returners of 1938

40.1 Alexander Orlov
1. "Scope of Soviet Activity in the United States. Hearing before the Subcommittee to Investigate the Administration of the Internal Security Act... 28 September 1955," Washington, 1955, p. 11.
2. Ibid., pp. 10, 12.

Endnotes 483

3. Tsarev O., Kostello Dzh. Rokovye illiuzii. Iz arkhivov KGB: Delo Orlova, stalinskogo mastera shpionazha, M., 1995, p. 355-356. [Oleg Tsarev & John Costello, Deadly Illusions, NY, 1993, p. 311.]
4. Ibid., pp. 356, 425.
5. Ibid., p. 359, 433.
6. Ibid., p. 453 [p. 389].
7. Ibid., p. 450.
8. Ibid., p. 437 [p. 376].

40.2 Fyodor Raskolnikov
1. "Proletarskaia revoliutsiia," 1923, № 10, p. 151.
2. Vospominaniia o V. I. Lenine, 3rd edition, Vol. 2, M., 1984, p. 266.
3. Trotskii L. D. Stalinskaia shkola fal'sifikatsii. Popravki i dopolneniia к literature epigonov, Berlin, 1932, pp. 20-21.
4. Raskol'nikov F. F. O vremeni i o sebe, L, 1989, p. 540.
5. Vlast' i oppozitsiia, p. 165.
6. Raskol'nikov F. F. O vremeni i o sebe, p. 541.
7. "Voprosy istorii KPSS," 1963, № 12, p. 94.
8. Reabilitirovan posmertno, p. 223.
9. "Kommunist," 1969, № 3, p. 75.
10. "Sotsialisticheskii vestnik," 1937, № 23-24, pp. 23-24.

41. Verdict of the Dewey Commission
1. Cited from: Volkogonov D. A. Trotskii, Politicheskii portret, Book 2, M., 1992, p. 279.
2. Trotsky Archive, № 8472.
3. Ibid., № 858.
4. *The Case of Leon Trotsky*, N.Y, 1938, p. 370.
5. Ibid., p. 435.
6. Ibid., p. 436.
7. Glotzer A. *Trotsky. Memoir & Critique*, N.Y, 1989, p. 262.
8. Ibid., p. 263.
9. Ibid., p. 265.
10. "Biulleten' oppozitsii," 1938, № 68-69, p. 2 ["Stalin and His Accomplices are Condemned"].
11. "Biulleten' oppozitsii," 1938, № 62-63, pp. 1-2 ["Verdict of the International Commission on the Moscow Trials"].
12. Ibid., pp. 3-4.
13. Ibid., pp. 5-6.

42. Bolshevism, Stalinism, Trotskyism
1. "Biulleten' oppozitsii," 1937, № 58-59, p. 4 [L. D. Trotsky, "Stalinism and

Bolshevism"].
2. "Biulleten' oppozitsii," 1938, № 68-69, p. 6 [L. D. Trotsky, "Their Morals and Ours"].
3. Ibid.
4. "Biulleten' oppozitsii," 1938, № 62-63, p. 11 [L. D. Trotsky, "The Spanish Lesson – A Last Warning"].
5. "Biulleten' oppozitsii," 1938, № 68-69, p. 11 [L. D. Trotsky, "Their Morals and Ours"].
6. Ibid., p. 12
7. "Biulleten' oppozitsii," 1937, № 58-59, p. 7 ["Stalinism and Bolshevism"].
8. Ibid., p. 8.
9. Ibid., pp. 8, 11.
10. Ibid., p. 13.
11. Ibid., p. 15.
12. "Biulleten' oppozitsii," 1938, № 65, p. 2 ["New Non-Returners"].
13. "Biulleten' oppozitsii," 1937, № 58-59, p. 17 ["Stalinism and Bolshevism"].
14. Ibid., p. 19.
15. Kestler A. Slepiashchaia t'ma, p. 164 [Koestler A. *Darkness at Noon*, NY, Bantam, 1966, p. 174].
16. Ibid., p. 134 [p. 142].
17. Ibid., p. 123 [p. 129].
18. Ibid., p. 153-154 [pp. 164-165].
19. Ibid., pp. 168-170 [pp. 182-184].
20. Ibid., p. 171.
21. Ibid., p. 177.
22. Ibid., p. 136.
23. Ibid., p. 134.
24. "Biulleten' oppozitsii," 1938, № 68-69, p. 19 ["Their Morals and Ours"].
25. "Biulleten' oppozitsii," 1938, № 66-67, pp. 22-23 [L. D. Trotsky, "Hue and Cry over Kronstadt"].
26. "Biulleten' oppozitsii," 1938, № 68-69, p. 19 ["Their Morals and Ours"].

43. "Hue and Cry over Kronstadt"
1. Doicher I. Trotskii v izgnanii, M., 1991, p. 467 [Deutscher, p. 436].
2. "Biulleten' oppozitsii," 1937, № 56-57, pp. 13-14 [L. D. Trotsky, "Answers to Questions from Wendelin Thomas," 6 July 1937].
3. "Biulleten' oppozitsii," 1938, № 66-67, p. 22 ["Hue and Cry over Kronstadt"].
4. Ibid., p. 23.
5. "Voprosy istorii," 1994, № 5, pp. 9-10.
6. "Voprosy istorii," 1994, № 4, p. 6; "Novyi mir," 1987, № 9, pp. 42-43.

Endnotes

7. "Voprosy istorii," 1994, № 4, p. 6.
8. "Voprosy istorii," 1994, № 5, p. 19.
9. Ibid., p. 21.
10. Drabkina E. "Velikii pereval," "Iunost'," 1987, № 10, p. 17.
11. Kuraev M. "Kapitan Dikshtein," "Novyi mir," 1987, № 9, p. 43.
12. "Voprosy istorii," 1994, № 5, p. 20.
13. "Voprosy istorii," 1994, № 7, p. 32.
14. "Biulleten' oppozitsii," 1938, № 66-67, p. 24 ["Hue and Cry over Kronstadt"].
15. Ibid., p. 25.
16. Ibid.
17. "Voprosy istorii," 1994, № 6, p. 26.
18. "Voprosy istorii," 1994, № 7, pp. 3-4.
19. Ibid., pp. 32-33.
20. "Biulleten' oppozitsii," 1938, № 66-67, p. 26 ["Hue and Cry over Kronstadt"].
21. "Biulleten' oppozitsii," 1939, № 70, p. 10 [L. D. Trotsky, "More on the Suppression of Kronstadt"].
22. Nicolaevsky Collection, Box 92, Folder 3.
23. "Voprosy istorii," 1994, № 5, pp. 5-6.
24. Nicolaevsky Collection, Box 92, Folder 3.
25. "Biulleten' oppozitsii," 1939, № 70, p. 10 ["More on the Suppression of Kronstadt"].
26. "Voprosy istorii," 1994, № 7, pp. 25.
27. "Biulleten' oppozitsii," 1939, № 70, p. 10 ["More on the Suppression of Kronstadt"].

44. "Their Morals and Ours"
1. "Pravda," 21 December 1994.
2. Bukharin N. Teoriia istoricheskogo materializma, M., 1923, p. 239.
3. Lenin V. I. Polnoe sobranie sochinenii, Vol. 41, p. 309 [Lenin, Collected Works, Volume 31, p.291].
4. Ibid., pp. 312, 313 [p. 294].
5. Ibid., p. 309, 310 [p.291].
6. "Biulleten' oppozitsii," 1938, № 68-69, p. 9 ["Their Morals and Ours"].
7. Ibid., p. 19.
8. Ibid., p. 9.
9. Shveitser A. Kul'tura i etika, M., 1973, pp. 271, 275.
10. "Biulleten' oppozitsii," 1938, № 68-69, p. 9 ["Their Morals and Ours"].
11. Kestler A. Slepiashchaia t'ma, p. 201.
12. Ibid., p. 121.
13. Ibid., p. 192.

14. Ibid., p. 200.
15. "Biulleten' oppozitsii," 1937, № 56-57, pp. 12-13 ["Answers to Questions from Wendelin Thomas"].
16. Drobnitskii O. G. Problemy nravstvennosti, M., 1977, pp. 201-202.
17. See: Filosofiia Kanta i sovremennost', M., 1974, p. 120.
18. "Molodaia gvardiia," 1922, № 3, p. 128.
19. "Biulleten' oppozitsii," 1938, № 68-69, p. 7 ["Their Morals and Ours"].
20. Ibid., p. 9.
21. Ibid., pp. 7-8.
22. Ibid., p. 18.
23. "Biulleten' oppozitsii," 1937, № 58-59, p. 17 ["Stalinism and Bolshevism"].
24. "Biulleten' oppozitsii," 1938, № 68-69, pp. 14-15 ["Their Morals and Ours"].
25. Cited from: Volkogonov D. A. Trotskii, Vol. 1, p. 284.
26. "Biulleten' oppozitsii," 1937, № 58-59, p. 4 ["Stalinism and Bolshevism"].
27. "Biulleten' oppozitsii," 1938, № 68-69, p. 17 ["Their Morals and Ours"].
28. Ibid., p. 13.
29. Baitalskii M. Tetradi dlia vnukov. Rukopis', p. 72.
30. "Biulleten' oppozitsii," 1938, № 68-69, p. 11 ["Their Morals and Ours"].
31. Ibid., p. 15.
32. Ibid., p. 19.

45. "The Old Man Would Find It Hard Without Sonny"
1. "Biulleten' oppozitsii," 1938, № 64, p. 2 [L. D. Trotsky, "Leon Sedov. Son, Friend, Fighter," 20 February 1938].
2. Ibid., p. 3.
3. Ibid., p. 5.
4. Trotsky Archive, № 17106.
5. "Biulleten' oppozitsii," 1938, № 64, p. 4 ["Leon Sedov. Son, Friend, Fighter"].
6. Ibid., p. 6.
7. "Biulleten' oppozitsii," 1939, № 74, p. 2 ["On the Anniversary of L. Sedov's Death"].

46. An Agent Known as "Tulip"
1. Volkogonov D. A. Trotskii, Book 2, pp. 134-135.
2. Ibid., p. 167.
3. Ibid., p. 198.
4. Ibid.
5. Ibid., p. 151.
6. Ibid., p. 135.

7. Ibid., pp. 313-314.
8. "Scope of Soviet Activity in the United States. Hearing before the Subcommittee to Investigate the Administration of the Internal Security Act," - February 29, 1956, Washington, 1956, pp. 93-94.
9. Volkogonov D. A. Trotskii, Book 2, pp. 141, 223, 274.
10. "Scope of Soviet Activity in the United States. Hearing...," February 29, 1956, p. 77.
11. Ibid., p. 80.
12. Ibid., pp. 88, 98-99.
13. Ibid., pp. 89-90.

47. The Death of Leon Sedov
1. "Stolitsa," 1992, № 39, p. 59.
2. Poretsky E. K. *Our Own People*, p. 238; Kudrova I. Gibel' Mariny Tsvetaevoi, p. 44.
3. "Biulleten' oppozitsii," 1938, № 64, p. 7 [L. D. Trotsky, "Leon Sedov. Son, Friend, Fighter," 20 February 1938].
4. "Biulleten' oppozitsii," 1938, № 68-69, p. 29 [L. D. Trotsky, "Investigation into the Death of My Son Lev Sedov," 19 July 1938].
5. Volkogonov D. A. Trotskii, Book 2, p. 167.
6. Trotskii L. D. Dnevniki i pis'ma, p. 164.
7. Trotsky Archive, № 780.
8. "Biulleten' oppozitsii," 1938, № 64, p. 8 ["Leon Sedov. Son, Friend, Fighter"].
9. Trotskii L. D. Dnevniki i pis'ma, p. 165.
10. Ibid., p. 164.
11. "Biulleten' oppozitsii," 1938, № 64, p. 7 ["Leon Sedov. Son, Friend, Fighter"].
12. "Biulleten' oppozitsii," 1938, № 68-69, p. 28 ["Investigation into the Death of My Son Lev Sedov"].
13. Ibid., pp. 29-30.
14. Ibid., p. 29.
15. "Biulleten' oppozitsii," 1939, № 70, pp. 14-15 [L. D. Trotsky, "Investigation into the Death of Lev Sedov," 24 August 1938].
16. Ibid., p. 13.
17. Ibid., p. 14.
18. Trotskii L. D. Dnevniki i pis'ma, p. 165.
19. "Biulleten' oppozitsii," 1939, № 70, p. 15 ["Investigation into the Death of Lev Sedov"].
20. Trotsky Archive, №№ 860, 15852.
21. "Scope of Soviet Activity in the United States. Hearing...," February 29, 1956, p. 92.

22. Volkogonov D. A. Trotskii, Book 2, p. 168.
23. Tsarev O., Kostello Dzh. Rokovye illiuzii, p. 532 [Tsarev & Costello, p. 469].

48. Trotsky in Mexico
1. Dallin, David J. *Soviet Espionage*, London, 1955, p. 420.
2. Volkogonov, D. A. Trotskii, Book 2, p. 212.
3. Ibid., p. 140.
4. Communication from V. B. Bronstein to the book's author. More detailed information about Trotsky's victimized relatives is contained in the following publications: Bronstein V. "Stalin and Trotsky's Relatives in Russia, in: *The Trotsky Reappraisal*, Edinburg, 1992; Bronshtein V. B. "Trotskii, ego blizhaishie i dal'nie rodstvenniki," Iz glubin vremen, Issue 4, S.- Pb, 1995.
5. "Biulleten' oppozitsii," 1938, № 70, p. 16 ["The Totalitarian Right to Asylum"].
6. Volkogonov D. A. Trotskii. Politicheskii portret, Book 2, p. 208.
7. "Biulleten' oppozitsii," 1937, № 62-63, p. 24 ["Investigation into the Murder of Comrade Ignaty Reiss"].
8. "Biulleten' oppozitsii," 1938, № 66-67, p. 32 ["The Life of L. D. Trotsky is in Danger"].
9. Volkogonov, D. A. Trotskii, Book 2, pp. 305-307.
10. Trotsky Archive, Ms 868, 869.
11. "Neva," 1989, № 3, pp. 204-205.
12. Trotsky Archive, № 17106.
13. Jean van Heijenoort, *With Trotsky in Exile*, London, 1978, pp. 101-102.
14. "Scope of Soviet Activity in the United States. Hearing..." September 28, 1955, Washington, 1962, pp. 2-3.
15. Tsarev O, Kostello Dzh, Rokovye illiuzii, p. 426.
16. Trotsky Archive, № 6137.
17. Tsarev O., Kostello Dzh. Rokovye illiuzii, pp. 369, 425-426, 544.
18. "Legacy of Alexander Orlov," Washington, 1973, p. 15.
19. Writing of Leon Trotsky. Supplement (1934-1940), N. Y, 1979, pp. 818-819.
20. "Legacy of Alexander Orlov," p. 16.
21. "Scope of Soviet Activity in the United States. Hearing..." March 2, 1956, pp. 137-138.
22. Writing of Leon Trotsky. Supplement (1934-1940), p. 950.
23. Tsarev O., Kostello Dzh. Rokovye illiuzii, pp. 368-369.

49. Murders Abroad
1. Volkogonov D. A. Trotskii, Book 2, p. 191.

2. Trotskii L. D. Prestupleniia Stalina, pp. 273-274.
3. Dallin David J. *Soviet Espionage*, pp. 415-416.
4. Serge V. & N. Sedova. *The Life and Death of Leon Trotsky*, p. 244.
5. "Biulleten' oppozitsii," 1938, № 68-69, pp. 27-28 [L. D. Trotsky, "On the Fate of Rudolf Klement," 3 August 1938].
6. "Biulleten' oppozitsii," 1939, № 73, p. 16 [L. D. Trotsky, "On the Murder of Rudolf Klement"].
7. Sudoplatov P. Razvedka i Kreml'. Zapiski nezhelatel'nogo svidetelia, M., 1996, p. 58.

50. Paris Intrigues
1. Nicolaevsky Collection, Box 628, Folder 10.
2. Ibid., Box 627, Folder 7.
3. Trotsky Archive, № 871.
4. Ibid., № 860.
5. Volkogonov D. A. Trotskii, Book 2, p. 306.
6. Trotsky Archive, № 860.
7. Volkogonov D. A. Trotskii, Book 2, p. 170.
8. Ibid., p. 227.
9. Ibid., pp. 169-170.
10. Tsarev O., Kostello Dzh. Rokovye illiuzii, p. 323.
11. Trotsky Archive, № 879.
12. Nicolaevsky Collection, Box 627, Folder 2.
13. Trotsky Archive, № 863.
14. Ibid., № 873.
15. Ibid., № 863.
16. Nicolaevsky Collection, Box 627, Folder 2.
17. Ibid., Box 628, Folder 10.
18. Ibid.
19. Poretsky E. K. *Our Own People*, p. 245.
20. Nicolaevsky Collection, Box 628, Folder 10.
21. Ibid., Box 627, Folder 2.
22. Trotsky Archive, № 860.
23. Ibid., № 7729.
24. Writings of Leon Trotsky [1937-1938], N. Y, 1970, pp. 338-339.

51. End of the "Yezhov Period"
1. "Voprosy istorii," 1990, № 6, p. 78.
2. Beriia: konets kar'ery, pp. 393-394.
3. Khlevniuk O. V. 1937-i: Stalin, NKVD i sovetskoe obshchestvo, pp. 243-244.
4. "Istoricheskii arkhiv," 1992, № 1, pp. 124-126.

5. "Voprosy istorii," 1992, № 2-3, p. 87.
6. Stalinskoe Politburo v 30-e gody, pp. 168-170.
7. Ibid., p. 168.
8. "Voprosy istorii," 1990, № 6, p. 81.
9. Yakovlev A. Tsel' zhizni, M., 1969, p. 509.
10. Simonov K. Soldatami ne rozhdaiutsia, M., 1981, pp. 609-610, 612.
11. Povartsov S. Prichina smerti – rasstrel, pp. 149, 151.
12. Shentalinskii V. Raby svobody, p. 67.
13. Ibid.
14. "Sovershenno sekretno," 1992, № 4, pp. 6-7.
15. "Argumenty i fakty," 1989, № 45.
16. "Oktiabr'," 1992, № 10, p. 132.
17. Efimov I. I. Ne sotvori sebe kumira, p. 391.

52. The Falsification of History
1. Volkogonov D. A. Trotskii, Book 1, pp. 82-83.
2. "Istochnik," 1994, № 6, p. 97.
3. Volkogonov D. A. Trotskii, Book 2, p. 282.
4. "Svobodnaia mysl'," 1993, № 10, p. 29.
5. Ibid., p. 30.
6. "Bol'shevik," 1937, № 9, p. 8.
7. "Golosa istorii," Vol. 22, Edition 1, M., 1990, p. 217.
8. Reabilitatsiia, p. 58.
9. Istoriia i stalinizm, pp. 75-76.
10. Ibid., p. 77.
11. "Pravda," 15 November 1938.
12. Ibid.
13. Istoriia VKP(b). Kratkii kurs, M., 1938, p. 332.
14. Trotskii L. D. Stalin, Vol. II, p. 274.
15. "Pravda," 15 November 1938.
16. Ibid.

Appendix I. From the History of the Exposure of Stalin's Crimes
1. "Voprosy istorii," 1992, № 6-7, p. 88.
2. Ibid., p. 83.
3. Ibid., p. 87.
4. Ibid., pp. 88-89.
5. Ibid., p. 81.
6. "Istoricheskii arkhiv," 1993, № 4, p. 81.
7. "Voprosy istorii," 1992, № 6-7, p. 83.
8. Ibid., pp. 84-85.
9. Chuev F. Так govoril Kaganovich, p. 99.

10. "Istochnik," 1994, № 2, p. 84.
11. Ibid., p. 81.
12. "Voprosy istorii," 1992, № 6-7, p. 84.
13. "Istoricheskii arkhiv," 1993, №4, p. 81.
14. "Istoricheskii arkhiv," 1993, № 6, p. 45.
15. "Istoricheskii arkhiv," 1994, № 1, p. 56.
16. "Istoricheskii arkhiv," 1993, № 4, pp. 62, 80.
17. "Istoricheskii arkhiv," 1994, №2, p. 41.
18. "Istoricheskii arkhiv," 1993, № 4, p.80.
19. "Istoricheskii arkhiv," 1994, № 1, pp. 8, 9.
20. "Istoricheskii arkhiv," 1993, № 3, p. 16.
21. "Istoricheskii arkhiv," 1994, № 1, p. 67.
22. "Istoricheskii arkhiv," 1993, № 5, p. 41.
23. "Istoricheskii arkhiv," 1994, № 2, p. 18.
24. "Istoricheskii arkhiv," 1993, № 5, pp. 41, 45.
25. "Istoricheskii arkhiv," 1993, № 3, pp. 44-45.
26. Ibid., p. 44.
27. "Istoricheskii arkhiv," 1994, № 1, p. 37.
28. "Istoricheskii arkhiv," 1993, № 3, p. 43.
29. "Istoricheskii arkhiv," 1993, № 4, p. 11.
30. "Istoricheskii arkhiv," 1993, № 4, pp. 16-17.
31. "Istoricheskii arkhiv," 1993, № 3, p. 43.
32. "Istoricheskii arkhiv," 1994, № 1, p. 9.
33. "Istoricheskii arkhiv," 1993, № 6, p. 66.
34. Ibid., p. 45.
35. "Istoricheskii arkhiv," 1993, № 3, pp. 19-20.
36. "Istoricheskii arkhiv," 1993, № 6, p. 38.
37. "Istoricheskii arkhiv," 1994, № 2, p. 41.
38. "Istoricheskii arkhiv," 1993, № 4, p. 62.
39. "Voprosy istorii," 1992, № 6-7, p. 88.

Appendix II. Statistics about the Victims of Mass Repressions
1. Bal'zak O. Sobranie sochinenii, Vol. 5, M., 1952, pp. 28-29.
2. Barmine A. *One Who Survived*, N.Y, 1945, p. 325.
3. "Novyi mir," 1988, № 8, p. 125.
4. "Novyi mir," 1990, № 3, p. 109.
5. Antonov-Ovseenko A. V. Portret tirana, M., 1994, pp. 270, 388.
6. Ibid., pp. 100, 426.
7. Medvedev R. A. O Staline i stalinizme, pp. 405, 455-456.
8. "Voprosy istorii," 1990, № 3, p. 82.
9. "Izvestiia," 3 June 1996.
10. "Istoriia SSSR," 1991, № 5, pp. 152-153.

11. "Izvestiia," 13 February 1990; "Nedelia," 1990, № 20, p. 11.
12. "Ivestiia," 3 August 1992.
13. Khrestomatiia po istorii Rossii. 1917-1940, M., 1994, pp. 385-386.
14. "Sotsiologicheskie issledovaniia," 1990, № 8, p. 45.
15. "Sotsiologicheskie issledovaniia," 1990, № 6, p. 17.
16. "Istoriia SSSR," 1991, № 5, p. 152.
17. Nekrasov V. F. Trinadtsat' "zheleznykh" narkomov, p. 90.
18. Shelestov D. Vremia Alekseia Rykova, M., 1990, p. 329.
19. "Sotsiologicheskie issledovaniia," 1991, № 7, p. 3.
20. Nashe otechestvo. Opyt politicheskoi istorii, Vol. 2, M., 1991, p. 419.
21. "Sotsiologicheskie issledovaniia," 1991, № 6, p. 10.
22. "Istoriia SSSR," 1991, № 5, p. 153.
23. "Sotsiologicheskie issledovaniia," 1991, № 6, pp. 14-15, 19.
24. "Istoriia SSSR," 1991, № 5, p. 152.
25. Ibid.
26. Reabilitatsiia, p. 34.
27. "Kommunist," 1990, № 8, p. 103.
28. "Istochnik," 1995, № 1, p. 120.
29. "Otechestvennye arkhivy," 1992, № 2, p. 28.
30. XX s"ezd KPSS i ego istoricheskie real'nosti, M., 1991, p. 54.
31. Nekrasov V. F. Trinadtsat' "zheleznykh" narkomov, p. 272.
32. "Sotsiologicheskie issledovaniia," 1991, № 7, p. 15.
33. XX s"ezd KPSS i ego istoricheskie real'nosti, p. 63.
34. Reabilitatsiia, p. 328; "Izvestiia," 3 August 1992.
35. "Pravda," 14 April 1991.
36. Reabilitirovan posmertno, p. 141.
37. "Voprosy istorii," 1995, № 11-12, p. 21.
38. "Voprosy filosofii," 1990, № 2, p. 13.
39. "Izvestiia TsK KPSS," 1990, № 1, p. 88.
40. Ocherki po istorii kompartii Ukrainy, Kiev, 1961, pp. 430, 452.
41. Trotskii L. D. Stalin, Vol. II, p. 261.
42. "Voprosy filosofii," 1990, № 2, p. 13.

Index
Photos are indicated by Boldface numbers

A

Abakumov, V. S. 313
Abbiate, Roland [Vladimir Pravdin] *320*, 323, 325, 398
Abel, Rudolf 335
Abramovich, R. A. 107, *240*, 244, 403
Adamova-Sliozberg, O. A. *233*, 237, 238, 248, 263
Adler, Friedrich 106
Afanasiev, B. *320*, 401
Agabekov, G. 340
Aksenov, P. V. 259, 260, 262
Akulov, I. A. 62
Aleksa-Agnaretis 316
Aleksandrovsky, M. K. 196
Alekseev 400
Alexander II 210
Alksnis, Ya. I. 198
Alliluyeva, N. S. 68
All-Russian Central Executive Committee (VTsIK) 28, 360, 364
Aminev 17
anarchists 9, 348, 350, 352, 357, 358
Andreev, A. A. 21, 130, 154, *155*, 156, 157, 169, 177, *184*, 196, 214, 216, 313, 315
  on Kosarev 217
  supports Trotsky during trade union debate 154
Andropov, Yu. V. 296
Aniashvili, P. 162
Antipov, N. K. 28, 171, 174, 414
Antonov-Ovseenko, A. V. 288
  Portrait of a Tyrant 442
Antonov-Ovseenko, V. A. 153
Anvelt, Jan 304
Apanasenko, R. I. 199
Aristov, A. B. 430, 433
Aronson 102
Arosev, A. Ya. 136, 137
Artuzov, A. Kh. 271
Avdeenko, A. O. 99, 180, 181
Avtorkhanov, A. 27, 169, 182, 183, 419

B

Babel, I. E. *71*, *225*, 226, 227, **440**
  correspondence with Malraux 228
  informant's report on 224
  "Lies, Treachery and Smerdyakovism" 221
  on Gorky 70
  on Khayutina 417
  prison testimony of 70, 227
  visits Souvarine 227
Badaev, A. E. 177

Bagirov, M. D. 18, 23, 161, 177
Bagliuk 282
Bagramian, I. Kh. 199
Bagritsky, E. G.
 "Thoughts About Opanas" 226
Baitalsky, M. 266, 378
Bakh, A. N. 229
Baklanov, G. Ya.
 July 1941 253, 257
Balabanova, Angelica 341
Balashov, M.
 "The Vorkuta Tragedy" 282
Balzac, Honoré de 441
 The Priest from Tours 441
Barmine, A. 31, 132, *330*, 331, 332, 408, 411, 441
 break with Stalin 328
 mixed feelings of 329
 One Who Survived 331
 on purge of Red Army 195, 329
Bauer, L. 308
Bauman, K. Ya. 175
Becher, Johannes 307
Beck, Colonel Jozef 90
Beilin, A. G. 259, 260
Beldyagin 419
Belevsky 306
Beloborodov, A. G. 131
Belov 304
Belov, I. P. 175
Benediktov, I. A. 294
Berdyaev, N. A. 374
Bergelson, D. R.
 "The People's Vengeful Sword" 221
Berggolts, O. F. *248*
Beria, L. P. 24, 130, 137, 139, 158, *162*, 164, 166, 177, 182, 211, 294, 297, 413, 418, 421
 against Ordzhonikidze 162
 and Postyshev 23
 as initiator of rehabilitations 429
 cult of in Georgia 161
 on Georgian oppositionists 30–31
 orders Kedrov's execution 155
 poisons Lakoba 163
 purges NKVD 416
 replaces Yezhov 416
Berman, B. 416
Berman, M. 416
Besedovsky, G. Z. 340
Bessonov, S. A. 39, 40, 71, 81, 82, 90, 99
Bezymensky, A. I. 221
Bliukher, V. K. *194*, 195, 199, 269
Bloch, J. P. 104
Blum, Léon 106
Bogdanov, A. A. 367
Bogomolov 112
Bogomolov, N. A. 28, 112
Bohr, Niels 270
Bolshevism 2, 3, 5, 124, 244, 345, 347–356, 357, 365, 383
 morality of 375
Boyarsky, V. A. 298
Braude 68
Brezhnev, L. I. 122, 141, 187, 292, 296, 298
Broido, G. I. 176
Bronstein, A. D. 397
Bronstein, B. A. *396*, 397
Bronstein, V. B. 397
Broué, Pierre 78
Brover, B. I. 285
Bruesse, G. 325, 326
Buber-Neumann, Margarete 311, 312
Bubiakin, V. 214
Bubnov, A. S. 174, 175, 269
Budenny, S. M. 146, 163, 177, *194*, 198, 199
Bukharin, N. I. 27, 31, 33, 34, 35, 36, 37, 39, 43, 44, *45*, 46, 47, 48, 49, 50, 51, 52, 53, 54, 55, 56, *57*, 58, 59, 60, 67, 71, 72, 75, 77, 80, 95, 99, 100, 101, 104, 107, 108, 111,

Index 495

122, 124, 134, 139, 140, 147, 149, 157, 169, 174, 223, 225, 242, 243, 261, 271, 303, *367*, 423, 425, 426, 434, 439
ABCs of Communism 366
and "Left Communists" 49–53
and prison writings 35
appeal for clemency 58–60
at Third Moscow Trial 43–46
conversation with Kamenev 76
letters to Stalin 35–36
letter to wife 37
meeting with Nicolaevsky 34
"Notes of an Economist" 47
on collective farms 46, 77
on confessions as evidence 55
on the "Riutin Platform" 47
Philosophical Arabesques 35
praised by Gorbachev 123
rehabilitation of 177
testimony of 45
Theory of Historical Materialism 366
Bulanov, P. P. 75, 76, 81
Bulgakov, S. N. 374
Bulganin, N. A. 24, 177
Bulin, A. S. 175
Bulletin of the Opposition 15, 78, 164, 180, 190, 309, 318, 326, 330, 381, 382, 383, 386, 393, 397, 400, 408, 411
Bure, Emile 42, 105
Burtsev, V. L. 421
Butenko 191
Bykin, Ya. B. 157
Bykov 17

C

Cachin, Marcel 317
Campo, Valentin 399
Capone, Al 65
Cárdenas, Lázaro 398

Catalonia 322
Central Committee 13, 20, 25, 34, 49, 73, 98, 103, 130, 132, 136, 139, 145, 163, 171, 173, 177, 179, 180, 185, 198, 200, 207, 217, 223, 225, 249, 291, 293, 297, 299, 339, 354, 362, 378, 418, 437, 442
and "mass operations" 7
December 1936 Plenum of 143, 148
decree of 17 November 1938 414–415
decree of 30 June 1956 436
decree on *Short Course* 424, 425, 426
February 1934 Plenum of 169
February 1935 Plenum of 169
February 1964 Plenum of 135
February-March 1937 Plenum of 129, 134, 147, 149, 169, 174, 205, 275, 289, 448
January 1938 Plenum of 15, 21, 170, 175
July 1953 Plenum of 167
June 1937 Plenum of 7, 174, 176, 206
June 1957 Plenum of 7, 120, 138, 142, 144, 147, 151, 166, 178, 208, 315, 434, 435, 439, 447
letter of 24 April 1936 19
letters to 413
of October 1917 134
of the KP(b) of Armenia 163, 284
of the KP(b) of Azerbaidzhan 161
of the KP(b) of Georgia 162, 294
of the KP(b) of Kazakhstan 182, 294
of the KP(B) of Ukraine 21, 158
of the KP(b) of Uzbekistan 154, 155, 294
Presidium of 37, 120, 147, 206, 430, 431, 433, 434, 438, 443
"On Studying Material of the Open Trials" 433

secretary of 143, 146, 154, 157, 164, 313, 416, 435
secret resolution of 17 November 1938 414–415
Central Committee of the VLKSM 211, 213, 214, 215, 216, 217, 283, 449
Cervantes 345
Chakovsky, A. B. 141
Chamberlain, Neville 90
Chattopadiaia 316
Chernenko, K. U. 141, 296
Chernousov, V. 414
Chernov, M. A. 76, 84, 175, 177
Chernov, V. M. 361
Chinese-Eastern Railway 9, 10
Chkalov, V. P. 293
Choibalsan, Kh. 316
Chubar, Tr. Ya. 171
Chubar, V. Ya. 19, 169, *170*, 171, *184*, 206
Chudov, M. S. 174
Chukovsky, K. I. 219, *220*
  on Stalin 220
Churchill, Winston 88, 91, 104
Chuvyrin, M. E. 176
Chuyanov, A. S. 413
Chuyev, F. I. 136, 137, 138, 139, 141, 148, 294, 431
Chvialev, E. D. 19
Ciliga, Anton 357
Civil War of 1918-1920 4, 238, 337, 352
Cohen, Stephen 58
collectivization 4, 73, 74, 76, 83, 129, 142, 213, 232, 233, 234, 249, 250, 271, 272, 287, 354, 444
Comintern 81, 88, 89, 107, 109, 112, 186, 245, 279, 299, 303, 304, 305, 306, 307, 308, 309, 311, 312, 315, 317, 318, 319, 321, 322, 344, 345, 395, 399, 451

Executive Committee of 304, 305, 306, 308, 309, 310, 312
Communist Parties
  founders of 303
  of Bulgaria 306, 313
  of France 5, 105
  of Germany 306, 310, 310–312, 311, 312
  of Hungary 314
  of Iran 316
  of Italy 432
  of Japan 317
  of Latvia 316
  of Lithuania 151, 315
  of Mexico 316, 398, 399
  of Palestine 318
  of Poland 306, 309–310
    disbanding of 310
  of the Soviet Union 2, 37, 103, 119, 120, 121, 122, 123, 125, 135, 141, 192, 223, 250, 292, 294, 295, 296, 298, 299, 300, 316, 318, 338, 339, 425, 427, 429, 430, 433, 439, 442, 443, 448. *See also* VKP(b)
  of the USA 404
  of Ukraine 449
  of Yugoslavia 307, 307–309
Conquest, Robert 96, 185
Cossacks 48, 226, 234, 237, 358, 377
Coulondre, Robert 87
CPSU. *See* Communist Parties: of the Soviet Union; *See also* VKP(b)

D

Daladier, Édouard 91
Damianov [Belov], G. 304
Dan, F. I. 42, 105, 108, *240*, 244, 326
Darkness at Noon. See Koestler, Arthur
Davies, Joseph E. 104
Deineka 282

Demchenko, M. S. 220
Deni (Denisov), V. N. 89
Deutscher, Isaac 285, 357
Deutsche Wehr 202
Dewey Commission 333, 341, 343, 345, 391
  Not Guilty 343
Dewey, John 341, 342, 343, 379
Dietrich, Isaak 312
Dimitrov, G. M. 163, 304, 305, 306, 309, 310, 313, *314*, 315, 317
Dingelshtedt, N. F. 285
Diukanov 294
Djilas, M. 308, 309, 379
Dmitrievsky, S. 340
Dobrushkin, D. B. 231
Domanevskaia, O. 244
Dombrovsky, Yu. O.
  The Department of Useless Things 441
Donbass 142, 145, 180, 181, 282
Dreitser, E. A. 226
Drobnitsky, O. G. 372
Duclos, Jacques 317, 395
Ducomet, Pierre 324
Durruti, Buenaventura 349
Dutt, R. Palme 122
Dzerzhinsky, F. E. 205, 271, 364

E

Eastland, Sen. James 335
Eastman, Max 357, 388
Eberhard, Hans. *See* Reiss, I.
Eberlein, Hugo *302*, 303
ECCI. *See* Comintern, Executive Committee of
Eden, Anthony 89, 90
Efron, S. Ya. 323, *324*, 325, 391
Eighteenth Congress of the VKP(b) 161, 169, 176, 289, 290, 291, 418, 431, 449
Eikhe, R. I. 19, 169, *170*, 171

Eisenstein, S. M. 227
Eismont, N. B. 31
Eitingon, N. I. 333
Eltsin, V. B. 285
Engels, Friedrich 34, 289, 312
Epstein, Shakhno 405
Erenburg, I. G. *218*, 222, 224, 259
  on Beria 162
  on Stalin 223
  on Stalin as demi-god 229
  People, Years, Life 229
Estrine, L. 331, 387, 388, 390, 395, 400, 402, 407, 408, 409, 410, 412
  on Barmine 330
ethnic purges 9–12, 414
Etienne. *See* Zborowski, M.

F

Fadeev, A. A. 250
Fainberg, E. L. 214
Fast, Howard 379
February-March 1937 Plenum. *See* Central Committee
Fedko, I. F. 198
Fedotov, G. P. *240*
  on Bukharin 56, 58, 108
  on moods against Stalin 77
  on Stalin 108
  on the Great Purge 242–243
Feldman 206
Feldman, B. M. 200
Feoktistov 336
Filippchenko, A. V. 272
Filippov 23
Filshtinsky, I. 261
Finerty, John 333, 342
Finnish War 200, 202
Fouché, Joseph 62

Fourth International 307, 318, 322, 326, 382, 388, 405, 408, 409, 412
Franco, Francisco 369
Frankel, Jan 399, 400
Frank, Jan 406
Freud, Sigmund 345
Frinovsky, M. P. *167*, 206, 316, 416
Frunze, M. V. 68
Furer 143
Furtseva, E. A. 433

G

Gachev, D. 306
Gaevsky, D. S. 226
Galkin 93
Galkin, S. M. 297
Galperin, D. I. 231
Gamarnik, Ya. B. 39, 77, 151, 152, 176
Germany
　Soviet relations with 74–75, 88, 90, 327
Gevorkian, S. A. 282, 283, 285
Gidazs, Antal 314
Ginzburg, E. S. 249
Gladun, A. F. 417
Glinsky, S. M. 334, 385
Gnedin, E. A. 99, 262
Goebbels, Joseph 61
Goethe 4, 345
Goglidze, S. A. 163, 208
Gogoberidze, L. 162
Goliakov, I. T. 98
Goloded, N. M. 164
Goltsman, E. S. 330
Gomez 316
Gorbachev, M. S. 123, 126, 179, 192, 256, 443, 452
Gorev, M. F. 419
Gorkic, Milan 307, 309

Gorky, A. M. 27, *29*, 51, 67, 69, *70*, 71, 72, 75, 190, 337, 409
　surrounded by NKVD 70
Gorodnichenko, T. Z. 298
Gorodovikov, O. I. 199
Gorshenin, K. P. 443
Gottwald, Klement 317, 319
Great Soviet Encyclopedia 94, 289, 451
Griaznov, I. K. 175
Grigoriev, N. 154
Grinko, G. F. 40, 81, 84, 175
Gromyko, A. A. *292*, 293, 296
Grossman, V. S. 2, 427
　Forever Flowing 427
　Life and Fate 427
Guchkov, A. I. 324
Günther 310

H

Halder, Franz 203, 204
Halifax, Lord 89
Heisler, Francis 341
　The First Two Moscow Trials 341
Hess, Rudolf 91
Hirsch 310
Hitler, Adolf 5, 69, 87, 88, 89, 90, 102, 109, 115, 123, 203, 204, 234, 239, 243, 245, 267, 268, 316, 327, 328, 342, 343, 348, 369, 408, 427
Hoover, J. Edgar 335
Hull, Cordell 104

I

Ignatov 22
Ikramov, A. I. 77, 78, 120, 154, 155, 252
Ilyasov 209
Ilyin, M.
　"Path to the Gestapo" 221

Index 499

Industrial Party 88
Inquisition 55, 94, 113, 115, 183
invalids
    execution of 9
Ioffe [Joffe], N. A. 237, 284
Irbe, V. A. *12*
Iskander, F. A. 235
Iskrov, P. 313
Iurenev, K. K. 28, 112, *113*
Iurkin, T. A. 176
Ivanovo 9, 145, 206, 298
Ivanov, V. I. 34, 101, 175
    testifies against Bukharin 44–45, 45
Ivanov, Vladimir 283
Ivanov, V. V. 226
Izotov, N. A. 143
Izvestiia 86, 88, 251

J

Jaurès, Jean 307
Jesuits 374, 375

K

Kaganovich, L. M. 18, 24, 41, 48, 62,
    128, 130, 131, 137, *142*, 144,
    145, 147, 149, 152, *155*, 157,
    169, 177, 182, *184*, 191, 208,
    214, 216, 266, 410, 431, 434,
    435, 437, 438
  and Furer 143
  at June 1957 Plenum 7
  attacks Postyshev 25
  letters to NKVD 143
  on love for Stalin 436
  on oppositionists 148
  on torture decree 151
  sanctions arrests of deputies 143
  threatens Rudenko 433
Kaganovich, M. M. 176, 293
Kaganovich, Yu. M. 190

Kahlo, Frida *398*
Kalinina, E. D.
    denounces Stalin 156
Kalinin, M. I. *128*, 130, *156*, *157*, 169,
    177, 272, 410
    arrest of wife 156
Kalinin, V. V. 272
Kalmanovich, M. I. 174
Kalnberzin, Ya. E. 316
Kameneva, O. D. 397
Kamenev, L. B. 29, 30, 46, 52, 61, 72,
    76, 83, 88, 149, 317, 322, 323,
    328, 383, 418, 425, 434
Kamenev, S. S. 199
Kamkov, B. D. 49, 50, 53
Kant, Immanuel 372, 374
Kapitsa, P. L. 270
Kaplan, F. 54, 205
Kapler, A. Ya. 54
Karakhan, L. M. 28, *112*
Kara-Murza, S. 3
Kardel, E. 309
Karelin, V. A. 49, 53, 54
Karklin 93
Karpinsky, V. A. 299
Karpov, G. G. 297, 298
Karpov, I. P. 297
Kashketin, E. I. 284, 285
Kataev, V. P. 227
Katkov 448
Kaverin, V. A. 222
Kavtaradze, S. I.
    freed by Stalin 31
Kazakhstan 13, 77, 182, 277, 294
Kazakov 146, 147
Kedrov, M. S. 155
    letter to Andreev 155
Keitel, Wilhelm 203
Kerensky, A. F. 421
Khandzhian, A. G. 163
Khayutina, E. S. 417, 418
Khlevniuk, O. V. 130

Khodzhaev, F. 74, 120
Khrushchev, N. S. 22, *118*, 120, 122, 125, 130, 131, 134, 135, 137, 140, 143, 147, 148, 151, 152, 160, 161, 167, 171, 175, 177, 179, *184*, 190, 206, 208, 259, 263, 290, 292, 293, 296, 298, 315, 317, 318, 415, 416, *432*, 434, 435, 436, 437, 439, 442, 447
   and June 1937 CC Plenum 7
   awe of Stalin 158
   on Andreev 154
   on Kirov's assassination 438
   on Molotov 433
   on NKVD 159, 210
   on purge of Red Army 204
   on purge of the party apparatus 185
   on report to Twentieth Congress 430–432
   on repression of Poles 11
   on Stalin 158, 191, 210
   on Trotsky 121
   on Trotskyists 119
   on Yezhov 413
   on Zinoviev's innocence 434, 438
   trip to Yugoslavia 429
Khrustalev-Nosar, G. 421
Kirov, S. M. 43, 61, 63, *64*, 67, 157, 169, 176, 212, 277, 300, 435, 438, 439, 444
Klement, Rudolf 150
   murder of 405–406
Klepinina, N. *324*
Klinger, Gustav *302*, 303
Kobulov, B. Z. 162, 163
Koestler, Arthur 27, 58, 59, 365, *371*, 379
   Darkness at Noon 353–355, 371
Kogan 35
Kolarov, V. 313
Kolchak, A. V. 294

Koltsov, M. E. 70, 99, 100, 225, 250, *251*, 252, 290, **440**
   on Mekhlis 165
   on the Moscow Trial 99–100
   Spanish Diary 250
Kolyma 37, 60, 275, 277, 279
Komarov 430
Komsomol 17, 18, 213, 214, 215, 216, 217, 220, 237, 281, 283, 288, 298, 367, 372, 381, 416, 432, 451
Kondratiev, V. 324
Konev, I. S. 199, 200
Korets 267, 269
Kork, A. I. 198
Korolenko, N. G. 108
Korotchenko, D. S. 161
Kosarev, A. V. 18, 206, 213, 214, *215*, 216, 217
Kosior, I. V. 176
Kosior, S. V. 17, 19, 53, 130, 153, 169, 170, 171, 206
   angers Stalin 171
Kosior, V. V. 170, 283, 285
Kosolapov, R. I. 126, 141
Kostiukov 146, 147
Kostrzewa, Wera 310
Kosygin, A. N. *292*, 293, 296
Kozlov, A. S. 298
Kozlovsky, A. N. 360
Kozub 273
Krebs, Hans 203
Krechinsky, M. V. 111
Kremlin 69
Krestinsky, N. N. 27, 33, *38*, 40, 42, 43, 57, 74, 80, 81, 89, 111, 112, *113*, 140
   and alleged meeting with Sedov 82
   arrest of 31
   denies pre-trial testimony 39
   reconfirms pre-trial testimony 41
Krinitsky, A. I. 310

Kriuchkov, P. P. 27, 70, 71, 75
Krivitsky, Walter 205, 322, 325, 326, *327*, 382, 388, 391, 399, 407, 408, 409, 411
  death of 328
  In Stalin's Secret Service 328
  on Stalin 328
Krivtsov, T. 282
Kronstadt 337, 339
Kronstadt rebellion 173, 356, 357–364, 365
  funeral procession of *363*
Kruglov, S. N. 443
Krupskaya, N. K. 176, 260
Krylenko, N. V. 93, 388
Krylenko, Ye. V. 388
Krzhizhanovsky, G. M. 176
Kuban 48, 74, 142, 213
Kubiak, N. A. 174
Kuibyshev, N. V. 197
Kuibyshev, V. V. 27, 53, 67, 68, 169, 176
kulaks 7, 8, 9, 46, 76, 83, 233, 238, 287, 288, 444
Kulik, G. I. 199
Kunaev, D. A. 294
Kun, Agnessa 314
Kun, Bela 314, *315*
Kun, Irina 314
Kupferstein, Hermann 310
Kurnik, N. 334
Kushchev 17
Kusonsky 241
Kuusinen, O. 316, 438
Kuzmichev, B. I. 226
Kuzmin, V. V. 275, 359

L

Lakoba, N. 162, 163
Lampe, General 241
Landau, Kurt 349, 403
Landau, L. D. 267, *268*, 269, 270
  prepares anti-Stalinist leaflet 267
Larina, Anna M. 35, 156, 237
Lashevich, M. M. 226, 227, 418
Latest News 242
Lavrentev, L. I. 174
Lazurkina, D. A. 250, 297
League of Nations 403, 404
Left Communists 49, 50, 51, 52, 53, 54
Left Opposition 5, 27, 30, 46, 50, 163, 178, 189, 226, 287, 299, 309, 351, 382
The Legacy of Alexander Orlov 335
Lenin, V. I. 44, 49, 50, 51, 52, 54, 55, 56, 69, 109, 112, 113, 119, 123, 125, 129, 141, 145, 153, 156, 158, 159, 178, 183, 205, 242, 250, 256, 261, 263, 266, 267, 274, 292, 299, 306, 328, 331, 336, 337, 338, 348, 349, 352, 353, 360, 368, 378, 418, 422, 423, 427, 438
  "amorality" of 377
  at First Congress of Comintern 303
  at Tenth Congress 173
  Materialism and Empirio-criticism 365
  on bureaucratization of Soviet regime 350
  on morality 367
  on Trotsky and Stalin 122
  slandered during perestroika 126
Lenski, Julian 310
Leonhard, Suzanne 281
Leonov, L. M. 226
Leow-Hofmann, Willi 310
Lepa, A. K. 164, 260
Lepeshinsky, P. N. *373*
  on morality 372–374
Le Temps 242
Levenzon 197
Levin, L. G. 67, 68, 69, 72, 75, 76

Lewis, F. 328
Lieber 397
Liebknecht, Karl 307, 383
Liebknecht, Wilhelm 383
Lincoln, Abraham 377
Linde, F. V. 263
Literary Gazette 221, 270
Litvinov, M. M. 89, 90, 99, 177, 404
Liubchenko, P. P. 176
Liubimov, I. E. 174
Liushkov, G. S. 400, 401, 415
Lominadze, V. V. 31, 213
Lomov, G. I. 134
Lozovsky, S. A. 177
Ludwig. *See* Reiss, I.
Ludwig, Emil 377
Lugovskoy, V. A.
  "Poetic Response" 221
Lukashov 161
Lukyanov, D. D. 214
Lunacharsky, A. V. 421
Luther, Martin 375
Luxemburg, Rosa 303, 307

M

Mac. *See* Zborowski, M.
Maclean, Donald 334
Magadan 264, 277, 278
Magid, M. 282
Maisky, I. M. 93
Makarov, I. G. 177
Makhno, N. I. 153, 358, 361
Maksimov-Dikovsky 27
Malenkov, G. M. 15, 16, 17, 18, 23, 130, 137, 152, 159, 163, 164, 167, 182, *184*, 196, 214, 216, 295, 304, 315, 434, 435, 437, 438
  report at January 1938 Plenum of CC 15
Malinovsky, R. Ya. 199

Mally, Teodor 334
Malraux, André *71*, 228
  visits Gorky 70
Malyshev, V. A. 293
Mandelshtam, N. Ya. 222, 229, 230
Manevich, L. I. 321
Mantsev, V. N. 49
Manuilsky, D. Z. 177, 304
Mao Tse-Tung 317
Marshak, S. Ya.
  "Path to the Gestapo" 221
Martignat, Charles 324
Martigny 398
Marty, Andre 317
Marx, Karl 34, 153, 263, 266, 289, 353, 360, 374
Mayakovsky, V. V. 256
Mdivani, B. 30, 226, 270
Medvedev, R. A. 185, 442
Mekhlis, L. Z. *165*, 177, *194*, 196, 201, 251, 294
  and purge of officers 165
Melnais, K. P. 283
Melnikov, B. 304
Mensheviks 9, 88, 93, 105, 348, 361, 408
  on the Great Purge 243–245
Menzhinsky, V. R. 53, 65, 67, 176
Merano 81
Mercader, Ramon 122, 401
Meretskov, K. A. 199
Merkulov, V. I. 162
  True Son of the Party of Lenin-Stalin 162
Meshik, P. Ya. 211
Mexico 81, 82, 341, 392, 397, 398, 399, 401
Meyerhold, V. E. **440**
Mezhlauk, V. I. 175, 190
Mezis 200
Mgeladze, A. I. 294
Miagkova, T. I. 276, *277*, 278

Mikhailov, M. 175
Mikhoels, S. M. 227
Mikoyan, A. I. 19, 23, 24, *128*, *153*,
    154, 164, 166, 169, 177, *184*,
    438
  criticizes *Short Course* 153
  on Rykov 120
  praises the NKVD 152
  support of Khrushchev 152
Milchakov, A. I. 211, 448, 449
Miletic, P. 308
Miliukov, P. N. 242, 357
Mink, George 399, 405
Minkov, M. I. 282
Mirzoyan, L. I. 182
Mishakova 216, 217
Mission to Moscow 104
Mitin, M. B. 289
Mitskiavichus-Kapsukas 316
Mogilevskaia 289
Molchanov, G. A. 205, 206
Molière 257
Molinier, Jeanne 385, 392, 394, 395,
    407
Molotov, V. M. 15, 18, 19, 24, 69, 75,
    98, *128*, 130, 131, 133, 134,
    135, 138, 140, 141, 142, 147,
    148, 149, 151, 152, 154, 156,
    169, 173, 177, 182, 196, 208,
    216, 223, 293, 355, 410, 418,
    424, 431, 432, 433, 434, 435,
    436, 437, 438, 439
  as Stalin's confidant 134
  defends Stalin 140
  depicted in film 141
  on Arosev 136
  on Bukharin 139
  on defendants' confessions 140
  on Rudzutak 136
  opposes rehabilitations 137
  opposes review of Moscow Trials 120
Morozova 18

Mosevich, A. A. 277
Moskatov 182
Moskvin 306
Mukardji 316
Münzenberg, Willi 104, *311*, 312
Mussolini, Benito 123, 267, 348
  on Stalin 109

N

Nagy, Imre 314, 315
Narokov, N.
  Imaginary Quantities 262
nationalities
  purge of 196
Nemtsova, Z. N. 238
Neumann, Heinz 311
Nevelson, M. 397
Nicolaevsky, B. I. 105, 281, 282, 387
  on meeting with Bukharin 34
Nietzsche 412
Nikolaenko 134
Nikolaev 75
Nikolaeva, K. I. 177
Nikolaev-Zhurid 416
Nikulin, L. V. 226
Nin, Andrés 349, 403, 406
Nineteenth Congress of the CPSU
    176, 177
NKVD 9, 10, 17, 23, 26, 31, 61, 68,
    69, 70, 75, 81, 95, 96, 102, 130,
    132, 134, 137, 143, 144, 145,
    146, 147, 151, 152, 155, 156,
    159, 161, 162, 166, 174, 182,
    183, 185, 190, 196, 199, 201,
    205, 206, 210, 211, 215, 216,
    230, 231, 238, 239, 262, 263,
    266, 268, 269, 276, 283, 284,
    285, 288, 297, 298, 300, 305,
    306, 311, 312, 314, 315, 317,
    322, 323, 324, 325, 326, 333,
    334, 335, 337, 339, 385, 386,

387, 388, 390, 391, 396, 397, 398, 399, 400, 401, 402, 403, 405, 406, 407, 408, 409, 410, 413, 414, 415, 416, 418, 419, 421, 426, 434, 443, 444, 445, 447, 448
and Kirov's assassination 63
and "mass operations" 7
and prisoners of war 304
and torture 136, 207
arrest of Latvians 11
arrest quotas 209
deportation of Koreans 13
infallibility of 19, 160, 252
number purged 212
privileges of 208
sadism of 273
nomenklatura 155, 158
non-returners 114, 183, 191, 270, 321, 326, 336, 338, 339, 340, 355, 382, 408, 410, 411
Nosaka 317

O

Okhotnikov, Ya. O. 226
Okudzhava 30, 31
Olesha, Yu. K. 227
  "Fascists Before the Court of the People" 221
Orakhelashvili, M. D. 162, 270
Ordzhonikidze, G. K. 68, 162, 163, 169, 176, 260, 270, 410
Orlov, Alexander 29, 79, 205, 333, 334, *335*, 336, 388, 415
  attempts to warn Trotsky 400–403
  letters to Yezhov 334
  on bureaucratic elite 187
  on food shortages 85
  on Vyshinsky 93, 95–96
  on Yagoda 62

The Secret History of Stalin's Crimes 335
Orlov, V. M. 198
Osinsky, V. V. 49, 52, 54, 451
Osipov, E. 300
Otwald 310

P

Paget, Lady 42, 105
Panferov, F. I. 232
Party Control Commission 16, 19, 26, 137, 166, 177, 182, 259, 416, 430, 448
Pasternak, B. L. *220*, 223
Pauker, K. V. 205, 206
Pavlotsky 144
Pavlovic, Zh. 309
  The Balance of the Soviet Thermidor 309
Paz, Madeleine 42, 105
Pelshe, A. Ya. 449
Peluso, Edmondo 303
  execution of 304
  torture of 303
perestroika 2, 123
Pergament, A. R. 279
Peshkov, Maksim 65
Petliura, S. V. 154
Petrichenko, S. M. 361
Petrov 334
Petrov, I. E. 60, 150
Petrovsky, G. I. 169, 171, 172, 176, 263, 264, 299
Philby, Kim 334, 336
Piatakov, Yu. L. 30, 46, 50, 83, 84, 88, 107, 112, 116, 177, 180, 222, 306, 321, 330, 418
Pieck, Wilhelm 305, 317
Pilniak, B. A. *218*, 226, 228
Pilsudski, Jozef 88, 91, 307, 310
Platonov, A. P.

Index

"Overcoming Villainies" 221
Platten, Fritz *302*, 303
Pletnev, D. D. *66*, 67, 68, 102
   torture of 68
Poliakov 277
Poliansky, D. S. 437
Pollitt, Harry 120, 317
Pompadourism 243
Ponomarev, B. N. 103, 296
Popov, Blagoi 313, *314*
Popular Front 89, 90, 106, 310, 349
Poretsky, E. 321, 322, 323, 326. See also Reiss, Elsa
Poskrebyshev, A. N. 177, 304
Pospelov, P. N. 122, 430, 433
Postel 209
Postyshev, P. P. 21, *22*, 23, 24, *25*, 26, 34, *128*, 169, 170, 182, 183
   arrest and execution of 26
   on Stalin and Yezhov 182
   reprisals in Kuibyshev 21–23
Pototsky, A. 165
POUM 322, 403
Poyntz, Juliet Stuart 404, 405
Poznansky, I. M. 283, 284, 285
Pramnek, E. K. 180, 181
Pravda 13, 49, 59, 67, 68, 87, 88, 97, 98, 99, 141, 166, 180, 187, 213, 214, 216, 221, 244, 250, 251, 328
Preobrazhensky, E. A. *367*, 451
   ABCs of Communism 366
   "Morality and Class Norms" 366
Primakov, V. M. 226, *227*
Prishvin, M. M. 187, 222
Pritt, D. N. 104
Problems of Leninism 17
Proletarian Revolution 336
Proshian, P. P. 50
Protestants 375
Prushitsky, S. 94
Pushin, G. E. 330

Putna, V. K. 198

Q

Questions of History 339

R

Radek, Karl 30, 31, 50, 83, 84, 90, 99, 107, 112, 225, 227, 303, 306, 321
   and Pilsudski 88
Rado, Alexander 321
Radomyslskaia, F. A. 285
Radzivilovsky, A. P. 10, 145, 206
Raikh-Johansson 78
Rakosi, Matyas 315, 319
Rakovsky, Kh. G. 27, 31, *32*, 33, 34, 40, 42, 75, 80, 90, 95, 96, 101, 105, 107, 108, 111, *112*, 113, 140, 225, 226, 227, 276
   death of 102
   denounces capitulators 41
   letter to Stalin 32
Rankovic, A. 308
Rappoport 105
Raskolnikov, F. F. 257, 336, *337*, 340
   At Battle Stations 339
   "How They Made Me an Enemy of the People" 338
   letter to Stalin 338
   rehabilitation of 338
Ravich, S. N. 299
Razumov, M. O. 28
Red Army 74, 75, 81, 109, 149, 150, 164, 165, 195, 196, 197, 198, 199, 200, 201, 202, 203, 204, 226, 242, 269, 273, 321, 329, 358, 362, 363, 376, 377, 399, 422, 446, 452
   suicides in 197
   rehabilitations 120, 299–302

Reichswehr 74, 75, 81
Reilly, Sidney 271
Rein, M. 399, 403
Reisner, Larisa 321
Reiss, Elsa 325, 409. *See also* Poretsky, E.
Reiss, I. 191, 252, 304, **320**, 321, 322, 323, 324, 325, 326, 329, 334, 388, 391, 392, 394, 398, 407, 408, 409, 410
  murder of 325
Remmele, Hermann 310
Ribar, I. L. 308
Riutin, M. N. 31, 47, 267
Rivera, Diego 345
Robotti, P. 316
Rodos, B. V. 206
Rogachevsky, I. G. 264
Rokossovsky, K. K. 198, 201
Rolland, Romain 70, 409
  letter to Bloch 104
Romm, M. I.
  Lenin in 1918 54
  Lenin in October 423
Romm, V. G. 330
Rosmer, Alfred 105
Rossi, Francois. *See* Abbiate, Roland
Rozenblium 33, 212
Rozengolts, A. P. 27, 31, 39, 40, 74, 75, 81, 82, **101**, 140, 177, 225
  addresses court 101
Rudenko, F. M. 144
Rudenko, R. A. 430, 433, 443
Rudzutak, Ya. E. 28, 39, 130, 136, 169, 170, 171
Rukhimovich, M. L. 136, 175
Rumiantsev, I. P. 28, 174
Rustaveli, Sh. 162
Rybakov, A. N. 238, 257
Rykov, Aleksei I. 13, 27, 31, 39, 40, 47, 58, 67, 71, 72, 75, 77, 80, 95, 108, 111, 120, 122, 123, 134, 139, 140, 147, 148, 169, 174, 175, 177, 225, 242, 271, 425, 434, 439
  final remarks at trial 100
  on collectivization 76
Rylsky, M. F. 159
Ryndin, K. V. 175

S

Sabo 266
sabotage 83–84, 234
  in agriculture 18, 84, 159
Sadaliuk 161
Sagidullin, G. 249
Sakharov, A. D. 449
  "Reflections on Progress, Peaceful Coexistence and Intellectual Freedom" 448
Saltanov, S. A. 214
samizdat 2, 427, 441, 452
Samoilov, F. N. 171, 423
Sarkisov, A. Kh. 160
Sarkisov, S. A. 180
Sartre, Jean-Paul 372
Sats, Natalia 410
Savich 259
Savinkov, B. V. 271, 362
Savko, I. A. 150
Savolainen 76
Sazonov, S. D. 199
Schildbach, Gertrude 323, 325
Schweitzer, Albert 370
Sedelnikov, A. I. 174
Sediakin, A. I. 175
Sedova, N. I. 81, 281, 328, **398**, 400
Sedov, L. L. 81, 82, 205, 323, 325, 326, 327, 330, 343, 379, **380**, 381, 382, 385, 386, 387, 388, 390, **393**, 394, 395, 396, 397, 399, 400, 401, 407, 408, 410
  death of 392

Index 507

on Tbilisi trial 31
Red Book on the Moscow Trial 383
surveillance of 391
Sedov, S. L. 281, *282*, 397
Seeckt, General Hans von 81
Seifullina, L. N. 226
Seifullin, S. 294
Semionov 8, 9, 10
Senin 406
Serbsky, S. N. *276*
Serebriakov, L. P. 98, 222, 226, 418
Serebriakov, P. V. 298
Serge, Victor 58, 77, 228, 346, 357,
    407, 408, 409, 410, *411*
  on Bukharin 56–57
  on collectivization 74
  on Rakovsky 42
  on Rudolf Klement 406
  The Life and Death of Leon Trotsky 58
Serov, I. A. 433, 435
Serpilin 417
Seventeenth Congress of the VKP(b)
    15, 47, 175, 176, 177, 179, 180,
    190, 198, 291, 431, 449
Shachtman, Max *398*
Shaginian, M. S.
  A History Question 423
  "Monstrous Mongrels" 221
Shakespeare 345
Shaposhnikov, B. M. 198, 199
Sharangovich, V. F. 45, 73, 74, 84, 225
Shatskin, L. A. 213
Shchadenko, E. A. 196, 197
Sheboldaev, B. P. 30, 74, 177
Shevarnadze, E. A. 192
Shkiriatov, M. F. 145, 166, *167*, 216,
    421
Shmidt, D. 226
Short Course of the History of the
    VKP(b) 54, 123, 153, 423–427,
    424, 425, 426, 427
  Serbo-Croatian translation of 308

Shreider, M. 9, 145, 147, 182, 206, 293
Shteingardt, A. M. 176
Shtern, G. M. 199
Shtrange, M. M. 324, 325
Shvarev 424
Shvarts, I. I. 176
Shvernik, N. M. 177, 430, 433, 447
Simkov 394
Simonov, K. M. 202, 278, 417
  Soldiers Are Not Born 417
  The Living and the Dead 278
Skrypnik, N. 21
Slepkov, A. N. 47, 48
Slutsky, A. A. 322, 326, 386
Šmeral, Bohumir 317
Smirensky, D. 324, 391
Smirnov 334
Smirnova
  Tales of Stalin's Childhood 422
Smirnov, A. P. 31, 76
Smirnova, S. 277
Smirnov, I. N. 226, 277, 418
Smirnov, V. M. 226, 275
Snechkus, A. Yu. 151, 315, 316
Sneevliet, Henk 323, 325, 388, 407,
    408, 410, 411
Snegov, A. V. 166
social equality 188, 368
Socialist Herald 79, 243, 244, 281, 340,
    357
Soifer, Ya. G. 164
Sokolnikov, G. Ya. 177, 225
Sokolovskaya, A. L. 397
Sokolovsky, V. D. 199
Soloviev 273
Solts, A. A. 93, 96, *97*, 98
  demands investigation of Vyshinsky
    97
  on Trifonov 97
Solzhenitsyn, A. I. 2, 260, 266, 267,
    281, 289, 442
  Cancer Ward 260, 289

First Circle 442
Gulag Archipelago 2, 266, 281
Sorge, Richard 321
Sorin, V. G. 422
Souvarine, Boris 105, 227, 357, 362
Sovietology 2–3
Sovnarkom 18, 19, 28, 50, 98, 162, 163, 176, 209, 234, 270, 293, 453
Spiegelglas, S. M. *320*, 323, 325, 334, 396, 399, 407
Spinoza, Baruch 115
Spiridonov, I. V. 299, 300
SRs [Socialist Revolutionaries] 8, 9, 49, 50, 51, 53, 54, 74, 361, 453
Stadniuk, I. F. 141
Stakhanov, A. G. 143
Stakhanovites 231, 293
Stalinism
  as social reaction 378
Stalin, I. V. 1, 2, 3, 4, 9, 17, 18, 19, 26, 28, 29, 30, 31, 32, 33, 34, 35, 36, 37, 41, 44, 45, 46, 49, 50, 51, 52, 56, 57, 58, 59, 60, 61, 62, 63, 64, 65, 68, 69, 70, 71, 72, 75, 77, 80, 83, 84, 87, 88, 89, 90, 95, 97, 98, 101, 102, 103, 104, 107, 108, 109, 111, 112, 113, 115, 116, 117, *118*, 119, 120, 121, 122, 123, 124, 126, *128*, 129, 130, 132, *135*, 136, 137, 139, 141, 142, 145, 147, 148, 149, 151, 153, 154, *155*, 156, *157*, 159, *160*, 161, 162, 163, *164*, 165, 166, 167, 170, 171, 172, 174, 176, 177, 178, 179, 180, 181, 182, 187, 188, 190, 191, *194*, 200, 201, 203, 204, 206, 208, 210, 211, 212, 214, 216, 217, 222, 224, 225, 226, 229, 230, 231, 235, 237, 239, 241, 242, 243, 244, 247, 248, 249, 250, 251, 252, 253, 254, 255, 257, 260, 261, 263, 265, 267, 268, 269, 270, 272, 273, 274, 275, 278, 281, 284, 285, 287, 289, 290, 294, 295, 297, 301, 304, 305, 311, 312, 313, 314, 315, 317, 319, 321, 322, 323, 324, 326, 328, 329, 331, 333, 334, 336, 340, 344, 345, 347, 351, 352, 353, 354, 355, 357, *366*, 375, 376, 378, 382, 383, 386, 388, 390, 391, 395, 396, 397, 400, 401, 403, 404, 409, 410, 413, 415, *417*, 418, 419, 421, 422, 423, 425, 427, 429, 430, 432, 433, 434, 436, 441, 442, 443, 445, 447
  abuses of power 140
  and ethnic purges 13
  and "mass operations" 7
  and Molotov 134
  and peasants 73
  and Postyshev 21, 23, 24
  and purge of the Komsomol 213
  and Red Army 74, 195, 196
  and the new constitution 114
  and Third Moscow Trial 27
  and trial of military officers 195
  and Trotsky 306
  as a "Trotskyist" 125
  as creator of collective farms 219
  as state criminal 125
  awards Yagoda 62
  blackmails Mikoyan 152
  bodyguards of 205
  Bonapartist aspirations of 186, 189
  correspondence with Molotov 134
  crimes of 135, 138, 152, 158, 183, 186, 223, 338, 339, 349, 426, 431, 435, 438, 439
  cult of, as secular religion 256
  devotion to 266, 318
  distrust of "non-Russians" 169, 196

distrust of Polish CP 309
envy of Trotsky 79
fear of Fourth International 307
glorification of 219
love of 307
negotiations with Hitler 327
notes on morality 365
on "cadre revolution" 292
on disbanding Polish CP 310
on Furer's suicide 143
on manuscript of *Short Course* 424
on number of people expelled from party 448
on torture 207
on Trotskyists 306
on Yegorov 175
on Yezhov 416
opposition to 76
orders beating of prisoners 131
panegyrics to 220
protects Shaposhnikov 198
rehabilitation of 296
repression of foreign communists 303, 307
signs execution lists 131
threatens Comintern 306
threatens Mikoyan 152
willpower of 133
Stasova, E. D. 299, 422
Stavsky, V. P. 222
Steiner, Renata *320*, 324, 325, 391
Sten, Ya. E. 289
Stepanov, M. O. 197
Stolypin, P. A. 210
Strogovich, M. S. 94
Struppe, P. I. 174
Struve, P. B. 374
Subotsky, L. M. 270, 271
Sudoplatov, P. A. 398, 406
Sulimov, D. E. 174, 175
Sultan-Zade, A. 316
Surits, Ya. Z. 338

Surnin 187
Suslov, M. A. 2, 135, 294, *295*, 296, 433, 449
Suvchinskaia (Trail), Vera 324
Sverdlov University 46
Sverdlov, Ya. M. 46, 50, 52
Syrtsov, S. I. 31, 213

T

Tagore, Rabindranath 317
Tal, B. M. 251
Tambov uprising 358
tamizdat 2, 347, 427, 441, 453
Tanev, Vasil 313, *314*
Tarov 408
Teleshko 272
Tell, William 369
Tenth Congress of the RKP(b) 173, 178, 360, 362
Thälmann, Ernst 310
Thermidor 192, 309, 310, 326, 350
Third Russia 242
Thirteenth Party Conference of the RKP(b) 178
Thomas, Wendelin 357, 371
Thorez, Maurice 120
Tikhonov, N. A. 296
Timoshenko, S. K. 199
Tito, I. B. 307, 308, 309, 429
  break with Stalin 309
  on arrest of wife 308
  "Trotskyism and its Accomplices" 308
Togliatti, Palmiro 312, 316, 317, 432
Toledano, Lombardo 398
Tolstoi, A. N. 250, 252, 273
  Grain 274, 423
  letters to, on repressions 272
Tolstoy, L. N. 379
Tomsky, M. P. 137, 176, 271
Tovstukha, I. P. 176

Trail, R. 324
Trail, Vera. *See* Suchinskaia, Vera
Trapeznikov, S. P. 339
Tregub 16, 17
Trepper, Leopold 203, 305, 317
   on repression of foreign communists 303, 305
Trifonov, V. A. 96
Trifonov, Yu. V. 98
Trilisser, M. A. 306
troika 8, 9, 131, 132, 163, 209, 211, 285, 443, 453
Trotsky, L. D. 22, 32, 34, 36, 40, 42, 52, 55, 58, 65, 67, 69, 72, 74, 75, 78, 79, *80*, 82, 87, 89, 91, 96, 100, 101, 102, 103, 104, 107, 109, 117, 119, 121, 122, 123, 125, 139, 154, 156, 157, 176, 180, 190, 192, 197, 198, 199, 205, 221, 225, 226, 234, 241, 242, 243, 254, 255, 261, 269, 274, 276, 283, 284, 306, 321, 322, 323, 324, 330, 331, 336, 340, 347, 359, 360, 361, 362, 364, 367, *376*, *380*, 385, 386, 387, 390, *398*, 399, 400, 401, 402, 403, 404, 405, 406, 407, 408, 409, 411, 412, 421, 422, 423
   and alleged conspiracy with Germany and Japan 88
   and alleged meeting with Krestinsky 81
   and alleged ties to England 90
   "Behind the Kremlin Walls" 29
   "Cain-Dzhugashvili Goes All the Way" 110, 111
   "Guiding Principles of Impending Policy in the Don" 377
   "Hue and Cry over Kronstadt" 358
   letter to Heisler 341
   letter to Wendelin Thomas 357–358, 371
   on analogies 348
   on anarchism 352
   on Bukharin 51
   on Bukharin's "plot" to arrest Lenin 50
   on Butenko 191
   "Once More on Comrades Sneevliet and Vereeken" 410
   on Civil War in America 4, 376
   on Comintern apparatus 305
   on common sense 370–371
   on degeneration of bureaucracy 188
   on Dewey Commission 343
   on extermination of Bolshevik Party 449
   on extermination of Old Bolsheviks 186
   on French-Soviet pact 349
   on Gorky's death 70–71
   on Hitler and constitution 342–343
   on Krestinsky's capitulation 41
   on Lenin 377
   on Lev Sedov 379, 381–383
   on Lev Sedov's death 392–395
   on masses 356
   on morality 368–372, 374–379
   on Moscow Trials 111–116
   on planned economy 353
   on Pletnev's sentence 68
   on Postyshev 21
   on purge of Red Army 201
   on Raskolnikov 337
   on reaction 348, 378
   on Reiss 326–327
   on revolutionary optimism 345
   on sabotage 84
   on *Short Course* 426
   on social inequality 189
   on Soviet bureaucracy 115
   on Stalin 34, 62, 72, 74, 111–115, 114, 124, 125, 133, 186, 188, 195, 307, 344, 345, 353, 375

Index

on Stalin's entourage 166
on state 342
on Toledano 398
on Tolstoy 379
on Voroshilov 149
on Vyshinsky 95
on Yagoda 61–64
on Yenukidze 29–30
on Yezhov 426
prognoses of 124
relatives persecuted 397
Revolution Betrayed 388
"Stalinism and Bolshevism" 348–353
"Super-Borgia in the Kremlin" 50
"Their Morals and Ours" 355, 365, 368
"The Totalitarian Right to Asylum" 398
"To the Garrison and Inhabitants of Kronstadt and the Rebellious Forts" 363
Troyanovsky, A. A. 93, 345
Tseshkovskaya 175
Tsintsadze, Kote 30
Tsvetaeva, M. I. 323, 325
Tukhachevsky, M. N. 39, 74, 77, 150, 154, *194*, 197, 198, 199, 202, 269, 271, 329, 349
Tulip. *See* Zborowski, M.
Tvardovsky, A. T.
  "By Right of Memory" 1
Twentieth Congress of the CPSU 1, 2, 119, 120, 121, 131, 152, 176, 177, 206, 263, 264, 270, 296, 299, 317, 427, 429, 430, 432, 433, 434, 442, 447
Twenty-Fourth Congress of the CPSU 177
Twenty-Second Congress of the CPSU 120, 121, 122, 152, 177, 250, 318, 338, 439

Twenty-Third Congress of the CPSU 177
Tynianov, Yu. N. 219
  "The Court's Verdict is the Country's Verdict" 221

U

Uborevich, I. P. 151, 200
Ulbricht, Walter 306, 317
Ulrikh, V. V. 39, *47*, 51, 56, 97, 98, 418
Union Bureau of Mensheviks 88
Union of Return to the Motherland 241, 323–324
Unshlikht, I. S. 174
Ushakov-Ushimirsky 416
Uspensky, A. I. 159, 160, 415
USSR Under Construction 418
Ustinov, D. F. 296
Utkin, K. P. 215, 216, 297
Uzbekistan 13, 120, 154, 294

V

Vaillant-Couturier, Paul 317
Vandervelde, Emile 106
van Heijenoort, Jean 399
Vareikis, I. M. 182, 183
Varga, E. 305, 314
Varshavskaia, M. 277
Vasetsky, N. A. 124
Vasilevsky, A. M. 203
Vasiliev, A. N. 145
Vatsetis, I. I. 421
VChK 359, 444, 447
Veinberg, G. D. 177
Vereeken, Georges 410
Verkhneuralsk 277
Vernadsky, V. I. *218*, 224, 295
Versailles Treaty 74, 75
Virabov, V. V. 284
Vishniak, M. V. 105

VKP(b) 2, 5, 10, 12, 15, 16, 19, 20, 23, 26, 73, 98, 109, 143, 153, 154, 157, 175, 176, 177, 190, 198, 200, 207, 217, 225, 272, 279, 284, 289, 291, 293, 305, 306, 310, 313, 321, 354, 423, 424, 425. *See also* Communist Parties: of Soviet Union
Voitolovskaia, A. L.
Tracing the Fate of My Generation 285
Volfovich 260
Volkogonov, D. A. 124, 395, 396, 397, 403, 442
Volkov, K. P. 298
Volkov, P. 397
Vorkuta 279, 281, 282, 283, 284, 285
Voronin 261, 262
Voronsky, A. K. 226, *227*, 418
Voroshilov, K. E. 61, *128*, 130, 131, 149, *150*, *157*, 169, 177, *194*, 195, 196, 198, 199, 201, 290, 410, 432, 433, 434, 435, 438
   denies endorsing torture 151
   letters to 150
   objects to Khrushchev's secret speech 430–431
   on Gamarnik 152
   on purge of Red Army 197
Vorozheikin 16
Voznesensky, N. A. 19
Vyshinsky, A. Ya. 39, 40, 41, 48, 49, 51, 52, *53*, 54, 55, 56, 59, 60, 61, 62, 63, 65, 69, 75, 77, 79, 85, 90, 92, *95*, 96, 97, 99, 100, 130, 131, 345
   as right-wing Menshevik 93
   compares Yagoda to Capone 64
   difficulty with Bukharin 43–47
   on confession as evidence 94
   on sabotage 86
   orders cases sent to troikas 211
   rewarded by Stalin 98

W

Wandurski, Witold 310
Warski, Adolf 310
Wehrmacht 202, 203
Weiss, Peter 104
Well, Roman 406
Wolf, Erwin 399, 403
Wrangel, P. N. 374
Wright, John G. 402

Y

Yagoda, G. G. 39, 43, 46, 61, *62*, 65, 69, 70, 71, 72, 75, 76, 81, 108, 123, 140, 205, 271, 329, 349, 376, 393
   and Kirov's assassination 63
   arrest of 62
   compared to Capone 64
   compared to Fouché 62
Yakhno 272
Yakir, I. E. 227, 349, 437
Yakovenko 47
Yakovin, G. Ya. 285
Yakovlev, A. N. 126, 192
Yakovlev, A. S. 158, 416
Yakovleva, V. N. 49, 51, 52
Yakovlev, Ya. A. 175
Yakubovich 9
Yalymov 294
Yaroslavsky, E. M. 18, 53, 143, 421, 422
Yashkevich 266
Yefimov, B. E. 165, 250, 252, 299
   caricature of Trotsky and Bukharin 100
Yefimov, I. I. 249, 299
Yefremova, M. I. 137
Yegorov, A. I. 175, 176, *194*, 195, 198, 269
Yeltsin, B. N. 192, 206, 256
Yenukidze, A. S. *28*, *29*, 30, 177, 282

Index 513

arrest of 29
shot without a trial 30
Yenukidze, L. 282
Yepanechnikov, D. S. 298
Yerbanov, M. N. 132
Yevdokimov, G. E. 226
Yezhov, N. I. 10, 23, 30, 33, 57, 58, 65, 69, 75, 76, 92, 111, 126, *128*, 130, 131, 132, 133, 135, 139, 149, 152, 155, 158, 159, 161, 163, 164, 166, *167*, 171, 181, 182, *184*, 195, 196, 201, 205, 206, *207*, 209, 211, 212, 215, 223, 238, 251, 271, 272, 273, 275, 297, 305, 324, 326, 327, 334, 345, 376, 386, 388, 401, 410, 413, *414*, *417*, *420*, 421
and "mass operations" 9
arrest of 418
execution of 419
letter to Stalin 415
on Sedov's death 396
removal from *Short Course* 426
replaced by Beria 416
Yurasov Card Index 11
Yusupov, U. Yu. 294

Z

Zaitsev, V. S. 339
"Hero of October and the Civil War" 339
Zakharian, E. T. *276*
Zakovsky, L. M. 212, 416
Zalman, V. P. *12*
Zapotocki 317
Zatonsky, V. P. 174
Zaveniagin, A. P. 176
Zborowski, M. 331, 334, 385, *386*, 387, 388, *389*, 390, 392, 395, 399, 400, 401, 402, 407, 408, 409, 410, 411, 412

Zelenskaia, A. G. 97, 98
Zelensky, I. A. 34, 73, 84, *85*, 86, 97
Zemskov, V. N. 238, 447
Zhdanov, A. A. 131, *157*, 158, 161, 169, 177, *184*, 190, 214, 216, 217
directs purge in Leningrad 157
Zhegalin, I. K. 144, 437
Zhu De 317
Zhukov, G. K. 198, 199, 200, 202, 435, 436, 437, 438
Zimianin, M. V. 296
Zimin 164
Zinger 285
Zinoviev, Alexander 3
Zinoviev, G. E. 29, 30, 49, 52, 58, 61, 72, 83, 88, 123, 148, 285, 299, 303, 311, 317, 322, 323, 328, 363, 383, 418, 425, 434, 438, 439
Ziuk, M. O. 226
Zorin, S. S. 226, 227
Zosimov, A. G. 359, 360
Zubarev, P. T. 76
Zverev, A. G. 293
Zweig, Stefan 62